UNION-MANAGEMENT RELATIONS IN A CHANGING ECONOMY

ALAN BALFOUR

University of South Florida

Prentice-Hall, Inc., Englewood Cliffs, New Jersey 07632

Library of Congress Cataloging-in-Publication Data

BALFOUR, ALAN.
  Union-management relations in a changing economy.

  Includes bibliographies and index.
    1. Industrial relations—United States—History.
  2. Collective bargaining—United States—History.
  3. Trade-unions—United States—History. I. Title.
  HD8066.B34 1987   331'.0973   86-30495
  ISBN 0-13-938804-4

Editorial/production supervision and
  interior design: *Judith R. Cornwell*
Cover design: *George Cornell*
Manufacturing buyer: *Harry P. Baisley*

Printed in the United States of America

10 9 8 7 6 5 4 3 2 1

ISBN 0-13-938804-4 01

Prentice-Hall International (UK) Limited, *London*
Prentice-Hall of Australia Pty. Limited, *Sydney*
Prentice-Hall Canada Inc., *Toronto*
Prentice-Hall Hispanoamericana, S.A., *Mexico*
Prentice-Hall of India Private Limited, *New Delhi*
Prentice-Hall of Japan, Inc., *Tokyo*
Prentice-Hall of Southeast Asia Pte. Ltd., *Singapore*
Editora Prentice-Hall do Brasil, Ltda., *Rio de Janeiro*

CONTENTS

THREE

DEVELOPMENT OF THE SYSTEM: HISTORICAL AMERICAN VALUES

FOUR

DEVELOPMENT OF THE SYSTEM: ADJUSTMENTS BASED ON EXPERIENCE

SEVEN

UNION POLITICAL ACTIVITY

EIGHT

UNION ORGANIZING CAMPAIGNS
AND RECOGNITION PROCEDURES

NINE

BARGAINING 166

TEN

IMPASSES AND STRIKES

ELEVEN

ECONOMIC ISSUES

SIXTEEN

UNION-MANAGEMENT COOPERATION   **403**

SEVENTEEN

EVALUATION OF THE SYSTEM   **423**

APPENDIX

PREFACE

Many observers believe that American labor relations are in a period of potential extreme change. Reduced employment in both the mass production industries and the unionized construction trades, changing technology, increasingly effective foreign competition, government intervention in business, and concerns for quality of product and quality of work life have raised serious questions concerning the appropriateness of our American industrial relations system. Lessons learned over the past fifty to one hundred years have to be reassessed. Much of what we learned in the past is still appropriate for the future, but some of it may not be. This book attempts to assess how we arrived at our current system, to explain how it operates, and to examine how the system copes with the sometimes new and different pressures of the 1980s.

The author believes that a major purpose of education is to help students understand their environment. For the purposes of this book, the environment is that of American union-management relations. Most of the readers will not pursue careers in a unionized environment. Fewer still will take positions in which they ever actually will negotiate a contract. Virtually none will be expected to become negotiators immediately. Accordingly, this book emphasizes an understanding of why the parties to collective bargaining act as they do. It does not attempt to make negotiators or labor lawyers out of students. Instead of stressing facts and data which are often not necessary for understanding, are memorized before exams and forgotten after, and often become out of date before the student graduates, this book tries to explain *why* we do what we do rather than merely describing what we do. It intentionally contains more philosophy, sociology, and psychology and fewer NLRB cases and economic data than other books in the field. The book's emphasis is on the behavioral impact of labor relations, rather than the economic or legal consequences of collective bargaining.

Hopefully, because of this emphasis on behavior and because of the subject's relevance to their own lives, students will find the book brisk and interesting—a valuable and thought-provoking guide to *understanding* (rather than describing) our contemporary labor relations system.

To facilitate class discussion and learning, each chapter ends with two types of questions: Discussion Questions and Statements for Comment. The Discussion Questions require a straightforward mastery of the material presented. The Statements for Comment are usually opinionated utterances taken from the real world. Reacting to them requires applying the principles developed in the chapter, rather than merely looking up answers given in the text. Each chapter also contains a series of Situations, which are hypothetical cases for which readers may make recommendations utilizing the principles developed in the chapter. Finally, a continuing Exercise runs throughout the book, beginning with a company involved in a union organizing campaign. It proceeds through a contract negotiation and a bargaining impasse and culminates in a pair of grievance arbitrations. Exercise assignments can be varied in length to fit the time permitted and can include role playing if desired.

ACKNOWLEDGMENTS

I wish to thank my colleagues Cynthia Fryer Cohen, Dick Dutton, and James J. Sherman for their input and critical review of materials. I also wish to acknowledge the very valuable contributions of research assistants Pamela Pautler, Suzanne Veczey, Mark Rose, Sharon James, and Brian Lindahl. Finally, I wish to thank Norma Walker for an excellent job of word processing.

ALAN BALFOUR

ONE

INTRODUCTION

Collective bargaining is about people, conflict, and power. It is a subject on which many Americans hold strong, easily voiced, ill-informed opinions. It is controversial, frustrating, irritating, and interesting. It affects the lives of all of us.

COLLECTIVE BARGAINING DEFINED

Collective bargaining is a process that obligates management and union representatives to negotiate in good faith in an attempt to reach agreement concerning a specified set of issues affecting employees. It also includes the application, interpretation, and enforcement of the agreed-upon contract.

INDUSTRIAL RELATIONS SYSTEM DEFINED

The *industrial relations system* consists of the interrelated needs and desires of employees, unions, managers, investors, nonunion companies, consumers, the government, and the public in general. Its purpose is to provide the greatest possible good for the greatest number of parties without overly harming any of them. How this "greatest good for the greatest number" is measured and accomplished is, of course, subject to debate. The pursuit of the goal is accomplished by attempting to balance the often competing and conflicting needs of the parties. While the system is not entirely perfect for any of its members, it is also not unacceptable to any. Like all systems, it is subject to pressures from the outside environment such as foreign competition, technological change, and the changing values and expectations of its participants.

The term "industrial relations" is historic and derives from a time when the primary source of employment in the United States was industrial. "Employment relations" or "labor-management relations" would be more appropriate terms for the changing nature of employment in America. Collective bargaining is a component of the industrial relations system.

PURPOSE AND GOALS OF A UNION

The purpose of a union is to get for employees what they could not get without one. Major goals of a union are (1) to improve employee wages and benefits, (2) to assure fair treatment of employees at the workplace, and (3) to allow employees input on decisions affecting them.

STUDY OF COLLECTIVE BARGAINING

The study of collective bargaining is complex. It may appear simple compared to other courses taught in college curricula because it is communicated in English prose rather than mathematical formulas, chemical symbols, or foreign languages. Many people underestimate its complexity and difficulty because it is a subject with which they are already somewhat familiar and about which they therefore feel qualified to express an opinion.

FIGURE 1-1   FACTORS AFFECTING THE INDUSTRIAL
RELATIONS SYSTEM

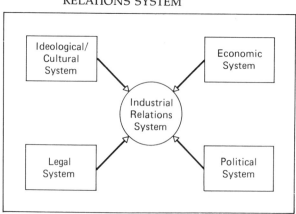

Complexity emerges when one considers the truly multidisciplinary nature of the field. A knowledge of sociology, psychology, economics, political science, history, philosophy, and law are all useful for understanding collective bargaining.

The study of collective bargaining is also inherently complex because it deals with people. People are a most variable unit of study. There are variances among groups, among individuals, and within the individual himself at different times. People do not behave with the consistency found in the laws of physics—or even accounting. This lack of consistency prevents the assertion of "exactly" right answers. Most situations provide several possible solutions, each valued differently by different people. The proposal of solutions to labor-management relations problems requires considerably more "art" than the solution of problems in the physical sciences.

The subject is still further confounded by the source of people's impressions. Industrial relations opinions in the real world are generally based on two sources—personal experiences (and anecdotes of the personal experiences of others) and media coverage. Because "news" is defined, at least partially, by what is special or not typical, impressions based on newspaper or television coverage of industrial relations events are likely to be "off-center." That is, newspapers cover strikes more than settlements, and corruption more than compliance. This is true despite the fact that agreement and honesty are far more common than their more publicized opposites. If the only time people are aware of unions is when they are doing something dramatic, unusual, or illegal, they will not have an accurate impression of what American unions are like. This problem is widespread throughout the population.

The subject is further confounded by the impressions of those studying it. Not only do different students have different values of what is "right" or "wrong"—or even "useful" in a given situation, they often cannot even agree on what the situation is. Any workplace is a great laboratory of discovery in the differences among people. Even when there is common agreement that a situation is bad, there are generally differences of opinion as to what is bad about it, why it is that way, and what should be done about it.

The compelling proof that collective bargaining is a complex, difficult subject and not given to "obvious" solutions is the fact that conflict between employers and employees (and their agents) continues to exist. If the solutions to these problems were all as clear-cut and obvious as some barroom patrons assert, the problems would have been solved long ago. Their continued existence demonstrates that solutions are not simple.

This book cannot provide concrete answers or "plug-in programs" to solve employment problems. It can, however, provide a framework for increased understanding that, coupled with experience, can provide improved (even if not perfect) performance for all who use it. To further enhance learning about the subject, a bibliography of related specialized readings is provided at the end of each chapter. Also, an Appendix at the end of this chapter contains sources of labor relations information and data.

METHODS OF DEALING WITH PROBLEMS
AT WORK

Whenever an employment relationship exists, conflict will occur. Employees have problems, regardless of whether or not they are unionized. The existence of a union merely presents one of several approaches to solving problems that arise in all workplaces.

When the nonunion employee confronts a displeasing event at work, he or she is presented with five choices or strategies to try to rectify the situation.

First, the employee can go to his or her supervisor and ask that person to remove the offending condition. This is a most natural response and is undoubtedly the way the vast majority of problems is handled. If the supervisor can grant relief and is inclined to do so, the issue will end with the employee being satisfied and believing that "the system works." If, however, the supervisor does not grant relief, the employee must resort to one of the other four remedies.

The second remedy is also a common one. It is to "lump it." The employee feels his or her situation has been worsened by the source of conflict, and that is dissatisfying. Employees are, however, also used to being dissatisfied. They realize they live in an imperfect world, one that is not organized solely for their benefit. They make compromises and concessions all the time. This situation represents one more dissatisfaction. Still, on the whole, the employee values the job more than any of the alternatives and continues to go about his or her work, although probably with less satisfaction and with more griping. This solution is used often for issues too trivial to fight more strongly over. However, if "lumping it" is not satisfactory, the employee must rely on one of the three remaining strategies.

The third method of expressing discontent in hope of getting a situation changed is to reduce one's productivity. This action escalates the confrontation considerably and makes it adversarial. By reducing performance, the employee reduces the organization's success. This outcome is intended to get the supervisor into trouble, thereby increasing the employee's bargaining power by trading off his or her restored productivity for concessions from the boss on the original conflict. This is a risky and damaging strategy to pursue, one that might result in discipline or discharge. An employee may be driven to it, however, because the only real bargaining *power* he or she possesses is to withhold services. The supervisor loses comparatively little in denying a mere request. The supervisor can, essentially, refuse for free. It begins costing the supervisor to disagree, however, when subordinates begin withholding or reducing their services. The supervisor's decision on whether to cooperate can be greatly influenced by a change in the cost of disagreeing. This strategy, when widespread, is often called a "morale problem."

The fourth remedy is a variation of the third. It is to form a union. This is similar to the withholding of services in that it is another mechanism for trying to impose costs on the employer for disagreeing. The ultimate threat of the union

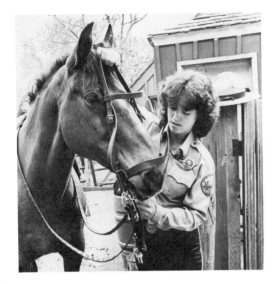 

 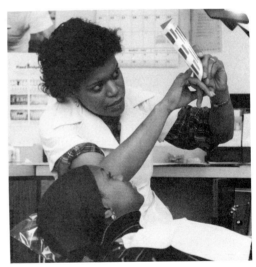

SOURCE: Laimute E. Druskis, Irene Springer, Alyeska Pipeline Service Co., Ken Karp.

would be to withhold the services of the entire workforce; i.e., strike. This represents a tremendous increase in the cost of disagreeing for the employer. But even without the threat of a strike, a union still presents a mechanism for voicing employee concern. In most jurisdictions, the employer legally *must* bargain with the union and attempt to resolve conflicts within the proper scope of bargaining. No individual employee enjoys imposing such an obligation on management. This strategy is severely limited, however, by the employee's need to have a majority of his or her co-workers join him or her to form a union.

The fifth and final strategy available to an employee unhappy with his or her job is to quit. This, of course, may result in trading one set of problems for another. It is pursued only when the discomfort is great and alternative jobs look better, or when the job is so little valued that nothing significant is lost by quitting. From an employer's standpoint, the quitting instead of fighting for change may produce fewer headaches but may also mean that the need for changes is not communicated to management.

One other method of seeking relief should be noted, even though it is outside the union-management focus of this book. It is for labor to approach the government to enact laws to protect the interests of all employees, not just those represented by unions. This form of intervention is particularly appropriate for problems widespread throughout the workforce, rather than being specific to a particular employer. Examples of governmental protection of employment interests include equal employment opportunity, occupational safety and health, pension protection, minimum wages, workers' compensation, unemployment compensation, and Social Security.

Only about 20 percent of the private-sector workforce[1] has opted for the fourth strategy—unionization—as a remedy for its problems at work. Whether an employee will choose to be included among those represented by a union depends on the answer to two questions:

1. Am I doing OK as it is? If not,
2. would a union help?

Employees who feel they are doing OK seldom press for unionization. Even those who feel they are not doing OK need to believe a union could cure their problem before they would wish to be represented by one. A central aim of this

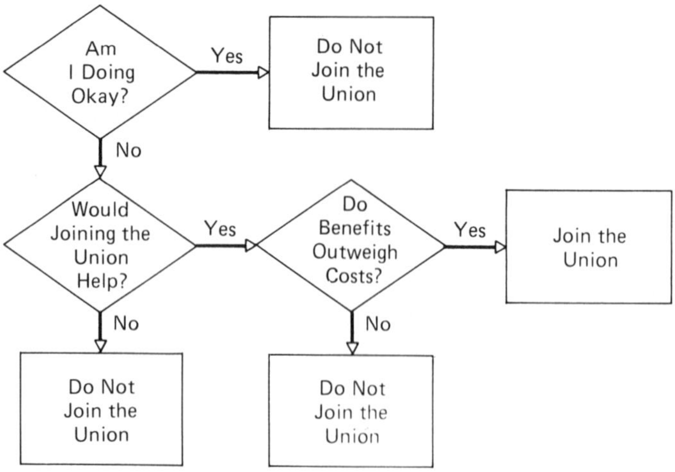

FIGURE 1-2 CIRCUMSTANCES UNDER WHICH A PERSON WOULD JOIN A UNION

book is the exploration of why some people perceive they are doing OK, why others perceive that they are not, and what leads some, and only some, employees to favor unionization as a method of resolving their employment problems.

INHERENT CONFLICT OF COLLECTIVE BARGAINING

The needs of employees and managers can, and do, come into conflict in the workplace. Employees seek good pay and benefits, job security, favorable working conditions, fair treatment, and a voice in the system. Employers seek to reduce costs and promote efficiency. Managers function between the cross pressures of the employers' demand for cost reduction and the employees' desire for ever-improving job conditions. The desire of employees to improve their position usually results in increased costs, which are generally resisted by employers. Managers, in attempting to reconcile these often conflicting goals, bring to a focus the employees' perceived need to protect their interests against their employers. The development of an adversary relationship is almost inevitable, despite many parties' claims of "cooperative purpose." Employees who form unions hope that they will do better collectively in their "struggle" than they would individually. Figure 1–3 shows an overall view of the activities inherent in the labor relations model that will be examined in the rest of this book.

FIGURE 1-3 THE LABOR RELATIONS MODEL

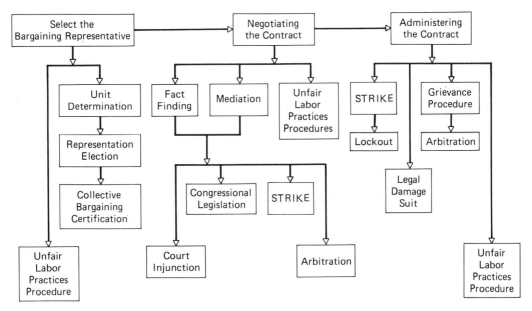

"ROOTS OF INDUSTRIAL RELATIONS" OR WHY THERE IS CONFLICT IN THE SYSTEM

Conflict between employees and employers was not always thought of as a problem. In ancient Greece, the aristocracy regarded work as unhealthy and demeaning. Therefore, aristocrats didn't work. Instead, they were served by the lower classes and slaves. This relationship was not so much one of employment conflict as it was one of oppression.

The growth of Christianity in the West changed attitudes toward work. In the Roman Catholic church, Thomas Aquinas viewed work as instrumental to a healthy soul. But the real leap forward occurred with Lutheranism and Calvinism. In these religions, work became a virtue in itself and a necessity to a full, complete, and virtuous life. The "Protestant Ethic" viewed work as a means of serving God. This viewpoint was extremely useful to the expansion of employment in an industrialized world and to accepting the roles of owners, managers, and hourly employees.

The outcomes of these new work relationships were often very harsh on the working class. The response of the scholars of the time was that this was a "natural" consequence of the laws of economics and that the "invisible hand" of the free enterprise marketplace would allocate resources in the most efficient manner.

While the free enterprise economy did allocate resources efficiently, it did not do so humanely. As was observed by Sidney and Beatrice Webb, two British labor scholars writing in the late 1890s:

If the capitalist refuses to accept the workman's terms, he will, no doubt, suffer some inconvenience as an employer. To fulfill his orders, he will have to "speed up" some of his machinery or insist on his work people working longer hours. Failing these expedients, he may have to delay the delivery of his goods, and may even find his profits at the end of the year fractionally less than before. But meanwhile, he goes on eating and drinking, his wife and family go on living, just as before. His physical comfort is not affected: He can afford to wait until the labourer comes back in a humble frame of mind. And that is just what the labourer must presently do. For he, meanwhile, has lost his day. His very subsistence depends on his promptly coming to an agreement. If he stands out, he has no money to meet his weekly rent, or to buy food for his family. If he is obstinate, consumption of his little hoard, or the pawning of his furniture, may put off the catastrophe; but sooner or later slow starvation forces him to come to terms. And since success in the higgling of the market is largely determined by the relative eagerness of the parties to come to terms—especially if this eagerness cannot be hidden—it is now agreed, even on this ground alone, that manual labourers as a class are at a disadvantage in bargaining.

Therein began the conflict still inherent in employment relationships: that the weaker party can be abused by the stronger (even classical economists would admit that) and that—for most people—this is not an acceptable consequence. Most observers living in the twentieth century agree that economics alone is not a sufficient criterion for resource distribution. When happiness, health, and participation in the benefits of society are at stake, human, as well as economic, factors must be considered. The system will not run properly on its own.

WHY EMPLOYEES JOIN UNIONS

Employees join unions under three conditions: (1) because they want to, (2) in order to go along with the group, (3) because it is sometimes required as a condition of employment.

The most important reason employees willingly join unions is a belief that their jobs should be improved and that unionization is an effective way to achieve that improvement. The specific improvement generally sought falls into three main categories: (1) wages (including supplemental benefits), hours, and working conditions; (2) fair treatment on the job; and (3) a voice in determining the policies that affect employees. Whenever there is a perception by the employees that management is not providing enough in any of these areas, and alternative ways of improving the situation are not perceived as working, employees become good candidates for unionization. On the other hand, where these needs are being met by management, employees are far less likely to join unions.

FAIR TREATMENT ON THE JOB AND LEGAL RIGHTS
OF NONUNION EMPLOYEES

The United States is a true bastion of the rights of private property. American employees are constantly amazed at how few job *rights* they have by law. In most instances this is not an important issue because good business practices (not legal requirements) dictate treating employees fairly and reasonably on the job. However, sometimes employees perceive they are not treated fairly. When this happens, they may form a union for the purpose of negotiating, through a contract rather than by law, protections and privileges they seek in their jobs.

Historically, an employer could fire an employee for a good reason, a bad reason, or no reason at all unless the parties had a contract specifying the duration of employment and grounds for termination. (After all, the employee could quit at any time, couldn't he or she?) Since such contracts were almost nonexistent in main-stream employment, employers realistically had the right to discharge at will.

A discharged employee had no right to know the reason for the dismissal, to present evidence on his or her own behalf, or to have an appeal. The employer was under no obligation to justify its decision. Needless to say, the potential for abuse was great. While it was administratively convenient not to have to justify decisions, it also allowed "miscarriages of justice" (by current standards) to occur.

Some famous examples of employees who sued to be reinstated to the jobs from which they were allegedly "wrongfully" discharged are:

Two accountants who gave truthful testimony under oath that proved damaging to the company in a federal investigatory case for the Securities and Exchange Commission.

(continued)

Two hourly employees who openly refused to follow their employer's orders to vote for George Wallace in a presidential election.

A male employee who refused to provide his wife, who was not an employee, for the sexual gratification of his employer.

All these employees were discharged for their failure to follow their employers' demands. All remained discharged under the "common-law" (based on case precedents rather than specific statutory language) right of the employer to discharge an employee without the reason being a concern of the courts.

The first enforceable statutory infringement of this "employment-at-will" right was the Wagner Act in 1935. It forbade discharging an employee because of his or her union activity. Title VII of the Civil Rights Act of 1964 and its subsequent amendments further restricted employer freedom by outlawing discharge based on race, color, sex, age, national origin, or handicap status. Finally, a common-law right to be free from discharge is emerging based on three exceptions to the employment-at-will doctrine: violation of public policy, implied contract, and the doctrine of good faith and fair dealing. How far these protections will be expanded remains to be seen, but it is clear that historically union-negotiated contract provisions provided far greater protection than was available solely through law.

Still, the examples given so far have been far-fetched and certainly not problems in most workplaces. If they were one of the major reasons employees joined unions, unions wouldn't be very large, especially considering that government protections against discrimination apply to all employees, union and nonunion alike.

One of the most important fair-treatment rights unions provide employees is to be free from the need to "brown-nose." In nonunion employment, the employer is free to assign the better jobs and offer promotions to those it sees fit. Ideally, those assignments will be made in response to merit. Realistically, they may be perceived as being allocated to the employees the supervisor likes best (for whatever reason), hence, the need to brown-nose to be favored by the supervisor. A union contract would substitute a consistent rule (such as seniority) for the boss's subjective judgment. To many employees, this is a great benefit to their personal dignity and may well be perceived as "fairer."

An employee's perception of being adequately treated is largely influenced by his or her perception of how others are doing and by how the employee has done in the past. A rapidly rising cost of living can add to the perception that individual bargaining is not working well enough. This is particularly true when highly publicized union-negotiated wage increases raise other employees' wages. Arbitrary and capricious treatment by supervisors, or the appearance of it, can increase the need for protection. Finally, when decisions affecting employees are made without their input, employees may feel powerless and unhappy. This is particularly true when the nature of the job does not provide much input or control.

When the attempt is made to recruit union membership, it appears that many employees are indifferent to joining or not joining and do not perceive that their lives will be greatly different because of unionization. These employees will join if key, visible leaders among the employees join. The strategy for getting these employees to join will be examined in Chapter Eight.

Last, some employees join unions because their place of employment has a contract with a union requiring that all employees, upon completion of their probationary period, join. The mechanism for this procedure is detailed in Chapter Twelve.

WHY EMPLOYEES DO NOT JOIN UNIONS

The vast majority of employees do not join unions. Probably the major reason for this is satisfaction with their job, or at least a belief that a union could not cure whatever problems do exist. If management is perceived as generally acting appropriately, there is no reason to band together to try to force a change in behavior. This is the basis of the modern "enlightened management" antiunion approach. It consists of appearing to do voluntarily what is right in employee relations.

A second deterrent to joining unions is that they cost money in the form of dues and initiation fees. In most unions this expense is usually not great (perhaps 1 or 2 percent of pay), but it still represents an additional expense that does not have to be incurred. This seems to be a sizable deterrent to many employees.

A third reason not to join is a fear of reprisal by the employer. Legally speaking, employers are not permitted to do this. Realistically, they do it every day. Assurances to employees that they will be protected by an agency of the federal government and that they will be beyond the reach of the employer's wrath are often just not true enough in the real world. Many employees have learned to keep their mouths shut, even when they are in the right, and make the best they can of an imperfect situation. Undoubtedly, there is a sizable percentage of the workforce that would like to be unionized but is afraid to act because it fears the consequences.

A fourth reason not to join is antiunion attitudes. Some employees believe that banding together is un-American and a rejection of a belief in individual responsibility. Others believe it will reduce their chances for recognition and promotion. Many are displeased with organized labor's reputation for corruption. Many also believe that union leaders might force them into untenable positions or call unwanted strikes.

A fifth reason not to join is it might make you unpopular with others.

While there may be social pressure to join a union, there is also often pressure not to join. Employees who do not have strong feelings personally about the advantages and disadvantages of unions may follow the example of influential others.

A sixth reason not to join is for religious or moral grounds. This affects only a tiny portion of the workforce, but occasional legal battles do arise over accommodating such interests.

Last, some employees don't join because unions don't want them. Historically, craft unions often refused admission on the basis of race or ethnicity. Presumably, that is no longer true. Today the principal reason unions do not organize some employees is because they form such a small group or are so widely scattered that the cost to the union to organize and represent them is greater than the dues dollars the group could generate.

WHY EMPLOYERS RESIST UNIONS

Employers generally resist the unionization of their employees. Their objection stems from three concerns—two pragmatic and one emotional. The first pragmatic concern is increased cost. The second pragmatic concern is reduced authority in making decisions. The emotional concern is philosophical.

Increased cost is expected to result from higher wages and better benefits and perhaps reduced productivity resulting from the employees' increased bargaining power. This is distressing to employers, because it results in increased expenses without an increase in revenues. That result, if not offset by increased productivity, may result in decreased profits.

Reduced authority is of particular importance to managers. Collectively bargained agreements often contain limitations on the assignment of work, promotion procedures, discipline, and other topics that restrict the manager's unilateral right to control, reward, and punish employees. This leaves the managers in the undesirable position of having the same responsibility they had before collective bargaining, but with considerably less authority to carry out their task. This can make their job much more difficult. Unions can also be an immense hassle to managers because reviewable actions must be supported by documentation rather than opinion. This can increase paperwork drastically for managers and sometimes reduce their incentive even to act.

The philosophical objection to employee unionization stems from two sources. One is a belief that collectivizing is contrary to the "American" ideal of self-reliance, with the emphasis on "self." People attracted to managerial positions often possess a great deal of this belief. The second is that the banding together of employees reflects a perception that managers are closer to enemies than to allies or helpers. This is generally an affront to managers who perceive themselves as leaders.

STATE OF UNIONS TODAY

Current Size and Distribution

Unions currently represent about one-fifth of the employees in America. This is down from a high of one-third in the mid-1950s.[2] (See Table 1–1A.)

Representation is not distributed evenly throughout the country. Unions are heavily represented in manufacturing, transportation, and mining; in the North; and in urban areas; and are proportionally under-represented in the white collar and service sectors, the South and Mountain states, and rural states. The widely held perception that unions have great power in the economy stems more from their location than from their absolute size. They are often located in the largest, richest, most powerful, most publicized, most troubled companies in America. What they do receives more than their share of attention. Furthermore, what they do often spills over into the non-union sector. Union negotiated benefits are often copied by non-union employers both to attract and retain employees and to discourage them from organizing. Data on union membership by organization are displayed in Tables 1–1B and 1–1C.

Reasons for Declining Membership

Several factors have contributed to the decline in the proportion of unionized employees in America. Some of the most important are (not necessarily in order):

Changes in the type and location of work. Employment is declining in the highly-unionized manufacturing industry and growing in the less-unionized service sector. This shift is a result of the transition of our business world to a service economy. It is not an anti-union movement, but it does have the effect of reducing union membership. The movement of jobs from the North to the South is, however, largely motivated by a desire to become or remain non-union and has undoubtedly had a significant impact on the decline of unions.

Activities of management. Management is working harder now than in the past to remain non-union. It does this two ways. One is by trying to provide a workplace that employees believe is fair and appropriate—one in which they do not perceive a need for a union to get for them that which they could not get for themselves. The other method is by more vigorously opposing union organizing campaigns when they do arise. Employer anti-union campaigns will be examined in detail in Chapter Eight.

Protections being provided by law for all employees. The federal government's increased protection of employment rights through legislation has provided an alternative source of employee protections. Protections formerly available only through union contracts are now available to everyone, unionized or not. These

TABLE 1–1A

	Employment by Industry				Membership of National Unions and Employee Associations by Industry		Approximate Percent of Industry as of 1978
	1950		1980		1978		
	Number of Employees*	Percent	Number of Employees*	Percent	Number of Employees*	Percent of Workforce	
TOTAL	54,979	100.0	93,966	100.0	24,377	100.0	26
Goods-Producing Industries							
Total	27,119	49.3	29,165	31.0	11,475	47.1	39
Agriculture	7,160	13.0	3,310	3.5	44	.2	1
Mining	929	2.0	1,025	1.1	428	1.8	42
Manufacturing	16,393	29.8	20,361	21.7	8,119	33.3	40
Construction	2,637	4.8	4,469	4.8	2,884	11.8	65
Service-Producing Industries							
Total	27,860	50.7	64,801	69.0	12,902	52.9	20
Transportation	4,226	7.7	5,156	5.0	1,748	7.2	34
Wholesale and Retail	9,742	17.7	20,573	21.9	1,713	7.0	8
Financial	1,956	3.6	5,165	5.5	51	.2	1
Services	5,547	10.1	17,741	18.9	2,893	11.9	16
Government	6,389	11.6	16,170	17.2	6,094	25.0	38
Other	—	—	—	—	402	1.6	—

In thousands.

SOURCE: *U.S. Bureau of Labor Statistics,* Monthly Labor Review, *May 1981, Table 8, 77; U.S. Bureau of Labor Statistics,* Directory of National Unions and Employee Associations, *September, 1980, Tables 16 and 17, pp. 61, and 69–70.*

TABLE 1–1B THE TEN LARGEST UNIONS (AS OF 1984)

Name	Membership
1. International Brotherhood of Teamsters, Chauffeurs, Warehousemen and Helpers of America ("Teamsters")	2,000,000
2. National Education Association ("NEA")	1,700,000
3. United Automobile, Aerospace, and Agricultural Implement Workers of America, International ("UAW")	1,500,000
4. United Food and Commercial Workers International Union ("UFCW")	1,300,000
5. United Steelworkers of America ("USW")	1,050,000
6. American Federation of State, County, and Municipal Employees ("AFSCME")	1,000,000
7. International Brotherhood of Electrical Workers ("IBEW")	1,000,000
8. International Association of Machinists and Aerospace Workers ("IAM" or "Machinists")	800,000
9. Communication Workers of America ("CWA")	650,000
10. United Brotherhood of Carpenters and Joiners of America ("Carpenters")	650,000

SOURCE: Labor Union Directory, *Bureau of Labor Statistics, United States Department of Labor.*

TABLE 1-1C   UNION MEMBERSHIP AS A PROPORTION OF NONAGRICULTURAL
             EMPLOYMENT BY STATES, 1976*

Rank	State	Membership as a Percent of Employees in Nonagricultural Establishments
1	West Virginia	38.9%
2	New York	37.1
3	Hawaii	37.0
4	Pennsylvania	36.4
5	Washington	35.6
6	Michigan	32.7
7	Illinois	32.2
8	Missouri	31.8
9	Ohio	31.5
10	Rhode Island	31.1
11	Indiana	30.7
12	Wisconsin	29.4
13	Alaska	29.1
14	California	26.3
15	Minnesota	25.3
16	New Jersey	25.3
17	Oregon	25.1
18	Connecticut	24.9
19	Kentucky	24.7
20	Massachusetts	24.6
21	Nevada ☆	24.6
22	Montana	23.9
23	Maryland/D.C.	21.2
24	Delaware	20.8
25	Alabama ☆	19.0
26	New Mexico	18.7
27	Iowa ☆	18.5
28	Tennessee ☆	18.3
29	Maine	17.9
30	Vermont	17.9
31	Colorado	17.4
32	Louisiana	16.2
33	Wyoming ☆	15.9
34	Arkansas	15.5
35	Arizona ☆	15.4
36	Nebraska ☆	15.2
37	Kansas ☆	15.0
38	Georgia ☆	14.2
39	Idaho	14.1
40	New Hampshire	13.7
41	Virginia ☆	13.6
42	Oklahoma	13.5
43	Utah ☆	13.4
44	Florida ☆	13.1
45	North Dakota ☆	12.1
46	Mississippi ☆	12.0
47	Texas ☆	12.0
48	South Dakota ☆	9.6
49	North Carolina ☆	6.8
50	South Carolina ☆	6.6

Legend:

▨ States without right-to-work laws

☆ States with right-to-work laws

*Although the above figures are somewhat dated, the relationship among states does not vary greatly over
time.*

SOURCE: *U.S. Bureau of Labor Statistics,* Directory of National International Labor Unions in the
United States, *1977, Bulletin No. 2044 (1979), p. 74.*

widespread improvements have reduced some of the reasons for needing a union.

Bad publicity for unions. In recent years much of what has been said about unions has been unfavorable. Internal corruption has been highly publicized and the legitimate successes of unions (such as wage raising) have sometimes been seen as not in the interest of the country.

Finally, *unions are apparently not trying as hard to organize the unorganized as they once did.*[3] Fewer elections are being called for and fewer organizing campaigns are begun. This may be a reflection of reduced concern for organizing or it may reflect an unwillingness to expend resources where the reduced probability of success does not warrant it.

Trends for the Future

Whether the decline in membership will continue, accelerate, stop, or reverse itself is uncertain. Growth in the past has been sporadic. Some of the periods of greatest growth followed periods of substantial decline—times in which it was believed that "unions were a dying institution." Membership in unions historically has been affected by cataclysmic changes such as the Great Depression, by changing employer attitudes, by government protection and regulation, and by the ability of employees to meaningfully affect their outcomes.

Almost certainly, if unions are to grow in the future they will have to expand in the areas of white collar and service employment. While employees in these areas have been relatively reluctant in the past to form unions, it is not clear what role technology and education will play in their job satisfaction—or dissatisfaction—in the future. This author is unwilling to posit a guess as to the future of union membership in the United States.

Appendix: Sources of Labor Relations Information and Data

Journals—The following is a list of some of the major journals in the field:

1. *Industrial and Labor Relations Review* (ILRR) Published by Cornell University since the 1940s. One of the most important journals in the field. Good source on collective bargaining, some international topics, and more recently, public sector labor relations.
2. *Industrial Relations* (IR) Published by the University of California, Berkeley. Similar coverage to ILRR.
3. *International Labor Review* (ILR) Published by the International Labor Office, Geneva. Essential source for foreign topics. Each issue includes a section on changes in labor legislation around the world.
4. *Journal of Human Resources* (JHR) Published by the University of Wisconsin. Focuses on manpower policy and labor markets rather than labor relations.

5. *Labor History* (LH) Important source on any historical topic, especially related to the history of labor organizations, mass movements, etc.
6. *Labor Law Journal (LLJ)* Important source on legal topics and arbitration. Articles cover legislation, NLRB policy and decisions, court decisions, etc.
7. *Monthly Labor Review* (MLR) Publication of the U.S. Bureau of Labor Statistics which focuses on labor and manpower policy and labor relations, and summarizes reports. Articles are shorter and less analytical than those in ILRR or IR.
8. Industrial Relations Research Association. *Proceedings of Annual Meetings.* Winter and Spring. These proceedings to date are a rich source of medium-length articles on all aspects of industrial relations.
9. In addition to the above journals, industrial relations articles often appear in economics, business, personnel, and sociology journals.

Newspapers—The following periodicals have good reporting of current labor issues: *New York Times, Wall Street Journal,* and *Business Week.*

Reporting Services—The following is a partial list of the reporting services available:

1. *Daily Labor Reporter* (DLR) A daily reporting service published by the Bureau of National Affairs, Washington, D.C., which contains short summaries of key labor events as well as full transcripts of important labor documents (legislation, key court and NLRB rulings, etc.). Indexed biweekly, with cumulative supplements.
2. *Labor Relations Reporter* (LRR) Bureau of National Affairs. An authoritative weekly report and analysis covering labor developments, legislation, current laws, and business practices. Includes reporting of: NLRB decisions, fair employment practices, arbitration, and wages and hours.
3. *Labor Law Reporter* (LLR) Commerce Clearinghouse, Inc. Weekly. Reports, analyzes, indexes, and provides editorial explanation of all pertinent federal and state statutes, regulations, court and NLRB decisions, and arbitration decisions. *A key source on NLRB decisions.*
4. Both the BNA and CCH publish other specialized reports (*White Collar Report, Government Employee Relations Report, Guidebook to Labor Relations,* etc.).

Union Publications—Several union publications are available. In addition to the *AFL-CIO News* and the *American Federationist* (publications of the AFL-CIO), the periodicals of many of the international unions are available. Many libraries also have an extensive collection of the proceedings of AFL-CIO and union conventions, constitutions, and collective bargaining contracts.

Labor Statistics—U.S.

1. U.S. Bureau of Labor Statistics. *BLS Handbook of Methods for Surveys and Studies.* (Bulletin 1910) Outlines data collection procedures for various studies conducted, and aids in interpretation of BLS charts, diagrams, and tables.

2. U.S. Bureau of Labor Statistics. *Employment and Earnings.* (Monthly) In addition to information implied by title, provides statistical data on characteristics of the unemployed, regional breakdowns, labor turnover, job vacancy rates, and uninsured employment.

3. ———. *Employment and Earnings Statistics for States and Areas.* (Annual) (Bulletin 1370) Provides data from the earliest available date to the present.

4. ———. *Employment and Earnings: United States.* (Annual) (Bulletin 1312) Provides data from the earliest available date to the present.

5. ———. *Handbook of Labor Statistics.* (Annual) Contains summary presentations of most BLS statistics. Tables list original source BLS Documents.

6. ———. *Monthly Labor Review.* (Monthly) Contains current employment, price, hours and earnings, productivity, and strike data.

7. U.S. President. *Employment and Training Report.* (Annual). Provides an extensive statistical section. It also contains the "official line" on recent developments in the labor market and manpower policy.

Labor Statistics—International

1. International Labour Office: *Bulletin of Labour Statistics.* (Quarterly)

2. ———. *Yearbook of Labor Statistics.* (Annual) Statistics on the world's labor force, prices, productivity, industrial disputes and accidents.

3. Organization for Economic Cooperation and Development. *Labor Force Statistics.* (Annual) Though primarily European in content, Australia, Canada, U.S., Japan, Iceland, and Turkey are included as well.

4. U.S. Bureau of Labor Statistics. *Handbook of Labor Statistics.* (Annual) Tables on "Foreign Labor Statistics" cover labor force and unemployment, earnings and hours, prices, and work stoppages.

In addition to statistics, the BLS publishes reports on developments in the labor market and labor relations. Their "Bulletin" series covers such topics as the following: "Characteristics of Agreements Covering 2000 Workers or More," "Characteristics of Agreements in State and Local Government," "Work Stoppages," etc. The BLS issues "Special Labor Force Reports" on developments in the labor market and "BLS Reports" on labor relations and other topics.

Indexes to the Literature

1. *Business Periodicals Index:* periodical articles.
2. *Journal of Economic Literature:* books, periodical articles.
3. *Index to Legal Periodicals:* periodical articles.
4. *Public Affairs Information Service Bulletin:* books, documents, pamphlets, articles.
5. *Social Sciences and Humanities Index:* includes foreign journals.
6. *Social Sciences Citation Index:* periodical articles.
7. *Work Related Abstracts:* theses and periodical articles.

Useful Subject Headings for I.R. Research.

1. Employment Statistics (by industry, trade, country, state, city)
2. Industrial Relations (by industry, trade, country)
3. Law and Legislation (by industry, trade, country)
4. Trade Union Law and Legislation (by country)
5. Trade Unions (particular unions)
6. Wage Statistics (by country, industry, occupation)

SOURCE: *Excerpted from Massachusetts Institute of Technology, Dewey Library, Industrial Relations Section,* Accessions Bulletin. *Laura Carchia, Librarian.*

Notes

1. Arthur A. Sloane and Fred Witney, *Labor Relations*, 5th ed. (Englewood Cliffs, N.J.: Prentice-Hall, Inc., 1985), p. 4.
2. Richard B. Freeman and James L. Medoff. *What Do Unions Do?* (New York: Basic Books, 1984), p. 221.
3. *Ibid.*, pp. 228–30.

Discussion Questions

1. Discuss why it is important to understand the industrial relations system.
2. Why is the study of collective bargaining complex? Why do many people underestimate its complexity?
3. Discuss in what ways employers and employees have common interests. In what ways do their interests conflict?
4. Analyze why some, and only some, employees join unions.
5. Analyze why employers generally resist unions.
6. Assess the state of unions today.

Statements for Comment

1. "Industrial Relations would be a good subject to take but I hear the professor grades very subjectively. I prefer accounting and calculus classes where there is only one right answer. It makes life a lot more fair."
2. "I don't believe in unions. I believe in taking care of myself."
3. "Form a union? If you don't like it here, you should quit!"
4. "Unions are OK for guys on assembly lines, but I'm a white collar technician. I don't think we need a union."
5. "Most managers are opposed to unions much more because of their intrusion on decision-making power than because of their effect on costs."

6. "American managers have a misguided sense of cause and effect. They think they got to where they are because they are better than other people."
7. "The South is not really antiunion. It just doesn't have much experience with industry. When industry which is unionized in the North moves South, Southern employees in those industries will join unions."

Situations

Case 1–1 Tyrone Jefferson is an employee of a fast food chain. He is 17 years old and works part-time after school and on weekends. Most of the time he fills orders for customers at the counter. Occasionally he helps with the cooking and also helps clean up the restaurant. He is one of the senior hourly employees at this location, having worked there a year and a half. He has always been a good and dependable worker.

The employer is concerned nationwide with missing product and cash-register shortages and has recently instituted a new policy. All hourly employees must be fingerprinted and submit to a lie detector test. Tyrone feels this is demeaning and probably a violation of his rights—and if it isn't, it should be.

What can Tyrone do? What should he do? What additional information might influence your recommendation?

Case 1–2 Doris Townsend is a 54-year-old office employee of a small manufacturing company in a large northern city. She does routine office work such as filing, typing, and answering the phone. She is not technically a secretary and does not take dictation. She has worked for the company for 12 years. She entered the workforce to give herself something to do once her children had grown up and left home.

During her 12 years Doris has been an ordinary performer, but because she has been on the job so long she has received many "merit" raises (which are really pretty much longevity raises). Yesterday her employer, Mr. Wilson, told her that she was being "permanently laid off" and that her services would no longer be needed after Friday.

Doris was crushed. She asked if her work had been bad. Mr. Wilson said no, but that business wasn't as good as it had been and the company had to cut expenses.

Two weeks later the company hired Jean Bolger, an 18-year-old girl straight out of high school with no experience, to do Doris's job. Doris's friends still working for the company were shocked and angered. They demanded to know why Doris had not been recalled if the job still had to be done.

Mr. Wilson said that the fact of the matter was that Doris's merit raises made him have to pay her a dollar more per hour than Jean, that anyone could do the job, and that "business is business." Other employees who know Mr. Wilson personally believe he fired Doris and hired Jean because Jean has better legs.

What should Doris do? Mr. Wilson? The other employees? Jean?

Case 1–3a Thomas Branscomb works as a truck loader at a small nonunion manufacturing facility. The employer works on a contract order basis, which causes alternating periods of overtime and slack. To reduce labor costs the employer likes to hire as few employees as possible and work them overtime as the occasion demands. Usually the overtime is short-lived, two weeks of 10-hour days at most. This summer business has been uncommonly good. Thomas has worked six 12-hour days per week (6:00 A.M. to 6:00 P.M., Monday through Saturday) for ten straight weeks. So far, this has been agreeable to Thomas because he is making a great deal of premium pay and he knows it won't always be this good financially. Other than a fear of coming down with mononucleosis, Thomas finds nothing to complain of.

Yesterday Thomas asked for the following Saturday afternoon off, from noon to 6:00 P.M. His supervisor refused, saying that he was the only truck loader and there would still be trucks to load. Thomas said he would take that afternoon off, even if the supervisor refused to authorize it, because "I can't be forced to work overtime." His supervisor warned him that if he did skip work he would be in trouble.

What should Thomas do? What should the supervisor do? Is there anything else you would want to know?

Case 1–3b That Saturday Thomas punched out at noon and left, saying goodbye to the supervisor as he went. The supervisor said, "You can't go." Thomas proved him wrong. When Thomas reported to work at 6:00 A.M. Monday, he found a pink slip paper-clipped to his timecard. It said, "See the Big Boss." Since the Big Boss didn't come in until 9:30 on Mondays, Thomas asked the supervisor what he should do. The supervisor said, "Load trucks." Thomas worked until 9:30 and went in to see the B.B.

The B.B. asked Thomas if he had worked Saturday afternoon. Thomas said he had not. The B.B. asked if he had permission to clock out. He said he did not. The B.B. asked why he took Saturday afternoon off. Thomas said to travel with his parents to his fiancée's family's house across the state to plan his marriage ceremony for the following Saturday (which he also, by the way, wanted off). The B.B. asked if the supervisor knew of this reason. Thomas said, "Not that I know of. He didn't ask why I wanted off."

What can the B.B. do? What should he do? What other recommendations would you make?

Bibliography of Related Readings

Biasatti, L. L., and J. E. Martin, "A Measure of the Quality of Union-Management Relationships," *Journal of Applied Psychology,* 1979, pp. 387–90.

Brett, J. M., "Why Employees Want Unions," *Organizational Dynamics,* 1980, pp. 47–59.

Cowan, P., and J. Miller, "Improving Employee Relations: A Four-Step Approach," *Personnel Administration,* February 1979, pp. 63–68.

Dabscheck, B., "Of Mountains and Routes Over Them: A Survey of Theories of Industrial Relations," *Journal of Industrial Relations,* 1983, pp. 485–506.

Farber, H. S., and D. H. Saks, "Why Workers Want Unions: The Role of Relative Wages and Job Characteristics," *Journal of Political Economy,* 1980, pp. 349–69.

Fulmer, W. E., "Labor-Management Relations in the 80s: Revolution or Evolution?" *Business Horizons,* 1984, pp. 26–32.

Ganez, J., "Resolving Conflict: A Guide for the Industrial Relations Manager," *Personnel,* 1979, pp. 22–32.

Gordon, M. E., and L. N. Long, "Demographic and Attitudinal Correlates of Union Joining," *Industrial Relations,* 1981, pp. 306–11.

Lippin, P. "Unions and the White Collar Worker," *Administrative Management,* July 1980, pp. 28–30.

Schrank, R., "Are Unions an Anachronism?" *Harvard Business Review,* 1979, pp. 107–15.

Strauss, G., et al., "A Symposium: The Future of Industrial Relations," *Industrial Relations,* 1984, pp. 1–57.

"Unions Growing in Public Sector, Census Reveals," *AFL-CIO News,* March 13, 1982, p. 6.

"Unless They Change, Labor Unions Face a 'Dreary' Future," *Management Review,* November 1981, pp. 29–30.

"Why Clerical Workers Resist the Unions," *Business Week,* May 2, 1983, p. 126.

$$==== \textbf{TWO} ====$$

THE TRADITIONAL SYSTEM
AND
FORCES FOR CHANGE

This chapter identifies the major characteristics of the American collective bargaining system, contrasts it with other systems, and examines the pressures for change upon our model.

AMERICAN SYSTEM

The American system uniquely focuses on the workplace, in contrast to European systems, which focus on the government.[1] Negotiations are predominantly limited to wages, hours, and working conditions, rather than attempts to run the company. Generally, only management and unions participate directly in the collective bargaining process; nonunionized employees, the government, and the public have only indirect input. Negotiations are adversarial and depend upon a balance of countervailing power.

  The goal of the union is to attain for the employees by collective power what they could not get on their own. Conflict and coercion are apparent everywhere. Benefits received are not freely given. Negotiations are conducted under the threat of increased costs resulting from strikes or lockouts, while grievances are resolved in arbitration proceedings declaring winners and losers. Demands made are settled by compromises and tradeoffs, rather than by searching for consensus. Union input is restricted to a limited area, while management jealously guards its prerogatives—areas of concern on which employee input will not be accepted.

Although unions directly represent only about one-fifth of the workforce, it is fair to include much of the remaining 80 percent in the industrial relations system. Nonunion employers may modify their behavior toward employees and adjust upward the benefits they pay in attempts to remain nonunion. In many instances, nonunion employees exert countervailing power by their implicit threat to form a union. The resulting changes in behavior are known as "spillover effects."[2]

Proponents of this system often claim it is cooperative because it provides a mechanism other than violence for resolving differences. Opponents argue that that is still somewhat short of true cooperation.

The limitation of bargaining to a two-party negotiation restricted to wages, hours, and working conditions was a conscious choice. The limited role of the government to represent the public in negotiations is consistent with our belief in laissez faire—at least, to the extent possible. The parties are free to negotiate whatever they wish, so long as it does not violate the law. The government does not prescribe the outcome. The system is based on the assumption that productivity will be maximized and cost minimized by the competitive pressures of the marketplace and that this mechanism will best serve the needs of the public as a whole. In important instances, however, this assumption may not hold true. Worse yet, the situation may be deteriorating rather than improving.

In some instances, large national unions bargaining with large oligopolistic employers have been able to "take wages out of competition." When a national union that represents all the major employers in an industry is able to impose the same wage burden on all the competitors, the employers are under less pressure to reduce costs or improve productivity. This holds true if there are no competitors outside the arrangement and the public will still buy the product.[3]

While this is a limited set of circumstances, it is a particularly important one. It applies to many of our largest, richest, most powerful, most troubled companies and their unions. This subset of manufacturers is arguably the particular group for whom our modern industrial relations system was designed.[4] These manufacturers also arguably affect the economic health of our entire nation through their impact on inflation, employment, productivity, and the ability to cope with foreign competition.

These industries have been the economic backbone of post-World War II America. It was historically believed that what was good for them was good for the country.[5] They have been characterized as high-paying (for the skill levels involved) but also, in some instances, as inefficient.[6] The inefficiency was sometimes attributed to a lack of economic incentive to resist wage demands or to establish efficient work rules. So long as one's only competitors were saddled with a similar burden, what need was there to improve?

The negotiation of work rules is a peculiarly American phenomenon. More than anywhere else, American collective bargaining focuses on job descriptions and workload—what is to be done and how much of it. While placing these agreements in the contract is a great protection to workers, it may also severely limit management's ability to cope with either planned or unplanned changes. Instead of doing what needs to be done at the moment, the contract compels doing what was required at the time of negotiation. The faster the work environment changes, the more difficult this is to live with. Nonunion employers often enjoy a large advantage in flexibility.[7]

It is exactly this deliberate constraint of bargaining issues to wages and work assignments that has made our labor relations both most proud historically and most attacked now. It has been argued by many that our labor relations system was created and nurtured for a particular type of industry—mass production manufacturing—and that that type of industry is no longer appropriate.[8] Furthermore, it is often alleged that the current labor relations system exacerbates the problem by making manufacturing too expensive, too inefficient, and too resistant to change.[9] Those who support these criticisms cite our labor relations system as a chief reason for our diminished capacity to resist foreign competition and for a transference of jobs from the union to nonunion sectors, both in type of production and in location. Allegations of this type have led many observers to question whether the system of post-Great Depression labor relations is appropriate in an arguably post-mass production manufacturing economy.[10] As the subject is developed in the remainder of the book, it will be up to the readers to determine for themselves the extent to which these allegations provide a convincing argument.

EUROPEAN SYSTEM

Our system is not the only labor relations model. Much can be learned about American labor relations by discovering what it is not. Labor-management relations in most of the Free World follow one basic model. The American system is an exception to that model.

While American labor relations focus on jobs and employers, those of Europeans focus on society and government. Although American unions do concern themselves with politics and European unions do concern themselves with collective bargaining, the two essentially have their priorities reversed. This outcome is attributable to cultural differences.[11]

Europe has a labor "movement." Today, the United States has no real equivalent.[12] The labor movement represents the interests of the working class in politics, employment, and society. The political thrust is much more direct than in the United States. In the United States, unions lobby for favorable rules for bargaining and occasional protection against cheap competition through tariffs, quotas, and minimum wage laws, and only occasionally for classwide social issues. In Europe, the Labor Party (or Parties) lobby for direct benefits for their constituents in the form of tax redistribution, socialized medicine, and nationalization of floundering companies. They also historically lobbied their governments for reform of society.[13]

Europe historically had a quite rigid class structure with significant barriers to upward mobility. The United States, on the other hand, prided itself on being the "land of opportunity"—the home of the "self-made man." It was useless to preach to a European worker to make something of himself when the system would not permit him to do so. These cultural and legal barriers arose from the feudal hierarchy of the Middle Ages and served to identify workers as a class.[14] Since the class members could not be expected to better themselves through individual initiative (since they were not allowed to), it made sense to attempt reform to benefit the entire class, rather than to attempt improvement through individual efforts. Hence, European workers readily joined unions because it was in no way a symbol of personal inadequacy. Americans, on the other hand, joined only when it became apparent that self-reliance would not succeed.

The European class-structured society, which originated in the feudal era and lasted until roughly World War I, in many ways disadvantaged working people. Besides having unequal voting rights and educational opportunity, workers were historically discriminated against in many ways not known in the United States. Not only were they not permitted in private clubs, but often they were not permitted in certain public theaters. They had to carry the equivalent of passports with their work record on them and were subject to police harassment. The response was to form their own counterculture with their own schools, night clubs, concert halls, and picnic grounds.[15] Working-class families worked together and they socialized together. They developed a class identification and loyalty. They harbored no realistic ambition of success in their own countries because their status at birth would not permit it. Getting a better job could not be a solution to the problem. Not surprisingly, they readily identified themselves as a group and attempted to gain influence over their government, not their employers, to enhance their benefits and eradicate the vestiges of class discrimination. Not inconsequentially, the belief that the government is their provider of benefits sometimes allows Europeans to show remarkably little concern for the prosperity of their employers.

Americans, on the other hand, have never identified themselves as members of a social class. The belief in upward mobility, no matter how unlikely for workers, could always be used as an excuse by the "haves" to justify the position of the "have-nots." Since wealth was supposedly acquired by merit rather than by birth (and this was certainly much more true in the United States than in Europe), Americans had more difficulty identifying with a working class. Being in the class might only be temporary and, besides, it was "your own fault." However simplistic the sociology behind this value system might have been, it was widely held. When American workers felt disadvantaged socially and legally, they approached their government individually as citizens, rather than as a class of workers. The pluralistic, pragmatic political parties of the United States adopted the demands of all groups and offered reform in small doses. As such, American workers never developed much of a governmental or social identity. They were workers only while at work, and for those limited purposes unions were to address only the "bread-and-butter" issues.

JAPANESE SYSTEM

A third system of collective bargaining has received much publicity in the 1980s—the Japanese. The rise of Japan's economy from the devastation of World War II has been admired by all industrialized nations. Many factors besides labor relations contributed to that success. Among them were the opportunity to start with all new capital investment; a favorable governmental policy on competition, foreign trade, and support of business; and a managerial emphasis on quality and long-term results. These features all played prominent roles in the resurgence of Japan, but the feature most popularized with the American public was labor relations.

The Japanese labor relations system is vastly different from either the American or the European model. Its most salient feature is that it is based on cooperation, rather than conflict. That cannot be said of either of the others. In the stereotypical Japanese manufacturing firm, workers are involved in local decision making and quality control. Employees are perceived as dedicated to the enterprise, diligent, and, most importantly, important in their own right. Their enthusiasm for the task is one reason for their high productivity. Their good attitudes contribute to high quantity and quality. Furthermore, they identify with the firm, rather than with their particular job (which is only part of the firm). This allows them to cooperate in efforts to be trained broadly and to switch rapidly from one position to another as production demands change. This is particularly valuable in a manufacturing world where production runs come more commonly in batches and less in long-run repetitions. The cooperative nature of the employee has also allowed the implementation of labor-saving automation without significant resistance from employees. (This feature may be a luxury of limited duration as Japan reaches the saturation of its markets and can no longer guarantee jobs to those displaced by machines.[16])

Within this system of cooperation, unions function mainly at the enterprise level and then as a channel of communication. They function to help keep employees and employers informed of each other's needs and to help reach consensus. If consensus cannot be reached, the employer generally prevails. Strikes are very rare. Confrontation is rare. In fact, conflict is apparently rare. It is clearly not the major purpose of the union to get for employees what they could not get on their own.

Many Americans, particularly employers, envy the Japanese system. They feel that American productivity would be enhanced if our workers pos-

JAPANESE EMPLOYEES PERFORMING ASSIGNED STRETCHING EXERCISES
ON BREAK TIME

SOURCE: AP/Wide World Photos

sessed the diligent and cooperative attitudes of Japanese employees. Undoubtedly, this is true, particularly in respect to diligence. (The value of cooperation
would be harder to prove, although its benefits from flexibility are clearly great.)
The problem is, those attitudes are not easily transportable. Calls for a rapid
conversion to cooperation, as if it were an attitude easily chosen and adopted,
are unrealistic.

Japanese employees and employers engage in cooperation partially because the system is compatible with their religion, philosophy, and culture but
mostly because the American military forced it upon them after World War II.
(This will be examined in more detail later in this chapter.) The Japanese reverence for family, honor, and organizations, coupled with an economic/polit-
ical/social need to add value to products in a nation with a large population and
few natural resources, leads individuals to pride themselves on how much they
can do to enhance the good name of their family and their employer. Since a
good name is achieved by subsuming oneself to the organization's goals, it is
not surprising that cooperation is widespread.

TABLE 2-1 GENERALIZED COMPARISONS OF THREE MAJOR SYSTEMS

Dimension	United States	Europe	Japan
Goals	Personal success	Class success	Company success
Loyalty	Self	Group	Organization
Focus	Job	Class	Company
Value	Efficiency	Preservation of group	Effectiveness
Decision-making authority	Authoritative	Political	Participative
Decision-making style	Confrontation	Consensus	Cooperation
Job mobility	High	Intermediate	Low
Society	Heterogeneous	Distinct classes	Homogeneous
Political value	Freedom and equality	Class dominance	Order and hierarchy

SOURCE: *Adapted from classroom materials of Professor Richard E. Dutton, University of South Florida.*

A synopsis comparing the American, European, and Japanese systems appears in Table 2–1.

THE CHANGING ENVIRONMENT

Has Labor Law Failed? Oversight Hearing on Question Is Scheduled

> A three-day oversight hearing will be devoted to the question of whether the nation's labor law has failed, William Clay, Chairman of the Labor-Management Relations Subcommittee of the House Committee on Education and Labor, announced. . . .
>
> In announcing the hearing, Congressman Clay noted that the "assertion has been made that there has been a collapse of the historic consensus forged by Congress in the 1930s when it passed the Wagner Act, a consensus that has served as the backbone of our system of labor-management relations and collective bargaining." Whether or not this system has failed and how it has failed will be addressed by the workers, academicians, and labor and management representatives scheduled to testify before the joint subcommittee.

SOURCE: *Reproduced with permission from LABOR LAW REPORTS Summary Letter No. 643 - Page 3, June 22, 1984, published and copyrighted by Commerce Clearing House, Inc., Chicago, Illinois 60646.*

Americans have been operating since 1935 under a set of assumptions and policies promoting collective bargaining and balanced countervailing power. The observations and value judgments expressed in Section 1 of the Wagner Act reveal the needs of the public as they appeared at that time:

> The inequality of bargaining power between the employees who do not possess full freedom of association or actual liberty of contract, and employers who are organized in the corporate or other forms of ownership association substantially

burdens and affects the flow of commerce, and tends to aggravate recurrent business depressions, by depressing wage rates and the purchasing power of wage earners in industry and by preventing the stabilization of competitive wage rates and working conditions within and between industries.

Experience has proven that protection by law of the right of employees to organize and bargain collectively safeguards commerce from injury, impairment, or interruption, and promotes the flow of commerce by removing certain recognized sources of industrial strife and unrest, by encouraging practices fundamental to the friendly adjustment of industrial disputes arising out of differences as to wages, hours, or other working conditions, and by restoring equality of bargaining power between employers and employees.

It is hereby declared to be the policy of the United States to eliminate the causes of certain substantial obstructions to the free flow of commerce and to mitigate and eliminate these obstructions when they have occurred by encouraging the practice and the procedure of collective bargaining and by protecting exercise by workers of full freedom of association, self-organization, and designation of representatives of their own choosing, for the purpose of negotiating the terms and conditions of their employment or other mutual aid or protection.

The 1980s are witnessing extensive short-term and long-term changes in work in America. The effect that these changes should and will have on the 50-year-old labor relations system is arguable, but there is little dispute as to their existence.

The short-term effects are largely political and are not fundamentally different from those in previous generations. Interpretations of laws and rules by the National Labor Relations Board and the federal court system often reflect the political preferences of the parties appointing their members and vacillate from pro-union to pro-management, depending on which party is in office. During the mid 1980s, Reagan appointees to the Board and to the Supreme Court issued many decisions and interpretations of the law which were pro-management. Democratic administrations seldom did so.

Also of a comparatively short-run nature are periods of economic prosperity and recession. Unions, and workers in general, historically have done better when labor supply is low and demand is high and have suffered when the reverse is true. The 1980s have experienced their share of economic fluctuation, with particular emphasis on recession. In fact, they produced an era of concession bargaining wherein unions gave up previously negotiated benefits—surely a short-term phenomenon. Still, economic fluctuations are not different from those in previous generations and would not raise concern for changing the labor relations system were it not for the suspicion that their economic causes are not cyclical but are instead permanent.

There are many indications in the 1980s of a permanently changed economy—one different from the manufacturing-based growth model of the post-World War II era. Changes are occurring in four major areas: (1) the markets that can be reached, (2) the method of producing goods and services, (3) the expectations of employees and employers, and (4) the role of the federal government.

Market Structure

Changing market structures are most noticeable in the declining growth rate of the domestic economy and the penetration of American markets by foreign competition, most notably Japanese. It is impossible to determine how severe and how permanent the reduced growth rate will be in the future. Past predictors were often terribly off-target in size and sometimes even in direction. Still, the petroleum shortages of the 1970s highlighted a current dependence on fossil fuels that affected not only consumption but also international banking and international affairs. Whether dependence on fossil fuels will be overcome remains to be seen. In the meantime, absolute growth will be harder to achieve for producers everywhere.

Of a more certain concern is the disappearing advantage of American technology. Prior to the 1980s, American productivity was extremely high by world standards, despite the absolutely high cost of labor in America. The United States could pay high wages and still sell its products competitively because our technology and managerial organization were vastly superior to those of the rest of the world. High wages could be tolerated because they were returned to the system in the form of increased purchases of American goods and services and because foreign products were either unavailable, inadequate, or comparatively expensive (despite lower labor costs) because of the lack of efficient technology. With the advent of increased dispersion of knowledge and communications throughout the industrialized world, American technological advantage is greatly reduced. This does not reflect a degeneration of America, but rather an increase in foreign capability. We can still be doing as well as in the past—or even better—but foreign producers backed by improved technology and aided by lower labor costs and governmental support can now compete better in their domestic economies and penetrate the American market. From a consumer standpoint, that is good news. From an employer or employee standpoint, however, that is bad news. American corporate sales may be less, both foreign and domestic. That could mean fewer dividends for stockholders, lower bonuses for managers, fewer and lower-paying jobs for employees, and a lot more strain on a labor relations system that did not anticipate a nongrowth economy. If American employers are to compete with a reduced technological advantage, they must reduce other costs and improve the desirability of their products.

Method of Production

Changes in the method of producing goods has had and will have a significant effect on employment patterns and practices. Unionization has been strong in the smokestack industries since the passage of the Wagner Act in 1935 and comparatively less strong in the service sector, which is largely white collar. Yet these highly unionized large manufacturing concerns for which our modern model of labor relations was largely constructed are experiencing long-range hard times. Some of this is probably caused by the American commitment to high wages and occasionally by restrictive work rules. The result is a perception that unionization increases cost and reduces flexibility. The remedy has been to try to escape its effects.

One way employers have tried to avoid the effects of unionization has been to avoid employment altogether. This has led to a continued effort to automate, with particular recent emphasis on robotics. As fewer people produce more goods, jobs are lost in the manufacturing sector. The result is a demise in traditional blue collar employment. The second method of coping with allegedly inappropriate unionization is to transfer the job to nonunion employees. This can be accomplished by subcontracting or by establishing employment in an area where a union will not organize the employees. This has traditionally meant in less urban areas or in the South. A third method of coping with the perceived high cost of unionization is to attempt to bargain with the union to be more "reasonable" in its demands. The extent to which this is successful depends largely on current economic conditions and on past experiences with management. As will be elaborated in Chapters 3 and 8, American union leaders are typically responsive to employer needs when those needs can be proven. The problem is made tougher if the employees have had reasons in the past not to believe all of management's claims.

Personal Expectations

The third major change in the environment is in the expectations people bring to the workplace. This applies to both employees and managers. The population as a whole is becoming more educated. More women have entered the workforce. The growth areas for employment are in the service sector. This means most of the jobs of the future will be white collar. Whether they will be challenging, satisfying, provide opportunity, and/or pay well remains to be seen. They will certainly not be, however, in areas in which unions have succeeded in the past. In the past, unions have had trouble organizing women, the highly educated, and white collar employees. Highly educated employees, in particular, might find bread-and-butter unionism addressing issues they can handle for themselves (pay and working conditions) and ignoring issues important to them (such as input and satisfaction). It is often alleged that employees now entering the workforce are demanding and expecting more intrinsic satisfaction from their jobs than their predecessors did, and that the traditional adversarial collective bargaining system is not designed to produce such results.

Changes in management attitudes and behavior are also challenging the traditional system. More and more employers are adopting more cooperative attitudes with subordinates at all levels. At the rank-and-file level, the solicitation of input, joint problem solving, and grievance procedures have become more widespread. While this change is partly aimed at keeping unions out, it is also believed by many managers (particularly young ones) to be good business in its own right. Certainly the Robber Baron mentality of previous generations that helped justify the organization of labor as a countervailing power group is less prevalent now than before.

Finally, many employee benefits such as pension protection, safety, and freedom from discrimination are being provided as a matter of law, reducing the need for employees to fight for them. Such legal requirements also lead employees to expect more from their jobs than did their predecessors.

Governmental Practices

A final challenge to our traditional labor relations system remains. It is the federal government's practice of bailing out large companies facing bankruptcy. The highly publicized aid requested by and/or granted the Penn Central Railroad, Lockheed Aircraft, New York City, and Chrysler Corporation all could be seen as providing examples to hourly employees that their jobs do not depend upon the profitability of their employer, but that the government will subsidize whatever inefficiencies exist within such organizations. This is particularly crucial in the United States, since our system presumes wages will be regulated by competitive pressure. Without having to depend upon employer profitability, employees need not show restraint. They could bankrupt their employer and still have a job—regardless of their cost. The result would be that the burden of providing for their needs would be transferred from the individual and his or her union to society and its government. While this is common in Europe, particularly in Great Britain, it would require a very different system in the United States. If the society as a whole were to accept the burdens of the cost of employment, the quasi laissez-faire system we have now would be inappropriate. Market pressures could not be assumed to regulate costs. Instead, the public would have to be represented in tripartite bargaining or outright political decision making. This is so foreign to traditional American values that no serious power group has ever dared suggest it. Certainly few would prefer it. The extent to which rank-and-file American employees have lost sight of the need for employer competitiveness is difficult to determine, but to whatever extent it exists, it strains the traditional labor relations system.

COOPERATION—AN ALTERNATIVE
TO COLLECTIVE BARGAINING

The conflict orientation of traditional collective bargaining has come under severe attack from outsiders during the 1980s. Many observers wish that something akin to the Japanese spirit of cooperation could become widespread in the United States. Actually, the United States does have substantial experience with cooperation in limited circumstances, both in the past and in the present. The current cooperative American system suggested as an alternative to collective bargaining does not have a particular form. Rather, it is a philosophy of and approach to decision making. It claims that the adversarial decision-making process creates many bad side effects. By parties competing for portions of a limited resource such as corporate income, what one gains the other loses. This can lead to hard feelings, inequitable distributions based on power rather than merit, and the conviction that the other party's interest is in opposition to yours. It certainly does not inspire trust or cooperation. Besides, it does not increase the size of the pie.

The distribution of limited resources among competing parties has been labelled a zero-sum game. Many observers claim that this may be less than an optimal system. Instead, they suggest focusing on ways to increase the size of the resource available so that all parties can benefit—presumably in their original proportions. The way to increase the value of the resource, they claim, is through cooperation.

In a business setting this would require involving hourly employees in decisions traditionally reserved for management. This is justified on the theory that such employees can make valuable contributions not previously realized by management. It also involves the employees more personally in the operation of the organization. This is supposed to result in greater productivity through reduced absenteeism, turnover, and scrap and in improved quality and quantity because of greater concern.

Many observers feel that only through a system such as this can Americans make quality products that are price competitive in a world of international markets. They fear that traditional reliance on high-wage concerns by unions and short-term bonuses for managers will lead to decisions not in the best interests of the parties or of the economy as a whole.

Scholars of organizational behavior have long lamented the American reliance on confrontation and countervailing power. They have instead urged cooperative decision making.[17] They have stressed employee input and mutual awareness of responsibility for outcomes. Rather than assign responsibility for employee benefits to unions and responsibility for profits to management, they would jointly make everyone responsible for everything. They claim this would not only be more satisfying to employees, it would be more productive and profitable for the company. In short, everyone would win. To back up their contentions they cite theories and case studies of varying degrees of persuasiveness.

Prior to the 1980s, the American business world was slow to adopt these notions. Skeptics claimed that the theory was hopelessly idealistic and would not work under "normal" conditions. Conditions became abnormal, however, during the eighties. For the first time in modern history America was afraid of being passed by the competition. For one of the few times in modern history, Americans asked how they went wrong and how they could do better. The example of the Japanese participative management style and cooperative workforce could not be ignored. The media called for American business and labor to abandon their adversarial posture and to join together in a cooperative effort to improve productivity, quality, and morale.

Given the vested interests of the union and management leaders in confrontation, and the historic success of the conflict-oriented system, it is not surprising that the United States has been slow to adopt cooperation. In fact, it appears that it will move from its confrontational stance only if forced to by outside competition. As long as all American competitors were ineffective in equal proportions under confrontation, market shares could be preserved and no one looked bad in performance-appraisal audits.

The United States experimented extensively with cooperation in the form of shop or works councils in the early 1900s. With the advent of World War I, the federal government imposed cooperative schemes upon many nationally important industries. In the 1920s these arrangements were repudiated by management and replaced with paternalism and company unions. As will be elaborated upon in Chapter 3, management regarded such an arrangement as intruding on rights that should be reserved solely for itself. One of the consequences of this managerially imposed differentiation of roles is the belief of many rank-and-file employees that profits are the responsibility solely of management. When employees are told their input is not welcome and when the company keeps secret its records on profitability, such a belief is not an irrational position. This arrangement—typical of the traditional system—makes it very hard to put moral pressure on employees to be concerned about outcomes on which they are not permitted input.

Although the practice of cooperation effectively died in America in the 1920s and was formally replaced with adversarial collective bargaining in the 1930s, Americans carried the idea elsewhere. In the post-World War II era, British and American armies of occupation were charged with rebuilding the economies of Germany and Japan. Allied advisors, cognizant of the experiences of the early 1900s and equipped with great power and an opportunity to start from the beginning, imposed cooperative models on Germany and Japan because it seemed like a good idea. The Germans had experienced cooperation before the war and adapted readily. The Japanese, surprisingly, had not had significant prior experience with cooperation in the business world. In fact, their history had been one of class confrontation. They were in no position, however, to resist, nor did they wish to (their last system had ended up costing them a great deal), and they also adopted the system. Obviously, it worked well for both of them.

LIKELIHOOD OF CHANGE

The first step in solving a problem is to realize that it exists. Our current labor relations system is certainly not beyond this stage. There are those who say that the impending changes are not fundamentally different from changes in the past and that the current system will muddle through because "It always has." Conspicuous believers in this position often are established professionals in the field. Surveys of high-level executives with labor relations responsibilities and high-level union officers often indicate a belief that current concerns with change are overdrawn and short-term and that things will return to normal in the future. Of course, the people holding tenaciously to these views are the prime beneficiaries of the traditional model, and this may bias their insights significantly.

Those who believe the future will require significant adjustments in labor relations often come from outside the practitioner ranks. This group is spearheaded by media reporters and editorialists, academics, and the American public. This is a group whose concern is presumably based less on self-interest and more on a concern for society as a whole.

The practitioners accuse the outsiders of ignorance of the situation and an overattention to atypical details. The commentators accuse the practitioners of tunnel vision and failing to learn new tricks. Practitioners cite media "mistakes" in analysis in the past in such areas as overconcern for the "blue collar blues." Commentators question the practitioners' occasional inability to see what others saw coming, citing as an example the plight of the auto industry. Which of these schools of observers will be correct—or what the blend of correctness will be between them—remains for the author and the readers to discover as the events of the future unfold.

Notes

1. Everett M. Kassalow, *Trade Unions and Industrial Relations: An International Comparison* (New York: Random House, 1969), chap. 1.
2. For an explanation of both positive and negative spillover effects, see Alan Balfour, "More Evidence That Unions Do Not Cause Higher Salaries for Teachers," *Journal of Collective Negotiations*, Vol. 3, No. 4 (Fall 1974).
3. Gordon T. Bloom and Herbert R. Northrup, *Economics of Labor Relations*, 9th ed. (Homewood, Ill.: Richard D. Irwin, Inc., 1981), p. 397.
4. Michael J. Piore, "Can the American Labor Movement Survive Re-Gomperization?" *Proceedings of the Thirty-fifth Annual Meeting, Industrial Relations Research Association* (Madison, Wis., 1983), pp. 34–37.
5. In the oft-quoted words of a General Motors President, "What's good for General Motors is good for America," and of Calvin Coolidge, "The business of America is business."
6. For an assessment on the conflicting evidence of unions' effects on efficiency, see Derek C. Bok and John T. Dunlop, *Labor and the American Community* (New York: Simon and Schuster, 1970), p. 270.
7. Obviously, contracts can be negotiated to attempt to preserve flexibility for management. Still, the very need to negotiate such flexibility, and perhaps without receiving it, is a limitation not placed on nonunion employers.
8. Piore, pp. 34–37.
9. Piore, pp. 34–37.

10. Piore, pp. 34–37.
11. Kassalow, pp. 7–10, p. 21.
12. Kassalow, pp. 7–10.
13. Kassalow, p. 14.
14. Kassalow, p. 8.
15. Kassalow, p. 10.
16. Jared Taylor, *Shadows of the Rising Sun: A Critical View of the Japanese Miracle* (New York: William Morrow, 1983), pp. 296–97.
17. Thomas A. Kochan and Michael J. Piore, "Will the New Industrial Relations Last? Implications for the American Labor Movement," *The Annals,* May 1984, p. 177.

Discussion Questions

1. Discuss the central characteristics of the American system.
2. Discuss the central characteristics of the European system.
3. Discuss the central characteristics of the Japanese system.
4. Analyze the ways in which the American system is being subjected to change.
5. Assess the philosophy of cooperation.
6. Why is cooperation uncommon in the United States? What is the likelihood of change?

Statements for Comment

1. "For such a small percentage of the labor force being unionized, Americans sure take collective bargaining seriously."
2. "The public is at the mercy of big companies and big unions. They can let the public be damned and get away with it."
3. "Marketplace pressures are a myth in much of American business. We don't have competition, we have collusion."
4. "The Japanese auto manufacturers certainly messed up a nice arrangement in Detroit."
5. "What's good for business is good for the country."
6. "American attention given to work rules was never a great idea, but we could live with it in the 40s and 50s. We won't be able to in the 80s and 90s."
7. "British auto workers didn't care if their employers went bankrupt. Let's hope American workers never feel that way."
8. "The Golden Era of Japanese labor relations will soon be ending. By the year 2000, they will have the same problems as America."
9. "The domination of the United States in world economics is over and will never return. The continued growth of the past is no longer possible."
10. "Treating employees well is good business."

11. ''Government bailouts of failing companies can have disastrous side effects. It should never be done.''
12. ''There is nothing wrong with American productivity that cooperation won't cure.''
13. ''It's management's job to make profits and it's the union's job to take care of the employees.''
14. ''Tomorrow will be different from yesterday. Labor relations will be facing their greatest challenge in decades.''
15. ''The more things change, the more they stay the same.''
16. ''Henry Ford's biggest contribution to American management wasn't the popularization of the assembly line, it was the realization that well-paid employees make good consumers.''

Situations

Case 2–1 In 1928 Selig Perlman, an early labor scholar, asserted in *A Theory of the Labor Movement* that:

> *The manual worker is convinced by experience that he is living in a world of limited opportunity; the businessman is an eternal optimist, sure that the world is full of opportunity. The former is not confident of driving a good bargain on his own, so he favors social control of opportunities; the businessman, of course, feels that he can drive a good bargain individually and so favors a ''laissez faire'' climate in which to operate. Unionism first became a stabilized movement in America only when the abundance consciousness of the pioneer days had been replaced in the mind of labor by a scarcity consciousness—the consciousness of job scarcity.*

Yesterday Bill Sherman and Dick Nash were imbibing after work at a local watering hole. Bill said that Perlman's observations show clearly the difference between workers and managers in America. Dick said he wasn't so sure and that maybe workers were more optimistic than Perlman realized.
What do you think?

Case 2–2 During a dream, whose causes you can't quite remember, you believe that you are President of the United States. You believe it is your duty to recommend the best possible policies for the country, all things considered. You are very concerned about the economy. Japanese imports have been taking an increasing share of the American market, resulting in layoffs in several key industries. Partisan lobbyists are urging you to do the following things:

Impose tariffs and quotas on imports

Not impose tariffs and quotas on imports

Subsidize American industry through tax breaks

Protect American jobs

Teach unions and management a lesson

Consider the plight of the "little man"

Remember "free enterprise"

Remember "free trade"

None of the above

What should you do? Why? How would it affect employers? Employees? Unions? Customers?

Case 2–3 Gil Prysbycki has been a unionized hourly worker in a steel mill in Pittsburgh for 25 years. Lately, times have been tough. Some mills in the area have closed altogether, and all have experienced layoffs. Only his extensive seniority has kept him working.

Gil's daughter Marie is a college student pursuing a degree in business administration. While home on summer vacation Marie tells Gil what she is learning about labor unions, costs, and international trade. Marie says that business is bad in Pittsburgh because steel costs too much to make there, both because the plants use outdated technology and because unionized work rules make the labor force less efficient. Therefore, sales are being lost to foreign producers (Japan, Sweden, and Germany) and to nonunion American firms in the South, whose production costs are lower. Unionized steel producers are so discouraged about the future, according to Marie, that they are investing company funds in real estate and resorts instead of the steel business because the rate of return promises to be better. Marie claims that unless the United Steel Workers take wage cuts and allow management to assign the workforce more efficiently (which will result in a loss of still more jobs), there will be no jobs at all.

Gil is distraught. He loves his daughter, no matter how great a heretic she may be. Also, he realizes while there may be truth in what Marie is saying, it is just not the "whole truth." Gil feels that Marie's views do not take into consideration other important points. For instance, without the protection of the union, steel workers were certainly abused by their employers in the past. He is not so sure the same thing wouldn't happen again if the unions were "weakened." Also, he's doing the same things now that he did 25 years ago when the company was making record profits. He can't help but feel that this is somehow the government's fault and the American workers ought not to have to lower their standard of living to that of lower-paid foreigners. He feels Americans should buy American products and preserve American jobs.

What advice can you offer in the name of Truth? Justice? Family Harmony?

Case 2–4 Irwin Daugherty, an American executive, is returning from a business meeting in Japan. Waiting for his plane in Haneta Airport, Tokyo, he strikes up a conversation with Carla Stafford, a 21-year-old American student returning from a visit to see her father, an Army sergeant stationed in Japan. The two comment on how different the Tokyo airport is from American airports.

Irwin (call me "Irv") points out how cooperative and efficient all employees are. He notes how the clerks behind the check-in counter run the two steps between the counter and the conveyor belt to load luggage to keep the line (which is a lengthy one) moving as quickly as possible. He also points out that the Tokyo subway runs exactly on time—to the minute. He says he sure wishes America could be more like Japan.

Carla says she's not sure it would be a good idea. She said it gives her the "creeps" to see everyone dressing and acting alike and to be squashed together like the lines in the airport, where the people stand so close that their shoulders touch people in the lines on either side and they are literally in contact with the person in front of and behind them. Besides, she says, they keep the subways on time by herding people on and wedging them in with sticks so the door will close. Finally, she says, "I don't know why they work that hard. It can't be fun to live like this."

Do you think we should become more like Japan?

Case 2-5 Kathy Puglisi is a teller for a large bank in Los Angeles. She graduated from college two years ago with a degree in business administration and sought a position as a management trainee. However, a depressed job market and a surplus of college graduates forced her to take her current position—one she could have had straight out of high school. So far she has rationalized her discouragement by observing that her best friend from college has two jobs—one as a clerk, the other as a waitress. Kathy at least has believed that her job has responsibility and opportunity.

Lately she has been less sure. There are 20 other tellers in her bank. They are almost all college graduates who are being paid substantially less than they had hoped to earn but who have aspirations of promotion to management. Unfortunately, as she has observed, very few ever are promoted. The employer keeps introducing new technology that seems to allow managers to function with fewer supporting staff. Perceptively and realistically she realizes this job is taking her nowhere. Worse yet, it's a pretty poor job currently. Working conditions are fine, but the job is boring, no one shows tellers any respect, and she feels lost on a personal basis.

Yesterday, she read in the newspaper that unionized grocery-store cashiers are making $6000 per year more than she. She feels outraged and repulsed. She considers her skills and training to be superior to a cashier's and feels that it "isn't fair."

What would you recommend Kathy do about her situation? What are the good points of your recommendation? What are the bad?

Case 2-6 While perusing a current issue of one of the national news magazines, David Cohen commented that our labor relations system was certainly undergoing a dramatic period of change. His friend Billy Bob Schwartz said that he felt that the claims of a changing environment were overdrawn.

Whom do you side with? What evidence supports your position?

Case 2-7 Both Democratic and Republican presidents have "bailed out" troubled enterprises in recent years. The author of this text has indicated that such behavior might be setting a bad labor relations example.

If you were president, would you bail out a large, unionized employer if it genuinely needed it? Why or why not?

Bibliography of Related Readings

"An Aging Work Force Strains Japan's Traditions," *Business Week*, April 20, 1981, p. 72.

Anderson, J., and M. Gundarson, *Union-Management Relations in Canada* (Don Mills, Ont.: Addison-Wesley [Canada] Ltd., 1982).

Blumberg, Paul, *Inequality in an Age of Decline* (New York: Oxford University Press, 1980).

Clegg, H. A., *The Changing System of Industrial Relations in Great Britain* (Oxford: Blackwell, 1979).

Cole, R. E., *Work, Mobility, and Participation: A Comparative Study of American and Japanese Industry* (Berkeley: University of California Press, 1979).

Cordova, E., "Workers' Participation in Decisions Within Enterprises: Recent Trends and Problems," *International Labor Review*, 1982, pp. 125–40.

Dickson, J. W., "Top Managers' Beliefs and Rationales For Participation," *Human Relations*, March 1982, pp. 203–17.

Guzda, Henry P., "Industrial Democracy: Made in the U.S.A.," *Monthly Labor Review*, May 1984, pp. 26–33.

Hanami, T., *Labor Relations In Japan Today* (New York: Harper and Row, 1979).

Industrial Democracy in Europe International Research Groups, eds., *European Industrial Relations* (Fair Lawn, N.J.: Oxford University Press, 1981).

Jain, H. C., "Workers' Participation Versus Management Control," *Journal of Contemporary Business*, 1980, pp. 137–52.

Kassalow, Everett M., *Trade Unions and Industrial Relations: An International Comparison* (New York: Random House, 1969).

Mroczkowski, T., "Japanese and European Systems of Industrial Relations—Which Model Is More Applicable for the U.S.?" *Industrial Management (United States)*, 1983, pp. 26–31.

Parker, P., "Industrial Relations in the USA: A British View," *Department Employee Gazette*, December 1979, pp. 1229–33.

Piore, Michael J., "Can the American Labor Movement Survive Re-Gomperization?" *Proceedings of the Thirty-Fifth Annual Meeting, Industrial Relations Research Association* (Madison, Wis., 1983).

Roberts, B. C., "Industrial Relations in Europe: Trends and Issues, Part I," *Personnel Journal*, September 1979, pp. 635–36.

Roberts, B. C., "Industrial Relations in Europe: Trends and Issues," *Personnel Journal*, October 1979, pp. 715–17.

Schienstock, G., "Towards a Theory of Industrial Relations," *British Journal of Industrial Relations,* 1981, pp. 179–89.

Sloane, Arthur A., and Fred Witney, *Labor Relations,* 4th ed., "Concluding Statement" (Englewood Cliffs, N.J.: Prentice-Hall, 1981).

Toffler, Alvin, *Future Shock* (New York: Random House, 1980).

Yoder, D., and P. D. Staudohar, "Rethinking the Role of Collective Bargaining," *Labor Law Journal,* May 1983, pp. 311–16.

Yoder, D., and P. D. Staudohar, "Assessing the Decline of Unions in the U.S.," *Personnel Administrator,* October 1982, p. 12.

THREE

DEVELOPMENT OF THE SYSTEM:

Historical American Values

In the eighteenth century there were no unions in America, nor was there a need for any. The perceived need for unionization developed during the nineteenth century—the Age of Industrialization. Prior to that time, employment in the colonial era was characterized by the "cottage industry" (see Figure 3–1). The typical work relationship consisted of master and apprentice. The arrangement was mutually beneficial and based on comparatively even bargaining power. The master was able to utilize the labor of his apprentices while they, in turn, acquired a skilled trade.

From an employee's standpoint, this was in many respects a golden era. Many needs that are difficult to meet in the twentieth century were well attended to then, and almost every condition in the eighteenth century was better than in the nineteenth century. The apprentice typically lived in the house of the master and shared his dinner table. Obviously, the employment relationship was close and personal. Products were often made from start to finish by one worker. Pride in workmanship and individual input and control were easily attainable. Financially, pay levels were the highest in the world, and an abundance of natural resources, coupled with a growing population, assured demand for products.[1] Job security was further enhanced by legislation protecting the rights of apprentices and by the irreplaceability of rare skills. Best of all, the apprentice could reasonably look forward to the day when he would become a

FIGURE 3-1 DEVELOPMENT OF THE AMERICAN LABOR RELATIONS SYSTEM CONFLICT RESOLUTION VALUES AND MECHANISMS

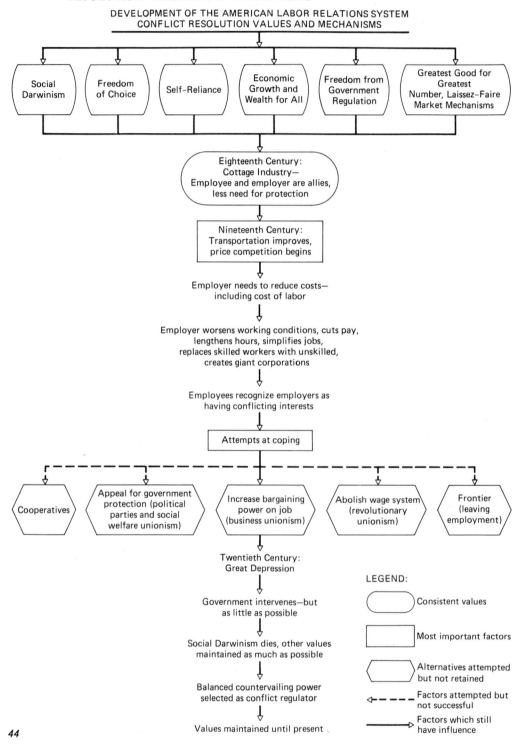

master and open his own shop. Whatever economic or social distance he might have felt from his employer was not only small, it was temporary. Under such conditions, employees had to believe they were doing adequately on their jobs and perceived no need for unions.

ORIGIN OF THE PROBLEM—PRICE COMPETITION

The nineteenth century destroyed much of this earlier satisfaction with employment in America. The problem was caused by the advent of price competition. In the colonial era, products were sold locally. Customers seldom had the opportunity to choose among suppliers. They were probably happy if they had any supplier at all. Improvements in transportation, however, drastically changed that situation.

As canals and roads were developed, it became possible to produce goods in one city and ship them to another for sale. When purchasers were given a choice of competitive products, all other things being equal, they chose the cheaper one. For employees, life has never been the same since. With price now becoming a more important determinant in sales, employers came under great pressure to reduce costs. One of the costs they sought to reduce was, of course, the cost of labor.

The desire to cut costs and improve efficiency began a transition to an entirely different world of employment. Despite the resistance of craftsmen and apprentices, job simplification was introduced. Instead of the satisfaction of making an entire product, the employee now often made only a small part. This task was not only less satisfying emotionally, it was a terrible setback economically. The assembly of interchangeable parts allowed the substitution of unskilled labor for skilled. That meant that women, children, immigrants, and convicts could replace the traditional male breadwinner of the time. Not only could these cheaper sources of labor replace many men, they competitively reduced wage rates for those still employed. Furthermore, employers lengthened hours and worsened working conditions at the same time they reduced pay.[2]

The new methods of manufacturing completely changed the employment relationship. Work was performed in factories and "sweat shops."[3] Employees no longer lived with their employer. On their meager incomes they moved into the cheapest housing possible. Slums arose, while owners lived in mansions on the other side of the tracks. Absentee owners hired professional managers to run their enterprises. Not only had a tremendous gap developed between employers and employees; it became apparent that employees were no longer likely to bridge that gap. An employee's dreams of one day owning his own company became much more unrealistic. For the great majority, the goal became survival. Employees could no longer say they were doing OK on their jobs.

TWENTIETH CENTURY CHILD LABOR IN AMERICAN FACTORY

SOURCE: *National Archives*

MARCH 25, 1911—LABOR'S DAY OF INFAMY

March 25th, 1981 will mark the 70th anniversary of the infamous Triangle Shirtwaist Fire.

Occupying three floors in a multi-storied loft building in New York City, a sweatshop garment firm had a fire break out that day on the eighth floor. Flames swept upward engulfing the three top floors which housed the sweatshop operation.

The exit doors were locked. Not closed, but locked. Two other doors that opened inward were soon rendered useless by piles of screaming and choking bodies stacked up behind the doors.

One hundred and forty six workers, nearly all of them young girls, many the children of immigrants, lost their lives in one of the worst tragedies in the scarred history of

American labor. They died in the burning building, or they died in desperate, panic-stricken leaps from the ninth floor to the ground.

The social conscience of the people was, of course, aroused, notably that of Frances J. Perkins who was later to become Secretary of Labor under President Franklin D. Roosevelt—the first woman cabinet member. Ms. Perkins watched the holocaust and ever after dedicated her life to promoting industrial safety.

The absolute horror of that fire is heightened by the fact that exit doors could have saved most or all of those lives. They had been locked deliberately, however, by the operators of the sweatshop to keep the victims locked into their workplaces. Management apparently feared that workers might have wandered between floors, possibly affecting the ill-earned profits of these exploiters of labor.

SOURCE: *Ben Zemsky, APWU Organization Director,* American Postal Worker, *March 1981, p. 17.*

By the late 1800s, the dream of becoming one's own employer was being lost as giant corporations became prominent employers. Ambition and talent were no longer sufficient to start a business. Now capital was required. Competition was truly ruthless. Equality of bargaining power between employer and employee became a myth. The worker needed the job much more than the employer needed any particular employee. The need to reduce labor cost had made the employer undisputably an enemy. The new form of corporate ownership made this enemy a powerful one. As workers watched their conditions worsen continually during the 1800s, many began to believe that the "invisible hand" of free enterprise was really a clenched fist.

An example of how badly working conditions had deteriorated is presented in the accompanying illustration, "Life in a Nineteenth-Century Coal Mine."

LIFE IN A NINETEENTH-CENTURY COAL MINE

Clarence Darrow is best remembered in American history as the lawyer for the defense in the Scopes Monkey Trial. He was, however, also an early champion of organized labor and human rights. These concerns were epitomized in the following scene from the Tony Award-winning production, *Clarence Darrow: A One-Man Play.* The scene captures the extremes to which unfettered capitalism ran.

(Entering the courtroom) In the whole country no one has it worse than the Pennsylvania coal miners. Men who work underground in twelve-hour shifts, 365 days a year, without Thanksgiving or Christmas off. Men whose ten-year-old daughters work in the mills next to the mines for three cents an hour!

The president of the Philadelphia and Reading Coal and Iron Company tells us "They

(continued)

don't suffer—why, they can't even speak English!''

(Darrow turns to him) You say you love children, sir? I have no doubt that you do. Just as the wolf loves mutton.

(The lights turn dark blue, suggesting that the entire stage is a coal mine—except for the spotlight on the witness stand, which Darrow now approaches) You're a breaker boy, Johnny McCaffery. That means they set you and a hundred others astradle the chute and as the coal comes rushing down, you pick out the slate?

What would you say that takes, Johnny? Quickness? You have to be quick to pick the slate out . . . ? Quick not to lose a finger, or a hand, or an arm?

Has that happened to any of your friends? How many of your friends?

Do they feed you, Johnny, before they send you into the breakers?

Do they give you anything besides the one potato to take down on your twelve-hour shift?

Do they let you see the sun, all day long?

Do they give you one day off, all year long?

You don't look very old to me. How old are you?

When will you be eleven? When's your birthday?

SOURCE: Excerpt from Clarence Darrow: A One-Man Play *by David W. Rintels. Copyright ©*
1975 by Dome Productions. Reprinted by permission of Doubleday & Company, Inc.

The emerging economic differences spilled over into social differences. Society began to have classes of ''haves'' and ''have-nots,'' and the mobility upward was much less than our American ideals would have one believe. In the workplace the distinction was particularly profound. A whole new class of employees—supervisors—was created which did no ''work.'' It merely made sure that others did. In such an environment, the development of distinct feelings of ''us'' and ''them'' became inescapable.

As employees began to see their interests as competing with their employer's, rather than being compatible, they began to perceive a need for protection. The pursuit of that protection took many forms.

A COMPARISON OF SELECTED CHARACTERISTICS
OF A WORKER'S SITUATION IN 1780 AND 1880

1780	1880
''Enriched,'' satisfying job	Pay reduced Hours lengthened Job ''simplified''
Job security high	Constant fear of losing job
Would own business in future	Needed capital to start business
Personal relationship with employer	Worked for a supervisor
Lived with employer	Lived in slums
High standard of living	Lived in poverty
Future optimistic	Future bleak

ATTEMPTS AT COPING

The miserable reality of nineteenth-century employment produced an entire continuum of responses ranging from fleeing employment altogether to placing ownership in the hands of the workers, with moderate steps in between designed to increase employee countervailing power or to regulate employer strength.

Frontier

At one end of the continuum is the classic free enterprise response to a miserable job—to quit. That solution was available to many people in the form of the frontier. However, it is not clear that the frontier was such a wonderful alternative. Clearing land, chasing off natives and bears, and exposing oneself to the capriciousness of Nature was not nearly as attractive a proposition as some schoolbooks might imply. This alternative was even less attractive to employees who had occupational and personal investments in employment in the city. Certainly some Americans left the cities and settled the frontier. In so doing, they often became self-employed or worked in a less competitive economy. This text and course is about those who remained in the competitive economy.

Cooperatives

At the other end of the continuum were employee ventures in taking over ownership of the enterprise. Such ventures usually took the form of worker cooperatives. Spurred by idealistic endeavors, liberal thinkers and philosophers gathered into mutual benefit enterprises. Generally, the hope was that everyone would contribute to the tasks of the enterprise, and the accumulated benefits would be shared by those who created them, rather than by those who invested in them.

Many cooperatives were formed in the 1860s by unionists who perceived them as a way to escape the wage system.[4] The efforts reached their zenith under the Knights of Labor (an early union) in the 1880s. All these efforts failed for the same reasons. They could not meet the cutthroat competition from the business community, antagonistic bankers would not grant them credit, and they lacked the managerial skill to be run efficiently.[5] The machine, mass production, and large-scale investment had made it impossible for workers to control the means of production by such simple expedients as producers' cooperatives.[6] There still needed to be some agreement or balance arranged between employees and employers. It was not realistically possible to bypass or eliminate the employer.

Appeals to the Government

Between the two ends of the continuum were the types of responses with which we are more familiar today. One type is direct appeals to the government to lessen the burdens of employment. This can be accomplished in either of two ways. One is to regulate employment to assure at least minimally acceptable working conditions and wages. The other is less direct. It is to redistribute the benefits of society along class lines through social welfare programs. Although both of these approaches were proposed at the state and federal level, neither was adopted as a solution during the nineteenth century.

Proposals to enact laws to limit hours, improve working conditions, or establish a minimum wage were all without success, although limitations on immigration were enacted in the latter part of the century. The resistance against protective legislation stemmed from a philosophical belief that enjoyed its fullest flower in America—*Social Darwinism.*

Charles Darwin's biological and zoological theories of evolution based upon survival of the fittest were widely popular in the Western world in the latter decades of the century. In the United States, the laws of physicial nature were readily (if not critically) transferred to the realms of economics and society. They made a wonderful justification for nonintervention. It was either Nature, Divine Providence, or God's Will that determined which people would lead and which would follow. Business success was used to identify those who "deserved" to be at the top. It was presumed that those who succeeded did so because they possessed the necessary and appropriate skills or characteristics for doing so. Conversely, the poor were poor because "they deserved to be." To attempt to adjust this outcome would be "messing with Mother Nature,"

GOD, MONEY, AND BUSINESS

The religious justification of success and appropriateness can be gathered from the following quotations from leaders of the period.

From Reverend Henry Ward Beecher (the leading Protestant theologian and spokesperson of the era):

*God has intended the great to be great and the little to be little.**

From John D. Rockefeller:

God gave me my money.

I believe the power to make money is a gift from God. . . . I believe it is my duty to make money and still more money. . . . †

From George T. Baer, President of the Philadelphia & Reading Coal Company, on the subject of leadership, when responding to a wife of a striking coal miner pleading with him to understand and sympathize with his workers' problems and show Christian mercy:

I beg you not to be discouraged. The rights and interests of the laboring man will be protected and cared for—not by the labor agitators, but by the Christian men to whom God in His infinite wisdom has given control of the property interests of this country.‡

SOURCES: *The Sermon of July 29, 1877, as reported in The New York Times, July 30, 1877. †Josephson, p. 318, and Litwack, p. 325. ‡Josephson, p. 374.

something that it is not wise to do. Consequently, the government found it philosophically inappropriate to intervene in the "natural" affairs of the economy.

The obvious fallacy in this system is that it presumes equal opportunity. It also presumes adequate opportunity—that there will be rewards for all those with talent and ambition. The second assumption was questionable in the nineteenth century; the first was totally inaccurate. Without even addressing the issue of subgroups such as slaves and women, it was apparent that being born poor had become a greater disadvantage than it had been previously—again, notwithstanding the mythology of American history. In fact, it was the romantic nature of this American mythology that allowed Social Darwinism to spread so wide and survive so long.

Social Darwinism (and its economic counterpart, laissez-faire) survived, despite the great misery it permitted for millions of people, because there was little organized opposition to it. The rich and powerful endorsed it for obvious reasons. The irony is that the poor also generally supported the concept. To a large extent, they apparently often agreed that they deserved to be poor. As a rule, even poor Americans supposedly believed that they controlled their own destiny—a simplistic notion more easily accepted before the era of mass industrialization and the popularization of sociology and psychology. Therefore, when they turned out to be poor, it was a result of a personal character flaw that should be overcome by self-improvement.

The acceptance of self-responsibility is an extremely American value. It is particularly important in its behavioral implications because it limited appeals to the government for aid and also reduced the inclination to coalesce into unions. The roots of this belief in self-responsibility not only supported Social Darwinism but also preceded and extended beyond it. Several factors contributed to the development of a national mentality that revered individuality and generally foreclosed class action. Some of those factors included the Protestant Ethic, the comparative lack of social classes based on birth, highly publicized success stories of rags-to-riches experiences (no matter how atypical they may have been), and the confidence/arrogance born of past successes.

The Protestant Ethic of hard work, diligence, and thrift was incorporated into the education system and the values of much of the population, regardless of their religious persuasion. The imported values of Methodism and Presbyterianism spread widely through the secular population because they seemed to make sense, obviously worked (at least on some occasions), and were probably already possessed in disproportionate conviction by people who chose to come to the United States. A person heard to complain that "the system is not fair" would probably have been chastised and counseled to redouble his personal efforts.

The comparative lack of a class structure based on birth was also an important justification for maintaining individual responsibility. This topic will be explored in the section explaining why Communism was not adopted in the United States.

Another reason the victims of nonintervention accepted their lot comparatively peacefully was that many believed they were not destined to remain that way. Regardless of how few working-class people rose to become captains of industry, they were aware that many of those captains had started with nothing. The popular literature of the late nineteenth century featured the stories of Horatio Alger, who, by dint of talent and hard work, rose from copy boy to publisher and set an example for all readers to follow him. Even though the probability of a worker's rising to such heights was extremely remote, one always had to consider that it was possible. In Europe, that would not have been true, and the significance of the difference is monumental. When one is *not permitted* to achieve, the fault lies in the system. When one is *unable* to achieve, the fault lies within the individual. The European worker could readily turn to his government to promote his personal interest. The American worker could not. The burden was individual.

Finally, Americans persevered in their conviction of their own omnipotence because, despite the misery of factory life, the economy was succeeding. The United States became the wealthiest nation in the world. As the century closed, the United States was becoming a first-class world power in trade, politics, and military might. However uncultured and unpedigreed we may have been, we were succeeding in developing the greatest business empire in the world and we were proud of it. We were reluctant to tamper with obvious success. The government believed in the rural adage, "If it ain't broke, don't fix it."

Reformist Unionism

Notwithstanding the general acceptance of Social Darwinism, there was still significant discontent among workers, who sought some form of organized expression. Fueled largely by recent immigrants of European extraction who were familiar with leftist labor movements on the Continent, the National Labor Union was formed in the 1860s. It was the first national union that included unskilled workers among its membership. It was not, however, a union of the type with which we are familiar today. Its interest was social reform rather than collective bargaining.

The National Labor Union sought a legislatively imposed eight-hour workday (with no reduction in wages), producers' and consumers' cooperatives, currency and banking reform, abolition of convict labor, restrictions on immigration, disposal of public lands only to actual settlers, and the establishment of a national government Department of Labor.[7] While these goals have obvious relevance to employment, their achievement is directed toward the government, rather than the employer. The organization lasted only until the death of its president, William H. Sylvis. Its format was to be revived 20 years later in the form of the Knights of Labor.

The Noble and Holy Order of the Knights of Labor rose to prominence in the 1880s. The Knights welcomed into membership workers from virtually every type of employment. The only exclusions were lawyers, bankers, doctors, drones, and professional politicians. It was the largest union of its time and engaged in several successful strikes, albeit without the approval of its president, Terence V. Powderly. In fact, many of goals of the membership and leadership were in conflict. The Knights held the same goals as the National Labor Union plus the prohibition of child labor, equal pay for the sexes, government ownership of railroads and telegraphs, and the adoption of a graduated income tax. Again, the achievement of these goals could be had only through the government, not through the employer.

A principal reason the Knights faded from existence was that workers were not primarily interested in unions servicing their citizenship needs. They sought union representation for their employment needs only. The goals of the Knights and NLU were not necessarily bad. The problem was that they could be achieved through other means. The Knights and NLU came to demonstrate that Americans favor narrow-purpose organizations. That is, the values that supported a belief in Social Darwinism prevented workers from coalescing into a class for purposes of social reform. Workers in America believed themselves to be employees only while at work. At home they were parents, neighbors, and citizens. Reform through government could be achieved through voting and political action, even though the success rate was not great at this time. This view was consistent with a belief in individual responsibility as long as taking such action was at all conceivable. American citizens did not believe they had to belong to an organization or to unite to approach their government. The jury was still out on what was needed to approach their employers.

Business Unionism

The difficulties of the Knights convinced Samuel Gompers that the needs of employees should be met by craft unions dedicated to bargaining with employers over wages, hours, and working conditions. In 1881, Gompers organized a group of craft unions into a federation. In 1886, the organization changed its name to the American Federation of Labor (AFL). This organization has remained remarkably consistent with its original goals.

The AFL's craftsmen were comparatively economically powerful because they possessed skills which were difficult to replace. The organization was opposed to radical unionism and believed reform of society to be beyond its goals. It made no effort to aid unskilled workers.

The AFL succeeded and flourished where others had failed for many reasons. Two of the most important are its focus on job conditions and its acceptability to employers. The AFL accepted the reality of a wage system and the necessity of employers. It did not try to eliminate or bypass them. Instead, it tried to make the existing system work better for employees by increasing the employees' bargaining *power*. It was never assumed that consensus would be reached by cooperation. Compromises reached would be the result of power exerted against employers to get them to do what they would not freely do. This system of countervailing power continues to the present.

The AFL's approach proved acceptable (though not popular) with employers because it was less radical than the alternatives of cooperatives, government intervention or control, or anarchy. The limited issues to which the AFL restricted itself (wages, hours, and working conditions) were areas over which employers had control and were willing to exercise it. They did not like Gompers, but they liked alternative forms of union representation less.

The AFL survived, to a large extent, because it was close to a manifestation of business as usual. That is, when Gompers negotiated an agreement, it was like any other contract to a businessman. Businessmen always negotiated with suppliers for a given amount of supplies, of a given quality, at a given price, for a given duration. They always expected to haggle with their suppliers and exact the best deal their position would allow. The only difference with the AFL was that its unions supplied labor in the form of individual workers instead of inanimate widgets. While this distinction did prove important for legal and philosophical reasons for some time after, pragmatic businessmen often sought to reach agreement with the AFL affiliates on acceptable terms rather than to destroy the union.

The AFL, then, represented a commitment to improving employees' lives by countervailing power, rather than through mutual goals or cooperation. It says a great deal about American vlaues that the form of improvement condoned was the *balanced* pursuit of *individual* self-interest, rather than the cooperative pursuit of mutual interest. It should also be remembered that the efforts of the AFL applied only to the very small portion of workers who were skilled craftsmen belonging to unions. The vast majority of employees were neither skilled nor represented.

LABOR DAY—A JOINT LEGACY OF THE KNIGHTS AND THE AFL

The holiday now celebrated on the first Monday of September honoring workers owes its origin to both the Knights of Labor and the AFL.

Labor Day is an important holiday in most industrialized countries, particularly the Socialist-Communist bloc. It is generally celebrated in other countries on May 1—May Day—rather than in early fall

as in the United States. The Soviet/European/Latin American date ironically derives from American history.

In 1890, the fledgling AFL decided to select a date each year to stage a general strike by one of its member unions to publicize demands for political issues such as the eight-hour day. (This was before the AFL established its principle of political noninvolvement.) The AFL pursued this strategy only twice, May 1 of 1890 and May 1 of 1891, before abandoning the idea as ineffective and inappropriate. European labor movements had observed this activity and, finding it more suitable to their political ideology than did Americans, embraced it vigorously. Now no longer a day necessitating a strike, Labor Day became a holiday honoring the working class.

The American date in September owes its genesis to the Knights of Labor, who had held annual parades in New York City around harvest time. To publicize their concerns, the Knights pressed states individually to create a Labor Day. In a short space in the early 1890s all states did. In 1894 the federal government standardized the date as the first Monday in September.

Congress also decided to honor labor in general, rather than a specific organization. Otherwise, they would have had to make Knight Day.

Radical Unionism

One other form of unionism was tried in the development of the American labor relations system: radicalism. Its principal proponent was the Industrial Workers of the World (IWW), or Wobblies, as they were known. Made up chiefly of western miners, lumberjacks, and migrant workers, they never constituted more than 60,000 members. They reached their heyday around the turn of the twentieth century. Their biggest contribution to the development of our current system was to make other forms of unions look good by comparison.

The Wobblies believed the capitalistic system was so bad that it had to be overthrown and replaced with employee ownership. One consequence of this goal was that the IWW did not wish to engage in collective bargaining.[8] That would have recognized the legitimacy of the employer's position. Instead, they sought to destroy the vestiges of employer "exploitation" by violent means. The stereotypical Wobbly was pictured as Clint Eastwood hanging from a railroad trestle by one hand with a bundle of dynamite in the other and a cigar in his mouth to light the fuse, waiting for the train to arrive.

PREAMBLE OF THE I.W.W. CONSTITUTION (1908)

The working class and the employing class have nothing in common. There can be no peace so long as hunger and want are found among millions of working people and the few, who make up the employing class, have all the good things of life.

Between the two classes a struggle must go on until the workers of the world organize as a class, take possession of the earth and the machinery of production, and abolish the wage system.

(continued)

We find that the centering of the management of industries into fewer and fewer hands makes the trade unions unable to cope with the ever growing power of the employing class. The trade unions foster a state of affairs which allows one set of workers to be pitted against another set of workers in the same industry, thereby helping defeat one another in wage wars. Moreover, the trade unions aid the employing class to mislead the workers into the belief that the working class have interests in common with their employers.

These conditions can be changed and the interest of the working class upheld only by an organization formed in such a way that all its members in any one industry, or in all industries if necessary, cease work when-ever a strike or lockout is on in any department thereof, thus making an injury to one an injury to all.

Instead of the conservative motto, "A fair day's wage for a fair day's work," we must inscribe on our banner the revolutionary watchword, "Abolition of the wage system."

It is the historic mission of the working class to do away with capitalism. The army of production must be organized, not only for the everyday struggle with capitalists, but also to carry on production when capitalism shall have been overthrown. By organizing industrially we are forming the structure of the new society within the shell of the old.

The extent to which Wobblies murdered foremen and blew up mines is difficult to tell from history. They certainly provoked a great deal of violent retaliation against themselves from the authorities. This lawlessness prompted the *San Diego Tribune* to write of the Wobblies' leaders,

> Hanging is none too good for them. They would be much better dead, for they are absolutely useless in the human economy; they are the waste material of creation and should be drained off into the sewer of oblivion there to rot in cold obstruction like any other excrement.[9]

While the revolutionary portion of the Wobblies was never more than a "lunatic fringe," the publicity and the disdain received served to emphasize that American values did not want and would not accept an overthrow of the economic system. If employees were going to receive better treatment, it would have to be through, not over, employers—at least under the values with which we began the twentieth century.

I.W.W. SOCIAL LIFE AND DEATH

The Wobblies certainly added to the color and folklore of the West. Their campfire songs included such poignant titles as, "Hallelujah! I'm a Bum!", "Casey Jones—the Union Scab," and "There Is Power in a Union." Some of the affairs of the composer of these songs, Joe Hill: I.W.W. song writer (1882–1915), are detailed below.

The I.W.W. sang its way to glory—and to eventual oblivion. But the demise of the or-

ganization, after the 1918 trial of 101 Wobbly leaders for subversive activities, did not
diminish the popularity of several of the
songs it inspired; and its most illustrious
and prolific song writer was unquestionably
the Swedish immigrant, Joel Emmanuel
Hagglund—known as Joe Hill. Arrested in
Salt Lake City in January 1914 on a murder
charge, he was executed nearly two years
later by a Utah firing squad. His guilt or innocence has long been disputed, even in la-

bor circles, as have his dying words—"Don't
waste time mourning. Organize." Nevertheless, he died an I.W.W. hero. Befitting the
cause to which he was attached, Hill's funeral procession in Chicago attracted
30,000 sympathizers, and, as he requested,
his body was cremated, the ashes placed
into thirty envelopes and sent to all parts of
the world—to all, that is, but the State of
Utah because Joe Hill "did not want to be
found dead there."

SOURCE: Leon Litwack, The American Labor Movement *(Englewood Cliffs, N.J.: Prentice-Hall,
Inc., 1962), p. 46.*

Marxism's Failure

One other coping mechanism remained possible—the workers' assumption of control of the government (and the economic system) through a political party. This never came close to occurring in the United States. The Socialist Party, led by Eugene V. Debs, did receive significant support in the early twentieth century but never won a national election, and the Communist Party never did more than "infiltrate" the CIO in the post-World War II years.[10]

This failure to win support in America is significant to understanding the American dedication to individuality rather than to cooperative efforts. Karl Marx had predicted that the United States should be particularly susceptible to class revolution because it suffered from the fullest development of capitalism. Ironically, it proved to be the most resistant economy to revolution. It turns out that Marx's economic predictions suffered because of a lack of understanding of sociology.

Marx hypothesized that capitalism would split the economy into two groups: a small, affluent bourgeoisie and a large, poor proletariat. What he had not accounted for was a belief that it was possible, even if not probable, to move up in class. So long as workers harbored that hope, they did not seek to destroy the system, they sought to benefit from it. For the reasons supporting Social Darwinism, this belief was strongly held in America, and appeals to class iden-tification had little effect. Further, the gradual improvements witnessed through union activity, government intervention, changes in employer attitudes, and economic growth, particularly in the twentieth century, served to defuse revo-lutionary fervor.

In Marx's defense, his personal observations of capitalism were largely European. What he did not realize was that European workers identified them-selves as a class (and Americans did not) because of social, not economic, fac-tors. Europeans were born to a class and could not escape it regardless of individual effort or merit. Americans, on the other hand, believed they could and should rise, no matter how unlikely such an occurrence might be. While the economic result of capitalism might be the same in either location, the preferred method of coping was vastly different. The failure of Marx in America can be attributed not so much to the benefits of capitalism but rather to a belief in individual improvement.

SELECTED CHARACTERISTICS OF THREE DIFFERENT TYPES OF AMERICAN UNIONIZATION IN THE NINETEENTH CENTURY

Knights of Labor
Broad membership
Wanted to reform society
Sought change through government
Felt working "class" should be aided
Programs co-opted by political parties
Died because workers did not see themselves as a class
Did not focus on job improvement

American Federation of Labor
Limited to skilled workers
Economic bargaining power derived from irreplaceability
Focused on wages, hours, and working conditions

No effort to form a political party
Pragmatic compromise, short-range goals
"Business unionism"
Accepted role of business as appropriate—worked within existing system

Industrial Workers of the World
Radical overthrow of capitalism
Business run by workers
Destroy capitalism to make way for its replacement
Angry reaction without improved solution
Never caught on with mainstream
Americans lacked class hatred necessary to be a Wobbly

MANAGEMENT RESPONSES TO EMPLOYEE EFFORTS

Our primary concern in this chapter thus far has been how employees attempted to cope with the inescapable realities of large capital, the wage system, and competition. Employers, however, by their reactions also helped shape our system and focus our values. Their responses were, generally speaking, attempts to preserve benefits they already had, rather than to gain more. They came in two major forms: (1) antagonistic attempts by economic force or law to defeat employee efforts, or (2) paternalistic attempts to provide conditions that would prevent employees from taking action against them.

Economic and Legal Force

American history prior to the 1920s reflects a long and serious conflict of interest between employers and employees. Union efforts to strike, particularly those by unskilled workers, met with the hiring of strikebreakers known as scabs, the use of "goon" squads to beat up union sympathizers, the issuance of injunctions to prohibit strikes, and the blacklisting of union sympathizers. Newly hired employees were forced to sign yellow-dog contracts pledging not to join or be in a union. Company spies audited the current workforce. Employers enjoyed judicial interpretations that decreed unions to be an illegal constraint of trade. In short, employer opposition to employee demands, particularly those of unions, was generally antagonistic and often violent. Prior to the twentieth century, there was no managerial indication whatsoever that the parties should ally themselves for any form of mutual benefit, and there was certainly no initiative on the part of management to cooperate. For it, the American goal was not to cooperate but to compete.

VIOLENCE AND EMPLOYER RETALIATION IN AMERICAN LABOR HISTORY

The following incidents portray some of the violence in American labor relations history. The first incident, the Haymarket Square riot in Chicago in 1886, reflected the hysterical response of the public to a tiny minority of anarchists in the labor movement of the time. The leading union of the era, the Knights of Labor, joined in the denunciation of the anarchists.

As described in *Labor in America* by Foster Rhea Dulles,*

A protest meeting was summoned for Haymarket Square the next evening, May 4, and some three thousand persons gathered to hear impassioned and inflammatory speeches by the anarchist leaders. But it was an entirely peaceful meeting for all these alarms (the mayor himself attended it and left upon finding everything so quiet), and when a cold wind began to blow gusts of rain through the square, the crowd gradually melted away. The meeting had, in fact, virtually broken up when a police detachment of two hundred men arrived and their captain peremptorily ordered such workers as remained to disperse. Suddenly there was a sharp explosion. Someone had hurled a bomb into the ranks of the police, killing one outright. They at once opened fire and there were answering shots from the workers. During the affray seven police in all

were either killed or fatally wounded, and some sixty-seven injured; four workers were killed and fifty or more injured.

Not only Chicago but the entire country was outraged by the bomb throwing. The anarchists were at once blamed and there was universal demand that they be hunted down and brought to trial. The police combed the city for suspects, and finally eight known anarchist leaders were arrested and charged with murder. In a frenzied atmosphere compounded equally of fear and the desire for revenge, they were thereupon promptly found guilty—seven of them sentenced to death and the eighth to fifteen years' imprisonment. There was no evidence whatsoever connecting them to the bombing. They were condemned out of hand for their revolutionary views and the incitements to violence which had supposedly caused the bombing. "Convict these men, make examples of them, hang them," urged the state's attorney, "and you save our institutions. . . . "

Two of the convicted men pleaded for executive clemency and were given life imprisonment. Six years later Governor John Peter Altgeld pardoned them, together with the eighth man who had been sentenced to fifteen years' imprisonment, on the ground that they had not been granted a fair trial.

(continued)

So violent was the feeling against the anarchists even at this late date, that Altgeld was assailed throughout the country for what has since been universally recognized as an act of simple justice. [Author's note: Of the seven others convicted, six were hanged and one committed suicide.]

In 1913, a strike of coal miners employed by the Colorado Fuel and Iron Company erupted into violence. Again, according to Dulles,

The principle of the open shop, often sustained with a conviction that went beyond all purely economic considerations, was used to justify or condone the most drastic measures in seeking to crush unions. This was perhaps most graphically illustrated in the suppression of the strike of employees of the Colorado Fuel and Iron Company in 1913. The real issue at stake in this dispute was recognition of the United Mine Workers, who had sent their organizers into the territory. Rather than make this concession, the company fiercely fought the strikers with hired detectives, special deputies and the state militia.

Open warfare continued for months in the Colorado mine fields and finally reached a bloody climax when the militia attacked a colony of the strikers at Ludlow. After several rounds of indiscriminate machinegun fire, the tents in which the workers' families were living were soaked in oil and put to torch. Women and children huddled in pits to escape the raging flames, and in one of them eleven children and two women were later found burned or suffocated to death. The nation was horrified by this massacre, but still the Colorado Fuel and Iron Company refused to consider negotiations with the unions to end the strike.

The company was controlled by the Rockefeller interests and in the investigation of the strike by the House Committee on Mines and Mining, John D. Rockefeller, Jr., was called to the witness stand. In reply to questions as to whether he did not feel that "the killing of people and the shooting of children" should not have led to efforts to re-establish labor peace, he implied that rather than give in to the miners, his company was prepared to go to whatever lengths were necessary.

Even after the passage of the Wagner Act violence continued. A Congressional Committee headed by Senator La Follette in 1937 investigated the Little Steel (smaller manufacturers) strike. The disclosure of the arsenals maintained by employers shocked America. As reported in Dulles,

The Youngstown Sheet and Tube Company had on hand 8 machine guns, 369 rifles, 190 shotguns and 450 revolvers, with 6000 rounds of ball ammunition and 3950 rounds of shot ammunition, and also 109 gas guns with over 3000 rounds of gas ammunition. The Republic Steel Corporation had comparable equipment, and with purchases of tear and sickening gas amounting to $79,000, was described as the largest buyer of such supplies—not excepting law enforcement bodies—in the United States. Senator La Follette declared that the arsenals of these two steel companies "would be adequate equipment for a small war."

Nor was the undermining of union activities limited exclusively to violence. In the La Follette investigation,

There was also brought to light one especially notorious example of industrial techniques in combating unionism, first developed by the Remington Rand Company and then widely publicized by the National Association of Manufacturers under the name of the Mohawk Valley formula. This formula blueprinted a systematic campaign to denounce all union organizers as dangerous agitators, align the community in support of employers in the name of law and order, intimidate strikers by mobilizing the local police to break up meetings, instigate "back to work" movements by secretly organizing "loyal employees," and set up vigilance committees for protection in getting a struck plant again in operation. The underlying purpose behind the Mohawk Valley formula was to win public support by branding union leaders as subversive and threatening to remove the affected industry from the community if local business interests stood by and allowed radical agitators to win control over workers otherwise ready and anxious to cooperate with their employers.

Finally there was the infamous "Battle at the Ford Overpass."

THE BATTLE AT FORD OVERPASS[†]

Henry Ford referred to unions as "predatory" organizations; his hostility toward labor organization and collective bargaining dictated his refusal to sign the NRA automobile code. Ford's private army— euphemistically called the Ford Service Department—made life unbearable for Ford workers and for union organizers. The incident described below by Walter Reuther and Richard Frankensteen occurred in May 1937—four years after the enactment of section 7a, two years after the Wagner Act was passed, and four years prior to Ford's final capitulation to the United Automobile Workers. As an "Ex-Ford Slave" indicated in a letter to the union newspaper, the bridge leading to the Ford plant, on which the Reuther-Frankensteen beating occurred, had become "the doorway to HELL."

The account that follows, given by a founder of the United Automobile Workers, Walter Reuther, is reprinted from *United Automobile Worker,* May 29, 1937:[‡]

I got out of the car on the public highway, Miller Road, near gate No. 4. Dick Frankensteen and I walked together over to the stairs. I got up the stairs and walked over near the center of the bridge. There a couple of minutes, then all of a sudden about 35 or 40 men surrounded us and started to

beat us up. I didn't fight back. I merely tried to guard my face. The men called me all sorts of names, of course. They picked me up about 8 different times and threw me down on my back on the concrete. While I was on the ground they kicked me in the face, head and other parts of my body. After they kicked me a while one fellow would say: "All right, let him go now." Then they would raise me up, hold my arms behind me and begin to hit me some more. They picked my feet up and my shoulders and slammed me down on the concrete. The process went on about 8 times.

Finally they got me next to Dick, who was lying on the bridge on the concrete, and with both of us together, they kicked us again and again. This lasted for quite a while. Then they picked me up and threw me down the first flight of steps. I lay there, and they picked me up and began to kick me down the total flight of steps. There are three flights.

There were about 150 men standing around us, ready to take up the fight, to take care of us and beat us up. I should say about 20 were doing the actual beating of us, but with this 150 standing around it is hard to say.

I never raised a hand. After they kicked me down all the stairs then they started to hit me at the bottom of the stairs, hit me and slugged me, driving me before them, but never letting me get away. The more we tried to leave the worse it was for us. They simply wanted to slug us out, not let us out. They drove me to the outside of the fence—almost a block of slugging and beating and hurtling me before them. I could never get away because the men surrounded me. If I ran it would make it all the worse. Finally they drove me to the other end. I was on the inside of the fence. While I was being driven down I had glimpses of women being kicked and other men being kicked.

When I got to the end of the fence I found Dick. In the meantime some newspaper photographers came along and they picked

(continued)

us up. We only managed to get away from
the thugs by getting into the car. The thugs
were still after us when we got into it. It is
the only way we could have escaped. . . .

I had the permit to distribute the leaflets in
my pocket but no one would look at that. I
might add that the police standing around
did nothing to prevent the slugging.

SOURCES: *LABOR IN AMERICA: A History, *Third Edition (Thomas Y. Crowell) © 1949, 1955,
1960, 1966 by Foster Rhea Dulles. Reprinted by permission of Harper & Row, Publishers, Inc.
†Headnote from Auerbach, p. 286. ‡Walter Reuther, *United Automobile Worker, *May 29, 1937.

Forced Cooperation

The period of the twentieth century beginning with the inauguration of President Theodore Roosevelt and ending with the United States' entry into World War I has been labelled the Progressive Era. The values of the public and of its government were changing. A liberal spirit pushed for political and social reforms, particularly aimed at special privilege. In the business world this became an effort to control the trusts, regulate the railroads, reform the monetary system, and reduce tariffs. At the state level, programs of economic and social reform sought to mitigate the evils of the slum, safeguard the health of women and children in industry, and generally improve factory conditions. Nineteenth-century concepts of laissez-faire were moderated by a belief that government had a social responsibility to deal with the problems of industrialization.[11]

These values, not generally shared by businessmen, resulted in the passage of child labor laws, maximum hours of work for women, and workers' compensation statutes.[12] These reforms were all achieved over the opposition of employers. The reforms also shared a common feature—they established standards or criteria that an employer must meet. They did not, however, attempt to tell management how to run its business or force it to seek the input of labor. That imposition arose with World War I.

American involvement in World War I required (as it would again in World War II) that capital and labor cooperate to create efficient production without the interruption of strikes in critical industries. To the progressive-minded President Woodrow Wilson and his Secretary of Labor William B. Wilson, this meant cooperation through plant-level advisory committees in addition to wage/price freezes and a prohibition on strikes. The government established a series of tripartite boards, the most important of which was the National War Labor Board, to enforce its rules, to mediate and arbitrate disputes, and to establish employee representation plans for their jurisdictions. It was hoped by Secretary Wilson that these forms of cooperative effort would carry over into peacetime.[13]

The War Labor Board ordered the creation of shop council plans in 88 major plants. The Shipbuilding Board ordered an additional 31 councils, and by the end of the war, government boards had created more than 225 shop councils. Private firms sometimes voluntarily created employee representation plans, and one Labor Department official remarked, "There was a deluge of works councils."[14] These councils gave workers, most for the first time, a definite voice in management.

That voice was not willingly accepted by management, however. Absolutely refusing to accept the philosophy or results of employee input, management did all it could to escape such responsibilities as soon as hostilities ended. Employers either unilaterally abolished the plans or converted them to company unions, admitting such sentiments as, "We would not have started the employees' committee had we not been forced to do so."[15] When similar efforts at cooperation were introduced during World War II, management rebuffed them with the candid comments of General Motors President Charles Wilson, who stated, "There will be none of this equal voice bunk at GM," and Ford Motor Company's response that "We have not been able to find any examples where labor has run manufacturing plants as well as management."[16] Succinctly put at a National Labor-Management Conference in 1945, "Management members cannot agree to joint management of enterprise. [It] has functions that must not and cannot be compromised."[17] In short, American management has not historically favored cooperation.

Paternalism and Company Unions

There is one major exception to management's historical opposition to cooperation—the Era of Human Relations that manifested itself in the paternalism and company unions of the 1920s. It was not really as much an era of cooperation as it was one of cooptation. Fueled by the belief that employee satisfaction helped increase productivity,[18] employers sought ways to ally themselves with labor without ceding control. This was generally accomplished by forming company-dominated unions that would serve in lieu of "real" unions beyond the control of management.

The creation of company unions was just one portion of the newly discovered "be kind to employees" attitude. Liberal personnel departments established profit-sharing plans, group insurance policies, old age pensions, free clinics, employee cafeterias and lunchrooms, picnics, glee clubs, dances, sports events, and company newspapers.[19] All these benefits were, of course, dependent upon the largesse of the employer, were totally unenforceable, and could be withdrawn at any time. While some of the benefits may have originated in response to employee suggestions or requests, they were never implemented without management's unilateral evaluation and approval. The system never really reflected a spirit of, or belief in, cooperation. Instead, it was merely a restructuring of the methods by which management unilaterally retained control to enhance the benefits of management. From the standpoint of employees and society in general, the new strategy was certainly more humanitarian in practice, even if it reflected no change in values.

Notes

1. Arthur A. Sloan and Fred Witney, *Labor Relations,* 4th ed. (Englewood Cliffs, N.J.: Prentice-Hall, 1983), p. 56.
2. Sloan and Witney, pp. 56–57.
3. For a detailed history of bad working conditions in America, see Leon Litwack, *The American Labor Movement* (Englewood Cliffs, N.J.: Prentice-Hall, 1962), Section I.
4. Foster Rhea Dulles, *Labor in America: A History* (New York: Thomas Y. Crowell Co., 1966), p. 109.
5. Dulles, pp. 109, 137.
6. Dulles, p. 113.
7. Dulles, p. 101.
8. Preamble of the IWW constitution, cited in Litwack, *The American Labor Movement,* p. 42.
9. Dulles, p. 214.
10. Although Communist agitation was alleged to be the cause of many strikes and may in reality have been a matter deserving significant concern, it never approached anything like a majority sentiment. This discussion is not exploring the likelihood of Communist success through subversion, but rather what the majority of the population's values were.
11. Dulles, p. 184.
12. Dulles, p. 201.
13. Henry P. Guzda, "Industrial Democracy: Made in the U.S.A.," *Monthly Labor Review,* Vol. 107, No. 5 (May 1984), p. 28.
14. Guzda, p. 29.
15. *Ibid.*
16. Guzda, p. 31.
17. *Ibid.*
18. This was the era which made the first systematic studies of the effects of employee attitudes and satisfaction on productivity. The early results, later modified by more sophisticated studies in the post-World War II years, indicated simplistically that making workers happy was a good business investment in its own right. Hence, employers changed their behavior toward employees without changing their values.
19. Dulles, p. 256.

Discussion Questions

1. Analyze why American employees came to regard employers as enemies—at least in some respects.
2. Discuss why business unionism succeeded while other forms of coping with conflict failed.

3. Analyze how employers reacted to the problems of employees.
4. Analyze why American employees reacted as they did.

Statements for Comment

1. a. "The past is prologue."
   b. "Those who do not understand history are condemned to repeat its mistakes."
   c. "History is bunk."
   d. "The best is yet to be."
2. "The Republican Party believes in Social Darwinism; the Democrats do not."
3. "The trouble with American unions is they lack a reformist goal. They only want more, more, more, now, now, now!"
4. "The Wobblies were reincarnated in the 1960s as the Students for a Democratic Society (SDS)."
5. "Current efforts by employers to be 'nice guys' are really lies. History proves they can't be trusted."

Situations

Case 3–1 "Remember, this is the most perfect of all possible worlds," Dr. Pangloss continually admonished Candide. Of course, Voltaire didn't believe it. Neither does anyone in labor relations. The real world is obviously an imperfect one, made up of compromises among lesser evils.

Mark Maine leaned back on the sofa in his apartment, put down his labor relations textbook, and wondered aloud, "How did we get into this mess?"

"What mess?" asked his close personal friend Vicki MacGregor.

"Our current labor relations system," he replied. "It's all fouled up. No one trusts anyone else. We compete when we should cooperate. We're paying for mistakes made generations ago and the Japanese are blowing our doors off. It's too bad we couldn't start over from scratch tomorrow and do it right this time."

Vicki, who had been around the block a few more times than Mark, replied, "Do you really think things would be different? Would it come out 'right' this time?"

What do you think? Support and attack your own position.

Case 3–2 "He's the only American buried in the Kremlin, you know." That information from the Academy Award-winning movie *Reds*, describing American journalist and advocate of the Industrial Workers of the World, Jack Reed, caused Tom Jolie to reflect over his morning coffee. "You know, Dear," he said to his half-awake wife, "I never realized how alienated American workers were in the early twentieth century. Nor did I realize how violently management resisted their demands. Times certainly have changed."

Dear looked up groggily from her cup (the movie ran 3½ hours and had kept the Jolies up well past their normal bedtime). "I'm not so sure," she said, "that things are all that different now. Oh, sure, companies don't hang union leaders any more, but I don't think the alienation is any less. We just cope with it in more civilized ways."

What do you think? What evidence do you see to support your conclusions? What evidence opposes your conclusion?

Case 3–3 "You know, it says here in this labor history book that Terrence V. Powderly wanted a shorter workday for—get this—extra time for workers to compose sonnets—you know, the 14 lines of rhyming iambic pentameter stuff. Can you believe that? What an airhead! If he had succeeded, we would be really messed up today," said Bubba Bristol.

Bubba's tutor, Janie Johnson, disagreed. She said, "That's what's wrong with mainstream America. They're all a bunch of crass materialists with the cultural appreciation of a pet rock, and American unions make it worse. Maslow never met an AFL-CIO bargainer. Those guys can never satiate Need Level Two. If they get a raise they buy a bass boat. Then they need another raise for a trailer for the boat. Then they need another raise for mag wheels for the boat trailer. America will be forever remembered as a nation whose greatest cathedrals were shopping malls. If people like Powderly had succeeded, we might have fewer dollars, but life would be more worth living. Really, how necessary is a jet ski?"

How valid are these accusations? How relevant are they?

Bibliography of Related Readings

Auerbach, Jerald S., *American Labor: the Twentieth Century* (Indianapolis: Bobbs-Merrill, 1969).

Bailey, M., "Joe Hill's Legacy: Don't Mourn . . . Organize!" *Allied Industrial Worker*, December 1978, pp. 6–8.

Brecher, J., "Uncovering the Hidden History of the American Workplace," *Review of Radical Political Economics*, Winter 1978, pp. 1–23.

Brody, David, *The American Labor Movement* (New York: Harper and Row, 1971).

Brommel, B. J., *Eugene V. Debs: Spokesman for Labor and Socialism* (Chicago: Charles H. Kerr Pub. Co., 1979).

Chandler, A. D., Jr., "Business History: What Is It About?" *Journal of Contemporary Business*, 1981, pp. 47–63.

Conlin, J. R., ed., *At the Point of Production: The Local History of the I.W.W.* (Westport, Conn.: Greenwood, 1981).

Cotkin, G. B., "The Spencerian and Comtian Nexus In Gompers' Labor Philosophy: The Impact of Non-Marxian Evolutionary Thought," *Labor History (United States)*, 1979, pp. 512–23.

Dobson, C. R., *Masters and Journeymen: A Prehistory of Industrial Relations, 1717–1800* (Totowa, N.J.: Rowman and Littlefield, 1980).

Dulles, Foster Rhea, *Labor in America: A History* (New York: Thomas Y. Crowell, 1966).

Eltis, W. "How Marx Maimed Britain," *Management Today,* August 1983, pp. 54–57.

Ficken, R. E., "The Wobbly Horrors: Pacific Northwest Lumbermen and the Industrial Workers of the World, 1917–1918," *Labor History (United States),* 1983, pp. 325–41.

Jacoby, S. M., "Union-Management Cooperation in the United States: Lessons from the 1920s," *Industrial and Labor Relations Review,* 1983, pp. 18–33.

Josephson, Matthew, *The Robber Barons* (New York: Harcourt Brace Jovanovich, 1962).

Kaufman, S. B., "Samuel Gompers vs. Horatio Alger: Defining The Work Ethic," *American Federationist,* February 1981, pp. 7–12.

Litwack, Leon, *The American Labor Movement* (Englewood Cliffs, N.J.: Prentice-Hall, 1962).

Nelson, D., "The Company Union Movement, 1900–1937: A Reexamination," *Business History Review,* 1982, pp. 335–57.

Neufeld, M. R., "The Persistence of Ideas in the American Labor Movement: The Heritage of the 1830s," *Industrial and Labor Relations Review,* 1982, pp. 207–20.

Ozanne, R., "Trends in American Labor History," *Labor History (United States),* 1980, pp. 513–21.

FOUR

DEVELOPMENT OF THE SYSTEM: Adjustments Based on Experience

BREAKDOWN OF THE SYSTEM

The Great Depression brought an end to employer-provided benefits. It also brought an end to whatever faith and trust employees might have developed in employers. The total crash of the entire system forced a reexamination of all the values that had helped form it. The spectacular demise of previously successful businessmen proved that the economic system was beyond the control of individuals and that ambition, talent, hard work, and capital were no longer sufficient to guarantee success.

The Great Depression was blamed on business. For the only time in American history, the public lost faith in the businessman. The unregulated laissez-faire system had turned into a disaster. No longer could poverty or unemployment be considered a character flaw. Social Darwinism died in the Great Depression.

The economy and society stood at a crossroads in the 1930s. It had become apparent that unregulated, pure laissez-faire capitalism would not and could not solve the problem. Some form of restructuring and intervention was obviously required. Exactly what form was not so obvious.

Several choices appeared available. The conservative monetarist, non-intervention-of-government theory had already been tried and proven a failure.

FOODLINES DURING GREAT DEPRESSION

SOURCE: AP/Wide World Photos

So had a toothless attempt at intervention in the form of the National Industrial Recovery Act.[1] What remained were radical or moderate solutions. Radical solutions ranged from nationalization of the means of production to bloody overthrow of the government. Moderate solutions ranged from the government's providing employment to changing the balance of power in employment by encouraging collective bargaining. No one suggested cooperation as a remedy for the Depression.

The threat of radical solutions was never a great one, at least not in the form of a revolution. The working class accepted the Depression with despair and apathy more than with anger.[2] They also observed that the suffering was universal. It was not limited to their class. For businessmen, the threat of a ''Red'' takeover was not very real, but government nationalization of the major means of production was. At least, businessmen had to believe it could happen. Germany, troubled by the same Depression, had already done so.[3] Whatever steps the government might take in a radical direction would certainly be resisted by the business community. Resistance to such steps, however, was less persuasive, now that business had been discredited. It became apparent that the interests of capital could be best protected from potential radical solutions by permitting moderate attempts at adjustment. That moderate attempt was the Wagner Act.

CHOICE OF BALANCED CONFLICT

Although the Wagner Act was not technically the first effort on the part of the government to aid unions,[4] it was the foremost. Its purpose was to help end the Depression with as little offense to the free enterprise system as possible. It was also intended to help promote the free flow of commerce by providing for union recognition based on secret-ballot elections rather than by forcing unions to strike for recognition.

The other major provisions of the National Labor Relations Act, as it was officially known, included the obligation of the employer to bargain in good faith over the limited subjects of wages, hours, and terms and conditions of employment[5] and not to discriminate against employees for their union activity.[6] The law also outlawed ''cooperation'' in the form of company unions as not being in the best interest of employees or the country.[7] In addition, the Act also established the National Labor Relations Board (NLRB) to conduct elections to determine if employees desired representation and to investigate and enforce unfair labor practice charges of failure to bargain in good faith and of discrimination against employees for union activity or maintaining a company union.[8]

It was hoped the Act would help end the Depression by giving greater bargaining power to employees. Hopefully, this greater bargaining power would result in higher wages which would serve as a stimulus to higher consumption, thereby generating a higher demand for labor which would reduce unemployment and end the Depression.

Although there is little to suggest that the Wagner Act worked as intended to end the Depression, there are those that claimed it had a tremendous influence on labor relations. According to Dulles,

> The advent of the New Deal [Wagner Act] was thus to prove a momentous watershed in the history of the labor movement. Age-old traditions were smashed; new and dynamic forces released.[9]

Richard A. Lester argues, on the other hand, that

> even with the New Deal . . . union development experienced, not a marked mutation, but a partial alteration and expansion in leadership, tactics, and ju-

---

THE CONSTITUTIONALITY OF THE WAGNER ACT

The Wagner Act was not the first law to attempt to assure employees the right to be represented by unions if they so chose. The Norris-LaGuardia Act of 1932 gave employees such a right, but there was no enforcement mechanism, and employers ignored that aspect of the law.

The National Industrial Recovery Act of 1933 also attempted to guarantee employees the right to be represented by unions. Utilizing the same language that now appears in Section 7 of the Taft-Hartley Act, employees formed unions. One employer, Schechter Poultry Corp., challenged the constitutionality of the law. The employer argued that the commerce clause of the Constitution allowed it to enter into contracts with other legal beings and, by implication, also permitted it not to enter into contracts it did not desire. In this case, the employer was choosing not to do business with agents of its employees. This, argued the employer, was a right protected by the Constitution that could not be abridged by a mere law. A majority of the Supreme Court, by a vote of 5–4, agreed, and the law was found unconstitutional in 1935.

President Roosevelt and his advisors found the decision unlivable. They believed that such a right was necessary to speed recovery from the Depression. Accordingly, the newly-passed Wagner Act contained exactly the same right of recognition for unions. This time, however, the President assured a more favorable interpretation of the constitutionality of the law by threatening to "pack" the Supreme Court.

The President's threat was a very believable one. The Constitution does not specify how many Supreme Court justices there shall be, and the number has ranged from 5 to 13 in the past. Justices are appointed to the Court by the President with the advice and consent of two-thirds of the Senate. FDR proposed adding a sufficient number of justices (selected solely on the criterion that they would find the Wagner Act constitutional) to assure its passage. He had the support of two-thirds of the Senate. The existing justices looked at the "handwriting on the wall" and this time, with one member changing his position, voted that the representation provisions were constitutional without any change in the language of the law or the Constitution.

risdiction. The adjustment in basic union philosophy was neither profound nor completely permanent.[10]

An analysis of these apparently contradictory conclusions proves informative. While the Wagner Act did prove to be a watershed in *who* was organized (the unskilled now joined by the millions, as employers were no longer permitted to replace them for their union activity) and in the government's accepting a responsibility to "interfere with and adjust" market mechanisms, it was not a watershed for determining who was responsible for what. The Act preserved the American value that all parties are responsible for their own self-interest, that the government will not provide their outcomes or benefits, and that maximum utility is provided when each party pursues its own self-interest. The only fine tuning required is to see that each party has enough countervailing power so that its pursuit of self-interest can be protected.

The Wagner Act passed because it was at least minimally tolerable to traditional American ideals. The limitation of mandatory subjects of bargaining to "wages, hours, and terms and conditions of employment" preserved the right of the employer to manage most aspects of the business without the intervention of the union. It guaranteed a system whereby employers, not the government, would run the businesses of the United States. It left the union focus of concern on jobs, not the government. It was still up to labor and capital to work out their own arrangements. The government would provide only a framework of rules for how bargaining would take place. Unlike European governments, it would not provide the benefits.[11] The commitment to private ownership, the wage system, and competititon was retained. The proposed solution was arguably as traditionally American as conditions would permit.

THE CONGRESS OF INDUSTRIAL ORGANIZATIONS (CIO)

The passage of the Wagner Act also made possible the next major development in the American labor relations system—the achievement of widespread *industrial unionism,* particularly in our giant, mass production industries.

The AFL had historically limited its membership to an elite minority of skilled craftsmen that were organized by occupation and blessed with comparative economic power. The legal (rather than economic) protection of organizing rights granted by the Wagner Act now made possible the unionization of the unskilled and semiskilled masses. When the existing AFL proved too slow in wanting to do this, John L. Lewis, President of the United Mine Workers, split from the existing federation and formed a competing alliance, the Congress of Industrial Organizations (CIO). The CIO retained, to a large degree, the AFL's emphasis on bread-and-butter business unionism, but it also added a substantial social welfare thrust to the labor movement. With the CIO, labor became actively involved in politics and purported to speak for the interests of all working people (not just unionists) on a wide range of liberal issues confronting society. The CIO also largely changed the focus of industrial relations in many instances from local and regional to national.

The emergence of the CIO met great resistance from both employers and the AFL. Despite theoretical legal protections of employee rights, employers countered with refusals to bargain and occasional violence.[12] The direction the development of the CIO would take was uncertain and chaotic.[13] From the start it was clear, however, that the CIO would not adopt the AFL's commitment to voluntarism—the avoidance of governmental regulation of items that could "voluntarily" be settled through bargaining. It immediately supported government involvement and the Democratic Party—although Lewis himself had a severe "falling out" with President Roosevelt.[14,15]

As the CIO began organizing the mass production industries, several important byproducts emerged. One was who was organized. Many new members were recognizable ethnic minorities who had recently emigrated from southern and eastern Europe. The common cause of the CIO's unions tended to promote greater harmony among workers than the AFL ever had—a sense of "we" that carried over into the political arena, creating a greater class consciousness than previously in the American labor movement.[16,17] The extent of this organizing and its widespread social and political effects also led to certain cities' being labelled "union towns."[18]

A second byproduct of the CIO's organizing efforts was the reaction it provoked from the AFL. Since the CIO organized along industry, rather than craft, lines, it occasionally recruited members in violation of the AFL's internally regulated jurisdictional boundaries. This caused the AFL to begin seeking out industrial members in retaliation. The result was that the AFL blurred its own jurisdictional lines as well as the lines between the jurisdictions of the two federations.[19,20] The AFL also became more active in organizing altogether. This merging of competing zones of interest ultimately paved the way for the AFL and CIO to merge in 1955, as they realized they had few differences and much in common, particularly a desire to combat management (rather than each other) and to ward off potential unfavorable legislation.

The third, and arguably most important, byproduct of the CIO's emergence is its effect on management. The CIO's lack of control of the supply of labor forced its concentration onto individual wages and work rules and their administration. This resulted in complex wage bargaining leading to the rationization of wage structures[21] and an intricate set of job descriptions and work assignments. This elaborate set of shop rules was enforced through grievance procedures terminating in determinations made, not by management, but by neutral outsiders.[22]

As the CIO organized the major portion of many of our largest oligopolies, many managements began to bargain on a national basis. Because oligopolies are less subject to the pressures of competition, unions became more accepted in these areas, as all competitors faced similar labor burdens.[23] Labor relations decisions were pushed upward in business organizations.[24] Pattern bargaining, where agreements in one company or industry are followed by others, emerged.[25] Small employers formed associations to negotiate with large industrywide unions.[26] Finally, large companies learned to blame large unions for price raises.[27]

COMMUNISM AND CORRUPTION

Two threats to the labor movement in the post-Depression era require comment. They are Communism and corruption. Communism is only of historical significance. It has no impact on current American labor relations. Corruption, however, remains a continuing problem in the labor movement.

Communists entered the CIO in the 1930s at the invitation of Lewis, who wanted to use their organizing skills.[28] He believed he personally would be able to remove them after they had served their purpose, but he resigned his presidency of the CIO in 1940 and left the problem to his successors, who found it difficult to solve.[29] The Communist influence grew in the postwar years to the point where the CIO finally had to expel several Communist-dominated affiliates in 1949 and 1950.[30] Other Communist-dominated unions withdrew voluntarily[31] and, serving no mainstream purpose, eventually faded from significance. No longer is there a serious issue of the Communist influence in mainstream American labor unions.

Corruption has been more difficult to eradicate. Corruption can take two forms. One is the misuse of union funds; the other is abuse of a union's internal democratic processes. The union most commonly associated with both types of corruption is the Teamsters. AFL-CIO-initiated campaigns to "clean up its own house" resulted in substantial improvement in many instances, but the Teamsters would not conform to the federation's requirements and were expelled for corrupt practices. The federal government added its muscle to solving the problem in 1959 by passing the Landrum-Griffin Act, regulating the collection and dispersal of union funds and the conduct of union elections.

REFINEMENT OF THE SYSTEM

Many events have taken place in labor relations since the New Deal, but few values have changed. Bargaining has continued as it did in the past, with unions demanding and management counteroffering until agreement is reached. Employers continue to resist the formation of unions, although they may have become more accommodating in attempts to reach agreement once they have accepted the existence of the union. The greatest reaffirmation of our faith in conflict and competition balanced by countervailing power has occurred in the field of law.

The Wagner Act was intended to encourage collective bargaining for the purpose of ending the Depression. Although it did not succeed in its task (World War II had a greater effect), the law was not repealed when the Depression ended. It had proved to be a good law for other reasons. Employees had greater protections, freedom, rights, and benefits at the same time the economy was enjoying great prosperity.

The public, however, had become somewhat disenchanted with unions. The businessman had regained his credibility by his contribution to American war productivity. Post-World War II union wage demands and strike activity alienated the public. The Wagner Act, which had been entirely prounion, was under attack for having swung the pendulum of economic power too far in the direction of unions. The response was typically, predictably, consistently American. It was to readjust the balance of countervailing power again. It was not an attempt to escape the system, to impose outcomes, or to discover harmony of interests. It was, instead, to have the parties fight it out on fairer terms.

The result was the Taft-Hartley (Labor Management Relations) Act of 1947. It incorporated and amended the Wagner Act. It added a list of union unfair labor practices (Section 8 (b)) and provided for protection of the public interest in national emergency disputes. Further undesired loopholes of union strength were closed with the passage of the Landrum-Griffin (Labor Management Reporting and Disclosure) Act of 1959. (The primary purpose of Landrum-Griffin was to assure that the internal affairs of unions were run honestly. It was not a collective bargaining bill per se, but did reflect a public concern that a healthy and honest labor union movement was useful for promoting the interests of the country.) Finally, the Labor Law Reform Bill of 1978, which would have adjusted the balance of power more in the direction of unions, was not passed. This could be interpreted as a recognition that the country is satisfied with the system as it now exists.

REASONS WE RETAIN THE SYSTEM

The set of values that has committed us to conflict rather than cooperation has come under much attack in the 1980s.[32] So far, it has weathered the attack well. Despite lamentations that we need to change our ways, we have not done so on any significant scale. The reasons require exploration.

The most obvious reasons are the self-serving ones. The people in charge—those who could institute such changes—are not inclined to do so. Union leaders and corporate executives with labor relations responsibilities have a vested interest in maintaining the status quo.

The interest of the union leader is fairly obvious. If cooperation works and management can be trusted, there will be little perceived need for a union. If cooperation eliminates the need for conflict, it largely eliminates the perceived need for the union president. Union leaders cannot be expected to voluntarily promote their own demise.

The interest of the executive is less blatant but not necessarily less strong. High-level executives rose to their positions by succeeding at their previous tasks. They have proven their worth at competitive collective bargaining. Now they are being asked to forego the game they have played and won and been rewarded for and to exchange it for a different task. It is not greatly different from saying, "We have found out who the best tennis player is. Now let's switch to golf." Unless the executive is very sure of his or her versatility, this may introduce a significant risk that one is not inclined to take unless one absolutely must. The problem is compounded if the executive is at a career point where change presents more risk than possible benefit.

Exercising even greater deterrence, although generally not admitted publically, are the perceived inherent liabilities of cooperation. Cooperation is egalitarian. Sharing and jointly making decisions is not the same as issuing orders to subordinates. Managers prepared and worked hard to rise to positions of power and influence. To now be asked to share that power with those over whom they have climbed will not commonly be greeted with genuine enthusiasm. This might not be a flattering view of managers, but it is a generally accurate one. Also, there is a genuine belief on the part of many managers that their subordinates really don't have much to contribute beyond that which management already knew and that their involvement will slow down and dilute the quality of the decision-making process. This view is not necessarily accurate, but it is widespread.

Lastly, there is the very real possibility that cooperation may not be attainable in America—that the goals of management and labor *really* are in conflict and that attempts to define their interests as mutual are unrealistic. Certainly many managers believe that at least some employees are not concerned with the competitive needs of the company, and many employees see no reason to believe that the company has their interests at heart. Recent dissatisfaction with "cooperative" concession bargaining indicates that a substantial portion of the rank-and-file is adamantly opposed to "helping out" the company when it comes at any expense to their paychecks. While this attitude may be frowned upon as "economic illiteracy," it nevertheless demonstrates that cooperation will not necessarily enlist all participants. Pessimists viewing these outcomes tend to place more belief in balanced countervailing power.

The third party of interest, the public, is not directly represented at the bargaining table. If cooperation is to replace conflict for the benefit of the public, the impetus will have to come from one of the other actors, unless extreme circumstances force a change in public policy.

In a different vein, a final reason for resisting cooperation is the change in social expectations it might require. Cooperation now works well in Japan in part because children there are raised to support the image of their family and their organization. Cooperation is consistent with self-actualization. In the United States it is often contrary. Americans are raised to be individualistic. We are taught to rely on ourselves. We do not generally see ourselves as a part of any integrated whole. Our religious institutions and school systems teach the importance of "standing up and being counted" and promote a willingness to "go against the crowd." Americans are expected to be different from one another. We not only tolerate diversity, we extoll it. We are proud to protect the minority from the tyranny of the majority, to permit all sides to be heard, to be allowed to be different.

When one's focus is the self, rather than the family, organization, or country, much more conflict is generated. Americans recognize that totally unrestrained individuality would produce chaos. We can and do compromise self-interest to attain group goals, but the compromise is generally only to the extent necessary and for the shortest duration possible. In the workplace, conformity is often required, but it is also often resisted. At all levels of employment, many Americans may fear that indulging in cooperation will not only reduce individual rewards and recognition but may also require conformity. Again, this belief is not necessarily accurate, but it is widespread. It is not surprising that when one is raised to be "treated like a person, not a number," it is uncomfortable to suppress that individuality for the gain of an employer. It can be done, but it is seldom done willingly.

CONCLUSION

Competition is as American as apple pie. Cooperation is not. Our choice of conflict regulated by countervailing power was a conscious one. It is consistent with a set of American values focusing on the self. Up to this point, the competitive pursuit of self-interest has brought us both the world's greatest prosperity and the world's greatest freedom. Whether the same values and system can continue to deliver such benefits in a changing world remains to be seen.

Notes

1. Foster Rhea Dulles, *Labor in America: A History* (New York: Thomas Y. Crowell Co., 1966), p. 273.
2. Dulles, p. 262.
3. Adolph Hitler had risen to power in Depression-wracked Germany on an anticapitalist fascist doctrine that nationalized the major means of production. The "captains of American industry" were aware of this and did not wish to see such outcomes repeated here.
4. The Railway Labor Act of 1926 encouraged collective bargaining in the limited sector of the economy to which it applied, and the Norris-La Guardia and National Industrial Recovery Acts of the New Deal attempted to extend a right of recognition to unions. Neither of these latter acts had sufficient enforcement power.
5. National Labor Relations Act, Sec. 8(d)1.
6. NLRA, Secs. 8(a)(1), 8(a)(3), and 8(a)(4).
7. NLRA, Sec. 8(a)(2).

8. NLRA, Secs. 9–12.
9. Dulles, p. 265.
10. Quoted in Arthur A. Sloane and Fred Witney, *Labor Relations.* 4th ed. (Englewood Cliffs, N.J.: Prentice-Hall, 1981), p. 97.
11. Many European countries reacted to the Great Depression by socialistically managing their economies.
12. Ben Fischer, "Collective Bargaining and Fifty Years of the CIO," *Proceedings of the 1985 Spring Meeting, Industrial Relations Research Association* (Madison, Wis., 1985), p. 659.
13. *Ibid.*
14. Irving Bernstein, "The Historical Significance of the CIO," *Proceedings of the 1985 Spring Meeting, Industrial Relations Research Association* (Madison, Wis., 1985), p. 656.
15. *Ibid.*, p. 657.
16. *Ibid.*, p. 656.
17. Edward L. Cushman, "Discussion: The CIO," *Proceedings of the 1985 Spring Meeting, Industrial Relations Research Association* (Madison, Wis., 1985), p. 664.
18. Bernstein, p. 655.
19. *Ibid.*
20. *Ibid.*, p. 657.
21. *Ibid.*, p. 658.
22. Fischer, p. 661.
23. Jack Barbash, "The Theory of Industrial Unionism," *Proceedings of the 1985 Spring Meeting, Industrial Relations Research Association* (Madison, Wis., 1985), 652.
24. Bernstein, p. 658.
25. Fischer, p. 660.
26. Bernstein, p. 658.
27. Fischer, p. 659.
28. Bernstein, p. 657.
29. *Ibid.*
30. Sloan and Witney, p. 82.
31. *Ibid.*
32. See R. Kohl et al., "Can America Increase Productivity to Compete with Foreign Competition?" *Management Science*, Vol. 27 (December 1981), pp. 1470–72; "Productivity: Key to Revitalizing American Industry," *Industry Week*, Vol. 20 (June 1, 1981) , pp. 64–68; "Productivity: What's America's Problem?" *Christian Science Monitor*, Vol. 75 (August 15, 1983), p. 23; "Productivity: Another Japanese Export," *Business*, Vol. 33 (October 1983), pp. 3–10; N. Hatvany and V. Puick, "Japanese Management Practices and Productivity," *Organizational Dynamics*, Vol. 9 (Spring 1981), pp. 4–21; J. E. Lapping, "Cooperation Is More Than Voluntary," *Engineering News Record*, Vol. 207 (November 5, 1981), p. 33; J. O'Toole, "How Management Hinders Productivity," *Industrial Week*, Vol. 210 (August 10, 1981), pp. 54–55; and J. Jenkins, "Participative Management: The New Wave," *Management World*, Vol. 10 (May 1981), pp. 8–10.

Discussion Questions

1. Evaluate the effect of the Great Depression on the American industrial relations system.

2. Analyze why balanced conflict of power was chosen over other forms of conflict resolution.
3. Discuss how the CIO constituted a major change in union philosophy. Discuss how it did not represent a major change in union philosophy.
4. Discuss the effects of Communism and corruption on the system.
5. Evaluate the extent of and reasons for changes in the conflict-resolution system in the past 30 years.

Statements for Comment

1. "Only dreamers believe American employers and employees can cooperate."
2. "The problem with motivation and cooperation today is it's been too long since the Great Depression."
3. "The Wagner Act is the source of our current problems. It interferes with market mechanisms in the allocation of resources."
4. "Labor relations are too important to be left to unions and companies."
5. "Cooperation won't really make us all alike."

Situations

Case 4–1 "American unions are Communistic. I don't mean controlled by Moscow, although God knows they may be. I mean they are opposed to the principles of free enterprise. They try to make everyone equal instead of recognizing everyone as individuals according to their merit," said Kathy Kubiak.

"I'm not sure that's a very good application of what Communism is about," said Brenda Johnson. "Besides, unions are like that because it's the only realistic way to be in situations of otherwise unequal bargaining power. Finally, I think Samuel Gompers demonstrated that American unions really are capitalistic, not Communistic. If you think of a union as a person—just like a corporation is a legal person—it acts just like any other capitalist."

Support and attack the positions taken by Kathy and Brenda.

Case 4–2 "Government support of unions is an example of what's gone wrong with the American economy. If workers want unions on their own, they should form them on their own and the government should stay out of business," said Warren Hilgert, President of the local Chamber of Commerce.

"Sir, I'm not sure you fully appreciate the potential consequences of your recommendations," said Norma Walton, an economics student at the local university. "I'm not sure you understand what life would be like without either protective government or protective unions. I think history provides us some lessons and that your rhetoric doesn't reflect them. In short, if you knew what you were talking about, you would change your position."

How defensible are the contentions of Warren and Norma?

Bibliography of Related Readings

Auerbach, Jerald S., *American Labor: The Twentieth Century* (Indianapolis: Bobbs-Merrill, 1969).

"Born in Battle—The UAW's Early Years," *Distributive Worker*, January 1980, pp. 9–10.

Chandler, A. D., Jr., "Business History: What Is It About?" *Journal of Contemporary Business*, 1981, pp. 47–63.

Erlich, M., "Peter J. McGuire's Trade Unionism: Socialism of a Trades Union Kind?" *Labor History (United States)*, 1983, pp. 165–97.

Gordon, M., "The Communists and the Drive to Organize Steel," *Labor History (United States)* 1982, pp. 254–65.

Klehr, H., "American Communism and the United Auto Workers: New Evidence on an Old Controversy," *Labor History (United States)*, 1983, pp. 404–13.

Levenstein, H. A., *Communism, Anticommunism and the CIO*, (Westport, Conn.: Greenwood Press, 1981).

MacLeod, Celeste, *Horatio Alger, Farewell: The End of the American Dream* (New York: Seaview Books, 1980).

Merry, R. W., "After The Fall: How Depression Gave a Boost to Big Labor, Changed Its Strategy," *Wall Street Journal*, September 20, 1979, p. 1.

Neufeld, M. R., "The Persistence of Ideas in the American Labor Movement: The Heritage of the 1830s," *Industrial and Labor Relations Review*, 1982, pp. 207–20.

Ozanne, R., "Trends in American Labor History," *Labor History (United States)*, 1980, pp. 513–21.

Shannon, David A., *The Great Depression* (Englewood Cliffs, N.J.: Prentice-Hall, 1960).

FIVE

LEGAL

FRAMEWORK

Laws often are not easy to read. They are even more difficult to apply. This is particularly true of our labor laws. They are generally worded in terms of conclusions or results, such as, "It shall be an unfair labor practice to fail to bargain in good faith," or "It shall be an unfair labor practice for an employer to discriminate, or for a union to cause an employer to discriminate, against an employee because of his union activity." The law seldom gives specific directions. For instance, it does not say whether employees may distribute leaflets in the parking lots of privately owned shopping malls. Whether such specific behavior is permitted requires an interpretation of the law.

Interpreting the law is the job of the National Labor Relations Board and the federal court system. They make decisions on a case-by-case basis—that is, they apply general principles of the statute and previous interpretations from other cases.

In each case, two concerns have to be resolved: (1) What actually happened? and (2) was what happened legal or illegal? The first concern requires a determination of the facts in the case. The second requires an application of the law.

Since the facts are always somewhat different (and somewhat alike) in the next case, labor lawyers get paid high fees to argue that their client is right under the law as applied to the new set of circumstances. Many, many cases get litigated each year. The accumulated decisions form the "case law" of labor relations. Although our main labor relations statute, the Taft-Hartley Act, is less than 50 pages long, the case law interpreting it runs thousands of pages per year.

In this textbook only the stated rules of the statutory law will be examined. Their interpretation is too complex to be approached in any synoptic fashion. Students seeking greater knowledge of application are encouraged to enroll in a specialized class in the subject or to read any of the texts recommended at the end of the chapter. It is the author's conclusion that more is lost than gained by having business students pursue labor law on a case-analysis basis. The risk in self-advisement is significant, and confusion and uncertainty are often promoted. This chapter will sacrifice some of the richness and complexity of interpretation for clarity and, hopefully, greater understanding of a less complicated subject.

TAFT-HARTLEY ACT

Policy

The role of law in American collective bargaining is to provide the rules of the game—not the outcome. It provides a framework for informing the parties of what they may do and what they must do. The success or failure of these actions is generally the concern only of the parties, not the government or the public. Practitioners like to talk in terms of "free collective bargaining" in the United States. "Free" in this sense is freedom from government interference.

Total freedom from government interference, however, proved unworkable historically. The great difference in bargaining power between employers and employees led to the passage of the National Labor Relations (Wagner) Act during the Great Depression. The Act was entirely prounion because that was the side the government and the public believed needed protection. Unions quickly lost their position of favor, however. Some highly publicized strikes by coal miners during World War II (when unions had been asked by the President not to strike because of the national emergency) and large numbers of strikes immediately after the war caused the public to reconsider its position. The result was the Labor-Management Relations (Taft-Hartley) Act of 1947. It was intended to swing the balance of power away from unions to a more moderate and—in the eyes of the public—more appropriate position.

The Taft-Hartley Act preserved the Wagner Act but added several amendments to it. The additional provisions were designed to protect the interests of nonunion employees as well as unionized employees, to strengthen and clarify management's rights, and to prevent abuses of union power by adding a section of union unfair labor practices. It also acted to protect the public's rights by providing procedures to end strikes threatening the nation's safety or health. This act, with slight amendments, remains the basic legal framework for collective bargaining today. Selected, annotated portions of the Act appear in the Appendix at the end of the book.

Coverage

The Taft-Hartley Act's provisions, with their subsequent amendments, apply to most businesses in the United States. There are two categories of exceptions to coverage: (1) by size of the employer and (2) by type of employment. The Act has "jurisdictional" provisions requiring that an employer be engaged in interstate commerce and do as much dollar volume of business as a set standard requires. The standard is adjusted from time to time to reflect inflation. Generally, all but the smallest businesses are covered, and those are often covered by state-enacted "little Taft-Hartley Acts" covering intrastate commerce. Overall, the provisions of the Act (or its state equivalents) apply to most businesses not subject to exclusion by type of employment. The jurisdictional standards appear in Table 5–1.

The exclusions for type of employment include several major categories, along with some minor exceptions not generally of importance in typical employment relationships. The major categories of employment not covered include managers and supervisors, government employees, and agricultural workers. Employees of railroads and airlines are covered by the largely similar Railway Labor Act.

TABLE 5-1   JURISDICTIONAL GUIDELINES OF THE NLRB

Type of Establishment	Annual Dollar Volume of Business
Nonretail operations	50,000
Retail enterprises	500,000
Office buildings	100,000
Transportation enterprises	50,000
Local transit systems	250,000
Newspaper enterprises	200,000
Local public utilities	250,000
Hotels	500,000
National defense	No minimum amount
Proprietary hospitals	250,000
and nursing homes	100,000
Private nonprofit universities and colleges	1,000,000
United States Postal Service	No minimum amount
Enterprises over which the Board does not assert jurisdiction:	
Racetrack enterprises	
Owners, breeders, and trainers of racehorses	
Real estate brokers	

SOURCE: *National Labor Relations Board,* Jurisdictional Guide *(Washington, D.C.: Superintendent of Documents, U.S. Government Printing Office)*

Exclusion from coverage means employees are not protected by the Act's provisions, nor are they bound by its restrictions. Generally, this is a liability for employees, since they may be discharged for their union activity. On one major occasion, however, it proved to be beneficial. In the 1960s, Cesar Chavez was attempting to organize farm workers in the western United States. Most of these workers were Hispanic, spoke little or no English, migrated from employer to employer as crops were harvested, and performed extremely difficult labor for very low wages. Their jobs had to be among the very worst in America. Previous attempts at unionization had been rebuffed by the grower-employers. Since the employees were not covered by the Act's provisions, the growers were legally free to discharge union sympathizers and were under no obligation to recognize any union, even if it represented a majority of the employees. But also because the workers were not covered by Taft-Hartley, the Act's prohibition of secondary boycotts did not apply to them.

Chavez had urged many growers to recognize his union and engage in collective bargaining. Citing the law, they refused, because they were not obligated to do so and certainly did not choose to do so. Chavez then urged a boycott by consumers of lettuce grown in nonunion fields. This was to be accomplished by picketing grocery stores and urging customers not to buy the lettuce sold there. Because Chavez was a genuinely charismatic leader, because the farm workers really were working under miserable conditions that anyone would feel sympathy for, and because a sense of ethnic pride (for all groups) was popular at the time, Chavez's campaign received a great deal of national publicity and effectively reduced the sale of nonunion lettuce. Unfortunately, that was not enough to win his fight.

Chavez's primary target was nonunion growers. He wanted to put pressure on them. One way he hoped he could do it was by getting grocery chains to stop buying nonunion lettuce. If the grocers would buy only from unionized suppliers, then growers would have to recognize the union to have a market for their product. Unfortunately, even though lettuce sales dropped under the boycott, grocers generally reflected on the loss of sales as a small one (certainly as a proportion of the total sales of a grocery store) and let the parties settle it on their own. (There may also have been some reluctance on the part of the grocers to cancel their contracts or change suppliers, since this would aid a union, and grocery chains are not known for a prounion stance on their own.) The union's request to grocers not to stock nonunion lettuce and to customers not to buy it may have been effective, but it did not cause enough pain to the grocers to get enough of them to change their behavior.

Chavez then escalated the confrontation. He changed the point of attack. Instead of trying just to hurt growers by reducing the sale of lettuce, he also began trying to hurt grocery store sales in general by picketing and requesting customers not to patronize grocery stores selling nonunion lettuce for any of their needs. This action had three effects: it transferred the dispute from the grower to the grocer, it hurt the grocers so badly they cancelled their nonunion lettuce contracts, and the growers were forced to recognize the union before a grocer would accept their product. In short, it worked.

The only problem with this classic example of a secondary boycott is that it would have been illegal under Taft-Hartley covered employment. Because the boycott was ultimately directed against a secondary employer (the grocer) with whom the union had no employment relationship, it would have been impermissible. After all, it was not the fault of the grocer that the grower would not recognize the union. Judging such activity not to be "fair play," secondary boycotts were made illegal in the sectors covered by the Taft-Hartlet Act. Ironically, the same absence of protection of the Act that had stifled unionization efforts in the past proved to be the avenue of success in this instance.

As an interesting footnote, California and Arizona passed state laws shortly thereafter regulating agricultural employment much the same as Taft-Hartley regulated mainstream employment. Also as an interesting footnote, the reason for the exclusion of agricultural employment should be mentioned. Many practical reasons can be advanced, such as, "Strikes at harvest time would create irreparable damage," or "Farm workers are generally migrants who don't have a continuing work relationship with one employer," or "It would make the cost of doing business prohibitive if agricultural workers were permitted to form unions, and since we all have to eat, it is not in the public's interest." Actually, none of these is the real reason. What really happened was Senator Wagner log-rolled a vote to get support for the entire Wagner Act. The Senators from Arizona and New Mexico originally opposed the Act. After all, in 1935 they had no industrial employee constituents to be concerned about. Their interest was in irrigation for the West. Wagner traded Eastern industrial votes in favor of Hoover Dam (a benefit to the Southwest) in exchange for Southwestern support for the Wagner Act. That support came with a proviso, however. Agricultural workers had to be exempted from coverage, since the Southwest did have politically powerful ranchers who would not have supported their Senators without such an exemption. This was acceptable to Wagner, because his allies had few agricultural workers and the industrial workers were anxious to get on with the Act. Hence, the law had an exemption based not on economic or business reality, but rather political reality.

Exemption of one of the other groups, however, was based definitely on business reality. No one ever objected to management's being exempted from coverage. After all, someone has to sit on the other side of the table and act as representative of the owners. A dispute arose, however, as to how low the exclusion from coverage should go. The original Wagner Act permitted supervisors to be represented by unions in bargaining units separate from their subordinates. Twelve years' experience with such an arrangement, however, convinced management to lobby for the exclusion of supervisors from the category of employees protected by the Act. Management claimed that although the supervisors' units were technically distinct from rank-and-file units, in reality they acted in concert. It was alleged that supervisors and subordinates were working together in opposition to higher management. It was also alleged that unionized supervisors would not enforce discipline against unionized subordinates.[1] Congress accepted these allegations and specifically excluded supervisors from coverage with the Taft-Hartley Act. The operational definition of who is a supervisor appears below.

> Sec. 2 (11) The term "supervisor" means any individual having authority, in the interest of the employer, to hire, transfer, suspend, lay off, recall, promote, discharge, assign, reward, or discipline other employees, or responsibility to direct them or to adjust their grievances, or effectively to recommend such action, if in connection with the foregoing the exercise of such authority is not of a merely routine or clerical nature, but requires the use of independent judgment.

The final major group excluded from coverage is public employees. Their legal status will be examined later in the chapter.

Unfair Labor Practices

Section 7 of the Wagner Act (now Section 7 of Taft-Hartley) guaranteed to workers the right to select representatives of their choosing (unions) to bargain for them collectively. To ensure that this right would be enforced, Congress prohibited certain activities that would interfere with accomplishing the goals of Section 7. These prohibitions are known as unfair labor practices. Section 7 appears below.

> RIGHTS OF EMPLOYEES. SEC. 7. Employees shall have the right to self-organization, to form, join, or assist labor organizations, to bargain collectively through representatives of their choosing, or to engage in other concerted activities for the purpose of collective bargaining or other mutual aid or protection, and shall also have the right to refrain from any or all of such activities except to the extent that such right may be affected by an agreement requiring membership in a labor organization as a condition of employment as authorized in section 8(a)(3).

The Wagner Act listed five employer unfair labor practices. They now make up Sections 8(a)(1) through 8(a)(5) of the Taft-Hartley Act. Sections 8(b)(1) through 8(b)(7) consist of union unfair labor practices. The original five unfair labor practices are clearly stated and easily understood, even if not so easily applied. Those unfair labor practices are statements of general policy. The union unfair labor practices, on the other hand, are often attempts to forbid specific types of behavior and are almost unreadable in their legal form.

Section 8(a)(1) prohibits the employer from interfering with the employees' rights of self-organization. While this includes the obvious prohibition on "punishing" employees for exercising their rights, it also prohibits "brib-

UNION MEMBERS PROTESTING EMPLOYER'S ALLEGED UNFAIR LABOR PRACTICES

SOURCE: AFL-CIO News

ing" them with benefits for voting against a union.[2] Section 8(a)(2) outlaws "company" unions—that is, unions established, maintained, and dominated by the employer. This device was very popular in the 1920s as a means of curtailing the organizing efforts of "real" unions. Employees were thought to be less likely to perceive a need for unionization if they already had a union. This type of violation is comparatively rare now.

Section 8(a)(3) is really a more specific statement of 8(a)(1). It prohibits discharging or discriminating against employees for supporting a union. Any violation of 8(a)(3) is also a violation of 8(a)(1). This section also prohibits promising benefits as well as threatening sanctions.

Section 8(a)(4) is an even more specific application of Section 8(a)(3). It prohibits discharging or discriminating against an employee for filing an unfair labor practice charge or testifying in an NLRB case. Typically, an 8(a)(4) violation is also an 8(a)(3) and an 8(a)(1).

Section 8(a)(5) is quite different. It requires the employer to bargain in good faith in an attempt to reach agreement over wages, hours, and working conditions. This section will be examined in detail in Chapter Nine.

Employers rarely admit to discharging an employee for union activity. They usually allege that the employee was terminated for cause. The employee, on the other hand, usually alleges that the charges were "trumped up" and that the real reason was union activity. In these "mixed-motive" discharges, the Board has to infer which explanation is more plausible. One of the all-time great cases demonstrating this problem appears below.

EDWARD G. BUDD MFG. CO. V. NLRB
UNITED STATES COURT APPEALS, THIRD CIRCUIT, 1943
138 F.2d 86, 13 LRRM 512
BIGGS, CIRCUIT JUDGE . . .

The complaint, as subsequently amended, alleges that the petitioner, in September, 1933, created and foisted a labor organization, known as the Budd Employee Representation Association, upon its employees and thereafter contributed financial support to the Association and dominated its activities. The amended complaint also alleges that in July, 1941, the petitioner discharged an employee, Walter Weigand, because of his activities on behalf of the union . . .

The case of Walter Weigand is extraordinary. If ever a workman deserved summary discharge, it was he. He was under the influence of liquor while on duty. He came to work when he chose and he left the plant and his shift as he pleased. In fact, a foreman on one occasion was agreeably surprised to find Weigand at work and commented upon it; Weigand amiably stated that he was enjoying it.[6] He brought a woman (apparently generally known as "the Duchess") to the rear of the plant yard and introduced some of the employees to her. He took another employee to visit her and when this man got too drunk to be able to go home, punched his time-card for him and put him on the table in the representatives' meeting room in the plant in order to sleep off his intoxication. Weigand's immediate

superiors demanded again and again that he be discharged, but each time higher officials intervened on Weigand's behalf because, as was naively stated, he was "a representative." In return for not working at the job for which he was hired, the petitioner gave him full pay and on five separate occasions raised his wages. One of these raises was general; that is to say, Weigand profited by a general wage increase throughout the plant, but the other four raises were given Weigand at times when other employees in the plant did not receive wage increases.

The petitioner contends that Weigand was discharged because of the cumulative grievances against him. But about the time of the discharge it was suspected by some of the representatives that Weigand had joined the complaining CIO union. (The court then describes the company's reasons for believing Weigand had joined the CIO union.)

The following day Weigand was discharged. As the court stated in National Labor Relations Board v. Condenser Corp. . . . 3 Cir., 128 F.2d at page 75, an employer may discharge an employee for a good reason, a poor reason or no reason at all so long as the provisions of the National Labor Relations Act are not violated. It is, of course, a violation to discharge an employee be-cause he has engaged in activities on be-half of a union. Conversely an employer may retain an employee for a good reason, a bad reason or no reason at all and the reason is not a concern of the Board. But it is cer-tainly too great a strain on our credulity to assert, as does the petitioner, that Weigand was discharged for an accumulation of of-fenses. We think that he was discharged be-cause his work on behalf of the CIO had be-come known to the plant manager. That ended his sinecure at the Budd plant. The Board found that he was discharged be-cause of his activities on behalf of the union. The record shows that the Board's finding was based on sufficient evidence. The order of the Board will be enforced. . . .

[6][Footnote numbered as in original.—Ed.] *Weigand stated that he was carried on the payroll as a "rigger." He was asked what was a rigger. He replied: "I don't know; I am not a rigger."*

Section 8(b)(1) parallels 8(a)(1). It makes it an unfair labor practice for a union to coerce or restrain employees in the exercise of their collective bargain-ing rights, one of which is to choose not to have a union.

Section 8(b)(2) prohibits a union from forcing an employer to discrimi-nate against or for an employee because of his or her union status.

Section 8(b)(3) requires the union to bargain in good faith. This provi-sion has its greatest effect on the employer's right to select its own represent-ative at the bargaining table. Unions have generally been anxious to proceed with bargaining, since it is one of their chief ways of delivering benefits to their constituents. On occasions, however, they have refused to bargain because they did not approve of management's representative (when, for instance, that per-son was a former union officer), or when the employer insisted on bargaining through an association. This provision requires that the union bargain with whomever the employer chooses, so long as that individual has the power to bind the employer.

Section 8(b)(4) is a very complicated and often-litigated section. It is di-vided into four subsections, 8(b)(4)(A) through 8(b)(4)(D). It is written in legalese that is all but unintelligible to the layman. (The reader is invited to compare any subsection of 8(a) with 8(b)(4). An oversimplified translation of 8(b)(4) follows.

Section 8(b)(4)(A) makes it illegal to use strikes or certain other economic pressures to force an employer to join a labor organization.

Section 8(b)(4)(B) contains the same prohibition when the object is to force recognition of a union. 8(b)(4)(C) makes it illegal to pressure an employer to recognize a union when it has already been organized by an NLRB-certified representative.

Section 8(b)(4)(D) forbids jurisdictional strikes. Jurisdictional strikes oc-cur when a union protests the assignment of work to a different group of em-ployees. In many instances the problem arises between unions representing dif-ferent crafts working for the same employer. Reasoning that these disputes are not the responsibility of the employer, the Act provides for arbitration as a substitute for strikes in this instance.

Section 8(b)(5) forbids excessive union initiation fees and dues.

Section 8(b)(6) prohibits "featherbedding"—payment for work not performed or not to be performed.

AMERICA'S BEST-KNOWN FEATHERBEDDING STORY

Although not technically within the jurisdiction of the Taft-Hartley Act, the following account is informative. The most widespread story of featherbedding in America is that of the railroad fireman. In the days of the steam-powered locomotive, the fireman shoveled coal from the coal car into the locomotive's boiler. When railroads converted to diesel-powered locomotives, there was no longer a need for a fireman—yet his position was not eliminated.

For roughly 30 years, firemen continued to ride, unneeded, next to the engineer. Rationalizations for his employment, such as, "He can stop the train if the engineer collapses from a heart attack," were provided, but everyone in the industry knew this was really only a device to continue employment for workers who would otherwise have been displaced.

The unneeded firemen continued to hold their jobs for so long because the union and employees desired it and management agreed to the practice despite its obvious economic waste. How this situation arose, why it prevailed for so long, and what brought it to an end require explanation.

The fact that a train moves has a profound influence on labor relations in the railroad industry. Unlike a factory, where a supervisor can constantly observe the workforce, a train crew cannot be continuously monitored. Therefore, the assurance that they are doing what they should must be accomplished by record keeping instead of observation. This meant that railroading developed an elaborate network of rules and procedures that delineated how and when the crew was to perform an operation.

Both on trains and in factories, procedures become outdated as technology and policies change. In a factory this outdating can be quickly adapted to, as supervisors can correct inappropriate behavior. For a moving workplace, the adaptation requires more attention to detail and records than in a stationary workplace. This problem became particularly bad in railroads, where management lacked an economic motivation to pay attention to such details.

Railroad economics were historically different from general business economics. Management did not perceive a compelling need to be efficient (and to eradicate outdated and inappropriate work rules) for two reasons:

1. *They were not in a competitive marketplace. The Interstate Commerce Commission regulated the rates carriers charged. The rate established took into consideration what costs were. So long as a cost was equal for all railroads (they all carried an unneeded fireman on every train) it was no burden to the railroad—the cost was passed along to the customer in the form of a consistently higher tariff.*

2. *Railroads were not in danger of losing total business because, historically, there was no other viable way to ship products across land.*

The consequence of these two factors was that profits were determined by volume carried, not by cost efficiency. The emphasis was placed on route allocation and, at its worst, kickbacks and bribes to receive rights-of-way and tonnage. The cost of the fireman was trivial compared to the other stakes. The waste of this featherbedding was permitted because of a combination of employee desire and benign neglect.

This situation did not continue forever, however (although 30 years is a long time to pay for something not needed). After World War II, improvements in American roads made trucking a more viable alternative to railroads than it had previously been. This meant that railroads now had competition that was not susceptible to the same cost (including the fireman) pressure. Any unnecessary cost had become a burden that needed to be eliminated. Under the pressure of competition from trucking, railroad management for the first time had a compelling need to be efficient.

One result was an attempt to reduce featherbedded expenses. The railroad unions resisted these attempts because of self-interest. The bargaining efforts of management and unions over this topic attracted great national attention, because the example created was so blatant. As the public became aware of the situation, it became appalled at union efforts to protect unneeded jobs. An eventual result was the legal prohibition of agreements to pay for work not needed.

One last caveat must be observed. Featherbedding is not usually a widespread problem, because most managements, unlike railroads, have competitive pressures forcing them to minimize cost. Featherbedding cannot exist without management cooperation. Such cooperation is seldom given.

Section 8(b)(7) places restrictions on picketing. The restrictions apply to its purpose, effect, and duration. The major goal is to assure that the NLRB election procedures are used, rather than economic pressure, to determine representation status.

The remaining portions of Section 8, subsections (c) through (f), clarify the rights and obligations of the parties. Section 8(c) permits the employer "free speech" rights in expressing its views on unions, so long as such expression contains no threat of reprisal or promise of benefit.

Section 8(d) clarifies bargaining obligations that will be examined in Chapter 9.

Section 8(e) bans "hot cargo" agreements, with exceptions for the construction and garment trades industries. Hot-cargo agreements are contract provisions in which the employer promises not to handle products that the union finds objectionable. The reason the union would find them objectionable is they had been produced by nonunion labor or at a plant on strike. The reason for making this provision illegal is that it expands a labor dispute beyond the contending parties to employers who are not really the cause of the problem. By implication, the same rules apply to secondary boycotts.

Section 8(f) provides additional special exceptions for the construction industry. It allows for recognition of a union without a demonstration of majority status, union shop enforceability after only seven days, and the use of union-operated referral or "hiring" halls, with provisions for nondiscriminatory referrals and without preference for union members.

These exceptions for the construction industry were made with the blessing of management in recognition of the realities of the construction business. Because construction is, by nature, a process of limited duration at a worksite, it is expected that the employer will seek business elsewhere upon completion of the project. Since this may be in another city, it is often infeasible for the contractor to relocate its workers each time a new project is begun. Instead, it is mutually beneficial for the employer and the employees to have the union train, certify, and refer competent employees to contractors at a location as they need them. It provides stability in the workers' lives and provides the employer with a source of adequately trained employees without having to sustain the cost of training them. Thus, the unusually symbiotic relationship between employers and unions in the construction industry historically supported a more "cozy" union shop relation than is usually tolerated.

The application of labor law in general is a difficult task. Questions of how the law applies to a particular set of facts keeps the NLRB very busy, labor lawyers highly paid, and takes us beyond the scope of this book. The average businessman's best response to labor law problems is probably to call a lawyer. It is an area in which it is dangerous to be self-advised.

NLRB Functions—Unfair Labor Practice Charges

The National Labor Relations Board was established by the Wagner Act and maintained under Taft-Hartley. It has two major functions: to conduct elections to determine if employees want union representation and to investigate and prosecute charges of unfair labor practices. Its members are appointed by the President (with the advice and consent of two-thirds of the Senate) and generally reflect the political preferences of the President appointing them.

When a party (usually an employee) files a complaint with a Regional Director, a field examiner from the Board's General Counsel is dispatched to gather evidence and determine if there are sufficient grounds for filing a charge. If there are sufficient grounds and the dispute cannot be conciliated, a formal charge is filed. At this point, the government becomes the plaintiff, since allegedly a law had been violated, and the employee becomes the complaining party. The defendant is called respondent. The prosecution of the case and its expenses belong to the government. A map of the NLRB's Regional Offices appears in Figure 5–1.

The case is tried at a hearing before an Administrative Law Judge (ALJ).

FIGURE 5-1 MAP SHOWING BOUNDARIES OF NLRB REGIONS, SUBREGIONS, AND RESIDENT OFFICES

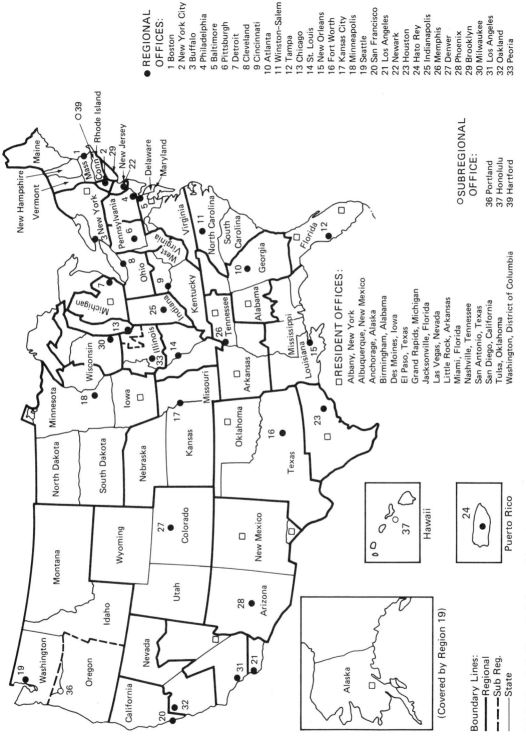

● REGIONAL OFFICES:

1 Boston
2 New York City
3 Buffalo
4 Philadelphia
5 Baltimore
6 Pittsburgh
7 Detroit
8 Cleveland
9 Cincinnati
10 Atlanta
11 Winston-Salem
12 Tampa
13 Chicago
14 St. Louis
15 New Orleans
16 Fort Worth
17 Kansas City
18 Minneapolis
19 Seattle
20 San Francisco
21 Los Angeles
22 Newark
23 Houston
24 Hato Rey
25 Indianapolis
26 Memphis
27 Denver
28 Phoenix
29 Brooklyn
30 Milwaukee
31 Los Angeles
32 Oakland
33 Peoria

○ SUBREGIONAL OFFICE:

36 Portland
37 Honolulu
39 Hartford

□ RESIDENT OFFICES:

Albany, New York
Albuquerque, New Mexico
Anchorage, Alaska
Birmingham, Alabama
Des Moines, Iowa
El Paso, Texas
Grand Rapids, Michigan
Jacksonville, Florida
Las Vegas, Nevada
Little Rock, Arkansas
Miami, Florida
Nashville, Tennessee
San Antonio, Texas
San Diego, California
Tulsa, Oklahoma
Washington, District of Columbia

Boundary Lines:
—— Regional
– – – Sub Reg.
—— State

SOURCE: *A Guide to Basic Law and Procedures Under the National Labor Relations Act* (Washington, D.C.: U.S. Government Printing Office, 1978), p. 56.

The ALJ hears testimony, receives briefs, and makes findings of fact and interprets and applies the law. If the ALJ rules that the respondent has committed an unfair labor practice, he or she may issue a cease and desist order to stop such behavior. The ALJ may not levy fines, bar employers from government contracts, or put anyone in jail. If an employee had been wrongfully discharged, the ALJ may order reinstatement with back pay plus interest, less setoff (the amount the employee earned in alternative employment while the case was pending). If an ALJ's order is not obeyed, the NLRB may appeal to a federal court for an injunction to enforce the order. If the order is still disobeyed, the federal judge issuing the injunction may find the guilty party in contempt of court and assess fines.

Either party losing the hearing before the ALJ may appeal the decision to the NLRB itself. The Board will not call witnesses or make determinations of fact. It merely reviews the record established at the hearing. It determines if the law was applied correctly and whether there is sufficient evidence to support the ALJ's findings of fact. It cannot substitute its findings of fact for the ALJ's. If it finds the law was not applied properly, or the facts are not supported by the record, it may reverse or amend the decision or remand the case to the ALJ for a new hearing in accordance with the Board's findings.

Either party losing at the Board level may appeal to the federal appeals court of proper jurisdiction, where a review similar to the Board's will take place. A final appeal may be made to the United States Supreme Court. The process obviously can be time-consuming and costly. Furthermore, a higher percentage of cases are probably appealed than would otherwise be the case because of the Board's notorious capacity to switch positions on issues as the membership changes—without any change in the law. The administrative organization of the Board and the processing of an unfair labor practice charge are depicted in Figures 5–2 and 5–3. Figure 5–4 is a chart depicting the enforcement of an NLRB order.

NLRB Functions—Conducting Elections

The other major function of the NLRB is to conduct representation elections. The rules and procedures it uses are covered in detail in Chapter Eight.

Emergency Disputes Procedures

The public was very concerned in 1947 about union strike power. It was particularly worried that a strike by a large union could cripple the entire country. The response was the passage of Title II of the Taft-Hartley Act—the National Emergency Disputes Procedures. The Procedures were established to operate as follows:

The President invokes Title II when a threatened or actual labor dispute (a strike or lockout) "will, if permitted to occur or continue, imperil the national

FIGURE 5-2 ADMINISTRATIVE ORGANIZATION OF THE NATIONAL LABOR RELATIONS BOARD

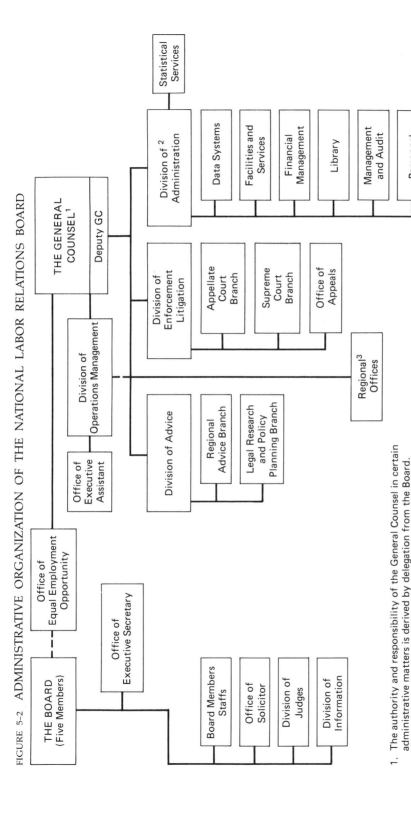

1. The authority and responsibility of the General Counsel in certain administrative matters is derived by delegation from the Board.
2. Division of Administration is also responsible to the Board for administrative support services required in the performance of Board functions.
3. Includes exercise by Regional Director of Board authority under Section 9 of the Act, in representation cases, by delegation from the Board.

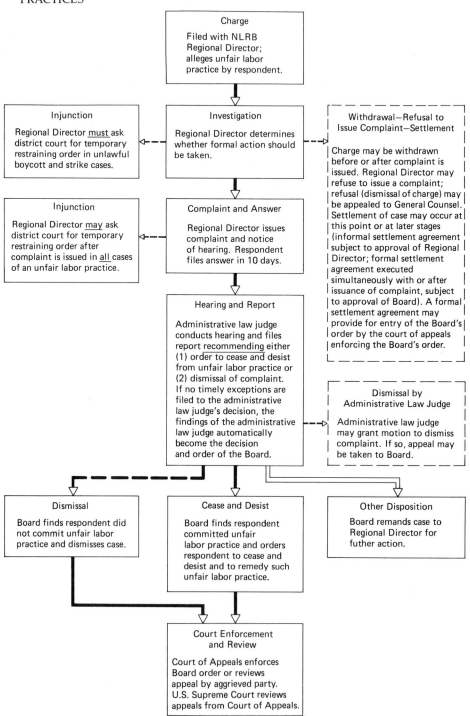

FIGURE 5-4   NLRB ORDER ENFORCEMENT CHART

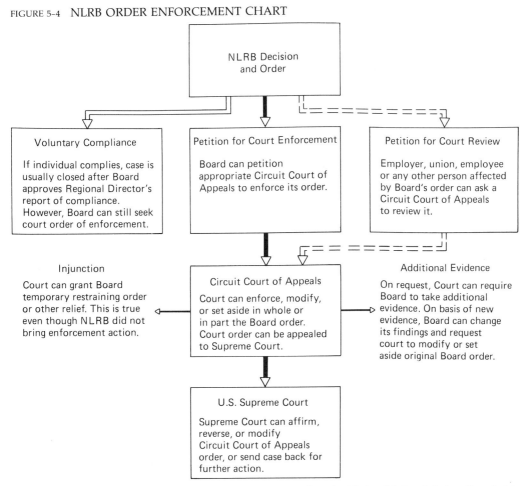

SOURCE: *Reprinted by permission from* How to Take a Case Before the National Labor Relations Board, *4th edition, by Kenneth C. McGuiness, page 307, copyright 1976 by the Bureau of National Affairs, Inc., Washington, D.C.*

health or safety." Having made such a determination, the President is required to appoint a "board of inquiry" to investigate and report back to him on the issues. The board is not permitted to make recommendations. The President may then direct the attorney general to seek an injunction in federal district court to prevent or terminate the strike (or lockout). While the injunction is in effect, the status quo on wages and working conditions is preserved. If a strike continues or begins, the strikers are, of course, subject to jail for contempt of the district court order. The employer and union are obligated to make efforts to resolve the dispute with Federal Mediation and Conciliation Service aid. If after 60 days the dispute is not resolved, the board of inquiry is reconvened to make an updated status report, again with no recommendations. The second report must indicate the employer's last offer for settlement, on which the NLRB must poll the employees within 15 days to see if they wish to accept the offer and certify the result to the attorney general within five days. After this step the injunction must be dissolved. The employees are then free to resume (or begin) the strike.

Since the passage of the Act there have been very few strikes that have genuinely threatened the nation's health or safety. In many of these instances, the President used extralegal methods to end the strike rather than using the specified procedures. Among these methods were personal suasion based on power of the President's office, implication that worse laws could be passed, suspending of federal contracts, and sequestering of the negotiators.[3] These extralegal methods are often effective because nobody wants to alienate the federal government with its power as a customer, regulator, and tax agent. The Title II procedures are probably more important as a statement to the public than they are as behavior modifiers. They are seldom used and seldom needed.

Other Legal Provisions

The Taft-Hartley Act has many provisions beyond unfair labor practices and emergency dispute procedures. Among them are the famous/infamous Section 14(b) which permits states to pass "right-to-work" laws, regulations establishing the scope of mandatory subjects of bargaining, restrictions on dues checkoff, direct presentation of grievances, unit determination criteria, and restrictions on certain types of strikes, along with the aforementioned election-procedure regulations and good-faith issues. Each will be dealt with in the chapters on the specific topics.

Role of the Federal Mediation and Conciliation Service

Sometimes the parties, despite their good-faith bargaining effort, fail to reach agreement on a contract. When such an impasse occurs, the parties are obligated to notify the Federal Mediation and Conciliation Service (FMCS) before a strike or lockout occurs. The FMCS is then given the opportunity to mediate the dispute in hopes of finding an agreement before the parties resort to "economic warfare." The techniques of mediation are described in Chapter 10.

The track record of the FMCS is very good. Historically, it has been involved in approximately 60 percent of all initial contracts and 45 percent of all renewals.[4] Of those submitted for mediation, settlement has occurred nearly 90 percent of the time.[5] It should be noted that the mediator has no power to compel the parties to agree or to impose a settlement of his or her own—that would be arbitration. The mediator's job is to find a way that the parties can agree on their own. The services of the FMCS are free to the parties.

Department of Labor

One other federal agency, though not technically a law maker, has substantial impact and visibility in this area. It is the Department of Labor. It was founded in 1913 as a cabinet department to promote the interests of working people. It is essentially the equivalent of management's interest in the Department of Commerce. According to its charter,

> The purpose of the Department of Labor is to foster, promote, and develop the welfare of the wage earners of the United States, to improve their working conditions, and to advance their opportunities for profitable employment. In carrying out this mission, the department administers more than 130 federal labor laws guaranteeing workers' rights to safe and healthful working conditions, a minimum hourly wage and overtime pay, freedom from employment discrimination, unemployment insurance, and workers' compensation. The department also protects workers' pension rights, sponsors job training programs, helps workers find jobs, works to strengthen free collective bargaining, and keeps track of changes in employment, prices, and other national economic measurements. As the department seeks to assist all Americans who need and want to work, special efforts are made to meet the unique job market problems of older workers, youths, minority group members, women, the handicapped and other groups.

The organization of the Department of Labor is shown in Figure 5-5.

RAILWAY LABOR ACT

The Railway Labor Act was passed in 1926, before the Great Depression and the New Deal. Its regulation of labor relations through government intervention was quite ahead of its time. But then so were the problems of the railroads. The railroads were highly unionized, very important to the commercial success of the country, and could be characterized as having highly volatile labor relations. Strikes and violence were common, and the consequences hurt the public as well as parties. Government nonintervention had proved incapable of handling the problem. The government (and the public) recognized earlier in this area than others the need to provide a formalized, civilized, equitable means of union recognition and collective bargaining. Hence, the passage of the Railway Labor Act and government intrusion on laissez faire prior to the general discrediting of business during the Great Depression. Employees of the airlines industry were later added to the Act's coverage.

The Railway Labor Act is largely similar to Taft-Hartley. Its principal difference is in the amount of direct government intervention in problem solving. Tripartite boards are established for the resolution of both bargaining impasses and grievances arising under negotiated contracts.

FIGURE 5-5   STRUCTURE OF DEPARTMENT OF LABOR

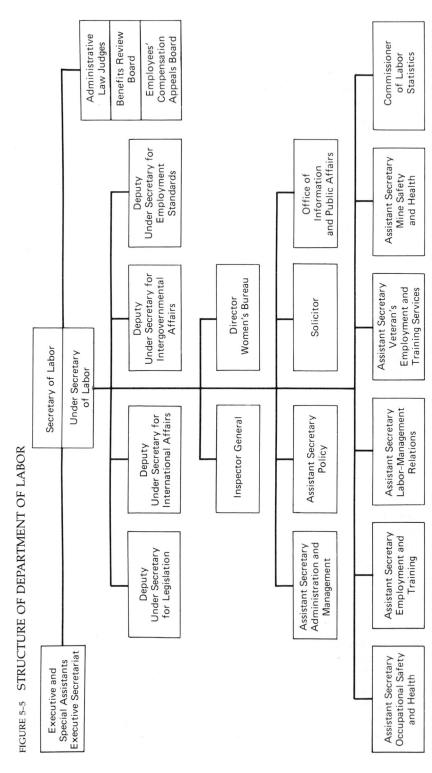

SOURCE: Office of the Federal Register, National Archives and Record Service, General Services Administration, U.S. Government Manual, 1983–1984 (Washington, D.C.: U.S. Government Printing Office, 1983), p. 828.

FIGURE 5–6 RAILWAY COLLECTIVE BARGAINING PROCEDURES AND "STATUS QUO" PERIODS UNDER THE RAILWAY LABOR ACT

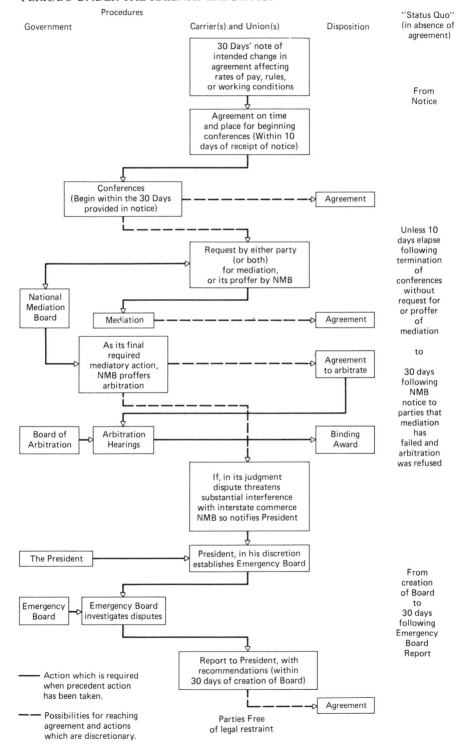

Procedures

Government | Carrier(s) and Union(s) | Disposition | "Status Quo" (in absence of agreement)

30 Days' note of intended change in agreement affecting rates of pay, rules, or working conditions

From Notice

Agreement on time and place for beginning conferences (Within 10 days of receipt of notice)

Conferences (Begin within the 30 Days provided in notice) — — → Agreement

Unless 10 days elapse following termination of conferences without request for or proffer of mediation

Request by either party (or both) for mediation, or its proffer by NMB

National Mediation Board

Mediation — — → Agreement

As its final required mediatory action, NMB proffers arbitration — — → Agreement to arbitrate

to

30 days following NMB notice to parties that mediation has failed and arbitration was refused

Board of Arbitration → Arbitration Hearings → Binding Award

If, in its judgment dispute threatens substantial interference with interstate commerce NMB so notifies President

The President → President, in his discretion establishes Emergency Board

From creation of Board to 30 days following Emergency Board Report

Emergency Board → Emergency Board investigates disputes

Report to President, with recommendations (within 30 days of creation of Board) — — → Agreement

——— Action which is required when precedent action has been taken.

— — Possibilities for reaching agreement and actions which are discretionary.

Parties Free of legal restraint

LANDRUM-GRIFFIN ACT

The Labor-Management Reporting and Disclosure (Landrum-Griffin) Act of 1959 is quite different in purpose from Taft-Hartley. Although a few of its provisions did close loopholes in Taft-Hartley, it is not its major purpose to regulate collective bargaining. Instead, it regulates the relationship between employees and unions. It attempts to ensure that unions are run honestly and fairly.

The Landrum-Griffin Act was passed in response to public indignation over highly publicized corruption and racketeering in union administration. A Senate committee headed by John L. McClellan in the late 1950s revealed misuse of funds and authoritarian control of major unions, particularly the Teamsters. When it became obvious that unions could not or would not administer themselves in a manner acceptable to the public, the government stepped in and legislated controls.

The Landrum-Griffin Act contains seven titles. The first six deal with the internal affairs of unions. Title VII amended the Taft-Hartley Act, closing loopholes on hot-cargo agreements, secondary boycotts, and recognitional picketing; provided the exceptions for the construction industry; and established jurisdictional limitations based on amount of sales. The following is a synopsis of Titles I through VI.

Title I—Bill of Rights

This title assures union members' rights within their organizations. It protects rights in voting in union elections and participation at meetings. It provides that fees cannot be increased without the consent of a majority. Members are protected against expulsion from the union unless due process is followed. This title also provides that a copy of the contract be made available to any member who requests it.

Title II—Required Reports

This title requires all unions to have their constitution and bylaws on record with the Secretary of Labor and to file detailed financial reports. The title also requires employers to file reports on money spent to influence employees in their choice of voting for or against unionization.

Title III—Trusteeships

This title attempts to provide guarantees that the use of trusteeships by national unions is restricted to appropriate circumstances. It requires the national to file a report with the Secretary of Labor detailing the reasons for the takeover.

Title IV—Elections

This title requires that international unions elect their officers at least every five years. Elections can be through referenda or by convention delegates who were selected by secret ballot. Local officers must be selected by secret ballot at least every three years. All members in good standing may participate in elections. Elections violating these provisions may be overturned.

Title V—Safeguards for Unions

This title requires that union officers be responsible for union assets and that they not have been convicted of certain felonies within the previous five years.

Title VI—Miscellaneous

This section outlaws extortionate picketing—where the purpose is to exact money from an employer as a condition of ceasing picketing—and prohibits unions from disciplining members for exercising their rights.

FIGURE 5-7   BARGAINING UNIT SELECTION PROCEDURES, BY SECTOR

The Labor Relations System	Legal Base	Unit Determination	Representation Election	Bargaining Certification
Private sector	National Labor Relations Act, as amended	National Labor Relations Board	National Labor Relations Board	National Labor Relations Board
Railway and airline sector	Railway Labor Act 1926	National Mediation Board	National Mediation Board	National Mediation Board
Postal sector	Postal Reorganization Act 1970	National Labor Relations Board	National Labor Relations Board	National Labor Relations Board
Federal sector	Civil Service Reform Act	Federal Labor Relations Authority	Federal Labor Relations Authority	Federal Labor Relations Authority
Public sector	Various state and local statutes	Varies	Varies	Varies

SOURCE: *Abridged from Eugene C. Hagburg and Marvin J. Levine,* Labor Relations: An Integrated Perspective *(St. Paul, MN: West Publishing Company, 1978), p. 274.*

PUBLIC-SECTOR LAWS

Employees of the federal, state, and local governments are exempted from the coverage of Taft-Hartley. Under the terms of the Postal Reform Act of 1970, Post Office employee relations became covered by the Taft-Hartley provisions, while retaining a prohibition on the right to strike. Other federal employees are covered by the provisions of the Civil Service Reform Act of 1978. The CSRA is very similar to Taft-Hartley and is administered by the Federal Labor Relations Authority, the equivalent of the NLRB. Strikes are prohibited. State and local government employees are covered by the laws (or not covered in the absence of laws) of their respective states. The legal aspects of public-employee collective bargaining will be examined in greater detail in Chapter Fifteen.

CONCLUSION

The public expresses its wishes for our labor relations system by passing laws. These laws try to keep government intervention to a minimum and leave the focus of responsibility on the parties. Laws are passed or amended from time to time to adjust the balance of countervailing power. The failure to change the rights of the parties may fairly be viewed as an assessment by the public that the balance of power is appropriate.

Notes

1. See Charles P. Larrowe, "A Meteor on the Industrial Relations Horizon: The Foreman's Association of America," *Labor History,* Vol. 2 (1961), pp. 259–94.
2. Bruce Feldacker, *Labor Guide to Labor Law,* 2d ed. (Reston, Va.: Reston Publishing Company, 1983), p. 119.
3. Arthur A. Sloane and Fred Witney, *Labor Relations,* 5th ed. (Englewood Cliffs, N.J.: Prentice-Hall, 1985), pp. 121–23.
4. *Thirty Fourth Annual Report,* Federal Mediation and Conciliation Service (Washington, D.C.: U.S. Government Printing Office, 1981), p. 7.
5. *Ibid.*

Discussion Questions

1. Why is labor law a difficult subject?
2. Discuss the purpose of American labor laws.
3. Discuss employer unfair labor practices.
4. Discuss union unfair labor practices.
5. Describe the function of the NLRB in unfair labor practices.

6. Describe the function of the NLRB in conducting representation elections.
7. Analyze Emergency Dispute Procedures.
8. Assess the purpose and content of the Landrum-Griffin Act.
9. Assess the role of laws governing collective bargaining by employees of local, state, and federal governments.

Statements for Comment

1. "The government is always meddling where it isn't needed or wanted. We need to go back to free enterprise."
2. "Collective bargaining may have been a desirable public policy 40 or 50 years ago, but times have changed."
3. "Section 8(a)(1) is wrong in spirit. If employers wish to prevent unions by improving jobs, no one should complain. Promising benefits for voting against a union ought not to be illegal."
4. "The Budd Mfg. case just demonstrates that it is impossible to fire a unionized worker, no matter how bad he is."
5. "The exceptions made for the construction industry were really a deal cut between unions and management. The nonunion worker got left out."
6. "The NLRB is far too political in its decisions and rulings. Its members should be selected on merit and tenured like judges."
7. "All the penalties the NLRB can assess are too lenient. The government can bar polluters and offenders of equal opportunity from bidding on government contracts. It should do the same to violators of labor law."
8. "Unions are more regulated than any other business entity in America. It's unfair and inappropriate."

Situations

Case 5–1 Everett Hall, supervisor of a unionized production department for an aerospace manufacturer, cannot believe what he sees every day. Many jobs in his department require much less than eight hours' work. In fact, he figures there are situations where a single employee could easily complete the requirements of two jobs every day. "This featherbedding makes me sick!" he exclaims to anyone who cares to listen.

Temporary summer employee and full-time college student Gilbert Maas begs to differ. "Pardon me, Chief, but this isn't featherbedding. It's merely underassignment and overpayment. We employees do perform the requirements of our job descriptions. This isn't illegal under the Taft-Hartley Act."

This observation hardly helps Everett feel better about the situation. He screams, "If it isn't illegal, it should be!"

Do you agree? Why or why not? What factors should be considered in making your recommendation?

Case 5–2 Patrick Bird is an American success story. He worked his way through college and received a B.S. in Management. He worked for a large company for three years before starting his own business supplying automotive parts to the Big Three manufacturers. Through hard work, talent, and good luck, his business has prospered. From his original 30 employees (all of whom he knew personally), the company has expanded to 900 employees.

Patrick has always wanted to be perceived as a good employer, a good citizen, and a good guy. Up till now, he has succeeded quite admirably. To keep up with modern methods, Patrick attends management seminars on employee relations. One idea he has been tempted to try is workers' councils, whereby his employees would form groups to meet with management representatives to discuss a wide array of topics ranging from quality, to input on decisions, to grievances. Over a luncheon cocktail at the lounge of the local Hook and Slice Club, Patrick describes his plan to his attorney, Julius Ewing. Julius believes the idea sounds all right in theory but may violate the Taft-Hartley Act, particularly Section 8(a)(2)—forming or abetting a company union. Patrick said that such a concern was "silly. Congress could not have intended such a constraint. I'm sure they never considered such a situation when they passed the law." Julius said he could tell that to the judge.

What do you say? Why?

Case 5–3 Patches, Inc., is a nationwide manufacturer of clothing. It has a large facility in San Antonio, Texas. The company is located there because costs, particularly labor, are low. The workforce is not unionized.

During a recent energy crunch, Elmer Haskins, an accountant in the front office, determined that the company could save $2000 a weekend by turning the plant air conditioning off from 3:30 on Friday to 7:30 on Monday when there was no production going on.

The management of the company implemented Elmer's "bright idea." What they did not anticipate was the workers' reaction on Monday morning. It can be very hot on August weekends in San Antonio. When the workers came in Monday morning it was 87 hot, stale degrees in the plant. It did not cool off to the customary 75 degrees until 11 A.M. The workers did not cool off at all. A group of them, led by Manuel Cepeda, approached their supervisor asking him to prevent the company from doing this next weekend. The supervisor said he would mention it to higher management but couldn't promise anything.

The following Monday the same situation occurred. The workers were steaming—in more ways than one. Manuel and 40 other employees stalked off the job, closing down their department and halting production entirely. Soon all the employees walked outside to the parking lot (where it was cooler) and said they would not return to work until the temperature reached 75 degrees.

Travis Westmoreland, the Vice-President of Personnel, came out to the parking lot and ordered the employees back to work, threatening to discharge anyone not at his workstation within five minutes. (This threat was realistic, since there was a large potential supply of labor in the area that could quickly assimilate the unskilled jobs.) The workers argued that the temperature was a health hazard and besides, the company couldn't fire them for exercising their legal rights.

Can Westmoreland legally fire these employees? What lessons might the company learn from this experience? What are the possible outcomes?

Bibliography of Related Readings

Atleson, J. G., *Values and Assumptions in American Labor Law* (Amherst, Mass.: University of Massachusetts Press, 1983).

Bakke, E. Wright, Clark Kerr, and Charles W. Anrod, eds., *Unions, Management, and the Public,* 3d ed. (New York: Harcourt Brace Jovanovich, 1967).

Cohen, Sanford, "An Analytical Framework for Labor Relations Law," *Industrial and Labor Relations Review,* April 1961, pp. 350–62.

Feldacker, Bruce, *Labor Guide to Labor Law,* 2d ed. (Reston, Va.: Reston Publishing Company, 1983).

Ferguson, T., and J. Rogers, "Labor Law Reform and Its Enemies," *Nation,* January 13, 1979, p. 1.

Justice, Betty W., *Unions, Workers, and the Law,* BNA Pub. (Washington, 1983).

Leslie, Douglas L., *Labor Law in a Nutshell* (St. Paul, Minn.: West Publishing Company, 1979).

McCulloch, Frank W., and Tim Bornstein, *The National Labor Relations Board* (New York: Praeger, 1974).

Wellington, Harry H., *Labor and the Legal Process (New Haven: Yale University Press, 1968).*

UNION STRUCTURE
AND
INTERNAL PRESSURES

This chapter examines how unions are structured, both by level and by function. It also examines the political pressures placed on union leaders by their need to be reelected, and the effect this can have on bargaining. Last, it examines the role of blacks and women in unions.

ORGANIZATION BY LEVEL

Employee representation needs occur at many levels, ranging from the local workplace to the nation's capital. At each of the various need levels, unions organize themselves into different forms with different purposes. To someone not acquainted with collective bargaining, the mass of union levels, units, and leadership titles may be confusing. It is therefore necessary to establish the purpose and procedures of the various levels of union representation.

Unions are typically organized at three levels: the local, the national (or international), and in affiliation with the AFL-CIO. Unions may also be divided into two major functional types: craft and industrial.

Local Union

In many ways the local union is the most important level. The local acts as a vehicle for grievance processing, dispenses advice on employer policies and labor laws, conducts social activities, and, in most instances, participates in collective bargaining. In craft unions, it also commonly negotiates the wage rate for a geographic area.

In amalgamated locals the president may appoint additional business reps to help handle the workload. The building trades often have a business agent who is a compensated, full-time employee of the union. The business agent travels to work sites to make sure the contract is being enforced and may refer candidates to job openings.

Since most union positions are not compensated, it is necessary to examine the motivation to become a union representative. Some employees certainly seek the position as an opportunity to make their views heard or to "crusade" for a cause. Others undoubtedly do it for ego gratification and the desire for power. Some employees seek the position as an opportunity for recognition and advancement in the union—or into the company. Effective union leaders are often recognized by their employers as people of managerial potential and are hired into employee relations jobs outside the bargaining unit. This is not entirely bad. It probably helps improve management's understanding of the employees' and union's situation. It also probably helps the union to attract quality officers. Finally, some employees are probably pressed into service as representatives by peer beliefs that they would be good at it and "It's a tough job, but someone's got to do it."

The local union is generally financed by collecting dues from its members. These dues are spent on administrative costs and for per capita taxes to the national union, if affiliated. In rare instances, dues are paid directly to the national, with the national redirecting a portion of the total back to the locals. Dues generally average about two hours' pay per month or one percent of total pay, although they are typically higher in skilled crafts unions. In some instances, again particularly in craft unions, the local and/or national may operate the employees' pension fund. This is typically done where the employee is likely to switch employers often, as in building construction where jobs are inherently of limited duration, and in situations where the union is bigger and more permanent than the employer. This is often the case in contracts with the Teamsters union. Problems with corruption and incompetence in the administration of these funds were significant reasons for the passage of the Landrum-Griffin Act.

National Union

The national (called "International" if it has Canadian affiliates) union is generally the center of union power. It charters locals and oversees their activities to insure that the local is complying with national requirements. If an affiliated local is not complying, it may be placed in "trusteeship" and administered by the national.

The national's chief functions are to aid the local in bargaining, grievance processing and arbitration, and legal matters. It also has the major responsibility for organizing the unorganized and maintaining and dispersing strike funds. It may take a very strong hand in determining that local contracts and conditions comply with the needs of the national at other locations. This can cause considerable friction between the national and the local.

The national is typically administered by full-time officers. Business is conducted and elections are held at the national convention. These conventions must be held at least every five years and are commonly held biennially. Officers are often elected by delegates to the convention rather than by direct vote of the membership. Since the national incumbents may have had a voice in appointing some of the delegates, abuse of the democratic process is sometimes possible. Those wishing to know the specific legal requirements for election timing, voter rights, and fiduciary responsibilities of union officers may find them in the Landrum-Griffin Act. An example of the organizational structure of a large union (the United Automobile Workers) appears in Figure 6-1.

Another area of common interest to the public is national union leaders' salaries. There is a common perception that they are highly paid. The term "highly," of course, depends on with what other group union leaders are being compared. Table 6-1 reports the total compensation packages of the 25 most highly paid union leaders.

One observation can readily be made from these data. Compared to the average American family income of $15,000-$17,000, union leaders are highly paid. That is not, however, necessarily a fair comparison to make. It may be argued that union leaders are poorly paid considering the responsibility of their positions. One way of determining whether or not they are underpaid is to compare them with company presidents. The data for the 25 most highly paid executives appears in Table 6-2. Note that the total compensation figures are stated in thousands of dollars. That is, the highest-paid executive in 1984 earned $13,229,000! Number 25 earned over $2 million.

Still, even these comparisons are not entirely fair. Besides the fact that the data aren't for the same years (a very small liability), the position of union president and corporation president are not exactly comparable. A fairer comparison would be with the executive with comparable labor relations responsibility—usually a vice-president. Compensation figures for such positions are not readily available, but even if vice-presidents earned only half as much as presidents (surely a low estimate), the corporate leader would still earn over ten times as much as his union counterpart!

In short, compared to the public as a whole, union presidents are highly paid. Compared to comparable executives in the business world, they are poorly paid. It is also interesting to note that union leader salaries are generally highest

FIGURE 6–1 STRUCTURE OF THE UNITED AUTOMOBILE WORKERS UNION

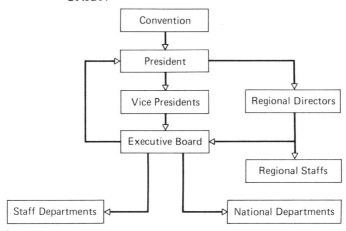

Staff Departments

Accounting
Arbitration Service
Auditing
Circulation
Community Action Program (CAP)
Community Services
Competitive Shop
Conservation and Natural Resources
Consumer Affairs
Education
Fair Practices and Anti-Discrimination
Family Education Center
International Affairs
Job Development and Training
Legal
Organizing
Public Relations and Publications
Recreation and Leisure Time Activities
Research
Retired Workers
Skilled Trades
Social Security—Health and Safety
Social-Technical-Educational Programs (STEP)
Strike Insurance
Time Study and Engineering
Veterans
Washington Office
Women's and Women's Auxiliary

National Departments

Aerospace
Agricultural Implement
American Motors
Bendix
Champion Spark Plug
Chrysler
Dana
Eltra
Ford
Foundry
General Motors
Independent Parts and Suppliers
Mack Truck
Technical, Office and Professional
   (TOP)

SOURCE: *Abstracted from* You and Your Membership in the UAW, *publication 383 (Detroit: United Auto Workers, 1978).*

TABLE 6-1 WHO GETS HOW MUCH IN ORGANIZED LABOR

	Salary	Allowance	Expenses	Total
1. Jackie Presser, Teamsters	$491,056	$ 4,850	$13,681	$509,587
2. Henry A. Duffy, Air Line Pilots	$246,557	$32,000	$42,737	$321,294
3. William H. Wynn, Food and Commercial Workers	$150,675	$13,250	$50,111	$214,036
4. Ed Garvey, Football Players	$146,154		$58,157	$204,311
5. Frank Drozak, Seafarers	$173,818		$29,145	$202,963
6. Jesse M. Calhoon, Marine Engineers	$195,500		$ 1,108	$196,608
7. Edward T. Hanley, Hotel and Restaurant Employees	$134,166	$15,860	$23,852	$173,878
8. Thomas W. Gleason, Longshoremen	$142,115	$10,170	$ 8,562	$160,847
9. J. C. Turner, Operating Engineers	$125,263	$23,600	$10,417	$159,280
10. Kenneth Moffett, Baseball Players	$120,721		$31,241	$151,962
11. Richard I. Kilroy, Railway Clerks	$125,000		$24,797	$149,797
12. Robert A. Georgine, AFL-CIO Building and Construction Trades	$115,416	$18,300	$10,757	$144,473
13. Shannon J. Wall, Maritime Union	$136,398		$ 6,686	$143,084
14. Angelo Fosco, Laborers	$129,875		$11,785	$141,660
15. Gerald W. McEntee, State, County and Municipal Employees	$125,000	$ 7,200	$ 8,148	$140,348
16. John H. Lyons, Iron Workers	$108,000	$23,450	$ 7,463	$138,913
17. S. Frank Raftery, Painters	$105,296	$18,250	$ 9,351	$132,897
18. Marvin J. Boede, Plumbers	$108,500	$21,500	$ 329	$130,329
19. Albert Shanker, American Federation of Teachers	$101,742		$27,835	$129,577
20. Edward J. Carlough, Sheet Metal Workers	$ 94,500	$34,825		$129,325
21. Charles H. Pillard, Electrical Workers (IBEW)	$124,770		$ 2,658	$127,428
22. John DeConcini, Bakery Workers	$100,000	$ 2,600	$16,955	$119,555
23. Sol C. Chaikin, Ladies' Garment Workers	$ 92,043		$27,493	$119,536
24. Lane Kirkland, AFL-CIO	$110,000		$ 7,609	$117,609
25. Patrick J. Campbell, Carpenters	$104,000	$ 9,100	$ 1,564	$114,664

SOURCE: *Reprinted from* U.S. News & World Report *issue of March 18, 1985. Copyright, 1985, U.S. News &* *World Report.*

when the members are more highly paid, e.g., airline pilots, professional athletes, and marine engineers. Following that same logic, migrant workers are the lowest-paid organized employees, and their president, Cesar Chavez, earns the least of any union president—$5,532 per year. Finally, not all prominent unions pay even as well as these figures indicate. At the time of this writing, the presidents of the United Automobile Workers, United Mine Workers, and United Steelworkers all were paid less than $100,000 per year.

AFL-CIO

The AFL-CIO is not a union and does not engage in collective bargaining. It is an association made up of member national unions. Other than resolving certain

TABLE 6-2 THE 25 HIGHEST-PAID EXECUTIVES

		Composition (in thousands of dollars)		
Executive	*Organization*	*Annual Total Compensation*	*Long-term Compensation*	*Total Compensation*
1. William S. Anderson, chmn.	NCR	$1,075	$12,154	$13,229
2. Phillip Caldwell, chmn.	Ford Motor	1,400	5,892	7,292
3. David Tendler, co-chmn.	Philbro-Salomon	2,080	4,841	6,921
4. Thomas S. Murphy, chmm.	Capital Cities	480	5,603	6,083
5. Daniel B. Burke, pres.	Capital Cities	455	3,894	4,349
6. William S. Cook, pres.	Union Pacific	905	3,396	4,301
7. Edward R. Telling, chmn.	Sears Roebuck	1,425	2,796	4,221
8. Gerard A. Fulham, chmn.	Pneumo	868	3,047	3,915
9. Donald E. Petersen, pres.	Ford Motor	1,140	2,643	3,783
10. George Weissman, chmn.	Philip Morris	1,115	2,603	3,718
11. James F. Beré, chmn.	Borg-Warner	470	3,235	3,705
12. Andrew S. Grove, pres.	Intel	488	2,907	3,395
13. Richard R. Rogers, pres.	Mary Kay Cosmetics	325	2,781	3,106
14. John F. Welch, Jr., chmn.	General Electric	1,158	1,673	2,831
15. James A. Wood, pres.	Pneumo	681	2,142	2,823
16. G. R. Simmonds, chmn. & pres.	Hercules Simmonds Precision Products	488	2,316	2,804
17. Ruben F. Mettler, chmn.	TRW	740	1,947	2,687
18. A. V. Shoemaker, chmn.	First Boston	1,500	1,168	2,668
19. D. S. MacNaughton, chmn.	Hospital Corp. of America	400	2,199	2,599
20. John C. Beasley, group v-p	Mary Kay Cosmetics	270	2,297	2,567
21. W. M. Caldwell, exec. v-p.	Ford Motor	871	1,669	2,540
22. F. R. Sullivan, chmn. & pres.	Kidde	689	1,831	2,520
23. W. A. Marquard, chmn.	American Standard	759	1,730	2,489
24. John R. Opel, chmn.	IBM	989	1,391	2,380
25. John G. Breen, chmn.	Sherwin-Williams	730	1,571	2,301

SOURCE: *Reprinted from March 22, 1985 issue of* Business Week *by special permission,* © *1985 by McGraw-Hill, Inc.*

types of disputes among its members, the main purpose of the AFL-CIO is to lobby Congress and state legislatures for the enactment of legislation favorable to unions. Its primary purpose is political rather than for collective bargaining. It also assumes some of the responsibility for the ''image'' of American unions by trying to reduce corruption and threats of Communistic takeover of the labor movement. Its structural organization is diagrammed in Figure 6–2.

FIGURE 6-2 AFL-CIO ORGANIZATION

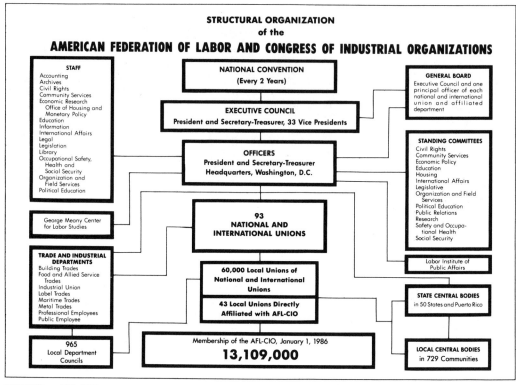

SOURCE: AFL-CIO

The AFL-CIO also has city and state councils to which local unions may belong. These organizations are lobbying, rather than collective bargaining, groups whose purpose it is to put pressure on elected officials for policies favorable to labor. They are generally active in attempting to create jobs for unionized labor and in addressing other issues of common concern.

The political activities of the AFL-CIO will be examined at greater length in the next chapter.

Activities by Union Level

Local
        Process grievances
        Participate in negotiations
        Channel communications to management
        Conduct social functions
National (or International)
        Aid local in negotiations
        Aid local in grievance arbitration

GEORGE MEANY AND WALTER REUTHER JOIN HANDS AS AFL AND CIO MERGE, DECEMBER 5, 1955

SOURCE: *Frank Alexander Collection, George Meany Memorial Archives*

> Organize new members
> Police locals for compliance with national's policies
AFL-CIO
> Represent labor's interests in political affairs
> Resolve disputes among affiliated member unions
> Police nationals for compliance with AFL-CIO policies

Activities by Union Officers

Local Rep or Shop Steward—Industrial Union
　　Listen to and file grievances
　　Enforce the contract
　　Communicate with management
Business Agent—Craft Union
　　Enforce the contract
　　Communicate with management
Local President—Industrial Union
　　Negotiate contract or plant supplement, depending on role of national union
　　Represent member in grievance arbitration
Local President — Craft Union
　　Represent craft in negotiations, perhaps in conjunction with other crafts
National President—Industrial Union
　　Negotiate national contract
　　Supervise locals
　　Organize new members
　　Represent union in AFL-CIO, if affiliated
National President—Craft Union
　　Supervise locals
　　Organize new members
　　Protect jurisdiction of union
　　Represent union in AFL-CIO, if affiliated
AFL-CIO President
　　Lobby politically for labor's interests
　　Resolve disputes among member unions
　　Promote labor's public image

ORGANIZATION BY FUNCTION

Major Types

Unions may be distinguished by function as well as level. The two major functional categories are craft and industrial. *Craft unions* are made up of employees performing the same type of work for different employers. *Industrial unions* are made up of employees performing different types of tasks for the same employer or type of employer. The Carpenters' Union is a typical craft union. One of its locals would likely consist of carpenters in a geographic area who work at different construction sites for different employers. The United Automobile Workers Union (UAW), on the other hand, is a typical industrial union. Its members perform a variety of tasks for employers in the automobile industry. (Ac-

FIGURE 6-3 INDUSTRIAL (VERTICAL) GROUPING COMPARED TO CRAFT (HORIZONTAL)

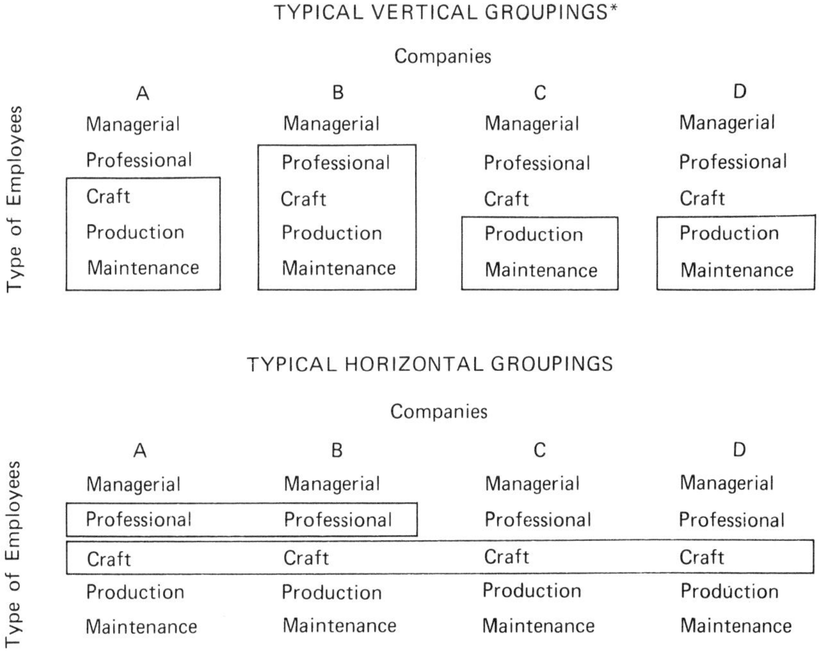

TYPICAL VERTICAL GROUPINGS*

Companies

	A	B	C	D
	Managerial	Managerial	Managerial	Managerial
	Professional	Professional	Professional	Professional
	Craft	Craft	Craft	Craft
	Production	Production	Production	Production
	Maintenance	Maintenance	Maintenance	Maintenance

Type of Employees

TYPICAL HORIZONTAL GROUPINGS

Companies

	A	B	C	D
	Managerial	Managerial	Managerial	Managerial
	Professional	Professional	Professional	Professional
	Craft	Craft	Craft	Craft
	Production	Production	Production	Production
	Maintenance	Maintenance	Maintenance	Maintenance

Type of Employees

*Vertical groupings may also extend across companies.

tually, the UAW also represents members in several additional related fields.) The term "industrial" union is a bit of a misnomer. Some craft unions function in industrial settings, and some industrial unions function in nonindustrial employment. The term "trade union" can denote either type.

The distinction between craft and industrial unions is often important. Generalizations about unions may not apply equally to each.

Craft Unions

Characteristics more typical of craft unions include the following.

They make up an "elite" minority of the workforce. They possess skills acquired through an apprenticeship program administered by the union. They are comparatively highly paid. Their source of power is their irreplaceability. They attempt to control the supply of labor by limiting admission to the apprenticeship program (generally the most acceptable way of learning the skill) and generating a demand to use union labor. They charge comparatively high dues and initiation fees and have historically been racially discriminatory. They may provide their own pension, and they operate hiring halls which refer employees to employers on an as-needed basis. Theoretically, the hiring hall operates without reference to whether a job applicant is a member of the union or not.

Craft unions negotiate their contracts locally or regionally. The locus of power is the local union. The contract will be comparatively brief, since it need not describe what jobs consist of or how they are to be done—that was determined in the apprenticeship training.

Craft unions jealously guard their jurisdiction against threats from other unions and from nonunion labor. They will strike over grievances arising from the administration of their contract, because there often is not time to submit such disputes to outside arbitration. Craft-union jobs are usually the "plums" of blue collar labor—at least while one is employed.

Industrial Unions

Characteristics of industrial unions are basically the opposite of those of craft unions. They typically include the following characteristics.

The vast majority of their members are unskilled or semiskilled, and they make up the large majority of the unionized workforce. They were recruited, selected, and trained by their employers and are often quickly and easily replaceable. They are paid comparatively less. Pension obligations are generally the responsibility of the employer, not the union. Contracts are long and complex because they must describe the method, amount of work, and rate of pay for each job. Because the union cannot control the supply of unskilled labor, it attempts to control the way the job is done. Work rules become very important. Dues and initiation fees are commonly low. Grievances arising from the administration of the contract are generally resolved through binding arbitration. Some of these unions are very large, representing virtually all the hourly employees in some of our largest oligopolies. Master contracts are often negotiated nationally, with local plant supplements. Power is typically greatest at the national union level.

GENERALIZED CONTRASTS BETWEEN
CRAFT AND INDUSTRIAL UNIONS

CRAFT	INDUSTRIAL
Minority of workforce	Majority of workforce
Skilled	Semi- and unskilled
Apprenticeship training	Employer training
Higher paid	Lower paid
Difficult to replace	Easy to replace
High initiation fees and dues	Low initiation fees and dues
Administer own pension funds	Employer provides pensions
History of racial discrimination	History of racial integration
Refers members to jobs	Employer recruits job applicants

CRAFT	**INDUSTRIAL**
Contract short and simple	Contract long and complicated
Contract local or regional	Contract may be national
Power at local level	Power at national level
Strike over grievances	Grievances arbitrated
Power: Control supply of labor	Power: Control how job is done

POLITICAL STRUCTURE: PRESSURES

Although unions are supposed to be democratic institutions, they are not pure democracies such as the traditional New England town hall meeting. In those meetings, all the citizens gathered to transact all business by majority rule. Union business, like that of companies and big government, is too continual, and sometimes too complicated, to have the members meet and transact all activities. For the sake of administrative efficiency, leaders are elected for a term of office. If the goals of the membership are not met by the officers, new leaders can be voted in to replace them, just as in government. This simple democratic check against the power of union leaders has very profound consequences on collective bargaining and employment relations.

The most important facet of internal union democracy is the need of the leader to "deliver." That is, the leader must make it appear that the union has obtained more for the employee than he or she would have received without collective bargaining. If opposed for office, the leader must also make it appear that he or she has delivered more than the rival would have. Furthermore, to have delivered in the past is not enough. The leader must continue to deliver or face challenge from someone else who will promise more.

This need to deliver often makes collective bargaining more difficult. A union leader may know, based upon experience, expertise, and wisdom, that a management proposal or policy is a sound one. However, sometimes the leader must oppose it because it is unpopular with the rank-and-file. While this representation of the rank-and-file is, of course, the very purpose of democracy, it is also very troublesome when the members' resistance is based on emotion or ignorance. Often the membership has neither the information nor the expertise to make well-informed decisions. To say that it is the leader's responsibility to "educate" the members on the wisdom of an unpopular position he or she has taken places a tremendous burden on the leader. The difficulty is evidenced by the fact that obviously management cannot make the sense of the position clear, or the employees would not be opposed to it. The union leader will often find it more expedient to side with the popular decision rather than the professional one.

The more democratic the union is—that is, the greater the likelihood of the leader's being voted out of office in favor of a challenger, the more troublesome the need to deliver becomes. Even if unchallenged for the position, the incumbent still must secure the ratification of contracts negotiated with management. Leaders must do this by convincing a majority of the employees to accept the package they have recommended jointly with management. Their mere word, handshake, or signature is not enough to bind the union. To secure the approval of the majority, the leader must "sell" the contract to the membership. This can be difficult, if only because the proposed contract never contains all that the membership wanted, and it may contain some unpopular features as well. Still, the leader believes it was the best package obtainable under the circumstances. If the leader has been elected by an overwhelming majority, it is probably safe to assume that the majority of the members will "take his or her word for it" that the contract proposed is the best they can get and will vote to ratify it.

On the other hand, if the leader's election to office was a close one, and the rival is still in the workplace, the ratification procedure can become much more difficult. If the leader won office by a margin of 55 to 45 percent, he or she can assume—at best—automatic support from only slightly over half the unit. The members who did not vote for the leader will, under the orchestration of the defeated candidate, argue that the contract is an inferior one, one not as good as would have been negotiated by their candidate. They may vote to reject as a showing of disapproval of the leader. They will certainly urge a critical examination of the proposed contract and emphasize the concessions made by the leader. This makes the securing of a majority much more difficult. If just 5 percent of the members are swayed to vote "no" because they do not believe the candidate they voted for obtained the best possible contract, the contract will fail. Obviously, it is much more difficult to obtain ratification under such circumstances, regardless of the true quality of the proposal.

This internal democracy problem carries over into grievance processing. Supposedly, a "responsible" union representative will inform a member that the member's complaint has no merit when such is the case. This is not a popular response and may well cause the member to vote for the other candidate in the next election, feeling that the rival will at least represent his or her dispute to management. It is bad enough to lose. It is even worse not to try. Union leaders who have to worry about being reelected often cannot afford to suppress unmeritorious grievances. They must process all grievances to maintain popularity. This problem is made even worse if there is not a checkoff procedure whereby union dues are deducted automatically (with the employee's consent) from the paycheck. If the union rep has to solicit dues periodically on a personal basis, the employee has great leverage to extort the rep into taking action on his or her demand. If the rep refuses to process the grievance, the member refuses to pay his or her dues. Obviously, it does not take such union leaders long to learn to process all grievances. The outcome of this behavior is to increase the amount of management time unnecessarily spent on grievances and to reduce the credibility of the union leader in the eyes of management.

The effects of union democracy make employment relations much tougher for both the union leader and management. Every time the leader is compelled to deliver, it must be at the "expense" of management. This can make it very difficult for managers who have bargained in good faith to get along with a union leader who constantly needs to demonstrate how much representation the members are getting.

A major factor in determining whether members will endorse a contract proposal, besides the salesmanship of the leader, is the members' perception of how "good" the offer is. "Good" is often determined by reference to others with whom the members compare themselves, rather than by some absolute value of the package. Employees often judge the merits of a contract by comparing it with conditions obtained by other employees, both unionized and non-unionized. Sometimes these comparisons are misguided, ill-informed, or absolutely "unfair." The conditions affecting different employers vary immensely and are not usually well known, let alone well understood, by employees elsewhere. Nevertheless, these perceptions are the basis for employees' determining the attractiveness of their offer. This can place the union leader in the very difficult position of either trying to obtain a settlement beyond the employer's means or accepting a "lesser," but appropriate, one that appears to the membership not to have been "delivered." The leader is again put into the position of having to educate the membership as to why their expectations are not appropriate. This is hard to do in a popular fashion and also requires making the employer look as if it has bargained appropriately. Sticking up for management on an unattractive contract offer does not generally help reelection possibilities. This was particularly true during the "concession bargaining" of the early and mid 1980s.

So far, all the union structure features examined make it difficult for the union leader to appear to have delivered. One very important structural feature, however, helps the union leader to appear to have succeeded in this respect. It is the "Great Turkey Dance." The Great Turkey Dance is the conventional form of collective bargaining in which the union demands more than it expects to receive, the employer initially offers less than it is prepared to give, compromises and tradeoffs take place, and a settlement is reached at some point between the parties' original positions. This bargaining strategy will be examined in greater depth in Chapter 9, but for now it is sufficient to recognize that when the employer starts low and then raises its offer, apparently in response to union pressure, the union appears to have delivered. One test union members will make in determining whether a proposed contract is a good one is to compare what is proposed as a settlement against what the employer originally offered. Under such conditions, the Great Turkey Dance almost always makes the union leader look good.

BLACKS AND WOMEN IN LABOR UNIONS

A final area of interest to many observers is the role of blacks and women in American labor unions. For both groups, the performance record of unions has been mixed.

The Role of Blacks

Union leaders have had a variety of emotions and actions regarding the organizing of blacks. In some instances, union leaders such as Powderly and Gompers espoused integration and equality.[1] In other instances, the AFL allowed discriminatory practices by its member unions to continue for decades.[2] In many situations there is an obvious conflict of interest between the racist sentiments commonly found in society as a whole and a self-serving interest in bringing blacks into unions.

The self-serving interest of unions dates from industrial employers' strike-breaking activities of the 1800s. It was a common practice for employers to attempt to replace striking white employees with blacks, who were willing to work under the conditions rejected by the whites—because even such jobs were often better than other opportunities available to them. The willingness of blacks to cross white picket lines and put whites out of jobs obviously did nothing to enhance relations between the races and helped spread ill-will and the perception of economic threats.

One potential solution to this problem was to attempt to enroll blacks into union membership. This was good for blacks, because it would presumably extend to them the benefits of unionization. It was also desirable for whites, because blacks receiving union wage rates and working conditions were not a source of low-cost labor competition.

Although there were obvious benefits to both sides, blacks made little progress in unions prior to the advent of the CIO. Craft-oriented AFL unions, practicing control of the supply of labor through their apprenticeship programs, were able to preserve jobs for whites while limiting the threat of low-cost black competition. They accomplished this in two ways. One was to require nomination to the apprenticeship program by a current union member. Since relatives and friends were usually recommended, this tended to perpetuate the already white composition of the membership. The other method of discrimination was to create segregated locals with rules requiring all members of the black local to be laid off before any members of the white local were. Vestiges of these two forms of discrimination have been a target of the reform practices of the Civil Rights Act of 1964 and the Equal Employment Opportunity Commission.

The industrially organized CIO has a considerably stronger record of equality and integration. Because industrial unions could not control who was hired for unskilled and semiskilled jobs, it was unambivalently in the union's interest to include blacks into membership. Since the unions had no control over hiring, any discrimination in entry-level jobs was caused by the employer. Once hired, blacks earned the same rate of pay as whites and moved into higher-paying and more desirable jobs at the rate their seniority, not their race, dictated. (CIO unions customarily negotiated contracts that attempted to allocate jobs by length of service rather than by managerial preference.) Since blacks were customarily assigned lower-paying and less desirable jobs by management, the CIO union-negotiated rules promoted truly equal, rather than discriminatory, treatment. Welcoming blacks into membership also was consistent with the CIO's broad-based political thrust. On the whole, industrial unions have been very good for black jobholders.

This is not to say that there are not race-related problems in industrial unions. One source of irritation to blacks in both craft and industrial unions is underrepresentation in leadership positions. This problem has been difficult to eradicate. One source of continuing friction is the fact that many blacks entered employment later than the white-dominated union hierarchy. This often creates a conflict between race-oriented concerns for blacks as comparatively new employees against seniority-dominated concerns which often favor whites disproportionately. This has led to continuing internal strife in many unions.

At the top administrative levels, much prointegration political activity has taken place. The AFL-CIO customarily supports the activities of civil rights groups and sponsors civil rights legislation. Within the AFL-CIO, the interests of minorities may be referred to its Civil Rights Committee. There is also a Coalition of Black Trade Unionists, made up of representatives of various member unions, that seeks to make the labor movement more relevant for the needs of both black and white workers. It also attempts to help blacks secure union leadership posts.

The Role of Women

The role of women in labor unions is, in several significant ways, quite comparable to that of blacks. Women, like blacks, have historically represented a source of cheap labor, thereby becoming a threat to union members' interests. They are typically underrepresented both in unionized jobs and in union leadership positions. They have also undoubtedly been discriminated against in the workplace by those (including Gompers) who believed a "woman's place was in the home."

Historically, women have been involved in organized labor for a long time. A group of women workers struck in 1828 to protest their employer's paternalistic work rules prohibiting gambling, drinking, or other "debaucheries" and requiring church attendance.[3] There was also a woman labor leader of national significance from the 1880s to the 1920s. Known as Mother Jones, she was a fiery spokesperson for mine workers and the Industrial Workers of the World.

Unions made up of women employees were generally short-lived in the 1800s, being formed prior to a strike and lasting only for its duration. The AFL did little or nothing to help them. Since women often performed jobs men didn't want, under conditions men would not accept, the AFL did not immediately perceive them as a threat. The advent of World War I, however, brought many women into the workforce in jobs they had never previously held. The threat of trained, experienced female employees who would work for less than males created a threat to the AFL. Out of economic expediency, the AFL began to attempt to organize women. The result has been a very modest (or perhaps a lack of) success.

Women are still underrepresented by unions both in membership and leadership positions. Explanations commonly given for low membership totals include more temporary attachment to the job than that of many men, lower-paying jobs that make it harder to afford dues, a preponderance of white collar positions, and a lack of women union organizers.[4] Explanations commonly given for lack of women in leadership positions include disproportionate family responsibilities away from the job; career interruptions caused by child-bearing, often occurring at the point union leaders assume their first position; a scarcity of women in high-visibility positions from which union leaders are often selected; and a belief by some men and some women that women are inappropriate for union office.[5]

The problems of women, like those of blacks, have led to internal reactions within organized labor. Particularly, the AFL-CIO has made specific attempts to address issues of concern to women such as child care, pay equity, and sexual harassment.[6] The AFL-CIO has also increased its attempts to organize women. The Service Employees International Union and the Working Women's National Association of Workers formed District 925 ("nine-to-five") to help promote the organization of office workers. Finally, the Coalition of Labor Union Women, made up largely of female officers of unions, works with other women's organizations to promote organizing and issues of concern to working women.

Notes

1. Sidney H. Kessler, "The Organization of Negroes in the Knights of Labor," *Journal of Negro History,* Vol. 37 (July 1952), pp. 248–75, and Mark Karson and Ronald Radosh, "The American Federation of Labor and the Negro Worker: 1894–1949," in Julius Jacobson, ed., *The Negro and the American Labor Movement* (Garden City, N.Y.: Doubleday Press, 1968), pp. 155–56.

2. Karson and Radosh.

3. John B. Andrews and W. D. P. Bliss, *History of Women in Trade Unions* (New York: Arno Press, 1974), p. 24.

4. William H. Holley and Kenneth M. Jennings, *The Labor Relations Process,* 2d ed. (Chicago: The Dryden Press, 1984), p. 350.

5. Karen S. Koziara and David A. Pierson, "The Lack of Female Union Leaders," *Monthly Labor Review,* May 1981, pp. 30–31.

6. "Kirkland Pledges AFL-CIO Support of Women's Rights as ERA Is Defeated," *Daily Labor Report,* No. 126 (June 30, 1982), Bureau of National Affairs, Inc. (Washington, D.C.), p. A–8.

Discussion Questions

1. Discuss the roles of the local union, the national (or international), and the AFL-CIO.
2. Analyze the differences between craft and industrial unions.
3. Assess the consequences of democratic procedures in the administration of unions.
4. Discuss the role of blacks and women in unions.

Statements For Comment

1. "Everyone would be better off if unions were more democratic."
2. "Union financial corruption would be reduced if members attended meetings more regularly."
3. "Craft unons ought to be made illegal because their control of the supply of labor through their apprenticeship programs is monopolistic. They are just like the trusts of the early 1900s and we had to make them illegal."
4. "Union presidents ought to be paid more, not less, than company representatives. They have a harder job."

Situations

Case 6–1 "Can you believe it?" said Clayton Worrell, Professor of Botany at Cactus State College. "Our Provost has decided to allocate additional faculty raises from his discretionary funds in accordance with his definition of merit—which to him is published research. That's not the criterion established by our union contract. We're supposed to be rewarded for teaching. Why doesn't our union do something about it? Are our leaders in bed with management?"

"Hold your horses, Big Guy," said Eric Oracle, Professor of Philosophy. "Why are you always griping about the union's leaders? Why don't you put up or shut up? You're eligible to run for office. Get yourself elected and run the union the way you think it should be run."

What factors should the Big Guy consider before running for office? After all, he might win.

Case 6–2 "I'm not sure this national contract negotiation is such a good deal," said Willard Lomax. "How can our national president know what we need here in Paducah? The company has 26 other plants for him to worry about and they can't all be alike. What's good for one isn't necessarily good for another. Besides, the union has become as big as the company. How can it represent us little guys?"

What can be said in defense of nationalized bargaining? Against it? Does it make a difference where Paducah is? Or where the other plants are?

Bibliography of Related Readings

Anderson, John C., "Local Union Participation: A Reexamination," *Industrial Relations*, Vol. 18 (Winter 1979).

Andrews, John B., and W. D. P. Bliss, *History of Women in Trade Unions* (New York: Arno Press, 1974).

Barbash, Jack, *American Unions, Structure, Government, and Politics* (New York: Random House, 1967).

"Building Trades Offer Guide on Fighting Union-Busters," *AFL-CIO News*, December 26, 1980, p. 3.

Cook, Alice H., *Union Democracy: Practice and Ideal* (Ithaca. N.Y.: New York State School of Industrial and Labor Relations, Cornell University, 1963).

Fritz, S., "Union Corruption: Worse than Ever," *U.S. News and World Report*, September 8, 1980.

Glick, William, Phillip Mirvis, and Diane Harder, "Union Satisfaction and Participation," *Industrial Relations*, Spring 1977.

Hickman, Charles W., "Labor Organizations' Fees and Dues," *Monthly Labor Review*, Vol. 100 (May 1977).

Hoyt, M., "Rebel Teamsters (Teamsters for a Democratic Union)," *The Progressive*, January 1982.

Hutchinson, John, *The Imperfect Union: A History of Corruption in American Trade Unions* (New York: E. P. Dutton & Co., Inc., 1972).

Jacobson, Julius, ed., *The Negro and the American Labor Movement* (Garden City, N.Y.: Doubleday Press, 1968).

Marshall, Ray, *The Negro and Organized Labor* (New York: John Wylie & Sons, 1965).

Nash, Allan, *The Union Steward: Duties, Rights and Status* (Ithaca, N.Y.: New York State School of Industrial and Labor Relations, Cornell University, 1977).

Perry, J. L., and H. L. Angel, "Bargaining Unit Structure and Organizational Outcomes," *Industrial Relations*, 1981, pp. 47–59.

Taft, Philip, "Internal Union Structure and Functions," in *The Next Twenty-five Years of Industrial Relations* (Madison, Wis.: IRRA, 1973).

SEVEN

UNION POLITICAL ACTIVITY

Before proceeding to the issues of how unions are organized and how they pursue collective bargaining, it is useful to examine their secondary function—political action.

Unions have been politically active in at least four areas of concern. They are (1) supporting legislation that favors the legal rights of unions, (2) promoting legislation and policies that benefit employees in general, (3) promoting social welfare legislation for the public as a whole, and (4) supporting candidates sympathetic to organized labor's position. The first concern is quite apparent. The results of that concern were examined in Chapter 5. The remaining issues will be examined in this chapter.

HISTORICAL NONINTERVENTION

The historical position of the AFL was one of ''voluntarism.'' This meant that rights and obligations between parties should be reached by bargained agreement, not by being forced upon the parties by law. Samuel Gompers philosophically favored ''free collective bargaining,'' meaning free of government intervention. In effect, it meant the AFL opposed *laws* protecting the rights of employees. Rather, it favored protection through contract negotiation. This attitude was a luxury available to AFL-affiliated skilled craftsmen, who possessed *economic* bargaining power because of their comparative irreplaceability. They felt they didn't need legal power.

EARLY AFL OPPOSITION TO PROTECTIVE LEGISLATION

The pre-New Deal AFL was opposed to all forms of legislative protections, including minimum wage laws for men, regulation of hours of work, unemployment benefits, and workers' compensation for injuries. The opposition stemmed from two sources: one, the AFL believed that because of its members' economic irreplaceability, it could get more through bargaining than through legislation; and two, if the government provided such protections, there would be less reason to join unions. The following statements are indicative of the AFL's philosophy:

In opposing action supporting workers' compensation, Gompers explained,

Sore and sad as I am by the illness, the killing, the maiming of so many of my fellow workers, I would rather see that go on for years and years, minimized and mitigated by the organized labor movement, than give up one jot of the freedom of the workers to strive and struggle for their own emancipation through their own efforts.

Opposing unemployment insurance at the 1930 AFL Convention, delegate Olander said,

Every system of unemployment insurance here contemplates supervision and control by both federal and state governments and will require registration, not only of aliens among the workers, but of all of us. . . . Have we lost courage to the point where we regard freedom as no longer the greatest essential of life and the most necessary element in human progress?

SOURCE: *Michael Rogin, "Voluntarism: The Political Functions of an Anti-Political Doctrine,"* in The American Labor Movement, *edited by David Brody. (New York: Harper & Row, 1971), pp. 102 and 112.*

Although in the Progressive Era of the early 1900s there had been government forays into protective legislation at the state level with child labor laws and laws protecting the rights of women, the New Deal legislation placed the government in the employment world in a big way. Social Security, minimum wage, and prevailing rate legislation were passed at the national level and workers' compensation and unemployment compensation statutes made inroads at the state level. These were to be followed in succeeding generations by liberalizing existing acts and passing new acts promoting full employment, equal opportunity, equal pay, occupational safety and health, and retirement protection. In the space of less than 50 years, the government went from a philosophy of noninterventionist Social Darwinism to one of significant involvement. The union movement joined the activity.

The splintering of the CIO from the AFL, coupled with the protections of the Wagner Act, provided the vast majority of American workers with the opportunity to form unions and affiliate with an organization not wedded to the AFL's historic principles. The CIO was, in fact, immediately politically active. Because it had no history (or likelihood) of survival without government assistance (the protections of the Wagner Act), the CIO had no opposition to political involvement. It supported government protection and the New Deal and effectively, if not formally, aligned itself with the Democratic Party. With the subsequent merger with the AFL in 1955, organized labor's commitment to political activity—as a secondary priority—continued, as did its informal allegiance to the Democratic Party.

LEGISLATION INTENDED TO BENEFIT EMPLOYEES IN GENERAL

The interest of unions in legislation benefiting all employees is a complicated one. Because the benefits of such "general" legislation apply to all employees, not just union members, it is not immediately clear what unions gain by sponsoring or supporting such legislation. On one hand, whatever benefits are extended by law to all employees are benefits that do not have to be won at the bargaining table. Therefore, this should decrease the incentive to join unions, since benefits can be received without incurring the costs of membership. Theoretically, unions should be opposed to such an outcome and not advocate such legislation.

On the other hand, unions stand to benefit in several subtle ways by overall improvements in employment. Of a direct benefit is gains achieved through legislation that were not achievable through bargaining. Many major health and safety provisions initiated by the Occupational Safety and Health Act probably belong in this category. Unions may also hope to be able to "ripple" upward through their ranks whatever benefits were accorded across-the-board to all employees. For instance, when the minimum wage is raised, unions may attempt to negotiate higher wages for those they represent to maintain preexisting differentials. Unions also probably perceive that they benefit from prosperity and consumption and therefore favor policies which promote demand and full employment. Examples of this kind of protection include the Full Employment Act and tariffs and quotas on foreign-made products.

The coverage and application of the above acts are beyond the scope of this text. The discussion that follows concentrates on how acts applying to all employees, unionized and nonunion alike, affect and are affected by, organized labor.

Protective Legislation

This category consists of child labor laws, historical laws regulating hours of work and working conditions for women, workers' compensation, unemployment compensation, Social Security, the Occupational Safety and Health Act

(OSHA), the Employment Retirement Income Security Act (ERISA), and protection against age and handicap discrimination. All these acts are generally supported by (if not sponsored by) the AFL-CIO. As a rule, organized labor's support of such legislation is largely humanitarian. That is, it supports such legislation not because it helps enhance organized labor's position, but because these laws are beneficial to all employees, including those who are unionized. Still, it is to union members' advantage to have nonunion "sweat shop" conditions improved, because it reduces the cost advantage available to nonunion competitors. This may help preserve union jobs.

NINETEENTH-CENTURY OPPOSITION
TO LEGISLATING SHORTER HOURS

The opponents of shorter hours advanced a number of arguments to support their position. During the first half of the nineteenth century, employers and the general public saw nothing wrong with urban workers following the agricultural working day of from dawn to dusk. The long working day was accepted by the public because it was the norm for employers, merchants, and retail clerks, and because of a prevailing, almost religious, conviction of the virtues of hard work. In 1822, for example, master builders in Boston considered the carpenters' demand for a ten-hour day "fraught with numerous and pernicious evils" because "altering the time of commencing and terminating their daily labor, from that which has been customary from time immemorial" would have an "unhappy influence" on apprentices "by seducing them from the course of industry and economy of time" and would expose the journeymen themselves "to many temptations and improvident practices" from which they were "happily secure" when working from sun to sun. The "gentlemen engaged in build-ing" were also concerned that the ten-hour movement might spread.

While some state legislatures were willing to regulate the hours of women and children, employers generally opposed this legislation. For example, some Massachusetts employers argued against an eight-hour law for children under 16 years of age on the grounds that "either the machinery and the adults must stop at the end of eight hours or we must discharge the children." The textile manufacturers regarded the employment of children "as a necessity to the building up and maintaining of a competent and adequate labor force for the textile industry" because it was "essential that the textile operative should begin his career in the mill at an early age . . . if he does not begin before 16 he has either come to look down on mill work or is an indifferent learner." It was also argued that "the hand must be trained to proper dexterity during the muscle-forming years, else the operative will always be clumsy and sluggish."

SOURCE: *Ray Marshall, Allan G. King, and Vernon M. Briggs, Jr.,* Labor Economics, *4th ed. (Homewood, Ill.: Richard D. Irwin, 1980), p. 463.*

LONG HOURS IN THE STEEL INDUSTRY

Early union demands for shorter hours stressed the need to increase leisure in order that workers might participate more effectively as citizens in a democracy. As industrialization proceeded, however, shorter hours were demanded as a means of combating unemployment and preventing injury to the workers' health.

The major industry that resisted longest the movement for shorter hours was the steel industry. By its nature, the production of steel requires continuous operations, 24 hours a day and seven days a week. The easiest way for management to meet the staffing requirements was to work two 12-hour shifts for seven days a week. In many steel firms the practice developed of rotating the day and the night shifts every two weeks. To do this, one shift worked a 24-hour shift—called "the long shift"—while the other shift would have a day off. It was not until 1923 that this practice was abandoned by the major steel firms, who then switched to eight-hour shifts. The change was a reluctant concession to mounting public pressure against the long hours. The most influential leader of the public action was Herbert Hoover, in his role as Secretary of Commerce during the Harding Administration.

SOURCE: *Marshall, King, and Briggs, p. 465.*

Wage Regulation

The federal government, prodded by the AFL-CIO, also supports wage regulation in several ways. These ways include the well-known minimum wage law (Fair Labor Standards Act), the establishment of "prevailing rates" on government construction projects (Davis-Bacon Act), provision for premium pay for overtime hours (but with no prohibition on compulsory overtime) for government suppliers (Walsh-Healy Act), and the Equal Pay Act requiring that women be paid equal to men when their jobs are essentially similar. The interest of the AFL-CIO in these functions goes beyond mere humanitarianism. In these areas, self-interest must also be considered.

The "noble" purpose of the minimum wage law is to assure that no one need live in poverty—provided, of course, that he or she has a job. Measuring the extent to which the law is successful or unsuccessful and whatever side effects it has should best be left to economists. What is of concern here is why unions support such legislation, especially considering how few of their members are employed at the minimum wage level.

As alluded to earlier, it is possible that unions support such legislation in the hope that increasing the pay at the bottom rung of the ladder can be used to "justify" demands by unions for increased wages at higher levels. The extent to which this rather imperfect connection succeeds is not clear. Of much more direct concern to unions is not how much one gets paid, but rather, *who* gets paid.

In the absence of minimum wage legislation, employers may offer as low a wage as needed to attract and retain a competent worker for a job. In many instances, applicants possessing characteristics not historically highly valued by employers (youth, minorities, women, immigrants) would offer their services at rates lower than white males, particularly unionized white males. If the "less desirable" worker could perform the job, the employer would have a significant economic incentive to overcome his or her own prejudices and preferences and hire the lower-cost option. If, however, the employer has to offer a wage closer to the rate commonly given to white males (or unionized employees of any age, race, or gender) he or she has less incentive to substitute "cheap" labor for "mainstream" labor. Whatever other motivations may be present, the union-serving characteristics of minimum wage laws cannot be overlooked.

Similar rationale justified the Davis-Bacon and Walsh-Healy Acts, two of the most controversial pieces of protective legislation. Davis-Bacon, in particular, can really separate the Democrats from the Republicans. Davis-Bacon was passed in the Depression. It requires that bidders for federal construction projects pay their workers the "prevailing rate" of the area. Interpreting exactly what that means varies from one political administration to another, but in its purest form it requires construction companies to pay union wage scales and realistically, to hire unionized workers, although that is not technically required.

From a union standpoint the provisions of the act keep the government, which generally awards contracts to the lowest bidder, from "exploiting" labor. It particularly discourages importing cheaper labor from other areas. For just this reason, conservatives oppose the law. They claim it adds unnecessary costs to government construction projects.

The Equal Pay Act also has hidden, but intended, consequences. On the surface, paying women equal to men for similar jobs has a modern, egalitarian appeal and can easily be justified on such grounds. However, paying women equal to men may have other consequences that are just as important as protecting women's rights and may have very different consequences.

Because women have historically (and currently) worked for less than men, they have formed a "cheap" source of labor of the type that minimum wage laws are supposed to suppress. The Equal Pay Act takes the minimum wage rationale one step further and requires equal pay for women. An expected consequence of such a regulation is that an employer who cannot hire a woman cheaper than a man would then prefer to hire a man, thereby preserving job opportunities for men and reducing opportunities for women. Again, the measurement of the extent to which such a displacement occurs is best left to labor economists. What is important here is that the support of such protective legislation may stem from mixed motives.

Increased Demand Policies

Organized labor's interest in stimulating demand is more straightforward. Increased demand (and decreased competition) increases job opportunities. From labor's perspective, this is good because it helps both employment and wage levels.

Increasing the demand for labor can be accomplished several ways. One way is, of course, to increase the total number of jobs available. This can be done by creating more demand for goods and services through higher standards of living and/or greater propensity to consume. Government policies consistent with these goals are often supported by labor. This can be seen in the AFL-CIO's strong interest in federal fiscal policy, including budgeting, interest rates, and the role of deficit spending. In particularly depressed times, organized labor will pressure the government to create jobs by becoming the "employer of last resort."

Job opportunities can also be enhanced by reducing the number of people competing for openings. Many of the techniques used to accomplish this goal are contract-oriented, rather than political, and will be addressed in subsequent chapters. However, the control of immigration, particularly that of illegal aliens, has been, and is, a major political concern of labor.

SOCIAL WELFARE LEGISLATION

In the post-Great Depression era, organized labor has been an active participant in the "liberal coalition of the left."[1] In some respects, this commitment is similar to European working class politics—that is, unions purport to speak for working people on all issues affecting their lives. While the AFL-CIO is still primarily, overwhelmingly oriented toward collective bargaining, it has expanded its political efforts to include issues having little or nothing direct to do with employment. In some cases, this commitment appears to go beyond the concerns of the membership and may be attributable more to the personal beliefs of the leadership. In many cases, organized labor's interest is not self-oriented but rather is based on philosophical concerns for the consumer (as contrasted to ownership) class.

Some social welfare legislation is also of vital importance in employment. Examples include the job rights of minorities and women. In many instances, though, social welfare legislation has only a tangential effect on employment. Examples include energy and the environment; health, education, and welfare; consumer protection; and foreign affairs. Some unexpected specific topics labor has addressed include drug regulation reform, tuition tax credits, education appropriations, no-fault auto insurance reform, the Panama Canal

LEADERS' AND MEMBERS' MOTIVATION
IN AFL-CIO SPONSORED LEGISLATION

The AFL-CIO legislative department, located in Washington, D.C., lobbies Congress actively not only on behalf of union-related measures, such as proposals concerning prevailing wage rates in federal construction projects, but increasingly on behalf of broad welfare and civil rights measures, many of which have little direct bearing on the lives of most union members and some of which may even be opposed by substantial numbers of unionists. In the mid-1960s, for example, a survey of white members of a large industrial union showed that 69 percent of the paid international staff thought that national progress in desegregating schools, housing, and jobs, was too slow, but only 21 percent of the rank-and-file members had that view; as a matter of fact, 30 percent of the rank-and-file felt that desegregation was moving too fast.

One consequence of the growth and institutionalization of union security agreements is that much of the political activity of unions can be directed toward ends that large numbers of union members either do not share or actively oppose. These political activities, once powerfully constrained by their incentive effect on members (localistic and job-oriented in the case of craft unionists, national and issue-oriented in the case of industrial unionists), now reflect, in all probability, more the interests of professional staff members and key union leaders and their active rivals. Insofar as politics has an incentive effect, it is more for the union activists than for the rank-and-file.

The same is probably true in some measure of the Committee on Political Education (COPE), the political action arm of the merged AFL-CIO. With a national staff of 20 and a large political fund, it became a leading force in the alliance that existed until the 1972 presidential campaign between organized labor and the liberal wing of the Democratic party. Aided by similar units at the state and sometimes the local level, COPE has to a degree routinized and bureaucratized union political activity and thus to an important degree has reduced the variation in that activity that once resulted from the differences among individual union leaders and their supporters over the value they attached to particular candidacies and causes. The convictions and interests of COPE staff members and their associated volunteers have become more determinative of union political activities than the views of those unionists primarily concerned with organizational maintenance and the advancement of economic interests.

SOURCE: From Political Organizations *by James Q. Wilson. Copyright © 1973 by Basic Books, Inc., Publishers, p. 136. Reprinted by permission of the publisher.*

Treaty, visas for Soviet representatives, the Mid-East jet sale, and international broadcasting.[2]

The genuine interest of labor (or at least its leaders) in these topics is not totally without collateral benefit, however. By actively supporting the liberal position on these issues, labor aids other liberal lobbyists in pursuit of their goals. These lobbyists may then feel some compulsion to aid labor in pursuit of its more particularist goals. In fact, it is possible that labor's particularist interests can be supported only when they are consistent with the broader interests of the liberal left.[3]

ELECTION ACTIVITIES

The AFL-CIO is very active in election campaigns. It is a very large contributor of dollars (almost always to Democratic Party candidates) and is a significant provider of volunteer helpers for distributing campaign literature and helping get people to the polls. It evaluates candidates based on their voting records and publicizes the candidates' positions. These activities are carried out by the AFL-CIO's political arm, the Committee on Political Education (COPE). COPE is funded by voluntary contributions of union members.

The Democratic Party often eagerly courts the AFL-CIO with promises of platform planks favorable to labor's position in exchange for money and volunteer help. What the AFL-CIO cannot promise to deliver, nor do candidates necessarily expect to receive, is a labor "bloc vote."

The AFL-CIO would like to tell a candidate that its endorsement (obtained in exchange for promising to help support unions) would guarantee the vote of the union member. Such is, however, not the case. American union members, like all American citizens, are independent. They don't like anyone to tell them for whom to vote. They will make the decision for themselves.

Determining whom to vote for is a complex process. Many factors impact on the decision. Some of the most common are income level, race, geography, religion, parents' voting behavior, and sometimes the merits of the candidates and the issues. The endorsement of a candidate by a union is just one of many other factors to be considered, and often a relatively minor one at that. The fact that union members do vote predominantly Democratic is as much attributable to characteristics they share in common with most Democrats as it is to union endorsement.

"TRACK RECORD" OF ORGANIZED LABOR

Considering the great expenditure of resources by organized labor, its political activity at the national level cannot be considered a major success. In areas of direct concern to labor, COPE has failed to repeal Section 14(b) of the Taft-Hartley Act authorizing state right-to-work laws, or to secure the passage of the Labor Law Reform Bill of 1978, or to enact a public employee collective bargaining bill. In fact, no legislation benefiting unions per se has been passed since the Depression. Neither have candidates endorsed by labor done particularly well. It certainly cannot be argued, in any informed way, that the AFL-CIO is

ORGANIZED LABOR PARTICIPATING IN THE "LIBERAL LEFT"

SOURCE: UPI/Bettman Newsphotos

running the country. In fact, it might be more appropriate to wonder, from a union member's point of view, whether labor is getting its money's worth out of politics.

At the local level, the track record is probably better. There the interest is not in securing legislation but rather in receiving more favorable treatment in the legal/political/economic system from local power brokers. The effectiveness of strikes may depend to a significant extent on the attitudes and activities of the local judiciary and law enforcement agencies. To the extent that they are subject to local political pressure, organized labor can have some effect on outcomes. In many large cities, the AFL-CIO and independent unions often work influentially behind the scenes to try to attract and retain jobs in the locale. This is particularly true of the pressure they exert to try to prevent plant closings.

On the whole, labor's involvement in politics has been aimed at enhancing the benefits of union members, of employees in general, and of society in general. It is also interested in protecting labor from attack by its enemies. Since no antiunion legislation has had a serious chance of passing since Landrum-Griffin in 1959, this does not appear too big a task. Still, as some employers have abused the Taft-Hartley Act's lack of enforcement provisions, labor has been unable even to close loopholes in existing legislation. Labor's track record as a liberal spokesperson for society is really quite good, both as to commitment and success. Its track record on behalf of itself is much less impressive. On the positive side of the ledger, it does appear that union-sponsored legislation protecting the rights of all employees has made a significant contribution to the quality of worklife in America and represents a fine return on investment.[4]

For labor's own assessment of its programs and those of President Reagan in a recent year, see "The AFL-CIO Program—1984."

THE AFL-CIO PROGRAM—1984

After three years of favoritism of the few at the expense of the many, American workers are looking for the redress of multiple grievances. The AFL-CIO, with 14 million members in 96 national organizations and 50,000 local unions, is the most inclusive cross-section of the American population that exists. Its members live in every community and work at every trade and occupation.

It is to that world of work that the current Administration has done its worst damage since it took charge.

Despite more than a year of recovery in the business world, recovery is not even in sight for the 8.5 million who are still unemployed. For those still holding a job, average real wages are 3.5 percent lower than they were four years ago.

The future for most of our children is grim. To reach full employment by 1990, defined as 3 percent joblessness, this country will have to generate 20 million more jobs. If jobs are created at a rate no greater than that of the last seven years, the shortfall will be 7.5 million jobs.

As for youngsters who have been forced to abandon the dream of higher education, this Administration proposes to throw them on that depressed job market at less than the minimum wage.

We believe the platforms of both major parties must also be concerned with the plight of the poor, working and non-working, who have been written off and deprived of the help and encouragement of their government for the past 3.5 years.

In early 1981 when the Reagan Administration's budget and tax proposals were unveiled, the AFL-CIO immediately responded that they posed a "high-risk gamble" with the lives of the American people.

That analysis grew from principles deeply held by American workers and their unions. The labor movement has always opposed the belief that piling more benefits on business and on the wealthy will allow enough to "trickle down" to satisfy America's working men and women.

The conservative economic and political thinking embodied in that "trickle-down" credo dominated the first century of America. That is what workers organized to overcome. Such economic doctrine, so thoroughly discredited by the Great Depression of the 1930s, was revived in the program President Reagan unveiled in early 1981. The opposition of unions was therefore immediate and total.

(continued)

Three years of the Reagan Administration's policies have confirmed that they were indeed high-risk gambles, with millions of workers losing their jobs and millions of dollars lost in production and tax revenue. In addition to widespread human misery in the short run, the long-run federal budget deficits produced by the Reagan Administration's policies threaten immense, permanent damage to the nation.

The Reagan economic policies have produced the highest levels of unemployment since the Great Depression, a half-century ago.

More than 23 million persons were unemployed at some time during 1981, 26 million in 1982 and the same number in 1983. The average duration of joblessness during those three years was 14 weeks and 20 weeks—3.5 to 5 months of lost jobs, lost income, lost health insurance and lost self-esteem.

Lost wages over those three years added up to $336 billion. Lost production amounted to $950 billion. The loss of the federal Treasury was $285 billion, enough to reduce the Reagan deficits quite substantially.

SOURCE: Introduction to The AFL-CIO Platform Proposals *presented to the Democratic and Republican National Conventions, 1984.*

Notes

1. Michael J. Piore, "Can the American Labor Movement Survive Re-Gomperization?" *Proceedings of the 35th Annual Meeting, Industrial Relations Research Association* (Madison, Wis., 1982), p. 34.
2. *Labor Looks at Congress: 1978* (Washington, D.C.: AFL-CIO, 1978).
3. Piore, pp. 37–39.
4. Richard B. Freeman and James L. Medoff, *What Do Unions Do?* (New York: Basic Books, 1984), p. 247.

Discussion Questions

1. Assess the reasons for the AFL's historical position of nonintervention in political activities. Contrast this with the policies of the National Labor Union and the Knights of Labor.
2. Assess the involvement of organized labor in legislation intended to benefit employees in general.
3. Evaluate labor's role in social welfare legislation.
4. Discuss labor's role in election activities.
5. Evaluate the political "track record" of organized labor.

Statements for Comment

1. "Unions belong in companies, not politics."
2. "Union demands for full employment and liberal spending are chief causes of inflation."

3. "If I were running for office, I wouldn't want the endorsement of the AFL-CIO."
4. "Union political activity is a key factor in the federal government's over-involvement in personnel administration."
5. "Union-sponsored protective labor legislation may hurt those it is intended to help."

Situations

Case 7-1 "Unions are sanctimonious, hypocritical, devious self-servers, just like everyone and everything in this world—except that some other types are more honest about their self-centeredness. Unions really don't do anything for anyone else's sake," said David Webster.

"My, my! We certainly have been reading our psychology and philosophy textbooks lately, haven't we?" said Sue Amherst, a devoted business student. "Is the whole world really as cynical as you think it is? I believe unions are often concerned for others and, by the way, so what if they're not? Who says anyone should be looking out for anyone else? It's the American way to take care of yourself."

To what extent are the above allegations valid? Do unions ever act to help others out of true humanitarianism? Is there such a concept as humanitarianism in a business school? Is Sue schizophrenic?

Case 7-2 "You know, I think the Republicans are missing a trick by always letting organized labor's money go to the Democrats. As union members become more comfortably middle class and lose their crusading interest, they're becoming more Republican in sentiment. They are more concerned about taxes than injunctions, and a large portion of them can't be liberals on civil rights. And, goodness knows, the membership can't give a flip about a lot of things COPE spends their money on. Finally, some, maybe even a lot, vote Republican at least some of the time. Besides, the Democrats have already proved you don't have to deliver anything in exchange for labor's support," said John MacNaughton.

"You may be right," said Martha Gonzalez, "but I doubt that such a thing would happen. Frankly, I don't think Republicans would want union members in their party. Not even for money."

"Not even for money! What better reason is there? That's why all business—I mean political—decisions are made," exclaimed John.

How realistic are the positions taken by John and Martha? How defensible is organized labor's political activity? Should labor try to barter its support to the highest bidder? Should the Republicans bid?

Bibliography of Related Readings

Labor Looks at Congress. Available for each Congress from the AFL-CIO (Washington, D.C., various years of publication).

Marshall, F. Ray, Allan G. King, and Vernon M. Briggs, Jr., *Labor Economics,* 4th ed. (Homewood, Ill.: Richard D. Irwin, Inc., 1980), Part IV, "Public Policy."

Piore, Michael J., "Can the American Labor Movement Survive Re-Gomperization?" *Proceedings of the Thirty-Fifth Annual Meeting, Industrial Relations Research Association* (Madison, Wis., 1982).

Rogin, Michael, "Voluntarism: The Political Functions of an Anti-Political Doctrine," in David Brody's *The American Labor Movement* (New York: Harper and Row, 1971).

EIGHT

UNION ORGANIZING CAMPAIGNS AND RECOGNITION PROCEDURES

This chapter examines how a union becomes the bargaining agent for a group of employees.

ORGANIZING CAMPAIGNS

There are two basic reasons to organize: (1) because a group of employees wants a union, (2) because a union wants a group of employees.

The motivation in the first instance is straightforward. At least some of the employees are unhappy with their current situation. Some portion of them believe they would be better off, or might be better off, if represented by a union. They typically contact a representative from an international union or the AFL-CIO and ask him or her to talk to them about organizing. The union responds by sending an organizer to talk covertly to those expressing an interest. The organizer assesses the probability that the bargaining unit can be won, how much it would cost to organize, and how much it would be worth to succeed.

Factors influencing these estimations include the proportion of employees known to be unhappy, the employer's attitude and its willingness and ability to oppose the union, the past history of organizing attempts at this workplace, the organizer's expenses, campaign propaganda costs, future costs to service

UNION ORGANIZERS DISTRIBUTING CAMPAIGN LITERATURE

SOURCE: *ILGWU-Justice Photo*

the unit, and the dues revenues the unit would generate based on the number of employees who could be expected to join the union. If the summation of these estimates indicates that the potential benefit is worth more than the potential cost, the organizer proceeds with his or her organizational efforts.

The first step the organizer usually takes is to meet secretly with key employees who are sympathetic to the union and who may be able to influence others. As more people become interested in the union, the campaign will certainly become known to management. At this time the campaign can come into the open. Union organizers distribute leaflets and buttons away from the workplace, while union-prone employees do the same in the workplace on non-working time. The union then distributes authorization cards to employees that state the employee's wish to be represented by the union. These cards will serve as a demand by the union to be authorized as the exclusive bargaining agent for that unit of employees.

In the second instance, where the union initiates the organizational effort, the scenario is somewhat different. The union has determined in advance that it wishes to represent the employees in question. The reason may be that it represents a large, potentially lucrative dues-paying membership, but that is not the most likely reason for organization. The most likely reason is that organizing this work site would protect the interests of bargaining units elsewhere already represented by the union.

For instance, if a multiplant manufacturer whose other facilities were already represented by the union opened a new plant, the union would want to organize it too—not just to bring in additional dues dollars but also to assure that management would derive no benefits from operating without a union. If the new plant remained nonunion, management could establish production standards and work rules unilaterally. Presumably, these would be more demanding than the standards established at all other plants by bilateral negotiations. If the nonunion plant operated more efficiently than the others, the employer would have an incentive to transfer work from the unionized plants to the nonunion plant. It might also open other plants, keep them nonunion, transfer production to them, and close the unionized plants, costing existing unionized employees their jobs. To prevent this from happening, a union will often attempt to organize a new plant and establish union-level production standards and work rules to keep the new plant from outproducing the old and being a threat to the old plant's employees' jobs.

The above organization effort is not for the benefit of the new, nonunionized employees, but rather for the benefit of the already unionized employees elsewhere. It may be thought of as a defensive campaign, and it will be engaged in with less regard to potential cost or probability of success. The actual mechanism for attempting organization will largely be the same.

LEGAL RULES AFFECTING ORGANIZING

Organizing campaigns often produce legal problems. The Taft-Hartley Act, as interpreted by the NLRB, requires that neither party coerce or intimidate the employees in choosing whether they wish to be represented.[1] The law also forbids employers to promise benefits to employees for defeating the union.[2] The Board's general inquiry is whether either party, judged by the totality of its conduct,[3] significantly distorted the "laboratory conditions necessary to determine the uninhibited desires of employees."[4] If the Board determines that a party's wrongful behavior during the campaign or election has affected the results, it may void the outcome and hold a new election.[5] In rare instances of widespread, pervasive unfair labor practices by an employer, the Board can order the employer to recognize the union and bargain in good faith despite the lack of the union's achieving majority support.[6] In such instances, the logic is that the employer's behavior prevented a fair election from ever being held, and the employer ought not to benefit from its illegal actions.

In the Board's determination of what constitutes illegal behavior in organizing campaigns, it has developed several general rules. The application of the rules to specific cases is a very difficult task over which highly trained labor lawyers can disagree. This text will merely state the rules as a matter of general policy.

Many of the rules deal with access to the employees. The employer may promulgate a "no solicitation, no distribution" rule at its workplace which bars all individuals and organizations (including unions) from entering the workplace to solicit membership or contributions.[7] The rule also bars the distribution of literature at the workplace by outsiders. To be legal, this prohibition must apply to everyone, not just unions. It does not apply to the company's own employees. They are free to discuss unionization and distribute literature on nonworking time. (There are some limitations on literature distribution where litter becomes a significant problem.[8]) Because the union organizer cannot generally enter the employer's workplace, the employer is obligated to provide the union with the names and addresses of all employees so that the union may contact them away from work.[9] In rare instances where it is totally impractical because of physical circumstances to contact the employees away from work, the union may be granted access to the workplace.[10]

There is no provision that the employer and the union have equal access to the employees. If the employer wishes to shut down production and hold a "captive audience" speech, it may do so with no corresponding right for the union to have "equal time." The only limitations on this rule are that the captive audience speech not be coercive, carry threats of reprisal or promise of benefits, contain significant distortions, or be made within 24 hours of the election, since the union would not have any reasonable opportunity to respond and rebut claims made.[11] The employer does have a free-speech right to tell how it feels about unions and point out their bad characteristics, so long as the comments made are not threatening or coercive.[12]

The question of how honest or accurate free-speech statements must be has proved a difficult one for the Board. It has changed its position on the matter several times in recent years, depending upon the political preferences of the membership at the time.

In the past the Board has set aside elections where there has been substantial misrepresentation, lack of time for the other party to reply, and reason to believe that the misrepresentation affected the outcome of the election.

As of this writing, the current position of the Board is not to involve itself in determining the truth or falsity of statements made during an election campaign. This conclusion was justified by claiming that policing of honesty resulted in an extensive analysis of campaign propaganda, restriction of free speech, . . . , increasing litigation, and a decrease in the finality of election results.[13]

DETERMINATION OF THE APPROPRIATE BARGAINING UNIT

For collective bargaining to take place, some group of employees must be collected. The employees grouped together to conduct a representation election constitute a *bargaining unit*. The term is a bit of a misnomer. Actually, the group should be called an *election unit*, since the bargaining unit (the group of employee positions covered by a contract) may be expanded beyond the election unit.

It is not always obvious which positions should be included within the bargaining unit and which should be excluded. The union and the employer both have partisan interests, of course, in wishing to include the groups of employees most likely to influence the election outcome in their favor.

Beyond mere partisanship, several factors need to be considered in unit determination. If the employees are so diverse that they don't want the same benefits from management, having them represented by a single agent may be no aid to the employees at all. If the union negotiates successfully for something one didn't want, little is gained. It is necessary for the employees to have a "community of interest." That is, the employees grouped together should reasonably be expected to want about the same benefits from the employer.

The grouping of employees by community of interest falls into two general categories: by common type of job or by common employer. (These are the same distinctions as between craft and industrial unions.) Employees grouped by similar jobs are said to be organized in *horizontal* bargaining units; those grouped by common employers are in *vertical* units. Horizontal units are common in the skilled trades; vertical units in manufacturing.

A conflict often occurs when craftsmen work in manufacturing situations. Craftsmen generally possess bargaining power by controlling the supply of labor; unskilled employees must rely on numbers for strength. Craftsmen do not generally need production and maintenance employees for power and do not generally wish to be grouped with them—for two reasons. One is that craftsmen often feel superior because of their more extensive training. The other is that they are less numerous and more privileged (higher paid). To be included in the same unit with a large number of production and maintenance employees might subject them to the "tyranny of the majority"—that is, the bargaining unit's members might decide, by majority vote, to negotiate disporportionate pay raises for the lower-paid but more numerous P & M employees. To avoid this potential conflict, the Board has rules that, in general, craftsmen may have a separate bargaining unit if they so desire.[14]

The Board also requires that plant guards not be in a unit represented by the union of the employees that they are supposed to police.[15] Professionals, like craftsmen, are permitted separate units.[16] The biggest exclusion of all, however, affects supervisors and managers. Because they are specifically defined by the Act as not being employees, they are excluded from representation altogether.[17]

If the parties can agree on the appropriate bargaining unit for an election, the Board will accept their determination and conduct a "consent" election. If they cannot agree, the Board will determine the appropriate unit. The Act requires that the Board try to effectuate to the greatest extent possible the desires of the employees.[18] In so doing it has applied the following criteria:

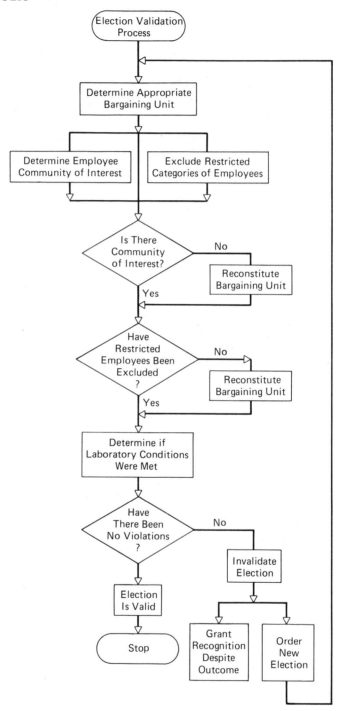

Community of interest

Geographical and physical proximity

Employer's divisions

Degree that the employer's operations are an integrated whole

Amount of employee interchange among work sites

Bargaining history

Employee desires

Extent of organization[19]

THE CAMPAIGN ITSELF

The organizational campaign is much like a political campaign. The parties make allegations of what it is like now and was like in the past, and make promises of how it will be in the future. Like political campaign promises, these statements don't always come true. Employees are not generally fools in these matters. In the past it was believed that they paid very little attention to the claims of *either* party. In fact, in one study of 33 election campaigns, it was found that on the day following the election, employees *remembered* only an average of three issues out of the average of 30 stressed by management. They averaged only two out of 25 on union-stressed issues.[20] It was reasonable to suppose they paid more attention to what had happened to them in the past than to what was predicted, in words, for their future. Still, the parties extend considerable effort, resources, and emotion in trying to win the employees to their side.

Recent findings and changes in managerial behavior, however, have led to new conclusions. In the 1980s, many managements have become much more aggressive in their antiunion campaigns, and indications are that these efforts are paying off.[21] The growth of "union-busting" consulting firms that recommend ways of defeating unions in elections (including illegal actions such as firing union sympathizers and taking the trivial legal consequences) and maintaining a union-free environment have become highly successful and have caused the AFL-CIO to seek redress through changes in the law. Provisions for changes such as speedier elections and heftier penalties for unfair labor practices were included in the Labor Law Reform Bill of 1978. The Bill failed to pass, however, and may be interpreted as a belief that the public is satisfied with the decreased effectiveness of union organizing campaigns.

One of labor's most difficult organizing campaigns—one that spawned much of its concern for the lack of enforceability of the Taft-Hartley Act—was waged against the J. P. Stevens Co., a southern textile manufacturer. A chronology of the events in this campaign is presented in the accompanying box. Particular note should be taken not only of the illegality of the employer's actions but also of the time consumed by the employer's violations and utilization of the legal process. Note should also be taken of the union's "corporate cam-

FIGURE 8–2   UNION ORGANIZING CAMPAIGN LITERATURE

THREE DIMENSIONAL STRENGTH

Hillsborough Classroom Teachers Association

4805 NORTH ROME AVENUE   TAMPA, FLORIDA 33603

DOLLARS

IN ADDITION TO SALARY, TEACHERS AND PARAPROFESSIONALS HAVE COLLECTIVELY BARGAINED FOR MORE EQUITABLE SALARY STRUCTURES BASED ON SENIORITY AND SELF-IMPROVEMENT.

UNORGANIZED SCHOOL EMPLOYEES "TAKE OR LEAVE" WHATEVER THE ADMINISTRATION GIVES THEM.

DIGNITY

TEACHERS AND PARAPROFESSIONALS HAVE PROTECTED THE DIGNITY OF THEIR JOBS AND SECURED INDIVIDUAL PROTECTION FROM INSENSITIVE SUPERVISORS THROUGH CONTRACT NEGOTIATIONS.

UNORGANIZED EMPLOYEES HAVE FEW AVENUES TO TAKE TO SAFEGUARD PERSONAL AND JOB-RELATED DIGNITY.

DUE PROCESS

TEACHERS AND PARAPROFESSIONALS HAVE BINDING ARBITRATION, LEGAL DEFENSE, AND GRIEVANCE PROCESSING BY TRAINED PROFESSIONALS TO GUARANTEE THE PROTECTION OF THEIR RIGHTS.

UNORGANIZED SCHOOL EMPLOYEES HAVE ONLY THEIR EMPLOYERS TO "PROTECT" THEIR RIGHTS.

CTA HAS COMMITTED ITSELF TO ORGANIZE ALL SCHOOL EMPLOYEES INTO ONE LOCALLY CONTROLLED, POLITICALLY AND CONTRACTUALLY POWERFUL UNION.

IF THE 3 D'S OF COLLECTIVE STRENGTH INTEREST YOU
CALL OR CONTACT

**STEVE FISCHER   238-7902
CLASSROOM TEACHERS ASSOCIATION**

FIGURE 8–3 UNION ORGANIZING CAMPAIGN LITERATURE

A UNION JUST FOR YOU

OR

MORE BROKEN PROMISES

Why *HSEF/AFL-CIO* is better than the Teacher's Association or no union...

AN AFL-CIO UNION MEANS:

- Earning higher salaries
- Making your own union decisions
- Electing your own officers
- Having expert negotiators
- Using political power
- Developing grievance procedures
- Voting on your dues rate
- Negotiating your own contract covering wages, job security, fringe benefits, job description, work rules and equal treatment

GET YOUR SHARE OF THE PIE

HSEF/AFL-CIO

Hillsborough School Employees Federation
AFT, FEA/United, AFL-CIO
Local 4154

10920 56th Street, Suite 205, Temple Terrace, Florida 33617 • (813) 985-6989

FIGURE 8-4 MANAGEMENT APPEAL IN UNION ORGANIZING CAMPAIGN

HILLSBOROUGH COUNTY PUBLIC SCHOOLS

P.O. BOX 3408
TAMPA, FLORIDA 33601-3408

October 20, 1983

SCHOOL BOARD

Cecile W. Essrig, Chairman
Joe E. Newsome, Vice Chairman
Roland H. Lewis
A. Leon Lowry
R. Sonny Palomino
Sam Rampello
Marion S. Rodgers

SUPERINTENDENT OF SCHOOLS
Raymond O. Shelton

SCHOOL ADMINISTRATIVE CENTER
901 East Kennedy Blvd. (Tampa)
(813) 272-4000
SUNCOM 571-4000

Dear School System Employee:

On Thursday, October 27, you will be given the opportunity to decide whether or not you will be represented by a union for purposes of collective bargaining. This is the second time in a little over two years in which you will be asked to decide this question. Before you vote, we ask that you keep the following things in mind:

Please vote! The clerical employees of the School Board will be represented by the Classroom Teachers Association by virtue of the election held recently in their group. Under State law, it is the majority of those persons <u>actually voting</u> who determine the results. In the case of the clerical employees, they will *all* be represented by a union even though a majority of those eligible did not select it.

Don't be fooled by the unions' scare tactics. Two years ago, union supporters told you many things. In particular, they said that a study being conducted by an accounting firm would mean the loss of jobs. *Well, the union lost and no one lost their job because of the study.* The same union tried to tell everybody that Civil Service was going to be done away with. *Again, the union did not win and Civil Service is still here.*

This year, the two unions - HSEF and CTA - are telling you that if the union is elected, then it will take the place of Civil Service and that it will be better for you. Just like the last time, unions are telling you things that aren't correct. The law of this State and a decision issued by the court which has jurisdiction over this area, both plainly state that a collective bargaining contract will <u>not</u> replace Civil Service. Any Civil Service system in place goes on and is unaffected by the fact that there is a union on the scene. Any of the subjects that are given by law to the Civil Service Board remain theirs and nothing about them can be changed without the consent of the Civil Service Board. Civil Service can only be done away with by law, over which the School Board has absolutely no control. When someone tells you that bringing in a union will displace the Civil Service Board, that person is telling you something that is contradicted by the very law that will govern all of us, regardless of whether or not there is a union.

Finally, keep in mind that both of the unions that want your vote are teachers' unions. The history of the AFT, with whom the Hillsborough School Employees Federation is affiliated, and the Classroom Teachers Association, both show that they are first, foremost and forever teacher organizations. They are dominated by teachers, they are organized by teachers; their officers, professionals and their staff are teachers. Such a union simply cannot give you the kind of representation that you want - no matter how much you pay in dues.

The School Board believes that the history of benefits given to you and your co-workers establishes beyond any doubt whatsoever that you have fared as well or better than those persons who have been represented by unions within our school system. We do not ask you to accept promises from us; we ask that you look at history. We believe we have done better for employees than the union has. We believe that we deserve to maintain the School Board free of further union entanglement and to operate the system in the best interest of everyone, indluding you.

PLEASE VOTE ! PLEASE VOTE **NO** !

Sincerely,

Raymond O. Shelton
Superintendent

paign,'' a strategy designed to inconvenience and financially injure members of the Board of Directors of the company. The union resorted to this strategy when conventional collective bargaining procedures were stifled by the company's actions. The corporate campaign consisted of using the union's and AFL-CIO's considerable clout in the financial community, where they had very large pension funds on deposit. This influence was used to have members of J. P. Stevens' Board deposed from directorships they held in other companies that did business with those financial institutions (the holding of such directorships is a common practice). Since these positions were very lucrative for the directors, there was significant personal pressure to change the company strategy.

A UNION AT J. P. STEVENS—ANATOMY OF A 17-YEAR STRUGGLE

1963: *The first union card is signed at J. P. Stevens, the world's second largest textile company. No one knew it would be 17 years before Stevens employees got their first union contract—but they knew it wouldn't be easy, because 100 union supporters were immediately fired after those first cards were signed. 1963 was the 150th year of Stevens, which started in New England but began moving South as early as 1946, making the major move of buying the Roanoke Rapids plants in 1956. That was already a milestone year in southern textile history because Roger Milliken shut down the Darlington Manufacturing Co. in Darlington, S.C., that year to show workers that unions would not be tolerated at textile mills. And 1963 was the year the Textile Workers Union (TWUA) selected Stevens as an organizing target because workers had worse working conditions and more union sympathies than other plants. The AFL-CIO Industrial Union Department pledges its resources to the campaign.*

1964: *TWUA charges Stevens with labor law violations before NLRB, including discharges for union activity, but also spying on union activity, and offering bribes for remaining anti-union.*

1964-1967: *Violations continue. Union supporters' jobs are downgraded and even relatives of union supporters are harassed and intimidated.*

1967: *Supreme Court orders reinstatement of 71 Stevens workers fired for union support. Stevens fires workers who testified in the case.*

1969: *Union is declared the bargaining agent at Stevens' Statesboro, Ga., plant, after NLRB sets aside a 1968 election.*

1972: *U.S. 2nd Circuit Court of Appeals holds Stevens in contempt for refusing to obey previous order enjoining it to stop violations.*

"Our system of justice cannot survive if litigants are seized with the notion that they can ignore the lawful orders of a court simply because they disagree with them," the court said. Court also rules that organizers can have access to company bulletin boards in Roanoke Rapids and make speeches in plants.

1973: *Crystal Lee Jordan, whose experiences became the basis for the movie "Norma Rae," and several other workers are fired for union activities during an organizing drive at Stevens's Roanoke Rapids, N.C., plant. In Wallace, N.C., where there are two Stevens plants, organizers discover Stevens is "bugging" their motel rooms. Two company officials indicted by federal grand jury; Stevens pays union $50,000 in settlement of suit.... By the end of this year, Stevens has paid more than $1 million in back-*

(continued)

pay and other settlements ordered by the NLRB and federal courts.

1974: On Aug. 28, a majority of the 3,500 workers in Roanoke Rapids vote union. Contract negotiations will drag on for 6½ years as Stevens refuses to discuss essentials like wages, seniority or arbitration.

1975: Stevens closes its Statesboro plant to avoid bargaining with the union.

1976: ACTWU is formed with the merger of TWUA with the Amalgamated Clothing Workers of America (ACWA). At the merger convention AFL-CIO President George Meany calls Stevens the "nation's No. 1 labor law violater." AFL-CIO mounts a nationwide boycott of Stevens consumer products to bring "this outlaw company" to the bargaining table.

1977: In March a coalition of labor, church and civil rights groups attends Stevens stockholders meeting at corporate headquarters in New York. A number of Stevens workers are also present to challenge company policies, the first action in the union's "corporate campaign."

In August the 2nd U.S. Court of Appeals again finds Stevens in contempt for continued violations of court directives. It orders the company to give union organizers access to all 63 Stevens plants in North and South Carolina and to educate its supervisors on the organizers' rights.

Also in August, congressional hearings on labor law reform take place at Roanoke Rapids Civic Center, where Lewis Harrel tells the poignant story of what it means to be the victim of "brown lung," a disease some textile company officials say doesn't exist.

1978: Boycott of Stevens consumer products gathers momentum. Support is pledged by student groups, city councils, women's groups and religious organizations throughout the United States and trade union movements from Japan, Israel and Australia endorse boycott. Stevens asks the union to discuss a possible settlement. Talks are held in 1978 and 1979, but don't really get going until 1980. . . . The Rev. Joseph Wil-

liams and Crystal Lee Jordan are re-instated to their jobs in Roanoke Rapids by Supreme Court order upholding an earlier court decision. Lewis Harrell dies of bysinossis.

Stevens Board Chairman James Finley resigns from board of Manufacturers Hanover after a union campaign to expose the bank's ties to the Stevens company. David Mitchell, head of Avon products, resigns from Stevens board. Later, R. Manning Brown, head of New York Life Insurance, resigns from Stevens board and Finley resigns from New York Life.

1979: Congressional leaders, retiree groups and community action councils pledge not to buy Stevens consumer products. . . . Release of the film "Norma Rae," by 20th Century Fox gives public at large awareness of the Stevens struggle . . . Workers vote for the union at Stevens plants in High Point, N.C., and Allendale, S.C. . . . Court orders Stevens to bargain in Wallace, N.C. . . .

In Milledgeville, Ga., evidence is uncovered of J. P. Stevens' 2½-year involvement in campaign of illegal surveillance of union organizers and its own workers—including wiretapping. The union takes Stevens to court in a $11.9 million civil rights suit.

Roanoke Rapids workers mark fifth anniversary of union election victory. . . . Company denies to its Roanoke Rapids workers the wage increases paid in other plants.

1980: Six southern Roman Catholic bishops endorse the Stevens campaign, saying that a union contract would be "an effective way of ensuring human dignity in the workplace." . . . 351 safety and health violations are discovered in Stevens's South Carolina plants. . . . 100 Stevens workers meet for leadership training classes in Spartanburg. . . . NLRB orders five illegally discharged workers reinstated in Stuart, Va. . . . The 4th U.S. Circuit Court says June 11 that Stevens has been bargaining in bad faith at Roanoke Rapids and, for second year, Stevens withholds wage increase from Roanoke Rapids workers while paying it in other plants.

Hundreds of trade unionists protest Sperry Corporation links with Stevens at Sperry stockholders meeting. . . . Whitney Stevens becomes chairman of the board and meets with ACTWU officials to negotiate a settle-ment to the long, costly campaign. . . . Oct. 19, settlement is agreed to and signed by company and ACTWU in New York. Contracts are ratified in 10 plants—and there is a union at J. P. Stevens.

SOURCE: *"A Union at J. P. Stevens" by Tom Herriman in* The AFL-CIO American Federationist, *December 1980. Reprinted by permission.*

An outside organizer who is employed by the union, rather than a fellow employee in the workplace, is at a disadvantage. The organizer is not known to the employees. He or she is an outsider who has something ''to sell.'' The organizer's credibility is not known. He or she will be treated suspiciously (at best) by many employees. To overcome this obstacle, the organizer needs to make converts of visible employees whom others will follow. Winning or losing may well depend on how many employees will ''go along with the gang.'' The organizer's campaign will generally be based on claims for better wages, hours, and working conditions, coupled with protection against arbitrary and capricious treatment by management.[22] The organizer will tell employees that the strength of the union will result in greater benefits and that the contract it will negotiate will include discipline and discharge only for just cause as well as the use of seniority (rather than managerial discretion) for filling job vacancies and for layoffs.

Management generally answers by claiming that it is already treating employees well (or at least fairly), that there is no guarantee that the union can negotiate a better deal, that unions cost dues and may cause a strike, and that they are outsiders who may have other people's interests at heart.[23]

The union sympathizers campaign by distributing authorization cards until they feel they can win an election. The NLRB requires at least a 30% ''showing of interest'' before it will conduct an election. Realistically, the union would want at least a majority before it made such an appeal.

When and if the union acquires cards from a majority of the employees in what it believes to be the appropriate bargaining unit, it presents them to the employer and demands to be recognized as the bargaining agent of the employees.

The employer then may voluntarily agree to recognize the union or it can dispute either the validity of the majority's feelings or the appropriateness of the bargaining unit. Since there may be great pressure to sign an authorization card in person, a secret ballot election is almost certainly a better measure of employee preference. The employer may request the NLRB to determine the appropriate bargaining unit and conduct such an election.

FIGURE 8–5 POSSIBLE SEQUENCE OF ORGANIZING EVENTS

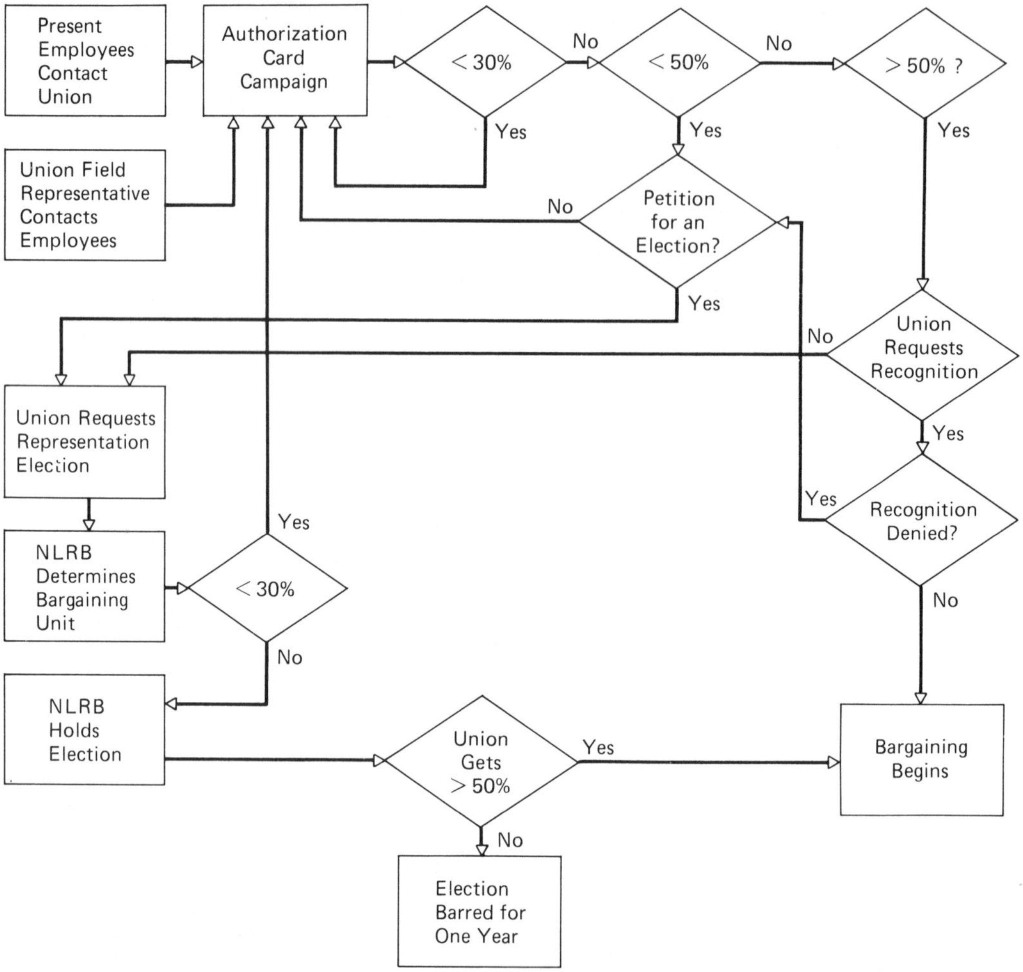

ELECTION AND CERTIFICATION

If the Board determines that it has jurisdiction for this campaign based on the type and size of business, it will conduct an election, generally within 30 to 90 days. If only one union is attempting to organize the unit, it need receive only a majority of the votes cast. If more than one union is involved in the election, and no one receives a majority from among the choices of each union and "no union," the Board will hold a runoff election among the top two finishers.[24] If a union wins, it becomes the exclusive bargaining agent of the employees for the next one year or until a contract agreement is reached, at which point the union will continue as the employees' agent until it is decertified.[25] If the employer wins, no union may call for an election in that unit for at least one year.[26] An NLRB sample ballot appears in Figure 8–6.

Increased management resistance to unionization is also making itself felt in the initial negotiation process. The Board has always assumed that the one-year certification right ought to be enough to negotiate a contract. In recent years, however, many managements, perhaps as many as one-third, have failed to reach an initial agreement with the union within a year, thereby negating its recognition and avoiding bargaining.[27] Again, this is an area where the lack of teeth in the Taft-Hartley Act hurts unions at the expense of employers who are willing to break the law.

In comparatively rare instances, a union may attempt to achieve recognition through picketing rather than authorization cards. In such an instance, the employer may voluntarily recognize the union or call for an election and the picketing must cease.[28] The same election rules apply.

It is also possible for employees to remove a union they selected by decertifying it. Using the same election rules, the Board will conduct an election to determine if the employees no longer wish to be represented by that union. A synopsis of NLRB involvement in elections appears in Figure 8–7.

FIGURE 8–6   SPECIMEN NLRB BALLOT

UNITED STATES OF AMERICA

National Labor Relations Board
OFFICIAL SECRET BALLOT

FOR CERTAIN EMPLOYEES OF

Do you wish to be represented for purposes of collective bargaining by

SAMPLE

MARK AN "X" IN THE SQUARE OF YOUR CHOICE

YES	NO
☐	☐

DO NOT SIGN THIS BALLOT. Fold and drop in ballot box.
If you spoil this ballot return it to the Board Agent for a new one.

FIGURE 8–7   NLRB INVOLVEMENT: PETITION TO ELECTION

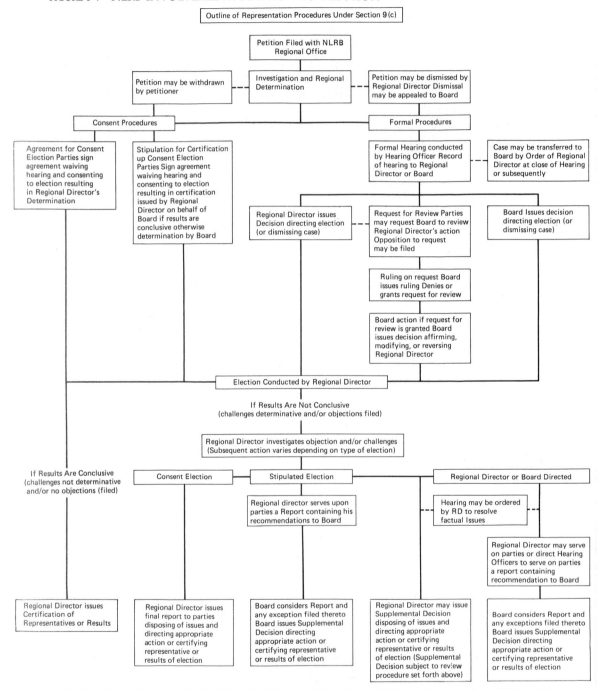

SOURCE: John A. Fossum, Labor Relations *(3rd Edition). (Plano, Texas: Business Publications, Inc., 1985), p. 124.*

EXCLUSIVE REPRESENTATION

Special attention should be drawn to the concept of exclusive representation. It is, for casual observers, one of the least understood concepts in labor relations. Specifically, exclusive representation obligates the union to represent *all* employees in the bargaining unit on matters within the scope of bargaining.[29] This includes, of course, representing its own members, but also includes representing those within the unit who are not members—even if they don't want to be represented. It also requires that nonmembers can no longer represent themselves in individual negotiations with management over wages, hours, and terms and conditions of employment, including job assignment, promotions, and pay.

This means that management may no longer reward high achievers (or personal favorites) preferentially unless the contract permits it. Motivation based on rewards for high performance may be lost. Since it is the motivation to please management that the employer seeks to cultivate, rather than the employees' nonunion status per se, the employer's prime interest is to defeat the union's organizational campaign, not to limit its membership. From an employee's standpoint, the question of joining a union may be trivial next to whether he or she has to be represented by one.

The winning of exclusive representation rights in an election does not give the union any claim on forcing the employees to join. Those who voted "no" for representation presumably will not join. However, it is also possible to vote "yes" for representation and not join the union. Those from both categories who derive the benefits of the contract but do not join the union and pay dues are known as "free riders." The union has a legal "duty of fair representation" to assure that nonmembers are treated the same as members.[30] Obviously, this is irritating and expensive to the union and encourages it to seek ways to compel nonmembers to join or pay their fair share of representation. This is usually accomplished through negotiating "union security" provisions into the contract. These will be discussed in detail in Chapter 13. It might also be suspected that unions might not try as hard to win the grievances filed by nonmembers, even though they are technically obligated to do so.

Despite its obvious irritations, it is clear that the principle of exclusive representation was elected by choice, albeit as a lesser of evils. On the negative side, it requires some employees to be represented by an agent they did not want, and it requires the agent to support constituents it might not want. The alternative, however, was thought to be worse.

Exclusive representation became the law with the passage of the Wagner Act in 1935. At the time of its enactment an alternative scheme was considered—representation for members only. Such was the existing policy in Europe, and the European experience showed that members-only representation was an even worse idea. Senator Wagner convinced the Congress that, although forcing representation upon unwilling employees was philosophically objectionable, allowing unions to represent only their members was unworkable.[31]

Citing the experience of France, Senator Wagner argued that it was necessary to have only one set of rules for all employees. This was convenient for the employer and avoided competition and strife among subgroups of employees. The French had found that with multiple representation by different unions (and a group of nonunion employees) the employer was constantly harassed with negotiations, could not administer its personnel policies in a consistent fashion, and was subject to "leapfrog" bargaining where each union wanted a little more than the one that had just completed negotiations. Wagner also observed that smaller representation units weakened unions because they were not as strong as one larger union would have been and they expended resources fighting among themselves.

As to the philosophical objection of being represented by an unwanted agent, it may be argued that voting for the losing candidate in an election doesn't get one out of paying the winner's taxes. Exclusive representation may be argued to be a reasonable concession to living in a democracy with majority rule—whether it be the country or the workplace.

Notes

1. Sections 8(a)(1) and 8(b)(1).
2. *The Great Atlantic & Pacific Tea Co., Inc.*, 166 NLRB 27 (1967).
3. *NLRB v. Virginia Electric & Power Co.*, 314 U.S. 469 (1941).
4. *General Shoe Corp.*, 77 NLRB 124 (1948).
5. *Ibid.*
6. *United Dairy Farmers Cooperative v. NLRB*, 633 F.(2d) 1054.
7. *Republic Aviation v. NLRB*, 324 U.S. 105 (1956).
8. *Ibid.*
9. *Excelsior Underwear, Inc.*, 156 NLRB 1236 (1966).
10. *Marsh v. Alabama*, 326 U.S. 501 (1946).
11. *Peerless Plywood, Inc.*, 107 NLRB 400 (1953).
12. Section 8(c).
13. *Midland National Life Insurance Co.*, 263 NLRB No. 24 (1982).
14. *Mallinckrodt Chemical Works*, 162 NLRB 48 (1966).
15. Section 9(b)(3).
16. Section 9(b)(1).
17. See Taylor and Witney, *Labor Relations Law*, 4th ed., pp. 347–359, for an extensive history of the decision to exclude supervisors from coverage.
18. Section 9(b).
19. See Fossum, *Labor Relations*, rev. ed., pp. 135–36.
20. Julius Getman, *Labor Relations* (Mineola, N.Y.: Foundation Press, 1978), pp. 82–96.
21. Richard B. Freeman and James L. Medoff, *What Do Unions Do?* (New York: Basic Books, 1984), pp. 233–39.
22. *Getman*, pp. 82–96.
23. *Ibid.*
24. Section 9(c)(3).

25. *Pacific Coast Assn. of Pulp & Paper Mfrs.*, 121 NLRB No. 134 (1958).
26. *Brooks* v. *NLRB*, 348 U.S. 96 (1954).
27. Freeman and Medoff, p. 240.
28. Section 8(b)(7)(c).
29. Section 9(a).
30. *Vaca* v. *Sipes*, 386 U.S. 171 (1967).
31. *Congressional Record*, 1935, Vol. 79, Part 7, p. 7571.

Discussion Questions

1. Discuss the reasons a union might wish to organize a group of employees and the factors which determine whether it might attempt to do so.
2. Describe the legal rules affecting organizing.
3. Describe the rules for creating and the significance of appropriate bargaining units.
4. Assess the critical issues of organizing campaigns.
5. Discuss the election and certification procedure.
6. Evaluate the significance and impact of exclusive representation.

Statements for Comment

1. "Unions shouldn't be allowed to campaign where the employees didn't invite them."
2. "Employers ought not to be forbidden to promise employees benefits for voting against a union, so long as they keep their promises."
3. "A union ought to be entitled to equal time and equal access to employees in election campaigns."
4. "Union organizers never made union members out of anyone. Management did."
5. "The Taft-Hartley unfair labor practice penalties are a farce. We're just lucky they work as well as they do."
6. "The NLRB has no business policing election claims for honesty. No agency polices presidential elections for honesty."

Situations

Case 8–1 Michael Elsey owns and manages a small (60 employees) nonunion manufacturing company in Jacksonville, Florida. He pays the prevailing wage rate and treats his employees well and fairly. He knows them all personally and seems to be genuinely concerned for their welfare. The company has been in business 20 years, and many of the employees have been with the company a long time. The company is consistently profitable, although it does not appear that Mr. Elsey is "rich."

Until recently, the employees had been as content, productive, and loyal as reasonably possible. Their attitude changed when a large unionized northern company in the same business opened a branch in their city and began paying the same wage rate in Jacksonville that it paid in Cleveland, Chicago, and Pittsburgh. This was almost $2 per hour more than Mr. Elsey pays. Suddenly, Mr. Elsey's employees feel underpaid and as if they are being, and have been, "had." There is talk, for the first time, of forming a union.

What should Mr. Elsey do and say? What should the workers do?

Case 8–2 "The NLRB's trying to police campaign claims for honesty is presumptuous and a waste of taxpayers' money," said Sheldon Maris. "After all, it's a well-known fact that neither side believes anything anyone tells them, so it doesn't matter what is said. It's also often impossible to determine what the 'truth' is in an election claim. Leave it to the parties to reveal each others' lies. It shouldn't be the government's job to interfere in what is essentially an internal affair of a company."

"Spoken like a true right-wing, conservative lawyer," said Mary Gray. "Your problem is you don't understand reality. The government has to intervene because it's sanctioning the election. Employees have to have faith that campaigns are conducted honestly and fairly. They can't be expected to ferret out the truth by evaluating evidence produced in an adversary process. Heck, lawyers and judges spend years training to make those decisions, and no one is overly impressed with that system. Some neutral expert, like the NLRB, has to run these affairs, and run them right. The parties sure can't do it on their own."

What portions of these arguments are persuasive? Which are not? Why? How analogous are union representation elections to governmental elections?

Case 8–3 "The reinstatement provisions of the Taft-Hartley Act for workers discharged for organizing are a travesty," claimed Sue Towers. "A Machiavellian employer will do a cost/benefit analysis and conclude that it's easily worth it to break the law by discharging agitators. If convicted, all the employer owes is back wages—less setoff [the amount the employee earned in other employment while the case was pending]—plus interest. In other words, a mere pittance. The employer can't even be fined for breaking the law. It's a rotten situation where it makes more sense to break a law than to comply with it. Something ought to be done about it."

Bill Zubrin disagreed. "I feel you have blown things all out of proportion" he said. "What evidence do you have that employers do exploit the law? I thought most of them complied almost all the time. Why get so upset over a few bad apples? The law works well for almost everyone, and no law can close every loophole. Let unions take care of such employers in other ways."

What do you think of the appropriateness of the current provisions? Why? Should the law be changed? If so, to what? What alternatives besides changing the law are possible?

Case 8–4 Elaine Wilson and Michelle Johnson both worked in the same area of a nonunion department store. When a supervisory opening occurred, Elaine was chosen and Michelle was encouraged to complete the college degree she was working on part-time. Michelle was told she would then be put into the managerial training program. In the meantime, Michelle continued to work in the department.

While Elaine was training for her new position, she heard store gossip to the effect that Michelle would "be out to get Elaine's job when she finished college" and that "to watch out for her in the meantime because she would try to make Elaine look bad."

As soon as Elaine completed her training program (at another location) she returned to the department and proceded to make Michelle look bad. Michelle's past evaluations had always been exceptionally good, but Elaine was able to catch Michelle (by watching her very closely) violating the following company policies: receiving "a few" phone calls on company time, being visited by a friend (whom she had not seen for one year) who dropped in, and speaking to another employee on company time. For these transgressions, Elaine put Michelle on probation.

Michelle was very upset. The things she was accused of were done by everyone in the store, and in greater amounts by almost everyone. She consulted her friend, Alan Rouflab, for advice. He suggested that she talk to Elaine and see if something could be worked out.

Michelle confronted Elaine, claiming she (Elaine) had "blown everything out of proportion." To Michelle's surprise, Elaine immediately backed down, tore up the probation slip, and told Michelle she was "going to give her another chance."

Michelle, surprised with her success, wonders what she should do next. She is sure she has won a battle, but she's not sure about the war. Meanwhile, other employees in the store (including those without supervisory aspirations) are aware of all that has gone on in this situation. Some are saying that, "It's crap like this that proves we need a union here."

What are the implications of a situation like this for a union organizer? For the employer? For the other employees? What should they do? Why?

Bibliography of Related Readings

Ahlburg, D. A., and J. B. Dworkin, "The Influence of Macroeconomic Variables on the Probability of Union Decertification," *Journal of Labor Research*, 1984, pp. 13–28.

Block, R. N., "Union Organizing and the Allocation of Union Resources," *Industrial and Labor Relations Review*, 1980, pp. 101–13.

Carney, C. F., "What Supervisors Can Do About Union Organizing," *Supervisory Management*, January 1981, pp. 10–15.

Craft, J. A., and M. M. Extejt, "New Strategies in Union Organizing," *Journal of Labor Research*, 1983, pp. 19–32.

Dickens, W. T., "The Effect of Company Campaigns on Certification Elections: Law and Reality Once Again," *Industrial and Labor Relations Review*, 1983, pp. 560–75.

Dougherty, James L., *Union-Free Management* (Chicago: Dartnell Press, 1968).

Fulmer, W. E., and T. A. Gilman, "Why Do Workers Vote for Union Decertification?" *Personnel*, 1981, pp. 28–35.

"High-Tech Organizing," *AFL-CIO News*, November 27, 1982, p. 5.

Leslie, Douglas L., *Labor Law in a Nutshell* (St. Paul: West Publishing Company, 1979).

"Organizing The Eighties," *Viewpoint*, 1981, pp. 1–10.

"Picket Line Gives Way to Sophisticated New Tactics," *Business Week*, April 16, 1984, p. 116.

Porter, A. A., and K. F. Murman, "A Survey of Employer Union-Avoidance Practices," *Personnel Administrator*, November 1983, pp. 61–71.

Sandver, M. H., "South-nonsouth Differentials in National Labor Relations Board Certification Election Outcomes," *Journal of Labor Research*, 1982, pp. 13–30.

"Study Bears Out Need for NLRA Reform," *AFL-CIO News*, July 17, 1982, p. 4.

Taylor, Benjamin J., and Fred Witney, *Labor Relations Law*, 4th ed. (Englewood Cliffs, N.J.: Prentice-Hall, 1983).

Voos, P. B., "Does It Pay to Organize? Estimating the Cost to Unions," *Monthly Labor Review*, June 1984, pp. 43–44.

Exercise

Sweet Swing, Inc., I and II   Sweet Swing, Inc., is a wholesale manufacturer of golf clubs retailed through sporting goods and department stores. It also has a very large contract with a mail-order catalog retailer of golf equipment. Its clubs are sometimes sold under its own brand name but more often under the name of the retailer. It also produces a smaller number of other sporting goods items such as ski poles and volleyball standards.

The company was founded in 1921 in St. Louis by Ian Douglass, an accomplished golfer of Scottish ancestry. Ian retired in 1958 and turned the business over to his son, Stuart, who is the current chief executive officer.

Originally, the manufacture of golf clubs was done by hand and required highly skilled club makers. Each iron club was individually forged, and the sets were quite expensive. As golf spread in popularity in the United States, the demand for clubs rose proportionately. Growth occurred particularly at the lower end of the economic scale, as play increased more on public courses than in country clubs. This created the desire on the part of manufacturers to mass-produce lower-cost clubs.

A breakthrough in technology (pioneered at another company) permitted this increase in production. It was called "casting." In casting, molten metal is poured into molds where it hardens to the desired shape. This process allows employees to produce many more clubs per day, reduces the cost (and perhaps the quality) of the finished product, and reduces the amount of skill necessary to be a club maker. It also increases the replaceability of employees and thereby suppresses the effectiveness of their demands for wage increases. It also takes the satisfaction of craftsmanship out of the job.

With the advent of casting and the big contract to supply the mail-order catalog supplier, the business has grown and changed dramatically under Stuart's leadership. When Ian owned and ran the company, he never had more than 20 club-makers and a support staff of four. Obviously, he knew everyone personally. Every-one who worked at Sweet Swing regarded it as a craft and a career. Pay was good, job security was excellent (demand was always exceeding supply), and "self-fulfillment" was high.

With the new technology, Stuart has been able to engineer a very efficient production process utilizing a sizable amount of capital and a large number (500) of unskilled and semiskilled workers. Production has grown so that Stuart employs all the latest techniques in the plant and in the office: computerized ordering and inventory control, his own research and design staff, and an aggressive team of manufacturer's representatives. The result has been an accumulation of wealth and problems.

The new jobs in production are, well—just jobs. A few old-timers remember the "good old days," but most of the employees are young and are not particularly put off by unskilled, monotonous work—that is what they expect from a job. What they are concerned about is job security and pay and benefit packages. These con-siderations take on increased importance in light of a lack of intrinsic satisfaction on the job.

Job security and pay increases have recently become a greater concern than in the past. There are two particular threats. One is a potentially decreasing market share. The Japanese, who dominate sales in the Eastern Hemisphere, are making a concerted effort to expand business in the United States. So far, most of their success has come in "new design" clubs made of graphite. These clubs sell at the high end of the market, but everyone in the American industry is concerned that if the Japanese continue to enjoy success in that market segment, they may broaden their sights. If the Japanese do aim at and hit the lower end of the market, pro-duction costs will become a greater problem, and the continued success of the company will not be nearly so certain.

The other threat the employees perceive is a form of automation. The current production process is partway between "long-run mass production" and "batch production." That is, the company makes several different styles of clubs at any moment in time (although it does make a great quantity of each style). It also changes quite regularly the type of club it makes, both in response to input from R & D and as a marketing strategy in a field some people characterize as "gim-micky." In recent years the company has produced shafts made of steel, light-weight steel, aluminum, fiberglass, and graphite. They have made iron clubheads solid, perimeter-weighted, and hollow. They have made "wood" clubheads of lam-inated maple, persimmon, "Pittsburgh Persimmon" (steel), fiberglass, and graphite. About the only consistent production feature is the club grips, and there are several styles of those. This fairly constant changing of the production process has, up until now, required that the workers be fairly broadly trained (to the extent that they are "trained" at all) and that they be flexible in their work assignments and duties.

A proposed new production process presents both a potential opportunity and danger. It is numerically coded production of forged irons. At this time, the company produces only token amounts of forged irons, utilizing a few of the old craftsmen clubmakers. It has been doing this mainly to protect patent and copy-right interests. Now Stuart is considering taking on the Japanese at their end of the market by producing a high-quality, high-priced, and, hopefully, relatively low-cost line of forged irons. The old form of technology, which required the clubmaker to forge, grind, mill, and polish the head and to insert the shaft at the proper depth and angle (not an easy task to do exactly right), would be (as it always was) prohibitively costly for widespread sales. But the new production process could polish heads and insert shafts at a greater level of consistent quality than even a skilled clubmaker, and at a fraction of the cost.

Stuart sees the new process as a potential boon both to the company and to the employees. It has the potential to increase sales and jobs. Stuart feels the employees ought to be happy. There are several catches, however. The new machinery is costly. Money spent on it is money that can't be spent on raises for employees. True, if this idea works, it will provide new jobs. It will not, however, provide very many of them—that is, after all, its great attraction. Lastly, there is no guarantee that the company can penetrate this portion of the market. There are already reputable manufacturers in the field and they, too, have the opportunity to use this technology.

Furthermore, this speculative venture is being considered at precisely the time the employees have become sensitized to job security issues for the first time in their company and within the economy in general. All the employees in St. Louis have friends or relatives or people that they know of who have lost jobs in the declining manufacturing economy. In some instances, it was believed by employees that the reduction in workforce was not handled properly—that management played favorites.

The employee unrest has been further kindled by Stuart's semiausterity program that has him openly conserving and marshalling resources for the new venture back into forged irons. While never exactly pleading hardship, Stuart has been reluctant to spend money on hourly employees (or anyone or anything else for that matter—he is not being discriminatory) that would detract from his "pet project." At least some employees feel that they are falling behind economically, that their job security may be in danger, that their needs are not being attended to, and that perhaps they need a union to remedy these problems. These employees are considering contacting a union to represent them—or at least to talk to them about the possible benefits of representation.

Assignment I

Recommend courses of action for:

1. The employees (all of them)
2. Stuart
3. Organizers of unions that might potentially represent these employees

Factors to consider:

Stuart's goals, needs, actions (and possible consequences thereof), and possible alternatives

Employee needs, benefits, probability of improvement, and other possible courses of action

Exercise

Sweet Swing, Inc., II Presume the United Molders wish to attempt to organize Sweet Swing because they are an industrial union, molded metal is used in the manufacture of the product, the union is fighting a declining membership in manufacturing, and the added revenue and membership would be appealing.

Assignment II

Prepare scenarios describing the likely activities of:

1. the union
2. the company
3. the employees

BARGAINING

All observers are aware that collective bargaining is supposed to produce benefits for employees in the form of improved wages, hours, and working conditions. However, to many observers, there appears to be no significant benefit for management—the best it can hope for is to hold its losses to a minimum. This is a misimpression. The benefit management receives from signing a contract is a guarantee of uninterrupted production at an agreed-upon quantity and price for the life of the contract. In other words, the union guarantees not to strike or ask for improvements in wages, benefits, or working conditions for the life of the contract. Nonunionized employees are always free to bargain for more and, in periods of rapid inflation, may well get raises more often than workers under a contract. The collective bargaining contract is very similar to any contract reached between the employer and any of its suppliers. The only difference is that the vendor in this case is supplying labor instead of raw materials. The contract is one of mutual benefit.

OBLIGATION TO BARGAIN IN GOOD FAITH

Once a union has acquired the right to represent a unit of employees, it begins collective bargaining. The central feature of collective bargaining is the obligation to bargain "in good faith" in an attempt to reach an agreement on issues within the scope of bargaining.

The failure of either party to bargain in good faith is an unfair labor practice. Section 8(d) of the Taft-Hartley Act (appearing in the accompanying box) defines the obligations of good faith and details the procedures to be followed prior to renegotiation of an existing contract.

TAFT-HARTLEY OBLIGATIONS FOR GOOD-FAITH BARGAINING

Section 8(d) For the purposes of this section, to bargain collectively is the performance of the mutual obligation of the employer and the representative of the employees to meet at reasonable times and confer in good faith with respect to wages, hours, and other terms and conditions of employment, or the negotiation of an agreement, or any question arising thereunder, and the execution of a written contract incorporating any agreement reached if requested by either party, but such obligation does not compel either party to agree to a proposal or require the making of a concession: Provided, That where there is in effect a collective-bargaining contract covering employees in an industry affecting commerce, the duty to bargain collectively shall also mean that no party to such contract shall terminate or modify such contract, unless the party desiring such termination or modification—

(1) serves a written notice upon the other party to the contract of the proposed termination or modification sixty days prior to the expiration date thereof, or in the event such contract contains no expiration date, sixty days prior to the time it is proposed to make such termination or modification;

(2) offers to meet and confer with the other party for the purpose of negotiating a new contract or a contract containing the proposed modifications;

(3) notifies the Federal Mediation and Conciliation Service within thirty days after such notice of the existence of a dispute, and simultaneously therewith notifies any State or Territorial agency established to mediate and conciliate disputes within the State or Territory where the dispute occurred, provided no agreement has been reached by that time; and

(4) continues in full force and effect, without resorting to strike or lockout, all the terms and conditions of the existing contract for a period of sixty days after such notice is given or until the expiration date of such contract, whichever occurs later. . . .

Note especially that the law does not require either party to make a concession—only that they make a good-faith effort to discover if they can find a settlement acceptable to each.

The determination of whether a party is bargaining in good faith is very difficult for two reasons. Obviously, the term "good faith" connotes a state of mind. Since a party's state of mind is never directly provable, the presence or absence of good faith must be inferred from the observable actions of the parties.

Furthermore, the term is imprecise and requires interpretation in light of the individual setting, the bargaining history of the parties, and "common law" meanings attached to the term. These conditions combine to make the obligation to bargain in good faith very difficult to determine and enforce.

Some elements of good-faith bargaining are specified in the law, such as the obligation to meet at reasonable times and places, to willingly discuss issues within the scope of bargaining, and to commit agreements reached to writing. Failure to abide by these requirements is a "per se" violation. A list of per se violations appears in the accompanying box.

PER SE VIOLATIONS OF GOOD FAITH BARGAINING

Management commits a per se violation whenever it:

refuses to meet with the union to negotiate its proposals,

insists to a point of impasse on a provision requiring that a secret ballot election be held before a strike can be called,

refuses to supply cost and other data relating to a group insurance plan, or

announces a wage change without consulting the union.

A union commits a per se violation when it:

insists on a closed shop or discriminatory hiring,

refuses to meet with a legal representative of the employer about negotiations, or

refuses to negotiate a management proposal involving a mandatory subject.

SOURCE: National Labor Relations Board, Guide to Basic Law, *pp. 28, 36.*

Often, the allegation that a party is failing to bargain in good faith is more difficult to substantiate and requires examination of more of the party's behavior. Other elements commonly observed, but not necessarily technically required as evidence of good faith, include the making of compromises and the offering of counterproposals. From actions of this type it can be inferred that the parties are bargaining in good faith. An absence of such behavior would cast suspicion that the party not participating in such activities is not really trying to reach agreement. In such cases the Board determines whether a party is bargaining in good faith based on its "totality of conduct." Some items found in the past to have been indicative of bad-faith bargaining in combination (but not necessarily alone) appear in the accompanying box.

It should be immediately apparent that the inferences drawn from these observations are subject to manipulation. A party wishing to escape reaching agreement could sit at meetings and offer concessions and counterproposals it knows won't be accepted (but are not blatantly unreasonable), thereby escaping both agreement and a charge of failure to bargain in good faith. Conversely, a

TOTALITY OF CONDUCT CONSIDERATIONS
OF GOOD-FAITH BARGAINING

Surface bargaining: *The party is willing to meet at length and confer but merely goes through the motions of bargaining. It includes making proposals which cannot be accepted, taking an inflexible attitude on major issues, and offering no alternative proposals.*

Concessions: *Although Taft-Hartley does not require the making of concessions, the term good faith certainly suggests a willingness to compromise and make a reasonable effort to settle differences.*

Proposals and demands: *Advancing proposals which open the doors for future discussions indicates good faith, whereas proposals that foreclose future negotiations and are patently unreasonable are reflectors of bad faith.*

Dilatory tactics: *Refusal to meet, unreasonable procrastination in executing the agreement, delay in scheduling meetings, willful avoidance of meetings, evasive tactics, delay in providing data for bargaining, and similar tactics are evidence of bad faith.*

Imposing conditions: *Attempts to specify conditions on bargaining or the administration of the agreement will be scrutinized closely to determine whether such conditions are onerous or unreasonable (for example, insisting that all grievances be re-solved before collective bargaining can start). In addition, the requirement of agreement on a specific item as a prerequisite to negotiating other issues reflects bad faith bargaining.*

Unilateral changes in conditions: *Such actions as changing the compensation or fringe benefits plan unilaterally during bargaining is a strong indicator of bad faith bargaining. Unilateral changes per se may not be illegal, but justification must be reasonable and accurate.*

Bypassing the representative: *Since the collective bargaining agreement supersedes the individual employee contract, the employer must not refuse to negotiate over mandatory issues. The duty to bargain is essentially equivalent to the duty to recognize the exclusive bargaining representative of the employees. Attempts to bypass this representative are evidence of bad faith.*

Commission of unfair labor practices: *Committing unfair labor practices (such as threatening to close the plant, promoting withdrawal from the union, reducing working hours, and engaging in discriminatory layoffs) during negotiations is indicative of conduct inconsistent with good faith bargaining.*

party unwilling to make concessions or counterproposals but still seeking to reach agreement (on its own terms) will be perceived as bargaining in bad faith when really it is not. Sophisticated bargainers can play games while still giving the appearance of bargaining in good faith, thereby rendering the NLRB's charge to prevent such behavior a very difficult task. Still, some parties take blatant enough positions to make unfair labor practice charges in these areas common.

SCOPE OF BARGAINING

Another source of charges of failure to bargain in good faith stems from whether an issue is properly within the scope of bargaining—that is, whether the parties are obligated to discuss it. When one side refuses to negotiate a subject, claiming it is not obligated to do so, the other party may file an unfair labor practice charge. The NLRB divides bargaining subjects into three categories: mandatory, voluntary, and prohibited. *Mandatory* subjects are those falling within the rubric of "wages, hours, and terms and conditions of employment." *Prohibited* subjects include certain practices directed at parties outside the labor dispute, racially discriminatory contracts, and the "closed shop"—the obligation to be a member of a particular union before one can be hired for a job in that bargaining unit. *Voluntary* subjects are those which are neither mandatory nor prohibited. The NLRB has ruled that the parties may discuss any voluntary subject, but it is an unfair labor practice to force an impasse over such issues. Again, sophisticated bargainers can usually escape this requirement by subtly conditioning acceptance of mandatory subject proposals upon negotiation of the voluntary subject.

A list of topics found to be mandatory subjects of bargaining in previous NLRB cases appears in Table 9–1.

The obligation to bargain in good faith does not end with the ratification of the contract. For matters not resolved by the contract the parties are obligated to continue to bargain during the life of the contract. This situation most commonly arises when management changes a production process or adds new types of work during the life of an agreement. Since the contract probably did not foresee these particular situations, it usually doesn't cover them. Although this matter can present some significant complexities in labor law, the general rule is as follows: If management wishes to make changes in areas not addressed by the contract, it must bargain in good faith with the union about them. If no agreement can be reached, management may implement its changes unilaterally and the union may strike. If the union has signed a no-strike clause in the contract (almost always the case), it may file a grievance concerning the changes and ultimately submit the dispute to binding arbitration.

Ironically, for all the attention given charges of failure to bargain in good faith, there is very little—actually, virtually nothing—the NLRB can do to punish offenders. It cannot fine parties or impose appropriate contract terms or bar offending companies from bidding on government contracts. All it can do is issue a cease-and-desist order telling the offending party to stop being naughty and start behaving.

FACTORS COMMONLY AFFECTING BARGAINING

Negotiations are very individual occurrences. They differ among parties and they differ among times with the same parties. They are a subject on which it

TABLE 9-1 ITEMS MANDATORY FOR BARGAINING

Wages	Cancellation of seniority upon relocation of plant
Hours	Discounts on company products
Discharge	Shift differentials
Arbitration	Contract clause providing for supervisors keeping seniority in unit
Holidays—paid	
Vacations—paid	
Duration of agreement	Procedures for income tax withholding
Grievance procedure	Severance pay
Layoff plan	Nondiscriminatory hiring hall
Reinstatement of economic strikers	Plant rules
Change of payment from hourly base to salary base	Safety
	Prohibition against supervisor doing unit work
Union security and checkoff	
Work rules	Superseniority for union stewards
Merit wage increase	Checkoff
Work schedule	Partial plant closing
Lunch periods	Hunting on employer forest reserve where previously granted
Rest periods	
Pension plan	Plant closedown and relocation
Retirement age	Change in operations resulting in reclassifying workers from incentive to straight time, or cut work force, or installation of cost-saving machine
Bonus payments	
Price of meals provided by company	
Group insurance—health, accident, life	
Promotions	Plant closing
Seniority	Job posting procedures
Layoffs	Plant reopening
Transfers	Employee physical examination
Work assignments and transfers	Union security
No-strike clause	Bargaining over "bar list"
Piece rates	Truck rentals—minimum rental to be paid by carriers to employee-owned vehicles
Stock purchase plan	
Workloads	Musician price lists
Change of employee status to independent contractors	Arrangement for negotiation
	Change in insurance carrier and benefits
Motor carrier—union agreement providing that carriers use own equipment before leasing outside equipment	Profit-sharing plan
	Company houses
	Subcontracting
Overtime pay	Discriminatory racial policies
Agency shop	Production ceiling imposed by union
Sick leave	Most favored nation clause
Employer's insistence on clause giving arbitrator right to enforce award	Vended food products
Management rights clause	

SOURCE: *Reed Richardson, "Positive Collective Bargaining,"* ASPA Handbook of Personnel and Industrial Relations, *Dale Yoder and H. G. Heneman, Jr., Editors. (Washington: BNA Pub., Inc., 1979) pp. 7–120 through 7–121.*

is definitely dangerous to generalize. Still, several factors influence bargaining strategies and styles (as opposed to outcomes) in many different situations. Some of the most significant factors are the personalities and training of the negotiators, the history of bargaining between the parties, the extent to which the union leader is secure in his or her position, and the size and composition of the bargaining unit.

The history of a bargaining relationship has a great influence on succeeding negotiations. If past relationships have been aboveboard, professional, and successful, the parties are likely to enter the next negotiation with as few hindrances to settlement as possible. On the other hand, if past negotiations have been conducted in bad faith, the parties don't trust one another, and "revenge" must be had, the current issues may be almost irrelevant and reaching agreement may be impossible. It should be apparent that agreeing is difficult enough on the issues themselves. Adding personal vendettas only makes it more difficult.

The less secure the union leader is in his or her position, the more difficult bargaining may be. As observed in Chapter 6 union leaders who are in danger of not being reelected must attempt to please all their constituents—an impossible task if they are to compromise any of their demands. This pressure can prevent a leader from making reasonable tradeoffs, thereby alienating management and making agreement even more difficult to achieve.

The size and composition of the bargaining unit also affect the ease with which agreement is reached. Very large units, particularly those which are geographically dispersed, make communication difficult for the negotiating team. This may, ironically, aid in reaching an agreement at the table (although not necessarily a ratification) by helping isolate the bargainers from the pressures of their constituents, at least momentarily. Diverse composition, however, is always a detriment to reaching agreement. When units contain many different job classifications or different types of employees, the divergent interests of the employees must be compromised not only with the employer but among internal employee interest groups. An employee leader who has to compromise demands within his or her constituency can less afford to compromise at the table, thereby complicating the negotiations.

PREPARATION OF DEMANDS AND OFFERS

In order for collective bargaining to produce an agreement, two main questions must be answered: (1) Where are we now? and (2) Where should we go from here? The preparation of demands and offers must anticipate answers to both of these questions.

Preparing for bargaining entails four main tasks: (1) formulating team membership and soliciting input from constituents, (2) gathering relevant data, (3) establishing goals and minimal acceptance points and, (4) devising a strategy.

Establishing goals and devising a strategy also obviously require estimating in advance the other side's goals and strategy.

Step 1 is extremely important to the long-range success of bargaining. Bargaining teams must be both politically and tactically well constituted. Politics requires that important constituencies be represented and in appropriate proportion to help enhance the success of proposed settlements. These delegates will represent their interest groups for input and will be expected to help "sell" the proposed agreement to their constituencies. Obviously, since members of the same bargaining team can be in conflict with one another, the balancing of competing interests may require a great deal of skill. Tactically, the team must be of convenient size for meeting, communicating, and maintaining confidentiality and must consist of individuals whose personalities are suitable for the demands of collective bargaining. Obviously, it is not easy to achieve all these goals simultaneously, especially for relative newcomers.

Once the team has been selected to represent various interest groups (the union team's composition may be dictated by its constitution), it becomes necessary to solicit input from and deliver communications to the constituencies. This, too, is no easy task. It requires both the facility to communicate well and the policy considerations of what information should be communicated. Frankly speaking, collective bargaining is not always an open, honest, straightforward exercise in communication—even with one's own team. Perhaps particularly not even with one's own team. Some information isn't communicated widely for fear of "leaks." Other information isn't communicated widely because the team is compromising a constituent's demand and doesn't want to hassle with both sides at the same time.

Even knowing what one wants to communicate or receive does not solve all the problems. All the usual human and physical barriers to communication continue to exist and may well be exacerbated by the heightened emotions of bargaining. How well communications with the constituencies are handled can have as important an impact on whether a proposal is accepted as the actual content of the contract itself.

Gathering relevant data is probably one of the more time-consuming but achievable tasks in preparing for bargaining. This phase is not so politically or personality-oriented as the others. If the parties can anticipate the issues to be discussed (not usually a hard task) and know where to look for information on these subjects, acquiring data becomes mostly a matter of effort.

A useful tactic that has gained some acceptance in recent years among sophisticated bargainers is the joint-study group. Made up of representatives from both parties, the joint-study group gathers data concerning comparative wage scales, cost of living, benefit coverages, etc. in anticipation of negotiations so that bargaining efforts will be well informed and directed as efficiently as possible at the question: "Where are we now?" Joint-study groups may also be used to study ongoing problems, such as accident prevention, during the life of the contract.

At this point it is useful to examine the role that facts play in bargaining. Facts help answer the question: "Where are we now?" If the facts are not known, the parties can only estimate each other's position. This restriction can complicate bargaining a great deal.

The employer is obviously the party in possession of relevant data on the company's financial position. Historically, employers have not willingly shared that information with the union, presumably on the assumption that the union would seek to capture whatever profits existed for wage increases. The failure to share that information has led, however, to some negative consequences. Consider the following typical scenario:

The union, because it does not have accurate information concerning the company's financial position, can only estimate the employer's ability to pay. Its estimate is that the company made a profit between 15 and 25 (add as many zeroes as you like) dollars last year. The employer is implying, although not proving, that the number is around 17. This claim is plausible because it falls within the 15–25 range. But the union also knows that management has an interest in portraying as weak an ability-to-pay position as possible. Therefore, that 17 figure is probably (although not necessarily) low. It is almost certainly a low figure if management hasn't proven its honesty in this area in the past.

The union is now confronted with a choice. If it accepts the comparatively low figure and it really is an understatement, raises will be lower than they might have been and management will have benefited from misleading the union. Both of these are bad consequences for the union.

To be on the safe side and to keep from being duped, the union leader must assume that the highest possible estimate was correct for the company until proven otherwise. This leads the union to make demands scaled to a profit level of 25. If there were really only a 20-level profit, the union demand is genuinely going to be an unreasonable one—one that will make agreement more difficult to achieve. It might even precipitate an otherwise avoidable strike.

Experienced parties to bargaining have realized many of the negative consequences of withholding facts and have sought to reduce the discrepancy in estimates by willingly providing factual evidence, rather than assertions, to support their positions. While this doesn't compel agreement from the other side, it does at least reduce some of the potential disagreement. At its most advanced state, it has led to the joint-study groups described above.

Establishing goals and minimal acceptance points is as much "art" as it is "science." There is no "exactly right" contract for a given set of demands and constraints. Different parties with the same bargaining expertise and power would reach different agreements simply because they attach different values to the terms of the settlement. Before beginning negotiations, the parties need to caucus among themselves and determine what they think they and their constituents need, what they would like to have, and what they feel they absolutely cannot give up. Empirical data on costs and comparisons are useful but not controlling. Unlike an organized debate where points are scored for the quality of an argument and its support, collective bargaining gives credit only for the settlement ultimately reached. Arguments that are well supported by data may be better received than those which are not, but what will be agreed upon still remains a political question. The merits of arguments are not always the persuasive issue. This is often difficult for highly educated bargainers to accept.

Particularly irritating to some parties is the propensity of unions to open bargaining with "outrageous" demands—demands they do not reasonably expect to attain. There are four main reasons for this: camouflage, tradeoffs, "seasoning," and "pet demands."

The presentation of a large number of demands, some of which certainly will not be granted, serves to disguise which ones are most valued by the union. Hopefully, as tradeoffs take place, management will make an important concession in exchange for a demand the union did not feel strongly about and was willing to concede. This could result in increasing the net value of the package.

Adding extra demands or making them overly extreme and then offering them as tradeoffs has less direct effect on increasing the value of a package. Unions have been known to make wage demands far in excess of what they expect to get, figuring that if a demand is compromised, they may as well start from far out so the settlement point will fall further in their direction. This logic would apply, however, only if the settlement point were the midpoint between the demand and offer. This is, however, obviously not the case. Certainly, a union demand for a 14 percent raise would not automatically result in a 7 percent increase. If this simplistic logic applied, unions would have no upper bound. A demand for a 100 percent increase would result in a 50 percent raise. Obviously, the settlement point is determined by factors other than the size of the demand. (The factors that do affect the settlement point for wage demands will be discussed in Chapter 10.) This logic applies to all demands incorporated for the purpose of being traded off. More demands do not change the settlement point.

Some early demands are offered by unions with the intention of compromising or abandoning them in the present negotiation but bargaining more earnestly about them in future years. Most benefits unions receive arose in this fashion. Seldom do they receive a new form of benefit the first time they ask for it.

Finally, "pet" demands are those even the union believes it should not receive but which were made by members whose support must be maintained. It is far easier for a democratically elected union leader to include an unreasonable demand and have management throw it out than for the leader to stand up and tell his or her constituent, "I'm not even going to try to get what you want."

In meeting to determine the team's goals, new negotiators often receive the first installment in one of the great lessons in life in collective bargaining— the "opponent" is not only the other side but may also be the other members of your own team. A particularly disturbing corollary to this observation is that internecine fights may well be worse than across-the-table fights. No matter how cooperative the members of the team may wish to be (and they may not wish to be cooperative at all, given the special interests that they represent and the experiences they have had with each other in the past), they are going to be forced to yield some of their own positions for those of others on the team. This is hard to do during goal setting; it is even harder to do in the presettlement negotiations. Again, the compromises reached may well be a product more of power than merit or reason.

A list of items for a management negotiator's preparations appears in the accompanying box.

MANAGEMENT ITEMS TO PREPARE FOR BARGAINING

The following items are illustrative of those prepared for negotiators by many companies:

1. *A summary of the previous collective bargaining negotiations with the union.*

2. *A book containing the existing collective bargaining agreement broken up into its separate clauses. A discussion of experience with each clause, pro and con, and changes to be proposed by the company is included. When it is possible to anticipate union demands for changes, these are also identified.*

3. *The internal data of the firm with respect to its labor costs, identified by clause of the contract, are summarized in a separate book.*

4. *Data regarding the labor costs of other firms, both competitors, wherever they are located, and noncompetitors in the same geographic area (compiled in yet another notebook).*

5. *Information about the union, its leadership, history, finances, and any other special circumstances bearing on the union's role in the negotiation.*

6. *A list of the union's expected demands and their impact on the company.*

7. *A list of resource people in the company who are most likely to know, or be able to ascertain quickly, the impact of proposed contract changes on the company's operations and costs.*

It is also useful to have an agreed-upon set of "ground rules" for bargaining. One example of such appears in the Appendix I at the end of the chapter. Appendix II contains an employer's tally sheet for estimating the cost of union demands.

PREPARATION OF STRATEGIES

The last step remaining in preparing for negotiations is to develop a strategy to obtain the goals set. The strategy selected depends heavily on bargaining power, the personalities of team members, and the past experiences between the parties. Strategies can range from total opposition to cooperation, with intermediate philosophies of power bargaining and accommodation.

Total opposition consists of making every legal effort (and sometimes illegal efforts as well) to refuse to bargain, to reach agreement, or even to recognize the other party. Unions, of course, are not likely to pursue this position, because they can achieve gains only by bargaining with management and reaching a favorable settlement. Management, on the other hand, may perceive benefits in such a strategy by avoiding agreement and maintaining the status quo. Total opposition has several significant deficiencies as a bargaining strategy. One is that it creates very bad relations with the employees which will certainly result in less than their best efforts at work. Another is that it fosters union militancy. Where the employer is uncompromising and hostile, the union may be more inclined to engage in a costly strike as the only way to receive benefits to which the employees feel entitled. Finally, it may well result in violations of the law in the form of unfair labor practices. It is certainly not a high-grade strategy designed to solve problems over the long run.

In *power bargaining*, the parties agree to play by the rules of the game, but each attempts to "win" by exerting power. Power bargaining does result in good-faith efforts to reach agreement but does so at the cost of substituting power for equity. When the criterion for settlement is what can be forced upon the other party, rather than what is appropriate, the resulting contract may not work well in application. Further, forced concessions may well provide a desire for revenge that will complicate future negotiations, particularly if the balance of power changes.

Accommodation is generally regarded as the most realistic of strategies. Here the parties accept each other and the rules of the game. They approach negotiations with an attitude of trying to reach a true agreement with a minimum of unnecessary games-playing. They are trying to reach an appropriate solution in this instance and also to lay the groundwork for future productive negotiations. Pragmatism generally reigns over philosophy or emotion.

Cooperation is a major step beyond accommodation. It requires that the parties perceive a mutual benefit in each other's existence. This situation, despite occasional public statements to the contrary, almost never occurs. It would require management to accept the union as a participant in running the organization. In America, management seldom considers giving the union a voice in operating the company—nor does the union want it. If the union were to be involved in joint decision making, it would be obligated to expand its responsibility from its constituents to the company as a whole and would create a perceived conflict of interest for its leaders. Further, if the parties could engage in productive cooperative efforts, the employees might well perceive less need for a union, thereby threatening the union leader's job. Given also that most managers, for ego reasons, are not favorably inclined to share their decision making with subordinates (despite whatever evidence might support the merits of such a strategy), and that union leaders have a vested interest in maintaining an adversarial relationship, it is not surprising that cooperation has appealed more to scholars and media commentators than it has to practitioners.

EMPLOYER BARGAINING POWER

Power is an important factor in bargaining. The outcomes it produces are not necessarily "fair" or "equitable." It has been said that collective bargaining is a process by which the lion receives the lion's share. Fortunately, it is not necessary that the parties' power be balanced exactly equally for the system to be workable. All that is required is that the weaker party be able to inflict sufficient cost or harm on the stronger party to make agreement more attractive than attack. Besides, neither party generally wishes to engage in a "war" with the other. The employer may wish to exterminate the union, but it does not benefit from unnecessarily alienating its own employees, while the union certainly does not want to bankrupt the company, which is, after all, the source of paychecks.

A main determinant of bargaining power is a party's willingness and ability to take a strike. The factors that influence this capacity are different for the parties.

For the employer the most important considerations are whether it can get along without production for a period of time and/or whether it can continue production without the employees who are on strike.

TAKING A STRIKE

Three of the major determinants of an employer's ability to wait out a strike are the timing of the strike, the ability of customers to stockpile the employer's product in advance, and the effects of competition.

A union would like to time its strike at the point the employer needs production the most, while the employer would wish it to occur when demand is least. Obviously, a toy manufacturer would rather have a strike occur in January than in November. These considerations can make the negotiation of contract expiration dates very significant.

Stockpiling can also relieve pressure on an employer. If a strike is impending, an employer can advise its customers to purchase product in advance in anticipation of interrupted supply. This has been a particularly valuable tactic to employers in the steel and coal industries whose product can be produced in advance and held in customer inventories as the union strikes. The pain of the strike for the union—no paychecks—is immediate, while the company suffers little reduced revenue: it sold its product in advance. In fact, an employer has very little incentive to settle if it has presold its product, since it cannot sell more to the same customers. Therefore, it is less likely to make concessions, since it does not want (cannot even use) production in the near future and can save labor costs during the almost inevitable strike. The employer will generally begin serious attempts to reach agreement only when its customers' inventories have been depleted and the potential for additional sales is again created.

Stockpiling obviously puts the employees at a great disadvantage. It is often asked by students why union members produce extra product in advance for use in defeating their own strike. The answer is because they are powerless to resist doing so. Remember, there is no *legal* right to refuse to work overtime, and very, very few contracts permit such a refusal. A refusal to work would be insubordination and subject the employees to discipline for just cause. The United Steel Workers found the employers' stockpiling tactic so successful that from the mid-1960s to the mid-1980s they operated under an Experimental Negotiating Agreement that substituted binding arbitration of negotiating impasses for the right to strike—which for them had been a very costly right. No other major union has agreed to such an arrangement.

The activities of competitors also affect an employer's ability to take a strike. If an employer who has lost production due to a strike can merely postpone (rather than lose) sales, it suffers less than if its competitors sell to its customers during the strike. Trucking companies have historically been vulnerable to demands of the Teamsters because of the effects of competition. Because over-the-road trucking historically consisted of many competitive firms, a strike by the Teamsters of one company was doubly painful. Not only was employer income reduced as deliveries were not made, those lost revenues could not be recovered in the future because customers shipped their freight through nonstruck competitors. Worse yet, customers often changed their allegiance to the competitors permanently. Obviously, the pressure on an employer to make a concession is much greater if its business competition can and will take advantage of its plight.

For a select few large companies—conglomerates—it may also be possible to take a strike by getting along without production in that phase of the business while continuing to operate the others. This weakens union bargaining power considerably.

CONTINUED OPERATIONS

A second facet of bargaining power is the extent to which an employer can continue to operate despite a strike. This depends largely on whether its nonunion employees can maintain operations (or a useful portion of them) for a period of time or whether replacements, either permanent or temporary, are available.

The ability of nonstrikers such as managers and supervisors and those hourly employees not respecting the picket line to operate a facility depends to a great extent upon the level of technology used. If a few managers can operate a largely automated production function (such as a telephone company), the union's bargaining power will be less. On the other hand, in a labor-intensive workplace, supervisors may not be physically able to do the work, and there almost certainly won't be enough of them. This gives bargaining power to the union—unless, of course, outside replacements are hired.

An employer's decision to attempt to replace its workers depends on the availability of replacements with suffcient skill to do the job. The more irreplaceable the employees are because few adequate substitutes are available, the more bargaining power the employees have. The factors affecting an employer's decision to attempt to continue operations will be examined in greater detail in Chapter 10.

A final factor can affect an employer's ability to take a strike. It is strike insurance. In situations where strikes are rare but severe (such as professional sports) the employers sometimes are able to insure their income against strike losses—in return for very high premiums.

UNION BARGAINING POWER

A union's ability to call a successful strike depends, of course, upon its bargaining power. Its power is usually the reverse of the conditions that favor management, plus the factors that affect the union alone. These additional factors include the availability of strike funds, the employees' past experiences (positive and negative) with strikes, and the political situation of the leader.

Local unions affiliated with national unions affiliated with the AFL-CIO generally have the best access to strike funds, particularly if they have not engaged in a costly strike recently. The workers' psychological willingness to strike may be based on their historical experiences and emotions rather than pure, rational economic analysis.

The political position of the union leader could cut either way. If he or she has nearly unanimous support, the leader can call a strike with more assurance that a picket line will be effective at keeping at least current employees away from work. On the other hand, a leader with only a small majority may wish to call a strike to "rally the troops around a common enemy" to solidify his or her position.

THE SCRIPT

Despite the obvious fact that each negotiation is unique, certain formats generally pertain. These are known as "the script." The most typical script consists of the union's making initial "outrageous" demands and management offering little or nothing in response. After much effort the parties compromise their positions and make tradeoffs as the period for negotiations comes to a close, agreement is reached, and the parties offer a public proclamation that, "It was very tough bargaining, but the parties have reached an agreement and are ready to move on together." Both sides shake hands and go away from the table with a sense of relief and accomplishment. This script then gives the constituents from both sides the impression that they have been well represented and that the contract, though imperfect, is the best they could have hoped for in an imperfect world.

The early stages of negotiations are not generally intended to be effective. Opening sessions are often attended by many representatives of both sides (beyond those on the formal bargaining committees) as well as representatives of the media and special interest groups. At these early sessions, everyone "talks tough" while the world is watching, waiting for the doors to be closed before the compromising begins.

Once the preliminaries have been dispensed with and the bargaining is turned over to the professionals, compromising, counterproposing, and trading-off begin. There is often not a great deal of rationality apparent at this time. Skillful negotiators learn to couch their positions and statements in a manner which minimizes personal conflict and retains flexibility. Astute negotiators have minutes taken of what was discussed at these sessions. This record can be very helpful in clarifying contract language in future disputes. The minutes of the previous session are generally reviewed, amended if necessary, and initialed by both parties before each subsequent session.

As the bargaining deadline approaches, the toughest decisions on what to compromise and what not to compromise must be confronted. If the parties fail to reach an agreement, the union may well announce a strike deadline, which will impose significant costs on both parties if agreement is not reached. Prior to the strike deadline, there is essentially no cost for disagreeing, and the parties are quite free to retain hard-line stances in hopes of getting as many of their demands as possible. When the cost of disagreeing goes up precipitously, however, the parties will reexamine their positions and make what compromises they can.

A final observation should be noted. Many bargaining experts have observed that the playing out of the script is largely a charade. They argue that the settlement point can be closely predicted before negotiations even begin by examining the economic position of the employer, making comparisons with employees working elsewhere, and examining the state of the economy. Arguably, the parties then engage in a great deal of pomp for very little effect. It appears that it is, indeed, a "Great Turkey Dance." While this may to some extent be true, it fails to highlight the fact that even if the bargaining ritual doesn't have a great effect on the value of the package, it will have a great effect on a different very important matter—the employees' perception of who delivers their benefits. By having the employer deliberately offer less initially than it is prepared to give ultimately and then raise its offer in response to the union's demands, the Great Turkey Dance script gives the impression that management will not do right voluntarily and that unions have a profound impact on the well-being of the employees. This perception, whether accurate or not, is always deduced from the way this script is played.

BOULWARISM

Perhaps to combat this perception, Lemuel Boulware, a labor relations executive with the General Electric Company in the 1940s to 1960s, developed a bargaining strategy that avoided the Great Turkey Dance. The strategy came to be known as ''Boulwarism.''

Boulware claimed that the process of traditional bargaining was a waste of administrative time. While it may well have been, the great damage to the employer that Boulware may have been trying to overcome was the perception that the union, not the employer, was the provider of the employees' benefits. Accordingly, as a general rule, Boulware began negotiations with a first, fair, firm, and final offer. This offer was the best the company was ever going to tender. It was produced without input from the union and was not adjusted in response to the union's demands. The company essentially offered it on a take-it-or-leave-it basis. Of course, the union did not generally wish to accept it, regardless of its merit, because it could claim no credit for it. To get the union to accept this offer, the company often communicated directly with the employees, urging them to pressure the union into acceptance. For such a strategy to work, it would help if the offer were perceived as an obviously generous one that the employees would willingly accept without alteration.

For many years Boulware was able to get his initial offers accepted by the union basically without modification. This was accomplished by a combination of the generosity of the offer, the effectiveness of his communicaiton of that generosity, and the relative inability of the unions involved to strike. (GE had several small bargaining units represented by different unions who had not historically cooperated with one another. No one standing alone could strike the company very effectively.) A probable result of this strategy was to convey to the employees the impression that it was the employer, not the union, that was providing their ''bread and butter.'' Many other employers would prefer to convey that image.

The unions involved obviously disliked this strategy. Their usefulness was being reduced merely to processing grievances—not a small task but certainly less important than grievance processing *and* negotiating. Upon protest from the union involved, the NLRB found Boulwarism to be an unfair labor practice because it dealt directly with the employees rather than with their bargaining agent. The Board ruled the company was not bargaining in good faith because, among other problems, it had not offered to compromise or produce counterproposals. Although such behavior is specifically not required under the Taft-Hartley Act, the Board claimed that the presence of such behavior would have supported the company's claim that it was bargaining in good faith. Without such activity, it is much harder to argue that bargaining is taking place. The company meanwhile maintained that bargaining really was taking place since an offer was made and was accepted voluntarily and only the unnecessary turkey dancing had been removed. It was, in the company's estimation, not only a form of bargaining in good faith, it was a superior form. This case was the origin of the NLRB's "totality of conduct" standard for good-faith bargaining.

The Board rejected the company's interpretation and sought to guarantee to the union the opportunity to appear to determine the benefit package jointly. Consequently, the use of compromises and tradeoffs as components of totality of conduct has become almost required as evidence of good faith, despite the irony that it obviously does not assure that a party is trying to reach agreement. Parties wishing to avoid agreement may merely make counterproposals that are not obviously bad but that they know won't be accepted and they will not be found guilty of a failure to bargain in good faith. Meanwhile, the making mandatory of the Great Turkey Dance assures to unions a format that makes the employer look unfair and makes the union appear an even greater protector of employee interest than it may be. This is certainly true to the extent that the employer's original offer is deliberately lowered in anticipation of negotiation so that it can be raised after compromising to the level the employer was originally willing to grant.

COMMITTING THE CONTRACT TO WRITING

Reaching agreement is obviously the most difficult task in bargaining. Still, two barriers remain to be surmounted even after agreement has been reached. They are (1) transforming the agreement into a written contract and (2) getting the necessary parties to ratify that contract.

Getting any verbal agreement into writing may be difficult. Getting a collective bargaining agreement into language appropriate for administering labor relations is always difficult. Someone has to draft a document which both reflects precisely the intentions of the negotiators and can be understood by those who have to use it. It is a common practice to have a lawyer perform this task. This concerns many practitioners, who believe that lawyers write contracts more for other lawyers than for employees and managers. Regardless of who performs the task, the contract must be readable by the practitioners. Therefore it is a good idea to have at least one supervisor and one union rep not involved in the negotiations read the contract for clarity and understanding before submitting it for ratification. It is also a good idea to have everyone on the bargaining teams read it for typographical errors, particularly in numerical data.

A COLLECTIVE BARGAINING AGREEMENT REACHED

SOURCE: UPI/Bettman Newsphotos

RATIFICATION

Ratifying a proposed contract generally requires that the union membership be consulted. The employer's representative at the bargaining table has the authority to bind the company.

Employee ratification is often a difficult matter. Generally speaking, the union bargaining team believes that the package it has negotiated is the best the employees will get and recommends that it be ratified. Complications arise when the employees either don't believe it is the best that can be had or do realize that fact but still deem it unacceptable. Disbelief that the recommended contract is the best possible one occurs particularly often when a vocal union member who is opposed to the incumbent officers tries to make the rank-and-file believe the offer is a poor one. Belief that the offer is the best possible one but still not good enough is an even more vexing problem. Employees may be dissatisfied because the contract is not as attractive as those of other employees with whom they compare themselves. This often happens when their employer is not as favorably situated economically as other employers. Failing to ratify the contract will not cure the problem and also puts a great strain on renewed negotiations.

A commonly suggested solution to these problems is to have the professional negotiators of both sides attempt to "educate" the rank-and-file more thoroughly to the economic facts of life. This is more easily urged than accomplished, particularly when an increasing proportion of the population has experienced comparatively few "hard times" and witnesses a federal government that tries hard to protect big private-sector employers from going out of business.

Another possible solution, albeit one not without liabilities, would be to allow the union leaders routinely to bind the rank-and-file with their agreement. This is not really such a radical or undemocratic idea. The public does not generally vote directly on legislation. Instead it elects representatives to pass laws. At periodic intervals those leaders stand for reelection. If their performance has been acceptable to the rank-and-file (the public), they are reelected. If not, they are replaced. The same logic could be applied to contract negotiation and administration. Understanding negotiating constraints requires awareness and sophistication beyond what can be expected of most constituents, who are uninformed and unskilled in their analysis. Giving them a right to veto their professionals' recommendations may be democratically appealing but it certainly isn't efficient. Besides, the origin of the common use of a ratification vote grew out of the 1950s' concern that the rank-and-file were "led like sheep" by their union leaders. In the 1980s the problem is more often that "the leaders are reasonable but the sheep can't be led."

VARIATIONS AND COMPLICATIONS

Up to this point bargaining has been assumed to take place between one employer and one union for the purpose of producing one contract. While this is generally the case, circumstances may cause the parties to bargain in other forms. These other forms include multitier, multiparty (coalition), coordinated, and pattern bargaining. Each has arisen in response to atypical needs.

Multitier Bargaining

This form of bargaining is common in industries where a large national company with many plants is organized by one union. A "master" contract is negotiated at the national level covering benefits standardized across all plants, such as wages, vacations, and health care coverage. Local "plant supplements" are negotiated at the various work sites covering local working conditions. The United

Automobile Workers and the "Big Three" auto manufacturers negotiate in this format.

Multiparty (Coalition) Bargaining

In this variation one or both of the parties form an association or coalition with others to negotiate with the opposing parties. A typical management example is a Freight Haulers Association made up of several trucking companies who bargain as a unit with the Teamsters to produce one contract applying to all members of the Association. A typical union example is a Building Trades Council made up of several craft unions who negotiate a contract with an association of contractors within a geographic region.

The formation of employer associations is generally motivated by a perceived mutual need to protect the members from a union. In the case of trucking companies, who are normally fiercely competitive and not cooperative or sympathetic to one another, the coalition was brought about by union "whipsaw" tactics. As alluded to earlier, freight haulers are particularly susceptible to strikes because of the effects of competition. The union was able to use this situation to whipsaw the employers one at a time by striking one company (often the weakest), forcing a quick and advantageous settlement from the employer, and then attempting to exact the same concessions (or better) from each of the remaining employers, one at a time.

Since the union suffered comparatively little during a strike of one company (the remaining Teamsters were working and contributing to the strike fund) while the employer suffered greatly, this tactic usually worked to the union's advantage. To prevent the union from whipsawing employers in sequence, the owners formed associations to bargain simultaneously with the Teamsters. If the Teamsters struck an association member, the others locked out their drivers. This caused more immediate harm to all the employers but less than they would have suffered in the long run, since the cost to the Teamsters was now much greater (they were all out of work) and the effects of competition had been neutralized. (It was, however, a greater inconvenience for customers, but they weren't represented at the bargaining table.)

The formation of employer associations presents many sticky legal questions about bargaining in good faith, particularly for a member that wishes to withdraw from the association and settle on its own. This situation commonly arises during a strike when the financially weakest member wants to settle because it can no longer sustain a strike. The other members object because it would weaken their bargaining position and again expose them to the perils of competition. Besides, they might not mind seeing some of their competition go bankrupt. (Collective bargaining can make strange bedfellows.) For those wishing to examine the legal ramifications of coalition bargaining in more detail, references are provided at the end of the chapter.

Union associations or councils more commonly arose out of convenience rather than mutual peril. The construction trades often bargain together because they have mutual needs from the employer and are not in competition with one another the way employing companies are. What disputes they do have over jurisdiction are resolvable through the AFL-CIO's internal procedures, if the unions involved are affiliated.

Coordinated Bargaining

A more difficult problem for unions emerges when one employer's operations are subdivided into multiple bargaining units represented by different unions who may, to some degree, be in competition with one another. Such was historically the case with the General Electric Company and in the copper mining industry.

In these instances the employer pursued, at least to some extent, a divide-and-conquer strategy. Since no individual union could close down enough of an operation to hurt the employer sufficiently to gain the concessions sought, the unions opted to band together in "coordinated" bargaining. In this format, each union negotiates its own contract but tries to include items agreed upon with the other unions, such as a common expiration date so they could strike simultaneously. The other unions might or might not appear at the bargaining table, but they would have no official voice. This format, too, provides difficult interpretations of labor law beyond the scope of this book.

Pattern Bargaining

A final variation occurs on a more informal basis. It is "pattern" bargaining. In this instance, settlements reached in one industry are used as a model or pattern in subsequent negotiations in the same or other industries. This has historically been the case in the closely similar contracts in the auto, steel, rubber, and allied industries. While the settlement reached in one is in no way technically binding on the others, it does have a great influence on what union members perceive they should get and on what a union leader will be able to get ratified. It is also important because pattern bargaining in these major industries can have a ripple effect across a substantial enough portion of employment to affect the national economy and psychology. But, most important, it may succeed in "taking wages out of competition."

Taking wages out of competition has long been an achieved goal of many major unions such as the United Automobile Workers. If a union has organized all the employers in an industry, it may be able to get them all to agree to the same wage-and-effort bargain. This is not objectionable to the employer because it can't be undersold (on labor cost) by its competition. Therefore, any labor cost increase can be passed along to the customer, so long as there are no producers outside the arrangement and so long as customers still purchase the product despite the higher cost. For years, the American auto industry allegedly operated in this fashion. The emergence of foreign competition not bound by the arrangement, together with overall tough times not related to labor problems, caused the system to break down in the 1980s.

Still, the goal of taking wages out of competition—and letting companies compete in all other areas—remains a goal of large unions in oligopolistic industries. It also remains a particularly poignant choice for priorities between the obvious human benefit of its application and the equally obvious affront it presents to classical economic market mechanisms.

A collective bargaining exercise appears on p. 197.

Appendix I: Ground Rules for Negotiations

1. Participation:
   a. Participation in negotiations at the bargaining table on behalf of the union shall be limited to appropriate representatives of that unit designated, which may include their attorney and two (2) representatives from the union.
   b. Active participation in negotiations on behalf of the employer shall be limited to the appropriate representatives, but shall not exceed five (5) representatives in number.
   c. Either party may have a limited number of additional personnel present in the negotiating room as observers. These observers shall not be allowed to disrupt the negotiating sessions. If either party desires to have its attorney present at any session, the other party shall be so notified at least twelve hours in advance of the negotiating session.

2. Negotiating Teams:
   a. The negotiating team for the employer shall be designated in writing and shall be comprised of at least three (3) and not more than five (5) individuals. One of the members will be designated as the Chief Spokesperson. At least one of the other members shall be designated as the Co-Chief Spokesperson. Each representative at the bargaining table shall have an alternate who is empowered to assume his or her role in his or her absence.
   b. The negotiating team for the union shall be designated in writing and shall be comprised of at least three (3) and not more than five (5) individuals. One of the members will be designated as the Chief Spokesperson.
   c. Direct communication is authorized only between the Chief Spokesperson of the employer and the union.
   d. Either party may designate a new Chief Spokesperson other than the one previously designated, provided due notification is given at the start of any negotiating session.

3. Negotiating Sessions:
   a. Negotiations between the aforementioned parties will commence on
      _____.

b. The time and commencement of each negotiation session shall begin at _____ and conclude at _____ . Additional time may be granted if such time is mutually agreeable to both parties. Meeting dates will be established at the conclusion of each negotiation session. Employees of the negotiating team for the union as defined in 2(b) above shall not suffer any loss of regular compensation while participating in negotiations.

c. Negotiating sessions will be held at _____.

d. The negotiating sessions will terminate upon the agreement to and proper execution of a Collective Bargaining Agreement.

4. Conduct of Sessions:
   a. The spokesperson for each party shall be responsible for the conduct of his or her negotiating team and observers.
   b. Adjournment of any session prior to the normal concluding time shall be by mutual consent of the Chief Spokespersons.
   c. The Chief Spokesperson for either party may call for a caucus of his or her team at any time for a reasonable length of time.

5. Records of Meetings:
   a. Secretarial assistance will be furnished by the employer to produce written minutes. Minutes of the negotiation sessions will not be recorded on a verbatim basis, but shall only include major points of discussion and agreement.
   b. At the commencement of each negotiation session, a copy of the minutes from the previous session will be furnished each individual on the negotiating teams, and an opportunity will be given to verify those minutes. If no omissions or corrections are noted in the minutes, they shall be initialed and stand approved as presented.

6. Press Releases:
   It is agreed that during the negotiating period, neither party will issue a statement to the news media on an individual basis. If such statements should become necessary, the contents of the news release must be mutually acceptable.

7. Submission and Discussion of Proposals:
   a. It is agreed that the negotiating team for the union will submit its list of proposals which it desires to have included in a Collective Bargaining Agreement. Additional proposals may be submitted only during the first ten (10) days after the initial proposals have been submitted.
   b. The negotiating teams for both parties will review these proposals and either agree to them, request modification of them, or submit appropriate counter proposals.
   c. Each proposal and/or counter proposal will be discussed. Either party is entitled to have a concise statement from the other party as to the meaning and proposed operation of specific provisions of a proposal submitted by the other party.
   d. In the interest of time, proposals may not necessarily be discussed in the same order as submitted. Some items may be deferred to a later point in the negotiations.

     e. If either party considers a proposal non-negotiable, it shall so state and provide specific reasons for that position.

     f. When tentative agreement on a proposal has been reached by both parties, it shall be initialed, dated, and timed by both parties.

8. Topics for Discussion:

     a. Discussion during negotiation sessions shall be limited to matters pertinent to proposals under consideration.

     b. Grievances and other employee relations matters shall not be made the subject of discussion during negotiating sessions.

9. Agreement and Execution:

     a. After all items which were timely submitted have been tentatively agreed upon by the negotiating teams, the final and complete document will be prepared by the employer.

     b. This final document shall be submitted to the union membership for ratification.

     c. The Collective Bargaining Agreement shall become final and binding when it has been ratified by the membership.

The foregoing Procedures for Collective Bargaining are hereby agreed to for implementation and compliance on the following date: _____ .

_____   _____

Chief Spokesperson   Chief Spokesperson
Employer   Union

SOURCE: *Florida Department of Community Affairs,* Collective Bargaining Negotiations, *Management Series No. 15.*

Appendix II: Tally Sheet for Contract Proposals

RE: FRATERNAL ORDER OF POLICE, LODGE 97

One Year Cost of Bargaining Demands

Item	Current Provision	Cost	New Demand	Cost	Additional Cost to City
WAGES	Average annual salary of $13,309 for 283 employees in the bargaining unit	$3,766,485	Average annual increase of $1,996, or 15% per employee (average annual salary of $15,305)	$4,331,458	$564,973
OVERTIME	Time and one-half hourly rate for work in excess of normally scheduled hours in the work day or work week	155,223	Same provisions with addition of overtime rate for all hours of court time in excess of normally scheduled work	184,438	29,215
PENSION	26.7% of payroll	1,005,651	26.7% of payroll, Pension Plan to be renegotiated within first six months of new contract	1,156,499	150,848
LONGEVITY	In accordance with the following schedule with percentage based on employee's first $6,000 of annual salary: Service Years / Rate 5–9 / 2% 10–14 / 4% 15–19 / 6% 20–24 / 8% 25 & over / 10%	53,760	Present schedule with % based upon the "F" step of salary range for employee's classification	141,523	87,763
VACATIONS	Service Years / Days 1–10 / 10 11–20 / 15 21 & over / 21	(189,147)[1]	Service Years / Weeks 6 mos.–1 / 1 1–5 / 2 5–10 / 3 10–15 / 4 15–20 / 5 20 & over / 6	(292,530)	(103,383)

(continued)

RE: FRATERNAL ORDER OF POLICE, LODGE 97 (Continued)

One Year Cost of Bargaining Demands

Item	Current Provision	Cost	New Demand	Cost	Additional Cost to City
COMPENSATORY TIME OFF	In lieu of cash payment for overtime hours worked, an employee is allowed compensatory time off at a rate of 1-1/2 times hours worked, except for time spent before Accident Review Board or while attending in-service training classes	$ (30,426)	Same provisions without exceptions	$ (45,639)	$ (15,213)
LIFE INSURANCE	$12,500 cash payment to beneficiaries of employees who die while not in course of service	12,500	$25,000 cash payment with double indemnity for accidental death	37,500	25,000
HOSPITALIZATION	Group hospital, medical, surgical insurance to all employees and employees' dependents	132,288	Additional coverage for dental, optical, hearing, drugs, mental and emotional disorders, and X-ray	233,081	100,793
CLOTHING	Basic issue of uniforms and $300 annual allowance to employees required to wear plain clothes	46,610	Basic issue, $450 plain clothes allowance, $150 annual cleaning allowance, summer weight jackets, summer shirts, $75 annual shoe allowance, winter parkas and winter hats	102,702	56,092
SICK LEAVE	6.4 days average usage	(92,713)	Assume similar usage at higher pay rate	(133,304)	(40,591)
SICK LEAVE PAY OFF	$1 per day of sick leave days up to 80 days, multiplied by retirement with over 10 years of service, $.50 upon resignation after 10 years of service	74 -0- 75 -0- 76 2,480	Pay off on total number of sick leave days employee has accumulated. Earning rate increase to 1 day for each month of service prior to 7/1/66. Potential cost increase upon payoff	74 -0- 75 -0- 76 4,495	2,015

LEAVE FOR LODGE CONFERENCE OR CONVENTIONS	28 man days per year	(1,433)	35 man days per year	(2,576)	(1,143)
FURNISH AND PROVIDE A PRIVATE OFFICE FOR LODGE	Not provided	-0-	Space and furnishings in Police Department	1,984	1,984
LIABILITY INSURANCE	None	-0-	$500,000 Professional Liability Policy to protect employees from any liability arising out of the course of employment	14,150	14,150
SPECIAL AUTOMOBILE AND MISCELLANEOUS EQUIPMENT	None	-0-	Air conditioned cars, shot gun mounts, flak-vests, cars with spot lights and flood lights, 38 caliber-2" revolvers, 3-cell flashlights, permanently mounted car radios and portable radios	141,759	141,759
COST OF LIVING ALLOWANCE	None	-0-	Cost indicated represents what the City would have to bear if cost of living had been provided during 1973	153,046	153,046
HAZARDOUS AND SPECIAL DUTY PAY	None	-0-	Motorcycle, riot, bomb squad, sniper, and diving duty	34,562	34,562
SHIFT DIFFERENTIAL	None	-0-	Additional 5% per hour for 4th shift, 10% per hour for 2nd & 3rd shifts, and 10% per hour for Vice, Juvenile and Detective officers on night shift	297,850	297,850
EDUCATION DIFFERENTIAL	30 hours $ 200/yr 60 hours 400/yr AA degree 500/yr AB degree 800/yr BA or MA in Police Adm. 1000/yr	43,300 (included in #1)	30 hours 300/yr 60 hours 500/yr AA degree 600/yr AB degree 900/yr BA or MA in Police Adm. 1200/yr	54,800	11,500

(continued)

RE: FRATERNAL ORDER OF POLICE, LODGE 97 (Continued)

One Year Cost of Bargaining Demands

Item	Current Provision	Cost	New Demand	Cost	Additional Cost to City
TWO MAN PATROLS	At the direction of the Police Chief	$ -0-	No employee shall be assigned to patrol duty unless the duty is done in the presence of another officer	$ 918,300 ×82.7% 1,677,734	$ 1,677,734
WORKMEN'S COMPENSATION	Supplemental wage payments for 26 weeks	37,324	Extend supplemental wage payments to 52 weeks	41,059	3,735
REST BREAKS	15 minute break each 1/2 shift	(184,806)	Similar provisions	(212,526)	(27,720)
LIFE INSURANCE FOR RETIREES	None	-0-	$5,000 cash payment to beneficiaries of retiree with double indemnity for accidental death	25,000	25,000

Total Police Demands in Money Costs: $3,376,004
Total Police Demands in Lost Productivity Costs: 295,858
Total Additional Costs of Police Demands: 3,671,862

[1]All parenthetical figures denote cost in lost productivity.
SOURCE: This report was furnished by Mr. Dean R. Mielke, Labor Relations Officer, City of Miami.

Discussion Questions

1. Discuss the obligation to bargain in good faith.
2. Discuss scope of bargaining.
3. Evaluate the factors commonly affecting bargaining.
4. Discuss the preparation of demands and offers.
5. Discuss the preparation of bargaining strategies.
6. Assess employer bargaining power.
7. Assess union bargaining power.
8. Describe the "script" and its significance.
9. Evaluate the consequences of Boulwarism.
10. Analyze issues to be considered in committing the contract to writing.
11. Analyze multitier and multiparty bargaining.
12. Analyze coordinated and pattern bargaining.

Statements for Comment

1. "Collective bargaining is both an art and a science."
2. "Bargaining power is certainly a poor way to determine a contract. It just perpetuates injustice—from either side."
3. "Union democracy is a major headache in negotiation. The more there is, the worse the headache."
4. "The obligation to bargain in good faith is a farce. The NLRB ought to give up trying to police it."
5. "Boulware really had it right. The *employees* weren't complaining. The Board and the courts blew it."
6. "Collective bargaining isn't really a zero-sum game. It's a cooperative effort to find solutions from which both parties will benefit."

Situations

Case 9–1 Marilyn McGraw is President and CEO of a middle-sized company that remanufactures used automobile engines. Her production and maintenance employees recently formed a union. She is now preparing to enter collective bargaining for the first time. At this point she is considering whom she should include on her bargaining team and why.

   You are an old friend from college days who is now a consultant in human resources management. She wants your input. What would you advise her?

Case 9–2 Fred Dryden is President of the newly formed union at McGraw Engine (Re) Works. The union's constitution does not specify who is to be on the negotiating team. Fred is essentially free to select his own membership. Whom should he select? What characteristics should he look for? What should he be trying to accomplish?

Case 9-3 Fred has completed selection of his team members and is now ready to begin formulating the union's demands. How does he know what to ask for? What are the strengths and liabilities of your recommendations?

Case 9-4 Bargaining has progressed as well as could be reasonably hoped between two beginners. Now, unfortunately, an impasse has been reached over a voluntary subject of bargaining. What methods are available for resolving this dispute?

Case 9-5 Porter Phillips is a high school physics teacher and is president of his union local. In two months he will engage in his first-ever bargaining session with the county superintendent of schools and Porter is preparing. He wants to represent his constituency as well as possible. One of the hurdles he has had to surmount is finding out exactly what his 700 members want in the upcoming contract. At a union membership meeting he explains what he has done to determine their desires and what he is going to bargain for:

"Ladies and gentlemen, I have processed the data from the questionnaires I sent out asking you to rank order your preference for each of the eight items we might demand. Using my home computer, I plotted a least-squares regression line of your composite desires and reached the conclusion that this is what we should demand, in order: 1) higher wages; 2) smaller classes; 3) more authority to have students permanently removed from classes for disciplinary reasons; 4) restoration of a within-the-schoolday planning period; 5) improved health care coverage; 6) improvements in the break area; 7) increased pay and merit consideration for extracurricular activities; and, lastly, 8) school-funded personal liability insurance.

"Rest assured, Gang, that I'm going to go out after the superintendent to get you exactly what you want—and I say that knowing that we have never before known so precisely, exactly what you want."

What reaction do you suppose Porter's speech received? What recommendations would you make?

Bibliography of Related Readings

Atherton, Wallace N. *Theory of Union Bargaining Goals* (Princeton, N.J.: Princeton University Press, 1973).

Bacharach, S. B., and E. J. Lawler, "Power and Tactics in Bargaining," *Industrial and Labor Relations Review,* 1981, pp. 219–22.

Bacharach, Samuel, and Edward J. Lawler, *Bargaining Power: Tactics and Outcomes* (San Francisco: Jossey-Bass Pub., 1981).

Barbash, J., "Collective Bargaining and the Theory of Conflict," *British Journal of Industrial Relations,* 1980, pp. 82–90.

Blum, Albert A., "Collective Bargaining: Ritual or Reality?" *Harvard Business Review,* November–December 1961.

Carlisle, J., "Successful Training for Effective Negotiators," *Human Resource Development,* 1980, pp. 8–10.

Clarke, J., ''Is There an Alternative to Adversary Bargaining?'' *Worklife,* 1981, pp. 16–17.

Granof, Michael H., *How to Cost Your Labor Contract* (Washington, D.C.: Bureau of National Affairs, 1973).

Hildebrand, George H., ''Cloudy Future for Coalition Bargaining,'' *Harvard Business Review,* November–December 1968, pp. 114–28.

Hoover, J. J., ''Negotiating the Initial Union Contract,'' *Personnel Journal,* September 1982, pp. 692–98.

Kaufman, B. E., ''Bargaining Theory, Inflation, and Cyclical Strike Activity in Manufacturing,'' *Industrial and Labor Relations Review,* 1982, pp. 333–55.

Kniveton, B., and H. Bonner, ''Emotion and Fact in Negotiating,'' *Industrial Relations Journal,* 1982, pp. 44–50.

Rubin, Jeffrey Z., and Bert Brown, *The Social Psychology of Bargaining and Negotiation* (New York: Harcourt Brace Jovanovich, 1975).

Skinner, Gordon S., and E. Edward Herman, ''The Importance of Costing Labor Contracts,'' *Labor Law Journal,* August 1981, pp. 497–507.

Smith, D., and D. Turkington, ''Problem-Solving in Collective Bargaining: A Comparative Study of Differences Between Union and Management Negotiators,'' *Industrial Relations Journal,* 1982, pp. 56–64.

Stevens, Carl M., *Strategy and Collective Bargaining Negotiations* (New York: McGraw-Hill, 1963).

Wagner, Lynn E., ''Multiunion Bargaining: A Legal Analysis,'' *Labor Law Journal,* December 1968, p. 737.

Whitney, Gary G. ''Before You Negotiate: Get Your Act Together,'' *Personnel,* July–August 1982.

Exercise

[This exercise may be undertaken now or at the end of the semester when the students have studied contract content.]

Sweet Swing, Inc., and United Molders, III The United Molders won the representation election. That was six years ago. They managed to negotiate a contract with Sweet Swing, Inc., for three years. Subsequently they negotiated another contract (contained herein) that is due for renegotiation.

One area of disagreement is the classic issue of cost. The employees claim they are underpaid (their rates of pay and other relevant data are included in the Appendix following the Agreement). At least some employees are worried, however, that if they receive a substantial raise, management might subcontract some of the bargaining unit's work. Whether it could or would is not known for sure, but the current contract does not clearly prevent such an action. The union is also worried that the employer is hiring an increasing number of part-time employees, who, besides not becoming union members, also cost the company less because they receive no supplemental benefits. In a nonexpanding economy, these employees may be taking jobs from union members.

The union is also concerned that with the company constantly changing product lines, layoffs in some departments might be "unfair." In particular, it has become fairly common to have junior employees in a prosperous department working while senior employees in a less prosperous department are on layoff. (Sizable swings in employment are common in the golf-club industry due to seasonal demand and fad buying by customers.) The union prefers a switch to plantwide seniority.

Other demands from the union include the following:

1. An increase in the company contribution to the pension fund;
2. A two-week layoff notice. If employees are not notified two weeks in advance of layoff, they are to be paid the difference between the length of notice given and two weeks' pay;
3. No further hiring of part-time help;
4. No subcontracting;
5. A company-paid dental plan;
6. A wage escalator clause with a five-cent-an-hour increase (adjusted quarterly) for every rise of one point in the Consumer Price Index; and
7. A substantial increase in the Long-Term Disability and Group Life Insurance Plan.

The employer, on the other hand, sees things differently. While still remaining prosperous overall, Stuart knows that both Japanese and American competition will be tough if costs get out of line. At the moment, he is probably "getting away with" low labor costs for the St. Louis area. The comparatively low rates that he is now paying were accepted by the union when it looked as if automation might displace some of its members. As things turned out, no one was laid off for automation and the company continued to grow. Whether this condition will continue is uncertain.

As for hiring lower-cost help, Stuart regards this as "merely good business" and is prepared to continue to do so in the future.

The company has not granted plantwide seniority for layoffs because it believes this will adversely affect productivity. The company is also "taking the offense" and questioning what it believes is an "overly generous" vacation policy. It has proposed retaining the current benefits but substantially reducing vacation time for employees hired after the effective date of this contract. In essence, it would be the beginning of a "two-tiered" compensation system. At the moment, the pension burden isn't too onerous because most of the employees will never qualify for it. Stuart's financial advisors like it that way.

Besides resisting the union's demands, management has proposed the following changes in the contract:

1. Promotions shall be determined by merit only;
2. The losing party shall bear the entire cost of arbitration; and
3. Management shall have the clear right to subcontract any work when it is cost-advantageous.

Assignment III

A. Form union and management bargaining teams of five or six members each. The union team shall consist of:

International Representative

Local President

Local Vice-President

Local Recording Secretary

At least one Local Steward

The management team shall consist of:

Vice-President—Human Resources

Compensation Analyst

Vice-President—Manufacturing

Vice-President—Accounting

Corporate Legal Counsel

Plus other representatives as needed to fill out team size

B. Before beginning negotiations, each team should construct its package of demands and counteroffers and their priorities. For each issue, determine a desired settlement position, an expected settlement position, and the lowest possible acceptance point.

C. Estimate the cost of all positions.

D. Develop a strategy to be used. Identify roles for each member in achieving these goals.

E. Establish ground rules.

F. Negotiate for the length of time permitted.

G. Estimate costs of agreement and disagreement.

H. Develop a strategy for getting your constituents to accept what has been agreed upon.

AGREEMENT
between
Sweet Swing, Inc.
and
United Molders, Local 127
St. Louis, Missouri

Effective ——————, ——————

TABLE OF CONTENTS

Article V – Hours of Work
    Section A – Hours of work defined
    Section B – Shift premiums and breaks
    Section C – Overtime premium and calculation
    Section D – Overtime distribution
    Section E – Holidays and premium paid
    Section F – Qualifications for holiday pay

Article VI – Wages
    Section A – Hourly rates
    Section B – Wage classification process
    Section C – Probationary rate
    Section D – Pay rates for change of assignment
    Section E – Reporting pay
    Section F – Call-in pay

Article VII – Part-time Help
    Section A – Employer's right to hire part-time help; employee benefit level
    Section B – Seasonal employees

Article VIII – Seniority
    Section A – Probationary period
    Section B – Plant seniority calculated
    Section C – Departmental seniority calculated
    Section D – Loss of seniority rights
    Section E – Effect of layoff on seniority
    Section F – Posting and bidding of job openings; use of seniority in filling
    Section G – Effects of transfer on seniority
    Section H – Departmental layoffs; bumping
    Section I – Recall from layoff
    Section J – Supervisors members of management

Article IX – Discipline and Discharge

Article X – Grievance Procedure and No-Strike Clause
    Section A – Appointment of stewards; no strikes
    Section B – Grievance procedure
    Section C – Effects of settling or dropping grievance
    Section D – Limitations on arbitrator

Article XI – Vacations
    Section A – Amount for years of service
    Section B – Pay rate for vacation
    Section C – Effect of holiday during vacation
    Section D – Employee notice of intent to take vacation
    Section E – Effect of discharge for cause on vacation
    Section F – Calculation of vacation time

Article XII – Sick Leave
    Section A – Eligibility
    Section B – Amount
    Section C – Pay rate
    Section D – Unused sick leave

Agreement

This agreement is entered into this _____ day of _____, 198_____, between Sweet Swing, Inc., hereinafter referred to as the "Company," and the United Molders, Local 127, hereinafter referred to as the "Union."

Article I

Purpose

It is the desire of the Company and the Union to promote mutual harmony and cooperation and to formulate rules in order to accomplish these objectives. The Company and Union have thus agreed upon the following provisions in order to establish rates of pay, hours of work, and other conditions of employment so that disputes may be settled peacefully.

Article II

Recognition

Section A—The Company recognizes the Union as the exclusive bargaining agent for all its production and maintenance employees. This excludes office, professional, supervisory, and guard personnel as defined in the Taft-Hartley Act.

Section B—The Union agrees that all members employed by the Company will work for the Company under the provisions set forth in this contract. The Company and Union agree that any employee who is a member of the Union on the effective date of the agreement shall, as a condition of employment, maintain his/her membership in the Union to the extent of paying dues. Any employee who is not a member of the Union on the effective date of this agreement, shall not be required to become a member, but shall be required to pay an amount equal to the Union's regular monthly dues.

Article III

Management Rights

The management of the plant and the direction of the workforce shall be vested exclusively in the Company. Included is authority over scheduling work, shift starting and stopping times, hiring and discharging of employees, and the transferring and laying off of employees as the Company deems necessary. In carrying out these activities, the Company agrees not to violate the following articles or the purpose of this agreement, nor will it discriminate against any member of the Union.

Article IV

Checkoff of Union Dues

Upon individual authorization from members, the Company shall be responsible for deducting the required amount from each member's first pay in each month. Such sums shall be forwarded by the Company to the Financial Secretary of the Union on or before the 15th day of each month.

Article V

Hours of Work

Section A—This article is intended to define the typical hours of work and how they should be scheduled and paid. It does not guarantee hours per day, or days per week.

Section B—The regular work week shall consist of five eight-hour days. Shift hours are from (1) 7:00 A.M. to 3:00 P.M. and (2) 3:00 P.M. to 11:00 P.M. Workers in the second shift will receive a twenty-cent-per-hour premium. Each worker will receive the following paid breaks: a 15-minute break two hours into the shift, a 30-minute break four hours into the shift, and a 15-minute break six hours into the shift.

Section C—All work performed after the conclusion of a worker's normal eight-hour shift will be considered overtime and receive a 50% premium based on the hourly wage rate. All hours in excess of the 40-hour week shall also be considered as overtime and receive the same premium. There shall be no pyramiding of overtime premium pay.

Section D—All overtime shall be distributed on an equitable basis within the department and decided upon by both supervision and Union representatives in the Department. Consideration will be given to seniority and ability to perform the work.

Section E—All work performed on the following holidays shall be paid a 100% premium based on the hourly wage rate: New Year's Day, President's Day, Memorial Day, Independence Day, Labor Day, Thanksgiving Day, and Christmas Day.

Section F—All eligible employees who do not work on the holidays listed in Article V, Section E, shall be paid for eight hours straight-time pay at their regular hourly base rate. In order to qualify, the employee must: have been employed by the Company for at least 30 days, work both the preceding scheduled work day and the next scheduled work day following the holiday, and must not be on any sort of disciplinary suspension.

Article VI

Wages

Section A—All hourly rates will be contained in the appendix.

Section B—The wage classification criteria used prior to the signing of this agreement shall continue in force during the life of this agreement. If a new job is established or the duties and responsibilities of an existing job have changed enough to warrant a new pay bracket, the job will be evaluated and rated in accordance to these methods used in the past. All ratings will be performed no later than 30 days from the time of request. The Union may object to new pay grades within seven days through the established grievance procedure.

Section C—New employees will be paid a probationary rate for the first 30 days of employment. After this time the employee shall receive the classified rate.

Section D—When an employee is permanently placed in a different job he/she will receive the level of pay corresponding to that job classification the first Monday on or after the assignment. If the assignment is temporary or part-time in nature, it will not be considered a change in classification. If the temporary or part-time assignment is in a classification with a higher pay grade, all hours in such pay grade will be paid the higher rate. If the temporary or part-time placement is in a lower wage class, the employee shall receive his/her regular hourly wage rate.

Section E—Should an employee report for work at the start of his/her regular shift and no work is available, and the Company failed to forewarn the employee that no work would be available, such employee will be granted four hours' pay at his/her straight-time base rate, unless the inability to work was beyond the control of the company.

Section F—Employees who have already completed their shift and have left the plant shall be guaranteed a minimum of four hours work if they are recalled to work. Such employees shall be paid a premium of 50% for all time actually worked, and their regular straight-time hourly rate up to four hours for these hours not worked.

Article VII

Part-Time Help

Section A—The Company retains the right to hire part-time employees whenever the need arises. Such employees will not be entitled to any supplemental benefits, nor will they receive any seniority standing.

Section B—The Company retains the right to hire seasonal employees as the need arises. Such employees may not be hired while regular employees are on layoff status. A seasonal employee is defined as an employee whose term of employment is no more than 120 consecutive days. All seasonal employees will be required to pay an amount equal to the Union's regular monthly dues after 30 days of employment.

Article VIII

Seniority

Section A—Employees who have worked less than 31 days shall be considered probationary employees.

Section B—Plant seniority will begin accumulating from the employee's earliest date of continuous employment with the Company and shall apply to divisional and plant layoffs and recalls.

Section C—Departmental seniority will begin accumulating from the employee's earliest date of continuous employment within the Department and shall apply to promotions, demotions, and reductions in the workforce within the Department.

Section D—An employee whose services are terminated either voluntarily or involuntarily shall lose all seniority rights.

Section E—If an employee is laid off and later returns at the Company's request, he/she shall retain all seniority time accumulated prior to the layoff. No seniority time may be gained during the layoff period.

Section F—The Company will be required to post notice of any job openings in the Department in which the position becomes available. Such notice shall remain posted for three working days. Any employee desiring to fill the vacancy must make written notice to the Company. Proper forms may be obtained in the Personnel Department. In filling the position, the Company will consider seniority, as well as qualifications and other experience.

Section G—Should an employee transfer from one Department to another, he or she shall retain all accumulated seniority in his/her original Department for a period of 90 days. If such employee chooses to return to the original Department, the request will be granted within 30 days. If no such request is made, all seniority rights in original Department will be forfeited.

Section H—All Departmental layoffs will be based upon seniority, providing those remaining are qualified to perform the work. If an employee is laid off, he/she may bump another employee in the same Department and claim the job of a less senior employee provided he/she is qualified to perform such work.

Section I—When it becomes necessary to recall employees, such recall shall be based upon Departmental seniority, provided returning workers have the qualifications to perform the work.

Section J—Supervisory employees are considered representatives of the Company and assignment of their duties, promotions, demotions, and transfers shall be determined by the Company, regardless of seniority.

Article IX

Discipline and Discharge

Section A—Discipline and discharge shall only be for just cause.

Article X

Grievance Procedure and No Strike Clause

Section A—The Union shall appoint Stewards in each Department for each shift to handle any grievances that may arise. All such grievances must be handled in accordance with the following procedure, and the Union and Company guarantee not to revert to a strike, lockout, slowdown or any other work stoppage during the life of this agreement.

Section B—The following steps must be taken to issue a grievance:

1. The employee and Steward must first take the problem up with the immediate Supervisor. If no settlement is reached within two working days, the grievance must be written on the appropriate form.
2. A copy of the written grievance must be presented to the General Supervisor and the Personnel Office. The General Supervisor must then hold a conference with the employee, the employee's immediate Supervisor, the Departmental Steward, and the Chief Steward. Such conference must take place within two days after receipt of grievance complaint.
3. If agreement is still not reached, the written grievance shall be presented to the Departmental Superintendent. Another conference will then be held including the Superintendent, General Supervisor, Supervisor, Employee, Chief Steward, Departmental Steward, Head of the Personnel Department, and the Union President. Such conference must take place within five working days of receipt of written grievance by Departmental Superintendent.
4. If settlment is still not reached, the Union Committee and a National Representative of the Union shall meet and try to resolve the matter with the Management Committee.
5. If the Union and Management Committees fail to settle the matter, it will be resolved by an arbitrator. The Union and Company may each elect a representative to decide upon the appropriate arbitrator. If an arbitrator has not been selected within five working days, a list of arbitrators will be requested from the Federal Mediation and Conciliation Service, and an appropriate person will be selected from said list. The decision of the arbitrator will be final and binding. All arbitration expenses will be shared equally by the Company and Union.

Section C—Should an agreement be reached at any point of the grievance procedure, the issue shall be dropped permanently and said agreement will be final and binding.

Section D—An arbitrator does not have authority to change or modify any of the terms or provisions of this contract.

Article XI

Vacations

Section A—The following table shall be used in determining the amount of vacation time each employee is entitled to in a year:

less than 12 months Company service—0 days

at least 12 months but less than 24 months—5 working days

at least 24 months but less than 120 months—14 working days

at least 120 months but less than 180 months—21 working days

at least 180 months but less than 240 months—28 working days

at least 240 months—35 working days

Section B—For each day of vacation time an employee is entitled to and chooses to take, he/she shall receive a sum of money equal to eight hours of pay at said employee's normal hourly base rate.

Section C—If a paid holiday occurs during employee's vacation period, he/she will receive an additional vacation day.

Section D—Employees must give a minimum of two weeks notice before using vacation time. The Company retains the right to refuse the vacation dates asked for if and only if plant operation could be seriously affected by the employee's absence at the requested time. The Company is expected to attempt to accommodate the employee in all such requests.

Section E—Any employee who is discharged for proper cause shall lose all rights to vacation pay.

Section F—A "year," for the purposes of computing vacation time, shall begin on the employee's first day of continuous employment and last 365 calendar days.

Article XII

Sick Leave

Section A—Employees with at least one year of continuous company service but less than five years shall be entitled to five days per year of paid sick leave. In order to qualify for such benefits, the employee must have been scheduled for work on the days in question, but unable to attend due to personal illness.

Section B—Employees with more than five years of continuous company service shall be entitled to ten days per year of paid sick leave. The rules for eligibility are identical to those in Section A of this article.

Section C—The rates of pay and derivation of one year are the same as those defined in Section B and Section E, respectively, of Article X.

Section D—Unused sick leave benefits may be carried forward and used in the next year. These days will be used only after the current year's benefits have been exhausted.

Article XIII

Long-Term Disability and Group Life Insurance

Section A—Employees with at least one year of continuous company service will be eligible to receive benefits from the Company's group life insurance plan. This entitles qualified employees to 60% of his/her regular base rate pay after a waiting period of one month and for a period of six months.

Section B—Subject to the provisions and qualifications of the Long-Term Disability Plan, employees are entitled to a monthly income benefit to begin after 26 weeks of continuous disability. Benefits shall continue until the time of recovery, the employee's 70th birthday, or death, whichever comes first. Amount of benefits and rules for eligibility may be obtained at the Personnel Office upon the employee's request.

Section C—The Company agrees to pay for the first $1,000 of group life insurance available to employees. Employees reserve the right to purchase additional insurance if they so desire.

Article XIV

Pensions

Section A—The Company agrees to contribute an amount equal to 5% of each employee's base rate pay in a retirement trust fund.

Section B—No vesting will actually begin until after the employee's 10th year of service, at which time vesting shall be 100%.

Section C—Any employee whose employment is terminated voluntarily or involuntarily prior to ten full years of continuous Company service forfeits all right to any pension benefits.

Article XV

Insurance Plan

Section A—The Company agrees to provide Blue Cross/Blue Shield Insurance to provide hospitalization to all employees. Coverage shall include all immediate family members living at home and not older than 21.

Article XVI

Safety

Section A—The Company agrees to take all measures possible to insure the safety of all employees during the hours of operation. Any equipment the Company deems necessary to protect employees shall be acquired by the Company at no cost to employees.

Article XVII

Nondiscrimination Agreement

Section A—The Company and the Union agree that the provisions of this article shall apply to all employees, and that neither will discriminate against any person on the basis of race, color, national origin, age, sex, or religion.

Article XVIII

Duration

Section A—This agreement shall take effect _____, and remain in effect until _____.

Appendix

The following tables show Sweet Swing's current employment situation, pay practices, and financial situation.

Table 1 presents a complete listing of job titles and base pay rates for all the positions in the bargaining unit. For the purpose of simplifying calculations, however, only the average wage rates of the 500 molders and finishers will be used for the rest of the problem.

TABLE 1 JOB TITLES, NUMBER OF EMPLOYEES, AND BASE WAGE RATES

Job Title	Number of Employees	Wage Rate
Tool and model maker	6	10.25
Tool and die maker	3	10.00
Systems control technician	2	9.85

(continued)

TABLE 1 JOB TITLES, NUMBER OF EMPLOYEES, AND BASE WAGE RATES
(Continued)

Job Title	Number of Employees	Wage Rate
Instrument maintenance technician	3	9.75
Electrician	2	9.75
Machinist	14	9.50
Welder	6	9.25
Precision grinder	8	9.40
Layout and setup worker	8	8.85
Machinist trainee	2	8.00
Metal fabricator	6	7.75
Grinder operator	6	7.75
Milling machine operator	5	7.75
Lathe operator	7	7.75
Blacksmith	1	8.85
Oiler	5	6.55
Material handler	6	6.50
Head stockroom clerk	1	7.85
Yard worker	7	6.55
Stock service worker	3	6.55
Truck driver	4	6.60
Experimental assembler	2	7.00
Tool crib attendant	1	7.00
Inventory clerk	3	7.00
Yard laborer	3	6.50
Janitor	5	7.00
Head molder B, Grade 1	7	7.30
Head molder B, Grade 2	28	8.30
Head molder B, Grade 3	50	9.30
Head molder B, Grade 4	20	10.30
Head molder B, Grade 5	18	11.30
Head molder A, Grade 1	8	7.10
Head molder A, Grade 2	23	8.10
Head molder A, Grade 3	41	9.10
Head molder A, Grade 4	29	10.10
Head molder A, Grade 5	22	11.10
Head finisher B, Grade 1	8	7.90
Head finisher B, Grade 2	29	8.90
Head finisher B, Grade 3	47	9.90
Head finisher B, Grade 4	21	10.90
Head finisher B, Grade 5	23	11.90
Head finisher A, Grade 1	7	7.70
Head finisher A, Grade 2	25	8.70
Head finisher A, Grade 3	42	9.70
Head finisher A, Grade 4	30	10.70
Head finisher A, Grade 5	22	11.70

Table 2 gives a breakdown of employees by seniority grouping.

TABLE 2   NUMBER OF EMPLOYEES PER YEAR OF SERVICE

Years of Seniority	Number of Employees	Cumulative Number
>10	105	105
6–10	125	230
3–5	145	375
1–2	75	450
<1	50	500

Table 3 gives probable turnover rates for the company, based on historical data.

TABLE 3   AVERAGE ANNUAL TURNOVER BY GRADE AND BY LENGTH OF SERVICE

Years of Service	Number of Employees	Turnover Rate	Total Turnover
Grade 1			
<1	15	.33	5
1–2	15	.33	5
Grade 2			
<1	25	.20	5
1–2	25	.20	5
3–5	55	.18	10
Grade 3			
<1	10	.00	0
1–2	35	.14	5
3–5	75	.13	10
6–10	50	.11	6
>10	10	.11	0
Grade 4			
3–5	15	.00	0
6–10	45	.00	0
>10	40	.13	5
Grade 5			
6–10	30	.00	0
>10	55	.27	15
TOTAL			71

The amount and distribution of overtime last year is reported in Table 4.

TABLE 4   AMOUNT AND DISTRIBUTION OF OVERTIME

Title	Average Hours of Overtime	Title	Average Hours of Overtime
Head Molder A		Head Finisher A	
Grade 1	26	Grade 1	24
2	48	2	46
3	40	3	43
4	45	4	42
5	55	5	54
Head Molder B		Head Finisher B	
Grade 1	24	Grade 1	22
2	50	2	48
3	47	3	50
4	44	4	41
5	48	5	47

Table 5 lists the average wage cost per employee per year. This cost is calculated by multiplying the average hourly wage by 2080 (52 weeks × 40 hours per week) and adding the average number of overtime hours (as shown in Table 4) multiplied by 1.5 times the base rate.

TABLE 5   AVERAGE WAGE COST PER EMPLOYEE PER YEAR

Title	Base Rate	Over-time	Total
Head molder A– 1	14,768	277	$ 15,045
2	16,848	583	17,431
3	18,928	546	19,474
4	21,008	682	21,690
5	23,088	916	24,004
Head molder B– 1	15,184	263	15,447
2	17,264	623	17,887
3	19,344	656	20,000
4	21,424	695	22,119
5	23,504	814	24,318
Head finisher A–1	16,016	277	16,293
2	18,096	600	18,696
3	20,176	626	20,802
4	22,256	674	22,930
5	24,336	948	25,284
Head finisher B–1	16,432	261	16,693
2	18,512	641	19,153
3	20,592	743	21,335
4	22,672	670	23,342
5	24,752	839	25,591
TOTAL			$10,435,658

Although pensions do not vest for employees until the tenth year of service, the company customarily sets aside the required sum in advance. Table 6 shows the probability of any employee vesting, given length of service.

TABLE 6 PROBABILITY OF VESTING GIVEN YEARS OF SERVICE

Years of Service	Number of Employees	Percentage of Workforce	Probability of Vesting	Number Vesting
>10	105	21	1.0	105
6–9	125	25	1.0	125
3–5	145	29	.85	123
1–2	75	15	.60	45
<1	50	10	.43	22
WEIGHTED PROBABILITY			.84	

By multiplying the probability of vesting by the wage costs given in Table 2, and utilizing a 5 percent contribution rate, total pension costs can be obtained. Table 7 gives total pension costs.

TABLE 7 TOTAL PENSION COSTS

Job Title	Number of Employees	Annual Wage	Pension Cost
Head Molder B			
Grade 1	7	15,447	$ 5,406.45
2	28	17,887	25,041.80
3	50	20,000	50,000.00
4	20	22,119	22,119.00
5	18	24,318	21,886.20
Head Molder A			
Grade 1	8	15,045	6,018.00
2	23	17,431	20,045.65
3	41	19,479	39,921.70
4	27	21,690	31,450.50
5	22	24,004	26,404.40
Head Finisher B			
Grade 1	7	16,293	5,702.55
2	25	18,696	23,370.00
3	42	20,802	43,684.20
4	30	22,930	34,395.00
5	22	25,284	27,812.40
Head Finisher A			
Grade 1	8	16,693	6,677.20
2	29	19,153	27,771.85
3	47	21,335	50,137.25
4	21	23,342	24,509.10
5	23	25,591	29,429.65
TOTAL CONTRIBUTIONS NECESSARY IF ALL EMPLOYEES VEST			$521,782.90

Since not all employees are predicted to vest, the company reduces its contribution in response to the projected likelihood of vesting. The overall probability of an employee vesting is .84 (Table 6). Therefore, the company deflates contributions to .84 of the possible total. This gives its actual contribution rate:

$$\begin{array}{r} \$521,782.90 \\ \underline{.84} \end{array}$$

ACTUAL CONTRIBUTION $438,297.64

It should be noted that for purposes of simplification, no allowance has been made for adjustments between present value and future value.

Other costs to consider are Social Security taxes, workers' compensation insurance, unemployment insurance, and health insurance. Assume that Social Security is 7.5% of payroll, unemployment insurance per worker is 4 percent on the first $8,000 of gross income, and workers' compensation costs are 1.2 percent of payroll. Health insurance costs average $180 per employee per year.

TABLE 8   TOTAL LABOR COST FOR LAST YEAR

Wages	$10,435,658
Social Security	782,674
Unemployment Insurance	160,000
Workers' Compensation Insurance	125,228
Health Insurance	90,000
Pension Plan	438,298
Training Expense[1]	56,800
Arbitration Expense[2]	60,000
TOTAL	$12,148,658

[1]The company estimates that it costs $800 to train a new employee. Projecting from the turnover rates in Table 4, the company estimates that it must train 71 employees in an average year. Multiplying 71 by 800 produces the yearly Training Expense.

[2]Arbitration expenses are shared equally by the employer and the union. They average $3000 per party per case. There were 20 cases last year. The company won 16 and the union won 4.

The overall financial situation of the company for the last three years is reported in Table 9. These data were taken from past financial statements presented to stockholders.

TABLE 9   OVERALL FINANCIAL DATA FOR THE LAST THREE YEARS

Sales	$507,190,600	$547,765,840	$608,020,260
Income before taxes	63,398,750	82,165,000	88,247,000
Provision for taxes	30,431,400	39,439,200	42,358,560
Net Income	32,967,350	42,725,800	45,888,440
Cost of plant and materials	334,746,060	345,091,950	364,812,000
Return on investment	14.5%	15.0%	15.5%

TEN

IMPASSES AND STRIKES

From reading headlines and watching the news on television, one would get the impression that almost all contract negotiations end in strikes. Actually, the converse is true. Historically, roughly only 10 percent of all negotiations have ended in strikes.[1] Over 90 percent end with the parties peaceably reaching agreement. Those that do not, however, generate a great deal of attention and concern. This chapter examines what happens when there is an impasse—an agreement by the parties that they cannot agree.

Impasses can result from either of two problems: (1) the settlement ranges of the parties do not overlap, or (2) the ranges overlap, but the parties, because of communication difficulties, are unable to find the area of mutual agreement.

POSSIBLE IMPASSE RESOLUTIONS:

Arbitration

When an impasse occurs, the parties generally turn first to mediation. If mediation is not successful, the parties then escalate the pressure for settlement by implementing a strike or lockout. They almost never submit their bargaining impasses to arbitration.

This decision to avoid arbitration is surprising, because, on the surface, arbitration of bargaining impasses (or "interests disputes" as they are sometimes called) possesses many attractive features. Having an expert, neutral outsider determine what the contract should contain would provide a speedy "fair and equitable" solution, prevent the interruption of production, and be inexpensive, at least compared to the cost of a strike. Experience and reflection have shown, however, that the arbitration of bargaining impasses contains significant costs not readily appreciated by outsiders.

Most prominently, experts generally agree that collective bargaining settlements achieved through voluntary means are the most workable and livable settlements. Arbitrated settlements, on the other hand, produce a set of rules made for the parties by someone else. When the inevitable difficulties in application arise, the parties may try to embarrass an "outsider's" contract, rather than trying to make "their own" work. The parties seem to feel that rules made for them by someone else are easier to break than rules made by themselves.

Also, the parties may not wish to submit a dispute to arbitration because the arbitrator might impose a condition they "could not live with." Theoretically, that cannot happen in agreed-upon contracts.

Less prominent but still significant are the effects arbitration has on negotiators, who are charged with important responsibilities and generally do not want to give up their control or power. Allowing an arbitrator to make a decision entails the risk that he or she may produce something you can't live with, and you certainly don't want to report to your constituents that you didn't make the decision for your side—some outsider did. It's not the best way to get a raise.

These problems are so great that in many instances the parties would rather sustain the cost of a strike than submit to such an imposed settlement. There is one major exception: in government employment, where strikes are often viewed as intolerable, arbitration of impasses is frequently found.

Mediation

In almost all instances, parties attempt to mediate their disputes before taking the more drastic measures of strikes and lockouts.

Mediation is the intercession of an impartial third person for the purpose of assisting the parties to resolve their differences voluntarily. The ultimate goal of a mediator is to help the disputants arrive at their own agreement. Often the term *conciliation* is used. This is a misnomer, in that technically conciliation is a much more passive form of third-party assistance. The conciliation process involves the conciliator only in procedural functions, such as scheduling, chairing, and recessing meetings and attempting to keep the parties bargaining on a face-to-face basis. Mediation is much more active in that the mediator is involved in substantive as well as procedural functions.

The virtue of mediation to be stressed is that it assists the parties in *reaching their own decision.* While the mediator facilitates the parties' efforts to reach agreement, he has no power to *compel* them to do so. He cannot force unreasonable parties to be reasonable or force reasonable parties to drop or modify unreasonable positions.

Because of this voluntary and nonbinding nature of the mediation process, mediation does less harm to the free collective bargaining process than other forms of third-party intervention such as arbitration or fact-finding. Since it is labor and management who must ultimately live within the confines of a negotiated labor agreement, it should be those two parties who determine the contents of that agreement. Mediation attempts to do just that.

The mediator is basically a listener, definer, and communicator. The mediator's functions can be separated into three areas: (1) procedural, (2) definition and communication, and (3) substantive. The procedural functions of a mediator involve the scheduling of meetings as well as selecting a neutral site for such meetings. This may seem a very insignificant duty, but in many cases, having a third party available to call a meeting can help both labor and management save face and avoid the stigma of weakness by requesting such a meeting. Another procedural function is that of meeting with the parties in separate caucuses in order to either defuse a very emotional situation or to counteract personality clashes. If negotiations seem to be bogged down as a result of exceptionally large bargaining committees, the mediator may establish subcommittees which break off from the main committee to negotiate separate issues and report back to the main committee for consensus of any tentative agreements. If the mediator notices that one or both party spokespersons seem to lack the necessary authority or seem to have a personal involvement that clouds their objectivity, he or she may make arrangements for one or both parties to bring additional representatives to the table. If no agreement has been reached as the strike deadline approaches, the mediator may suggest that the parties extend their agreement to allow for additional negotiations or may request that the union present the employer's "final offer" to the employees for a secret ballot vote.

Most of the mediator's defining and communicating functions are conducted when meeting with the parties separately. It is in these meetings that the mediator probes and analyzes to determine what the real issues are, what the parties' priorities are, and to determine what flexibility, if any, the parties have on these unresolved issues. In many cases the parties' impasse may have occurred not over their bottom-line positions, but as a result of their failure to communicate their positions to each other effectively. Thus the mediator often spends considerable time explaining the real positions of the parties to each other and assisting in "feeling out" the parties on possible compromises. The mediator's ability to try out alternative solutions—without officially destroying either party's bargaining position—allows the parties to indicate to the mediator flexibility or movement that they would never indicate in a face-to-face meeting with the other party. In some instances the mediator's defining and communicating role essentially boils down to explaining to the parties the cost of agreement compared to the cost of disagreement. This may involve the mediator's drawing from his or her experience and explaining what the parties will likely experience in a work stoppage.

Substantive functions performed by the mediator include duties such as assisting the parties in structuring their counterproposals or package proposals, providing advice as to the proper timing of proposals and/or concessions, and in some special situations could even include formally recommending a settlement for all the unresolved issues. It is in the area of *substantive duties* that the mediator can be most helpful in bringing about a resolution to the parties' dispute. For example, the timing of a proposal or concession is often as important as the content of that proposal or concession. It is a well-established principle in all forms of bargaining that parties will not consider any compromises or alternatives as long as they feel they can achieve their complete proposal. Until that point is passed, concession is perceived as inappropriate.

Since mediation is usually voluntary and always nonbinding, it is essential that the mediator gain the respect and cooperation of both parties in order to fulfill his or her duties effectively. This requires convincing them that the mediator understands and appreciates the problems confronting them and is sincerely interested in helping them resolve these problems while leaving the basic decision in the hands of the parties themselves.

Mediators are usually assigned on an ad hoc basis and are normally full-time employees of a state agency or of the Federal Mediation and Conciliation Service. These mediators are paid a salary by the state or U.S. government and are furnished at no direct charge to the parties. Very little mediation is performed by private mediators employed by the parties themselves. Most state and federal mediators are professionals who at one time in their careers have been at the bargaining table as advocates for either management or labor. They are believers in the free collective bargaining process. Sometimes a negotiator will be concerned about a mediator's background or the possibility that a mediator might be pro one party or the other. Since a mediator's success depends upon his or her mutual acceptability to the parties, no chosen mediator is likely to be biased. Even if the mediator were, it would not matter, because he or she could not force any outcome not acceptable to *both* parties.

Mediation usually ends when both parties indicate they feel no further progress can be made in mediation or when the mediator determines that further efforts would be fruitless. Obviously, mediation will also cease when the parties reach a total agreement.

Mediation is most likely to be successful when the parties are inexperienced and somewhat inept at finding possible solutions, or when past and/or current events have created personal animosities which stand in the way of settlement. In rare instances, where these conditions are not present, it may be bypassed.

If Mediation Fails

One difficulty in resolving impasses through mediation is that the process is essentially free. The parties are sustaining no significant costs and are imposing little burden on each other or themselves. In such a situation it is not surprising that parties may cling adamantly to positions. There is essentially no cost to disagreeing. This creates the necessity of the strike deadline. If a strike occurs, both parties will suffer substantially, and compromises that previously were unacceptable become acceptable under the newly applied cost/benefit analysis.

If mediation has not succeeded and an existing contract has expired, any of several avenues of action may be taken. With the consent of both parties, the employees may continue to work under the provisions of the old contract while negotiations continue. This, of course, tends to reduce both the cost of disagreement and the pressure to settle. Whether any improvements reached in the new contract will be made retroactive to the expiration of the old contract is subject to negotiation.

Another alternative is that the employees will refuse to work without a contract and will go on strike. Most often, the employer will accept this conclusion and do without production while attempting to outwait the union.

A final alternative is that the employer will attempt to hire replacements under the conditions of the offer it has made that the union has refused to accept. This last alternative, although legal, is not commonly used. It requires the availability of a labor force willing and able to do the employer's work on the employer's terms. Even if successful, it would often present monumental training problems. It also tends to promote violence on the picket line as permanent employees attempt to prevent "scabs" from replacing them on their jobs. Lastly, it is not generally good public relations to undercut long-time employees.

The factors affecting an employer's decision on which of these avenues to pursue are largely measures of bargaining power, as described in Chapter Nine.

WHAT IS A SCAB?

After God had finished the rattlesnake, the toad, and the vampire, he had some awful substance left with which He made a scab. A scab is a two-legged animal with a corkscrew soul, a water-logged brain, and a combination backbone made of jelly and glue. Where others have hearts, he carries a tumor of rotten principles.

When a scab comes down the street, men turn their backs, and angels weep in heaven, *and the devil shuts the gates of Hell to keep him out. No man has a right to scab as long as there is a pool of water deep enough to drown his body in, or a rope long enough to hang his carcass with. Judas Iscariot was a gentleman compared with a scab. For betraying his Master, he had character enough to hang himself. A scab hasn't.*

Esau sold his birthright for a mess of pot-
(continued)

tage. Judas Iscariot sold his Savior for thirty pieces of silver. Benedict Arnold sold his country for a promise of a commission in the British Army. The modern strikebreaker sells his birthright, his country, his wife, his children, and his fellowmen for an unfulfilled promise from his employer, trust, or corporation.

Esau was a traitor to himself, Judas Iscariot was a traitor to his God. Benedict Arnold was a traitor to his country. A strikebreaker is a traitor to his God, his country, his family, and his class!

SOURCE: *Philip S. Foner,* Jack London, American Rebel *(New York: Citadel Press, 1947), pp. 57–58.*

TYPES OF STRIKES

There are several different types of strikes. The one of interest for this chapter is the strike intended to resolve a bargaining impasse. The National Labor Relations Board labels this type of action an ''economic strike,'' even if its purpose is to improve working conditions. Another major type of strike is the unfair labor practice strike. This may or may not occur during negotiations. Its purpose is to force the employer to cease committing what the union believes to be unfair labor practices. Obviously, the NLRB is supposed to be preventing unfair labor practices, but sometimes unions feel they need a more powerful and immediate cure. The legal rights of employees are somewhat different in these two types of strikes.

Three other types of strikes are the wildcat, the jurisdictional, and the sympathy. *Wildcat strikes* are those indulged in by groups of workers without the authority and consent of the union. Sometimes they occur during the life of an existing agreement in contravention of a pledge not to strike. They are often caused by a schism within the union, where subgroups of workers don't feel their union is representing their interests adequately. They are particularly common in large multiplant companies that have centralized negotiations. In such instances, local employees may not feel that the national bargainers understood their particular problems. (One way this problem is commonly treated is to use multitier bargaining, as described in Chapter 9.)

Wildcat strikes are particularly troubling to management—and to union officials also for that matter. They can be terribly disruptive of production and can destroy good-faith bargaining. An employer can rightfully complain that if it bargained in good faith for a package of wages, hours, and working conditions, it ought not to be extorted through wildcat strikes to yield more after negotiations are complete. Of course, wildcat strikes are sometimes for the purpose of assuring that what was agreed to in negotiations is delivered in the workplace.

STRIKING MEMBERS OF THE INTERNATIONAL ASSOCIATION OF MACHINISTS
WALK A PICKET LINE

SOURCE: *AP/Wide World Photos*

Wildcat strikes often arise in response to local working conditions, rather than dissatisfaction with pay levels. In the United States, such complaints during the life of the contract are generally referred to the grievance procedure and no interruption of work occurs. In Europe and Great Britain, however, local complaints often result in wildcat strikes that can greatly cripple efficiency in mass production industries such as automobiles.

Jurisdictional strikes have either of two purposes—to pressure an employer to assign work to the members of one bargaining unit rather than another or to pressure an employer to recognize one union as representative of its employees when it is already recognizing another. *Sympathy strikes* are refusals by one union to work for its employer to pressure another (or the same) employer in its dealings with a second union. A typical example might be a refusal of the employees of one bargaining unit in a company to work while another unit of employees is on strike.

LOCKOUTS

The employer's equivalent of a strike is a lockout. In this situation the employer may try to place pressure on the union to accept its bargaining position by refusing to allow any bargaining-unit employees to work until an agreement has been reached with their bargaining agent. An employer can legally engage in a lockout only if the existing labor agreement has expired and there is truly an impasse in contract negotiations. However, in utilizing the lockout, the employer must lock out all employees in the bargaining unit—nonmembers as well as union members—and cannot allow individual members the right to return to work. Such a lockout must be for the purpose of advancing or protecting an employer's legitimate economic interests and not for the purposes of discouraging union membership or to eliminate a union as the bargaining agent.

A lockout is most frequently used in situations where the union is stalling to drag negotiations into a busy or prime season or where the union otherwise could "whipsaw" employers by striking only one member of an employer association. The employer's purpose in implementing a work stoppage is to allow the pressure emanating from a cessation of work to occur at a time more advantageous to the employer than to the union.

FACT-FINDING

A final impasse resolution procedure remains: fact-finding. It is commonly used in the public sector, but in the private sector is generally used only in very specialized cases involving strikes (or potential strikes) that might harm the public. The basic purpose of fact-finding is twofold: (1) to help determine facts disputed in negotiation so that areas of disagreement can be reduced and, (2) to publicize these findings so that the party "in the wrong" under the facts will feel public pressure to concede to a more reasonable position.

The procedure generally involves the appointment of a panel of neutrals, which conducts a hearing in which both parties present evidence and data supporting their positions on the unresolved issues. The fact-finding panel then issues a public statement of its findings and sometimes issues a recommendation for the solution of those issues presented during the hearing. When the process involves a recommendation for settlement of issues, it is technically misnamed, because the neutral third party's function exceeds that of merely finding and establishing facts. This process is distinguished from the arbitration process in that the fact-finder's recommendations are nonbinding upon the parties. In the fact-finding process the parties are free to accept or reject any part or all of the fact-finder's recommendations. This process, particularly in the public sector, may also be referred to by other names, such as "special master" process, "board of inquiry," or "advisory arbitration."

Fact-finding in the private sector has been around for a long time. The

Railway Labor Act of 1926 permitted the appointment of a presidential emergency board when there was the likelihood of a serious interruption in rail or air transportation arising out of a labor dispute.[2] The Labor Management Relations Act of 1947 (Taft-Hartley) also provided for the appointment of a board of inquiry to perform fact-finding tasks in those labor disputes which might imperil the national health or safety.[3] When the health-care amendment to the Labor Management Relations Act was passed in 1974, it provided for the appointment of an impartial board of inquiry in those health-care disputes that would substantially interrupt the delivery of health care in the locality concerned. These boards generally functioned as fact-finders and issued written recommendations concerning the settlement of unresolved issues involved in disputes. Other than these statutory requirements, the private sector has been rather reluctant to utilize the fact-finding process. This reluctance stems from the private-sector parties' conception that the nonbinding nature of fact-finding makes it impotent and from the lack of need to sell the ''rightfulness'' of their position to the general public. Public-sector use will be examined in greater detail in Chapter 15.

MECHANICS OF INSTITUTING A STRIKE

In order for a union to initiate a strike following an impasse in contract negotiations, it must usually meet certain procedural requirements contained in its constitution and bylaws. In most unions the strike must be approved by a two-thirds secret-ballot vote of the membership, and the union must obtain sanction from its international union (if affiliated) before setting up any picket lines. A few unions must also utilize the mediation process prior to obtaining strike authorization from the international union.

After meeting all these procedural requirements, a union will often inform the employer of its strike authorization in hopes that this threat will break loose stalled negotiations, thus avoiding the actual implementation of the strike weapon. If the impasse is not broken and the deadline arrives, the union will set up picket lines and request all bargaining-unit employees to withhold their services until a settlement is reached and the picket lines are removed. Individual bargaining-unit employees may decide to cross the picket lines and report to work. Most unions' constitutions authorize the union to fine any *member* who crosses a legal picket line, and that fine is usually equal to at least one day's pay for each day the member crosses the picket line. The possibility of this fine, along with peer-group pressure, makes it a very difficult decision for unionized employees to cross a picket line. The Supreme Court eased this burden somewhat in 1985 by ruling that workers could renounce their union membership during a strike and return to work without being fined, since the union no longer had organizational rights against them.[4] The extent to which this will occur has yet to be determined.

LAWS AFFECTING ECONOMIC AND UNFAIR
LABOR PRACTICE STRIKES

The Taft-Hartley Act, as interpreted by the NLRB, distinguishes between economic and unfair labor practice strikes.[5] In both instances, an employer may hire replacements (if it is willing and able to do so) and attempt to continue production. At the end of an unfair labor practice strike, the employer must reinstate its original employees.[6] After an economic strike, it is not obligated to do so.[7] It is true that replaced workers must be rehired preferentially as openings occur for up to one year,[8] but the very real possibility exists that economic strikers will have lost their jobs permanently to their replacements. Obviously, the likelihood of actually losing one's job by engaging in a strike is a risk that must be carefully weighed against potential benefits. Replacement is not common because of the problems it presents to the employer, but it is legal and it is a possibility.

The replacement of a majority of the workforce during a strike can also present difficulties in representation. In the past, employers have called for de-certification elections after replacing their workforce on the grounds that the union did not represent a majority of *that* group of employees. Not surprisingly, the new employees usually voted the union out. Machiavellian employers discovered that they could escape union recognition by precipitating an economic strike, hiring replacements, and calling for a decertification election. To combat this problem the NLRB now permits strikers as well as replacements to vote in decertification elections for up to a year after a strike begins.[9]

NLRB and court rulings also define the legality of picketing. Generally speaking, when the purpose of the picket line is to discourage employees and/or replacements from going to work during a strike, the law limits pickets to informing others that the employer is on strike and to urging people not to cross the line.[10] Technically speaking, pickets are not allowed to prohibit entry to those seeking to cross the line. However, since a great deal may be riding on the union's effectiveness at maintaining the line, pickets may imply or use force illegally to prevent entry. How well this may be accomplished in the real world depends to a great deal on the effectiveness of the police and the sympathy (or lack of it) of local authorities. On "orderly" picket lines, nonmembers of the bargaining unit such as managers, supervisors, and clerical employees are permitted to enter with a minimum of hassle.

One other legal feature of picketing should be noted. Pickets who are themselves breaking the law by threatening or using force or by defying an injunction limiting their number or positioning are still citizens protected by rights common to everyone in society. A picket who is illegally trespassing on company property, violating a court order, disturbing the peace, and making threatening overtures may not legally be shot by management or run over by a scab. The enforcement of picket-line law rests with the authorities, not with the owners, the public, or nonsympathizers. Those who take action into their own hands are legally liable for the consequences.

Finally, provisions for dealing with strikes imperiling the nation's health and safety were detailed in Chapter 5.

An account of an eleven-year-long labor dispute is reported in the accompanying box.

KOHLER AND U.A.W. END DISPUTE THAT STARTED WITH STRIKE IN '54

MILWAUKEE, Dec. 17, 1965 (AP) —The Kohler Company and the United Automobile Workers union ended 11½ years of bitter strife today as the company agreed to pay $4.5 million in back pay and pensions.

The awards stemmed from an acrimonious six-year strike marked by violence and a union-sponsored nationwide boycott of goods produced by the sprawling Kohler, Wis., plumbingware plant.

The central characters in the long feud, Emil Mazey, U.A.W. secretary-treasurer, and Lyman C. Conger, Kohler vice president and general counsel, sealed the pact with a handshake at a news conference after the signing.

They also announced agreement on a new labor contract to be submitted to the union membership tomorrow night.

Terms of the final agreement were worked out in a series of sessions that came to a head at the A.F.L.-C.I.O. convention in San Francisco earlier this week. The conditions are subject to approval by the National Labor Relations Board and the United States Circuit Court of Appeals in Washington, before which a contempt action against the company is still pending. Dismissal will be sought.

$3 Million to Strikers

Approximately 1,400 former strikers will receive a total of $3 million back pay in individual amounts ranging up to $10,000. The

restoration of pension rights will account for $1.5 million.

Mr. Mazey said the strike had cost the U.A.W. $12 million in strike benefits.

The dispute began on April 5, 1954, when members of Local 833, accusing the family-owned Kohler concern of union-busting tactics, walked out.

Union security was the main issue. Arbitration machinery, seniority rights and wages were secondary items.

The plumbingware factory remained closed for eight weeks as pickets marched at plant gates in increasing numbers. The company obtained an injunction banning mass picketing, then opened the gates in a recruitment drive.

That was the signal for the first of what later became sporadic outbreaks of violence. Incidents ranged from fist fights to full-scale rioting with more than 300 arrests. The biggest battle involved efforts to block the unloading of shipments of clay aboard Norwegian vessels and consigned to the Kohler plant.

The company listed more than 1,000 acts of vandalism that it said were connected with the strike, including damage to a construction project being built for it at Sheboygan.

A by-product of the hiring of non-striking workers, many of whom commuted long distances daily to and from the plant, was bitterness among hundreds of families in the Kohler-Sheboygan area.

(continued)

More than six years after the strike began, the union scored its first major victory. The N.L.R.B., after four years of hearings, ruled that Kohler had prolonged the strike through unfair labor practices, which included refusal to bargain in good faith. The board ordered reinstatement of all remaining strikers—estimated by the union to total 1,700—but upheld the dismissal of 78 workers on charges of misconduct.

Early in 1960, the union charged that the company was not complying with the directive because 300 workers had not been offered employment. A Federal court found the company in contempt for refusal to reinstate all remaining strikers with back pay and pension rights restored. The company appealed to the Supreme Court for a review but was turned down.

On Sept. 28, 1962, the company and union negotiated the first contract in eight and a half years. This expired only recently but was extended from day to day pending negotiations.

RATIONALE FOR ALLOWING STRIKES

Many beginning observers of labor relations are often troubled by the seeming wastefulness of strikes. After all, the employees, the employer, and the customers all suffer. In some instances, the strike lasts so long that the employees cannot regain in raises what they lost in forgone wages. To many, such activity seems needlessly wasteful—if not worse. Yet the fact remains that it is the legal/economic/political/sociological policy of the United States to permit the right to strike and to constrain that right under only the most dire of circumstances. To understand why, it is necessary to give greater attention to the benefits of strikes and to assess more accurately their costs.

It is generally agreed that the right of employees to form unions is necessary or, at the very least, highly convenient in creating in employers the desire to treat their employees well. Without an effective right to strike, the threat of unionization would be far less imposing on employers.

Without the right to form unions and thence to strike, there really is no significant pressure on management to make concessions or to bargain reasonably. If employees were dissatisfied with the final offer of the employer, they could do nothing but accept it. A Machiavellian employer that relied on the employees' inability to strike need never bargain in good faith—so long as it maintained proper appearances. Without the right of the employees to withhold their only bargaining chit—their services—collective bargaining would truly become "collective begging."

This fact makes the auditing of the economic benefits of strikes more difficult. The gains—or losses—of any individual strike must be balanced against what the outcomes might be if there never were any effective strikes. When this was essentially the case in the nineteenth century, employers did not treat employees very well. It is impossible to measure precisely how much benefit all employees gain by having the right to unionize and to strike, but any reasonable person would have to concede that it is substantial. Furthermore, it is not safe to assume that all gains for employees are losses for employers. A very significant portion of whatever improvements in the standard of living that the right to strike has provided are undoubtedly returned to employers in the form of greater consumption of goods and services.

The right to strike may also be justified on human as well as economic grounds. The freedom to help determine one's outcome is a hallowed American tradition. It takes on much greater probability of success for many employees with the right to strike. It also helps promote a sense of self-worth and reduces feelings of helplessness in a very large and often hostile world. Finally, the parties' own experiences with strikes have demonstrated that they prefer the occasional costs to the alternatives of neutral intervention or grossly unequal power.

Notes

1. Richard B. Freeman and James L. Medoff, *What Do Unions Do?* (New York: Basic Books, 1984), p. 218.
2. Railway Labor Act, Sec. 10.
3. Sections 207–210.
4. *Food and Commercial Workers Local 506* (Facciola Meat Company), 274 NLRB No. 211.
5. *Labor Law Course*, 24th ed. (Chicago: Commerce Clearing House, 1979), par. 1605, p. 1600.
6. *Ibid.*, p. 1601.
7. *NLRB* v. *Mackay Radio & Telegraph Co.* (1938), 304 U.S. 333.
8. *Labor Law Course*, par. 2221, pp. 1839–1840.
9. *Ibid.*
10. *Ibid.*, par. 1772, pp. 1720–1721.

Discussion Questions

1. Describe the causes of and possible means of resolving impasses.
2. Assess the benefits and liabilities of interests arbitration.
3. Evaluate the usefulness of mediation.
4. Discuss types of strikes.
5. Assess the purpose and effectiveness of economic strikes.
6. Discuss fact-finding.
7. Discuss the laws affecting strikes.
8. Assess the rationale for allowing strikes.

Statements for Comment

1. "There are no unsolvable bargaining impasses, just communication difficulties."
2. "Mediation is a waste of time, Without the mediator being able to bind anyone, neither side will give in. The only thing worse would be to allow the mediator to bind the parties."
3. "More American companies should hire scabs during a strike. It would teach the employees a lesson."
4. "Employers should take the offensive in bargaining more often. They should use the lockout more."
5. "Fact-finding will never work because neither side cares what the public thinks."
6. "Employers would treat their employees well even without the right to join unions or to threaten to strike. Just look at nonunion employers."

Situations

Case 10–1 Clarence Steinbridge, owner of a medium-sized steel fabricating company, pondered what to do next. Bargaining with the union representing his employees had reached an impasse, and the contract was due to expire that evening. As his CEO, you are called into his office for a briefing on the options available to the company and the respective strengths and weaknesses of the options.

   What would you advise Mr. Steinbridge to do? What do your recommendations depend upon? What additional information do you need to know about this situation?

Case 10–2 Giuseppe Jones is between a rock and another rock. He is a member of the union at Mr. Steinbridge's plant. It looks like the union will be on strike tomorrow. Giuseppe is busted, disgusted, and can't be trusted. He needs his paycheck. He is chronically behind in his installment payments. One more missed payment and he will lose his television, his car, and maybe his lease. He is considering crossing the picket line tomorrow.

   What advice would you give Giuseppe? What else do you need to know about this situation?

Case 10–3 The impasse didn't break and the union has thrown a picket line around the plant. Giuseppe still hasn't make up his mind what he's going to do. He has arrived at the plant in time for his normal shift to begin. There he runs into his old high school football teammate, Jim "Freight Train" Smith.

   "Giuseppe, old buddy, old pal, it sure is great to see you down here to work the picket line with us. Great to see a quarterback 'getting dirty.' Remember how us big guys used to block for you?" said Freight Train. "Boy, we're going to close this place up tighter than a drum! *No one* is going to cross this picket line! This is fun!"

   What should Giuseppe do now? What should Freight Train do?

Bibliography of Related Readings

Cabot, S. J., and J. R. Cureton, "Labor Disputes and Strikes: Be Prepared," *Personnel Journal*, February 1981, pp. 121–23.

Creigh, S. W., et al., "Differences in Strike Activity Between Countries," *International Journal of Manpower*, 1982, pp. 15–23.

Fantasia, R., "The Wildcat Strike and Industrial Relations," *Industrial Relations Journal*, 1983, pp. 74–86.

Gerhart, P. F., and J. E. Drotning, "Dispute Settlement and the Intensity of Mediation," *Industrial Relations*, 1980, pp. 352–59.

Imberman, W., "Who Strikes—And Why," *Harvard Business Review*, 1983, pp. 18–20.

Jackson, C. N., and D. C. King, "The Effects of Representatives' Power Within Their Own Organizations on the Outcome of a Negotiation," *Academy of Management Journal*, 1983, pp. 178–85.

Kaufman, B. E., "Interindustry Trends in Strike Activity," *Industrial Relations*, 1983, pp. 45–57.

Kaufman, Bruce E., "The Determinants of Strikes in the United States, 1900–1977," *Industrial and Labor Relations Review*, July 1982, pp. 473–90.

Kennedy, Thomas, "Freedom to Strike Is in the Public Interest," *Harvard Business Review*, Vol. 48 (July–August 1970), p. 57.

Kolb, D. M., "Roles Mediators Play: State and Federal Practice," *Industrial Relations*, 1981, pp. 1–17.

Kolb, Deborah, M., "Roles Mediators Play: Contrasts and Comparisons in State and Federal Mediation Practice," *Industrial Relations*, Winter 1981, pp. 1–17.

Mauro, M. J., "Strikes as a Result of Imperfect Information," *Industrial and Labor Relations Review*, 1982, pp. 522–38.

Nicholson, N., and J. Kelly, "The Psychology of Strikes," *Journal of Occupational Behavior*, October 1981, pp. 275–84.

Perry, C. R., et al., *Operating During Strikes* (Philadelphia: University of Pennsylvania, 1982).

Simkin, William E., *Mediation and the Dynamics of Collective Bargaining* (Washington, D.C.: Bureau of National Affairs, 1971).

Exercise

Sweet Swing, Inc., and United Molders, IV Presume the negotiations carried out in the previous exercise look like they may result in an impasse despite the already utilized efforts of the FMCS. Switch teams from your bargaining exercise and prepare a strategy for your new side, should an impasse result. Detail the factors that influenced the strategy you chose and justify it to your constituents. Estimate the benefits and costs of the strategy selected and explain why it was better than other possible choices. Develop a plan of implementation.

ECONOMIC

ISSUES

The next three chapters deal with the content of collective bargaining agreements. Issues covered in contracts fall into three main categories: economic, administrative, and institutional. *Economic issues* include wages and supplemental benefits. *Administrative issues* detail how the work is to be allocated and performed. *Institutional issues* concern the rights and responsibilities of management and the union to protect and maintain their positions. Major economic issues include base wage rates, differentials, premium pay, and supplemental benefits. Major administrative topics include production standards, seniority, and discipline. Major institutional topics include management's rights and the union's membership requirements. A final major provision of the contract is the grievance procedure. Its use is intended to assure that when management takes action, it does so in accordance with the provisions agreed upon in the contract. The grievance procedure will be examined separately and in detail in Chapter 14. Contract clause examples and related data are interspersed throughout the next three chapters.

COMPONENTS OF WAGE AND BENEFIT DEMANDS

The following discussion of wage and benefit issues focuses on how compensation administration is affected by unionization. Basic compensation factors that are affected only tangentially, if at all, by unions are not addressed. Students seeking a more complete understanding of compensation procedures in general are invited to consult the specialized readings recommended at the end of the chapter or the wage and benefit section of any textbook in personnel or human resources management.

Economic issues, while complicated and of obvious importance, are not necessarily the most difficult with which to deal. Because they concern money, rather than principles, wage demands and offers can be comprised with comparative administrative ease and without general references to "rights" or "prerogatives"—issues which might produce much more emotional responses. Furthermore, a wealth of relevant data is usually available. Given the availability of relevant data, commonly agreed-upon methods of wage determination, the ability to compromise the subject, and the general agreement that both sides can see the other's needs, it would seem that professional negotiators could handle these issues comparatively easily. The major stumbling block to agreement in this area arises not from an unwillingness to understand the issue but rather from either a lack of money or a disagreement as to appropriate shares.

Wage-Determination Standards

Three main standards are commonly used by employers and unions to justify the basic wage rate: (1) comparative wage norms, (2) standard of living, and (3) employer ability to pay.

Comparative Wage Norms. Comparative wage norms (also known as equity considerations) seem a particularly attractive method for determining appropriate wage levels. The worth of a job can be inferred by comparing pay rates for jobs in the bargaining unit with equivalent jobs in other places of employment. These comparisons, standing alone, provide a psychological and economic opportunity reference but obviously do not take account of differences in employer efficiency or ability to pay. The conceptualization of wage comparisons is easy, but the application is surprisingly difficult for four reasons. The first problem is that it is usually impossible to find exactly equivalent jobs elsewhere. Given the fact that jobs that are being compared are different, room is left to dispute the importance of the differences. Second, the method of compensation in other places of employment may well be different from that of the bargaining unit; certainly the mix of wages and supplemental benefits will be different. This makes compensation comparison very difficult. Third, it may be difficult to obtain appropriate data on other jobs from which to make valid comparisons. Last, and most important, both sides have partisan interests in with whom the comparisons are made. In general, the union would be expected to seek comparison with the highest-paid members of the job classification, employers with the lowest.

Standard of Living. Standard-of-living arguments are more value-laden than wage comparisons and cannot be as persuasively argued based on data. Standard-of-living arguments assert that employees ought to be able to live at certain levels, and that the amount of wages required to do this is determined by the cost of living—an issue over which neither side has control and which is in no way related to the employees' productivity or value to the employer. Because of these two features, many employers feel standard-of-living arguments ought to be irrelevant in establishing the wage rate. Still, the standard of living may well be the most compelling issue to employees in wage determination and cannot be shunted aside. The issue takes on particular emphasis in periods of rapid inflation, during which the employees need raises ''just to stay even.''

Employer Ability to Pay. Employer ability to pay may be the most significant of the three standards in ultimately determining the wage rate. Much hard bargaining takes place over this subject, because it is both highly significant and highly variable from negotiation to negotiation. If the employer has had a prosperous period, the employees may be able to share in it. If it did not, there is probably little that they can bargain for.

Without regard to the previous years' prosperity for an individual company, there are two ability-to-pay factors that impact on all employers. They are the proportion of labor cost to total cost and elasticity of demand.

All other things being equal, if the *proportion of labor cost to total cost* is low, the employer can afford a pay raise more easily than can an employer whose proportion of labor cost to total cost is high. For instance, if in the capital-intensive petroleum industry the proportion of labor cost to total cost at a refinery were 10 percent, a wage increase of 10 percent would result in only a 1 percent increase in total cost (10 percent × 10 percent). On the other hand, in the labor-intensive textile industry, if the proportion of labor cost to total cost were 90 percent, a 10 percent wage increase would result in a 9 percent increase in total cost. Obviously, on just this feature alone, it is difficult for labor-intensive industries to pay high wages. It is also a reason they move to low-labor-cost areas such as the South and outside the country. It is also a reason they often fight unions vehemently.

A feature closely related to the proportion of labor cost to total cost is *value added.* Value added is a measure of how much an employee contributes to the value of the product. Two factors are important here: how much value is added and how much the employee costs. If an employee can make a significant increase in the value of the product by his or her inputs, there is a significant opportunity for the employer to make more money. This, in turn, provides the opportunity for the employer to profit and afford a wage increase at the same time.

In application, value added by employees is generally increased significantly in either of two ways. One is by adding more effective machinery or improving the efficiency of the process by better layout or insight. The other is by removing restrictions to effectiveness such as the performance of unnecessary procedures (sometimes union-negotiated work rules). Large gains are seldom accomplished by getting employees to work *harder*.

In collective bargaining, value added is commonly addressed as "productivity bargaining." That is, if the production process becomes more efficient (through suggestion programs, for instance) or less inefficient (through concessions on restrictive work rules), prosperity for both parties can be enhanced. Value added also results in a lowering of the proportion of labor cost to total cost. Under these circumstances, expensive employees can be afforded if they are highly productive. Then the entire economy benefits. In traditional collective bargaining, the responsibility for increasing value added rests heavily on management. Large breakthroughs in this area provide one of the best opportunities for high profits for owners and significant wage enhancement for employees.

Elasticity of demand describes how much sales are reduced if the price of a product is raised. When demand is highly elastic, a small rise in price will result in a large loss of sales. In a highly inelastic demand situation, even a large rise in price will not reduce sales. The consumer just has to ante up more and keep on buying.

From the consumer's standpoint there are two important questions to be answered. (1) If my supplier raises its prices, can I find a cheaper substitute from another supplier? (2) If I can't find a cheaper alternative, can I get along without it?

In answer to the first question, unions attempt to "take wages out of competition" by organizing entire industries or product markets and impose the same wage-cost burden on all employers. This is livable for employers if the entire industry is unionized and total demand can be maintained through advertising or necessity or any other method. It is less livable for unionized employers in partially unionized industries. In those situations, union-negotiated wage increases are very difficult to pass along in the marketplace because the nonunion employers can increase their market shares by selling at lower cost. When all employers have the same cost, no employer gets hurt so long as total sales for the industry remain high. Only the customer gets hurt.

In recent years, wage levels that previously were largely standardized across industries by pattern bargaining or master contracts with plant supplements have eroded. Increasing economic competition from foreign suppliers and deregulation have made it more difficult for employers to maintain proportional parity. This has lead to concessions in older, less-efficient plants to avoid shutdowns.[1]

Nothing in any of these three wage-determination standards makes any of them either essentially prounion or promanagement. Wage comparisons are raised by employees when wages are low. They are brought up by employers when wages are high. Likewise, the standard-of-living argument would be raised by employees during periods of inflation and by employers during periods of

FIGURE 11-1   WAGE DEMAND COMPONENTS

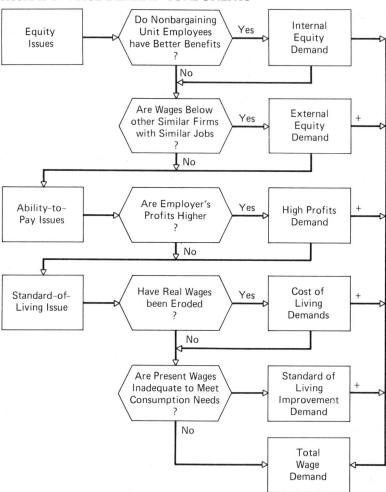

SOURCE: *John A. Fossum,* Labor Relations: Development, Structure, Process *(3rd Edition). (Plano, Texas: Business Publications, Inc. 1985), p. 190.*

deflation, should any ever happen to exist. Ability to pay is raised by unions when profits are high and by employers when profits are low. A synopsis of wage demand components appears in Figure 11-1.

Applying the Standards

Once the basic wage rate has been established, many complications arise in applying it to specific jobs and specific circumstances. The first issue to be addressed is wage differentials among jobs—that is, how much more or less one job pays than another, and for what reasons. An additional issue is how compensation will be awarded for shift work, overtime, and in terms of supplementary benefits such as holiday pay. The final set of specific circumstances deals with adjustments for individuals based on merit or longevity.

Wage differentials among job classifications are generally justified on the basis of differing requirements for education, experience, effort, and responsibility. Since there is no perfect way to measure these differences or even to agree upon their significance, there is a great deal of room for bargaining. This area can become extremely politicized in *collective* bargaining, because evaluations made in one classification affect the availability of funds for other classifications. While this is also true in nonunion situations where management establishes differentials unilaterally, in collective bargaining one subgroup of employees will be pitted against another, despite their being represented by a common agent. In general, lower-paid employees may oppose giving substantial raises to higher-paid employees because they perceive less "need" for these individuals. The money "saved" can then be allocated to lower-paying jobs. Because the collectively bargained distribution is based on popularity rather than necessarily on merit, and because lower-paid employees are usually more numerous, wage differentials may be more subject to political pressures than to merit in collective bargaining. It can also potentially subject a minority of employees to the tyranny of the majority.

Special Pay Situations

In many work situations, premium pay is awarded for overtime and shift differentials. In situations where work is routinely performed on shifts beyond the conventional workday, a premium differential is usually bargained for the "less desirable" shifts.

SHIFT PREMIUM CLAUSE

SHIFT DIFFERENTIAL

Section 1: An employee whose work shift consisting of $7\frac{1}{2}$ or 8 work hours on a scheduled work day begins before 6:00 a.m. or at or after 12:00 noon will be paid a shift differential of 35 cents per hour for all such hours worked on that shift.

Section 2: Any employee who works overtime on his/her work shift as described in Section 1 will receive the applicable shift differential for all overtime hours worked.

Section 3: Employees who are called in to work a shift on their scheduled day off and who worked not less than a full $7\frac{1}{2}$ or 8 hours shift which begins before 6:00 a.m. or at or after 12:00 noon shall receive, in addition to the appropriate rate, the shift differential as set forth in Section 1 for all such hours worked.

This is seldom an area of extreme controversy. Overtime, on the other hand, can be more troubling.

OVERTIME DISTRIBUTION

Overtime shall be distributed commencing in order of seniority as equally as practicable to all employees, but excluding those who have not yet earned seniority rating.

Almost all contracts provide for premium pay for overtime, but the amount of premium depends upon what is negotiated. Sometimes "excessive" premiums are really designed to discourage employers from assigning work on Sundays and holidays.

OVERTIME PREMIUM PAY

All overtime hours worked will be paid for at one and one-half (1½) times the rates set forth in Exhibit "A" for each classification, and employees shall not be required to take time off to offset overtime hours worked. In this connection the following hours of labor shall be deemed overtime hours:

1. All work on holidays or rest days.
2. All hours over eight (8) per day.
3. All hours over forty (40) per week.
4. All off-schedule work, including all work in the forty-eight (48) hours next following a change in schedule, where proper notice of change in schedule is not given.
5. For each call-out, a minimum of two (2) hours at time and one-half pay.

(f) Employees designated in Exhibit "A" as "S" shall be scheduled employees and assigned to work on irregular but definite assigned schedules of five (5) eight (8) hour days per work week, consecutive where possible (special provision is made in Exhibit "A" for Garage Department employees), provided, however, that schedules may be changed upon forty (40) hours' advance notice, except that this notice shall not be required where change in schedule is made necesary by absence of an employee. No holiday work will be regularly scheduled for such non-shift employees. All overtime hours worked will be paid for at one and one-half (1½) times the rate set forth in Exhibit "A" for each classification, and employees shall not be required to take time off to offset overtime hours worked. In this connection, the following hours of labor shall be deemed to be overtime hours:

1. All work on holidays or rest days.
2. All hours over eight (8) per day.
3. All hours over forty (40) per week.

Step increases based on longevity or merit are also subject to bargaining. Unions have an established track record of wishing longer-service employees to be paid more while management has an established track record of wanting to reserve significant funds to be distributed as merit increases. Each side finds flaws in the priorities of the other, but both generally agree that both positions have some merit. Generally, bargaining significantly affects the basic wage rate (either across-the-board or by percentage) and diminishes the proportional importance of merit.[2]

Two other wage provisions found in many contracts are call-in pay and reporting pay. *Call-in pay* provides pay for a minimum length of time (often four hours) to employees who are called into work at times other than their normal shift, regardless of how briefly they work. *Reporting pay* guarantees the employees a set minimum number of hours pay (also commonly four hours) if the employer has no work for them but did not notify the employees before they reported to work.

CALL-IN PAY PROVISION

ARTICLE XV
CALL-IN PAY - REPORT PAY

Section 1: An employee who is called in to work at a time when he-she is not regularly scheduled to report for work shall receive a minimum of four (4) hours work at his-her regular rate of pay.

Section 2: An employee who reports to work at the start of his-her regular shift shall receive a minimum of four (4) hours of work at his-her regular rate of pay unless the employee was notified in advance of his-her reporting that less than four hours work was available in which case, the employee will be paid at straight time for the hours he-she was authorized to work.

Section 3: An employee will not be paid under the above when the failure by the County to provide work is due to causes or conditions beyond the County's control, such as, but not limited to, extreme weather conditions or power failure. Notification to county employees not to report for work may be by mail to the person's last address; by telephone; in person, or when appropriate or necessary, by news media.

A less obvious economic issue is the length of the workday. Unions have occasionally pushed for a 35- or even 30-hour workweek. This is not generally an attempt to increase leisure but rather an indirect form of a pay raise. If the employer continues to utilize employees for the traditional number of hours, the hours above 35 (or 30) will be calculated as overtime and compensated at a premium rate. Since the employer usually still needs employees 40 hours (or more) per week, the shorter workday will not reduce hours but will increase pay.

Some requests for reduced hours are sincere, however. In some instances there is a genuine desire for more leisure. More often the desire is to "spread the work" across more employees in times of job scarcity. A 35-hour workweek can support one-eighth more employees—a reduction in unemployment of $12\frac{1}{2}$ percent—albeit at an equal expense in reduced earnings for all those still employed.

TABLE 11-1 PAYMENTS COMPENSATING WORKERS FOR INCONVENIENCE AND UNPLEASANTNESS (FREQUENCY EXPRESSED AS PERCENTAGE OF CONTRACTS)

Overtime provisions (see note)		Frequency
1. Daily overtime	87%	
a. For work after eight hours		92%
b. At time and one-half		84
2. Weekly overtime	64	
a. For work after forty hours		93
b. At time and one-half		95
3. Premium pay for weekend work	92	
a. For Saturday—not part of regular work week		62
b. For Sunday—not part of regular work week		84
c. For Saturday—part of regular work week		3
d. For Sunday—part of regular work week		12
4. Premium pay for work on holidays	82	
a. Double time		12
b. Double time and one-half		45
c. Triple time		30
Reporting pay	78	
1. Two-hour guarantee		25
2. Four-hour guarantee		56
3. Eight-hour guarantee		9
Call-in/Call-back pay	53	
1. Four hour guarantee		61
2. Rate of pay		
a. Straight time		48
b. Time and one-half		35
Shift differential	83	
1. Money differential		77
2. Time differential		13

Note: When interpreting the percentages, the left column is based on all contracts studied. The right column is based on those contracts having the contract provision in question. For example, 87 percent of all contracts provide for daily overtime. Among those contracts providing for daily overtime, 92 percent pay overtime after eight hours' work, and in 84 percent of these contracts the overtime rate is time and one-half.

SOURCE: U.S. Department of Labor, Characteristics of Major Collective Bargaining Agreements— *January 1, 1980 (Washington, D.C.: U.S. Government Printing Office, May 1981), Bulletin 2095.*

Incentive Plans

Up to this point it has been assumed that pay is based on an hourly wage. This is not always exclusively the case. Approximately one-third of all contracts call for some form of incentive pay based on performance.[3] Unions do not generally favor individual incentive plans because they may promote competition among employees. Group incentive plans, often adopted in accordance with a management-union cooperation scheme, have proved more palatable to unions.[4]

Wage Adjustments During the Life of the Contract

Generally speaking, the parties wish to reach agreement on issues for as long as their situation won't change. The more items agreed to for the longer the period of time, the more stability, the less administrative hassle, and the less chance of a strike. However, sometimes situations change rapidly, and the parties do not wish to obligate themselves to contract provisions that might be unlivable under changed circumstances. Particularly in periods of rapid inflation, the parties may be unwilling to lock themselves into wage obligations that may be inappropriate in the particularly unpredictable future. In such a situation they may agree to adjust the wage rate at later times through either of two methods: escalator clauses (cost-of-living adjustments) or wage-reopener clauses.

Cost-of-living adjustment (COLA) or *escalator* clauses are automatic adjustments in wages at agreed-upon intervals (usually quarterly) in response to changes in some measure of the cost of living (usually the Consumer Price Index). Floors and ceilings on the amount of adjustment may be negotiated. *Wage reopeners* are clauses allowing the contract to be reopened at some agreed-upon point (usually the midpoint) for the purpose of renegotiating only wage issues. Each of the methods has its virtues and flaws.

The virtues of the escalator clause are that it is highly popular with employees, requires almost no administrative hassle, and may well be paid for out of increased revenues. (The Consumer Price Index goes up if there is an aggregate increase in the price of goods and services. If the employer is inflating its prices at or above the national rate, this system will not hinder return on investment. If, on the other hand, the employer's price raising is not keeping pace with the national inflation rate, an escalator clause could prove expensive and would probably be avoided by an employer who anticipated such an occurrence.)

The liabilities of the escalator clause are that it has no motivational value and it is a less predictable cost than bargained wage rates. Because the employees receive their escalator adjustment regardless of their personal performance or the company's profitability, COLAs have virtually no motivational value except whatever might spill over from having "happy" employees. Managers in charge of motiviation through financial rewards may not favor such systems.

The funding of escalators can also cause problems. Because it is impossible to forecast the rate of inflation (which is why one has a COLA in the first place), and because wage payments are very liquid debits, financial planners must budget the highest amount they might have to spend in a given period to cover possible expenses. If this amount isn't consumed, valuable resources (corporate cash) have been tied up in less-than-optimal usage. Financial planners don't like this.

ESCALATOR CLAUSE

1. Effective August 6, 1986, an adjustment will be made in basic weekly rates in each wage schedule. The amount of the adjustment shall be 50¢ plus .6% of the scheduled rates applicable during the first year of the agreement, rounded to the nearest 50¢, for each full percent increase in the U.S. Bureau of Labor Statistics National Consumer Price Index (1967 = 100) for May 1986 over May 1985. A partial percent increase shall be applied proportionately.

2. Effective August 5, 1987, a second adjustment will be made in basic weekly rates in each wage schedule. The amount of the adjustment shall be 50¢ plus .6% of the scheduled rates applicable during the second year of the agreement, rounded to the nearest 50¢, for each full percent increase in the U.S. Bureau of Labor Statistics National Consumer Price Index (1967 = 100) for May 1987 over May 1986. A partial percent increase shall be applied proportionately.

3. In no event shall a decrease in the CPI result in a reduction of any basic weekly wage rate.

4. In the event the Bureau of Labor Statistics does not issue the appropriate Consumer Price Indexes on or before the dates referred to in (1) or (2) cost-of-living adjustments required by such appropriate indexes shall be effective at the beginning of the first payroll week after receipt of the indexes.

The virtue of a wage reopener is that the new wage rate can be established in accordance with criteria appropriate to the specific parties at the specific time. Its liability is that it requires additional bargaining, thereby increasing administrative burden and the possibility of a strike. Worse yet, the limitation of the scope of bargaining to only wages can be easily avoided.

Legally speaking, the employer is not obligated to discuss issues other than those provided for in the reopener clause,[5] and that restriction has significant value to management. However, union leaders have learned how to get around the restriction.

The NLRB has ruled that it is an unfair labor practice for a party to bargain to impasse over an issue that is not a mandatory subject of bargaining.[6] Since the contract, not the law, restricts bargaining in this instance to only wages, the union should be foreclosed from raising any other issue (such as subcontracting). The union, however, might pursue the following strategy: Offer to settle for a 5 percent raise and satisfactory resolution of the subcontracting question or, if management refuses to negotiate the subcontracting issue (which it may legally refuse to do), hold out for a 20 percent raise. Under such conditions, management may "voluntarily" agree to expand the scope of bargaining to reduce the breadth of disagreement. Such a tactic obviously has the potential effect of cutting the entire contract in half, if all issues the union didn't get before and now wants can be included. The wage reopener may become an entire contract reopener and yet not be an unfair labor practice, since the impasse was theoretically caused by disagreement over the wage rate—the permissible issue for bargaining.

WAGE REOPENER

This Agreement shall become effective March 1, 1986 and shall remain in full force and effect until March 1, 1990, however, it is expressly understood and agreed that this Contract shall be reopened thirty (30) days prior to the beginning of the fourth (4) year of this Agreement solely for the purpose of discussing adjustment in the wage rates, including cost-of-living and for no other purpose whatsoever. Wage rates shall include night shift differentials, extra work differential and split shift and short-shift differentials.

VACATIONS

(a) Vacations for each individual employee for the current year shall be determined by the length of service with the Company on December 31st of the previous year in accordance with the following schedule:

Length of Service on December 31st of Previous Year	*Accrued Vacation Allowance*
Less than one month	One Week
One month or more, but less than seven years and one month	Two Weeks
Seven years and one month or more, but less than seventeen years and one month or more	Three Weeks
Seventeen years and one month or more, but less than twenty-six years and one month or more	Four Weeks
Twenty-six years and one month or more	Five Weeks
Effective January 1, 1983:	
Seventeen years and one month or more, but less than twenty-four years and one month	Four Weeks
Twenty-four years and one month or more	Five weeks

In the event that an employee, who has an accrued but unused vacation allowance under the above schedule and conditions, leaves the service of the Company, such employee shall be entitled to pay in lieu of such vacation if, at the termination of employment date, such employee shall have completed at least six months of continuous service with the Company.

Newly employed regular full-time employees shall be entitled to one week vacation in the first calendar year of employment after completion of six months continuous employment and providing requirements of the Company's operation will readily permit such vacation scheduling. In the event of termination of employment during such first calendar year, vacation allowance (if vacation has not previously been taken) shall be paid if six months continuous employment has been completed prior to date of such termination.

(b) A week of vacation shall consist of forty (40) hours, for which employee will be paid his regular straight-time rate of pay.

(c) Vacation shall, in the case of a week, be taken in a single period but in the case of two (2), three (3), four (4) or five (5) weeks may be taken in two periods and will, insofar as practicable and subject to the requirements of the Company's operations, be granted at the time most desired by the employee, giving preference to company wide seniority.

If an employee splits his vacation, he will be allowed only one choice of dates, taking his remaining vacation after other employees, in order of company wide seniority, have exercised their choice of dates.

(d) If an enumerated holiday occurs during an employee's vacation, such vacation shall be extended for one (1) additional day.

(e) If the operations of the Company make it impossible for an employee to take his scheduled vacation he will receive straight time pay in lieu of the vacation. Vacations shall not be cumulative nor shall any employee receive more than five (5) weeks vacation in any one calendar year.

Economic Issues—Supplemental Benefits

Supplemental benefits deal with three main categories: insurance coverage, pensions, and pay for time not worked. As a group, these can make up a very sizable expense. In 1981, supplemental benefits averaged 37.3 percent of payroll costs.[7]

Insurance coverage can be as creative and expensive as the parties wish to make it. Many contracts have health-care coverage for the employee and dependents. The division of the cost of premiums is subject to negotiation, as is who is to be the carrier. In general, the more people covered by a contract, the lower the per unit cost.

Pension expense can also be substantial. Forecasting the cost of pensions requires actuarial predictions as to the number of claimants and the likely duration of their claims. Care must be taken that whatever provisions are agreed upon comply with the Employment Retirement Income Security Act. Other issues include the rights of survivors and the effect of early retirement.

Pay for time not worked commonly includes vacations, holidays, and sick and personal leave. Contracts generally specify the number of weeks of vacation employees are entitled to by length of service. They also specify how the amount to be paid is calculated. It is generally 40 hours pay at the employee's basic wage rate per week, but alternatives such as $\frac{1}{52}$ of average annual pay per week can be negotiated. The number of paid holidays is also negotiable.

TABLE 11-2 MOST COMMONLY OBSERVED HOLIDAYS (FREQUENCY EXPRESSED
AS PERCENTAGE OF CONTRACTS)

Holiday	Frequency
Thanksgiving	98%
Labor Day	98
Christmas	98
Independence Day	97
New Year's Day	97
Memorial Day	96
Good Friday	50
Day after Thanksgiving	49
Christmas Eve	47
Washington's Birthday	36
New Year's Eve	27
Employee's Birthday	22

SOURCE: Bureau of National Affairs, Basic Patterns in Union Contracts, 9th ed. (Washington, D.C.: BNA, Inc., 1979), p. 20.

Provision also needs to be made for payment when employees work on holidays or through their vacations. Working on holidays almost always entitles employees to premium pay unless their job classification typically works continuously (hospitals, hotel, and restaurant employees). It is a common contract provision to require employees to work the days before and after a holiday to qualify for holiday pay.

HOLIDAYS

(d) Each employee covered by the Agreement shall be entitled to eleven (11) holidays with pay each year as enumerated below:

New Year's Day	Thanksgiving Day
Gasparilla Day	The Day After Thanksgiving
Memorial Day	Christmas Eve Day
Fourth of July	Christmas Day
Labor Day	Employee's Birthday
Good Friday Holiday	

(1) If a holiday falls on Sunday, the following Monday shall be observed as a holiday. If a holiday falls on Saturday, the preceding Friday will be observed as a holiday; however, the Company at its option may give the employee Monday off in lieu of Friday provided seven (7) calendar days notice is given.

(2) Employees working on a holiday shall be compensated for actual work on such holiday at one and one-half (1½) times their respective regular hourly rates and shall receive additional compensation computed at their respective regular hourly rates for a period of eight (8) hours, such additional compensation representing the holiday to which the employee was entitled but did not receive.

TABLE 11-3 PROVISIONS PERTAINING TO PAY FOR TIME NOT WORKED
(FREQUENCY EXPRESSED AS PERCENTAGE OF CONTRACTS)

	Frequency
Vacation pay (percent specifying length)	72%
1. Maximum length vacation	
a. Under four weeks	7%
b. Four to five and one-half weeks	73
c. Six weeks or longer	20
2. Modal length of service for various vacations	
a. One weeks' vacation—one year of service	
b. Two weeks' vacation—three years of service	
c. Three weeks' vacation—ten years of service	
d. Four weeks' vacation—twenty years of service	
e. Five weeks' vacation—twenty-five years of service	
f. Six weeks' vacation—thirty years of service	
Paid holidays	84%
1. Eight holidays with pay	6%
2. Nine holidays with pay	12
3. Ten holidays with pay	25
4. Eleven holidays with pay	22
5. Twelve holidays with pay	11
Other payments for time not worked	
1. Funeral leave	69%
2. Jury duty	67
3. Court witness	25
4. Military service	30
5. Paid meal periods	31
6. Paid rest periods	42
7. Paid wash-up, clean-up, and clothes-changing periods	24

See Note, Table 12.4

SOURCE: U.S. Department of Labor, Characteristics of Major Collective Bargaining Agreements—
January 1, 1980 *(Washington, D.C.: U.S. Government Printing Office, May 1981), Bulletin 2095.*

Sick leave and personal leave generally have specified upper limits. Sick
leave claims may require proof under some contract provisions. Of less universal
application, some contracts provide for time off with pay for bereavement (with
specific limitations on the relationship to the deceased to qualify for payment)
and jury duty.

BENEFIT PLANS

Section 1. Health Benefits

The Employer will continue its contribution to the cost of the health insurance program of 75 percent based on the present method of computation. The term "present
method of computation" refers to the following:

A. The bi-weekly contributions by the Employer for employees shall be an amount equal to 75 percent of the average of the subscription charges in effect on the first day of the first pay period of January 1984 for employees of the United States as defined in 5 U.S.C. 8901, with respect to self alone or self and family enrollments, as applicable, for the highest level of benefits offered by—

(1) the service benefit plan;
(2) the indemnity benefit plan;
(3) the two employee organization plans with the largest number of enrollments as determined by the Office of Personnel Management; and
(4) the two comprehensive medical plans with the largest number of enrollments, as determined by the Office of Personnel Management.

B. The amount of contributions by the Employer for employees shall be readjusted beginning on the first pay period of January 1985 in accordance with the annual readjustment of the average by the Office of Pesonnel Management as provided above or in other words, 75 percent of said adjusted average.

C. The amount of contributions by the Employer for employees shall be readjusted beginning on the first pay period of January 1986 and January 1987 in accordance with the annual readjustment of the average by the Office of Personnel Management as provided or in other words, 75 percent of the newly adjusted average.

D. There shall be withheld from the pay of each enrolled employee and there shall be contributed by the Employer, amounts, in the same ratio as the contributions of the employee and the Employer which are necessary for the administrative costs and reserves provided for by 5 U.S.C. Section 8909 (b).

E. The amount necessary to pay the total charge for enrollment after the Employer's contribution is deducted shall be withheld from the pay of each enrolled employee.

F. The limitation in 5 U.S.C. Section 8906(b) upon the Employer's contribution for any individual employee shall bear the same ratio to the Service's percentage contribution, as stated above, as 60 bears to 75.

G. The Postal Service, the APWU, and the NALC shall establish a joint Task Force which shall investigate the possibility of establishing a Postal Service Employee Health Benefit Plan, based upon the USPS's Request for Proposal, to be jointly administered by the Unions and USPS (on either a single Union or joint Union basis, as may be agreed upon).

Section 2. Life Insurance
The Employer shall maintain the current life insurance program in effect during the term of this Agreement.

Section 3. Retirement
The provisions of 5 U.S.C. Chapter 83 and any amendments thereto, shall continue to apply to employees covered by this Agreement.

Section 4. Injury Compensation
Employees covered by this Agreement shall be covered by subchapter I of Chapter 81 of Title 5, and any amendments thereto, relating to compensation for work injuries. The Employer will promulgate appropriate regulations which comply with

applicable regulations of the Office of Workers' Compensation Programs and any amendments thereto.

Section 5. Health Benefit Brochures

When a new employee who is eligible for enrollment in the Federal Employee's Health Benefit Program enters the Postal Service, the employee shall be furnished a copy of the Health Benefit Plan brochure of the Union signatory to this Agreement which represents the craft in which the employee is to be employed.

SICK LEAVE

Section 1.   Employees shall be entitled to earn and accrue sick leave while on active pay status on the following basis:
  a. Scheduled fifty-six (56) hour employees shall earn fourteen (14) hours of sick leave for every calendar month worked.
  b. Scheduled forty (40) hour employees shall earn eight (8) hours sick leave for every calendar month worked.
Employees shall be eligible for sick leave after one (1) month of service. For services rendered prior to this Agreement, employees shall not forfeit any unused sick leave accumulated since their initial date of employment.

Section 2.   Sick leave may be accumulated to a maximum of nine hundred sixty (960) hours by scheduled forty (40) hour employees and one thousand three hundred forty-four (1344) hours by scheduled fifty-six (56) hour employees.

Section 3.   The sick leave incentive award will be given to employees who use little or no sick leave during a one year period. The eligibility for the incentive award is to be based on:
  a. anniversary date of employment
  b. the amount of sick leave used in previous anniversary year
The incentive award will be credited as personal leave hours and may be taken with the annual vacation leave. The incentive award is computed on the following basis for each anniversary year:

Sick Leave Used	Personal Leave Time Awarded
0–23 hours	24 hours
24–47 hours	12 hours
More than 47 hours	None

Section 4.   An employee incapacitated and unable to work shall notify the on-duty shift commander at least fifteen minutes before his scheduled reporting time as designated by the department, stating the nature of his illness and expected period of absence. This procedure shall be followed for each day the employee is unable to work, unless prior approval is given by the department.

Section 5.   If, and whenever, sick leave may appear to be abused, or when an employee consistently uses his sick leave as it is earned, the employee claiming/requesting such sick leave may be required to furnish competent proof of the necessity for such absence. The Employer reserves the right in all cases of illness, or reported illness, to require the employee to furnish a doctor's certificate. Departmental Management shall notify the employee within 24 hours of the reported illness that a doctor's certificate will be required.

Section 6.   Employees may not use any accumulated sick leave for contagious or infectious disease or injury sustained while engaged in outside employment.

Section 7.   Sick leave used under this Article shall be charged as used in increments of one hour.

Section 8.   Employees using sick leave are expected to be found at their respective homes, physician's office, hospital, or enroute to one or the other of these locations. An employee may go elsewhere provided he obtains the approval of the Fire Chief or his designee.

Section 9.   Employees covered by this Agreement may use three (3) days sick leave in the event of a death in his immediate family. The employee's immediate family shall be defined as: father, mother, sister, brother, spouse, spouse's brother and sister, stepfather, stepmother, stepchildren, father-in-law, mother-in-law, child, grandparents, spouse's grandparents.

Section 10.   Should an employee require additional funeral leave other than provided in Section 9 of this Article, he may request the additional time from the Fire Chief. Upon approval by the Fire Chief, any additional time used may be charged to vacation or sick leave if the employee has hours accrued that can be charged.

Section 11.   If requested, the employee shall furnish proof of death in his immediate family.

Section 12.   In the event an active employee should die, any unused sick leave which he has accumulated as of the time of death will be paid on the basis of one (1) day's pay for each three (3) days' leave to the deceased employee's beneficiary.

Section 13.   Sick leave will be granted upon approval of department management for reasons of the employee's health which shall include medical, dental or optical treatment which is necessary during working hours.

A fringe benefit found in a few contracts is SUB—Supplemental Unemployment Benefits. Found primarily in the automobile and steel industries, this benefit supplements workers' incomes while on layoff. In some highly publicized instances, some workers could receive 95% of their take-home pay while on layoff.[8]

At first blush, such a provision appears to be a "lazy man's dream foisted upon helpless big business by overly powerful unions bent on getting paid without working." Actually, the exact opposite may be closer to the truth.

Periodic layoffs had long been the bane of hourly employees in the auto industry. All attempts to have themselves placed on salary or some form of guaranteed annual wage failed. Eventually, the UAW convinced the Big Three auto manufacturers to agree to SUB—most likely as an incentive for the employers to continue offering them opportunities to work. After all, if an employer has to pay someone it has laid off, it will do all it can to prevent such a layoff.

Since the employers agreed to SUB, it can be presumed they thought they could manage with it. Unfortunately, massive layoffs in the auto industry occurred anyway, caused not by traditional cyclical fluctuations in demand, but by massive changes in buyer behavior such as shifting to smaller and foreign cars.

TABLE 11-4   PROVISIONS PROVIDING PROTECTION WHEN NOT WORKING OR
             UNABLE TO WORK (FREQUENCY EXPRESSED AS PERCENTAGE
             OF CONTRACTS)

Unemployment[a]	Frequency
1. Severance pay	34%
2. Supplemental unemployment compensation	14
Sick leave[a]	30
Insurance[b]	
1. Life insurance	95
2. Accidental death and dismemberment insurance	65
3. Sickness and accident insurance	81
4. Long-term disability insurance	35
5. Hospitalization insurance	91
6. Surgical insurance	84
7. Major medical insurance	71
8. Dental insurance	41
9. Prescription drugs	24
Pension plans[b]	
1. Retire at sixty-five	87
2. Noncontributory plans	92
3. Benefit formula	
a. Flat monthly amount per year of service	59
b. Percentage of employee earnings multiplied by years of service	12
c. Choice of a or b, whichever is greater	9
d. Benefits depend on contributions to employee's retirement fund	22

[a]*SOURCE: U.S. Department of Labor, Characteristics of Major Bargaining Agreements—January 1, 1980 (Washington, D.C.: U.S. Government Printing Office, May 1981), Bulletin 2095.*
[b]*SOURCE: Bureau of National Affairs, Basic Patterns in Union Contracts, 9th ed. (Washington, D.C.: BNA, Inc., 1979), pp. 41–50 and 68–72.*

The high cost to employers and the failure to protect against layoffs in the auto and steel industries have greatly lessened the potential expansion of SUB plans. An example of how complicated a SUB clause can be is contained in Appendix II at the end of this chapter.

Determining the Distribution of Benefits

A final note should be taken not only of the value of the wage and supplemental benefit package but also how its distribution is determined. The issue can be more complicated than it appears on the surface.

If the negotiators are highly competent and relevant data are available to both sides, the total value the employer can arguably afford to pay can be determined. It is not generally possible to expand the value of this package. Increases in one benefit will require decreases in another. Noncontributory (for employees) health-care coverage appears to be a significant benefit to employ-

EMPLOYEE ENJOYING AN EMPLOYER-PROVIDED SUPPLEMENTAL BENEFIT

SOURCE: Bobbie Kingsley/Photo Researchers

ees. Actually, the entire cost of the wage and supplemenal benefit package is always borne by the employer. In the past, if employees contributed to health-care coverage, the employer was spared that particular expense but then had those funds directed to other benefits. On the other hand, if the union at a later time negotiates full contributions from the employer, the employer just has that much less available to pay in other benefits, including wages. The distribution of the benefit package in many respects approaches a zero-sum game. Unless the amount of the *package* can be changed, bargaining in this area will reflect only preferences, not value or cost.

A major exception to the generalization that wages and benefits are equivalent tradeoffs is the effect of taxes. Wages received by employees are subject, of course, to federal income tax. Benefit coverages (of presumably equal value to the employee and equal cost to the employer) are not subject to federal taxes. Therefore, a supplemental benefits dollar may go further than a wage dollar because it is less heavily taxed. This result will, in many instances, incline some unions to press for supplemental benefits increases rather than direct wage increases.

Two other factors complicate this apparently otherwise easily fungible distribution of resources. One is that it is not always an easy task for the union to determine its members' priorities for benefits. The other is that for the employer, wages and supplemental benefit expenses are not always fungible if employment levels vary.

The determination by the union of priorities for benefit distribution may be a difficult task. Because different workers may have different needs (young married employees with small children may seek medical coverage for dependents while older employees might opt for increased pensions), it becomes apparent that if the employer can't offer everything for everybody, what one employee interest group gains, another loses. This presents the union with the difficult job of satisfying competing needs within its own membership.

How the union determines its members' needs is a tough communication problem. How it accommodates them is a tough political problem.

Theoretically, in a pure democracy, all members of the unit should be allowed to be heard on the subject of what they want. The resolution of conflicting interests for limited benefits should then be resolved by popular vote, with each member's vote being equal. One problem with unions' formulating demands this way is that it is difficult for everyone to be heard or even surveyed. Another difficulty is that, realistically, not everyone's vote counts the same. Members who are influential in maintaining support for incumbents may have more voice. Lastly, a tyranny of the majority is a possibility. If pure popularity determined the outcomes, it would be possible for the most numerous employee interest group to outweigh smaller subinterests and take all the benefits for itself (provided the employer was not getting involved in the issue).

Realistically, the union's demand for the benefit package is probably significantly moderated by expectations based on settlements elsewhere, what the leaders have communicated to the rank-and-file, and the union leaders' and employer's desire to attempt to maintain a sense of appropriate balance and stability.

Generally, the union leader may try to achieve an "appropriate" distribution of benefits by pursuing the strategy examined in Chapter 9. That is, the leader, for political purposes, may initially submit all members' demands and let management (with the selective acquiescence of the union leader) throw out those which are inappropriate. In such a fashion, the conflict among competing interest groups within the bargaining unit appears to be minimized.

For the employer, the tradeoff between wages and benefits is generally not exactly equal. Supplemental benefits can carry with them two potential concealed costs. One is that bargained benefits usually provide for coverages, not costs. Since the employer generally provides for health-care coverages through some insurance plan, the employer's carrier can (and often does) raise premiums to the employer during the life of the collective bargaining agreement. The second problem is that supplemental benefits are not reducible when there are

TABLE 11-5   PERCENT OF FULL-TIME EMPLOYEES BY PARTICIPATION[1] IN
EMPLOYEE BENEFIT PROGRAMS, MEDIUM AND LARGE FIRMS,[2] 1983

Employee Benefit Program	All Employees	Professional and Administrative Employees	Technical and Clerical Employees	Production Employees
Paid:				
Holidays	99	99	100	98
Vacations	100	100	100	99
Personal leave	25	31	35	17
Lunch period	11	4	5	17
Rest time	74	58	76	80
Sick leave	67	92	91	42
Sickness and accident				
insurance	49	29	34	67
Noncontributory[3]	41	22	26	57
Long-term disability				
insurance	45	66	58	28
Noncontributory[3]	34	47	42	23
Health insurance for				
employee	96	98	95	96
Noncontributory[3]	65	62	54	71
Health insurance for				
dependents	93	95	91	92
Noncontributory[3]	43	42	35	47
Life insurance	96	97	95	95
Noncontributory[3]	80	79	78	81
Retirement pension	82	86	84	79
Noncontributory[3]	75	79	79	72

[1]*Participation is defined as coverage by a time off, insurance, or pension plan. Employees subject to a minimum service requirement before they are eligible for a benefit are counted as participants even if they have not met the requirement at the time of the survey. If employees are required to pay part of the cost of a benefit, only those who elect the coverage and pay their share are counted as participants. Benefits for which the employee must pay the full premium are outside the scope of the survey. Only current employees are counted as participants; retirees are excluded even if participating in a benefit program.* [2]*See Appendix A for scope of study and definitions of occupational groups.* [3]*All coverage in the benefit program is provided at no cost to employee. Supplemental life insurance and pension plans, not tabulated in this bulletin, may be contributory.*

SOURCE: *U.S. Bureau of Labor Statistics. Employee Benefits in Medium and Large Firms, 1983. Bulletin 2213, p. 16.*

layoffs. Although wages will be reduced by the number of hours not worked, benefit costs continue at the same level.

Table 11-5 displays the portion of contracts containing various benefit clauses.

ECONOMIC EFFECTS OF WAGE AND BENEFIT DEMANDS

Because the focus of this text is on behavior and motivation, rather than the measurement of economic consequences, the following discussion of the eco-

TABLE 11-6 COST OF EMPLOYEE BENEFITS AS A PERCENT OF PAYROLL
DOLLARS: 1980

Type of Benefit	Percent of Payroll
Legally required payments (employer's share only)	8.9%
Pension, insurance and other payments (employer's share only)	12.6
Paid rest periods and lunch periods	3.5
Payments for vacations, holidays, and sick leave	9.9
Profit-sharing payments and bonuses	2.2
Total	37.1%
Total employees' benefits as dollars per payroll hour	$ 2.96
Total employees' benefits as dollars per employee per year	$6084.00

SOURCE: *Reprinted with the permission of the Chamber of Commerce of the United States of America from* Employee Benefits 1980, *p. 8.*

nomic effects of unionization on pay and benefits will be stated largely in terms of conclusions. For those who wish to pursue the justification of the conclusions, references are provided at the end of the chapter. In many instances the conclusions drawn are particularly dependent upon definitions, samples, and methods of measurement. Labor economists, with more time and skill than permitted here, find the subject one on which it is difficult to generalize.

The most relevant wage question for most observers is whether unionized employees earn more than nonunion employees. The answer is yes. According to one study, when other factors such as firm size and location are held constant, wage differentials range from 5 to 10 percent.[9] This figure is probably lower than that which would be estimated by the proverbial "person on the street." It is the author's opinion that the difference between the two estimates is probably attributable to the public's developing an inflated notion of union wage effects based on a select few nontypical examples highly publicized in the media. It is also probably due to the public's failure to account carefully for differences in firm size, labor-to-total-cost ratio, market monopolization, and other factors that affect the employer's ability to pay. It may also be partially attributable to atypically powerful union wage effects for the decade from the mid-sixties to the mid-seventies. During this period unions may have raised wages as much as 24 percent,[10] although this differential appears to be returning to more "normal" rates during the eighties.[11]

It should also be noted that measuring the difference between union and nonunion wages overlooks a perhaps powerful contribution of unionization—the spillover effect. It has been demonstrated that some nonunion employers (usually large, professionally managed ones) raise their wages to prevent too great a gap from developing between their employees' wages and those of unionized competitors in the labor market.[12] They do this both to attract employees and to decrease their employees' incentive to form a union. In this sit-

FIGURE 11-2   UNION WAGE DIFFERENTIAL OVER TIME

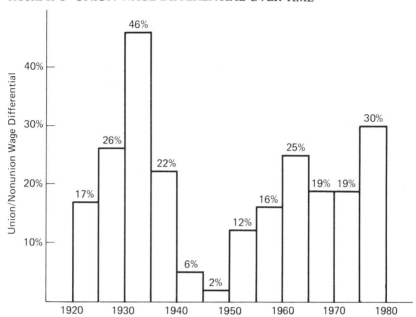

SOURCE: *George Johnson, "Changes Over Time in the Union/Nonunion Wage Differential in the United States" (University of Michigan, February 1981, mimeographed), table 2. Approximate percentage differentials were calculated as antilogs of estimated union coefficients in semilog regression models.*

uation, both organized and unorganized employees receive wage benefits from unionization.

Unionization has also been shown to decrease the variance of wages within the bargaining unit (as compared to nonunion organizations).[13] This is not surprising, since unions commonly favor raises granted across-the-board, prefer seniority over merit for differentials, and oppose competition among members of the bargaining unit.

Unions appear to have a particularly profound effect on supplemental benefits. One study found they significantly increased the value of pensions, insurance, vacations, and holidays and decreased the use of overtime, sick leave and bonuses.[14] Another found that unionization increased the value of the benefit package for blue collar workers by an average of 28 to 36 percent.[15]

Table 11-7 is a synopsis of the overall effects of unionization on pay and benefits.

An appendix describing how to evaluate labor costs for a collective bargaining agreement appears at the end of this chapter.

TABLE 11-7 RECENT EVIDENCE ON UNION/NONUNION DIFFERENCES BASED ON CROSS-SECTIONAL DATA

Variable	Finding
Wage rates	All else (measurable) the same, union/nonunion hourly wage differential is between 10% and 20%.
Fringes	All else the same, union/nonunion hourly fringe differential is between 20% and 30%. The fringe share of compensation is higher at a given level of compensation.
Wage dispersion	Wage inequality is much lower among union members than among comparable nonmembers, and total wage dispersion appears to be lowered by unionism.
Wage structure	Wage differentials between workers who are different in terms of race, age, service, skill level, and education appear to be lower under collective bargaining.
Cyclical responsiveness of wage rates	Union wages are less responsive to labor market conditions than nonunion wages.
Determinants of compensation differential	Other things equal, the union compensation advantage is higher the greater the percent of a market's workers who are organized. The effects of market concentration on wage differentials is unclear. The differentials appear to be very large in some regulated markets. They appear to decline as firm size increases.

SOURCE: *Richard B. Freeman and James L. Medoff, "The Impact of Collective Bargaining: Illusion or Reality?", U.S. Industrial Relations 1950–1980: A Critical Assessment (Madison, Wis.: Industrial Relations Research Association, 1981), p. 50.*

Notes

1. John A. Fossum, *Labor Relations*, 3d ed. (Plano, Tex.: BPI Pub., 1985), p. 188.
2. William H. Holley and Kenneth M. Jennings, *The Labor Relations Process*, 2d ed. (Chicago: Dryden Press, 1984), pp. 404–405.
3. Fossum, p. 203.
4. *Ibid.*, p. 204.
5. Holley and Jennings, p. 417.
6. Betty W. Justice, *Unions, Workers, and the Law* (Washington, D.C.: BNA Books, 1983), p. 89.
7. Holley and Jennings, p. 417.
8. Fossum, p. 204.
9. Daniel J. B. Mitchell, *Unions, Wages and Inflation* (Washington, D.C.: Brookings Institution, 1980), pp. 80–83.
10. William J. Moore and John Raisian, "The Level and Growth of Union/Nonunion Relative Wage Effects, 1967–1977," *Journal of Labor Research*, Winter 1983, pp. 65–79.
11. Richard B. Freeman and James L. Medoff, *What Do Unions Do?* (New York: Basic Books, 1984), pp. 56–57.
12. Susan Vroman, "The Direction of Wage Spillovers in Manufacturing," *Industrial and Labor Relations Review*, October 1982, pp. 102–112.

13. Richard B. Freeman, "Union Wage Practices and Wage Dispersion within Establishments," *Industrial and Labor Relations Review,* October 1982, pp. 3–21.

14. Fossum, p. 209.

15. Richard B. Freeman and James L. Medoff, "The Impact of Collective Bargaining: Illusion or Reality?" in Jack Stieber et al., eds., *U.S. Industrial Relations 1950–1980: A Critical Assessment* (Madison, Wis.: Industrial Relations Research Association, 1981), pp. 53–54.

Discussion Questions

1. Discuss and evaluate wage-determination standards.
2. Describe and evaluate incentive plans.
3. Evaluate the strengths and weaknesses of the various methods of wage adjustment during a contract.
4. Assess the role and effect of supplemental benefits.
5. Describe how the distribution of benefits is determined.
6. Discuss the effects of wage and benefit demands.

Statements for Comment

1. "Big unions and big business have been in bed together at least since the end of World War II."
2. "Escalator clauses are not a cause of inflation—they are a reaction to it."
3. "Having a union is certain to decrease the emphasis on merit pay."
4. "Improved employee benefits are in competition with increased employment."
5. "An obvious solution to COLA problems is to shorten the duration of contracts."

Situations

Case 11–1 Pamela Webster, cost accountant for a large insurance company, was reviewing the demands of its unionized clerical employees for wage adjustments during bargaining. The union has requested double-time pay for work on Saturdays (employees currently receive time and one half) and triple time on Sundays and holidays (up from the current double time). The union has also requested a reduction in the length of the workday from eight hours to seven.

How should Pamela treat these demands? What questions should management be asking itself and the union? What else do you need or want to know?

Case 11–2 Melvin Johnson, the personnel manager of the insurance company, is troubled by the union's demand for across-the-board pay raises based on positions rather than on the performance of the individual in that job. This emphasis comes as no surprise to Melvin and he is prepared for it.

What arguments should Melvin make, what tactics should he pursue, and what results should he expect?

Case 11-3 Michael Stokes, vice-president of human resources administration for a large, unionized manufacturing company, has come up with a new job enrichment program that will greatly increase employee smiles per hour. The problem is, it won't quite pay for itself—even after considering all the arguments for improved morale, reduced turnover, improved quality, etc. Still, he thinks it is a good idea and would like to do this for the employees' benefit.

"Chief, I have an excellent idea that would be a great human gain for us but it won't quite pay for itself," said Michael to Suzanne Simmons, the company president. "May I implement it?"

What should Suzanne ask him? Are there circumstances in which a company might forego some level of profit increase in exchange for making employees happy? What if those employees are executives? Does it matter if the company is unionized? Why or why not?

Case 11-4 William Reston is vice-president of human resources for Scooter Craft, Inc., a large manufacturing company with plants in several states. All the production and maintenance employees are represented by a union. None of the other employees are.

The union, of course, bargains over wages and benefits for the employees it represents. In recent years the union's efforts have been, in everyone's opinion, highly successful. The employees represented by the union have been very grateful for that success. Ironically, so have the nonunion personnel.

The company, like many others, pursues a policy of "tandem" raises. That is, whatever benefits are won by the union are passed along automatically to the nonunion personnel from the clerical level through the managerial level. When vacation or health-care benefits are improved in the contract, the company also extends those benefits to the nonunion personnel. When wages are raised, similar raises are extended to the others both to preserve perceived parity and to negate the perceived need for a union.

Lately, Mr. Reston has become concerned with what he perceives to be some adverse side effects of his policy. Namely, it has come to his attention that many of his nonunion employees (including some supervisors) are "rooting" (and some not too subtly) for the union against the company in its bargaining efforts. This distresses Mr. Reston greatly.

Can you recommend to Mr. Reston ways to change the nonunion employees' perceptions without causing more harm than good? Identify the goals of your salary program and how they would be achieved.

Bibliography of Related Readings

Alpert, W. T., "Unions and Private Wage Supplements," *Journal of Labor Research,* 1982, pp. 179–99.

Babson, Stanley M., Jr., *Fringe Benefits—The Depreciation, Obsolescence and Transience of Man* (New York: John Wiley & Sons, 1974).

Cooper, R. D., "Employee Benefits in the 1980s," *Compensation Review*, 1981, pp. 57–61.

Dunlop, John J., *Wage Determination Under Trade Unions* (New York: Augustus M. Kelly, Inc., 1950).

Fosu, A. K., "Impact of Unionism on Pension Fringes," *Industrial Relations*, 1983, pp. 419–25.

Freedman, Audrey, *Security Bargains Reconsidered: SUB, Severance Pay, Guaranteed Work* (New York: Conference Board, 1978).

Freeman, R. B., "Union Wage Practices and Wage Dispersion Within Establishments," *Industrial and Labor Relations Review*, 1982, pp. 2–31.

Garbarino, Joseph W., *Wage Policy and Long-Term Contracts* (Washington, D.C.: Brookings Institution, 1962).

Kwoka, J. E., Jr., "Monopoly, Plant, and Union Effects on Worker Wages," *Industrial and Labor Relations Review*, 1983, pp. 251–57.

Long, J. E., and A. N. Link, "The Impact of Market Structure Wages, Fringe Benefits, and Turnover," *Industrial and Labor Review*, 1983, pp. 239–50.

Patten, Thomas H., *Pay: Employee Compensation and Incentive Plans* (New York: The Free Press, 1977).

Sherry, R. L., "The Economics of Collective Bargaining: A Literature Review Essay," *Labor Studies Journal*, 1980, pp. 99–105.

Appendix I

CALCULATING WAGE AND BENEFIT COSTS:[1]
INTRODUCING THE PROBLEM

"Compensation" consists of both salaries and/or wages and fringe benefits. It encompasses all forms of wage payments (including, for example, bonuses, commissions, and incentive payments) as well as the cost to the employer of all types of fringes.[2] Obviously, the higher-paid, senior employees in the bargaining unit tend to enjoy higher compensation, while the compensation of those at the opposite end of the salary and seniority spectrums tends to be lower.

For bargaining purposes, the most relevant statistic is the unit's average compensation or, more specifically, its *weighted* average compensation. The weighted average compensation (hereafter "average compensation" or, simply, "compensation") is merely an expression of how much it costs the employer, on the average, for each person on the payroll. It is this figure which presumably will be increased through negotiations.[3]

Although precision in computing these compensation costs depends very much on detailed data usually available only in the employer's payroll records, it is possible to develop some reasonably accurate approximations even without such detailed information. . . .

These computations (to repeat) are not performed simply to engage in a mathematical exercise. The reason for seeking out this type of information is its usefulness at the bargaining table.

The value of salaries and fringe benefits must be known so that the value of any bargaining offer or settlement can be judged. Logically, therefore, the base compensation costs as of the point in time of negotiations—or, more accurately, immediately prior to the receipt of any increase—must be known.

The information that is needed in most cases in order to compute compensation costs is (a) the salary scales and benefit programs, (b) the distribution of the employees in the unit according to pay steps, shifts, and length of service, and (c) for purposes of some medical care programs, the employees' coverage status. If this information is in hand, just about all but one item of compensation can be readily computed.

The sole exception is the cost of the overtime premium. Overtime is apt to vary widely from week-to-week or month-to-month. Consequently, the data for any one pay period are an inadequate gauge where overtime is concerned. Simply by chance, it may cost the employer more one week than the next. It is common practice, therefore, to cost-out the overtime premium by averaging the cost of that benefit over the prior 12 months.

So far as the other elements of compensation are concerned, however, it is not necessary to study a full year's experience. With salaries, vacations, holidays, etc., the costs can be based on a snapshot taken at a fixed point in time on the basis of the provisions in the current collective bargaining agreement and the current distribution of the employees in the bargaining unit. That snapshot of compensation costs should be made as of the time the parties are at the bargaining table.

The purpose of this Appendix is to provide guidance on how to perform those computations, as well as the computations to determine the cost—the value—of an *increase* in compensation. The development of such compensation information gives the parties a basis for weighing the value of any particular wage and fringe benefit package.

Before the value or cost impact of any increase in compensation—whether in salaries, fringes, or both—can be gauged, the first step is to develop the base, or existing, compensation figure. A pay increase of $500 per employee, for example, means something different for a bargaining unit whose existing salary and fringe benefit cost per employee amount to $20,000 per year than for a unit whose compensation is $10,000. In the latter case, it represents an increase of 5 percent, but on a base of $20,000 it amounts to only 2½ percent. Thus, the base compensation figure is essential in determining the percentage value of any increase in compensation.

In order to demonstrate the computation methods for arriving at the base compensation figure, a Sample Bargaining Unit of firefighters has been constructed and certain levels of employment, salaries, fringe benefits and hours of work have been assumed.

Sample Bargaining Unit

(a) Employment and Salaries

Classification	Number of Firefighters	Salary
Probationary		
Step 1	5	$10,100
Step 2	10	11,100
Private	65	12,100
Lieutenant	15	13,500
Captain	5	14,500
	100	

(b) Longevity Payments

Longevity Step	Number of Firefighters	Longevity Pay
Step 1	20 Privates	$ 500
Step 2	10 Privates	1,000
Step 2	15 Lieutenants	1,000
Step 2	5 Captains	1,000

(c) Hours of Work. The scheduled hours consist of one 24-hour shift every three days (one on; two off), or an average of 56 hours per week and a total of 2,912 hours per year.

(d) Overtime Premium. All overtime hours are paid at the rate of time-and-one-half. The sample bargaining unit is assumed to have worked a total of 5,000 overtime hours during the preceding year.

(e) Shift Differential. The shift differential is 10 percent for all hours between 4 P.M. and 8 A.M. However, ten members of the unit work exclusively on the day shift, from 8 A.M. to 4 P.M.

(f) Vacations

15 employees—(probationers) 5 shifts

35 employees—(privates) 10 shifts

50 employees—(all others) 15 shifts

(g) Holidays. Each firefighter is entitled to 10 paid holidays, and receives 8 hours pay for each holiday.

(h) Clothing Allowance. $150 per employee per year.

(i) Hospitalization

Type of Coverage	Number of Firefighters	Employer's Monthly Payment
Single	15	$20.00
Family	85	47.00

(j) Pensions. The employer contributes an amount equal to 6 percent of the payroll (including basic salaries, longevity, overtime, and shift differentials).

Average Employee Compensation in Unit

On the basis of the foregoing information on employment, salaries and benefits, we are now in a position to compute, for the Sample Bargaining Unit, its average base compensaton—in essence, the cost of compensation for the average employee.

(a) Average Straight-time Salary

(1) Classification	(2) Number of Firefighters	(3) Salary	(4) Weighted Salaries (2) × (3)
Probationary			
Step 1	5	$10,100	$ 50,500
Step 2	10	11,100	111,000
Private	65	12,100	786,500
Lieutenant	15	13,500	202,500
Captain	5	14,500	72,500
	100		$1,223,000

Average annual basic salary = $1,223,000 ÷ 100; or $12,230 per year

(b) Longevity Pay

(1) Longevity Step	(2) Number of Firefighters	(3) Longevity Pay	(4) Total Longevity Pay (2) × (3)
Step 1	20	$ 500	$10,000
Step 2	30	1,000	30,000
			$40,000

Average annual longevity pay = $40,000 ÷ 100;* or $400 per year

*Since the unit is trying to determine its average base compensation—that is, all the salary and fringe benefit items its members receive collectively—the total cost of longevity pay must be averaged over the entire unit of 100.

The combined average salary cost and average longevity cost amount to $12,630 per year. On an hourly basis, this comes to $4.337 ($12,630 ÷ 2,912 hours). This hourly rate is needed to compute the cost of some fringe benefits.

(c) Average Cost of Overtime. Overtime work for the Sample Bargaining Unit is assumed to be paid for at the rate of time-and-one-half. This means that part of the total overtime costs is an amount paid for at straight-time rates and part is a premium payment.

	(1) Annual Cost	(2) Number of Firefighters	(3) Average Annual Cost (1) ÷ (2)
Straight-time cost (4.337 × 5,000 overtime hours)	$21,685.00	100	$216.85
Half-time premium cost (½ × $21,685.00)	10,842.50	100	108.43
Total overtime cost	$32,527.50		$325.28

It can be seen from these overtime-cost calculations that the half-time premium is worth $108.43 per year on the average, while the straight-time portion is worth $216.85. This means, of course, that total pay at straight-time rates amounts to $12,846.85 ($12,630 plus $216.85) per firefighter.

(d) Average Cost of Shift Differential. The Sample Bargaining Unit receives a shift differential of 10 percent for all hours worked between 4 P.M. and 8 A.M. But 10 members of the unit who work in headquarters are assumed to work hours that are not subject to the differential. This leaves 90 employees who receive the differential.

Since the differential is paid for hours worked between 4 P.M. and 8 A.M., it is applicable to only two-thirds of the normal 24-hour shift. It, therefore, only costs the employer two-thirds of 10 percent for each 24 hours. That is the reason for column (5) in the following calculation. Each employee receives the differential for only two-thirds of his 24-hour tour.

(1) Classification	(2) No. on Shift Pay	(3) Salary	(4) 10% of Col. (3)	(5) .667 of Col. (4)	(6) Total Cost (2) × (5)
Probationary					
Step 1	5	$10,100	$1,010	$ 674	$ 3,370
Step 2	10	11,100	1,110	740	7,400
Private					
Longevity—0	35	12,100	1,210	807	28,245
Longevity—1	17	12,600*	1,260	840	14,280
Longevity—2	7	13,100*	1,310	874	6,118

(continued)

(1) Classification	(2) No. on Shift Pay	(3) Salary	(4) 10% of Col. (3)	(5) .667 of Col. (4)	(6) Total Cost (2) × (5)
Lieutenant	12	14,500*	1,450	967	11,604
Captain	4	15,500*	1,550	1,034	4,136
	90				$75,153

Average annual cost of shift differential = $75,153 ÷ 100;† or $751.53 per year

*Basic salary plus longevity pay.
†Since the unit is trying to determine its average base compensation—that is, all the salary and fringe benefit items its members receive collectively—the total cost of the shift differential must be averaged over the entire unit of 100.

(e) Average Cost of Vacations. Vacation costs for the unit are influenced by (a) the amount of vacations received by the employees with differing lengths of service, and (b) the pay scales of those employees.

(1) Classification	(2) Number of Firefighters	(3) Hourly Rate*	(4) Hours of Vacation†	(5) Total Vacation Hours (2) × (4)	(6) Total Vacation Costs (3) × (5)
Probationary					
Step 1	5	$3.468	120	600	$ 2,080.80
Step 2	10	3.812	120	1,200	4,574.40
Private					
Longevity—0	35	4.155	240	8,400	34,902.00
Longevity—1	20	4.327	360	7,200	31,154.40
Longevity—2	10	4.499	360	3,600	16,196.40
Lieutenant	15	4.979	360	5,400	26,886.60
Captain	5	5.323	360	1,800	9,581.40
	100				$125,376.00

Average annual vacation cost = $125,376 ÷ 100; or $1,253.76 per year

*Derived from annual salaries (including longevity pay), divided by 2,912 hours (56 hours × 52 weeks). The 10 firefighters who do not receive shift differential would be on a regular 40-hour week and would, therefore, have a different hourly rate and vacation entitlement. The impact on cost, however, would be minimal. It has, therefore, been disregarded in this computation.
†Since each firefighter works a 24-hour shift, the hours of vacation are arrived at by multiplying the number of work shifts of vacation entitlement by 24 hours. For example, the figure of 120 hours is obtained by multiplying 5 shifts of vacation × 24 hours (one work shift).

(f) Average Cost of Paid Holidays. Unlike vacations, the number of holidays received by an employee is not typically tied to length of service. Where the level of benefits is uniform, as it is with paid holidays, the calculation to determine its average cost is less complex.

In the Sample Bargaining Unit, it is assumed that each firefighter receives 8 hours of pay for each of his 10 paid holidays, or a total of 80 hours of holiday pay:

1. Average annual cost of paid holidays = $346.96 (80 hours × $4.337 average straight-time hourly rate), or
2. Total annual cost of paid holiday hours per year = 8,000 (80 hours × 100 employees)

Total annual cost of paid holidays = $34,696.00 (the unit's average straight-time hourly rate of $4.337 × 8,000 hours)

Average annual cost of paid holidays = $346.96 (34,696.00 ÷ 100 employees)

(g) Average Cost of Hospitalization

(1) Type of Coverage	(2) Number of Firefighters	(3) Yearly Premium Cost to Employer	(4) Total Cost to Employer (2) × (3)
Single	15	$240	$ 3,600
Family	85	564	47,940
	100		$51,540

Average annual cost of hospitalization = $51,540 ÷ 100; or $515.40 per year

(h) Other Fringe Benefits

1. Pensions cost the employer 6 percent of payroll. The payroll amounts to $1,370,723 (salary cost—$1,223,000; longevity cost—$40,000; overtime cost—$32,528; and shift differential $75,195). Six percent of this total is $82,243, which, when divided by 100, yields $822.43 as the average cost of pensions per firefighter, per year.
2. The yearly cost of the clothing allowance is $150 per firefighter.

Recapitulation

As the recapitulation below indicates, total compensation—salary plus fringes—for each firefighter averages $16,795.78 per year.

Once having determined the base compensation costs, it is now possible to compute the value—or cost—of any increase in the items of compensation. The methods used to make these computations are essentially the same as those used to compute the base compensation data.

Average Annual Base Compensation for the Sample Bargaining Unit

(a) Straight-time earnings	$12,846.85	(b) Fringe benefits	$ 3,948.93
Basic salary	$12,230.00	Overtime premium	$ 108.43
Longevity pay	400.00	Shift differential	751.95
Overtime	216.85*	Vacations	1,253.76
		Holidays	346.96
		Hospitalization	515.40
		Clothing allowance	150.00
		Pension	822.43
		(c) Total	$16,795.78

This is only the straight-time portion of overtime pay. The premium portion appears with the fringe benefits.

COMPUTING THE COST OF INCREASES IN ITEMS OF COMPENSATON

In order to demonstrate how to cost-out any increases in compensation, it will be assumed that the Sample Bargaining Unit negotiates a settlement consisting of the following package:

An increase of 5 percent in basic salaries;

Two additional shifts of vacation for all those at the second step of longevity;

An improvement in the benefits provided by the hospitalization program, which will cost the employer an additional $4.00 per month for family coverage and $2.50 for single coverage.

The cost of this settlement—that is, the amount of the increase in compensation that it represents—would be computed in the manner presented below, starting first with the cost-impact of the salary increase. As will be noted, the objective of the computation is to find the *average* cost of the increase—that is, the cost per firefighter, per year.

(a) Increase in Cost of Salaries

The increase in average annual basic salary (0.05 × $12,230) is $611.50. The cost of longevity pay does not increase. This is because longevity increments for the unit are fixed dollar amounts. If these payments were based on a percentage of salary—that is, if they were linked to the pay scales—then the cost of the longevity payments would also have risen by 5 percent. However, as a fixed dollar amount, these payments remain unaffected by the increase in basic salaries.

As a result, the increase in the unit's total average salary ($12,230 in basic salary plus $400 in longevity) is, in reality, not 5 percent, but only 4.8 percent ($611.50 ÷ $12,630).

This difference is important because of the way in which pay increases impact on the cost of fringe benefits. This is commonly referred to as the ''roll up.'' As salaries increase, so does the cost to the employer of such fringes as vacations, holidays, overtime premiums, etc. This increase in cost comes about even though the benefits are not improved.

Some fringes, however, are not subject to the roll up. This is the case with respect to those fringe benefits that are not linked to pay rates. Examples of this type of fringe benefit include shift differentials that are stated in cents-per-hour (in contrast to a percentage of salary), a flat dollar amount for clothing allowance, and most group insurance programs.

(b) Cost Impact of the "Roll up"

The increase in average straight-time pay (basic salary plus longevity pay) of the Sample Bargaining Unit was shown to be 4.8 percent. This means that the average cost of every benefit linked to salary will likewise increase by 4.8 percent. In our example, therefore, the average cost of compensation will go up by $611.50 per year in salaries, *plus* however much this adds to the costs of the fringe benefits as a result of the roll up.

But there is more. For our example, it is also to be assumed that the Sample Bargaining Unit will gain a vacation improvement—two additional shifts at the second step of longevity—and an improved hospitalization program.

The employer's contribution for the hospitalization program of the Sample Bargaining Unit is a fixed dollar amount and is, therefore, not subject to any roll up. Thus, we need in this instance be concerned only with the costing-out of the improvement in that benefit.

This is not the case with the vacations. Here the cost-increase is double-barreled—the cost of the improvement *and* the cost of the roll up.

None of the other fringe benefits of the Sample Bargaining Unit will be improved. Consequently, so far as they are concerned, we need only compute the increases in cost due to the roll up. The fringes which fit this category are overtime premiums, holidays, sick leave, shift differentials, and pensions.

(1) Fringe Benefit	(2) Base Average Annual Cost	(3) Roll-up Factor	(4) Increased Cost (2) × (3)
Overtime			
Straight time	$216.85	0.048	$ 10.41
Premium	108.43	0.048	5.20
Shift differential	751.95	0.048	36.09
Holidays	346.96	0.048	16.65
Pensions	822.43	0.048	39.48
			$107.83

As is indicated in the table, column (3)—the added cost due to the roll up—is obtained by multiplying the base (presettlement) cost by 0.048. Obviously, if shift differentials and/or pensions were based on a set dollar (or cent) amount (instead of a percentage of salary), there would be no roll-up cost associated with them. The only increase in cost that would result in such a situation would be associated with an improvement in the benefit item.

Having performed this computation, we can now begin to see the impact of this roll up factor. As a result of the increase in pay, the four fringe benefit items will together cost the employer an additional $107.83 per firefighter, per year.

(c) Increase in Cost of Vacations

As noted earlier, the vacation improvement of two shifts—48 hours (2 shifts × 24 hours)—is to be limited to those whose length of service is equal to the time required to achieve the second step of longevity in the salary structure. Thus, it will be received by 30 members of the unit—10 privates, 15 lieutenants, and 5 captains.[4]

The first step in the computation is to determine the cost of the *new* benefit under the *existing* (old) salaries—that is, before the 4.8 percent pay increase:

(1) Number of Firefighters	(2) Hours of Increased Vacation	(3) Total Hours (1) × (2)	(4) Existing Hourly Rates	(5) Cost of Improvement (3) × (4)
10 Privates	48	480	$4.499	$2,159.52
15 Lieutenants	48	720	4.979	3,584.88
5 Capatins	48	240	5.323	$1,277.52
				$7,021.92

The calculation thus far reflects only the additional cost of the vacation improvement based on the salaries existing *prior to* the 4.8 percent pay raise. In other words, if there had been no pay increase, the vacation improvement would result in an added cost of $7,021.92. But there was a pay increase. As a result, the base-year vacation costs—including now the added cost of the improvement—must be rolled up by the 4.8 percent factor. Every hour of vacation—the old and the new—will cost 4.8 percent more as a result of the pay increase:

(1) Classification	(2) Existing Vacation Costs	(3) Increase in Cost	(4) Adjusted Base Costs (2) + (3)	(5) Roll-up Factor	(6) Increased Cost from Roll up (4) × (5)
Probationary					
Step 1	$ 2,080.80	—	$ 2,080.80	0.048	$ 99.88
Step 2	4,574.40	—	4,574,40	0.048	219.57

(1)	(2)	(3)	(4)	(5)	(6)
	Existing Vacation	Increase	Adjusted Base Costs	Roll up	Increased Cost from Roll up
Classification	Costs	in Cost	(2) + (3)	Factor	(4) × (5)
Private					
Longevity—0	34,902.00	—	34,902.00	0.048	1,675.30
Longevity—1	31,154.40	—	31,154.40	0.048	1,495.41
Longevity—2	16,196.40	$2,159.52	18,355.92	0.048	881.08
Lieutenant	26,886.60	3,584.88	30,471.48	0.048	1,462.63
Captain	9,581.40	1,277.52	10,858.92	0.048	521.23
	$125,376.00	$7,021.92	$132,397.92	0.048	$6,355.10

By adding the two "new" pieces of cost—$7,021.92, which is the cost of the improvement, and $6,355.10, which is the cost due to the impact of the wage increase—we obtain the total increase in the cost of vacations. It amounts to $13,377.02. In order to figure the *average* cost, this total must be divided by the number of firefighers in the Sample Bargaining Unit. The increase in the average cost of vacations, therefore, is

$$13,377 \div 100, \text{ or } \$133.77$$

Had the vacation improvement been granted across-the-board, to everyone in the unit, the calculation would have been different—and considerably easier. If the entire unit were to receive an additional 48 hours of vacation, the total additional hours would then be 4,800 (48 hours × 100 employees). These hours would then be multiplied by the unit's old average straight-time rate ($4.337), in order to arrive at the cost of the additional vacation improvement which, in this case, would have come to $20,817.60 (4,800 hours × $4.337). And, in that case, the total cost of vacations—that is the across-the-board improvement, plus the impact of the 4.8 percent salary increase—would have been computed as follows:

(a) Roll up of old vacation costs ($125,376 × 0.048)	= $ 6,018.05
(b) Cost of vacation improvement	= $20,817.60
(c) Roll-up cost of improvement ($20,817.60 × 0.048)	= $ 999.24

These pieces total to $27,834.89. When spread over the entire Sample Bargaining Unit, the increase in the average cost of vacations would have been $278.35 per year ($27,834.89 ÷ 100 employees).

This latter method of calculation does not apply only to vacations. It applies to any situation where a salary-related fringe benefit is to be improved equally for every member of the unit. An additional paid holiday would be another good example.

(d) Increase in Cost of Hospitalization

In this example, it has been assumed that the Sample Bargaining Unit has negotiated as part of its new package an improvement in its hospitalization plan. As with most hospitalization programs, the one covering this unit is not linked to salaries.

This improvement, it is assumed, will cost the employer an additional $4.00 per month ($48 per year) for family coverage, and $2.50 per month ($30 per year) for single coverage. Thus, based on this and previous information about the breakdown of employees receiving each type of coverage the calculation of the increase in hospitalization costs is as follows:

(1) Type of Coverage	(2) Annual Number Covered	(3) Total New Cost of Improvement	(4) Cost (2) × (3)
Single	15	$30	$ 450
Family	85	48	4,080
			$4,530

The unit's average hospitalization cost will be increased by $45.30 per year ($4,530 ÷ 100 employees).

THE TOTAL INCREASE IN THE AVERAGE COST OF COMPENSATION

At this point, the increase in the costs of all the items of compensation which will change because of the Sample Bargaining Unit's newly negotiated package have been calculated. All that is left is to combine these individual pieces in order to arrive at the total increase in the unit's average cost of compensation. This is done in the tabulation which appears on page 267.

As the recapitulation shows, the average increase in salary costs amounts to $621.91 per year, while the average increase in the cost of the fringe benefits (including *new* benefit costs, as well as *roll-up* costs) comes to $276.49, for a total increase in average annual compensation of $898.40 per firefighter, per *year*. That is the total annual cost of the settlement per firefighter.

There remains one final computation that is really the most significant—the *percent* increase that all of these figures represent. The unit's average base compensation per year was $16,796. The total dollar increase amounts to $898. The percent increase, therefore, is 5.3 percent ($898 ÷ $16.796), and that is the amount by which the unit's package increased the employer's average yearly cost per firefighter.

INCREASE IN AVERAGE ANNUAL COST OF COMPENSATION FOR SAMPLE BARGAINING UNIT

(a) Straight-time earnings	$621.91	(b) Fringe benefits	$276.49
		Overtime premium	$ 5.20
Basic salary	$611.50	Shift differential	36.09
Longevity pay	—	Vacations	133.77
Overtime (straight-		Holidays	16.65
time portion)	10.41	Hospitalization	45.30
		Clothing allowance	—
		Pensions	39.48
		(c) Total increase in average annual cost of compensation	$898.40

COMPUTING THE HOURLY COST OF COMPENSATION

The increase in the cost of compensation per *hour* will be the same. The approach to the computation, however, is different than that which was used in connection with the cost per year. In the case of the hourly computation, the goal is to obtain the cost per hour of *work*. This requires that a distinction be drawn between hours worked and hours paid for. The difference between the two is leave time.

In the Sample Bargaining Unit, for example, the employee receives an annual salary which covers 2,912 regularly scheduled hours (56 hours per week, times 52). In addition, he works an average of 50 hours of overtime per year. The sum of these two—regularly scheduled hours and overtime hours, or 2,962—are the total hours paid for.

But they do not represent hours worked, because some of those hours are paid leave time. The Sample Bargaining Unit, for example, receives paid leave time in the form of vacations and holidays. The number of hours actually worked by each employee is 2,600 (2,962 hours paid for, minus 362 hours[5] of paid leave).

The paid leave hours are, in a sense, bonuses—hours paid for, above and beyond hours worked. Thus, in order to obtain the hourly cost represented by these "bonuses"—that is, the hours of paid leave—the annual dollar cost of these benefits is divided by the annual hours *worked*.

It is the same as if we were trying to compute the per-hour cost of a year-end bonus. The dollar amount of that bonus would simply be divided by the total number of hours worked during the year.

So it is with *all* fringe benefits, not only paid leave. In exchange for those benefits the employer receives hours of work (the straight-time hours and the overtime hours). Consequently, the hourly cost of any fringe benefit will be obtained by dividing the annual cost of the benefit by the annual number of hours *worked*. In some instances that cost is converted into money that ends up in the employee's pocket, as it does in the case of fringe benefits like shift differentials, overtime premiums and clothing allowances. In other instances—such as hospitalization and pensions—the employee is provided with benefits in the form of insurance programs. And in the case of paid leave time—holidays,[6] vacations, sick leave, etc.—the return to the employee is in terms of fewer hours of work.

The average annual costs of the fringe benefits of the Sample Bargaining Unit were developed earlier in connection with the computations of the unit's average annual base compensation. They appear in column (2) under average annual cost.

15 firefighters × 120 hours (five 24-hour shifts)	=	1,800 hours
35 firefighters × 240 hours (ten 24-hour shifts)	=	8,400 hours
50 firefighters × 360 hours (fifteen 24-hour shifts)	=	18,000 hours
		28,200 hours

This averages out to 282 hours of vacation per firefighter (28,200 ÷ 100), which, together with 80 holiday hours, totals 362 paid leave hours.

In order to convert the costs of those fringe benefits into an average hourly amount, they are divided by 2,600—the average hours worked during the year by each employee in the unit. As can be seen, the hourly cost of all fringe benefits amounts to $1.518.

(1)	(2)	(3)	(4)
			Average
	Average	Average Hours	Hourly Cost
Fringe Benefit	Annual Cost	Worked	(2) ÷ (3)
Overtime premium*	$ 108.43	2,600	$0.042
Shift differential	751.95	2,600	0.289
Vacations	1,253.76	2,600	0.482
Holidays	346.96	2,600	0.133
Hospitalization	515.40	2,600	0.198
Clothing allowance	150.00	2,600	0.058
Pensions	822.43	2,600	0.316
	$3,948.93		$1.518

Includes only the premium portion of the pay for overtime work.

In addition to the fringe benefit costs, compensation includes the basic pay. For our Sample Bargaining Unit this is $12,630 per year (average salary plus average cost of longevity payments). On a straight-time hourly basis, this comes to $4.337 ($12,630 ÷ 2,912 hours). Even with the straight-time portion for the year's overtime included ($216.85), the average straight-time hourly rate of pay will, of course, still remain at $4.337 ($12,846.45 ÷ 2,962 hours).

A recapitulation of these salary and fringe benefit cost data produces both the average *annual* base compensation figure for the Sample Bargaining Unit and the average *hourly* figure:

	Hourly	Yearly
Earnings at straight time	$12,846.85 ÷ 2,962 =	$4.337
Fringe benefits	3,948.93 ÷ 2,600 =	$1.519
Total compensation	$16,795.78	$5.856

As indicated, on an annual basis, the average compensation cost comes to $16,795.78, a figure that was also presented earlier. And on an hourly basis, the average compensation of the unit amounts to $5.856.

Essentially the same process is followed if the *increase* in compensation is to be measured on an hourly (instead of an annual) basis.

The 5 percent pay increase received by the Sample Bargaining Unit would be worth 21 cents ($12,230 × 0.05 = $611.50; $611.50 ÷ 2,912 = $0.21). The annual increase in the unit's fringe benefit costs per firefighter—$276.49 for all items combined—works out to 10.6 cents per hour ($276.49 ÷ *2600* hours).

Together, these represent a gain in average compensation of 31.6 cents per hour, or 5.4 percent ($0.316 ÷ $5.856). This is one-tenth of a percentage point off from the amount of increase (5.3 percent) reflected by the annual data— a difference due simply to the rounding of decimals during the computation process.

Notes

1. Excerpted from a U.S. Department of Labor publication entitled, *The Use of Economic Data in Collective Bargaining*, as written in 1978 by the Labor-Management Services Administration.
2. Technically, employee compensation may also include the cost of legally required employer payments for programs such as social security, unemployment compensation, and worker's compensation. These items are disregarded in this analysis.
3. It is also referred to as the "base" compensation—that is, the compensation figure against which the cost of any settlement will be measured in order to determine the value of the settlement.
4. In costing out an improvement in vacations, the computation should cover the cost impact in the first year *only*. There is no need to be concerned with the impact in subsequent years when, supposedly, more and more employees become eligible for the improved benefit. For computational purposes, it must be assumed that the average length of service in the unit remains constant. This constancy is caused by normal personnel flows. As the more senior staff leave because of retirement or death, the staff is replenished by new hires without any accumulated seniority. Thus, for this type of computation, it must be presumed that the proportion of the workforce which benefits from the improved vacation will be constant year after year.

It should be noted that an improvement in vacations (or any other form of paid leave) that is offset by corresponding reductions in on-duty manning does not represent any increase in cost to the employer.

5. Each firefighter receives 80 hours in paid holidays per year. The average number of hours of vacation per year was derived as follows.

6. Typically, of course, firefighters do not receive time off, but are paid an extra day's pay for working a holiday.

Appendix II Amended Agreement on Supplemental Unemployment Benefits

TABLE OF CONTENTS

THIS AGREEMENT made this 30th day of April, 1982, by and between THE GOODYEAR TIRE & RUBBER COMPANY (hereinafter referred to as the "Company") and THE UNITED RUBBER, CORK, LINOLEUM & PLASTIC WORKERS OF AMERICA, AFL-CIO-CLC, International Union, and the Local Unions thereof executing this Agreement (hereinafter referred to as the "Union").

WHEREAS: The parties hereto established a Supplemental Unemployment Benefits Plan by an "Agreement on Supplemental Unemployment Benefits"

dated September 11, 1956, as heretofore amended, and

WHEREAS: The parties now desire to extend and to provide for further modifications and amendments of the Plan.

NOW, THEREFORE, IT IS MUTUALLY AGREED THAT SAID AGREEMENT AS HERETOFORE AMENDED IS HEREBY EXTENDED AND FURTHER AMENDED AS FOLLOWS:

SUPPLEMENTAL UNEMPLOYMENT BENEFITS PLAN

ARTICLE I
ELIGIBILITY FOR BENEFITS

Section 1 — Eligibility for a Regular Benefit

An Employee shall be eligible for a Regular Benefit for any Week beginning on or after the effective date of this Agreement if with respect to such Week he:

(a) was on a qualifying layoff, as described in Section 4 of this Article, for all or part of the Week;

(b) received a State System Benefit not currently under protest by the Company or was ineligible for a State System Benefit only for one or more of the following reasons:

(1) he did not have prior to layoff a suf-

SOURCE: The Bureau of National Affairs, Inc.

ficient period of employment or earnings covered by the State System;

(2) exhaustion of his State System Benefit rights;

(3) the amount of his pay (from the Company or otherwise) for the Week (and in New York State for the period he worked in the week);

(4) he was serving a State System "waiting week" while temporarily laid off out of line of Seniority pending placement under the terms of the Collective Bargaining Agreement; provided that the provisions of this item (4) shall not be applicable to 1. plant rearrangement, 2. inventory layoffs, 3. when he has refused or delayed placement to a job to which his Seniority entitles him.

(5) the Week was a second "waiting week" within his benefit year under the State System, or was a State System "waiting week" immediately following a week for which he received a State System Benefit, or occurring within less than 52 weeks since his last State System "waiting week";

(6) he refused a Company work offer which he had an option to refuse under the Collective Bargaining Agreement or which he could refuse without disqualification under Section 4(b)(3) of this Article;

(7) he was on layoff because he was unable to do work offered by the Company while able to do other work in the Plant to which he would have been entitled if he had had sufficient Seniority;

(8) he failed to claim a State System Benefit and his pay received or receivable from the Company for the Week was not less than his ESSEL minus $2;

(9) he was receiving pay for military service with respect to a period following his release from active duty therein;

(10) he was entitled to statutory retirement or disability benefits which he received or could have received while working full time;

(11) he was denied a State System Ben-

efit and it was determined that, under the circumstances, it would be contrary to the intent of the Plan to deny him a Benefit;

(12) he was required to take work under the state law paying less than 80% of his "Weekly Straight Time Pay";

(13) he took outside work paying less than 80% of his "Weekly Straight Time Pay";

(14) in the event of a complete plant closure, he took outside work paying less than 100% of his "Weekly Straight Time Pay";

(c) was actively seeking work or had accepted outside work which paid less than 80% of his "Weekly Straight Time Pay", had not failed or refused to accept work deemed suitable under the applicable State System and has met any registration and reporting requirements of an employment office of such applicable State System, except that this subsection does not apply to any Employee who was ineligible for a State System Benefit or "waiting week" credit for the Week only because of the amount of pay (or New York State only, period of work), or his failure to claim a State System Benefit when Company pay was not less than ESSEL minus $2 (as specified, respectively in items (3) and (8) of subsection 1(b) above);

(d) had to his credit a Credit Union or fraction thereof;

(e) did not receive an unemployment benefit under any contract or program of another employer or under any other "SUB" plan of the Company (and was not eligible for such a benefit under a contract or program of another employer with whom he has greater seniority than with the Company nor under any other "SUB" plan of the Company in which he has credit units which were credited earlier than his oldest Credit Units under this Plan);

(f) was not eligible for an Automatic Short Week Benefit;

(g) has made a Benefit application in

accordance with procedures established by the Company hereunder.

Section 2 — Eligibility for a Special Short Week Benefit

An Employee shall be eligible for a Special Short Week benefit for any Week beginning on or after the effective date of this Agreement, if:

(a) during such Week he performed some work for the Company or performed Compensated Work for the Union or was otherwise compensated by the Company for a day or part thereof but his Compensated or Available Hours were less than the number of hours in his Standard Work Week (but not to exceed 40 hours), except that during a week of scheduled shutdown, compensation for a holiday or holidays (but only with respect to an employee laid off in a reduction of force in accordance with the applicable local plant Supplemental Agreement), for vacation or for work for the Union or a combination thereof, shall not of itself qualify him for a benefit hereunder;

(b) with respect to such Week his Company pay and any Company pay which he would have received for hours scheduled for or made available to him but not worked did not equal or exeed his ESSEL; and (in New York State only) work was made available to him by the Company on less than 4 days within the Week; and

(c) with respect to such Week he satisfied all of the eligibility conditions for a Regular Benefit.

Section 3 — Eligibility for an Automatic Short Week Benefit

(a) An Employee shall be eligible for an Automatic Short Week Benefit for any Week beginning on or after the effective date of this Agreement, if;

(1) During such Week he performed some work for the Company or performed Compensated Work for the Union or was otherwise compensated by the Company for a day or part thereof but his Compensated or Available Hours were less than those in his Standard Work Week (but not to exceed 40 hours), except that during a week of scheduled shutdown, compensation for a holiday or holidays (but only with respect to an employee laid off in a reduction of force in accordance with the applicable local plant Supplemental Agreement), for vacation or for work for the Union or a combination thereof, shall not of itself qualify him for a benefit hereunder;

(2) he had at least 1 Year of Seniority as of the last day of such Week;

(3) he was on a qualifying layoff, as described in Section 4 of this Article, for some part of such Week;

(4) with respect to such Week his Company pay and any Company pay which he would have received for hours scheduled for or made available to him but not worked, equaled or exceeded his ESSEL: or (in New York State only) work was made available to him by the Company on 4 or more days within the Week; and

(5) he did not have a period or periods of layoff in the Week and in the preceding or following Week occurring in such sequence as to constitute a "week of unemployment" (as defined under the applicable State System) which included some part of the Week; provided, however, that when an Employee has a period of layoff with respect to which he has established such a State System "week of unemployment", which starts on a day other than Sunday or Monday, he will be entitled (if otherwise eligible) to receive a partial Automatic Short Week Benefit with respect to any hours of layoff on days within a Work Week which are not included in such (or any other) established State System "week of unemployment."

(b) No application for an Automatic Short Week Benefit, other than a partial Automatic Short Week Benefit, will be required of an Employee. However, if an

Employee believes himself entitled to an Automatic Short Week Benefit for a Week which he does not receive on the date when such Benefits for such Week are paid, he may file written application therefore in accordance with procedures established by the Company.

(c) An Automatic Short Week Benefit payable for a Week shall be in lieu of any other Benefit under the Plan for that Week, except that this provision does not apply to a partial Automatic Short Week Benefit.

Section 4 — Conditions with Respect to Layoff

(a) A layoff for the purposes of this Plan is any layoff which occurred in a reduction of force (medically restricted Employees awaiting suitable placement will be considered on a layoff occurring in a reduction in force) or temporary layoff, including a layoff because of the discontinuance of an operation or plant, except that an Employee who accepts a Service Award, a Special Distribution or a Pension (except a Deferred Vested Pension) under the Pension and Insurance Agreement shall not be eligible for a Benefit.

(b) An Employee's layoff for all or part of any Week will be deemed qualifying for Plan Purposes only if:

(1) such layoff was from the Bargaining Unit;

(2) such layoff was not for disciplinary reasons, and was not a consequence of; not in military service or on a military leave.

(i) any strike*, slowdown, work stoppage, picketing (whether or not by Employees), or concerted action, at a Company Plant or Plants, or any dispute of any kind involving Employees or other persons employed by the Company and represented by the Union whether at a Company Plant or Plants or elsewhere,

*At the end of any legal strike by Employees, the Company and the Union shall mutually agree as to the period of time necessary for normal start-up which shall be incorporated as part of any strike settlement memorandum. After such period of time an Employee will not be disqualified for S.U.B. solely because of such strike.

(ii) any war or hostile act of a foreign power (but not government regulation or controls connected therewith),

(iii) sabotage or insurrection, or

(iv) any act of God, provided, however, this subsection (iv) shall not apply to the first two weeks of layoff resulting from such cause;

(3) with respect to such Week the Employee did not refuse to accept work when recalled pursuant to the Collective Bargaining Agreement and did not refuse an offer by the Company of other available work, which he had no option to refuse under the Collective Bargaining Agreement; provided, however, that when maintenance Employees refuse production work it will not disqualify them from Benefits under this Section 4(b)(3).

(4) with respect to such Week the Employee was not eligible for and was not claiming;

(i) any accident or sickness or any other disability benefit (except a Social Security disability benefit to a medically restricted Employee waiting suitable placement under the rules set forth in the applicable local Supplement Agreement or except a benefit which he received or could have received while working full time); or

(ii) any Company pension or retirement benefit; and

(5) with respect to such Week the Employee was not in military service or on a military leave.

(c) If, with respect to some but not all of his regular work days in a Week, an Employee is ineligible for a Benefit by reason of subparagraph (b)(2) or (b)(4) of this section, (and is otherwise eligible for a Benefit), he will be entitled to a reduced Benefit payment as provided in Section 1(c) of Article II.

(d) The determination of eligibility under this Article shall be based upon the reason for the Employee's last separation from the Company.

Section 5 — Disputed Claims for State System Benefits

(a) With respect to any Week for which an Employee has applied for a Benefit and for which he:

(1) has been denied a State System Benefit, and the denial is being protested by the Employee through the procedure provided therefore under the State System, or

(2) has received a State System Benefit, payment of which is being protested by the Company through the procedure provided therefore under the State System,

and the Employee is eligible to receive a Benefit under the Plan except for such denial, or protest, the payment of such Benefit shall be suspended until such dispute shall have been determined.

(b) If the dispute shall be finally determined in favor of the Employee, the Benefit shall be paid to him if and to the extent that he had not exhausted Credit Units subsequent to the Week to which the State System Benefit in dispute is applicable.

Section 6 — Vacation Shutdowns

It is understood that an Employee who is eligible for weeks of paid vacation in an amount not less than the period of scheduled plant vacation shutdown, will not be eligible to receive a Benefit under the Plan for the period of plant shutdown, regardless of whether he has taken his vacation prior to or is deferring his vacation until after the shutdown, and regardless of his eligibility for State Unemployment Compensation under these circumstances.

An Employee who has taken vacation during a week or weeks when he otherwise would have been scheduled off in a curtailment of production shall not be disqualified from Benefits under the Plan, as provided above, to the extent of such week or weeks so taken.

ARTICLE II
AMOUNT OF BENEFITS

Section 1 — Regular Benefits and Special Short Week Benefits

(a) The Regular Benefit payable to an eligible Employee for any Week beginning on or after the effective date of this Agreement shall be an amount, which, when added to his State Benefit and Other Compensation, will equal 80% of his Weekly Straight Time Pay for each Week for which he is eligible for a Regular Benefit.

In the event of a complete plant closure, if wages or remuneration are received or receivable by the Employee from employers other than the Company as set forth in Section 3 of this Article II, the Regular Benefit payable to an eligible Employee whose employment is terminated, shall be an amount, which, when added to his State Benefit, and Other Compensation, will equal 100% of his Weekly Straight Time Pay for each Week for which he is eligible for a Regular Benefit.

(b) The Special Short Week Benefit payable to an eligible Employee for any Week beginning on or after the effective date of this Agreement, shall be an amount which, when added to the Employee's State Benefit and Other Compensation (excluding the amount of any pay received or receivable from the Company) will equal the product of the number by which his Standard Work Week (but not to exceed 40 hours) exceeds his Compensated or Available Hours, counted to the nearest tenth of an hour, multiplied by

80% of his Short Work Week Average Hourly Earnings provided, however, that a Regular Benefit shall be payable for the Week if the amount of such Regular Benefit is equal to or greater than the amount of the Special Short Week Benefit.

(c) An otherwise eligible Employee entitled to a Benefit reduced, as provided in subsection 4(c) of Article I, because of ineligibility with respect to part of the Week, will receive the greater of:

(1) 1/5 (or 1/6 if his Standard Work Week is 6 days) of a Regular Benefit computed under subsection (a) of this section for each work day of the Week for which he is eligible under this Plan, provided, however, that there shall be excluded from such computation any pay which could have been earned, computed, as if payable, for hours made available by the Company but not worked during the days for which he is not eligible for a Benefit under subsection 4(c) of Article I; or

(2) any Special Short Week Benefit computed under subsection (b) of this section for which he may be eligible.

Section 2 — Automatic Short Week Benefit

(a) The Automatic Short Week Benefit payable to any eligible Employee for any Week beginning on or after the Effective date of this Agreement, shall be an amount equal to the product of the number by which the number of hours in his Standard Work Week (but not to exceed 40 hours) exceeds his Compensated or Available Hours, counted to the nearest tenth of an hour, multiplied by 80% of his Short Work Week Average Hourly Earnings.

(b) An eligible Employee entitled to a partial Automatic Short Week Benefit with respect to certain hours of layoff not included in a State System "week of unemployment", as provided in Section 3(a)(5) of Article I, will receive an amount computed as provided in subsection 2(a)

above, based on the number by which the hours for which the Employee would regularly have been compensated exceeds his Compensated or Available Hours, with respect to the days within the Work Week not included in such State System "week of unemployment."

Section 3 — State Benefit and Other Compensation

(a) An Employee's State Benefit and Other Compensation for a Week means:

(1) the amount of State System Benefit received or receivable by the Employee for the Week or the estimated amount which the Employee would have received if he had not been ineligible therefore solely as set forth in item (8) of Section 1(b) of Article I (concerning a Week for which his pay received or receivable from the Company was not less than his ESSEL minus $2); plus

(2) All pay received or receivable by the Employee from the Company (including Holiday Pay but excluding pay-in-lieu of vacation) and except in determining the amount of a Special Short Week Benefit, any amount of unearned pay computed, as if payable, for hours made available by the Company but not worked after notice consistent with existing practices made under the Collective Bargaining Agreement has been given for such Week; and provided, that if wages or remuneration are received or receivable by the Employee from employers other than the Company and are applicable to the same pay period as hours made available by the Company, only the greater of (a) such wages or remuneration in excess of $10 from other employers, or (b) any amount of pay which could have been earned, computed, as if payable, for hours made available by the Company shall be included; and further provided, that any pay received or receivable for a shift which extends through midnight shall be allocated:

(i) to the day on which the shift started if he was on layoff with respect to the corresponding shift on the following day,

(ii) to the day on which the shift ended if he was on layoff with respect to the corresponding shift on the preceding day, and

(iii) according to the pay for the hours worked each day, if he was on layoff with respect to the corresponding shifts on both the preceding and the following days; plus

(3) all wages or remuneration, as defined under the law of the applicable State System, in excess of $10 received or receivable from other employers for such Week (excluding such wages or remuneration which were considered in the calculation under subsection (a)(2) of this Section); plus

(4) the amount of Social Security Benefits and benefits in the nature of compensation for unemployment received or receivable under any State or Federal System (such as, for example, the so-called readjustment allowances which were payable under federal laws to veterans of World War II).

(b) For purposes of subparagraph (a)(1) above, the estimated amount of the State System Benefit which would have been received by the Employee shall be equal to whichever of the following amounts is applicable:

(1) if he has an established and currently applicable weekly benefit rate under the State System, such benefit rate plus any dependents allowances, or

(2) in all other cases, the State System Benefit amount which would apply to an individual having the same number of dependents as the Employee and having weekly earnings equal to the Employee's Weekly Straight Time Pay.

(c) If the State System Benefit actually received by an Employee for a state week shall be for less, or more, than a full state week (for reasons other than the Employee's receipt of wages or remuneration for such state week), because

(1) he has been disqualified or otherwise determined ineligible for a portion of his State System Benefit for reasons other than set forth in Section 1(b) of Article I,

(2) the applicable state week includes one or more "waiting period effective days," or

(3) of an underpayment or overpayment of a previous State System Benefit, the amount of the State System Benefit which would otherwise have been paid to the Employee for such state week shall be used in the calculation of "State Benefit and Other Compensation" for such state week.

(d) If the State System Benefit applies to a period of less than 7 days due to commencement or termination of unemployment other than on the first or last day of the normally applicable state week, the 7-day period of the normally applicable state week will be used in calculating State Benefit and Other Compensation for such state week.

Section 4 — Definition of Scheduled and Unscheduled Short Work Week

(a) For purposes of the Plan, a Scheduled Short Work Week with respect to an Employee is a Short Work Week which Management schedules in order to reduce the production of the Plant, department, or other unit in which the Employee works, to a level below the level at which the production of such Plant, department or unit would be for the Week were it not a Short Work Week, but only where such reduction of production is for the purpose of adjusting production to customer demand.

(b) For purposes of the Plan, an Unscheduled Short Work Week with respect to an Employee is any Short Work Week:

(1) which is not a Scheduled Short Work Week as defined in subsection 4(a) above;

(2) in which an Employee returns to work from layoff to replace a separated or absent Employee (including an Employee failing to respond or tardy in responding to recall), or returns to work, after a full Week of layoff, in connection with an increase in production, but only to the extent that the Short Work Week is attributable to such cause.

(c) The Company will advise a designated Union Representative, or Representatives, of the Local Union at the time of layoff of the reason or reasons causing any Short Work Week involving a substantial number of Employees.

Section 5 — *Insufficient Credit Units for a Full Benefit*

If an Employee has to his credit less than the full number of Credit Units required to be canceled for payment of a Benefit for which he is otherwise eligible, he shall be paid the full amount of such Benefit and all remaining Credit Units or fractions thereof to his credit shall be canceled.

Section 6 — *Effect of Low Trust Fund Position*

Notwithstanding any of the other provisions of the Plan, if, and as long as the applicable Trust Fund Position for any week shall be less than 4%, no Benefit for such week shall be paid.

Section 7 — *Benefit Overpayments*

(a) The Company may reasonably request an applicant under procedures set forth in Article V, Section 1, to sign a statement acknowledging that the Trustee has the right to collect the amount of any overpayment.

(b) If the Company or the Board determines that any Benefit(s) paid under the Plan should not have been paid or should have been paid in a lesser amount, written notice thereof shall be mailed to the Employee receiving the Benefit(s) and he shall return the amount of overpayment to the Trustee, provided, however, that no repayment shall be required, if the cumulative overpayment is $3 or less or if notice has not been given within 120 days from the date the overpayment was established or created, except that no such time limitation shall be applicable in cases of fraud or willful misrepresentation.

(c) If the Employee shall fail to return such amount promptly, the Trustee shall arrange to reimburse the Fund for the amount of overpayment by making a deduction from any future Benefit (not to exceed $15 from any one Benefit except in cases of fraud or willful misrepresentation) or Separation Payment otherwise payable to the Employee, or by requesting the Company to make a deduction from compensation payable by the Company to the Employee (not to exceed $25 from any one pay check except in cases of fraud or willful misrepresentation), or both. The Company is authorized to make such deduction from the Employee's compensation and to pay the amount deducted to the Trustee.

Section 8 — *Withholding Tax*

The Trustee shall deduct from the amount of any Benefit (or Separation Payment) any amount required to be withheld by the Trustee or the Company by reason of any law or regulation, for payment of taxes or otherwise to any federal, state, or municipal government.

Section 9 — *Minimum Regular Benefit*

Whenever an Employee performs no work for the Company or any employer other than the Company in the Week and his Regular Benefit computed under paragraph (a), Section 1 of this Article provides no Benefit, or a Benefit less than $10 for the Week, he shall be paid an amount sufficient to bring his Benefit for the Week up to $10.

Section 10 — Deduction of Union Dues

(a) The Trustee shall deduct Union Membership Dues in such amount as may be fixed by the Local Union from benefits payable under the Plan to those employees who have signed a written authorization consenting to such deduction.

(b) The Local Union shall submit to the Trustee or its agent, following the procedure outlined under Article IV, Section 4(b) of the Collective Bargaining Agreement, a list of its members and the amount of deductions for dues to be made from the payment of each member for the month. The Trustee shall deduct such amount from one Supplemental Unemployment Benefit payment each month (as specified by the Local Supplement) of each of those employees whose name has been furnished by the Local Union as provided above, and who has executed an assignment and authorization, and remit the same to the Local Union Treasurer. Modification of this procedure may be made on a local plant basis.

ARTICLE III
CREDIT UNITS AND DURATION OF BENEFITS

Section 1 — General

Credit Units shall have no fixed value in terms of either time or money, but shall be a means of determining eligibility for and duration of Benefits.

Section 2 — Accrual of Credit Units

(a) For Work Weeks commencing on or after the effective date of this Agreement, Credit Units shall be credited at the rate of ½ of a Credit Unit for each Work Week for which an Employee receives any pay from the Company and for Work Weeks for which he does not receive pay from the Company but for which he receives a Leveling Week Benefit.

(b) For the purpose of accruing Credit Units under this Section:

(1) pay in lieu of vacation shall be considered as pay for the Work Week in which it is paid; and

(2) back pay shall be considered as pay for each Work Week to which it may be allocable; and

(3) Sickness and Accident payments, Workers' Compensation Payments, and Supplemental Workers' Compensation Payments shall be considered as pay for the Work Week for which they are paid; and

(4) time lost when excused for Local Union business and a Leave of Absence for Local Union business shall be included in determining a Work Week under this Section.

(c) No Employee may have to his credit in the aggregate at any one time more Credit Units under this Plan and under any other "SUB" Plan of the Company than the applicable maximum number of Credit Units as shown in the following table:

MAXIMUM NUMBER OF CREDIT UNITS

Seniority of Employee at Layoff	Maximum Credit Units
less than 5	52
at least 5 but less than 10	78
at least 10 but less than 15	104
at least 15 but less than 25	130
at least 25 and over	208

However, any Employee who has at any time to his credit in the aggregate under this Plan and any other "SUB" Plan of the Company more Credit Units than the applicable maximum number of Credit Units shown above and who would otherwise accumulate additional Credit Units in the Bargaining Unit in which he is currently employed, may direct that such additional Credit Units shall be credited to him and a corresponding number of Credit Units accumulated under this plan in any other Bargaining Unit or under any other "SUB" Plan of the Company, shall be cancelled, so long as the aggregate of his Credit Units at any one time does not exceed the applicable maximum number of Credit Units under this Plan.

(d) No Employee shall be credited with any Credit Unit prior to the first day on which he:

(i) has at least 1 year of Seniority; and

(ii) is on the Active Payroll in the Bargaining Unit (or was on such Active Payroll within 45 days prior to such first day) but as of such day he shall be credited with Credit Units for weeks subsequent to his Company service date at the rates specified in Paragraph (a) of this Section.

For the purposes of this subparagraph only, an Employee is on the Active Payroll in any pay period for which he draws pay while in a Bargaining Unit or is on authorized leave of absence which is limited, when issued, to 90 days or less, during the first 90 days of continuous absence due to illness or injury or disciplinary layoff; absent without leave up to 7 calendar days from his last day worked.

(e) An Employee who has Credit Units as of the last day of a Week shall be deemed to have them for all of the Week.

(f) At such time as the amount of any Benefit overpayment is repaid to the Fund, except as otherwise provided in the Plan, the number of Credit Units, if any; theretofore canceled with respect to such overpayment of Benefits shall be restored to the Employee, except to the extent that such restoration would raise the number of his Credit Units at the time thereof above the applicable maximum, and except as otherwise provided with respect to Credit Unit forfeiture under Section 3 of this Article.

Section 3 — Forfeiture of Credit Units

A person shall forfeit permanently all Credit Units with which he shall have been credited if at any time:

(a) he shall incur a break in his Seniority;

(b) he shall be on layoff from a Bargaining Unit for a continuous period as determined by the following table:

Years of Seniority	Months of Layoff
Less than 15	24
15 but less than 25	30
25 or more	48

(c) he shall willfully misrepresent any material fact in connection with an application by him for Benefits under the Plan.

Section 4 — Credit Unit Cancellation on Payment of Benefits

The number of Credit Units to be canceled for any Benefit shall be determined in accordance with the following table on the basis of:

(a) the Seniority of the Employee to whom such Benefit is paid; and

(b) the Trust Fund Position applicable to the Week for which such Benefit is paid.

If the Trust Fund Position Applicable to the Week for which such Benefit is paid is:	*If the Seniority of the Person to whom such Benefit is paid is:*				
	1 to 5 Years	5 to 10 Years	10 to 15 Years	10 to 20 Years	20 Years & over
	The Credit Units cancelled for such Benefit shall be:				
80% or over	1.00	1.00	1.00	1.00	1.00
70–79.99%	1.15	1.00	1.00	1.00	1.00
60–69.99%	1.30	1.15	1.00	1.00	1.00
50–59.99%	1.50	1.30	1.15	1.00	1.00
40–49.99%	2.00	1.50	1.30	1.15	1.00
30–39.99%	2.50	2.00	1.50	1.30	1.15
20–29.99%	3.33	2.50	2.00	1.50	1.30
10–19.99%	5.00	3.33	2.50	2.00	1.50
4–9.99%	7.50	5.00	3.33	2.50	2.00
Under 4%	-No Benefit Payable-				

If the Trust Fund Position Applicable to the Week for which such Benefit is paid is:	*If the Seniority of the Person to whom such Benefit is paid is:*				
	1 to 5 Years	5 to 10 Years	10 to 15 Years	10 to 20 Years	20 Years & Over
	The Credit Units cancelled for such Benefit shall be:				

Exceptions to the Credit Unit Cancellation Rates in the above table are as follows:

(1) ½ of the above number of Credit Units will be canceled for an Unscheduled Automatic Short Week Benefit payable for 3 or more hours; and

(2) No Credit Units shall be canceled when an Employee receives:

(i) an Automatic Short Week or Special Short Week Benefit for a Scheduled Short Work Week;

(ii) a Leveling Week Benefit; or

(iii) an Automatic Short Week Benefit for an Unscheduled Short Work Week payable for less than 3 hours.

Section 5 — Armed Services

An Employee who enters the Armed Services of the United States directly from the employ of the Company shall, while in such service, be deemed, for purposes of the Plan, to be on Leave of Absence and shall not be entitled to any Benefit or Separation Payment, and all Credit Units credited to the Employee at the time of his entry into such service or which would have been earned by him but for such service shall be credited to him upon his reinstatement as an Employee.

Section 6 — Transfer Out of Bargaining Unit

If an Employee is transferred out of the Bargaining Unit to a job which is not covered by a similar Supplemental Unemployment Benefit Plan of the Company, his Credit Units shall be canceled. They shall be reinstated, however, if he is transferred back to the Bargaining Unit with, or after he acquires, at least 1 year's Seniority therein.

Section 7 — Exhaustion of Credit Units

On exhaustion of an Employee's Credit Units he shall not be entitled to further Benefits.

Section 8 — Cancellation of Credit Units

When an Employee's Credit Units are canceled under the provisions of Section 3 of this Article, he shall be entitled to no further Benefits until he shall have been credited with Additional Credit Units.

ARTICLE IV
SEPARATION PAYMENTS

Section 1 — Separation Payments

Upon the terms and conditions set forth in this Article IV and subject to the other provisions of this Plan, an Employee who meets the conditions specified in Section 2 of this Article shall become eligible for a Separation Payment in an amount determined as provided in Section 3 of this Article.

Section 2 — Eligibility

(a) No person shall be eligible for a Separation Payment unless and until he shall have made due application therefore in accordance with the procedure established by the Company hereunder and shall have met the eligibility requirements of subsection (b) of this Section.

(b) An Employee shall be eligible for a Separation Payment, if:

(1) Employee is on layoff and has recall rights;

(2) the Employee's layoff was not the result of any of the circumstances specified in Section 4(b)(2) and (3) of Article I of the Plan;

(3) the Employee's layoff has continued for at least 1 year (except that recall to work for a period of less than 3 months' duration shall not interrupt the running of the 1 year period of continuous layoff and that the Company may determine on the basis of the Employee's prospects of reemployment by the Company to permit earlier application);

(4) Employee had on the last day on which he was on the Active Payroll not less than 1 year of Seniority;

(5) Employee has not received and is

not eligible for a Service Award or Special Distribution under the applicable Agreement on Employee Benefit Programs.

Section 3 — Amount of Separation Payment

(a) Subject to the provisions of Section 4 of this Article, the amount of the Separation Payment payable to an eligible Employee shall be the following:

(1) 1 year of Seniority but less than 2 years—His Average Hourly Earnings multiplied by 50;

(2) 2 years of Seniority but less than 3 years—His Average Hourly Earnings multiplied by 70;

(3) 3 years of Seniority but less than 4 years—His Average Hourly Earnings multiplied by 100;

(4) 4 years of Seniority but less than 5 years—His Average Hourly Earnings multiplied by 135;

(5) 5 years of Seniority but less than 10 years—One Week of Straight Time Pay multiplied by his years of continuous service to the nearest ¼ year;

(6) 10 years of Seniority but less than 15 years—1¼ weeks of Straight Time Pay multiplied by his years of continuous service to the nearest ¼ year;

(7) 15 years of Seniority but less than 20 years—1½ Weeks of Straight Time Pay multiplied by his years of continuous service to the nearest ¼ year;

(8) 20 or more years of Seniority—2 Weeks of Straight Time Pay multiplied by his years of continuous service to the nearest ¼ year.

(b) For the purposes of Separation Payment years of Seniority in (a)(1), (2), (3), (4), (5), (6), (7) and (8) above shall be the Seniority of the Employee at the time of his layoff.

Section 4 — Effect of Pension or Other Benefit on Separation Payment

The amount of any Separation Payment payable to an eligible Employee un-der Section 3 of this Article shall be reduced by the single sum present value of any pension or other benefit for which he is eligible, at the time his application for a Separation Payment is made, under any Pension Plan financed by or to which the Company has contributed as an Employer. If such single sum present value equals or exceeds the amount of Separation Payment, such Employee shall not receive any Separation Payment under this Plan.

Section 5 — Effect on Seniority and Benefits

An Employee upon acceptance of a Separation Payment shall be deemed to have terminated his Seniority with the Company and shall be deemed to have forfeited any and all insurance and other rights under any Employee Benefit Plan, other than any Pension Plan, financed by or to which the Company has contributed as an Employer.

Section 6 — Method of Paying Separation Payment

(a) Separation Payments shall be payable from the Fund only when the applicable Trust Fund Amount for the Week in which the Payment becomes payable is equal to or in excess of $240 and the amount of all Separation Payments so paid from the Fund shall be deducted from the value of the assets of the Fund for purposes of computing the Trust Fund Amount.

(b) At all times when the applicable Trust Fund Amount for the Week in which the Payment becomes payable is less than $240, Separation Payments shall be paid by the Company directly rather than from the Fund established under the Plan. Separation Payments paid by the Company directly shall not be charged against the Fund for purposes of computing the Trust Fund Amount or otherwise and the Company shall not take credit for such payments against the contributions to the Plan then or thereafter falling due.

Section 7 — Re-employment

If an Employee who has received a Separation Payment is subsequently re-employed by the Company, there shall be no obligation to repay the Separation Payment except for overpayments and then only as specified in Section 8 below, and prior Seniority of the Employee shall not be reinstated.

Section 8 — Overpayments

If the Company, or the Board of Appeals, determines, after issuance of a Separation Payment that the Separation Payment should not have been issued or should have been issued in a lesser amount, written notice thereof shall be mailed to the former Employee and he shall return the amount of the overpayment to the Trustee.

Section 9 — Armed Services

An Employee who enters the Armed Services of the United States directly from the employ of the Company shall, while in such service, be deemed, for purposes of the Plan, as on Leave of Absence and shall not be entitled to any Benefit or Separation Payment.

ARTICLE V
APPLICATION AND DETERMINATION
OF ELIGIBILITY

Section 1 — Applications
(a) Filing of Applications

An application for a Benefit or Separation Payment may be filed either in person or by mail in accordance with procedures established by the Company. Such procedures shall require the applicant to apply for a Benefit within 60 days after each week for which he is claiming Benefits except that if the Employee's State System Benefit is delayed because

of a protest, application for a Benefit will be accepted for two full weeks after the protest has been settled. Under such procedures an Employee applyling for a Benefit shall be required to appear personally at a location designated for this purpose to register as an applicant and to supply needed information at the time of, or prior to making his first application following layoff.

(b) Application Information

Applications filed for a Benefit or a Separation Payment under the Plan will include:

(1) in writing any information deemed relevant by the Company with respect to other benefits received, earnings and the source thereof, dependents, and such other information as the Company may require in order to determine whether the Employee is eligible to be paid a Benefit or Separation Payment and the amount thereof; and

(2) with respect to a Regular or Special Short Week Benefit, the exhibition of the Employee's State System Benefit check or other evidence satisfactory to the Company of either—

(i) his receipt of or entitlement to a State System Benefit; or

(ii) his ineligibility for a State System Benefit only for one or more of the reasons specified in Section 1(b) of Article 1; provided, however, that in the case of State System Benefit ineligibility by reason of the pay received from the Company (and in New York State the period worked) or otherwise (item (3) of Section 1(b) of Article 1), State System shall not be required.

Section 2 — Determination of Eligibility
(a) Application Processing by Company

When an application is filed for a Benefit or Separation Payment under the Plan and the Company is furnished with the evidence and information required, the

Company shall determine the Employee's entitlement to a Benefit or a Separation Payment. Company shall advise the Employee of the number of Credit Units canceled for each Benefit payment and the number of Credit Units remaining to his credit after such payment.

(b) Notification to Trustee to Pay

If the Company determines that a Benefit or a Separatoin Payment is payable, it shall deliver prompt written notice to the Trustee to pay the Benefit or Separation Payment. In each Plant, the payment of Benefits or Separation Payments under the Plan may be made by, and the return of amounts of overpayments may be made to, the representatives of the Trustee appointed by it for such purpose in such Plant. Such representatives may be employees of the Company.

(c) Notice of Denial of Benefits or Separation Payment

If the Company determines that an Employee is not entitled to a Benefit or to a Separation Payment, it shall notify him promptly, in writing, of the reason(s) for the determination.

(d) Union Copies of Applications and Determinations

The Company shall furnish promptly to the Local Union SUB Representative a copy of each application for a Separation Payment and a copy of all Company determinations of Benefit or Separation Payment ineligibility or overpayment.

ARTICLE VI
ADMINISTRATION OF THE PLAN
AND APPEAL PROCEDURES

Section 1 — Powers and Authority of the Company

(a) Company Powers

The company shall have such powers and authority as are necessary and appropriate in order to carry out its duties under this Article, including, without limitation, the following:

(1) to obtain such information as the Company shall deem necessary in order to carry out its duties under the Plan;

(2) to investigate the correctness and validity of information furnished with respect to an application for a Benefit or Separation Payment;

(3) to make initial determinations with respect to Benefits or Separation Payments;

(4) to establish reasonable rules, regulations and procedures concerning;

(i) the manner in which and the times and places at which applications shall be filed for Benefits or Separation Payments, and

(ii) the form, content and substantiation of applications for Benefits or Separation Payments.

(5) to designate an office or department at each Plant, or in the alternative a location in the general area of the Plant, where Employees laid off from such Plant may appear for the purpose of complying with the Plan requirements; it being understood that a single location may be established to serve a group of Plants within a single area;

(6) to determine the Maximum Funding of the Fund and the Trust Fund Position;

(7) to establish appropriate procedures for giving notices required to be given under the Plan;

(8) to establish and maintain necessary records; and

(9) to prepare and distribute information explaining the Plan.

(b) Company Authority

Nothing contained in this Plan shall be deemed to qualify, limit or alter in any manner the Company's sole and complete authority and discretion to establish, regulate, determine, or modify at any time levels of employment, hours of work, the extent of hiring and layoff, production schedules, manufacturing methods, the products and parts thereof to be manufactured, where and when work shall be done, marketing of its products, or any other matter related to the conduct of its business or the manner in which its business is to be managed or carried on, the same manner and to the same extent as if this Plan were not in existence; nor shall it be deemed to confer either upon the Union or the Board of Appeals any voice in such matters.

Section 2 — Appeals Procedure
(a) First Step Appeals

At each local Plant, the Company shall designate one person to serve as its representative for the consideration of appeals by applicants and the Local Union shall designate a representative for the same purpose. The Employees designated as the representative of the Local Union shall be paid for time lost from work in attending meetings with the Company representative for the consideration of such appeals. Such payments shall be made directly by the Company.

Any person who shall have been determined by the Company not to be entitled to a Benefit or Separation Payment, who shall have been determined to be entitled to be paid a Benefit or Separation Payment that is lesser in amount than the amount to which such person believes he is entitled, who questions the number of Credit Units credited to him at the time of layoff, who has had more of his Credit Units canceled than he believes correct or who is determined to be ineligible for a Benefit or Separation Payment which determination is disputed by him, may appeal such determination by presenting an Appeal (other than determinations made in connection with Section 1(b)(11) of Article I), on a form to be provided for that purpose, either to the Company representative or to the Union representative. In situations where a number of Employees had filed applications for Benefits or Separation Payments under substantially identical conditions, an appeal may be filed with respect to one of such Employees and the decision thereon shall apply to all such Employees. If there is no Local Union or Plant SUB Representative at any Plant because of a discontinuance of such Plant, the appeal may be filed directly with the Board of Appeals. Appeals concerning determinations made in connection with Section 1(b)(11) of Article I (contrary to intent of Plan) shall be made directly to the Board. Such written Appeal must be filed within 30 days following the date of notice of such determination or denial or reduction of such Benefit or Separation Payment to such person, or within 30 days after the date of mailing of a check of such smaller amount by the Trustee to such person. The respresentative who receives said written Appeal will promptly furnish one copy to the representative of the other party.

If either the Company representative or the Union representative shall find that such Appeal is justified, he shall so notify the other representative and the Company representative and Union representative shall meet within 10 days from the date of the Appeal (or such extended time as may be agreed upon) to determine the disposition of such Appeal.

In the event the two parties cannot agree upon the disposition of the Appeal, either representative may refer the matter to the Board of Appeals for disposition, on a form to be provided for that purpose.

(b)(1) Within 20 days after disposition of an Appeal by the Company and Union representatives at the local level, the Union representative may request a ruling by the Board of Appeals. Such a request shall be in writing, shall specify the respects in which the Plan is claimed to have been violated and shall set forth the facts relied upon as justifying a reversal or modifications of the determination appealed from. A copy of said request will be furnished to the Company representative. The Board of Appeals shall have no jurisdiction to act upon an Appeal made after the time specified above or upon an Appeal which does not otherwise comply with this subparagraph. Subject to the limitations of subparagraph (2) set forth below, the handling and disposition of such a request to the Board of Appeals shall be in accordance with the regulations and procedures established by the Board. The Union representative at the local Plant level, or the Union members of the Board of Appeals may withdraw any Appeal to the Board at any time before it is decided by the Board.

(2) In ruling upon Appeals the Board shall have no authority to waive, vary, qualify, or alter in any manner, the eligibility requirements set forth in the Plan, the procedure for applying for Benefits or Separation Payments set forth therein, or any other provision of the Plan, and shall have no jurisdiction other than to determine, on the basis of the facts presented and in accordance with the provision of the Plan:

(i) whether the first step Appeal and the Appeal to the Board were made within the time and in the manner specified in this Section;

(ii) whether the Employee is an eligible person with respect to the Benefit or Separation Payment involved and, if so,

(iii) the amount of any Benefit or Separation Payment payable;

(iv) whether the accrual or cancellation of Credit Units was properly determined.

(v) any question by either the Company or the Union concerning the interpretation or application of this Plan unless specifically excluded from the Appeals Procedure.

(3) There shall be no Appeal from the decision of the Board of Appeals. It shall be final and binding upon the Union, its members, the Employee involved, the Trustee, and the Company. The Union will discourage any attempt of its members to appeal and will not encourage or coop-erate with any of its members in any Appeal to any court or labor board from any decision of the Board, nor will the Union or its members by any other means attempt to bring about a settlement of any claim or issue on which the Board is empowered to rule hereunder.

(c) Applicability of Appeals Procedure

The Appeals procedure set forth in this Section may be employed only for the purposes specified in the Plan. Such procedure shall not be used to protest a denial of a State System unemployment benefit or to determine whether or not a Benefit should have been paid under a State System (Appeal procedures under State law being the exclusive remedy therefor).

The Board of Appeals shall have no power to determine questions arising under any Collective Bargaining Agreement, even though relevant to the issues before the Board. All such questions shall be determined through the regular procedures provided therefore by the applicable Collective Bargaining Agreement, and all determinations made pursuant to such Agreement shall be accepted by the Board.

No questions involving the interpretation or application of the Plan, except to the extent otherwise specified in Section 2 of this Article, shall be subject to the grievance procedure provided for in the Basic Labor Agreement.

(d) Composition and Procedure—Board of Appeals

(1) There shall be established a Board of Appeals consisting of 4 members, 2 of whom shall be appointed by the Company (hereinafter referred to as the Company members) and 2 of whom shall be appointed by the Union (hereinafter referred to as the Union members). The Company and the Union shall each appoint two alternates. In the event a member is absent from a meeting of the Board, one of his alternates may attend, and, when, in at-

tendance, shall exercise the powers and perform the duties of such member. Either the Company or the Union at any time may remove a member appointed by it and may appoint a member to fill any vacancy among the members appointed by it. The Company and the Union each shall notify the other in writing of the members respectively appointed by it before any such appointment shall be effective.

(2) The members of the Board shall appoint an impartial chairman, who shall serve until requested in writing to resign by 2 members of the Board. The person so appointed shall be a member of the Panel of Arbitrators named in the collective Bargaining Agreement and shall be selected for appointment in the manner specified in the Collective Bargaining Agreement. The impartial chairman shall be considered a member of the Board, but shall attend meetings and shall vote only in matters within the Board's authority to determine, and only when the other members of the Board shall have been unable to dispose of a matter by majority vote, except that the impartial chairman shall have no vote concerning determination made in connection with Section 1(b)(11) of Article I (contrary to intent of Plan).

(3) At least 1 Union member and 1 Company member shall be required to be present at any meeting of the Board in order to constitute a quorum for the transaction of business. At all meetings of the Board, the Company members shall have a total of 2 votes and the Union members shall have a total of 2 votes, the vote of any absent member being given to the member present, appointed by the same party. Decisions of the Board shall be by a majority of the votes cast.

(4) The Board shall not maintain any separate office or staff, but the Company and the Union shall be responsible for furnishing such clerical and other assitance as its respective members of the Board shall require. Copies of all Appeals, reports and documents to be filed with the Board pursuant to the Plan shall be filed in duplicate, one copy to be sent to the Company members at the address designated by them and the other to be sent to the Union members at the address designated by them.

Section 3 — Determination of Dependents
  (a) Regular Benefits

In determining an Employee's Dependents for purposes of Regular Benefit determinations, the Company shall be entitled to rely upon the official form filed by the Employee with the Company for income tax withholding purposes, and the Employee shall have the burden of establishing that he is entitled to a greater number of withholding exemptions than he shall have claimed on such form.

  (b) ESSEL

In calculating an Employee's ESSEL, the Company shall be entitled to rely upon such information as may be available listing dependents. The Employee shall have the burden of establishing that he is entitled to a different number of dependents than that being used by the Company.

Section 4 — To Whom Benefits and
  Separation Payments are Payable
  in Certain Conditions

Benefits and Separation Payments shall be payable only to the eligible Employee, except that if the Company shall find that the Employee is deceased or is unable to manage his affairs for any reason, any Benefit or Separation Payment payable to him shall be paid to his duly appointed legal representative, if there be one, and if not, to the spouse, parents, children, or other relatives or dependents of the Employee as the Company in its discretion may determine.

Any Benefit or Separation Payment so paid shall be a complete discharge of any liability with respect to such Benefit or Separation Payment. In the case of death, no Benefit shall be payable with respect to any period following the last day of layoff immediately preceding the Employee's death.

Section 5 — *Nonalienation of Benefits and Separation Payments*

Except for a deduction specifically provided for under this Plan, no Benefit or Separation Payment shall be subject in any way to alienation, sale, transfer, assignment, pledge, attachment, garnishment, execution or encumbrance of any kind and any attempt to accomplish the same shall be void. In the event that such an attempt has been made with respect to any Benefit or Separation Payment due or to become due to any Employee, the Company in its sole discretion may terminate the interest of the Employee in the Benefit or Separation Payment and apply the amount of the Benefit or Separation Payment to or for the benefit of the Employee, his spouse, parents, children, or other relatives or dependents as the Company may determine, and any such application shall be a complete discharge of all liability with respect to the Benefit or Separation Payment.

Section 6 — *Applicable Law*

The Plan and all rights and duties thereunder shall be governed, construed and administered in accordance with the laws of the State of Ohio, except that the eligibility of an Employee for, and the amount and duration of, State System Benefits shall be determined in accordance with the State laws of the applicable State System.

ARTICLE VII
FINANCIAL PROVISIONS

Section 1 — *Establishment of Fund*

The Company shall maintain the Fund in accordance with this Supplemental Unemployment Benefit Plan, with a qualified bank or banks or a qualified trust company or companies selected by the Company as Trustee. The Company's contributions shall be made into the Fund, the assets of which shall be held, invested and applied by the Trustee, all in accordance with the Plan. Benefits shall be payable only from such Fund. The Company shall provide in the contract with the Trustee that the Fund shall be held in cash or invested only in general obligations of the United States Government or in other investments fully secured by such obligations.

Section 2 — *Maximum Funding and Trust Fund Position*
(a) Maximum Funding

There shall be a Maximum Funding of the Fund for each calendar month (and for each pay period when required by the provisions of subsection (c) of this Article). Commencing with the month following the month in which the Plan becomes effective and for any month thereafter the Maximum Funding of the Fund shall be determined by multiplying the sum of the number of Employees on the active payroll and the number of laid off Employees from work who are not on the active payroll but who have Credit Units (both numbers shall be as determined by the Company as of the latest date for which the figures are available prior to the first Monday in the month for which the Maximum Funding is being determined or prior to the pay period if the Maximum Funding is being determined for a pay period) by the applicable amount as shown in the following table:

MAXIMUM FUNDING FACTORS

(1) For the month of August, 1976, and succeeding months—$375

(2) For the month in which the Trust Fund Amount first reaches $375, and succeeding months—$400

(3) For the month in which the Trust Fund Amount first reaches $400, and succeeding months—$425

(4) For the month in which the Trust Fund Amount first reaches $425, and succeeding months—$450

(5) For the month in which the Trust Fund Amount first reaches $450, and succeeding months—$475

(6) For the month in which the Trust Fund Amount first reaches $475, and succeeding months—$500

(7) For the month in which the Trust Fund Amount first reaches $500, and succeeding months—$525

(8) For the month in which the Trust Fund Amount first reaches $525, and succeeding months—$550

(9) For the month in which the Trust Fund Amount first reaches $550, and succeeding months—$575

(10) For the month in which the Trust Fund Amount first reaches $575, and succeeding months—$600

(11) For the month in which the Trust Fund Amount first reaches $600, and succeeding months—$625

(12) For the month in which the Trust Fund Amount first reaches $625, and succeeding months—$650

(13) For the month in which the Trust Fund Amount first reaches $650, and succeeding months—$675

(14) For the month in which the Trust Fund Amount first reaches $675, and succeeding months—$700

(15) For the month in which the Trust Fund Amount first reaches $700, and succeeding months—$725

(16) For the month in which the Trust Fund Amount first reaches $725, and succeeding months—$750

(b) Trust Fund Amount

There shall be a Trust Fund Amount for the Fund for each month commencing with the month of August, 1970. The Trust Fund Amount for any particular month shall be determined by dividing the cur-

rent market value of the total assets in such Fund as of the close of business on the Friday preceding the first Monday of such month, as certified by the Trustee, by the sum of (i) the number of employees on the Active Payroll and (ii) the number of persons laid off from work who are not on the Active Payroll, but who have Credit Units, such total number to be that used in determining the Maximum Funding for such month in accordance with Paragraph (a) of this Section. The Trust Fund Amount for the Fund for any particular month commencing with August 1970 shall be applied in connection with such Fund for all purposes under the Plan to each of the pay periods beginning within such month.

(c) Trust Fund Position

There shall be a Trust Fund Position (stated as a percentage) for the Fund for each calendar month commencing with the month of July 1957. The Trust Fund Position for the Fund for any particular month shall be determined by dividing the current market value of the total assets in such Fund as of the close of business on the Friday preceding the first Monday of such month, as certified by the Trustee, by the Maximum Funding of such Fund for such month. The Trust Fund Position for the Fund for any particular month shall be applied in connection with such Fund for all purposes under the Plan to each of the pay periods beginning within such month; provided, however, that after July 1, 1957, whenever the Trust Fund Position for the Fund for any particular month is less than 10%, such Trust Fund Position shall be applied in connection with such Fund for all purposes under the Plan only to the first pay period beginning within such month, and thereafter there shall be determined a Trust Fund Position (stated as a percentage) for such Fund for each pay period until the Trust Fund Position for a particular pay period equals or exceeds 10%. When the Trust Fund Position for a particular pay period equals or exceeds such percentage such Trust Fund Position shall be applied in connection with such Fund for such purposes to each pay period until a Trust Fund Position for the following calendar month shall be applicable pursuant to this Section. The Trust Fund Position for the Fund for a particular pay period shall be determined by dividing the current market value of the total assets in such fund as of the close of business on the Friday preceding such pay period, as certified by the Trustee, by the Maximum Funding of such Fund for such pay period.

(d) Finality of Determinations

No adjustment in the Maximum Funding, Trust Fund Amount or the Trust Fund Position of the Fund shall be made on account of any subsequently discovered error in the computations or the figures used in making the computations, except (i) in the case of an error in bad faith, or (ii) in the case where after discovery of an error adjustment is practicable, and then the adjustment shall only be prospective in effect, unless such adjustment would be substantial in the opinion of the Company. Nothing in the foregoing shall be construed to excuse the Company from making up any shortage in its contributions to the Fund.

Section 3 — Contributions by Company
(a) Company Contributions

(1) Commencing with the pay period beginning April 23, 1979, and with respect to each pay period thereafter, for which the applicable Trust Fund Amount is less than the figure shown in Column A; the Company shall make a contribution to the Fund of an amount to be determined by multiplying the applicable figure in Column B by the total number of hours for which Employees shall have received pay from the Company for such pay period (or such lesser amount as will bring the total

market value of the Fund to the then applicable Trust Fund Amount in Column A, in which case the remainder of said total number of hours shall be multiplied by the next lower figure in the applicable Column B).

COLUMN A	COLUMN B
$150	$.17
300	.15
450	.13
550	.11
650	.09
750	.07

(2) In addition to the contributions otherwise required by this Article, the Company shall contribute to the Fund the amount of any Automatic Short Week and Special Short Week Benefits paid from the Fund as Scheduled Short Work Week Benefits for any pay periods for which the Trust Fund Amount is less than $180.

(3) Notwithstanding any other provisions of this Agreement, the Company shall not be obligated to make any contribution to the Fund with respect to any pay period for which the applicable Trust Fund Amount is more than $750, and no contribution to the Fund for any pay period shall be in excess of the amount necessary to bring the total market value of the assets in such Fund up to $750.

(b) When Contributions are Payable

Contributions by the Company shall be made on or before the close of business on the first regularly scheduled work day in the third calendar week following the pay period with respect to which the contribution is being made.

In periods in which the Trust Fund Position equals or exceeds 10% weekly contributions may be accumulated and made on or before the close of business on the first regularly scheduled work day of the calendar week in which the Friday used for determining the Trust Fund Position falls.

(c) Reductions from Contributions

The contributions required by the provisions of Section 3(a) of this Article shall be reduced by the following:

(1) the cost of providing Hospital-Medical and Prescription Drug Benefits for laid-off Employees as specified in the applicable Welfare and Pension Agreements, less the period following layoff for which the Company pays otherwise;

(2) the amounts of any Benefits and Lump Sum Payments paid by the Company during the period to separated Employees under other agreements dated July 16, 1979, between the Company and the Union which specifically provide that the amount of such Benefits and Lump Sum Payments to be paid thereunder will be deducted from contributions required under the Plan;

(3) the amount of money added to each vacation check at the time written due to Short Week Benefit payments, consistent with Article IX, Section 2(a) of the Collective Bargaining Agreement;

(4) the amount of reductions to Separation Payments under Section 4 of Article IV which otherwise would have been payable from the Fund under Section 6(a) of Article IV during the period;

(5) if contributions to the Fund are not required for any period, or if the contributions required are less than the amounts to be offset under this Paragraph (c), then any subsequently required contribution shall be reduced by the amount not previously offset against contributions;

Any such amount not previously offset against contributions shall be deducted from the Market Value of the assets in the Fund in determining Trust Fund Position and the relationship of the Fund to Maximum Funding;

(6) if the Company at any time shall be required to withhold any amount from any contribution to the Fund by reason of any federal, state or municipal law regulation, the Company shall have the right to deduct such amount from the contribution and pay only the balance to the Fund.

(d) Separation Payment Liability

(1) Separation Payment shall be payable from Fund only when the applicable Trust Fund Amount for the Week in which the Payment becomes payable is equal to or in excess of $240.

(2) At all times when the applicable Trust Fund Amount for the Week in which the Payment becomes payable is less than $240, Separation Payments shall be paid by the Company directly. Such direct payments paid by the Company shall not be charged against the Fund and the Company shall not take credit for such payments against any contributions to the Plan then or thereafter falling due.

Section 4 — Liability

(a) The provisions of these Articles I through IX constitute the entire Plan. The provisions of Article IV and VII express, and shall be deemed to express, completely each and every obligation of the Company with respect to the financing of the Plan and providing for benefits and payments. Without limiting the foregoing, no Benefit or Separation Payment shall be payable from the Fund except as stated in the Plan, and except as provided in Article IV hereof, the Company shall not be obligated to provide for any Benefit or Separation Payment not provided for in the Plan, or to make any contribution to the Fund not specifically provided for in the Plan, even though the assets in the Fund should be insufficient to pay Benefits and Separation Payments to which eligible persons would have been entitled under the Plan were the assets of such Fund adequate to pay such Benefits and Separation Payments; and the Union shall not, except as provided in Article IV hereof, call upon the Company to make or provide for any such Benefit or Separation Payment. The Company shall not be obligated to make up, or to provide for making up, any depreciation, or loss arising from depreciation, in the value of the securities held in the Fund (other than as contributions by the Company may be required under the provisions of Article VII, when the Trust Fund Position of the Fund is less than one hundred percent (100%); and the Union shall not call upon the Company to make up, or to provide for making up, any such depreciation or loss.

(b) The Company, the Trustee, and the Union, and each of them, shall not be liable because of any act or failure to act on the part of any of the others, and each is authorized to rely on the correctness of any information furnished to it by an authorized representative of any of the others.

(c) Notwithstanding the above provisions, nothing in this Section shall be deemed to relieve any person from liability for willful misconduct or fraud.

(d) The Trustee shall not be liable for the making or retaining any investment or for realized or unrealized loss thereon whether from normal or abnormal economic conditions or otherwise.

Section 5 — No Vested Interest

No Employee shall have any right, title, or interest in or to any of the assets of the Fund, or in or to any Company contribution thereto.

Section 6 — Reports

(a) Reports by the Company

(1) The Company shall notify the International Union monthly (weekly when the Trust Fund Position is less than 10%) of the amount of Maximum Funding, Trust Fund Amount and the Trust Fund Position for the Fund as determined by it under the Plan, and shall furnish a statement showing the number of Employees on the Active Payroll and the number of laid-off Employees having Credit Units upon which the Trust Fund Position determination was made.

(2) On or before May 1 of each year, beginning with the year 1957, the Company shall furnish to the International Union a statement certified by a qualified independent firm of Certified Public Accountants selected by the Company:

(i) showing the number of hours for which Employees drew pay from the Company and with respect to which the Company shall have made contributions to the Fund during each period of the preceding year; and

(ii) verify the accuracy of the information furnished by the Company during the preceding year pursuant to subsection (a)(1) of this Section.

(3) The Company will comply with reasonable requests by the International Union for other statistical information on the operation of the Plan which the Company shall compile. Such information will include the following:

(a) The number of Employees on layoff monthly;

(b) the amount monthly of Regular Benefits paid, Special and Automatic Short Week Benefits paid and Separation Payments;

(c) the duration of the Regular Benefits;

(d) the number of Employees who have exhausted their Regular Benefits each calendar year;

(e) the number of Employees laid off and ineligible for Regular Benefits because of having less than 1 year of Seniority,

(f) the total number of Employees who received one or more Regular Benefits, Special and Automatic Short Week Benefits, and Separation Payments;

(g) the amount of the Reductions monthly from contributions reduced by the provisions of (c) of Section 3 of this Article and the amounts under each category listed in (c);

(h) the amounts of Company contributions made to the Special Account each month;

(i) the total assets in the Special Account reported monthly;

(j) the Distribution of the Special Account annually;

(k) the number of employees who drew more than 52 Credit Units during a continuous period by designated Seniority brackets each calendar year;

(l) on or before January 31st of each year, the Company shall furnish to each Employee the amount of Benefits received by him under the Plan;

(m) the Company will comply with reasonable requests by the International Union for other statistical information on the operation of the Plan which the Company may have compiled.

(b) Reports by the Trustee

(1) Within 10 days after the commencement of each month, beginning with the month in which the Company shall have made its first contribution under the Plan, the Trustee shall be required to furnish to the International Union and the Company a statement showing the amounts received from the Company for the Fund during the preceding month.

(2) Not later than the second Tuesday following the first Monday of each month, the Trustee shall furnish to the International Union and the Company (i) a statement showing the total Market Value of the Fund as of the close of business on the Friday following the last Monday of the preceding month, and (ii) a statement showing the amounts, if any, paid as Benefits from the Fund each week during the preceding month.

Section 7 — Cost of Administering the Plan

(a) Expense of Trustee

The costs and expenses incurred by the Trustee under the Plan and the fees charged by the Trustee shall be charged to the Fund.

(b) Expenses of Board

The Compensation of the Impartial Chairman, which shall be in such amount and on such basis as may be determined by the other members of the Board, shall be paid from the Fund.

Reasonable and necessary expenses of the Board for forms and stationery required in connection with the handling of appeals shall be borne by the Fund. The Company Members and the Union Members of the Board shall serve without compensation from the Fund.

(c) Cost of Services

The Company shall be reimbursed each year from the Fund for the cost to the Company of Bank fees and auditing fees.

Section 8 — Benefit and Separation Payment Drafts Not Presented

If the Trustee has segregated any portions of the Fund in connection with any determination that a Benefit or Separation Payment is payable under the Plan and the amount of such Benefit or Separation Payment is not claimed within a period of 2 years from the date of such determination, such amount shall revert to the Fund.

ARTICLE VIII
MISCELLANEOUS

Section 1 — General

(a) Purpose of Plan

It is the purpose of this Plan to supplement State System Benefits and not to replace or duplicate them.

(b) Receipt of Benefits and Separation Payments

Neither the Company's contributions nor any Benefit or Separation Payment paid under the Plan shall be considered a part of any Employee's wages for any purpose. No person who receives any Benefit or Separation Payment shall for that reason be deemed an Employee of the Company during such period, and he shall not thereby accrue any greater right to participate in, accrue credits or receive Benefits under any other employee benefit plan to which the Company contributes than he would if he were not receiving such Benefits or Separation Payment.

Section 2 — Effect of Revocation of Federal Rulings

In the event any ruling required under Section 6 or Section 7 of this Article having been obtained shall be revoked, modified or nullified in such manner as no longer to be satisfactory to the Company, all obligations of the Company under the Plan shall cease and the Plan shall thereupon terminate and be of no further effect (without in any way affecting the validity or operation of the Basic Labor Agreement or the Local Supplements thereto) except that assets of the Fund at the time of termination shall be held and distributed as provided in Section 4(d) of Article VIII.

Section 3 — Alternate Benefits

In the event it is determined that the receipt of a Benefit in any state would have the effect of reducing State System Unemployment Benefits to which the applicant would otherwise be entitled, payment of such Benefits shall cease in such state and the parties shall attempt to develop an alternative method of accomplishing the purpose of this Plan in such states. Benefits payable under any such alternative method shall be known as "Alternate Benefits". Any alternative method agreed upon shall not apply to an Employee who is ineligible to receive a State System Benefit only for one or more of the reasons stated in Section 1(b) of Article I of the Plan. Such Employee, if otherwise eligible, may apply for and receive a Weekly Supplemental Benefit under the Plan. Automatic Short Week Benefits will be payable to eligible Employees in such state.

Section 4 — Amendment and Termination of the Plan

(a) So long as the Collective Bargaining Agreement of which this Supplemental Unemployment Benefit Plan as amended is a part shall remain in effect, the Plan shall not be amended, modified, suspended or terminated, except as may be proper or permissible under the terms of the Plan or the Collective Bargaining Agreement. Upon the termination of the Collective Bargaining Agreement, the Company shall have the right to continue the Plan in effect and to modify, amend, suspend or terminate the Plan, except as may be otherwise provided in any subsequent Collective Bargaining Agreement between the Company and the Union.

(b) Upon termination of the Plan, the Plan (Articles I-IX) shall terminate in all respects except that the assets then remaining in the Fund shall be subject to all of the applicable provisions of the Plan as then in effect and shall be used until exhausted to pay expenses of administration and to pay benefits to eligible applicants laid off, or thereafter laid off, in the order, each week, of the respective dates as of which they were laid off, and to pay Separation Payments to eligible applicants in the order of dates of filing due application therefor. Section 7 of Article II shall not apply in the event the Plan is terminated, and for the period of 24 months following termination the Trust Fund shall be deemed to be 100%. In the event at the expiration of such 24-month period there are any assets in the Fund after all of the above payments have been made, the parties shall negotiate an agreement for the distribution of remaining assets of the Fund for the employee benefits not inconsistent with the purpose of the Plan, subject only to the limitation that neither party shall receive any part of such assets under the agreed upon distribution.

(c) Notwithstanding any other provisions of the Plan, the Company, with the consent of the International Union, may make such revisions in the Plan not inconsistent with the purpose, structure, and basic provisions thereof as shall be necessary to obtain or maintain any rulings required under the Plan. Any such revision shall adhere as closely as possible to the language and intent of the Plan.

(d) This Agreement and the obligation of the Company to continue the Plan without change or modification (except as permitted thereunder) during the life of the Collective Bargaining Agreement of even date herewith shall be deemed supplemental to and a part of such Collective Bargaining Agreement and during the term thereof neither the Company nor the Union shall request any change in, deletion from or addition to the Plan or this Agreement except as provided for in the Plan with respect to the payment of Alternate Benefits.

Section 5 — Effect of Amended Agreement

When this Agreement becomes effective, the amendments of the Plan provided for herein shall take effect and amend the original Agreement on Supplemental Unemployment Benefits concluded between the parties September 11, 1956, as from time to time previously amended. However, until such time as this Agreement becomes effective, the Plan shall be continued and governed in all respects by the terms of the original Agreement of September 11, 1956, as heretofore amended.

Section 6 — Federal Income Tax Rulings

This Agreement shall not become effective unless the Company shall have received from the Internal Revenue Service a currently effective ruling or rulings satisfactory to the Company holding that the amendments of the Plan accomplished hereunder do not modify, alter or change in any manner the rulings previously issued by the Service with respect to the Plan, including, particularly, the determination that Company contributions to the Plan constitute currently deductible business expense of the Company under the Internal Revenue Code of 1954, as amended, and that Company contributions to the Plan do not constitute taxable income to the trust which implements the Plan under any applicable Federal income tax law.

Section 7 — Department of Labor Rulings

This Agreement shall not become effective unless and until the Company shall have received from the U.S. Department of Labor a currently effective opinion satisfactory to the Company indicating that the amendments of the Plan accomplished hereunder do not modify, alter or change in any respect the opinions previously given by the Department with respect to this Plan, including, particularly, the determination that no part of the Company contributions to the Plan shall be included in the regular rate of any employee for purposes of computing overtime compensation.

Section 8 — Ratification

Further, this Agreement shall not become effective unless and until this Agreement and the Collective Bargaining Agreement executed concurrently herewith shall both have been ratified and approved by a majority of the Local Unions representing a majority of the membership and also by the International Executive Board of the International Union and written notice of such ratification and approval shall have been received by the Company.

Section 9 — Company Applications for Rulings

The Company shall apply promptly for any required rulings from the Department of Labor and the Internal Revenue Service. Copies of all correspondence concerning such rulings shall be mailed to the International Union and the Local Union or Unions party to this Agreement.

Section 10 — Union Identification on Benefit Checks

All checks payable for any Benefit or Payment under the Plan shall indicate that the Benefit or Payment is being made in accordance with the Agreement on Supplemental Unemployment Benefits between the Company and the Union.

ARTICLE IX
DEFINITIONS

As used herein:

(1) "Active Payroll"—An Employee is on the Active Payroll in any Period for which he draws pay while in a Bargaining Unit;

(2) "Average Hourly Earnings"—The maximum hourly rate or the job wage level of the applicant's regular operation—the applicant's individual hourly rate for Employees on incentive plans at the Lincoln, Nebraska; and Plant C Akron Plants—plus any cost of living allowances and the night shift differential to which his scheduled shift entitled him,

(a) For the purpose of computing continuing Regular Benefits and Separation Payments only the applicant's highest rate during the six-month period preceding layoff shall be the rate applied. To determine the highest applicable rate, the Company will compare the applicant's rate for the pay period preceding layoff with that of the pay period 173 days prior thereto, and the higher of the two will be used unless the Employee when first applying for Benefits shall designate an intervening third pay period for comparison. If so, the rate for such third pay period shall also be compared by the Company and shall be the rate applied if it is the highest of the three.

(b) For the purpose of computing continuing Regular Benefits only Average

Hourly Earnings shall be adjusted for the amount of any general wage increase and cost of living allowance effective after the day or period used to establish his Average Hourly Earnings. In such event the amount of increase shall be the amount applicable to the job classification in which the Employee worked either on the day, or the last day of the period, for which his Average Hourly Earnings were determined as defined above. The Average Hourly Earnings adjustment due to the increase shall be effective with respect to Benefits which may be payable for and subsequent to the Week in which such increase became or becomes effective.

(c) "Short Work Week Average Hourly Earnings" for the calculation of Automatic Short Week Benefits and Special Benefits means the maximum hourly rate, the job wage level, or the individual's hourly rate as defined above for the week for which the Benefit is paid.

The above shall be adjusted to include the amount of any general wage increase and cost of living allowance effective prior to or during the pay period of the Short Work Week, even though it has not become payable.

(3) "Bargaining Unit" means a unit of Employees covered by the Collective Bargaining Agreement;

(4) "Benefit" means an Alternate Benefit, Automatic Short Week Benefit, Regular Benefit, Special Short Week Benefit, or any or all four as indicated by the context:

(a) "Alternate Benefit" means the Benefit payable to an eligible Employee, in certain circumstances, in a State which does not permit Supplementation;

(b) "Automatic Short Week Benefit" means the Benefit payable to an eligible Employee for a Short Work Week for which his Company pay and any Company pay which he would have received for hours scheduled for or made available to him but not worked equaled or exceeded his ESSEL or (in New York State only) work was made available to him by the Company on 4 or more days within the Week;

(c) "Leveling Week Benefit" means the weekly Supplemental Benefit payable to an eligible Employee for all or part of a Week because, with respect to the Week, he was serving a State System, "waiting week" and during such Week or part thereof he was temporarily laid off out of line of Seniority pending placement in accordance with the terms of the Collective Bargaining Agreement;

(d) "Regular Benefit" means the Benefit payable to an eligible Employee for a week of layoff in which he performed no work for the Company, or in which he performed no work for the Company but neither the period worked nor the pay received was sufficient to disqualify him for a State System Benefit and the amount of the Special Short Week Benefit calculated for such Week was less than the Regular Benefit amount;

(e) "Special Short Week Benefit" means the Benefit payable to an eligible Employee for a Short Work Week for which his Company pays and any Company pay which he would have received for hours scheduled for or made available to him but not worked did not equal or exceed his ESSEL, or (in New York State only) work was made available to him by the Company on less than 4 days within the Week;

(f) "Weekly Supplemental Benefit" means either a Regular Benefit or a Special Short Week Benefit, payable under the Plan;

(5) "Board" means the Board of Appeals;

(6) "Collective Bargaining Agreement" means the currently effective Basic Labor Agreement between the Company and the Union which incorporates this Plan by reference;

(7) "Company" means the Goodyear Tire & Rubber Company;

(8) "Compensated or Available Hours" for a Week shall be the sum of:

(a) all hours for which an Employee receives pay from the Company (including call-in pay and holiday pay, but excluding pay in lieu of vacation) with each hour paid at premium rates to be counted as 1 hour;

(b) all hours scheduled for or made available to the Employee by the Company but not worked by him after notice consistent with existing practices under the Collective Bargaining Agreement (including any period on leave of absence). When work is offered and refused, hours charged will not exceed hours made available and such hours will be charged in the following order:

(i) to the Employees who actually perform the work offered,

(ii) to Employees who signified intention to work and then failed to report,

(iii) to Employees who first refused the opportunity for the work in the event that insufficient Employees offered to work the hours available (includes absent. Employees who otherwise would have been offered the work).

When work is offered (as opposed to scheduled) on Saturday and/or Sunday, hours worked will not be charged; and

(c) all hours not worked by the Employee because of any of the reasons disqualifying the Employee from receiving a Benefit under subsection 4(b)(2) of Article I; and

(d) all hours not worked by the Employee which are in accordance with a written agreement between Local Management and designated Local Union Representatives; and

(e) all hours which are attributable to absenteeism of other Employees, providing such absenteeism was not caused by an act of God; and

(f) with respect to any Employee whose regularly scheduled Work Week is less than the standard Work Week (not to exceed 40 hours) for the shift on which the Employee works, the number of hours by which such Employee's regular Work Week is less than the standard Work Week (not to exceed 40);

(g) all hours not worked by the Employee because of work sharing required by the Collective Bargaining Agreement except:

(i) where the Union is not asked by the Company to waive the work sharing provisions; or

(ii) when the Union refuses to waive the work sharing provisions and the Company, after the work sharing period, fails to lay off;

(h) all hours not worked by the Employee because of a change in shift resulting from a request of the Employee.

(9) "Credit Units" means the units determining duration of any Employee's Benefit which are credited to him generally by reason of his Weeks of Active Service and cancelled at specified rates for the payment of certain Benefits;

(10) "Dependent" means a spouse or a person recognized as a dependent under the Internal Revenue Code for establishing the Employee's withholding tax exemptions;

(11) "Employee" means an employee of the Company while during the life of this Agreement, he is in a collective bargaining unit as defined in and covered by the Collective Bargaining Agreements; or in any other bargaining unit represented by a Local Union which is a party to this Agreement to which the parties may extend the Plan;

(12) "ESSEL" (Estimated State System Earnings Limit) means the amount if any, of an Employee's remuneration which is disregarded in determining whether he is unemployed during a week under the law

of the applicable State System, plus the first item in the following amounts which is applicable:

(a) if the State System law applicable to the Employee is that of New York State, the maximum state weekly benefit rate under that law plus 1;

(b) if the Employee has had established under the State System a currently applicable weekly benefit rate for a week of "total unemployment", an amount equal to such benefit rate (plus any applicable dependents' allowances if such allowances are considered under the State System in determining whether an individual is unemployed);

(c) if the Employee is ineligible for State System benefits because of exhaustion of his Benefit rights under the State System, an amount equal to the Weekly Benefit rate for a Week of "total unemployment" which applied to the most recent Week for which he received a State System Benefit (plus any applicable dependents' allowances if such allowances are considered under the State System in determining whether an individual is unemployed); or

(d) for any other Employee, an amount equal to the State System weekly Benefit rate for a Week of "total unemployment" which would be payable to an individual having the same number of dependents as the Employee and having weekly earnings equal to the Employee's Weekly Straight-Time Pay (plus any applicable dependents' allowances if such allowances are considered under the State System in determining whether an individual is unemployed);

(13) "Fund" means the Trust Fund established under the Plan to receive and invest Company contributions and to pay Benefits and Separation Payments;

(14) "Plan" means the Supplemental Unemployment Benefit Plan established by "Agreement on Supplemental Unem-

ployment Benefits" between the Company and the Union dated September 11, 1956, as from time to time amended and as continued under this Agreement;

(15) "Plant" means any of the Company's Plants which are covered by the Collective Bargaining Agreement;

(16) "Plant rearrangement" for the purposes of Article 1, Section 1(b)(4) are those physical rearrangements of machinery and/or equipment which affect all or substantially all of the operations in a department, division or plant;

(17) "Seniority" means seniority status under the Collective Bargaining Agreement; and "Break in Seniority" means any break in or loss of Seniority pursuant to the Collective Bargaining Agreement;

(18) "Separation Payment" means a lump sum amount payable to an eligible person by reason of qualified layoff;

(19) "Short Work Week" means a Work Week during which an Employee performs some work for the Company or performed Compensated Work for the Union or was otherwise compensated by the Company for a day or part thereof but his Compensated or Available Hours for such Week are less than his Standard Work Week (but not to exceed 40 hours), except that during a week of scheduled shutdown, compensation for a holiday or holidays (but only with respect to an employee laid off in a reduction of force in accordance with the applicable local plant Supplemental Agreement), for vacation or for work for the Union or a combination thereof, shall not of itself qualify him for a benefit hereunder;

(20) "State System" means any system or program established pursuant to any state or federal law for paying Benefits to persons on account of their unemployment under which a person's eligibility for Benefit payments is not determined by application of a "means" or "disability" test; including any such system or program established for the primary purpose

of education or vocational training where such programs may provide for training allowances;

"State System Benefit" means an unemployment benefit payable under a State System, including any dependency allowances and training allowances (excluding any allowances for transportation, subsistence, equipment or other cost of training). If an Employee receives a Workers' Compensation benefit while working full time and a higher Workers' Compensation benefit while on layoff from the Company, only the amount by which the Workers' Compensation benefit is increased shall be included;

(21) "Supplementation" means recognition of the right of a person to receive both a State System Benefit and a Weekly Supplemental Benefit under the Plan for the same Week of layoff at approximately the same time and without reduction of the State System Benefit because of the payment of the Weekly Supplemental Benefit under the Plan;

(22) "Trustee" means the Trustee or Trustees of the Fund established under the Plan;

(23) "Trust Fund Position" means the percentage position of the Fund as determined periodically pursuant to the provisions of Article VII;

(24) "Union" means the International Union of the United Rubber, Cork, Linoleum and Plastic Workers of America, AFL-CIO-CLC, and certain Local Unions thereof—namely, Local Union No. 2, Akron and Stow, Ohio; Local Union No. 147, Gadsden, Alabama; Local Union No. 18, Jackson, Michigan; Local Union No. 200, St. Marys, Ohio; Local Union No. 286, Lincoln, Nebraska; Local Union No. 289, Windsor, Vermont; Local Union No. 290, New Bedford, Massachusetts; Local Union No. 307, Topeka, Kansas; Local Union No. 831, Danville, Virginia; Local Union No. 835, Madisonville, Kentucky; Local Union No. 843, Marysville,

Ohio; Local Union No. 878, Union City, Tennessee; and Local Union No. 904, Sun Prairie, Wisconsin; each acting as the sole and exclusive representative of the Employees in the respective bargaining unit as provided in the Collective Bargaining Agreement.

(25) "Week" when used in connection with eligibility for and computation of Benefits with respect to an Employee means;

(a) a period of layoff equivalent to a Work Week;

(b) a Work Week for which a full-time Employee shall have been scheduled or offered work for less than 27 hours including hours paid for but not worked, if on a standard 8-hour day or less than 25 hours including hours paid for but not worked, if on a standard 6-hour day; or

(c) a Short Work Week.

"Week of layoff" shall include any such Week; provided, however, that if there is a difference between the starting time of a Work Week and of Week under an applicable State System, the Work Week shall be paired with the State System Week which corresponds most closely thereto in time; except that if an Employee is ineligible for a State System Benefit because of any of the reasons set forth in Section 1(b) of Article I (excluding the reasons under items (3) and (4) thereof) for the entire continuous period of layoff, the Week under the State System shall be assumed to be the same as the Work Week. If an Employee becomes ineligible for a State System Benefit because of the reasons set forth in Section 1(b) of Article I (excluding items (3) and (4) thereof), during a continuous period of layoff, the Week under the State System

shall be assumed to continue to be, for the duration of the layoff period during which he remains so ineligible, the 7-day period for which a State System Benefit was paid to the Employee during such continuous period of layoff. Each Week within a continuous period of layoff will not be considered a new or separate layoff. Notwithstanding the foregoing provisions of this definition, if an Employee is ineligible for a State System Benefit because of the reason set forth in item (3) of Section 1(b) of Article I, the Week under the State System shall be assumed to be the 7-day period which would have been used by the State System if the Employee had applied for a State System Benefit on the first day of partial or full layoff in the Work Week and had been eligible otherwise for such State System Benefit;

(26) "Weekly Straight Time Pay"—an amount equal to an Employee's Average Hourly Earnings (as determined for a Weekly Supplemental Benefit) multiplied by 36 if on a Standard 6-hour day and 40 if on a Standard 8-hour day;

(27) "Work Week" or "Pay Period" means 7 consecutive days beginning on Monday at the regular starting time of the shift to which the Employee is assigned, or was last assigned immediately prior to being laid off.

IN WITNESS WHEREOF THE PARTIES HERETO HAVE HEREUNTO SET THEIR HANDS THIS 30TH DAY OF APRIL, 1982.

THE UNITED RUBBER, CORK, LINOLEUM AND PLASTIC WORKERS OF AMERICA, ALF-CIO-CLC

THE GOODYEAR TIRE & RUBBER COMPANY

TWELVE

ADMINISTRATIVE ISSUES

Administrative issues, while not as visible to outsiders as economic issues, are still tremendously important. They have a profound economic impact through their effect on productivity, they may well be more important to many employees than wage levels, and they can create great aggravation for supervisors and great protection for employees. The topics covered in this chapter include production standards, job descriptions, seniority, scheduling, discipline and discharge, and job security issues including automation and subcontracting.

FUNDAMENTAL CONFLICT— EFFICIENCY VS. JOB SECURITY

Anyone even vaguely familiar with American collective bargaining is aware of the generalizations that management is interested in optimal efficiency and that unions are interested in preserving the greatest number of jobs possible and that these two goals sometimes/often come into conflict. Some advanced students of organizational behavior and/or economics believe that the two goals are not necessarily in conflict. That is, greater efficiency could produce greater wealth, which could result in increased consumption, which would create rather than eliminate jobs. Some practitioners have little faith in this conclusion, however. As union leaders point out, jobs eliminated in one place and created in another do their constituents little good—regardless of their effect on the economy as a whole—and if management didn't think a labor-saving service was going to reduce the cost of (and probably the need for) labor, it wouldn't institute it.

The issue which brings this conflict to the fore is production standards—the determination of how much achievement is a "fair day's work for a fair day's pay." The issue is not a simple confrontation of greed against laziness. Union efforts to reduce the amount each worker must produce are far more often intended to increase the number of union members needed than to protect sloth and indolence. Highly energetic, highly productive employees (unionized and nonunion alike) may "kill the job." Hence, there is often a continuing battle between the need to be productive and competitive and therefore nonwasteful, and the need to continue the demand for one's services, especially when paid by the hour.

At their very worst, union demands for employment opportunities result in "featherbedding." Featherbedding is, in its technical definition, the requirement of payment for work not performed. Such an extreme requirement is illegal under the Taft-Hartley Act and was discussed in Chapter 5. More commonly, union pressure results in the division of labor among more workers than is absolutely necessary to get the job done. To that extent, there is a conflict between economic waste and employment gain.

Economists point out that, in aggregate, real wages can grow only when productivity increases faster than wage rates and that this has been the source of the long-term rise in our standard of living. They also point out that advances in technology create more jobs than they destroy—that the automobile created far more positions for mechanics than the reduction in horse travel cost jobs to blacksmiths. Sometimes it takes a long time for these changes to occur, but "in the long run" the result is a gain. Cynics point out that "in the long run we are all dead," and realists point out that the jobs created in the growth sectors of the economy may not be as desirable as those that are being lost. This is very often true in the area of wages. For those who don't see the goals as mutually attainable, the conflict basically pits "efficiency experts" against "breadwinners."

EFFECTS OF UNIONIZATION ON PRODUCTIVITY

The extent to which unions hinder or enhance productivity (there are arguments on both sides) is very difficult to measure. Clearly, the stereotypical belief is that unions restrict productivity. Equally clearly, unionized companies are, on average, more productive and efficient than nonunion competitors.[1] Careful attention must be paid to how both these conditions can be true.

One well-known package of arguments claims unions reduce efficiency through the above-cited featherbedding, reduced flexibility, restrictive work rules, emphasis on seniority, and resistance to technological change. On the other side of the ledger are claims that unions increase productivity by causing management to plan better, by encouraging the substitution of capital for labor, and by reducing turnover by providing effective voice on matters affecting employees.

In an attempt to assess the cumulative influence of these competing factors, one extensive well-documented study came to the conclusion that unions are, on the whole and with exceptions, good for productivity.[2]

That perhaps surprising conclusion requires careful examination. One ''exceptional'' situation in which restrictive work rules could survive was that where the employer was sheltered from competition, as railroads or the steel industry have historically been. This exception may be significant in major blue collar unions. The study also claimed that union resistence to technology was never widespread and was often exaggerated.[3]

Even allowing the questionable assertions that wasteful work restrictions will be eliminated by increasing competition and that resistance to technological change is not a significant problem, it is still questionable whether it is fair to conclude that unions enhance productivity. The fact that managers manage better under union pressure says more bad about management than good about unions. The fact that management comes under more cost pressure to do its job well because of unions does not excuse its failure to do so without unions. Likewise, high expense and inefficiency caused by unions that make

FIGURE 12–1   POSSIBLE RELATIONSHIPS BETWEEN UNIONIZATION
AND PRODUCTIVITY

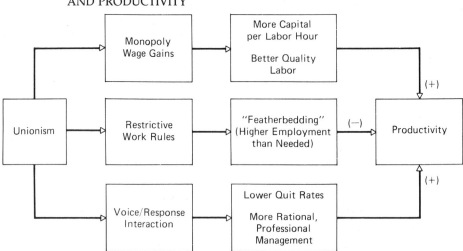

SOURCE: *Richard B. Freeman and James L. Medoff,* What Do Unions Do? *(New York: Basic Books, Inc. 1984), p. 163.*

palatable the substitution of capital for labor can hardly be considered an improvement in productivity. If the human resource is so costly or inefficient that it gets eliminated, it is not a triumph for employees. To the extent that unionization helps promote worker satisfaction and reduces turnover, it can be concluded that unionization does enhance productivity. That, in the author's opinion, is as much as unions can take credit for. The improvements in managerial performance ought not to be credited to unionization.

JOB-CONTROL UNIONISM

A traditional source of union power is to control how a job gets done. This is particularly true if the union cannot control access to the hiring function through an apprenticeship program. It then attempts to exert control through a "web of rules" at the workplace level. These rules are the main component of administrative clauses.

Typically, the system requires precisely described jobs assigned to particular workers. An employee's rights on his or her specific job are determined by contract language, customs arising from "the common law of the shop," and precedents established in that particular workplace. The rules also include the employee's obligations to the employer. Strict lines of jurisdiction determine which workers are assigned which task and generally forbid supervisors from performing bargaining-unit work. Wage rates are attached to specific jobs. Seniority considerations are applied for filling job vacancies and laying off employees. Disputes over the application of rules are resolved through the grievance procedure and arbitration, with great stress on specific rights, procedures, and obligations.

This determination of employee rights by the web of rules requires that jobs be strictly defined and that changes be strictly limited. Otherwise, it is meaningless to attach specific wages and employment rights to each job, because the rights would be too ambiguous to be administered effectively through the grievance procedure. The outcome of this procedure is to limit management's flexibility to adapt to changing conditions. This form of job-control unionism is cited by critics as an impediment in competing with nonunion employers.

In defense of unions accused of creating this impediment, it should be noted that collective bargaining has only codified a set of practices largely initiated by management. It was industrial engineers who originally broke larger jobs into clearly defined sets of tasks. It was management, through time and motion studies, that linked specific wage rates to specific jobs. Work standards, disciplinary procedures, and appeals processes had been formalized and codified by higher management to assert control over supervisors and workers. Unions merely accepted management's existing methods and sought to apply them fairly and uniformly through contract rights.

JOB DESCRIPTIONS AND PRODUCTION STANDARDS

A primary administrative issue in contract negotiations is the combined effect of job descriptions and production standards. Job descriptions dictate what duties a job encompasses. Without a union, job descriptions are created unilaterally by management. With a union, they are often collectively bargained. Production standards then dictate how much achievement there must be of the duties in the job description.

WORK AND/OR TIME STANDARDS

A. The principle of a fair day's work for a fair day's pay is recognized by all parties to this Agreement.

B. The Employer agrees that any work measurement systems or time or work standards shall be fair, reasonable and equitable. The Employer agrees that the Union or Unions concerned through qualified representatives will be kept informed during the making of time or work studies which are to be used as a basis for changing current or instituting new work measurement systems or work or time standards. The Employer agrees that the National President of the Union may designate a qualified representative who may enter postal installations for purposes of observing the making of time or work studies which are to be used as the basis for changing current or instituting new work measurement systems or work or time standards.

C. The Employer agrees that before changing any current or instituting any new work measurement systems or work or time standards, it will notify the Union or Unions concerned as far in advance as practicable. When the Employer determines the need to implement any new nationally developed and nationally applicable work or time standards, it will first conduct a test or tests of the standards in one or more installations. The Employer will notify the Union at least 15 days in advance of any such test.

D. If such test is deemed by the Employer to be satisfactory and it subsequently intends to convert the test to live implementation in the test cities, it will notify the Union at least 30 days in advance of such intended implementation. Within a reasonable time not to exceed 10 days after the receipt of such notice, representatives of the Union or Unions and the Employer shall meet for the purpose of resolving any differences that may arise concerning such proposed work measurement systems or work or time standards.

E. If no agreement is reached within five days after the meetings begin, the Union may initiate a grievance at the national level. If no grievance is initiated, the Employer will implement the new work or time standards at its discretion. If a grievance is filed and is unresolved within 10 days, and the Union decides to arbitrate, the matter must be submitted to priority arbitration by the Union within five days. The conversion from a test basis to live implementation may proceed in the test cities, except as provided in Paragraph I.

F. The arbitrator's award will be issued no later than 60 days after the commencement of the arbitration hearing. During the period prior to the issuance of the arbitrator's award, the new work or time standards will not be implemented beyond the test cities, and no new tests of the new standards will be initiated. Data gathering efforts or work or time studies, however, may be conducted during this period in any installation.

G. The issue before the arbitrator will be whether the national concepts involved in the new work or time standards are fair, reasonable and equitable.

H. In the event the arbitrator rules that the national concepts involved in the new work or time standards are not fair, reasonable and equitable, such standards may not be implemented by the Employer until they are modified to comply with the arbitrator's award. In the event the arbitrator rules that the national concepts involved in the new work or time standards are fair, reasonable and equitable, the Employer may implement such standards in any installation. No further grievances concerning the national concepts involved may be initiated.

I. After receipt of notification provided for in Paragraph D of this Article, the Union or Unions shall be permitted through qualified representatives to make time or work studies in the test cities. The Unions shall notify the Employer within ten (10) days of their intent to conduct such studies. The Union studies shall not exceed one hundred fifty (150) days, from the date of such notice, during which time the Employer agrees to postpone implementation in the test cities for the first ninety (90) days. There shall be no disruption of operations or of the work of employees due to the making of such studies. Upon request, the Employer will provide reasonable assistance in making the study, provided, however, that the Employer may require the Union to reimburse the USPS for any costs reasonably incurred in providing such assistance. Upon request, the Union representative shall be permitted to examine relevant available technical information, including final data worksheets, that were used by the Employer in the establishment of the new or changed work or time standards. The Employer is to be kept informed during the making of such Union studies and, upon the Employer's request the Employer shall be permitted to examine relevant available technical information, including final data worksheets, relied upon by the Union.

COLLECTIVELY BARGAINED JOB DESCRIPTION: ASSISTANT DRIVER-LOADER

DEFINITION:

This is work performing refuse collection activities and alternating as a refuse collector driver.

NATURE OF WORK

An employee in this class of work is responsible for performing a variety of refuse collection activities of routine difficulty on a task basis following established collection routes. Responsibilities include performing curbside, alley and special backdoor service in the collection of refuse as well as alternating in the operation of an assigned vehicle. These employees are expected to be physically and mentally able to perform collection activities during all types of weather at a rate and in a manner that will not upset work schedules or cause damage or injury to

(continued)

persons or property. When alternating as driver, employees are expected to be careful in operating the assigned vehicle. During the probationary period, employees having no prior experience in the operation of rear-loading sanitation vehicles will participate in a formal training program. Under general supervision, employees receive instructions both orally and in writing and are required to exercise only limited initiative and independent judgment in completing assignments. Work is reviewed through continuous observation while in progress and results obtained.

EXAMPLES OF DUTIES

Performs curbside and alley service, and special backdoor service for handicapped or disability cases in the collection of refuse; alternates in driving a residential refuse collection packer truck on an assigned collection route; operates packing and unloading mechanism; alternates in driving to assigned route, to landfill and back to storage facility.

Shares in completing daily vehicle inspection and reporting of maintenance requirements discovered; shares in completing daily collection route information reports.

Assists in cleaning and performing minor maintenance on assigned vehicle to include checking tire air pressure, motoroil level, fuel, and hydraulic oil, and bleeding brake air tanks; receives on-the-job training in vehicle safety, operating procedures and maintenance.

Performs related work as required.

DESIRABLE KNOWLEDGE, ABILITIES AND SKILLS

Some knowledge of operation and maintenance characteristics of packer-type refuse collection trucks.

Some knowledge of occupational hazards and appropriate safety precautions.

Ability to read, and to understand and follow simple and specific oral and written instructions.

Ability to interpret route maps.

Ability to operate mechanisms requiring physical coordination.

Ability to perform work requiring physical strength and endurance during all types of weather.

Ability to establish and maintain effective working relationships with others.

Skill in the operation and maintenance of packer-type refuse collection trucks.

TRAINING AND EXPERIENCE

Completion of the eighth grade and some experience in performing heavy physical work and driving medium weight automotive equipment; or an equivalent combination of training and experience.

*SPECIAL REQUIREMENTS

All sanitation vehicle operators must complete a supplemental vehicle operator training course prior to the end of their probationary period.

LICENSES OR CERTIFICATES

Possession of a valid Florida Chauffeur's License.

3810 - Assistant Driver-Loader

Job duties and effort and achievement levels can produce very hard bargaining. In the above mentioned stereotyped extremes, management wishes to require the highest performance levels possible, while the union wishes to establish the lowest that would still permit the employer to continue in business.

Compromising between these points may not be as easy as compromising between wage demands and offers. There is no empirically correct effort level. In fact, it is even hard to find comparative data.

The formalizing of job descriptions has been the bane of supervisors in blue collar settings. One of the greatest aggravations supervisors of unionized employees encounter is trying to direct an employee to perform a task and being rebuffed with, "It's not in my job description." This makes planning more important—and more difficult—and makes optimal efficiency far harder to attain. Worse yet, some unions are known to pursue a deliberate strategy of negotiating severely restricted job descriptions that ultimately require the use of extra employees for small, irregularly occuring jobs that really do not justify employing (or calling in on overtime) an extra person. Unions also often protect this labor-preserving (or labor-creating) tactic further by negotiating a provision that forbids supervisors from doing routine bargaining-unit work. (Exceptions are generally allowed for training and emergencies.) A great deal of irritation is caused by these clauses of the contract, although generally less so as the bargaining unit becomes composed more of white collar employees who generally have greater latitude on how the job gets done.

RESTRICTION ON SUPERVISOR WORKING CLAUSE

Section 8. It is not the intention of the Employer to have supervisory or managerial employees perform bargaining unit work. Bargaining unit work will not be assigned to the aforementioned employees except for the following:

a. Emergency situations where regular employees are not immediately available for assignment and where the assignment would not extend past a reasonable period of time.

b. Training, instruction, testing, or demonstration of current or new work projects, systems, or equipment.

However, none of the aforementioned acts shall be used to deprive an employee from working his normal weekly schedule.

Production standards have become a highly publicized feature of bargaining in recent years. Often referred to as "productivity bargaining," management has taken the offensive at the bargaining table with demands that increased wages can be justified only by increased employee productivity. Historically, the source of America's increased productivity has always been more efficient organization of jobs or the installation of machinery that helps make human labor more effective. It certainly has not come through successive generations of Americans each putting forth greater physical effort than their forebears. Therefore, the introduction of labor-saving machinery may be resisted by unions despite the fact that it often results in less physically demanding employment.

PRODUCTIVITY BARGAINING CLAUSE

ARTICLE VIII: PRODUCTIVITY AND PERFORMANCE

Delivery of municipal services in the most efficient, effective and courteous manner is of paramount importance to the City and the Union. Such achievement is recognized to be a mutual obligation of both parties within their respective roles and responsibilities. To achieve and maintain a high level of effectiveness the parties hereby agree to the following terms:

Section 1. Performance Levels

(a) The Union recognizes the Department of Sanitation's right under the New York City Collective Bargaining law to establish and/or revise performance standards or norms notwithstanding the existence of prior performance levels, norms or standards. Such standards, developed by usual work measurement procedures, may be used to determine acceptable performance levels, prepare work schedules and to measure the performance of each employee or group of employees. For the purpose of this section the union may, under Section 1173-4.3b of the New York City Collective Bargaining Law, assert to the Department of Sanitation and/or the Board of Collective Bargaining during the term of this agreement that the Department of Sanitation's decisions on the foregoing matters have a practical impact on employees, within the meaning of the Board of Collective Bargaining's Decision No. B-9-68. The Department of Sanitation will give the Union prior notice of establishment and/or revision of performance standards or norms hereunder.

(b) Employees who work at less than acceptable levels of performance may be subject to disciplinary measures in accordance with applicable law.

Section 2. Supervisory Responsibility

The Union recognizes the Department of Sanitation's right under the New York City Collective Bargaining Law to establish and/or revise standards for supervisory responsibility in achieving and maintaining performance levels of supervised employees for employees in supervisory positions. For the purposes of this Section, the Union may, under Section 1173-4.3b of the New York City Collective Bargaining Law, assert to the Department of Sanitation and/or the Board of Collective Bargaining during the term of this agreement that the Department of Sanitation's decisions on the foregoing matters have a practical impact on employees, within the meaning of the Board of Collective Bargaining Decision No. B-9-68. The Department of Sanitation will give the Union prior notice of establishment and/or revision of standards of supervisory responsibility hereunder. Employees who fail to meet such standards may be subject to disciplinary measures in accordance with applicable law.

JOB ASSIGNMENT

A second major administrative issue is job assignment—the determination of which employee holds which job. This can be a problem in two respects: (1) the filling of routine single-person openings and (2) the assignment of work to members of a particular craft or work jurisdiction.

The first major requirement is how to fill routine position openings. Unions and employers can generally agree on the value of a "post and bid" system. In this arrangement all job vacancies within the bargaining unit are posted in a conspicuous spot. Employees desiring to fill the posted vacancy submit bids to receive the position. This method of publicizing openings is designed to reduce favoritism on the part of management in selecting replacements without other employees ever being aware of the openings. The criteria by which candidates are evaluated can, however, produce substantial disagreement. The critical variable is usually seniority.

PROVISION FOR FILLING JOB VACANCY

ARTICLE XLII
POSTING OF VACANCIES

Whenever a vacancy arises or is anticipated, the Superintendent shall post notice of the same for no less than two (2) weeks, if possible, before the position is filled, and notify the Union representative. Vacancies shall be filled on the basis of experience, competency, qualifications of the applicant and other relevant factors. Any new position shall be posted with accompanying job description, qualifications, and salary minimum. All factors being equal, the employees within the system shall be given priority when filling a position.

POSTED BID

ELECTRICIAN II
$7.85 - $10.57

Must have a minimum of four years experience working with low and medium voltage (440-4160 volts), switch-gear, motors, transformers and control systems. Applicants must have or be able to obtain a Pinellas County Journeyman's Electrician License at the time of appointment. Apply in person at the Employment Office. Closing date for applications is February 20, 1987.

SENIORITY

Once the bids are received, employers and unions may well part company over the selection process. Employers have generally favored awarding jobs to the most able candidate. Unions, on the other hand, generally favor selecting the senior bidder capable of doing the job. Often contracts result in language calling for some combination of ability and seniority, with seniority commonly receiving the greater emphasis in application.

Unions have developed their great reverence for seniority through experience. In situations where "merit" was used to fill positions, unions often argued that the subjective nature of assessing merit really resulted instead in favoritism. Worst of all, the favoritism, it was sometimes alleged, was often a result of "brown-nosing" the boss—a notion considerably more repugnant to rank-and-file employees than to managers. Since merit is often difficult to determine, measure, and demonstrate, and because not everyone reaches the same conclusion even while examining the same data, even the most scrupulously run merit system is subject to attack by those who favor an objective criterion such as seniority. Given the inherent difficulty of merit selection and its often obvious misuse historically, it is not surprising that many unions have pushed for its removal.

What is surprising is the extent to which management verbally objects to but tacitly acquiesces in the use of seniority principles in job allocation. Opponents of seniority may argue vigorously that it creates two unlivable problems: (1) every job in the bargaining unit could be filled with less than the most capable person; and (2) a great deal of motivation could be destroyed because employees would realize that outstanding performance could not be rewarded with job promotions.

On the surface, these appear to be terribly damning criticisms. Upon closer examination, however, it is revealed that seniority principles may not be inappropriate at all in some situations and may actually result in greater productivity through improved morale.

The selection of the most senior applicant over the most meritorious is damaging to the employer only if there are important merit differences among the applicants. In many instances there are no important differences. This is really not too surprising. Employees seldom produce in proportion to their aptitude (which might differ significantly among applicants) or to their training (which probably does not differ as significantly, since minimal criteria are established to be eligible to bid on the vacancy). Instead, employees often perform at about the same level. This is caused by a combination of managerial practices and employee social norms.

Management's own behavior creates a great deal of the uniformity in performance. Paying everyone the same rate for the same job has a great leveling effect on performance. American management has not often been known for highly motivational incentive schemes, and merit pay is seldom great enough, nor is it commonly allocated differentially enough, to produce motivational differences. Further, management often gives everyone the same "tools" and "one best method" for carrying out the task. When everyone is doing a job the same way, it is not surprising that the outcomes are similar. Add to this a common American desire in many work situations to be "one of the gang," and one finds that in many situations almost all the employees produce about the same amount. In such a situation, using seniority as the selection criterion is absolutely superior to merit, since there are no important merit differences and any selection based on them will be perceived as favoritism.

In short, the loss to management caused by using seniority is often small or nonexistent.

ELABORATE SENIORITY CLAUSE

ARTICLE XV: SENIORITY DEFINITIONS AND LOSS OF SENIORITY

Section A. Definitions

For the purposes of this agreement, the following definitions shall apply:

1. "Seniority" means uninterrupted employment with the University beginning with the latest date of hiring with the University and shall include periods of University employment outside the bargaining unit, layoffs and other periods of absence authorized by and consistent with this agreement.

2. "Unit" means a functional area of patient care or service under the direction of the same supervisor.

Section B. Loss of Seniority

An employee shall lose seniority and no longer be an employee if:

1. The employee resigns or quits;

2. The employee is discharged or terminated;

3. The employee loses, or otherwise does not maintain a State of Michigan Nursing license;

4. The employee retires;

5. The employee does not return to work from layoff at the scheduled return time, provided the employee is given not less than seven (7) calendar days notice to return by certified or registered mail or by telegram addressed to the employee at the employee's last address filed with the University Personnel Office, except when the failure to return to work as scheduled is due to circumstances beyond the control of the employee, the University has been so notified, and an acceptable alternate return date is agreed to by the University.

6. The employee does not return to work at the expiration of a leave of absence, unless circumstances beyond the control of the employee prevented the return, except that continuation of the reasons for which the leave was granted shall not be such a circumstance. If the employee was able to (1) seek a leave extension, if available, prior to the leave expiration, or (2) notify the University that the return would not be timely, but did not, this exception to termination shall not apply;

7. The employee has been on layoff for a period of time equal to the employee's seniority at the time of the employee's layoff or two (2) years, whichever is greater; or

8. The employee is absent from work for three (3) consecutive days without notifying the University, except when the failure to notify and work is due to circumstances beyond control of the employee. After such absence, the University shall send written notification to the employee at the employee's last known address that the employee has lost seniority and the employee's employment has been terminated.

A grievance involving compliance with this Section shall begin at step three of the grievance procedure, and may be processed through the Grievance and Arbitration Procedures by the Association only for an employee who has lost seniority and is no longer an employee, provided it is submitted in writing at step three of the grievance procedure within one hundred sixty-eight (168) hours after facts have occurred giving rise to the employee's grievance.

The failure to put the best person on the job isn't important if the other applicants produce the same amount. (Actually, there is no "best" candidate in such a situation.) Furthermore, apparently the loss of the motivation to produce highly to earn a promotion is often not a big loss in the real world. The fact that most of the employees were already producing at about the same level indicates that they weren't motivated to perform differentially before and that union seniority provisions were not the cause of the problem.

The above generalizations do not, of course, apply when there are true differences among candidates. There are always a few "rate busters" and a few malingerers, but they can be treated separately by promotions to management (supervisory positions are generally outside the bargaining unit and therefore are not subject to the restrictions of the contract) and by disciplining the unacceptable performers. More importantly, some job classifications do not tend to produce equality of performance. Certainly most managerial and many professional jobs fit into this category. This is caused by the variety of problems confronted, the wide range of possible responses, the nonrepetitive nature of the task, and common group norms to excel rather than to "blend." For these groups of employees, seniority is far less appropriate and much more damaging to management. Furthermore, managers and professionals seem to be more motivated by the possibility of promotion than most other employees and need to perceive the opportunity of reward in exchange for performance. For these groups, seniority principles are not commonly used.

Transfers

Provision must also be made for filling positions on a temporary or training basis and to establish rules for transferring to other units. These are all negotiable items. Management generally wishes to preserve as much flexibility for itself as possible through use of temporary assignments and transfers. In general, unions do not regard these as highly emotional issues. A much more serious problem for them in job assignment is reduction of the workforce or layoffs.

Layoffs

How to determine which employees to lay off has become an important subject of bargaining. Management purists, at least theoretically, maintain that the decision should be made on merit. Unions again favor seniority, this time in reverse order. Bargaining generally results in emphasis on seniority, both because the union favors it and because management realizes its appropriateness. Management people also realize that it minimizes a lot of headaches for them by eliminating the need to defend merit assessments that they know are less than perfect and whose consequences would definitely be fought over. It is also much easier to tell the laid-off employee that the decision wasn't personal, rather than having to say, "I've selected you as one of our twenty worst employees," and dealing with the consequences of such a conclusion.

The use of seniority systems for layoffs and for the filling of job vacancies has had side effects on equal employment opportunity and Affirmative Action programs of employers. Because minorities were historically underrepresented in many employment situations, recent efforts to balance their participation have resulted in a disproportionate number of minorities occupying recently filled positions. When a layoff occurs, the utilization of a union contract's reverse seniority principle has the effect of reducing minority employment disproportionately. This tends to negate the effects of an Affirmative Action program. Not to follow reverse seniority, however, would violate the contract's provisions and result in reverse discrimination. The way in which employers are expected to cope with this "damned if you do, damned if you don't" dilemma has varied with the "liberality" of the enforcement agencies and the judiciary.

As of January 1985, the federal government had applied the following rule to situations involving equal employment and seniority systems: unless intent to discriminate can be shown, a seniority system that results in an adverse impact is still valid.[4]

The reverse-order-of-seniority principle can provide other problems in its application during layoffs. Sometimes layoffs in one area of an operation can result in situations where a junior employee is retained in Department B while a senior one in Department A is laid off. Unions dislike this occurrence and like to negotiate the widest seniority unit possible for "bumping" purposes—that is, the right of a senior person scheduled for layoff to displace a junior employee still working.

In bumping situations management wishes to assure that senior employees bumping into jobs not normally their own will be competent to perform those jobs and that there will be as few employees working out of classification as possible. Examples of different bumping plans are given in the accompanying box.

BUMPING

What sounds simple in principle may become quite complicated in application. Consider the following two examples, one made up of departmentwide seniority units and the other made up of plantwide units, and the differing effects they would have on the same workforce.

The workforce is divided between two departments, A and B, with a need to lay off three employees in Department A. The numbers in each column are the years of seniority for each employee.

Department A	Department B
20	6
15	5
10	4
9	3
8	2
7	1

(continued)

If bumping rights are limited to departmentwide, the following layoff will occur:

Department A	Department B
20	6
15	5
10	4
9 out	3
8 out	2
7 out	1

This outcome will satisfy management's need for efficiency but will obviously irritate the employees laid off, since they are senior to everyone still retained in Department B.

On the other hand, consider the effect of a plantwide seniority unit for bumping:

Department A		Department B	
20		9	6 down
15		8	5 down
10	b u m p	7	4 down
9	b u m p	6	3 out
8	b u m p	5	2 out
7		4	1 out

This scheme results in the junior employees being bumped, but it also results in everyone in Department B working outside his or her normal job classification. Since all sensible systems require that an employee must be able to perform a job onto which he or she has bumped, it can be assumed that Department B will continue to function. It can also be assumed, however, that it probably won't function as efficiently as it did when everyone was doing his or her normal job. For this reason, and because multiple bumping produces an administrative hassle, most employers seek to limit bumping rights to the narrowest unit possible.

LAY-OFF AND "BUMPING" CLAUSE

D. Lay-off, reduction of hours worked and recall:

1. *The department head shall give written notice of any pending layoff to the employee and the Union. Such notice shall state the reasons therefore and shall be submitted at least one week before the effective date.*

2. *Any lay-off or reduction of the hours worked shall be based on seniority, the least senior employee to be affected first. Employees with less than ninety (90) days and federally funded employees will be included on the seniority list for the purpose of lay-off.*

3. *In the event a lay-off by seniority should result in the loss of an employee whose*

duties *cannot be performed by the remaining employees, such cases shall be taken up by special conference of the YCUA and Union Committees and every effort will be made to reach a settlement satisfactory to all parties involved.*

4. *Employees on lay-off shall continue to accumulate seniority during lay-off. However, recall from lay-off shall be governed by paragraph 6 of Section D of Article 7.*

5. *Notice of recall from lay-off shall be sent by certified mail to the employee's last known address. The employee shall have three (3) days to report for work after receiving proper notice of recall. Any employee who does not report for*

duty after notification shall waive all rights. It shall be the employee's responsibility to keep Management informed of any change of address.

6. Seniority employees shall have the right to recall from lay-off for a period not to exceed their total seniority but Section 4 above shall in no way entitle an employee to be recalled after he has been laid-off for a period in excess of his actual time worked prior to being laid-off.

7. Recall from lay-off shall be made in the order of seniority.

8. No new employee shall be hired to fill a position while a regular employee is laid-off and elects to take such position, if qualified.

9. In the event of a lay-off or elimination of a position resulting in a lay-off, employees will be allowed to bump into a lower classification or to an equal classification, provided they are qualified to do the job and have the requisite seniority. Employees bumping into the office staff from outside must pass the tests required of new hires coming into the office staff before being allowed to bump into the group. Employees will be allowed to bump into a higher classification only if they have previously held that job while in the employ of YCUA, Ypsilanti Township Water and Sewer Department or City of Ypsilanti Water and Sewer Department. Employees will be allowed a five (5) day trial period in which to demonstrate their ability to perform the job into which they have bumped. Employees who are unable to perform the task they have bumped into will then be placed on lay-off status.

Superseniority

A final application of seniority principles is "superseniority." Superseniority is a status that can be granted by the labor agreement to union officers to place them at the top of the seniority list for avoiding layoffs. The rationale for such a privilege is that the application of the contract carried out by the union officers is beneficial for all parties and it is therefore necessary to have the experts on hand to see that the job is done right. Superseniority does not apply for bidding on job vacancies.

Craft Assignment

The assignment of work can also be a problem on an aggregate basis, without regard to seniority, particularly if there are multiple craft unions present. Craft unions jealously guard their jurisdictions and will fight to have work assigned to the members of their craft rather than to some other group of employees. As mentioned in Chapter 6, unions affiliated with the AFL-CIO have an internal plan for resolving their jurisdictional disputes, but this relieves employers of aggravation only by preventing strikes over work assignment. It may not relieve the employer from having "to use an electrician to screw in a light bulb." At times, job descriptions and assignments may require utilizing a highly trained employee whose specialized skills are not needed. When the work could be done by somebody more easily available and cheaper, management gets aggravated.

SCHEDULING

Most contracts contain clauses affecting the scheduling of the workforce for such occasions as overtime, vacations, holidays, shifts, and breaks. These are not generally hotly contested issues. The employer is usually interested in assuring that a qualified employee is available when needed, but beyond that, is relatively indifferent as to whether overtime (for instance) is distributed on a seniority-first or rotating basis, or by any other method that can be agreed upon. It should be remembered at all times that employees have no *legal* right to refuse overtime, and few contracts provide such a right. Most contracts merely prescribe rules to determine which employees will work if not all of them are needed. For vacations, management must assure itself of an adequate supply of adequately trained employees at all times, including peak vacation-demand periods. Again, management is fairly indifferent to the method used to select vacation times, so long as its staffing needs are met. Shift assignments are subject to similar constraints.

DISCIPLINE AND DISCHARGE

This is one of the most important and controversial administrative issues. The better the job, the more the employee wishes to protect himself or herself against losing it. In unionized workplaces, an employee's *rights* to retaining his or her job are *much* greater than in the nonunion workplace. In most states, employment-at-will is still the basic rule. That is, either party (obviously including the employer) may cease the employment relationship at any time for any or no reason (so long as the reason isn't an illegal one) if there is no contract stating for how long the employment shall be or that there be justifiable reasons for terminating it. A union contract can provide such protections. Furthermore, it also provides for an enforcement mechanism through the grievance procedure and provides professional advice and advocacy through the union's representation.

PROHIBITED REASONS FOR DISCHARGE

The following is a *complete* list of reasons for which an employer is not permitted to discharge an employee. Note that it does not contain such items as length of hair, personal beliefs unrelated to the job, etc., nor does it require that the reason for discharge be a good one.

1. *Race or ethnicity*
2. *National origin*
3. *Religion*
4. *Sex*
5. *Age between 40 and 70*
6. *Certain handicap situations*
7. *Union activity*
8. *"Whistleblowing" on employer violations of certain federal acts*

A few states have laws creating additional employee rights, but they are the exception, not the rule. A few states are also beginning to modify the employment-at-will doctrine to prohibit three types of discharge: (1) where an implicit contract exists; (2) where the discharge is contrary to public policy (such as firing an employee for serving jury duty); and (3) where the purpose of the discharge is to avoid "the benefits of the bargain"—for instance, to fire a salesman after a large sale so as to avoid paying the commission. At this time, these restrictions should be viewed as exceptions to the rule.

Most contracts provide for discipline or discharge only for "just cause." This is a very substantial benefit for employees. Not only does it assure them protection against arbitrary or capricious supervisors, it also relieves them of having to be popular with the supervisor. This undoubtedly reduces "brown-nosing." It also probably reduces cooperation. "Just cause" also requires definition on a case-by-case basis. Experienced negotiating parties realize that there are so many extenuating and mitigating circumstances in discipline cases that it is seldom feasible to concretely apply rules written into contracts. Instead, rules are established either by management or bilaterally. Decisions made by management to discipline employees may then be appealed through the grievance procedure to determine if there was "just cause" in light of past interpretations of that phrase.

Discipline and discharge cases generally fall into two major categories—discipline for behavior and discipline for poor work performance. Certain kinds of behavior may result in immediate discharge if substantiated. Included in this category are such acts as fighting, carrying weapons, using drugs on the job, major theft, gross insubordination, violations of important safety practices, etc. These categories may be listed in the contract or they may be interpreted through the "common law of the shop." Discipline for poor performance is generally treated more procedurally and with greater emphasis on trying to rehabilitate the employees or reassign them more properly.

"Progressive" discipline is based on the belief that poor-performing employees should be improved rather than removed. It gives employees notice of their shortcomings and the opportunity to improve, rather than facing summary discharge. Without question this makes it more difficult to fire an employee and lets employees "play games" with the system. It also results in much aggravation for first-line supervisors, who now must document, over time, what they could formerly do swiftly and with only their judgment. Requirements for administering progressive discipline and tests it must withstand in the grievance procedure are given below.

PROGRESSIVE DISCIPLINE PROCEDURE

Section 1. Principles

In the administration of this Article, a basic principle shall be that discipline should be corrective in nature, rather than punitive. No employee may be disciplined or discharged except for just cause such as, but not limited to, insubordination, pilferage, intoxication (drugs or alcohol), incompetence, failure to perform work as requested, violation of the terms of this Agreement, or failure to observe safety rules and regulations. Any such discipline or discharge shall be subject to the grievance-arbitration procedure provided for in this Agreement, which could result in reinstatement and restitution, including back pay.

Section 2. Discussion

For minor offenses by an employee, management has a responsibility to discuss such matters with the employee. Discussions of this type shall be held in private between the employee and the supervisor. Such discussions are not considered discipline and are not grievable. Following such discussions, there is no prohibition against the supervisor and/or the employee making a personal notation of the date and subject matter for their own personal record(s). However, no notation or other information pertaining to such discussion shall be included in the employee's personnel folder. While such discussions may not be cited as an element of prior adverse record in any subsequent disciplinary action against an employee, they may be, where relevant and timely, relied upon to establish that employees have been made aware of their obligations and responsibilities.

Section 3. Letter of Warning

A letter of warning is a disciplinary notice in writing, identified as an official disciplinary letter of warning, which shall include an explanation of a deficiency or misconduct to be corrected.

Section 4. Suspensions of 14 Days or Less

In the case of discipline involving suspensions of fourteen (14) days or less, the employee against whom disciplinary action is sought to be initiated shall be served with a written notice of the charges against the employee and shall be further informed that he/she will be suspended after ten (10) calendar days during which ten-day period the employee shall remain on the job or on the clock (in pay status) at the option of the Employer.

Section 5. Suspensions of More than 14 Days or Discharge

In the case of suspensions of more than fourteen (14) days, or of discharge, any employee shall, unless otherwise provided herein, be entitled to an advance written notice of the charges against him/her and shall remain either on the job or on the clock at the option of the Employer for a period of thirty (30) days. Thereafter, the employee shall remain on the rolls (non-pay status) until disposition of the case has been had either by settlement with the Union or through exhaustion of the grievance-arbitration procedure. A preference eligible who chooses to appeal a suspension of more than fourteen (14) days or his discharge to the Merit Systems Protection Board (MSPB) rather than through the grievance-arbitration procedure shall remain on the rolls (non-pay status) until disposition of the case has been had either by settlement or through exhaustion of his MSPB appeal. When there is reasonable cause to believe an employee is guilty of a crime for which a sentence of imprisonment can be imposed the Employer is not required to give the employee the full thirty (30) days advance written notice in a discharge action but shall give such lesser number of days advance written notice as under the circumstances is reasonable and can be justified. The employee is immediately removed from a pay status at the end of the notice period.

Section 6. Indefinite Suspension—Crime Situation

A. The Employer may indefinitely suspend an employee in those cases where the Employer has reasonable cause to believe an employee is guilty of a crime for which a sentence of imprisonment can be imposed. In such cases, the Employee is not required to give the employee the full thirty (30) days advance notice of indefinite suspension, but shall give such lesser number of days of advance written notice as under the circumstances is reasonable and can be justified. The employee is immediately removed from a pay status at the end of the notice period.

B. The just cause of an indefinite suspension is grievable. The arbitrator shall have the authority to reinstate and make the employee whole for the entire period of the indefinite suspension.

C. If after further investigation or after resolution of the criminal charges against the employee, the Employer determines to return the employee to a pay status, the employee shall be entitled to back pay for the period that the indefinite suspension exceeded seventy (70) days, if the employee was otherwise available for duty, and without prejudice to any grievance filed under B above.

D. The Employer may take action to discharge an employee during the period of an indefinite suspension whether or not the criminal charges have been resolved, and whether or not such charges have been resolved in favor of the employee. Such action must be for just cause, and is subject to the requirements of Section 5 of this Article.

Section 7. Emergency Procedure

An employee may be immediately placed on an off-duty status (without pay) by the Employer, but remain on the rolls where the allegation involves intoxication (use of drug or alcohol), pilferage, or failure to observe safety rules and regulations, or in cases where retaining the employee on duty may result in damage to U.S. Postal Service property, loss of mail or funds, or where the employee may be injurious to self or others. The employee shall remain on the rolls (non-pay status) until disposition of the case has been had. If it is proposed to suspend such an employee for more than thirty (30) days or discharge the employee, the emergency action taken under this Section may be made the subject of a separate grievance.

Section 8. Review of Discipline

In no case may a supervisor impose suspension or discharge upon an employee unless the proposed disciplinary action by the supervisor has first been reviewed and concurred in by the installation head or designee.

In associate post offices of twenty (20) or less employees, or where there is no higher level supervisor than the supervisor who proposes to initiate suspension or discharge, the proposed disciplinary action shall first be reviewed and concurred in by a higher authority outside such installation or post office before any proposed disciplinary action is taken.

Section 9. Veterans' Preference

A preference eligible is not hereunder deprived of whatever rights of appeal such employee may have under the Veterans' Preference Act; however, if the employee appeals under the Veterans' Preference Act, the employee thereby waives access to any procedure under the Agreement beyond Step 3 of the grievance-arbitration procedure.

Section 10. Employee Discipline Records

The records of a disciplinary action against an employee shall not be considered in any subsequent disciplinary action if there has been no disciplinary action initiated against the employee for a period of two years.

Upon the employee's written request, any disciplinary notice or decision letter will be removed from the employee's official personnel folder after two years if there has been no disciplinary action initiated against the employee in that two-year period.

Obviously, not all steps need to be followed in extremely serious offenses. Also, provision is often made for removal of evidence of discipline if an employee keeps "a clean record" for a stated period of time.

ITEMS AN EMPLOYER MAY HAVE TO PROVE IN ARBITRATION TO SUSTAIN A DISCHARGE FOR POOR PERFORMANCE

Employee and union were aware of the reason for the discharge	Employee was properly trained
Standard is fair	Employer offered reassignment to a less demanding task
Employee was aware of the standard	Employee received progressive discipline
Employee is aware that performance is below standard	Mitigating circumstances do not excuse the performance level
Standard is enforced consistently over time and among employees	No alternative to discharge exists

---

Obviously, sustaining this proof not only imposes a substantial administrative burden but may also be difficult to sustain on the facts. It will also certainly take a long time.

JOB-SECURITY PROVISIONS

Besides an interest in the number of people necessary to do a job, unions also have an interest in the number of jobs available. There are three major threats to the continued existence of jobs: (1) automation, (2) subcontracting, and (3) reduced production. To decrease these dangers, unions often attempt to negotiate guarantees that jobs will not be abolished during the life of the contract.

Automation—the replacement of a person by a machine—has been with us since humans began using tools. In different eras it has been known by different names, such as industrialization, cybernetics, and robotics. By whatever name, two features combine to continue to push forward the replacement of humans: (1) people continue to cost more, and (2) machines are continually invented to do more things.

If a machine exists that can do a person's job, it is necessary that the person work for less cost than the automated alternative. The more an employee's wages and benefits are raised, the greater the employer's incentive to replace him or her. As machines become available and cost-effective, they will be used. They also possess other characteristics desirable to many employers, such as not forming unions.

The opportunity to mechanize jobs presents an employer with a formidable offensive weapon in bargaining. A credible threat to automate can certainly act to suppress demands for wage increases and may even result in concessions by the union. To prevent this from happening, particularly in decaying industries, unions will often forego other demands to extract a guarantee that the employer will not reduce or eliminate currently existing benefits.

It should be noted that unions do not always oppose technological innovation. One reason is that it often makes the job easier. Another is that it doesn't necessarily cost employees jobs. If the improvements in technology result in greater efficiency, employer sales may increase and employment will expand in other places in the company. If the displaced workers can be absorbed, no harm is done and everyone benefits. If, however, the displaced workers cannot be assimilated into the organization elsewhere, unions may try to resist the advance of technology. In such situations they often negotiate clauses to cushion its blow. Provisions found in some contracts include severance pay, retraining, advance notice of plant shutdown, and aid in placement elsewhere.

Subcontracting presents another major threat to high-cost labor. If an employer can hire work done by another employer cheaper than it can do it itself, it is in its economic interest to do so. This situation may arise when an employer's own unionized employees cost it more than the sum of some other entrepreneur's (probably nonunion) labor cost plus profit. If the subcontractor can meet quality and production standards, the union is in big trouble. To try to avoid this, unions often attempt to negotiate restrictions on the subcontracting of work that could be performed by members of the bargaining unit. Obviously, the employer would agree to such limitations only in exchange for comparable benefits elsewhere.

TYPICAL SUBCONTRACTING CLAUSE

ARTICLE XXV: SUBCONTRACT WORK

Section 1

Nothing contained within this agreement shall limit the County's right to enter into contracts for the performance of work by persons not covered by this agreement, except as follows:

(A) County shall give notice in writing to the Union of its intention to enter into a contract with the third party to perform work at the time of the notice being performed by employees covered by this agreement, which written notice shall be given at least three weeks prior to the entry into the contract with the third party.

(B) County shall not enter into any such contract unless the agreement with the third party shall provide that the third party and its successors shall be bound by the obligations of the County under this agreement.

(C) The County shall not subcontract as long as they have capable employees available to do all County work.

ELABORATE SUBCONTRACTING CLAUSE

ARTICLE 46: PRESERVATION OF BARGAINING UNIT WORK

Section 1. Managerial and supervisory employees, independent contractors, other state employees, and agents, will not be assigned to perform bargaining unit work so as to cause the layoff, downgrading, or to prevent the return to work of an available competent employee. This Agreement will not be construed to prevent managerial and supervisory employees from performing bargaining unit work for the purpose of instruction, illustration, lending an occasional hand, experimenting, developing, in emergency situations, or where necessary, carry out the functions and programs of the Employer, or maintain the Employer's standards of service.

Section 2. Effective December 1, 1983, the provisions of Section 1 above shall be superceded by the following:

a. Managerial, supervisory and other state employees will not be assigned to perform bargaining unit work so as to cause the layoff, downgrading or to prevent the return to work of an available, competent employee. This Agreement will not be construed so as to prevent managerial, supervisory or other state employees from performing bargaining unit work for the purpose of instruction, illustration, lending an occasional hand, experimenting, in emergency situations, or where necessary, carrying out the functions and programs of the Employer, or maintaining the Employer's standards of service.

b. Independent contractors and agents may be assigned bargaining unit work which may cause the layoff, downgrading or prevent the return to work of an available competent employee where the assignment is for legitimate operational reasons resulting in cost savings or improved delivery of services to the taxpayers. The Employer shall provide the Union with as much advance notice as is possible of such an assignment upon request of the Union, the Employer agrees to meet and discuss with the Union concerning the reasons for the proposed assignment and recommendations submitted by the Union regarding relevant alternative methods of achieving the Employer's desired result which may include the possible use of attrition, reassignment, transfer or voluntary furloughs.

If after meeting and discussing as provided above, the Employer decides to assign the work to an independent contractor or agent resulting in a furlough, the placement procedure provided for in Article 29, Section 10, shall be expanded to provide the following:

1. Placement rights shall begin at the time the employee's completed placement

questionnaire is received by the central agency personnel office of the appropriate agency and will continue for twelve (12) months from the date of furlough.

2. An employee shall be eligible for placement in a budgeted, available, uncommitted vacancy in a classification covered by this Agreement provided the vacancy is at the same or lower pay range of the classification held by the employee prior to being laid off; the employee is qualified and there are no seniority claims to the vacancy in question.

3. If an employee is not placed within the first six (6) months of the one (1) year placement period, the employee shall have a one-time right to alter the pay range below which the employee will not accept placement as well as the designated work locations.

4. The placement period may be extended if the Employer and the Union agree.

The final threat, reduced production, is a potentially fatal result of high-cost labor. If an employer cannot make a satisfactory return on investment, it may go out of business. Certainly this is the case if it goes bankrupt, but it is also the case in such examples as the steel industry, where employers have invested company earnings in real estate development rather than in expanded steel production because the return on investment promises to be better.

For unions, the line between protecting existing jobs and promoting their value can be a very thin one. It may also be very difficult to detect. It depends on an accurate assessment of what opportunities are available to the employer and what the employer can afford to pay. Miscalculations in this area can cause a union to attempt to force an employer into an unworkable contract. Unfortunately, the chances of such a problem's arising are exacerbated by typical collective bargaining tactics, because management historically has tried to give unions the impression things were worse off financially than they were. Then, when union restraint was genuinely needed, management's claims were not heeded, because it had "cried 'Wolf!'" too often in the past and had destroyed its credibility. Given management's self-interest in understating its financial position, it is not surprising or shameful that unions do not always accept what may seem to be reasonable pleas from employers.

SAFETY AND HEALTH

Many contracts contain specific provisions to promote safety and health in the workplace. Often these goals are pursued through joint committees and do not produce significant disagreement in bargaining. Exceptions do exist, however. Sometimes union demands for a safer workplace can be extremely costly, or sometimes there is disagreement as to the danger present.

In the 1970s it was anticipated that this area of bargaining would be reduced in importance because of the passage of the Occupational Safety and Health Act (OSHA). OSHA was supposed to provide safe workplaces but has encountered a great deal of managerial and political opposition. In the 1980s, federal enforcement of the Act has been greatly reduced. Still, many unionized

SAFETY PROTECTION REQUIRED BY WORK RULES

SOURCE: *Charles Gatewood*

employees may be receiving its benefits by having the Act's provisions incorporated into the labor agreement. In this way, the worker receives protection through the grievance procedure rather than depending on the federal government to enforce the law. An area that has received increased attention in recent years is that of employees with substance abuse problems, both on and off the job. While not primarily a union-management relations issue, many contracts have begun addressing the subject. A typical cooperative problem solving clause appears below.

ALCOHOL AND DRUG RECOVERY PROGRAMS

Section 1. Programs

The Employer and the Unions express strong support for programs of self-help. The Employer shall provide and maintain a program which shall encompass the education, identification, referral, guidance and follow-up of those employees afflicted by the disease of Alcoholism. When an employee is referred to PAR by the Employer, the PAR counsellor will have a reasonable period of time to evaluate the employee's progress in the program. The parties will meet at the national level at least once every six months to discuss existing and new programs. This program of labor-management cooperation shall support the continuation of the PAR Program at the current level. In addition, the Employer will give full consideration to expansion of the PAR Program where warranted.

An employee's voluntary participation in such programs will be considered favorably in disciplinary action proceedings.

Section 2. Joint Committee

In offices having PAR Programs the status and progress of the program, including improving methods for identifying alcoholism at its early stages and encouraging employees to obtain treatment without delay, will be proper agenda items for discussion at the local regularly scheduled Joint Labor-Management Committee meetings as provided for in Article 17, Section 5. Such discussion shall not breach the confidentiality of PAR participants.

Section 3. Pilot Program and Referrals

The Employer agrees to continue the pilot project regarding a self-help program to assist users of non-hard core drugs. And the Employer will meet periodically with the National Union(s) to discuss the status of the pilot project. Additionally, in postal installations having professional medical units, the Employer will insure that the professional staffs maintain a current listing of all local community federally-approved drug treatment agencies for referring employees with such problems.

JOB ENRICHMENT, QUALITY OF WORKLIFE, AND THE ROLE OF COOPERATION

One other administrative issue—quality of worklife—has received a great deal of attention in the 1980s. Because of the nontraditional nature of this topic, its unclear outcomes, and its perhaps peculiar effect on labor-management relations, a separate chapter has been devoted to this and related topics.

Notes

1. Richard B. Freeman and James L. Medoff, *What Do Unions Do?* (New York: Basic Books, 1984), p. 162.
2. *Ibid.*, pp. 162–180.
3. *Ibid.*, p. 173.
4. Kenneth L. Sovreign, *Personnel Law* (Reston, Va.: Reston Publishing Company, 1984), p. 94.

Discussion Questions

1. Assess the fundamental conflict in administrative issues.
2. Discuss the effects of unionization on productivity.
3. Discuss the methods and importance of job-control unionism.
4. Discuss job descriptions, production standards, job assignment, and scheduling.
5. Evaluate the role played by seniority in union-management relations.
6. Discuss discipline and discharge as administrative issues.
7. Discuss job-security issues and solutions.
8. Discuss how safety and health are treated as administrative issues.
9. Assess the role of unions in job enrichment, quality of worklife, and cooperative problem solving.

Statements for Comment

1. "From an employee's viewpoint, administrative issues are the most important subjects in the contract."
2. "Low operating costs are not the only consideration in employment. Sometimes economics must also accommodate human needs. Sometimes employment should be continued even if it's not the cheapest possible alternative."
3. "Production standards may well be more important to management than wage rates."
4. "On assembly lines, any reward criterion other than seniority is favoritism."
5. "Other than in sales positions, it is often difficult to measure merit."
6. "Discipline only for just cause makes better managers."
7. "Job-security concerns are management's greatest offensive weapon in bargaining."

Situations

Case 12–1 "It's a crying shame," muttered Harold Cox, aerospace engineer. "With a team of five engineers, we can tear down, inspect, service, and reassemble one of these jet engines in 10 hours, yet the company is paying 30 unionized mechanics to do the job—and they take 20 hours! I've gone to the CEO with my findings and all he tells me is, 'There's nothing we can do. We don't want to antagonize the union.' I think that's a pretty rotten response."

Presuming the facts in this case to be correct, what might account for the company's position? For the union's? What, realistically, might be done? What pressures are there to change? Not to change? How did such a situation develop?

Case 12–2 "I can't stand it anymore! I'm sick of turkeys, leakers, and weenies!" screamed first-line supervisor Cathy Pinero. "I've got three good-for-nothing loafers in my department who produce nothing but I can't fire them because of this damn union."

"But surely you can fire them for poor performance, can't you? After all, that is 'just cause,' isn't it?" queried Cathy's college-student son Carl.

"You've been spending too much time in the library again, Carl," said his mother. "Get into the real world and realize the difference between theory and reality. I'm going to have to find something else to do."

How justified is Cathy's cynicism? What alternatives does she have? How do most supervisors in unionized workplaces handle such situations? What would you do? Why?

Case 12–3 "Bill Robinson is a lot younger and stronger than Hank Richards and I'm sure he'd do a better job. Loading trucks is hard work. The job might kill Hank. Unfortunately, Hank wants it and he's senior to Bill. The contract says that when merit is equal, seniority shall prevail. I wonder which one I should give the job to?" mused Walter Krinski, supervisor of the loading dock.

Which would you give it to? What do you need to know? What factors are relevant? What might be the reaction to your decision? Are there any other alternatives?

Case 12–4 "Coal mining has always been a dangerous job. It's part of the folklore," said Frank Jones, West Virginian coal miner. "I remember when no one wore gas masks. They existed, all right, but no one here had one. The President of the country had some Mine Safety Board that was supposed to inspect mines and see that safety equipment was being used properly, but we never saw any inspectors. In fact, I heard that none of the Board members had ever been in a coal mine, and that half of them had never been to West Virginia. I'm sure our mine was operated in violation of the regulations and, for many years, our union did nothing about it. It's only been lately that these safety rules and equipment are being used."

Assume that what Frank says is basically correct. How would you account for the absence of safety provisions? How about the composition of the Board and its behavior? The role of the union? Why is the situation better now? Are the issues faced here typical of many employment situations—that is, are they just more dramatic as a matter of degree, or are they fundamentally different?

Case 12–5 "Here, use this to sweep the floor," said Mr. May, handing Tom Riley a broom. Tom was dumbfounded. He didn't know what to do or say. Finally he said, "But I'm a college graduate!"

Mr. May told Tom to wait a minute because he was busy, but when he was finished, he would show Tom how to do it.

May the employer do this? Is there anything else you need to know? Why did Mr. May do it? Should Mr. May do it? Should Tom do it?

Bibliography of Related Readings

Addison, J. T., "Are Unions Good For Productivity?" *Journal of Labor Research*, 1982, pp. 125–38.

Bacow, Lawrence S., *Bargaining for Job Safety and Health* (Cambridge, Mass.: MIT Press, 1980).

Baer, Walter E., *Discipline and Discharge Under the Labor Agreement* (New York: American Management Association, 1972).

Bernhardt, H. N., "Subcontracting During the Term of a Contract: A Clash Between the NLRB and Arbitral Principle," *Arbitration Journal*, 1982, pp. 45–49.

Blau, F. D., and L. M. Kahn, "Unionism, Seniority, and Turnover," *Industrial Relations*, 1983, pp, 362–73.

Gersuny, Carl, "Origins of Seniority Provisions in Collective Bargaining," in *Proceedings of the 1982 Spring Meeting, Industrial Relations Research Association* (Madison, Wis., 1982).

Levine, H. Z., "Corporate Responsibility During Layoffs," *Personnel*, 1983, pp. 55–58.

Medoff, James R., "Layoffs and Alternatives under Trade Unions in U.S. Manufacturing," *American Economic Review*, June 1979, pp. 380–95.

"Pressure Grows for Shorter Hours," *Personnel Management*, December 1983, p. 9.

Rones, P. L., "Response To Recession: Reduce Hours or Jobs?" *Monthly Labor Review*, October 1981, pp. 3–11.

Somers, Gerald, ed., *Collective Bargaining and Productivity* (Madison, Wis.: Industrial Relations Research Association, 1975).

"Workplace: Preparing for Automation," *Worklife/IR Research Reports*, 1983, pp. 17–18.

THIRTEEN

INSTITUTIONAL ISSUES

Institutional issues address the rights of the parties to exist and to act. Topics include the union's pledge not to strike, management's reserved rights, union membership requirements, union prerogatives and obligations, the union's duty of fair representation, and contract duration.

Contrasted to other subjects of bargaining, institutional issues may cause more than their share of aggravation. Many of them take on a philosophical taint that makes them difficult to compromise. They are often perceived in terms of, ''I'm right and you're wrong,'' rather than, ''How much do we each need?''

NO-STRIKE CLAUSE

Virtually all contracts contain a clause obligating the union not to strike during the life of the agreement and to submit all disputes arising under the contract to the grievance procedure. Occasionally, specific issues are exempted from this broad coverage and the union retains the right to strike over that issue only. An example is the United Automobile Workers' reservation of the right to strike during the life of the contract over assembly-line speed-ups.

NO-STRIKE CLAUSE, WITH EXCEPTIONS

The Union agrees not to strike during the life of this agreement except if the Employer fails to pay wages or contribute to the agreed upon funds, or fails to implement the award of an arbitrator.

The pledge of the union not to strike during the life of the contract—nor to seek additional improvements in wages, hours, and working conditions—is the quid pro quo for management's concessions in bargaining. The continued utilization of the employees' services under the agreed-upon conditions is the one valuable commodity that the union can offer. Everything else that the union offers is usually a reduction in a demand for some additional benefit it sought. In other words, in most situations, management doesn't gain anything, it just loses less. The pledge not to strike does not fall into that category and is commonly of sufficient value to produce an agreement.

MANAGEMENT'S RESERVED RIGHTS

Taken very seriously and emotionally by the parties is the issue of management's rights. This section of the contract attempts to determine which rights are reserved for management and which for the union and employees. There are two basic contract forms to cover the problem—the long clause and the short clause.

The *long clause* basically attempts to list all the rights reserved exclusively for management. These will be areas in which management is specifically permitted to act and to formulate policy without negotiating with the union. Management does, of course, have to negotiate with the union over which issues are to be included on the list. The danger of listing specifically which rights management possesses unilaterally becomes apparent when an issue arises which does not appear in the contract. This could happen either because the parties considered the issue but couldn't agree on whether to include it or because no one ever considered the issue during negotiations. If the list attempts to be exhaustive, all other issues are arguably subject to joint determination.

MANAGEMENT RIGHTS CLAUSE, LONG

The rights of the City, through its management officials, shall include, but shall not be limited to, the right to determine the organization of City Government; to determine the purpose of each of its constituent departments; to exercise control and discretion over the organization and efficiency of operations of the City; to set standards for service to be offered to the public; to direct the employees of the City, including the right to assign work and overtime; to rehire, examine, classify, promote, train, transfer, assign, and schedule employees in positions with the City; to suspend, demote, discharge, or take other disciplinary action against employees for proper cause to increase, reduce, change, modify or alter the composition and size of the work force, including the right to relieve employees from duties because of lack of work or funds; to determine the location, methods, means and personnel by which operations are to be conducted, including the right to determine whether goods or services are to be made or purchased; to establish, modify, combine or abolish job pay positions; to change or eliminate existing methods of operation, equipment of facilities; and to establish, implement and maintain an effective internal security program.

The *short clause* attempts to avoid this problem. Its theory is based on the assumption (and probably even the direct statement) that, "All rights not specifically conveyed to the union by this contract are reserved to management." This treatment of the subject reflects a belief of many managers that all rights initially belong to the owner of the enterprise as "property rights" and that the owner's rights are diminished only as he or she chooses to bargain them away. Following this logic, unions and employees have no rights (other than those arising under laws) that cannot specifically be found in the contract.

MANAGEMENT RIGHTS CLAUSE, SHORT

All managerial and administrative rights and functions, except those which are abridged by this Agreement, are vested exclusively in the University's Administration.

The problem with this logic is that it is based on an erroneous assumption of what the owner "owns." Management, as agent of the owners, may use the employer's *capital* as it sees fit because property is owned. Employees, however, are not *owned* by the employer and may be utilized only in accordance with the contract between the employee and management. In nonunion situations, the contract is seldom committed to writing and is generally offered on a "take it or leave it" basis. The fact that the employer almost always has the economic advantage over the employee to dictate the terms of the agreement does not give it the *right* to do so, but merely the *power*. In industrialized America, many employers have lost sight of (if they ever had sight of) this distinction.

The common belief that the employer can tell the employees what to do because it owns the enterprise is wrong—theoretically, legally, and morally. The employer doesn't own the employees. It must reach agreement with employees for services and prices just as it does with customers and suppliers. In unionized situations, these bargains are reached after joint negotiations and are specifically committed to a written contract which reflects for employees not greater *rights* but rather greater *power.*

Having observed that there is no theoretical basis for management's reserved rights, it must also be observed that the union can, at least theoretically, create such rights for management by specifically agreeing to such an arrangement in the contract. The caveat "at least theoretically" was used because it appears that in grievance arbitration rulings, employees may occasionally be the recipients of rights not specifically provided for them, even under a reserved rights clause. The limitations on even reserved rights will be noted in Chapter 14.

UNION SECURITY ARRANGEMENTS

Union "security" deals with the extent to which the union can compel membership in the organization or require payment of dues in support of its activities for those in the bargaining unit.

Historically, the strongest form of union security was the "closed shop." It required that a job applicant be a member of the union before being hired. This provision was made illegal in 1947 for contracts covered by the Taft-Hartley Act.[1] In many instances, management objected to such a demand because it severely restricted who they could hire. Nonunion employees also objected because they were often caught in a double bind. Besides not being eligible to be hired, they also often could not get into the union. (The unions that used closed shops often had very restrictive admissions policies.) Some vestiges of the closed shop still exist, most notably in the construction industry, maritime trades, printing, entertainment, and garment industry. In these areas, unions often still operate hiring halls from which applicants are referred to available jobs. Before Taft-Hartley, one had to "have his union card" (be a member of the union with jurisdiction over his type of work) to use the hiring hall. Since Taft-Hartley, the hiring hall is theoretically obligated to refer qualified job seekers without reference to union status.[2]

Hiring halls arose in these industries because of the temporary nature of the work. In construction, for instance, a contractor will bid on a job, perform its services, and go on to another work site—perhaps in another city or state. In such a situation it was advantageous to the *employer* to have the union perform the hiring function. It wasn't feasible for employers to transport skilled workers from town to town or to relocate them constantly. It made more sense for the contractor to obtain a bid in a city and then contact the local hiring hall for the number of apprentices, journeymen, and master craftsmen required. Normally, an employer wishes to make hiring decisions itself, rather than leaving them to a union, but in these instances, it was not a problem. Since craft unions conducted apprenticeship training programs (which, incidentally, removed the cost of training from employers), the union could guarantee the quantity and quality of work. It would be equal to "union standards." Therefore, the employer did not particularly care *which* craftsmen were referred to the job. In such a situation, the hiring hall was beneficial not only to the union, but also to the employer. In recognition of this symbiotic relationship, Congress liberalized the restriction on union shops and the length of probationary periods in the construction and garment trades industries so that they more approximate closed shops.[3]

The next strongest form of union security is the "union shop." It is a common way of doing business in highly unionized states. In the union shop, the union *and the employer* negotiate a provision into the contract that all employees are required to join the union as a condition of keeping their jobs. This obviously infringes on the rights of individual employees, but then so do most employment arrangements. It can be justified on the grounds that since, under the principle of exclusive representation, the union is compelled to represent all employees in the bargaining unit, all employees should have to share in the burdens of representation to share in its benefits. Besides, the union was elected by majority vote, just like our political candidates. Voting for a losing candidate in an election does not excuse a citizen from obeying laws passed by the majority—or to refuse to pay taxes to support them. It is basically a compromise justified by living in a pluralistic legal system.

The Taft-Hartley Act requires that a probationary period must be completed before an employee can be compelled to join a union.[4] The period must be at least 30 days, but can be longer if the parties so agree. During this period, the employee cannot join the union nor is he or she protected by it. The doctrine of employment-at-will prevails. An employer may discharge an employee during this period without having to show just cause or document its reasons and the union cannot and will not intervene.

UNION SHOP CLAUSE

All employees covered by this agreement shall be members of the Association and must maintain their membership in good standing as a condition of employment. New employees may be hired by the employer without regard to Association, provided that such persons tender their application for membership in the Association within 30 days from the date of their employment.

The purpose of the probationary period is to protect the interest of the employer. This creation of decidedly "second class" rights for probationary employees reflects the realities of working life. Since the selection process in many workplaces is chancy at best, employers need the right to "weed out" obvious misfits without having to justify and document every case for employees whose relationship with the company was very ephemeral.

Not everyone agrees with the rationale justifying union shops. Actually, some of the opposition to them by employer and political action groups is probably more pragmatic (meaning they just want to make things difficult for unions) than philosophical. The controversial nature of union shops led to the inclusion of the famous/infamous Section 14(b) of the Taft-Hartley Act, which allows each state to individually ban union shops in the state by passing a "right-to-work" law. Actually, these laws do not entitle anyone to a right to work. They merely permit the right to work without having to join a union. Twenty states, mostly in areas low in industry, have passed such laws. Almost all public-sector jurisdictions have "right-to-work" provisions which forbid the union shop.

STATES WITH RIGHT-TO-WORK LAWS (AS OF 1982)

Alabama	Nevada
Arizona	North Carolina
Arkansas	North Dakota
Florida	South Carolina
Georgia	South Dakota
Iowa	Tennessee
Kansas	Texas
Louisiana	Utah
Mississippi	Virginia
Nebraska	Wyoming

Still, when not outlawed, union shops are the most common security arrangement for employees represented by unions. It is therefore necessary to examine the reasons for their popularity. As noted earlier, this arrangement cannot come into existence without the agreement of management. On the surface, this would seem contrary to management's best interest. Closer examination, however, reveals significant benefits for the employer. Obviously the union has a strong desire for the union shop. That makes granting it a valuable bargaining chit for management. Further, to grant it costs nothing in dollars, or more surprisingly, performance. Compelling nonunion sympathizers to join will probably alienate them from both parties (although generally only temporarily), but

UNION MEMBERS LOBBY AGAINST RIGHT-TO-WORK LAW

SOURCE: AFL–CIO News

it won't affect the *motivation* of nonunion employees. Because the principle of exclusive representation requires the equal application of the contract's provisions to members and nonmembers alike, nonmembers no longer can be rewarded for culling management's favor. Therefore, their motivation, at least as affected by job promotions, will be removed. Forcing them to *join* the union is no big obligation after they have already been forced to abide by the contract. Finally, and probably foremost in management's mind, a union that can compel membership does not need to be constantly "showing off," trying to prove to the membership and free riders that they should support the organization. This makes life much simpler for management.

The beginning union security arrangement is no security at all. It is the "open shop." In this situation, a union represents the bargaining unit, but no one can be compelled to join it or to pay dues. The union, in winning the right to represent the unit, must represent nonmembers without being able to force them to share in the costs of representation. This is obviously a fine arrangement for people willing to take advantage of it, and in some workplaces free riding is fairly widespread. Some managers feel "smug" about this feature, realizing what a burden it is to the union. They feel less smug when they realize what a burden it becomes for them, as the union constantly must give the appearance of delivering, both to try to recruit new members and to prevent current members from resigning.

Another form of union security is most commonly found in public employment and in right-to-work states. It is the "agency shop." In this arrangement, no employee is required to join the union, but everyone in the bargaining unit is required to pay a fee, usually equal to dues, to the union for his or her share of the costs in representation. This is representation which he or she may or may not have wanted but had to receive under exclusive representation. In some instances, the fee may go to a charity instead of the union. This form of union security seems a sensible compromise between freedom of choice and the unfairness of free riding. Employees with moral objections to joining unions are accommodated, while those who merely sought to obtain benefits without paying for them are not.

LAW AUTHORIZING AGENCY SHOP

2a. Notwithstanding any other provisions of law to the contrary, the majority representative and the public employer of public employees in an appropriate unit shall, where requested by the majority representative, negotiate concerning the subject of requiring the payment by all non-member employees in the unit to the majority representative of a representation fee in lieu of dues for services rendered by the majority representative. Where agreement is reached it shall be embodied in writing and signed by the authorized representatives of the public employer and the majority representative.

AGENCY SHOP CLAUSE

All employees in the collective bargaining unit for more than thirty (30) days who do not become, or do not remain members, shall, during any such period of nonmembership, as a condition of employment, pay to the Union a service fee equivalent to the dues uniformly required of its members.

A great convenience to union security is the dues checkoff precedure. It permits the union to have dues deducted, with the employee's consent, directly from the employee's paycheck, rather than having the union rep go around and solicit them. The administrative expense to the employer is gen-

---

LEVELS OF UNION SECURITY

Open Shop	Union represents bargaining unit, but no employee is compelled to join or pay dues.
Agency Shop	Members of bargaining unit are required to pay dues or representation fee but are not required to join. Legal in some right-to-work states, illegal in others.
Union Shop	Members of bargaining unit are required to join union. Illegal in all right-to-work states.
Closed Shop	Potential employees must already be members of the union to be hired. Illegal wherever Taft-Hartley Act applies.

---

erally compensated by the union. Again, some employers believe resisting a checkoff demand will weaken the union, since it will make its revenues more uncertain. On the other hand, a very pronounced way to increase the number of grievances filed is to make the rep talk to every employee every dues period and have him or her be extorted to press the employee's personal grievance or not receive the dues. Many experienced managers find it more convenient to have the union be as secure as possible. Fat cats are less aggressive than hungry ones.

TYPICAL DUES CHECKOFF CLAUSE

During the term of this agreement, and to the extent the laws of the State of Michigan permit, and as provided in this Article, the University will deduct current Association dues, or the representation-service fee from the pay, if any, of each employee who voluntarily executes and delivers to the University the following deduction authorization forms: . . .

ELABORATE DUES DEDUCTION CLAUSE

ARTICLE 4: DUES DEDUCTION

Section 1. The Employer agrees to deduct the Union bi-weekly membership dues and an annual assessment, if any, from the pay of those employees who individually request in writing that such deductions be made. The amounts to be deducted shall be certified to the Employer by the Union, and the aggregate deductions of all employees shall be remitted together with an itemized statement to the Union by the last day of the succeeding month, after such deductions are

(continued)

made. This authorization shall be irrevocable by the employee during the term of this Agreement. When revoked by the employee in accordance with Article 3, the agency shall halt the check-off of dues effective the first full pay period following the expiration of this Agreement.

Section 2. The employee's written authorization for dues payroll deductions shall contain the employee's name, social security number, agency in which employed, work location (institution, district, bureau, etc.), Union name and local number.

Section 3. Where an employee has been suspended, furloughed or discharged and subsequently returned to work, with full or partial back pay or has been reclassified retroactively, the Employer shall, in the manner outlined in Section 1 above, deduct the Union membership dues that are due and owing for the period for which the employee receives back pay.

Section 4. The dues deduction provisions of this Article shall continue to pertain and be complied with by the Em-

ployer with regard to those employees who are promoted into or demoted from a unit of first level supervisors represented by the Union or when any employee is transferred from one position to another position covered by this Agreement. Dues deductions will be resumed for employees upon their return from leave of absence without pay or recall from furlough.

Section 5. The Employer shall provide the Union, on a quarterly basis, a list of all employees in the bargaining units represented by the Union. This list shall contain the employee's name, social security number, address, agency in which employed, class code, work location (institution, district, bureau, etc.) and whether the employee is a member or non-member.

Section 6. The Union shall indemnify and hold the Employer harmless against any and all claims, suits, orders, or judgements brought or issued against the Employer as a result of the action taken or not taken by the Employer under the provisions of this Article.

FIGURE 13–1 DUES CHECKOFF FORM

W/L	P/R	EMP. NO.	NAME		DATE

HILLSBOROUGH CLASSROOM TEACHERS ASSOCIATION, INC.
PAYROLL DEDUCTION ENROLLMENT CARD

I authorize and request the School Board of Hillsborough County to deduct Hillsborough Classroom Teachers Association clerical dues from my bi-monthly pay, and to transmit these amounts to the Association office.

I also understand the School Board will discontinue dues deduction upon written notification to the Association and Board.

S.S.# _____   NEW ☐   RENEWAL ☐

Name ___MR.___
        MRS.
        _____   Worksite _____
        MISS   PRINT OR TYPE
        MS.
Address _____   Signature _____

City _____ Zip_____   Date _____

RETURN INTACT TO CTA OFFICE 4505 N. Rome Ave. Tampa, Fla. 33603

UNION PREROGATIVES AND OBLIGATIONS

Much union business is conducted with management during normal business hours. This is particualy true of grievance processing. Since union reps are regularly employed by the employer rather than the union, this activity takes them away from their normal work duties. How they are compensated for this time and how much of it they are allowed is commonly subject to negotiation. Most contracts call for payment at the employee's normal rate with a limitation on the number of hours spent per week on grievances.

REPRESENTATION BY UNION OFFICIALS

Section 1. Stewards
Stewards may be designated for the purpose of investigating, presenting and adjusting grievances.

Section 2. Appointment of Stewards
A. Each Union signatory to this Agreement will certify to the Employer in writing a steward or stewards and alternates in accordance with the following general guidelines. Where more than one steward is appointed, one shall be designated chief steward. The selection and appointment of stewards or chief stewards is the sole and exclusive function of each Union. Stewards will be certified to represent employees in specific work location(s) on their tour; provided no more than one steward may be certified to represent employees in a particular work location(s). The number of stewards certified shall not exceed, but may be less than, the number provided by the formula hereinafter set forth.

Employees in the same craft per tour or station	
Up to 49	1 steward
50 to 99	2 stewards
100 to 199	3 stewards
200 to 499	5 stewards
500 or more	5 stewards plus additional steward for each 100 employees

B. At an installation, a Union may designate in writing to the Employer one Union officer actively employed at that installation to act as a steward to investigate, present and adjust a specific grievance or to investigate a specific problem to determine whether to file a grievance. The activities of such Union officer shall be in lieu of a steward designated under the formula in Section 2.A and shall be in accordance with Section 3. Payment, when applicable, shall be in accordance with Section 4.

C. To provide steward service to installations with twenty or less craft employees where the Union has not certified a steward, a Union representative certified to the Employer in writing and compensated by the Union may perform the duties of a steward.

D. At the option of a Union, representatives not on the Employer's payroll shall be entitled to perform the functions of a steward or chief steward, provided such representatives are certified in writing to the Employer at the regional level and providing such representatives act in lieu of stewards designated under the provisions of 2.A or 2.B above.

E. A steward may be designated to represent more than one craft, or to act as a steward in a craft other than his/her own, whenever the Union or Unions involved so agree, and notify the Employer in writing. Any steward designations across craft lines must be in accordance with the formula set forth in Section 2.A above.

Section 3. Rights of Stewards

When it is necessary for a steward to leave his/her work area to investigate and adjust grievances or to investigate a specific problem to determine whether to file a grievance, the steward shall request permission from the immediate supervisor and such request shall not be unreasonably denied.

In the event the duties require the steward leave the work area and enter another area within the installation or post office, the steward must also receive permission from the supervisor from the other area he/she wishes to enter and such request shall not be unreasonably denied.

The steward, chief steward, or other Union representative properly certified in accordance with Section 2 above may request and shall obtain access through the appropriate supervisor to review the documents, files and other records necessary for processing a grievance or determining if a grievance exists and shall have the right to interview the aggrieved employee(s), supervisors and witnesses during working hours. Such requests shall not be unreasonably denied.

While serving as a steward or chief steward, an employee may not be involuntarily transferred to another tour, to another station or branch of the particular post office or to another independent post office or installation unless there is no job for which the employee is qualified on such tour, or in such station or branch, or post office.

If an employee requests a steward or Union representative to be present during the course of an interrogation by the Inspection Service, such request will be granted. All polygraph tests will continue to be on a voluntary basis.

Section 4. Payment of Stewards

The Employer will authorize payment only under the following conditions:

Grievances:
> Steps 1 and 2—The aggrieved and one Union steward (only as permitted under the formula in Section 2.A) for time actually spent in grievance handling, including investigation and meetings with the Employer. The Employer will also compensate a steward for the time reasonably necessary to write grievance. In addition, the Employer will compensate any witnesses for the time required to attend a Step meeting.

Meetings called by the Employer for information exchange and other conditions designated by the Employer concerning contract application.

Employer authorized payment as outlined above will be granted at the applicable straight time rate, providing the time spent is a part of the employee's or steward's (only a provided for under the formula in Section 2.A) regular work day.

Contracts also often specify the provision of an office on the premises for the union to conduct business and the use of specified bulletin-board space to post announcements of upcoming meetings, social events, etc. There are usually limitations against posting propaganda. The use of the employer's facilities for these purposes is justified on the grounds of management's being a joint beneficiary of a mutually negotiated contract.

BULLETIN BOARD PROVISION

ARTICLE XXVIII - BULLETIN BOARDS

The Union may post notices on bulletin boards in places and locations where notices usually are posted by the Employer for employees to read. All notices shall be on Union stationery, shall be used only to notify employees of matters pertaining to Union affairs, and shall not contain any derogatory or inflammatory statements concerning the City, the Department, or personnel employed by either entity.

The contract may also impose some specific obligations on the union. There may be a section on the union's obligations during a strike, such as requiring that valuable machinery be shut down and maintained properly. Many contracts will also contain a clause in which the union specifically agrees to conduct its activities without reference to race, color, creed, sex, age, or national origin. This antidiscrimination disclaimer, of course, merely restates obligations already imposed by law. Adding the provision is not completely redundant, however. It does serve to give more attention to the matter and allows use of the grievance procedure as an additional remedy for wrongdoing.

NON-DISCRIMINATION CLAUSE

SECTION 4 - NON-DISCRIMINATORY CLAUSE

The provisions of this agreement and the wages, hours, terms and conditions of employment set forth herein shall be applied without regard to race, creed, religion, color, national origin, age, sex or marital status.

DUTY OF FAIR REPRESENTATION

A union obligation that has received increased attention in recent years is the "duty of fair representation." It requires the union to represent all employees in the bargaining unit fairly under the contract, regardless of their membership status or favor within the union.[5] If an employee is not fairly represented by the union, the union may be liable for damages. The authority for this responsibility lies in the interpretation of the Taft-Hartley Act given in recent years by the NLRB and the courts.[6]

Besides obvious requirements, such as a union's not treating constituents in a racially discriminatory manner and not deliberately losing the grievances of nonsupporters, recent decisions are also requiring that union grievance investigations be not only unbiased but also competent.[7] Previously, all that was required of the union was that it investigate grievances in good faith. No measure of competency was required, so long as all members of the bargaining unit were treated equally. Now, the union can be held liable for damages if it doesn't investigate a grievance well enough, and a further case has established the principle that the union's share of damages can be very great. When an employee is wrongfully discharged (which is the employer's fault) and the employee was not fairly or competently represented in the grievance procedure (which is the union's fault), the employee may be reinstated with back pay. The employer will be liable for back pay up to the time of the arbitration hearing (usually less than one year), and the union can be liable for the remainder up to the time the case is resolved in the courts (perhaps several years!).[8]

CONTRACT DURATION AND EXPIRATION DATE

Contract length and expiration date are subject to negotiation. Factors affecting the desired duration of a contract generally impact the parties approximately equally. That is, the parties desire a contract that will stabilize their relationship on satisfactory terms for as long as it won't become seriously outdated. This reduces administrative burdens and expense for both sides, reduces the threat of harmful strikes for both sides, and increases predictability of outcomes for both sides. At some point, however, this "locked-in" predictability may become detrimental to one or both sides in a changing environment. The more rapidly the environment changes or the more unpredictable the future, the shorter both sides desire the contract to be. Conversely, stable environments allow lengthier contracts. In a comparatively stable economy, contracts of three years' duration are relatively common.

Expiration dates are not as readily agreeable a subject as duration. There are tactical advantages to be gained by one side over the other in the timing of a contract's expiration. As noted in the discussion on strike power in Chapter 9, *when* a strike occurs can have a significant influence on the strength of the parties to deal with it. Since economic strikes may generally occur legally only when a contract has expired, the negotiation of the expiration date may have a significant effect on the parties' bargaining power.

Notes

1. Sec. 8(a) (3).
2. Sec. 8(f).
3. Sec. 8(f).
4. Sec. 8(a) (3).
5. *Vaca* v. *Sipes*, 386 U.S. 171 (1967).
6. *Miranda Fuel Co.*, 140 NLRB 181 (1962).
7. *Hines* v. *Anchor Motor Freight, Inc.* 96 S.Ct. 1048 (1976).
8. *IBEW* v. *Foust*.

Discussion Questions

1. Evaluate the significance and consequences of no-strike clauses.
2. Describe and assess management's reserved rights.
3. Describe and evaluate union security arrangements.
4. Discuss the duty of fair representation.

Statements for Comment

1. "Even if management's reserved rights are not based on law, they should be. It's the only sensible way to run a business."
2. "Right-to-work laws are directed at the wrong target. They should exempt employees from having to be bound by the contract (if they don't want to be), rather than from having to join the union."
3. "Agency shops are the proper way of doing business. Union shops just reflect unfair bargaining power."
4. "The whole principle of exclusive representation is unfair."
5. "The only legitimate excuse for outlawing union shops is to protect members who are dissatisfied with the leadership."

Situations

Case 13-1 "You know, it sure seems to me that agency shop is the best of both worlds," said Susie Smithson, a management major at a state university. "After all, the principle of exclusive representation requires the parties to extend the benefits of the contract even to nonmembers of the union, so there is justification for billing them for the services they receive, yet it still permits those who don't wish to be affiliated the right not to join. Although imperfect, it seems to me to be the least evil solution to a complex problem, particularly when considering the needs of *all* parties. I wonder why it isn't more popular than union shop arrangements."

What insight can you provide Susie on this situation? If agency shops are so good, why aren't they more popular than union shops where both are permitted?

Case 13–2 "I'm really disappointed in this union we voted in," said Ruth Allen. "It's costing me dues and, as far as I can tell, we're no better off than before. If I had it to do over again, I wouldn't vote for the union. I wonder if there's anything I can do to get out of this mess."

What would you advise Ruth to do? What avenues are open to her? Are there any other facts you need to know? How practical and effective are the solutions you have recommended? Does it make a difference why she is unhappy? If so, why?

Bibliography of Related Readings

Bennett, J. T., and M. H. Johnson, "Free Riders in U.S. Labour Unions: Artifice or Affliction?" *British Journal of Industrial Relations*, 1979, pp. 158–72.

Haggard, Thomas R., *Compulsory Unionism, the NLRB, and the Courts* (Philadelphia: University of Pennsylvania Press, 1977).

Hunt, J. C., and R. A. White, "The Effects of Right-To-Work Legislation on Union Outcomes: Additional Evidence," *Journal of Labor Research*, 1983, pp. 47–63.

Kuhn, James W., "Right to Work Laws: Symbols or Substance?" *Industrial and Labor Relations Review*, July 1961.

Lumsden, Keith, and Craig Petersen, "The Effect of Right-to-Work Laws on Unionization in the United States," *Journal of Political Economy*, December 1975.

Muthuchidambaram, S., "Union's Duty of Fair Representation: Evolution Of Jurisprudence in North America," *Indian Journal of Industrial Relations*, 1983, pp. 21–44.

Prasow, Paul, "The Theory of Management Reserved Rights—Revisited," in Gerald G. Somers, ed., *Proceedings of the Twenty-Sixth Annual Winter Meeting, Industrial Relations Research Association* (Madison, Wis., 1974).

Rubin, M., "To Cross or Not To Cross: Picket Lines and Employee Rights," *Industrial Relations Law Journal*, 1981, pp. 419–47.

Zemke, R., "Corporate Resonsibility: The Perils of Becoming Thy Brother's Keeper," *Training*, October 1981, pp. 50–51.

FOURTEEN

GRIEVANCE PROCESSING AND ARBITRATION

The rights gained through collective bargaining are of no value unless they can be enforced. The standard mechanism for enforcing these rights is the grievance procedure. When an employee believes he or she has not been treated as well as required by the contract, the remedy is to file a grievance. Normally, if the grievance is not settled, it may ultimately be appealed to an impartial arbitrator. This system of enforcement is an alternative to the much more costly mechanisms of strikes and law suits.

The processing of grievances is one of the greatest benefits unions provide for their members. The contract provides more rights than unrepresented employees have, and the union's expertise helps assure that employees receive those rights. Further, this protection of employee rights may also bring substantial benefits to management, and at a cost considerably lower than the alternatives. The grievance procedure may help management by providing a forum through which problems can be both communicated and solved. A grievance procedure gives management a formal means of discovering and addressing employee needs (not always an easy task in large organizations) before they become bigger through neglect. Further, this problem solving takes place without disruption of production and in an atmosphere more likely to promote cooperation and a sense of fair play than would strikes or law suits to enforce the contract.

REASONS WHY A GRIEVANCE PROCEDURE
IS NEEDED

After a contract is negotiated, it must be applied to events that occur in the workplace. This means that the language of the contract must be interpreted for use in particular situations. In many instances this is not easy. There are two principal reasons for this: (1) the contract doesn't address the issue in dispute directly, (2) the issue is addressed, but the meaning of the contract language is subject to different interpretations. Either situation can cause disagreements as to the rights of the parties.

Most grievances arise when management takes some action that the union believes (and the employer does not believe) violates the contract. (There are very few grievances where management alleges that the union violated the contract, because the union or the employee seldom has the authority to initiate any decision or action.) If the union believes that the contract has been violated, it has three basic remedies to rectify such a breech: (1) strike to place economic pressure on the employer to comply with the union's interpretation of the contract, (2) sue for enforcement of the contract and for damages in a court of law, or (3) submit the dispute to the grievance procedure.

The first remedy, to strike, is direct, quick, and perhaps forceful, but it is also terribly expensive to both sides and is usually very inappropriate. Shutting down operations over disputes that may affect only a single individual or a small portion of the workforce makes little sense. Since Americans on both sides of the table recognize the general inappropriateness of striking to enforce contracts, the union generally agrees to a no-strike provision for the life of the agreement in exchange for a grievance procedure with outside arbitration. The British, on the other hand, have not generally discovered the wisdom of this tradeoff and continue to be plagued with disruptive strikes during the life of their contracts.[1] British businesspeople are often heard to envy the practicality of American dispute resolution in the workplace during the life of the contract. This is in sharp contrast to the often more bitter and hostile contract *negotiations* in the United States compared to Western Europe.[2]

The second remedy, a law suit, is also flawed. Law suits are expensive and time-consuming and are (some unions believe) tried in a promanagement court system. Law suits also do not tend to promote harmonious relations among people who will have to continue to work together in the future.

The third remedy, the grievance procedure, is almost always favored by both parties. In the typical situation, management (in the eyes of the union) assigns an employee to do something not in accordance with the contract or allocates a benefit wrongly. When this occurs, under American common-law rules, the employee must "work now and grieve later." If review of the decision upholds the grievant, the employee will be made whole. If management is upheld, no harm was done. Either way, production was carried on for the benefit of all parties while the rights of individuals were being processed fairly and efficiently.

There are three common-law exceptions to the doctrine of "work now and grieve later." An employee may temporarily refuse a supervisory order pending discussion with his or her union representative if the action to be taken is arguably either

1. illegal,
2. immoral, or
3. dangerous.

These exceptions are generally granted in recognition of the difficulty of "making whole" an employee who was wronged in these areas.

In the eyes of much of the rest of the industrialized world, the fair, quick, and inexpensive resolution of grievances is one of the great triumphs of American industrial relations.[3]

TYPICAL GRIEVANCE PROCEDURES

Grievance procedures can consist of whatever the parties negotiate. Although there is some variety among them, most follow a basic model. The typical procedure consists of a series of steps at different levels, usually three or four, before terminating in binding arbitration of unresolved grievances by a jointly selected neutral outsider.

At the first level usually the local representative and immediate supervisor try to resolve the grievance. If they are unsuccessful, the grievance is appealed to the next level specified in the contract with higher-ranking representatives from each side. Again, if resolution cannot be had, another level of appeal takes place. This continuing review at higher levels may help produce agreement, as people less personally and emotionally involved examine the case. Finally, if there is still no agreement, the case will be referred to arbitration.

GRIEVANCE FORM

UNION GRIEVANCE AND APPEAL
STEP 1
CITY OF ST. PETERSBURG

EMPLOYEE NAME_____INDENT. NO._____DATE_____

CLASSIFICATION____SHIFT_____LOCATION_____

STEP 1 – GRIEVANCE (Submit within three (3) working days of supervisor's verbal decision)

Statement of Grievance:_____

_____
_____
_____
_____
_____

Date, Details and Facts upon Which Grievance is Based: _____

_____
_____
_____
_____
_____

Article_____Section_____of the Labor Agreement Alleged to have been violated.
Action, Remedy or Solution Requested:_____

_____
_____
_____
_____
_____

_____ _____ _____ _____
UNION Representative's Signature   Date   Employee's Signature   Date
   (if applicable)

IMMEDIATE SUPERVISOR'S RECEIPT OF GRIEVANCE:

NAME_____ TITLE_____ DATE/TIME_____

DIVISION CHIEF'S RESPONSE _____ :

Review and Analysis of Alleged Violation:_____

_____
_____
_____
_____
_____

Grievance is Granted or Rejected Based on the Following:_____

_____
_____
_____
_____
_____

Remedy or Solution Recommended:_____

_____
_____
_____

IMMEDIATE SUPERVISOR'S SIGNATURE   DATE

Receipt Acknowledgement of Answer: DIVISION CHIEF'S SIGNATURE   DATE

Employee's Signature   Date/Time

Union Representative's Signature   Date/Time
Distribution: Prepare Original and 4 copies

Original	– Division Chief	
Copy	– Employee Receipt	
Copy	– Answer to Employee	
Copy	– Answer to Labor Relations	Form – UG I
Copy	– Answer to Department Director	R/7–76

Grievance procedures generally require time limits for filing complaints and for answers. This prevents the filing of stale complaints, which are harder to investigate, and requires management to give timely answers, rather than stalling or ignoring the problem. Steps in a typical grievance procedure are portrayed in Figure 14–1 on page 350.

ELABORATE GRIEVANCE PROCEDURE

17.100   Definition of a Grievance

   A claim by a teacher or the Association that there has been a violation, misinterpretation, or misapplication of any provision of this Agreement, may be processed as a grievance as hereinafter provided.

17.200   Grievance Procedure

   17.210   In the event that a teacher believes there is a basis for a grievance, he/she shall first discuss the alleged grievance with his/her appropriate administrator either personally or accompanied by his/her Association representative.

   17.220   If, as a result of the informal discussion with the appropriate administrator, a grievance still exists, it shall be reduced to writing within five (5) work days after discussion with the administrator or in any event not later than fifteen (15) work days after the occurrence of the alleged violation and submitted to the appropriate administrator, on the form set forth in annexed Appendix B. The grievant shall sign the grievance.

   17.230   Within three (3) work days of receipt of the grievance, the administrator shall meet with the grievant and the Association representative in an effort to resolve the grievance. The administrator shall indicate his/her disposition of the grievance

FIGURE 14-1 STEPS IN A TYPICAL GRIEVANCE PROCEDURE

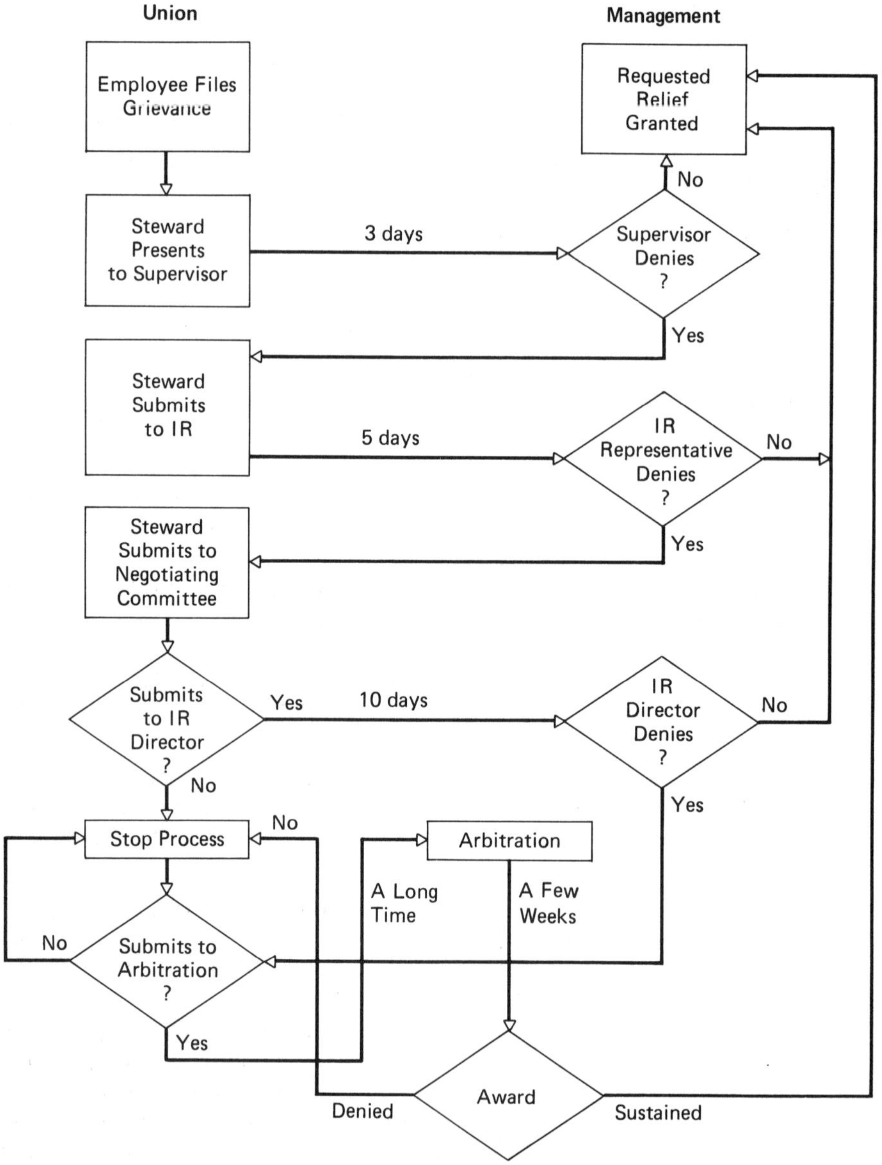

Union   **Management**

in writing within three (3) working days of such meeting, and shall furnish a copy thereof to the grievant and the Association.

17.240   If the aggrieved teacher or the Association is not satisfied with the disposition of the grievance, or if no disposition has been made within three (3) work days of such meeting (or six (6) work days from the date of the filing, whichever shall be later), the grievance may be transmitted to the Superintendent. Within five (5) work days, the Superintendent or his/her designee shall investigate the grievance, including giving the aggrieved teacher and the Association a reasonable opportunity to be heard and shall indicate his/her disposition of the grievance in writing within nine (9) work days of such meeting. A copy of his/her decision shall be furnished to the teacher involved and the Association.

17.250   If the grievance is not resolved at Sec. 17.240 of the Grievance Procedure and if it involves an alleged violation of a specific Section of this Agreement, either party may, at its option, submit the grievance to the American Arbitration Association for appointment of an arbitrator; by written notice delivered to the superintendent or the local Association President, as the case may be, and the American Arbitration Association twenty (20) days after receipt of the Superintendent's answer in Sec. 17.240. The written notice shall identify the provisions of the Agreement allegedly violated, shall state the issue involved, and the relief requested. If no such notices are given within the twenty (20) day period, the Superintendent's answer shall be final and binding on the Association, the employee or employees involved, and the Board.

   17.251   Powers of Arbitrator

      It shall be the function of the Arbitrator, and the Arbitrator shall be empowered, except as powers are limited below, after due investigation, to make a decision in writing, setting forth findings and conclusion in a case of an alleged violation of a specific Section of this Agreement.

      17.251.1   The Arbitrator shall have no power to add to, subtract from, alter, or modify any of the terms of this Agreement.

      17.251.2   The Arbitrator shall not make any decision which requires the Board to reinstate or reemploy any probationary teacher.

      17.251.3   The Arbitrator shall not make any decision on any case in which the grieving party has alleged any violation of statute.

      17.251.4   The Arbitrator shall have no power to establish wage scales or change any wage.

   17.252   At the time of the Arbitration Hearing, both the Board and the Association shall have the right to examine and cross-examine witnesses. Upon request of either the Board or the Association or the Arbitrator, a transcript of the Hearing shall be made and furnished the Arbitrator with the Board and the Association having an opportunity to purchase their own copy. The requesting party shall secure the services of an official transcriber. At the close of the Hearing, the Arbitrator shall afford the Board and the Association a reasonable opportunity to furnish briefs.

17.253 The fees and expenses of the Arbitrator and the fees and the expenses of the Arbitration, including the expense of a transcript, if any, shall be shared equally by the Board and the Association. The expenses of and the compensation for each and every witness and representative for either the Board or the Association shall be paid by the party producing the witness or having the representative.

17.254 The Arbitrator's decision, when made in accordance with the jurisdiction and authority established by this Agreement, shall be final and binding upon the Association, the employee or employees involved, and the Board.

17.255 The termination of probationary teachers or the placing of a probationary teacher on a third year of probation shall not be subject to arbitration. However, in the termination of a probationary employee, the Association may file within five (5) work days of the Board's action, a request for the Superintendent and/or his/her designated representatives to meet with the teacher and representative of the Association to review the action. A written response shall be given to the teacher with a copy to the Association within five (5) work days following said meeting.

17.260 The time limits provided in this Section shall be strictly observed but may be extended by written agreement of the parties. In the event a grievance is filed after May 15 of any year and strict adherence to the time limits may result in hardship to any party, the Board shall use its best efforts to process the grievance prior to the end of the school term or as soon thereafter as possible.

17.270 Other provisions regarding grievances.

17.271 Grievances arising under this Section shall be processed during non-teaching hours unless mutually agreed otherwise.

17.272 Any appeals not processed within the applicable time periods shall be considered settled on the basis of the last answer given by the respective school authority. Any grievance not answered by the respective school authority within the time limits prescribed in this Section may be processed to the next level.

17.273 Claims involving financial liability will be limited in retroactivity to a period of five (5) work days from the date on which the grievance was filed, except in the case of a payroll error, or in bona fide cases where affected individuals could not have had knowledge of the cause for complaint.

17.274 No grievance shall be filed or continue to be processed by any teacher after the effective date of his/her resignation.

17.275 Any grievance occurring during the period between the termination date of this Agreement and the effective date of a new Agreement shall not be processed.

17.276 The following matters shall not be the basis of any grievance filed under the procedure outlined in this Section:

17.276.1 The termination of services or failure to reemploy any probationary teacher.

17.276.2 The placing of a nontenure teacher on a third year of probation.

17.276.3 Any matter subject to the procedures specified in the Teacher Tenure Act (Act 4 of Public Acts, Extra Session of 1937, of Michigan, as amended).

Both sides generally agree on the virtues of settling grievances short of arbitration. In this way the parties retain control of the outcome for themselves and avoid the often substantial costs of arbitration, which are generally shared equally by the parties. In a typical system, the great majority of cases are settled short of arbitration.[4]

TYPES OF ARBITRATION COMPARED AND CONTRASTED

Interests Arbitration—To *establish* the terms of a contract when the parties cannot agree.

Almost never used in private sector because of weaknesses detailed in Chapter 10.

(continued)

Commonly found in public sector (employees who work for some unit of the government), where strikes are generally not available to resolve bargaining impasses.

Decision not always binding in some jurisdictions.

Grievance or Rights Arbitration—To apply the language of a contract *agreed*

upon by the parties in a dispute as to how it should be applied.

Commonly found in both private and public sectors.

Arbitrator merely interprets what parties intended in their contract; he or she does not create the parties' responsibility.

Decision of arbitrator is virtually always final and binding.

STRATEGIES FOR PROCESSING GRIEVANCES

Each contract may be thought of as delineating certain rights that unarguably belong to management and other rights that unarguably belong to the union. There is also a band between the two clear sets of rights that may be thought of as a "zone of ambiguity." Deciding which grievances to take to arbitration can reflect a range of strategies.

"Aggressive" strategists will take any grievance to arbitration, rather than settle or compromise, if the dispute is over any provision not clearly the other's right. In this strategy the aggressive party attempts to extend the range of its rights by capturing portions of the ambiguous zone. Such a strategy is costly in terms of finances expended on arbitration and in bad relations. It also results in a larger number of lost decisions than any other strategy.

"Defensive" strategists, on the other hand, wish to lose as few cases in arbitration as possible. This is particularly true of management. To achieve few reversals, defensive strategists compromise or settle all claims they are not confident of winning. This can be costly in giving away rights in grievance processing to which they may have been entitled from negotiations. Defensive grievance processors concede the entire zone of ambiguity to the other side, in exchange for producing impressive records in arbitration.

"Legalistic" grievance processors wish to apply the contract requirements precisely, without substantial regard for what is to be gained or lost from the way the grievance is treated. They do receive that to which they are entitled, but they sustain a loss in opportunity cost. This becomes apparent when considering the "bargaining" style of grievance processing.

In the bargaining style, the parties consider, in addition to their estimated probability of winning or losing on the merits, what it would cost the other side to settle the grievance, and what could be gained in exchange for settling. Sometimes grievances are raised that management can gain more from by settling than by winning in arbitration. If settling would be highly valued by the union and would cost the employer relatively little, a bargaining grievance processor might offer to settle both as a gesture of cooperation and to create an obligation on the part of the union, which now owes management a favor. These IOUs can prove very valuable at times when other leverage is not readily available. This bargaining strategy, of course, has the effect of continually renegotiating the contract. Many legalists regard this as dreadful. Many managers, on the other hand, regard it as the appropriate way to do business. Certainly it does increase flexibility and cooperation at the expense of uncertainty and increased administrative burdens.

There are two other competing interests in grievance-processing strategies: the desire to resolve the issue at as low a level as possible and the desire to maintain consistent application of the contract.

It is often recommended that grievances be resolved at the lowest level possible. This reduces costs and administrative burdens for both sides and places responsibility for administration of the contract in the hands of those who have to make it work.

On the other hand, decentralizing managerial authority on contract administration can result in different supervisors' reaching different conclusions as to what is required. This can result in different departments having different rules under the same contract. As will be demonstrated in a later section, this inconsistency can cause management to lose rights in arbitration.[5] To guard against this, some employers automatically deny grievances until they reach a level where a professional contract interpreter can review them for consistency. The liability of this strategy is that the supervisor may appear to the rank-and-file to have little authority or discretion, which may lead to bypassing him or her entirely in the process.

One other conflict can arise in grievance-processing strategies. Either party, but particularly the union, can play ''political games'' with the system. That is, grievances are used to obtain outcomes other than the resolution of contract violations. Most commonly this takes the form of the union's ''stuffing'' the grievance procedure with many frivolous complaints. The requirement to answer this large number of grievances places a tremendous administrative burden on management. The union then hopes to bargain with the employer by dropping the grievances in exchange for concessions on some matter not related to the grievance procedure. Less commonly, management can misuse the procedure by taking all grievances to arbitration. While this creates large financial costs for both sides, the burden generally falls more heavily on the union, since it is usually less able to afford it. A Machiavellian management can then force the union to make concessions to keep from being bankrupted by arbitration costs.

PREPARATION FOR ARBITRATION

There are three major steps in preparing for arbitration: (1) researching the case, (2) selecting the arbitrator, and (3) preparing the presentation.

Researching the Case

Arbitrators are bound to base their award on their interpretation of what the contract calls for, not on what would be fair or appropriate.[6] To get the best estimation of how an arbitrator would rule, it is useful to know how similar cases in the past have been interpreted and decided. This information can help in three ways. First, it will allow a more informed estimate of one's chances of winning. If the information indicates the chances are not good, one may wish to settle before incurring the expenses of arbitration. Second, if one does, however, decide to proceed, examining other cases can help one structure one's argument most effectively. While arbitrators, unlike judges, are not technically bound by previous decisions,[7] they may be influenced by them, and the logic that prevailed in previous instances is probably still appropriate. Last, researching the case may also help in determining which arbitrator to select. Each party would like to select an arbitrator who appears to be sympathetic to the type of issues it will raise. Many professionals believe they can determine those sympathies by researching potential arbitrators' previous decisions.

Researching a case requires locating and reading decisions on cases similar to the one pending or reading past decisions of the arbitrators being considered to hear the case. The Bureau of National Affairs, Inc. (BNA) and the Commerce Clearing House (CCH) each compile published arbitration decisions. The volumes containing these cases are indexed by subject matter and by arbitrator. Evaluating the relevancy of past cases to the present grievance is a great portion of the "art" of grievance arbitrating and is a matter of the researcher's skill. Often the parties are able to obtain expert opinions as to the value of these cases by relying on support from their affiliated organizations (unions, from their national or the AFL-CIO if appropriate; management, from employer associations or consulting firms) or by hiring an attorney.

Throughout the researching of previous decisions, the parties are implicitly developing "a theory of the case"—that is, constructing a set of arguments that, if proven to the arbitrator's satisfaction, would render a ruling in its favor. Each side, of course, has a theory of the case from the very beginning. The union has the position initially taken by the grievant and the employer has the supervisor's reason for rejection. Both of these positions were originally taken on the basis of the information at hand at the time and may have been based more on emotion than was appropriate. As the grievance travels upward, subsequent reviewers are more likely to examine the case not only in terms of contract language but also for employer consistency and past practice. As this information is added, the theory of the case may be refined or even redefined. Finally, upon a wholesale "academic" investigation of the case based upon previously unconsidered decisions, it might be necessary to again redefine the case's theory. Such an outcome is more common than might be expected, because the final redefinition is directed at convincing the *arbitrator,* not the *other party,* of the position and may require different arguments.

Selecting the Arbitrator

Most grievance arbitrator selection is performed ad hoc. That is, an arbitrator is selected to hear only that particular case and has no continuing employment relationship with the parties. In contrast, in some established bargaining relationships the parties agree to use the same arbitrator for all their cases arising during a specified period. Arbitrators serving in this capacity are sometimes referred to as "permanent umpires." The use of ad hoc procedures results in delays caused by the selection process, additional effort (and risk) in acquainting the arbitrator with the parties and their relationship, and the potential of inconsistent decisions from different arbitrators. Umpires, on the other hand, may be resorted to too often, since the cost does not increase per case.

AD HOC ARBITRATOR SELECTION PROCEDURE

The arbitrator is to be selected by the parties jointly within seven working days after the notice has been given. If the parties fail to agree on an arbitrator, either party may request the Bureau of Mediation to submit a list of seven possible arbitrators.

The parties shall, within seven working days of the receipt of said list, meet for the purpose of selecting the arbitrator by alternately striking one name from the list until one name remains. The Employer shall strike the first name.

Each case shall be considered on its merits and the collective bargaining agreement shall constitute the basis upon which the decision shall be rendered. The decision at Steps I, II, and III shall not be used as a precedent for any subsequent case.

The arbitrator shall neither add to, subtract from, nor modify the provisions of this Agreement. The arbitrator shall be confined to the precise issue submitted for arbitration and shall have no authority to determine any other issues not so submitted.

The decision of the arbitrator shall be final and binding on both parties, except where the decision would require an enactment of legislation, in which case it shall be binding only if such legislation is enacted. The arbitrator shall be requested to issue the decision within 30 days after the hearing or receipt of the transcript of the hearing.

In the interest of expediting the resolution of grievances involving discharges, shift preference and the denial of annual or personal leave requests, the parties agree to utilize alternative approaches and methods, including such procedures as the use of preselected arbitration panels, advance scheduling of fixed hearing dates with individual arbitrators, scheduling; multiple cases with a single arbitrator on the same day, waiving the preparation of written briefs, and providing for the issuance of decisions within reduced periods of time including bench decisions.

All of the time limits contained in this Section may be extended by mutual agreement. The granting of any extension at any step shall not be deemed to establish precedence.

(continued)

All fees and expenses of the arbitrator shall be divided equally between the parties except where one of the parties of this Agreement requests a postponement that results in a settlement of the grievance in which event the postponement charge shall be divided equally between the parties. A postponement charge resulting from a joint postponement request shall be shared equally by the parties. Each party shall bear the costs of preparing and presenting its own case. Either party desiring a record of the proceedings shall pay for the record and make a copy available without charge to the arbitrator.

PERMANENT ARBITRATOR SELECTION PROCEDURE

. . . the parties during the term of this Agreement, may agree to mutually select a permanent arbitrator. In the event either party withdraws its approval of the agreed upon permanent arbitrator they may mutually select and agree upon another permanent arbitrator.

Most people serving as arbitrators do so on a part-time basis. Generally they hold full-time positions as lawyers or college professors. Although there are no specific qualifications for becoming an arbitrator, useful background includes a presumption of neutrality, a knowledge of law (particularly rules of contract interpretation), and experience on both sides of the bargaining table. In modern arbitration, with its emphasis on legalistic matters rather than equity, expertise in the field is definitely required. An open mind and unquestioned integrity are no longer sufficient preparation. The parties place a great deal of emphasis on previous experience as an arbitrator.

The parties usually select arbitrators from three sources; the Federal Mediation and Conciliation Service (FMCS), the American Arbitration Association (AAA), and the National Academy of Arbitrators (NAA). The FMCS refers panels (lists) of potential arbitrators for free. The AAA, a private nonprofit organization, charges a service fee for providing a list of arbitrators and will also perform related services such as arranging meeting rooms and times. The NAA, made up of the most-utilized arbitrators, merely provides the names of its members, and the parties must arrange for their services on their own.

The arbitrator must be mutually acceptable to the parties—at least before the case. If the parties can sit down and agree on the candidate, and the candidate is available, there is no problem. However, the parties often cannot agree. For these situations, the parties must negotiate into the contract a mechanism to produce a selection. The two most common methods are the alternate striking procedure and the use of a limited number of panels.

In the alternate striking procedure, a list of five names may be solicited from the FMCS. If the parties cannot agree on which to choose, a coin is flipped. The winner can either strike one name from the list or have the other party do so. The parties then alternate strikings until only one name remains. In this "least of evils" procedure, it is definitely advantageous to be the second party to strike.

In the limited number of panels method the parties may request a panel of three names from AAA. If no agreement is reached, a second and ultimately a third panel may be requested. If there is still no agreement, the parties often provide for AAA to appoint the arbitrator. Since neither side generally wishes to assume the substantial risk of having an unacceptable arbitrator appointed by an outsider, agreement can almost always be reached on the third panel. In fact, if AAA is providing the panels, agreement may be reached even earlier, since each request for a new panel increases the cost of the proceeding.

Preparing the Presentation

Although arbitration hearings are not as formal as legal cases, they do follow the same format. The parties introduce documents and evidence by presenting witnesses and examining them through the question-and-answer method. The other party, of course, has the opportunity to cross-examine these witnesses. This means the persuasiveness of a party's case may be influenced not only by its "academic" strength but also by how it is presented. This is particularly true when presenting issues of fact (proof of what happened in the incident) as contrasted to issues of contract interpretation (whether such an action, if it occurred, would be permissible).

The best preparation for a presentation is a rehearsal. In the rehearsal the presenter of the case arranges the order of witnesses and asks them the questions he or she will ask in the hearing. Surprising answers can be dealt with safely, and adjustments in both questions and answers can be made. Since being a witness can produce anxiety, the rehearsal can help reduce some of this tension. Elaborate rehearsals even include mock cross-examination to prepare the witnesses for the type of questions to anticipate, the type of answers to give, and type of demeanor to exhibit.

NATURE OF THE HEARING

As noted earlier, arbitration hearings are similar in form to courtroom cases but are less bound by technical rules of procedure. Arbitrators generally accept all evidence into the record "for what it is worth."[8] The "common law" rules of grievance arbitration are applied unless there is a specific reason not to do so. In general, the burden of proof is on the union to convince the arbitrator, by a "preponderance of the evidence," that the action taken by management violates the contract.[9] An exception to this rule is discharge cases, where there is a presumption of innocence which the employer must generally overcome "beyond a reasonable doubt."[10]

A GRIEVANCE BEING ARBITRATED

In the hearing the parties attempt "to build a record" upon which the arbitrator can find for its side. Since the arbitrator will be bound by the submission agreement (a statement of the issues the parties wish to have decided) and the record only,[11] it is imperative that the parties make all their relevant arguments and make them as well as they can. Theoretically, at least, the arbitrator is not supposed to help the parties build their cases or base his or her decision on relevant, but unpresented, data. This is particularly important because grievance arbitration is final and binding—there is no avoiding the outcome and there is no appeal. If a party is dissatisfied with a decision, it can only wait until the next negotiation and hope to get the offending contract language altered. It can also refuse to use that arbitrator again in the future, but that, of course, provides no remedy for the original case. An exception to the final and binding rule is civil rights cases, which may be pursued at law after an unfavorable ruling in arbitration.[12]

The submission agreement serves to establish the range of authority of the arbitrator and to determine the issue he or she is to decide. Any portion of a decision going beyond the issue stated in the submission agreement or exceeding the arbitrator's scope of authority is unenforceable.[13] Because the way in which the issue is stated can greatly influence the outcome of the arbitration, the construction of the submission agreement requires a great deal of care and skill.

Often the parties cannot agree on what the issue is. There are three basic remedies to this problem. One is to rely on the statement in the grievance as originally filed. The disadvantage here is that this statement may often be poorly worded, unclear, or not fully representative of the issues in dispute. A second remedy is to have the parties stipulate to the issue at some point in the hearing after enough evidence has been presented to help clarify the dispute. The final remedy is to allow the arbitrator to determine the issue. Management may perceive here a danger that the arbitrator is free to expand the scope of his or her authority beyond the limits to which management would wish to restrict the arbitrator.

In the hearing, both sides generally make brief opening statements about what they will attempt to prove to support their cases. They may also present stipulations of facts upon which they can agree and will not need to prove. The more that can be stipulated, the more expeditious and relevant the hearing will be. Historically, stenographic transcripts of hearings were seldom taken. As more attorneys have begun representing the parties, transcripts have become more common. Arbitrators generally feel competent to take their own notes and often feel such transcripts are unnecessary. Certainly, they are always very costly and always necessitate a delay between the close of the hearing and the time at which the arbitrator can begin final consideration of the case.

Closing statements are generally presented by both sides. These recapitulate what the parties perceive as the issue to be considered and their arguments in support of their position. Post-hearing briefs are also sometimes filed, particularly in cases in which at least one side is represented by a lawyer. These are also generally expensive and can be very time-consuming.

COMMON ERRORS

AAA has observed that the parties often hurt themselves in arbitration with the following errors:

1. Overemphasis and exaggeration of the grievance.
2. Reliance on a minimum of facts and a maximum of arguments.
3. Using arguments where witnesses or exhibits would better establish the facts.
4. Concealing essential facts; distorting the truth.
5. Holding back books, records, and other supporting documents.
6. Tying up proceedings with legal technicalities.
7. Introducing witnesses who have not been properly instructed on demeanor and on the place of their testimony in the entire case.
8. Withholding full cooperation from the arbitrator.
9. Disregarding the ordinary rules of courtesy and decorum.
10. Becoming involved in arguments with the other side. The time to try to convince the other party was before arbitration, during grievance processing. At the arbitration hearing, all efforts should be concentrated on convincing the arbitrator.[14]

RULES OF CONTRACT INTERPRETATION

Contracts need to be interpreted when their wording is subject to multiple meanings. When language, or its absence, creates different possible conclusions, arbitrators rely on established contract interpretation rules from law. Some of the most commonly used rules follow.

The first test in determining the meaning of language is to determine what it meant *to the parties* using it.[15] If it has some other meaning to some other group, that is irrelevant. Furthermore, the meaning of each portion of the contract must be construed within the context of the entire contract.[16] Interpretations that would produce harsh or unworkable results are to be avoided.[17] Where there is conflict between specific and general language, specific governs.[18]

Precontract negotiations can play a significant role in contract interpretation. Generally speaking, if a party attempted to incorporate a specific provision into the contract during negotiations and failed, arbitrators will not confer that right through the interpretation of ambiguous language.[19] Offers of compromise or concession made during the processing of the grievance, however, should be given no weight.[20] The less experienced and expert the draftsmen were, the more liberally construed the language will be. If all other attempts to resolve the ambiguity fail, the ambiguity will be resolved against the party providing the language in question.[21]

ROLE OF CUSTOM AND PAST PRACTICE

An entire subset of contract-interpretation rules that seems to fascinate arbitrators is provided by past practice and custom. These practices can be introduced for either of two purposes: (1) to help interpret ambiguous contract language or (2) to assert a right not deriving from the contract itself.

The use of past practice in interpreting contract language is not controversial. The best way of determining what the parties meant by the language they used is to see how they applied it in the past. If the parties' actions and practices help clarify the meaning of their language, interpretation is made more easily and accurately.

The use of past practice to establish rights existing outside the contract is considerably more controversial. Many managers assert the proposition that the only rights employees possess, beyond their legal rights, are those specifically conveyed to them under the contract. Arbitrators have found otherwise, however. In instances where employees have asserted the right to continuance of employer-provided benefits not specified in the contract (nor denied by the contract), arbitrators have granted, under certain conditions, the recognition and continuation of those benefits until the contract is reopened for negotiation.[22] The rationale behind such a decision is that the union, during negotiations, assumed such benefits would be continued and did not attempt to bargain for their preservation. According to this rationale, once agreement had been reached, it would be inequitable to allow management to reduce the value of the package without the union's having the right to negotiate on the matter.

The tests for which practices fall into the protected past-practice category are complicated and often apparently contradictory between cases. The basic measures of whether a past practice will be preserved are: (1) Was it long established and consistent? (2) Was it open and well known? (3) Was it a significant benefit to employees? (4) Did it affect management's right to direct the workforce?[23] Practitioners and students wishing to know more details on the application of these principles are invited to consult the recommended readings listed at the end of the chapter.

DISCIPLINE AND JUST-CAUSE CASES

One topic of contract interpretation requires specific attention. It is the subject of discipline for just cause. Almost all union-negotiated contracts call for employee discharge or discipline "only for just cause," or the equivalent. *Just cause* then has to be interpreted in light of the facts of each individual case. Arbitrators have developed an extensive common law of what constitutes just cause.

Four essential tests must be met to satisfy an arbitrator that discipline was for just cause. They are:

1. Did the alleged behavior actually occur?
2. If so, is such behavior prohibited by the contract?
3. Was the discipline applied consistently among individuals and over time?
4. Did the punishment fit the "crime," considering possible mitigating circumstances?

If management fails to satisfy the arbitrator in any of these areas, its discipline may be modified or overturned.

Some cases hang particularly on the facts. That is, everyone agrees that if the employee behaved in the manner alleged, he or she would be subject to discipline. This is commonly true in the "moral turpitude" cases such as theft and intoxication. Here management's most crucial task is to convince the arbitrator that the employee behaved in the prohibited fashion. These cases turn on the abilities of the parties to prove their facts, rather than on interpretation of contract language.

The second question, on the other hand, requires just the opposite test. The facts are not generally in dispute. Rather, the parties are concerned whether such activity is prohibited by the contract. This will require a careful analysis of contract language and the rules for its interpretation. Arbitrators generally put a stringent burden on management to make clear what is not permitted. Good-faith doubts are generally resolved in favor of employees. The first time a new form of arguably prohibited behavior arises, management would be well advised not to discipline the employee but rather to ask the employee to cease such behavior and then promulgate and publicize a rule specifically prohibiting such behavior in the future. If the union believes that such a rule is not permitted by the contract, it may grieve.

In response to the third question, management is always under the burden of applying discipline consistently. Two tests must be met in this regard. The first is that the rule must be applied equally to all employees. The second is that the rule must be applied equally all the time. If the union can demonstrate that management selectively enforced the rule against the grievant but let such behavior slide with other employees, the discipline will almost certainly be overturned in its entirety. Failure of the second test may result in a complete overturning of the discipline or a reduction in its severity. If it can be shown that management only occasionally enforces a rule, many arbitrators are sympathetic to grievants who argue that they knew they were violating a rule but did not think management took it seriously because they had not "cracked down" in the past. This situation comes up often in regard to tardiness. In this instance, if management does want to begin enforcing a preexisting rule, it is well advised to announce its intention loudly in advance and not to discipline anyone prior to the announcement.

The fourth test is the most subjective of all. Many times a grievant will be able to argue that, even if guilty, the discipline imposed is too severe for the offense. This is particularly true when there are mitigating circumstances involved. A common form of mitigating circumstances involves fighting on the job when the other person started it or insubordination when the supervisor's behavior was not exemplary. Arbitrators place a great deal of weight in these cases on how other cases of this type, within this bargaining unit, were decided. Decisions on cases that occurred in other settings carry considerably less weight. A common outcome in arbitration hearings on this issue is for the arbitrator to sustain the employer's right to discipline, but to reduce the severity of the punishment.

The question of severity is also partially contingent upon the type of offense. In some cases, discharge may be suitable on the first offense.[24] Assaulting a supervisor would fit into this category. Failure to meet production standards, on the other hand, is almost never dischargeable on the first offense but must be subjected to progressive discipline.[25]

The concept of progressive discipline has been known to aggravate many supervisors. A series of offenses, not singly meriting discharge, may be accumulated for purposes of discipline. Enforcing discharge via this method can often be very vexing for management. Contracts usually have statutes of limitation barring the use of previous offenses after a stated period of time and under certain restrictions. A Machiavellian employee (which an employee involved in cumulative discipline may be) can play games with the system by behaving well enough long enough to expunge his or her record. The employee can then revert to his or her original irritating behavior and begin the cycle again.

PROGRESSIVE DISCIPLINE

Discipline, dismissal or non-renewal of contract of non-probationary employees shall be for just cause. Except in cases that constitute a real and immediate danger to the district, progressive discipline shall be applied as follows.

1. Verbal reprimand—(with notation of action placed in the site file).
2. Written reprimand.
3. Suspension with or without pay.
4. Suspension without pay.
5. Dismissal.

An even more difficult aspect of progressive discipline for many managers is the amount of documentation required to prove a case in arbitration. The sustaining of a progressive discipline case in arbitration requires a great deal more record keeping than many managers are used to. In the most extreme case of discharging an employee for poor performance, arbitrators have been known to require management to meet all of the following tests:

1. Was there an objective, quantifiable standard that the employee did not meet? If there is no standard, management will have a very difficult case.
2. Was the standard fairly set?
3. Did the employee know what the standard was?
4. Did he or she know his or her performance was below it?
5. Was it his or her own fault that he or she was below standard, or were there mitigating circumstances?
6. Were other employees similarly below standard disciplined?
7. Was he or she given the opportunity to improve through extra training?
8. Was he or she offered reassignment?
9. Was he or she disciplined progressively?

If the answer to any of these questions is "no," management may lose its case. To assure that discipline is carried out according to contract, management must accomplish two tasks. It must keep sufficient records to document its case, and it must apply rules uniformly or not at all. The failure to apply rules consistently can result in reversals of discipline in arbitration hearings that cause management to lose rights it had clearly gained in bargaining.[26] As for documenting the case, supervisors will have to keep more elaborate records than they might otherwise have, and they must learn not to "fly off the handle" when irritated, because they may have to spend a long time building a case. This is not entirely bad. Besides providing greater justice for employees, it probably makes better managers out of the supervisors. Unfortunately, some supervisors are unable to cope with the complexities of the union-negotiated grievance procedure and remedy their problems instead by transferring discipline-prone employees to other managers.

Some contracts attempt to eliminate some of the subjectivity inherent in the determination of just cause by prescribing a list of disciplinable offenses. These lists, however, run the same risks as lengthy management-rights clauses. If a specific behavior does not appear on the list, an argument can be made that it is permitted. Furthermore, the subjectivity involved in mitigating circumstances is still present. A diagram of the elements of processing a discipline case appears in Figure 14-2.

DISCIPLINE LIST

CAUSES FOR DISCIPLINE SPECIFIED

"Any action which reflects discredit upon the service or is a direct hindrance to the effective performance of the City government functions shall be considered good cause for disciplinary action. The following are declared to be good cause for disciplinary action against any employee, though charges may be based upon causes and complaints other than those listed:

"(a) Habitual use of alcoholic beverages to excess or the use of narcotics;

"(b) Has been adjudged guilty of a crime involving moral turpitude, or infamous or disgraceful conduct;

"(c) Partaking of intoxicating beverages; or intoxication while on duty;

"(d) Use of abusive or improper treatment to a person in custody, provided the act committed was not necessarily or lawfully done in self-defense or to protect the lives of others, or to prevent the escape of a person lawfully in custody;

"(e) Offensive conduct or language toward the public or toward City officers or employees;

"(f) Insubordination;

"(g) Incompetence to perform the duties of his position;

"(h) Negligence in the care and handling of City property;

"(i) Violation of any lawful and reasonable official regulation made or given by his superior officer, where such violation or failure to obey amounted to an act of insubordination or a serious breach of proper discipline or resulted, or might

FIGURE 14–2 SCHEMATIC DIAGRAM INDICATING ELEMENTS OF DISCIPLINE

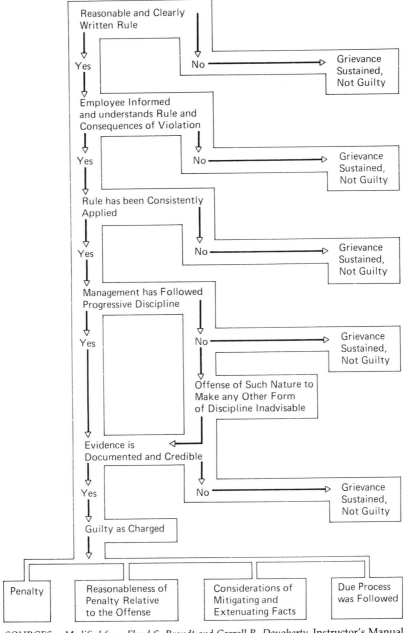

SOURCES: *Modified from Floyd S. Brandt and Carroll R. Daugherty,* Instructor's Manual for Conflict Cooperation: Cases in Labor-Management Behavior *(Homewood, Ill.: Richard D. Irwin, 1967), p. 6. © 1967 by Richard D. Irwin, Inc. Used by permission.*

reasonably have been expected to result, in loss or injury to the City, to prisoners of the City, or to the public;

"(j) Commission of acts or omissions unbecoming an incumbent of the particular office or position held, which render his reprimand, suspension, demotion of discharge necessary or desirable for the economical or efficient conduct of the business of the City or for the best interest of the City government;

"(k) Willful violation of any of the provisions of the City Charter or any of the rules promulgated thereunder;

"(l) Has induced or attempted to induce any officer or employee in the City service to commit an illegal act or to act in violation of any lawful and reasonable departmental or official regulation or order, or has participated herein;

"(m) Solicitation or receipt from any person, or participation in, any fee, gift, or other valuable thing in the course of work, when such fee, gift or other valuable thing is given in the hope or expectation of receiving a favor or better treatment than that accorded other persons;

"(n) Use or attempted use of political influence or bribery to secure an advantage in an examination or promotion;

"(o) Failure to pay just debts due or failure to make reasonable provision for the future payment of such debts, thereby causing annoyance to the City or his superiors or embarrassment to the service;

"(p) Absence from duty without leave contrary to the provisions in this agreement, or failure to report after leave of absence has expired, or after such leave of absence has been disapproved or revoked and cancelled by the proper authority;

"(q) Change of residence to a location outside the City of Omaha.

"Violation of the provisions of this section shall be punishable by reprimand, suspension, demotion, and/or discharge. A copy of this section with any amendments thereto, shall be submitted to each department head to be posted in such manner as will bring it to the attention of all employees of such department."

Finally, in many instances provision is made for a union representative to be present (at the employee's request) at any hearing from which discipline may result.

RIGHT OF UNION REPRESENTATIVE TO BE PRESENT
AT DISCIPLINARY HEARING

"No member of the Bargaining Unit shall be discharged, suspended or taken out of service of the employer unless a preliminary hearing was held. A preliminary hearing shall be held prior to a hearing on the merits of the alleged charges, brought against the member by the supervisor, who is making said charges.

"The preliminary hearing shall consist of an oral explanation being given by the supervisor as to the grounds or reasons for said charges; and said oral explanation shall be made in the presence of a Union Steward; the employee must be furnished by the supervisor with a written statement as to the grounds or reasons for said charges being brought against said employee. In the event a Union

Steward is not available a copy of the statement will be given to the Union within 24 hours.

"It is further provided that said preliminary hearing shall be held or written statement furnished to the employee, prior to the employee leaving the premises or work area where the employee is assigned for duty, when said charges are made against the employee."

ARBITRATION OF UNFAIR LABOR PRACTICE CHARGES

Occasionally the action precipitating a grievance may also constitute an unfair labor practice charge. This situation presents a dilemma, because the two charges should be made in different forums—the grievance to an arbitrator and the unfair labor practice charge to the NLRB. Because it is cumbersome to present the same case twice and there exists a risk of inconsistent verdicts, economics and logic dictate that there should be only one case, provided that minimal standards for both forums are maintained. The NLRB has handled this problem by deferring unfair labor practice charges to grievance arbitration so long as the parties agreed in the contract to be bound by the arbitrator's decision, the proceedings were fair and regular, and the results were not inconsistent with the law.[27]

ARBITRABILITY

One final issue remains in administering a labor agreement. Up to this point it has been assumed that disputes arising under the contract would be referred to the grievance procedure and, ultimately, to arbitration. This is not always the case. Sometimes one of the parties, usually management, refuses (or attempts to refuse) to submit a complaint to arbitration. This can occur in either of two ways. The first is an assertion that the grievance was not filed properly according to the rules of the contract and therefore cannot be submitted to arbitration. This could occur because previous steps of the grievance procedure were not complied with properly, or because the grievance was not filed in a timely fashion. Failure to file a grievance within the contractually stipulated time limits, or failure to appeal within proper limits, generally will serve as a defense against having the grievance heard on the merits, provided that management was not a contributing factor to the delay.[28]

The other justification for failing to submit to arbitration is more argumentative. It claims that the issue in dispute should not be submitted to arbitration because it is not a subject about which the employee is entitled to grieve. This could arise when the dispute falls within a category that the parties have, by contractual agreement, specifically removed from the grievance process, or when management asserts that the subject is one over which management has unilateral control by nature of its "inherent" rights that it has not specifically ceded under the contract.[29]

The question of whether an issue is properly grievable can, of course, be subject to dispute. The legal rule for resolving disputes regarding arbitrability is to have an arbitrator determine whether the issue is grievable.[30] If the arbitrator determines that it is not, he or she dismisses the case. If the arbitrator determines that it is, the case may then be presented on its merits. The rule for determining whether an issue is arbitrable is, "All issues not specifically removed from the grievance procedure are arbitrable."[31]

Notes

1. Everett M. Kassalow, *Trade Unions and Industrial Relations: An International Comparison* (New York: Random House, 1969), p. 158.
2. Kassalow, p. 152.
3. Peter Feuille and Hoyt N. Wheeler, "Will the Real Industrial Conflict Please Stand Up?" in *U.S. Industrial Relations 1950–1980: A Critical Reassessment*, Jack Stieber, ed. (Madison, Wis.: Industrial Relations Research Association, 1981), p. 279.
4. Arthur A. Sloane and Fred Witney, *Labor Relations*, 5th ed. (Englewood Cliffs, N.J.: Prentice-Hall, 1985), p. 235.
5. Paul Prasow and Edward Peters, *Arbitration and Collective Bargaining*, 2d ed. (New York: McGraw-Hill, 1983), chap. 8.
6. Sloane and Witney, p. 245.
7. Maurice S. Trotta, *Arbitration of Labor-Management Disputes* (New York: AMACOM, 1974), p. 23.
8. Trotta, p. 93.
9. Prasow and Peters, p. 280.
10. Prasow and Peters, p. 281.
11. Prasow and Peters, p. 19.
12. *Alexander* v. *Gardner-Denver Co.*, 415 U.S. 36 (1974).
13. Prasow and Peters, p. 20.
14. Frank Elkouri and Edna Asper Elkouri, *How Arbitration Works*, 4th ed. (Washington, D.C.: BNA Publications, 1985), p. 293.
15. Prasow and Peters, chap. 5.
16. Prasow and Peters, chap. 5.
17. Elkouri and Elkouri, p. 354.
18. Prasow and Peters, p. 104.
19. Prasow and Peters, p. 207.
20. Trotta, p. 97.
21. Dennis R. Nolan, *Labor Arbitration Law and Practice* (St. Paul: West Publishing Company, 1979), p. 169.
22. Prasow and Peters, p. 150.
23. Condensed from Prasow and Peters, chaps. 6–9.
24. Sloane and Witney, p. 452.
25. Sloane and Witney, p. 452.
26. Prasow and Peters, p. 165.

27. *Collyer Insulated Wire Co.*, 192 NLRB 150 (1971).
28. Sloane and Witney, 4th ed., pp. 242–47.
29. Sloane and Witney, pp. 271–79.
30. *United Steelworkers* v. *American Mfg. Co.*, 363 U.S. 464.
31. *United Steelworkers* v. *Warrior & Gulf Navigation Co.*, 363 U.S. 574.

Discussion Questions

1. Why is a grievance procedure needed?
2. Describe a typical grievance procedure. Why is it structured that way?
3. Analyze the various strategies for processing grievances.
4. Describe how to research a case for arbitration.
5. Discuss the selection of an arbitrator.
6. Discuss how to prepare and present an arbitration case.
7. Explain the primary rules of contract interpretation.
8. Describe the role of past practice and custom.
9. Describe the arbitration considerations of discipline and discharge cases.
10. Discuss the arbitration of unfair labor practice charges.
11. Discuss the issues of arbitrability.

Statements for Comment

1. "The major benefit of unionization is improving job rights."
2. "Arbitrators, like judges, should be bound by previous decisions."
3. "The legal rules of evidence protect both parties. They ought to apply to arbitration cases as well as court cases."
4. "Arbitrators can make wrong decisions. There ought to be a right of appeal."
5. "The legalizing of arbitration cases is a sad mistake."
6. "Just-cause procedures really hurt efficiency."

Situations

Case 14–1 "I hear that some large nonunion companies are instituting grievance procedures that use 'juries' of equal numbers of managers and employees instead of using outside arbitrators," said Rita Hall. "It seems like a good idea to me."

What do you see as the advantages and disadvantages of such a system?

Case 14–2 "From what I learned in my labor law class, I thought an arbitrator's decision could not be overturned, even if it was wrong. Now I hear that if the grievant claims that a Title VII of the Civil Rights Act of 1964 provision was violated, the employee can lose the grievance and turn around and still sue the employer anyway in a legal action. That seems to me to defy the finality of arbitration and emasculate the grievance procedure. It also seems to give the grievant 'two bites of the apple,'" said Terry Kierpa.

To what extent are Terry's allegations justified? How can they be reconciled with the general rules? How big a threat of opposing decisions is there?

Case 14–3 "Delays in arbitration are becoming outrageous," moaned Harold Williams, vice-president of industrial relations for a large chemical company. "The selection process takes time, and scheduling delays waiting for the arbitrator we've agreed upon to become available are running to half a year. Then the hearing takes two days with all the legalistic motions, then we have to wait a week or sometimes more for the transcript to be available, then another two weeks to a month for post-hearing briefs to be filed, and then another month for the decision—if we're lucky. It's getting as time-consuming and expensive as law suits and is defeating the purpose of arbitration. For that matter, it's become so legalistic that I'm not certain the therapeutic value hasn't been hurt."

What would you recommend to solve these problems—without creating other worse ones?

Bibliography of Related Readings

Abrams, R. I., "A Theory for the Discharge Case," *Arbitration Journal*, September 1981, pp. 24–27.

Baer, Walter E. *Practice and Precedent in Labor Relations* (Lexington, Ky.: Lexington Books, 1972).

Bowers, M. H., "Grievance Mediation: Another Route To Resolution," *Personnel Journal*, February 1980, pp. 132–36.

Elkouri, F., "Informal Observations on Labor Arbitration Today," *Arbitration Journal*, 1980, pp. 41–45.

Elkouri, Frank, and Edna Asper Elkouri, *How Arbitration Works*, 4th ed. (Washington, D.C.: Bureau of National Affairs, 1985).

Gannon, J. S., "How to Handle Discipline Within the New National Labor Relations Board Requirements," *Personnel Administrator*, March 1981, pp. 43–47.

Kagel, Sam, *Anatomy of a Labor Arbitration* (Washington, D.C.: Bureau of National Affairs, 1961).

Knight, T. R., "The Impact of Arbitration on the Administration of Disciplinary Policies," *Arbitration Journal*, 1984, pp. 43–56.

Lawson, Eric W., Jr., "Arbitrator Acceptability: Factors Affecting Selection," *Arbitration Journal*, December 1981.

Loewenberg, J. J., "Structure of Grievance Procedures," *Labor Law Journal*, January 1984, pp. 44–51.

Marx, H. L., Jr., "Arbitration as an Ethical Institution in Our Society," *Arbitration Journal*, 1982, pp. 52–55.

Nelson, N. E., and E. M. Curry, Jr., "Arbitrator Characteristics and Arbitral Decisions," *Industrial Relations*, 1981, pp. 312–17.

Prasow, Paul, and Edward Peters, *Arbitration and Collective Bargaining,* 2d ed., (New York: McGraw-Hill, 1983).

Raffaele, J. A., "Lawyers in Labor Arbitration," *Arbitration Journal,* 1982, pp. 14–23.

Robinson, J. W., "Some Modest Proposals for Reducing the Costs and Delay in Grievance Arbitration," *Personnel Administrator,* February 1982, pp. 25–28.

Trotta, Maurice S., *Arbitration of Labor-Management Disputes* (New York: American Management Association, 1974).

Wrong, E. G., "The Social Responsibility of Arbitrators in Title VII Disputes," *Labor Law Journal,* September 1981, pp. 621–26.

Zirkel, P. A., "A Profile of Grievance Arbitration Cases," *Arbitration Journal,* 1983, pp. 35–38.

Exercise

Sweet Swing, Inc., and United Molders, V and VI The following two grievances appealing discharges (excerpted from actual case transcripts) could not be settled short of arbitration. The facts are presented (from each side's viewpoint) for your consideration. Depending upon your instructor's preferences, you may be assigned either to decide the case as an arbitrator or to present the case as an advocate of one side in a mock hearing.

The following is a list of activities you may wish to utilize to prepare for a mock hearing. After each grievance, several questions are presented to help focus preparation of "the theory of the case" for the parties.

Items to Consider for Role-Playing Arbitration Cases

1. Assign roles for each side. The union is commonly represented by its president or the international representative. The company is commonly represented by its attorney.
2. Research case for precedent and argument.
3. Develop a "theory of the case."
4. Meet with other side to see what can be stipulated.
5. Determine issue, if possible.
6. Prepare a prehearing brief.
7. Rehearse case. Include opening and closing statements. Examine witnesses.
8. File post-hearing brief (if required).

Grievance #1

There is agreement on certain essential facts. The grievant was hired in March of 1983 as a Material Handler and served in that capacity until the time of his discharge.

The reason for his discharge was described in a letter dated July 19 as follows:

This is to advise you that the Company has completed its investigation. As a result of that investigation, your suspension is corrected to discharge for your misconduct in the plant on the night of June 7 and the morning of June 8, and for the violation of the following rules:
Section II, Paragraph C—Misconduct on Company Premises

1. Employees shall not fight with anyone on Company premises.
2. Employees shall not threaten, intimidate, interfere with the work of, or assault anyone on Company premises.
Section III—Paragraph A—Work Conduct
2. Employees shall not refuse or fail to complete a job assignment.

The present grievance protests this discharge as being without proper cause within the meaning of that term in Article IX of the current labor agreement.

Position of the Company   The Company contends that the grievant's discharge was for proper cause. It supports this contention by pointing to the testimony of all persons with knowledge of the incident. It characterized this testimony in a post-hearing brief as follows:

Late on the night of June 6, Foreman Paul Goulet was working in the dock area of the shipping department when he was approached by Ronnie Torrez, an Inventory Clerk. Torrez, who audits orders before they are shipped to the stores, informed Goulet that the order for Store 880 was missing a sizable amount of product, according to his computer printout of the store order and his audit of what had been actually pulled and placed on pallets in the dock area for shipment. Torrez asked if Goulet had already loaded part of the Store 880 order on the waiting trailer. Goulet checked the trailer, determined that the missing portion of the store order had not been loaded, and told Torrez to check again what had been pulled to make sure he, Torrez, had not overlooked it.

Torrez later informed Goulet that the missing product was nowhere to be found. Together they determined that the missing portion of Store 880's order had not yet been pulled, although the second of the two pallet loads of product already assembled was tagged "2 ALL." (The Material Handler writes the number of the store on each pallet. If the store's order comprises more than one pallet, each pallet is also marked "2," "3," etc., with the last pallet bearing the notation "ALL," indicating that the entire order is completed so that it may be audited at one time and thereafter loaded in one place on the truck trailer.)

Thereupon Goulet asked Chester Colbert, the Material Handler who had pulled the two pallets for Store 880, if there was another pallet of product for the store and, if so, where was it. Colbert replied that the order of Store 880 was "two all baskets," meaning that the store order contained only "baskets" and that the entire order had been pulled. Goulet pointed out, however, that one of the pallets also had "boxes" on it; therefore, Store 880's order was not "baskets" alone, some of the remaining portion of the order may not have been pulled, and, if so, the second pallet should not have been marked "2 ALL" because there were more than two pallets to the order.

Colbert then stated that he had not finished the order and Goulet replied, "Well, fine. Just go ahead and finish the order." Becoming irritated, Colbert "insisted on telling" Goulet that he had not finished the order because someone had removed his portion of the Store 880 computer printout order from his clipboard before he was finished. (When a Material Handler completes a Store order he removes the computer-generated slip from his clipboard and places it near the plant office for Torrez or another Inventory Clerk to see so that the entire order can be audited.)

Goulet listened and then said, "Chester, go back and finish pulling the order and make it 100 percent." But Colbert, "getting more excited and angry," refused to leave, saying, "I don't have to do what you say. I don't have to go back and do that. I don't have to take this shit." Whereupon Goulet again ordered him to "go back and finish pulling the order for store 880." At that point Colbert, who was standing on his pallet jack, jumped down, rushed Goulet and, putting his finger in his supervisor's face, told him that he, Goulet, "(can't) tell (me) what to do" . . . (I do) not have to take this kind of shit. . . . " Goulet replied, "Chester, if you don't go back and pull this order, I will suspend you for insubordination." Colbert retorted that Goulet "(can't) tell (me) what to do," he was not "his boy," "I could just take you out and beat the shit out of you and not do this work either," and that he was "going to get" Goulet.

With that Goulet summoned Union Steward David Washington, another Material Handler working in a different area of the plant, and ordered Colbert to accompany him to the shipping office. In the presence of Washington and Torrez, Goulet asked Colbert to repeat what he had said on the dock. Colbert said that Goulet had heard what he had said and, "(I don't) need to repeat it." Washington then asked Torrez to relate what Colbert had said, but before Torrez could respond, Colbert interjected: "You don't have to lie to Paul just because he is your boss. Tell him (i.e., Washington) what happened. Tell him that he (i.e., Goulet) spit on me. Tell him that he harassed me." With the meeting "getting out of control," Goulet told Colbert that he was being suspended pending further investigation and that he should punch out and leave the premises. Colbert continued, "really getting into it," telling Washington to be sure that he wrote down that Goulet had spat on him and that he wanted to file a grievance. Washington "attempted to calm" Colbert, telling him that he should leave and that he and Colbert could discuss it the next day.

Goulet then told Washington to lead the way upstairs to the lockerroom. With Washington in the lead, Colbert behind him, and Goulet last in line the three men walked down an aisle toward the stairway leading upstairs. On the way Colbert came back to Goulet, saying that he knew his way. Goulet replied that it was his responsibility to see to it that Colbert punched out and left the premises. Washington, apparently overhearing some of the conversation, "insisted" that Colbert leave and assured him that he, Washington, would call the Union in the morning.

When they reached the door leading to the stairway Washington, still in the lead, opened the door for Colbert and Goulet. But Colbert motioned for Washington to resume the lead, which he did. When Washington was at or near the landing at the top of the stairs, Colbert, who was about four steps in front of Goulet, stopped and turned around, facing Goulet. Nothing was said; Goulet, noticing Colbert, stopped and looked at him; then Colbert turned and proceeded up the stairs. Washington, when he got to the top of the stairs, again held the door, which opened toward him, and again Colbert motioned him to go first. Washington proceeded down the corridor leading to the lockerroom as Colbert crossed the threshold with Goulet close behind.

Suddenly, Colbert turned on his heels and shoved Goulet into the wall, saying, "You don't have to push me, motherfucker." Goulet, stunned by the unexpected assault, regained his balance, and when he straightened up he saw Colbert standing in front of him with a fire extinguisher in his right hand. (The extinguisher had been fastened on the opposite corridor wall.) From the end of the hallway Washington, having heard the commotion, implored Colbert to "put it down." Once Colbert had done so and started down the corridor, Goulet picked up his hardhat, which had flown off when Colbert struck him. Washington and Goulet accompanied Colbert to the timeclock and then to the lockerroom where Colbert removed his belongings and threw his hat down. Washington retrieved the hat and the three men started down another flight of stairs to the parking lot. All the while Colbert was "ranting and raving," saying that he wanted to file a grievance because Goulet had pushed him and spat on him.

As they had reached the bottom of the stairway Colbert turned to Goulet, and, in the latter's words:

"Colbert pulled out a wad of money and stuck it in my face and said he had plenty of this, and as long as he had plenty of this, that the boys would take care of me. He said that no one could treat him like this and get away with it, and it wouldn't be the last time that I saw him."

Washington, who had already proceeded outside, called out for Colbert to leave the plant. With Washington's help Colbert got his car started and left the parking lot.

Goulet then returned to the plant and phoned Plant Manager Gary Lawn to relate what had happened. Later, following an investigation of the matter, Colbert and the Union were advised that the suspension had been converted to discharge. Thereafter, the instant grievance was filed.

Position of the Union The Union contends that the grievant's discharge was not for proper cause. It supports this contention by pointing to the grievant's version of the incident, which it submits is more credible than that which Management relied upon in assessing the penalty of discharge. The grievant's version of the incident was described in the post-hearing brief as follows.

On June 8, the grievant was working the second shift at the Plant. Shortly after lunch, the grievant was approached on the loading docks by his supervisor, Paul Goulet. Goulet accused him of failing to finish an order for Store 880. The grievant attempted unsuccessfully to explain that the Inventory Clerk had completed the order. As a result, Mr. Goulet became angry and ordered the grievant to "take your ass back to fab" while putting his finger on the grievant's nose. The physical effect of the supervisor's words was to place spit on the grievant's face. Additionally, the supervisor threatened to have the grievant fired.

After asking the supervisor to remove his finger, the grievant told the supervisor that he was not a child and, as such, did not need to be treated as one. After this response, the grievant started to go to fab; however, the supervisor ordered him to go home.

Goulet escorted the grievant out to his car. On the way to the clock, which was upstairs, the supervisor followed the grievant too closely. On the third step from the top, the supervisor kicked the grievant's heel or overran him. The effect was to cause the grievant to stumble.

The supervisors' overrunning of the grievant's heel had two immediate effects. It caused the supervisor to lose his balance and his hat. It further caused the grievant to fall into the fire extinguisher causing it to fall from the wall. At no point in time did the grievant push, intimidate, or threaten his supervisor.

After the grievant clocked out, Goulet followed him to the lockerroom and then out to his car in the parking lot. On the way down the back stairs, the supervisor reiterated that he was going to get the grievant's "black ass fired." The supervisor further disparaged the grievant by stating that he was a "broke ass nigger."

Factors to Be Considered in the Theory of the Case   If a grievance turns on facts, and the testimony pits the word of the supervisor against the grievant as to what happened, how should the arbitrator decide? Why? How should you prepare your case to favor such a result?

Grievance #2

There is agreement on certain essential facts. The grievant was hired September 11, 1978, as an LSM Operator and later bid and was awarded a position as Clerk in the front office, where she served until the time of her discharge. The reason for her discharge was explained in a letter from the Personnel Manager dated August 21 as follows:

> You are hereby notified that you will be discharged from Sweet Swing, Inc. effective thirty (30) days from your receipt of this notice. The reasons for this action are:
>
> Charge 1. You are charged with physically grabbing an acting supervisor in a threatening manner. Part 2 of the Employee and Labor Relations Manual requires that employees be honest, reliable, trustworthy, courteous, and of good character and reputation. It further requires that employees maintain satisfactory personal habits so as not to be obnoxious or offensive to other persons or create unpleasant working conditions.
>
> Specifically, on August 16, at approximately 11:00 A.M. Ms. Harriett Drury, Shipping Supervisor, and Mr. Pete Alex came into my office. Ms. Drury was visibly upset and I told her to sit down. I inquired as to what the problem was and Ms. Drury stated that she had borrowed a pair of fingernail clippers from your husband, Mr. James Hilton, a molder, to cut a hangnail. She said further that you came by and saw that she had your husband's keys with the nail clippers. Ms. Drury stated that you grabbed her by the upper right arm and told her something to the effect that you "were tired of her fucking your husband." Ms. Drury stated that you also called her a bitch.

After obtaining information from Ms. Drury, I discussed this matter with you, and you denied grabbing Ms. Drury or calling her a bitch; however, you did state to me in a very loud tone that Ms. Drury was sleeping with your husband. You further stated that you would settle this another way if she did not stop.

I also interviewed your husband, and I asked him what had transpired. He stated that Ms. Drury had asked to borrow his fingernail clippers, and he had let her use them. He further stated the encounter was over nothing. He also indicated that he has gotten accused of this before.

Ms. Drury's arm was checked by Ms. Rose Hammond, and Ms. Hammond indicated that the right arm had a welt on it, but the skin was not broken.

The above-described events are highly serious and go to the very heart of the supervisor/employee relationship. Such a situation cannot and will not be condoned and is sufficiently serious to warrant your discharge from Sweet Swing, Inc.

The Union protests this discharge as being without just cause.

Position of the Employer   The employer contends the grievant's removal was for just cause. It supports this contention by pointing to the testimony of the witnesses, some of whom saw the incident, others who heard the grievant's accusatory and threatening language immediately following the incident, and still others who saw the results of the grievant's assault upon Supervisor Drury, namely, a bruise on her upper arm. Management contends such evidence more than satisfies its burden of proof, and having proved that the grievant committed an unprovoked assault upon Ms. Drury, it follows that the removal action was justified. Finally, it should be emphasized that Management testified, and the Union did not, and could not validly, deny, that Management in this facility has been consistent in its handling of cases involving an assault upon a supervisor. Whenever such an offense has been proven, the penalty has been discharge. Moreover, this disciplinary policy has been a successful one in that this type of misconduct has been extremely rare. Accordingly, it is requested that the Arbitrator uphold this policy and Management's action in this instance by denying the grievance.

Position of the Union   The Union contends the grievant's discharge was not for just cause. It supports this contention by pointing to the evidence, which it characterizes as essentially circumstantial and lacking in credibility. The Union submits the grievant's version of the incident is clearly more credible, and her testimony was corroborated by the testimony of several impartial witnesses.

The Union asserts Supervisor Drury took a simple misunderstanding and blew it all out of proportion by claiming to be injured. Then, rather than making an unbiased and thorough investigation of Ms. Drury's allegations, Tour Superintendent Daley accepted her version of the incident and enlisted the help of others to support the charges. The record shows that this entire investigation took less than two hours, and Superintendent Daley convinced himself that the grievant was guilty and deserving of the ultimate economic penalty.

Finally, with respect to the long list of cases referred to by Management, wherein an employee's removal has been upheld based upon his/her assaulting a supervisor, the Union states simply that each case must be judged on its own facts. The facts in the instant case are, this was a personal matter between two women, one of whom was seized by a momentary feeling of jealousy because another woman (Ms. Drury) was seen returning a set of keys to her (the grievant's) husband. So, she did what most women (or men) would do, she demanded to know what was going on. But, as the grievant testified, she addressed this question (accusation) to her husband, and Ms. Drury, believing it was addressed to her, began to explain. At this point, it appeared to the grievant that Ms. Drury was providing the explanation which she wanted to hear from her husband. So, the grievant simply told Ms. Drury not to interfere, that this was a family matter. The point is, Management treated the instant case as though it were the same as the customary removal for assault on a supervisor. In the customary case the employee is charged with some form of misconduct arising out of the management/employee relationship—one in which the employee's conduct could properly be viewed as challenging the authority of Management. In brief, even if the evidence supported Management's version of the incident, which the Union adamantly denies, the penalty would have to be considered excessive under the unique circumstances of this case. Accordingly, the grievant should be reinstated and compensated for all lost pay.

Factors to Be Considered in the Theory of This Case

What would you like witnesses for your side to be able to testify to?

In what ways is this a "normal" supervisory assault case?

In what ways is it not?

How credible are the charges of either side?

How well are these charges substantiated by the evidence?

FIFTEEN

COLLECTIVE
BARGAINING
IN PUBLIC
EMPLOYMENT

The public sector (employees of the federal, state, and local governments) is one of the few union growth areas since 1960. This chapter examines the causes of this growth and assesses how applicable the system we have been studying is to this somewhat different employment relationship.

DEVELOPMENT AND GROWTH OF PUBLIC-EMPLOYEE UNIONISM

Historically, collective bargaining (and especially the right to strike) was generally seen as inappropriate and illegal in public employment. Much of the objection arose from the "sovereignty doctrine." The sovereignty doctrine argues that elected officials must be responsible to the public and do what the laws require of them. Particularly, it is their job to decide how to spend taxes, and if the public doesn't like the way the spending is done, it can pressure the officials or vote them out of office. In theory, this means that you can't have collective bargaining in good faith, because that would require the public employer to share its decision-making authority with someone not elected by the public—a sharing arguably not permitted even if the government were willing. This theoretical constraint was largely overcome in the 1960s and 1970s by pragmatic concerns in employment relationships.

Government jobs traditionally contained benefits not common in the private sector, such as protection against layoffs, perceived status, more leave time, an absence of timeclocks, and grievance procedures for protection from arbitrary treatment. Ironically, these features of a "government job" arose because government employment had in the past been much worse than private employment in one respect—patronage.

Patronage, or the "spoils system," arose with President Andrew Jackson, who filled all federal jobs under his discretion not with experts on the job, but with people who helped get him elected. His rationale was that honesty and fairness were the only requirements for holding the job. He did not perceive a need for expertise or experience. Obviously, a modern government cannot run well on pure patronage. (It is not clear how well Jackson's ran.)

The patronage model became the standard for government employment at all levels for the next 100 years. It also became apparent that it was a poor way of getting the job done. To combat this, Civil Service and merit systems became widespread, starting in the Progressive Era of the early twentieth century. These systems removed most job appointments from elected officials and replaced them with a professional personnel program with selection based on applicants' qualifications. It also provided rules and policies similar to modern labor agreements and provided employees with a grievance procedure to assure them of their rights.

Within these merit systems there often developed organizations known as "employee associations," rather than "unions." Associations provided services similar to unions but did not engage in collective bargaining with the employer. Instead, they served as pressure groups, approaching their legislative bodies to *lobby* (rather than bargain) for better financial benefits, and acted as employee representatives in the grievance procedure over the application of rules. They also had professional and social functions.

Management generally liked associations as a vehicle of communication and encouraged supervisors to join and assume leadership roles. In many ways, associations were like company unions.

For the next half-century or so, this arrangement proved satisfactory for public-sector personnel issues. But in the 1960s things began changing dramatically. The previously perceived advantages of a "government job" had been eroded by gains made by unionized blue collar employees in the private sector, who were now enjoying similar benefits and higher pay. Raises for government employees were not keeping up with inflation. Furthermore, job security was becoming a concern. A perception arose that others had passed government employees by means of their unionized bargaining power—a tactic not available to public employees. It was also perceived that employee associations and merit systems were not effective enough at promoting the interests of public employees, especially compared to their unionized counterparts in the private sector. Public employees, particularly federal, began clamoring for the same right as all other citizens—the right to be represented by unions if they so chose.

In response to a campaign promise, President Kennedy in 1962 issued Executive Order 10988 authorizing a rudimentary form of unionization and collective bargaining (but without the right to strike) in the executive branch of the federal government. This gesture was perceived by public employees at all levels as a sign that it was all right to form unions—the President said so. In the next 15 years, states passed laws enabling state and local employees to organize, and federal employee rights were liberalized in a series of executive orders culminating in the passage of a law, the Civil Service Reform Act of 1978, that now governs collective bargaining for federal employees. (The Post Office, pursuant to the Postal Reorganization Act of 1970, is covered by the Taft-Hartley Act, although the employees are forbidden to strike.)

The passage of legislation allowing government employees to unionize also resulted in an increase in strikes, despite the fact that they were illegal in all jurisdictions at the time. These highly publicized strikes appalled the public but also demonstrated to employees how successfully they could bargain for themselves—at least at that time. This realization undoubtedly also helped speed union growth in the sector.

The changes in membership in public-employee unionism for the period 1960–1985 are portrayed in the accompanying table. It should be remembered that this growth was occurring at the same time that unions were losing ground in the private sector.

PUBLIC-EMPLOYEE ORGANIZATION MEMBERSHIP

	1960	1970	1980	1985
National Education Association (NEA)	713,994	1,082,108	1,600,800	1,600,800
American Federation of State, County, and Municipal Employees (AFSCME)	200,000	400,000	1,200,000	1,200,000
American Federation of Teachers (AFT)	50,772	125,000	555,000	580,000
American Nurses Association (ANA)	174,000	200,000	182,000	180,000
International Association of Fire Fighters (IAFF)	95,000	120,000	175,000	170,000
Fraternal Order of Police (FOP)	55,000	80,000	147,000	163,552
Amalgamated Transit Union (ATU)	150,000	130,000	130,000	160,000

SOURCE: *Excerpted from ENCYCLOPEDIA OF ASSOCIATIONS: 1960, 1970, 1980, 1985 edited by Denise S. Akey (Copyright © 1959, 1961, 1964, 1968, 1970, 1972, 1973, 1975, 1976, 1977, 1978, 1979, 1980, 1981, 1982, 1983, 1984 by Gale Research Company; reprinted by permission of the publisher), Gale Research, 1985.*

APPROPRIATENESS OF THE SYSTEM

A common topic of discussion in industrial relations circles is the uniqueness, or lack of uniqueness, of public-sector collective bargaining. While some differences do exist between the public and private sectors, what can be disputed is the significance of these differences, whether they are growing or shrinking, and what actions should be taken because of them. This section identifies the primary differences between the sectors and evaluates the significance of each difference.

THE DIFFERENCES BETWEEN PUBLIC
AND PRIVATE EMPLOYMENT

Eleven characteristics make public employment different from private employment. Some of these differences are very important; others may have little significance. That is, in some cases the private-sector model is not very appropriate; in others it can be readily adapted. The special characteristics of public employment are:

1. Employer is often very labor-intensive.
2. Strikes are usually illegal.
3. Use of interests arbitration.
4. Division of decision-making authority.
5. Determination of appropriate bargaining units.
6. Scope of bargaining.
7. Supervisors' sympathies.
8. Employer is a monopoly.
9. Employers may depend upon the support of the employees for their jobs.
10. Employer is not in business for a profit.
11. Lack of a uniform labor law.

DIFFERENCES THAT ARE PARTICULARLY SIGNIFICANT

In the author's opinion, nine of these commonly observed differences are particularly significant and two are somewhat "overrated." The important differences are examined below.

Employer Is Often Very Labor-Intensive

Government provides services much more than products. The provision of services generally requires human labor more than capital technology. Many service jobs would be difficult to mechanize at reasonable expense. This has two main effects. First, it tends to provide job security for employees (unless there is a threat of subcontracting or reduction of services). Second, and more important, it also tends to make the employer more wage and human-efficiency conscious than its private-sector counterpart in the capital-intensive sector—for two reasons. First, as labor cost becomes a bigger proportion of total cost, the need to control it closely becomes greater. Second, without machinery, it is difficult to achieve any great increase in productivity.

These constraints have forced public-sector managers to adjust in an era of financial restraint. Assumptions that "the employer cannot go out of business" started receiving closer scrutiny as government services, particularly municipal, were reduced in response to tax-revenue shortages. A particularly well-publicized example was California's Proposition 13, limiting the power to tax and to spend. The public's vehement opposition to taxes and, collaterally, to employees and unions served as a warning to other public employees that it *was* possible for the government to go out of business if that was what the public wanted.

Another adjustment made by management to avoid high labor costs was to subcontract to private business some traditional governmental services. This was particularly true of trash removal. This alternative became feasible if a private contractor could perform the job equally well at a cost below the government's, yet still high enough to make an attractive profit. A large component of this probability was whether the contractor could get greater productivity per manhour and/or pay lower wages. If the contractor could do either of these, the public employee was sometimes bypassed. If a union had negotiated inefficient work rules or unreasonably high wages, this possibility took on increased likelihood.

Strikes Are Usually Illegal

In the private sector a strike may, theoretically, only mildly inconvenience the consumer, forcing him or her to purchase from a nonstruck alternative supplier. When that alternative supplier does not exist in public employment services, and the continuation of services is highly critical, as in police and fire protection, the situation becomes much worse. This difference has been cited by most observers as being so significant as to justify banning strikes in public employment.

This distinction may exist more in theory than in reality. A closer examination reveals less difference between the sectors in practice than exists in theory. Many of the private sector's significant labor relations are conducted through coordinated bargaining, which can, and sometimes does, result in entire industries being shut down, depriving customers of the possibility of purchasing from alternative suppliers. The public's fear of such a potential danger resulted in the passage of the National Emergency Disputes procedures in the Taft-Hartley Act of 1947 to protect the public's "health and safety."

Labor relations in that sector, history has shown, have turned out to be manageable, at least from the "flow of products to the consumer" perspective. The public has never been "brought to its knees" by a strike in the sector. Occasional highly publicized stoppages, such as the coal strike of 1977-78, have never resulted in the widespread hardship forecast for them. Resolution has

NATIONAL FEDERATION OF FEDERAL EMPLOYEES PICKET IN FRONT OF THE
WHITE HOUSE TO PROTEST BUDGET CUTS

SOURCE: *AP/Wide World Photos*

always been had before the direst of consequences resulted. This is attributable
to some degree both to the emergency dispute procedures and to governmental
ad hoc actions and, to a larger degree, to the adaptability of the parties. One
adaptation private employers learned was to produce in advance and "stockpile" their customers in anticipation of a strike.

    This adaptation, however, is often less available in the public sector. It
is impossible to stockpile police or fire protection in advance. Further, the private-sector response of doing without the product for the duration is more easily
accomplished than in the public sector, where going without police protection
is not a mere matter of belt-tightening. On the other hand, this is not true of
all governmental services. The public can probably do without libraries indefinitely.

    At the beginning of the seventies it was believed by virtually everyone that strikes in public employment were completely unmanageable and must be banned as a matter of law. The experience of the seventies provided at least three lessons: (1) banning strikes did not eliminate them, (2) the consequences of some strikes were very dire indeed—much more so than those of their private-sector counterparts, and (3) management could minimize the effectiveness of strikes by preparing for them.

Recently, managers in the public sector who deal with militant unions have come to rely less on legal provisions to deter strikes[1] and more on contingency plans both to minimize the impact on the public and to discourage the union from going on strike in the first place. These contingency plans include providing replacement personnel from management and from similar services in other jurisdictions along with recommendations to the public on how to provide the missing services for themselves.

Despite these alternative pressures in response to possible strikes and the fact that some jurisdictions have legalized some strikes under some conditions, the overwhelming sentiment is still to prohibit strikes. This prohibition is also commonly abided by. This requires a significantly different form of impasse resolution and leads to the next important difference in the public sector.

Use of Interests Arbitration

Because strikes are forbidden in almost all jurisdictions, and because impasses do arise, some way of dealing with them must be provided. There are two typical responses. One is to leave the employees without further recourse other than begging the employer to improve jobs. If the employer does not do this, the employees' only options are to accept the offer or quit. These solutions have obvious shortcomings both as conflict-resolution mechanisms and as problem-solvers. The other typical solution is to permit interests arbitration. In *interests arbitration* an expert, neutral outsider considers the positions, situations, and needs of the parties and prescribes the contract for them. The arbitrator's decision may or may not be binding, depending upon the law of that jurisdiction. The decision reached may be based on the arbitrator's perception of equity rather than purely on the bargaining power of the parties.

Chapter 10 examined in detail the reasons why arbitration is not favored for resolving interests disputes (lack of commitment to the result, inability to take credit for the outcomes, and fear of loss of control). Despite its shortcomings, interests arbitration is often utilized in public employment because the alternatives—powerless employees or potentially devastating strikes—are considered even worse.

Some observers also have been concerned that conventional interests arbitration can have a ''chilling'' effect on negotiations. If the parties fear that an arbitrator might split the differences between them, it is in their interest to have made as few concessions before arbitration as possible. That is, if an arbitrator is going to select a *midpoint,* it is in the parties' interest to stick to outrageous demands. It will move the midpoint in one's own direction. This strategy could not, of course, be expected to move the parties closer to mutual agreement and should result in more arbitration and fewer settlements than would otherwise result—thus the "chilling effect on bargaining." Incuring the costs of a strike would, however, presumably have moved the parties to settle on their own.

To counteract the potential chilling effect, some jurisdictions provide for "final-offer arbitration." In this arrangement, the arbitrator must select the final offer of one of the parties and reject that of the other. The arbitrator may not compromise between them. Obviously, the arbitrator is expected to select the more appropriate (or less inappropriate) offer. For a party to enhance its chance of having its offer selected, it is necessary to formulate a proposal the arbitrator will perceive as appropriate. Outlandish proposals, such as those that might be presented in conventional arbitration in preparation for splitting the differences, will not be selected. Therefore, there is great pressure to move toward appropriateness, rather than away. This theoretically creates a situation in which the parties will minimize their distance from the arbitrator's perception of appropriateness and will collaterally move closer to each other. When and if this occurs, it becomes easier for the parties to settle the issue themselves, rather than resorting to outsiders. If final-offer arbitration worked perfectly, it would never need to be invoked.

Division of Decision-Making Authority

Lack of finality in negotiations presents problems in both sectors. The problems are worse in the public sector. In private negotiations the company representative has the power to bind the employer with his or her signature. The union representative, however, generally must submit proposed agreements to the entire membership for ratification. If the rank-and-file reject the proposed settlement, the offer must be "sweetened" or an impasse will occur. While this is a problem in both sectors, and an increasing one at that, it may be decidedly minor compared to lack of managerial finality in the public sector.

The "separation of powers" doctrine found throughout American government dictates that the administrative functions of the executive branch be separate from the budgeting function of the legislative branch. This means that the managers who have responsibility for administering the employment relationship (the executive branch) cannot, generally, agree to pay for it. Bargains reached in negotiations are subject to funding approval by the legislative arm. This can cause profound problems in transferring the private model to the public sector.

A principal tenet of collective bargaining is that the parties meet in a good-faith effort to reach agreement. When the parties know that the agreement reached may well not be the final one, this awareness puts a substantial burden on their good faith. The problem can be a two-way street. On one side of the street, executive branch managers, who can be assumed to desire the support of their subordinates and who do not have to fund the cost of their agreements, may be willing to settle for more than the legislature will provide. Legislative rejection or reduction then leaves the employees disappointed and frustrated at the inability of their union to influence the financial decision maker. To tell the union to lobby the legislature like other interest groups then denies to the union its principal reason to exist—to bargain collectively. Further, a Machiavellian executive could escape good-faith bargaining by agreeing to demands popular with the rank-and-file and then covertly influencing the legislature not to fund them, thereby placing the blame for the employees' dissatisfaction on a party outside the bargaining relationship.

On the other side of the street, the union is sometimes able to play this lack of finality to its advantage. In early collective-bargaining relationships it was often believed that some unions benefited from "two bites of the apple." They would first reach agreement with an executive department administrator, who gave all he or she could in good faith, and then proceed to lobby the legislative branch (with whom they had considerable clout) to sweeten the agreement. This result had a very deleterious effect on the management bargaining team, which would now probably withhold a portion of benefits in anticipation of the union's "end run" to the legislature.

Another major problem associated with the separation of powers is the lack of clarity in determining which manager is responsible for which issues. This is especially true when a strong merit system impinges on the scope of bargaining. Sincere managers, believing they are unable to bargain on the issues, may shuttle union negotiators back and forth. Machiavellian managers may deliberately avoid bargaining and stall by claiming that the issues are in someone else'e bailiwick. Often the parties genuinely do not know who is responsible for what. The union's goal is to bargain with the manager who may say "I will" or "I won't" rather than "I can't." This particular problem is best handled when addressing the related question of bargaining-unit determination, discussed below.

Determination of Appropriate Bargaining Units

In the private sector, the NLRB generally determines bargaining units. The criteria it utilizes are extremely cursory. The special interests of supervisors, professionals, craftsmen, guards, and confidential employees are provided for, but beyond that, the Board is merely charged with providing for the employees' "community of interest" and bargaining history. Unit-determination problems are further reduced by the Board's willingness to allow the parties to expand the bargaining unit by their own consent to facilitate mutually advantageous bargaining structures.

In the public sector, the criteria for determining a community of interest take a much wider significance. This is caused by two factors: the split of managerial authority and the need for the employer to provide standardized benefits. Bargaining units must be structured in the public sector to coincide with the scope of bargainable issues. In the private sector, the employer representative at the bargaining table holds the authority to discuss and agree to all issues not forbidden by law. It is therefore quite simple to match the employer and the scope of bargaining issues in a private-sector bargaining unit. In the public sector, it is common for the executive branch employer to control working-conditions issues and for the legislative arm to control pay and benefits. Therefore, units organized along agency or departmental lines to negotiate working conditions may be inappropriate for discussing wage and benefit issues. This problem is made more difficult by laws that commonly require standardization of benefits—for instance, in state employment, a requirement that vacation policies be uniform across all departments. With this requirement, it makes sense to have broad bargaining units in public employment to facilitate negotiations with the administrator who controls all agencies. To create bargaining units of narrower jurisdiction causes great difficulties in maintaining standardization.

This problem is often a bad one, because much public-sector bargaining arose through departmental units, rather than governmentwide units. These narrow-purpose units were suitable for discussing working conditions but not pay and benefits. As the scope of bargaining expanded (see below), these units became much less appropriate for maintaining standardization. The problem was made worse by the fact that there were often a very large number of these units. The problem was still further worsened by the fact that the unions representing the existing units had no guarantee of winning representation rights in newly constructed larger units. Therefore, in at least some instances, they opposed the creation of more appropriate bargaining units.[2]

Scope of Bargaining

Where private-sector employees have chosen to be represented by a union, the rulings of the NLRB have encouraged the broadest range of problem solving through collective bargaining, at least as long as it concerns employee wages, hours, and terms and conditions of employment. Only a few items of direct interest to unions are forbidden topics. These include the closed shop, "hot cargo" agreements, and secondary boycotts. This is quite different from the public-sector model, where the scope of bargaining may be severely restricted by the presence of an alternative system of employee protection—a civil service or merit system.

With the exception of referral unions in the trades, American unions, both public and private, have expressed relatively little interest in the hiring process. However, once employees have entered the system, unions see it as their opportunity and duty to represent the employees on matters of how a job is to be done and who is selected to perform it. Merit systems, however, also deal with these topics. When there are parallel mechanisms for providing resolution to the same problems, efficiency generally dictates that only one should be followed. The determination of which system will resolve these topics—a merit system or a union contract—must be determined by the legislative body for the jurisdiction. In many instances, the decision to favor merit-system coverage of these topics results in a restriction of bargainable issues on which the union can appear to deliver. The outcome of such a restriction is to place greater emphasis on the resolution of matters that can be negotiated and to reduce the latitude of the parties to trade off.[3] This can make bargaining considerably more difficult.

The private sector experienced the difficulties of restricted bargaining from the mid-thirties to the fifties. During that time the parties learned two lessons. First, it is difficult to exclude topics the other side wishes to negotiate. The Taft-Hartley Act makes it an unfair labor practice to force a bargaining impasse over a voluntary issue—that is, one that is not mandatory. However, the distinction between mandatory and voluntary can easily be avoided. The party that wishes to force consideration of the nonmandatory issue merely indirectly makes the other side aware that acceptance of the mandatory issues is contingent upon negotiation of the nonmandatory. This avoids the unfair labor practice charge and broadens the scope of bargaining extralegally. The second lesson learned is that this is not all bad. Historically, private employers fought through the courts to preserve the limitation on mandatory bargaining issues, opposing consideration of such issues as pensions and health-care coverage.[4] As employers lost these decisions in courts (it was ruled that these issues were included in the mandatory scope of bargaining), they began to reassess whether it was necessary or desirable to restrict the scope of bargaining. They generally concluded that it was not. Unions expressed little interest in managerial decisions not directly affecting employees, and the increased scope permitted more opportunities to manage the outcome.

The public-sector conflict is not so simply resolved. Even if management were willing to bargain over merit-system issues, doing so is usually illegal and there is someone to complain if they do—the merit-system bureaucrats who have a vested employment interest in preserving the distinction. Still, as collective bargaining has come to be more accepted, even if not more popular, the scope of bargaining has been increased to where it is more comparable to that in the private sector.

Supervisors' Sympathies

In the United Sates, collective bargaining is commonly expected to consist of two parties—management and the union. It is further expected that the interests of the two sides will often be in conflict (a safe assumption), that each side will be internally united against the "opposition" (a far less safe assumption), and that one knows which side he or she is on. For a large number of employees carrying the title of supervisor in the public sector, it is difficult to determine on which side of the table they belong.

In the private sector the line between management and rank-and-file is reasonably clear. First-line supervisors and those above them are excluded from the coverage and protection of the Taft-Hartley Act. The Act defines "supervisor" basically by the activities and responsibilities of the position. Chief characteristics of supervision include the right to direct the workforce, answer grievances, and exercise independent judgment. These responsibilities differentiate "true" supervisors from workleaders or "straw bosses." There is a gray area for managers who meet the supervisory definition but have little authority over personnel. This area has not, however, proved very troublesome. On the whole, the distinction between management and rank-and-file is fairly easily drawn.

Unfortunately, the public sector seldom enjoys such agreement. Several characteristics of public-sector supervision combine to make the identification and treatment of supervisors more difficult: the public sector's liberal use of the title (often in lieu of a pay raise), the lack of status differentiations from lower-level employees, and the carrying of a workload of the same nature as the subordinates' (for instance, a social services supervisor who carries a caseload of a few of the most difficult cases in the agency). This blurring of the lines between supervisor and subordinate seldom occurs in the unionized private sector. In fact, it is a common union contract provision to forbid a supervisor from doing bargaining-unit work.

The difficulty of treating supervisors' problems evolves from the differences in role and expectations between the two sectors. Private-sector supervisors are expected to share an undivided community of interest with higher management. In the public sector, that assumption requires closer scrutiny. Several factors lead to arguments for treating supervisors differently from their private-sector counterparts. Among them are the absence of the opportunity to climb to the top of the hierarchy (these positions are usually elective or appointive); the presence of formalized promotion policies that may reward seniority more than merit, at least compared to the private sector; the common failure to be able to negotiate one's own wage and working conditions; and a likelihood of having been promoted from the rank-and-file one now supervises.

These factors combine to create a viewpoint much more like that of one's subordinates than is generally true in the private sector. This often leads public supervisors to seek union representation—an almost unheard-of private-sector sentiment—and to be represented by the union of their subordinates. To deny the right of representation to these supervisors because it is not permitted in the private sector ignores the important differences between the two. On the other hand, permitting representation also causes problems.

The principal ill in not allowing representation is the possiblity of failing to recognize and account for the needs of these employees. If that occurs, it can be expected that the positions will be filled with lower-quality personnel than they would otherwise be. If representation is permitted, then there is a risk that higher-level management's orders will not be carried out as zealously "against" organizational cohorts as they would be absent such representation. Permitting organization also creates significant difficulties with grievance processing and, perhaps, stifling of internal commentary in the union when the "boss" is present.[5]

Employer Is a Monopoly

Most often the government is the only supplier of the services it renders. This is important for two reasons. First, a disruption in production—i.e., a strike—would leave the consumer/taxpayer totally without the services of that function. Second, the absence of price competition makes it difficult to determine what a service should cost. In the private sector the consumer generally benefits from price competition. More efficient producers can sell at lower prices, thereby increasing their market share. Less efficient producers are ultimately driven out of business. In an inelastic-demand monopoly situation, either private or public, the pricing mechanism is not available to insure efficiency. Inefficient producers will be maintained because of the absence of cheaper alternatives. Theoretically, this should lead to unreasonable bargaining power on the part of unions, because the employer need not be efficient. However, this phenomenon is largely mitigated by the financial constraints cited below in "the employer is not in business for a profit."

Still, the monopoly condition is an important difference, because alternative mechanisms must be provided to assure continuation of services and financial restraint.

Employers May Depend upon the Support of the Employees for Their Jobs

In the private sector, managers' rewards and promotions depend upon their pleasing their superiors. In the public sector, elected employers may depend, to a large extent, upon the approval of their subordinates. In the simplest sense this is because of the different organizational structures. The private company appoints managers from above. The government elects leaders from below. Public employees, especially at the local level, can form a very important power base in these elections.

Local officials are particularly subject to their employees' demands in the political arena—for several reasons. First, any sizable bloc of voters is worth considering if elections are at all close. The public-employee bloc is particularly powerful for its size. American voting preferences are a product of many considerations, such as age, income, race, education, occupation, and family history. These factors may cause employees working for the same government agency to vote differently in national political elections. However, in a local election, where one candidate is proemployee and the other is not, and especially if jobs are at stake, public employees can be expected to suppress their usual political variances and unite behind their employment interest. Further, they are highly likely to vote, and may bring along their relatives and friends, who would not want to see them out of work. In municipal elections that commonly have very light voter turnouts, this group becomes proportionally much larger and can wield power far beyond its apparent size. While a private-sector manager does not want to antagonize his employees, it is a rare public official at the local level who can dare to.

ARITHMETIC OF LOCAL ELECTIONS

The following hypothetical example, using realistic percentages, demonstrates how a small group of city employees, voting as a bloc, could influence the outcome of a much, much larger election unit.

BACKGROUND FACTS

Population of city	275,000
Number of city employees	4,000
Percent of population who are city employees	1.5%

VOTING BEHAVIOR OF PUBLIC	Percent	Number
Population of eligible voting age and status	70	192,500
Population of eligible to vote who are registered	55	105,875
Registered voters voting in city elections	15	15,881
Absolute number of votes needed to win	(50 + 1)	7,941

VOTING BEHAVIOR OF CITY EMPLOYEE BLOC	Percent	Number
Voters for candidate favoring city employees' job	100	4,000
"Allies" (spouses, dependents, etc.—approximately one per employee) voting with bloc	—	4,000
Total bloc vote		8,000

CONCLUSION

The city-employee bloc is not only significant and influential, it may be controlling. In this instance, 1/69 of the population could determine the outcome of the election.

Even the remarkable "arithmetic of local elections" figures in the accompanying illustration may understate the influence of the bloc, because they make no allowance for non-city employees who would also vote for the candidate. If the candidate would ordinarily receive 40 percent of the other votes, the bloc becomes that much more powerful.

Some cautions should be noted, however. The generalizations used in the example, while valid in many typical instances, can be off substantially if the municipal election is, for instance, a "hot one" on some other issue, if the employees affected are from traditional nonvoting groups, or if it is part of a Presidential election, when turnout is always higher.

DIFFERENCES THAT ARE LESS SIGNIFICANT

Employer Is Not in Business for a Profit

This is one of the most commonly cited differences between the private and public sectors, yet it is one of the least significant. Because the government is not trying to make money, many observers fear that it will be too generous in granting wage demands to unions. That would result in either higher taxes or reduced services. In reality, the public employer acts very much like its private counterpart in trying to reduce labor costs.

The private-sector need for profits has always been viewed as a mechanism that created an upper bound on union demands. Theoretically, a union could raise wages at the expense of profits only to the limit of the employer's next best opportunity for investment. Further, if high wages forced costs above the level of competition, all other things being equal, the employer's market share in a competitive economy would diminish and union jobs would be lost. Since a high wage rate for a job one no longer possesses is worthless, it is assumed that unions will, in general, seek to constrain their wage demands in line with the employer's ability to pay and its alternative investment opportunities. This model would not, of course, be true for monopolies or oligopolies that are uniformly unionized and have a highly inelastic demand for their product. In such a situation an increased wage cost, or any other increased cost, could be passed along to the consumer.

The absence of a profit motive, the monopolistic nature of many government services, and a supposed near-inelastic demand for services might be expected to make the public employer an "easy mark" for union wage demands. In theory, the employer has little reason to resist union wage demands, since it will continue in business regardless of cost.

This assumption is, however, grossly misrepresentative, as any public employee union can attest. Public employers are often more, not less, parsimonious with the purse strings than their private-sector counterparts. The private employer is often able and willing to grant wage increases (although not as high as the union has demanded) and recover the costs through improved efficiency and increased revenues resulting in part from price increases that can be passed along in the marketplace.

The public employer, on the other hand, is up against some imposing financial constraints not faced in private employment. The passing along of the cost of a wage increase through an increase in the cost of the product—i.e., taxes—is always politically undesirable to elected officials and is occasionally illegal as well. Many local government functions have state constitutional limitations on taxing powers, whether they be over property or income, and most are forbidden to operate at a deficit. Further, the public employer is likely to be a hard bargainer on finances for the following reasons:

1. Executive agency bargainers must receive funding from their respective legislative arms. Legislators generally oppose any budget necessitating a tax increase. Since the legislature does not work directly with government employees, it may be under even less pressure to consent to a wage demand than private-sector managers, because it is more isolated from the employees' displeasure.
2. Elected officials fear being voted out of office because of a rise in taxes more than private managers fear losing their jobs over a cost increase, especially if the cost increase can be more than compensated for by increased revenues and/or efficiency.
3. Excessive government spending in any area leads to the formation of interest groups to oppose it. Highly visible gains for employees are likely to produce the formation of antiunion interest groups.
4. Giving raises to employees is a poor way for a bureaucrat to spend money. He or she would rather spend the same amount on physical facilities or services, returning something visible to the public for its taxes. Pay increases for employees with no concomitant increase in services is seen as a ''no return'' investment for the taxpayer.
5. Most public managers, like most private managers, want to do a good job. They philosophically oppose ''giving away'' tax dollars undeservedly.[6]

One other characteristic of overconcern remains: that of the absence of a uniform labor law.

Lack of a Uniform Labor Law

Most private-sector labor relations are governed by one law, the Wagner Act as amended by Taft-Hartley. The public sector is much more fragmented. Federal labor relations are now largely covered by the Civil Service Reform Act of 1978. Each state is free to legislate, or not to legislate, its own rules for state and local employees. It may, in fact, prescribe different rules for different groups of employees—for instance, teachers and firefighters—within the same state. The complexity is compounded by municipalities' also occasionally legislating collective bargaining ordinances in addition to state law. The situation is compounded even further by the application of common-law principles in areas in which the states have not legislated. With 50 states, multiple laws for different job classifications, and additional city ordinances, labor law in the public sector becomes very complex.

This complexity caused by a lack of uniformity was seen as a liability in the early seventies.[7] Coupled with a common lack of specificity in some laws, it was seen to create confusion for the parties, particularly in knowing what they could or could not do. In the private sector, 40 years' experience with one national law had greatly reduced the confusion in that area. Practitioners in the public sector, on the other hand, in order to make progress had to wait for the accumulation of decisions in their own jurisdiction, and that accumulation came more slowly as the activities of other states were of little precedent value.

Organized labor has, from time to time, called for a standardized collective bargaining law to be passed by the federal government and to be applied to all the states.[8] Such a law has not been passed. In the 1970s its chances received a substantial setback with the Supreme Court's decision in *National League of Cities* v. *Usery* that it was unconstitutional for the federal government to apply the Fair Labor Standards Act (the minimum wage law) to the states.[9] Although that decision was overruled in 1985 in *Garcia* v. *San Antonio Metropolitan Transit Authority*, no law appears imminent. However, a more important issue is whether there is a need for a uniform law.

The fact that the rules are not the same among states is not inherently offensive so long as the parties know the rules for their own jurisdiction. Unfortunately, not even this is always the case. The "minimal legislation" approach common in some states means that the court system, rather than the legislature, creates the rules for the parties to live by. This can be time-consuming, expensive, and very disruptive to stable labor relations.[10]

A synopsis demonstrating the variety of state laws appears in Table 15-1.

CONCLUSIONS AS TO THE APPLICABILITY OF THE PRIVATE-SECTOR MODEL

Before collective bargaining came to public employment, many observers felt that the differences between the sectors justified the exclusion of unions for governmental employees. Twenty-five years of experience with unions has tended, however, to reduce the differences between the sectors and to increase the adaptability of public management. While there still are discernible differences, the behavior of the parties on both sides of the table has become surprisingly similar to that of their private-sector counterparts—at least, judged by preunionization days.

Recently, public managers have taken a more aggressive strategy to the bargaining table in the form of demands for increased productivity, subcontracting, reduction of services, and mechanization. These have lead to restraint on union demands that the theorists for the seventies seldom imagined. The worry about "untrammeled" union power based on inelastic demand has proved largely unjustified. Public employers are becoming ever more successful at elasticizing the demand for their employees' services.

TABLE 15-1   STATUS OF COLLECTIVE BARGAINING RIGHTS FOR STATE AND LOCAL GOVERNMENT
EMPLOYEES AS OF JANUARY 1, 1985

State	Bargaining Statute[a]	Right to Bargain	Mandatory Bargaining	Third-Party Intervention	Exclusive Representation	Antistrike Provisions
Alabama	1967[b]	Yes	—	—	—	Yes
Alaska	1978[c]	Yes	Yes	Yes	Yes	Yes[d]
Arizona	—	No	—	—	—	—
Arkansas	—	No	—	—	Yes	—
California	1968[e]	Yes	No	Yes	Yes	—
Colorado	—	No	—	—	—	—
Connecticut	1975[f]	Yes	Yes	Yes	Yes	Yes
Delaware	1970[g]	Yes	Yes	Yes	Yes	Yes
Florida	1974	Yes	Yes	Yes	Yes	Yes
Georgia	1971[h]	Yes	No	No	Yes	Yes
Hawaii	1970	Yes	Yes	Yes	Yes	Yes[i]
Idaho	1971[j]	Yes	Yes	Yes	Yes	Yes
Illinois	1983[hh]	Yes	Yes	Yes	Yes	Yes[k]
Indiana	1973[l]	Yes	Yes	Yes	Yes	Yes
Iowa	1974	Yes	Yes	Yes	Yes	Yes
Kansas	1971[m]	Yes	No	Yes	Yes	Yes
Kentucky	1972[d]	Yes	Yes	Yes	Yes	Yes
Louisiana	—	Yes	—	—	—	—
Maine	1969[n]	Yes	Yes	Yes	Yes	Yes
Maryland	1978[o]	Yes	Yes	Yes	Yes	Yes
Massachusetts	1973	Yes	Yes	Yes	Yes	Yes
Michigan	1980[p]	Yes	Yes	Yes	Yes	Yes
Minnesota	1971	Yes	Yes	Yes	Yes	Yes[q]
Mississippi	—	No	—	—	—	—
Missouri	1967[r]	Yes	No	No	Yes	Yes[t]
Montana	1973[s]	Yes	Yes	Yes	Yes	Yes[t]
Nebraska	1969[u]	Yes	Yes	Yes	Yes	Yes
Nevada	1969[v]	Yes	Yes	Yes	Yes	Yes
New Hampshire	1975	Yes	Yes	Yes	Yes	Yes
New Jersey	1968[w]	Yes	Yes	Yes	Yes	—
New Mexico	1972[x]	Yes	Yes	Yes	Yes	Yes
New York	1967	Yes	Yes	Yes	Yes	Yes
North Carolina	—	No	—	—	—	—

(continued)

TABLE 15-1 (Continued)

State	Bargaining Statute[a]	Right to Bargain	Mandatory Bargaining	Third-Party Intervention	Exclusive Representation	Antistrike Provisions
North Dakota	1969[y]	Yes	Yes	Yes	Yes	Yes
Ohio	1983[ii]	Yes	Yes	Yes	Yes	Yes[d]
Oklahoma	1971	Yes	Yes	No	No	Yes
Oregon	1973	Yes	Yes	Yes	Yes	Yes[d]
Pennsylvania	1976[z]	Yes	Yes	Yes	Yes	Yes[aa]
Rhode Island	1958[bb]	Yes	Yes	Yes	Yes	Yes
South Carolina	—	No	—	—	—	—
South Dakota	1969[cc]	Yes	Yes	No	Yes	Yes
Tennessee	1978[dd]	Yes	Yes	Yes	Yes	Yes
Texas	1973	Yes	Yes	Yes	Yes	Yes
Utah	—	No	—	—	—	Yes
Vermont	1969[ee]	Yes	Yes	Yes	Yes	Yes
Virginia	—	No	—	—	—	Yes
Washington	1967[ff]	Yes	Yes	Yes	Yes	Yes
West Virginia	—	No	—	—	—	—
Wisconsin	1966[gg]	Yes	Yes	Yes	Yes	Yes
Wyoming	1965	Yes	Yes	Yes	Yes	—
District of Columbia	1978	Yes	Yes	Yes	Yes	Yes

(a) Following dates are for laws currently in effect. Some laws may supersede earlier statutes. (b) Refers only to firefighters. (c) Refers to state and local employees only; separate statutes cover teachers, elected or appointed officials, noncertified employees of a school district. (d) Refers only to safety forces. (e) Refers to state and local employees only; separate statutes cover firefighters, public school employees, and employees of higher education. (f) Refers to state employees only. Separate statutes cover teachers and municipal employees. (g) Refers to state and local employees, separate statutes cover transit workers and teachers. (h) Refers only to firefighters. State employee strikes prohibited by separate statute. (i) Without compliance of impasse procedures. (j) Refers to teachers only. (k) Refers to security employees only. (l) Refers to teachers only. (m) Mandatory bargaining provided for in separate statute covering teachers. (n) University employees, state and municipal employees covered by special statutes. (o) Refers to teachers only. Noncertified public school employees covered by separate statute. (p) Refers to state civil service employees. Local government employees and safety forces covered by separate statutes. (q) Refers only to essential employees. (r) Teachers and policemen excluded. (s) Nurses covered by special statute. (t) Refers only to firefighters. (u) Teachers covered by separate statute. (v) Refers only to local government employees. (w) Compulsory arbitration for safety forces provided for in a separate statute. (x) Refers only to classified state civil service employees. (y) Refers to teachers only. Mediation of impasses for all public employees covered in separate statute. (z) Safety force provided for in special statute. (aa) Refers only to court employees, prison and mental hospital guards. (bb) Refers to state employees only. (cc) Refers to teachers only. State employees covered in separate statute. (dd) Refers to safety forces only. Teachers covered in separate statute. (ee) Refers to state employees only. (ff) Refers to state civil service employees. Local government employees and teachers covered by separate statutes. (gg) Refers to state employees only. (hh) Became effective July 1, 1984. (ii) Signed July 6, 1984. (ii) Became effective in part on October 6, 1983, fully effective April 1, 1984.

SOURCE: Ron M. Portaro, "An Empirical Study of Ohio Impasse Resolution Procedure," Journal of Collective Negotiations in the Public Sector; Vol. 15, No. 2; 1986; pp. 168–70.

One result is that public-employee unionization appears to be in a second generation. In the 1980s, after two decades of strenuous activities, growth and conflict both seem to have subsided. Debates as to the appropriateness of public-employee unions have given way to quieter internal problem solving. The similarities to and differences from private-sector experiences have been noted by practitioners and largely adjusted to.

Notes

1. For an examination of the limited effectiveness of laws, see Alan Balfour and Alexander B. Holmes, ''The Effectiveness of No Strike Sanctions for Public School Teachers,'' *Journal of Collective Negotiations in the Public Sector*, Vol. 10, No. 2 (1981), pp. 133–44.
2. For a more detailed examination of the conflicting needs in bargaining-unit determination, see Alan Balfour, ''Appropriate Bargaining Units for State Employees,'' *State Government*, Fall 1976.
3. According to interviews with Wisconsin practitioners in 1975, the state formerly had a restricted scope of bargaining that did not include wages until 1972. At that time, both management and labor successfully petitioned the legislature to broaden the scope of bargaining to include wages and to reduce union demands in areas more commonly reserved for managerial prerogative.
4. See Herbert L. Sherman and William P. Murphy, ''Subjects of Bargaining,'' in *Labor Relations and Social Problems* (Washington, D.C.: BNA Publishing, 1975), pp. 119–43.
5. For a more detailed examination of the problems of supervisory representation, see Alan Balfour, ''Rights of Collective Representation for Public Sector Supervisors, *Journal of Collective Negotiations in the Public Sector*, Vol. 4, No. 3, pp. 257–66.
6. This list has been paraphrased from James A. Belasco, ''Municipal Bargaining and Political Power,'' in *Collective Bargaining in Government* by J. Joseph Loewenberg and Michael H. Moskow (Englewood Cliffs, N.J.: Prentice-Hall, 1972), pp. 245–46.
7. See Harold W. Davey, *Contemporary Collective Bargaining*, 3d ed. (Englewood Cliffs, N.J.: Prentice-Hall, 1972), pp. 353–56.
8. *Ibid*, p. 356.
9. *National League of Cities* v. *Usery*, 426 U.S. Supreme Ct., 1976.
10. For an example of the consternation caused the parties by the minimal-legislation approach, see Alan Balfour and Sandra Jennings, ''Chaos in Union Recognition Procedures: A Case History of Oklahoma's School Teacher Bargaining Law,'' *Journal of Collective Negotiations in the Public Sector*, Vol. 11, No. 1 (1982), pp. 77–88.

Discussion Questions

1. Describe the conditions leading to the growth of unionization in the public sector.
2. Evaluate the appropriateness of collective bargaining in the public sector.
3. [(a) through (k)] Discuss the significance of each of the special characteristics of public employment.

Statements for Comment

1. "Unions are the cause of our screwed-up private sector. They should be banned from the public sector before they make things even worse there."
2. "The sovereignty doctrine is bad theory and bad law. Besides, it won't work."
3. "All illegally striking public employees should be fired and put in jail."
4. "Without the right to strike, collective bargaining is collective begging."
5. "State and local governments have a harder time passing along a price increase than any other monopolist."
6. (a) "The differences between the public and private sectors are overrated."
   (b) "The differences between the public and private sectors are underrated."

Situations

Case 15–1 "You know, public employees are, in many ways, second-class citizens. Their right to run for office is restricted and they often don't have effective collective bargaining rights. And, for sure, they don't have nice perquisites. Local government buildings are so spartan, and even the managers don't get carpeting, drapes, or wall paneling. I don't know why anyone would want to be one—at least anyone who could get any other job," said Susie Schuster.

"My dear, they do it out of loyalty and public service!" said Barry Simon, her boyfriend. "Besides, the jobs are cushy and they don't have the stress to get the job done that exists in the competitive world."

"Oh, don't give me that Boy Scout crap, Barry—and I hardly think the jobs are any cushier than private-sector counterparts, in fact, they look a lot alike to me. I'm afraid that leaving pay and benefit matters to legislatures will result in government jobs being staffed by those who can't get other jobs, and I don't want my city, state, and country being run by losers. We've got to make public employment comparable to private," said Susie.

What do you say? Are Barry and Susie right on their facts and their goals? Cite evidence to support your conclusions.

Case 15–2 "The problem with studying public-employee collective bargaining," said Patti Prentice, "is that you find yourself being forced into one of two camps—either you believe public employees should be limited to lobbying, with all its attendant liabilities, or you believe they should be allowed collective bargaining with all its attendant liabilities. It may be possible that there is a third choice."

"Pray tell, what might that be?" queried Manny Hall.

"To automatically tie benefits to benchmark equivalent jobs in the private sector. As pay and benefits change in the private sector, public jobs would be adjusted. If the cost of doing business went up, the legislature would automatically have to fund the wage increases and shuffle their budgets elsewhere," said Patti.

"Actually, that sounds like a very attractive idea, but if I'm not wrong, I believe the federal government's pay policies are already supposedly operated that way, and no one would hold them up as a model of perfection," said Manny.

What benefits do you see to such a scheme? What liabilities?

Case 15-3 "Democracy is a lousy way to run anything you want to be efficient. Nobody suggests running a company that way. The operation of the government should be run like a business, and that includes personnel policy. Leaving important personnel matters to the public's elected representatives is a disaster. At best, politicians are not experts in personnel administration. At worst, they accurately reflect the ignorant inclinations of the public. The only thing the public is concerned with is holding down taxes, and they think it's smart, efficient, and necessary to hold down wages while still expecting performance and then griping all the time about the perceived high cost and low efficiency. If war is too important to be left to the generals, running the government is too important to be left to the public. The public should prioritize the programs it wants carried out, but professional administrators should deliver those services in accordance with business practices, not public sympathy. The public is, frankly, not qualified to judge," said Steve Tillotson, management consultant.

"You elitist snob," said Carl O'Meara. "You underrate the common sense of the American public. The reason they are so concerned about government cost is that there is so much waste in government spending. In defense of the public, it's much easier for them to protest public employee pay levels than it is for them to find waste in contracts for suppliers of the government."

"That may be exactly the reason for not leaving managerial decisions to amateurs. The public may focus on the wrong target out of frustration. A professional manager would go after the contractors rather than trying to rip off the people whose performance and cooperation he needs. If, however, the employees were part of the problem, a good manager would go after them, too," said Steve.

What voice should the public have in personnel decisions? Why?

Case 15-4 "You can't put us in with them!" exclaimed Don James, a physical therapist at the state hospital.

"You don't want to be put in with a thousand nurses?" queried Raymond MacMillan, Chairman of the State Public Employee Relations Board.

"Not in a bargaining unit, I don't," said Don. "There are only 100 of us therapists, and we'll be tyrannized by the majority. It's no secret that professional groups don't like one another, and if it ever comes down to splitting up limited resources— and it always does come down to that—we'll be outvoted 1000 to 100 on every issue, and they'll take everything for themselves. We need to have a bargaining unit of just physical therapists."

"But, Don, be reasonable," said Raymond. "If we give the physical therapists their own unit, we'll have to have one for x-ray technicians, dieticians, LPNs, and every other identifiable subgroup. For administrative convenience, we have to have only one unit of professionals."

"I'd rather not be represented at all than be submerged under all the others," said Don.

Is there any way out of this dilemma? What do you recommend? Why?

Bibliography of Related Readings

Cunningham, R. M., "Labor-Management Relations in the Federal Sector: Democracy or Paternalism?" *Labor Law Journal,* October 1980, pp. 636–44.

McGarry, S. J., "Public Sector Collective Bargaining and the Contract Clause," *Labor Law Journal,* February 1980, pp. 67–75.

Methe, D. T., and J. L. Perry, "The Impacts of Collective Bargaining on Local Government Services," *Personnel Administration Review,* 1980, pp. 359–71.

Nelson, W. B., "An Economic Analysis of Public Sector Collective Bargaining and Strike Activity," *Journal of Labor Research,* 1981, pp. 77–98.

Smith, R. L., and A. H. Hopkins, "Public Employee Attitudes Toward Unions," *Industrial and Labor Relations Review,* 1979, pp. 484–95.

Spero, Sterling, and John M. Capozzola, *The Urban Community and Its Unionized Bureaucracies* (New York: Dunellen Publishing Company, 1973).

Stanley, David T., *Managing Local Government Under Union Pressure* (Washington, D.C.: Brookings Institution, 1972).

Sterret, G., and A. Aboud, *The Right to Strike in Public Employment* (Ithaca: ILR Press [New York State School of Industrial and Labor Relations, Cornell University], 1982), 2d ed., p. 59.

Stieber, Jack, *Public Employee Unionism* (Washington, D.C.: Brookings Institution, 1973).

Wellington, Harry H., and Ralph K. Winter, *The Unions and the Cities* (Washington, D.C.: Brookings Institution, 1971).

SIXTEEN

UNION-MANAGEMENT COOPERATION

Up to this point, union-management relations have been characterized as a balanced conflict of self-interest. That is not always the case, however. In some limited but often highly publicized instances, employers and unions do engage in cooperation. This chapter explores the situations leading to the use of cooperation rather than competition, what forms cooperation may take, the conditions required for its implementation, its limitations, the views of participants, the effects of cooperation, and its implications for employers, employees, and unions.

SITUATIONS CAUSING COOPERATION

Cooperation is generally resorted to only after adversarial methods have been shown not to work well enough.[1] It is generally implemented for one of three reasons. One is to improve the quality of worklife. Another is to share in potential gains created by mutual problem solving. The third is to share potential losses so that both parties can hope to survive. The first incentive is generally characterized as Quality of Work Life; the second as productivity bargaining; the third as concession bargaining.

LABOR AND MANAGEMENT REPRESENTATIVES ENGAGED IN MUTUAL
PROBLEM SOLVING

SOURCE: *Stephen L. Feldman/Photo Researchers*

FORMS OF COOPERATION

Cooperation comes in three main forms, corresponding roughly to the three
purposes. One is where the employer and union work together in some form
of employee participation to improve worker satisfaction. These participation
processes are known by such titles as Quality of Worklife, Quality Circles, Employee Involvement, Labor-Management Participation Teams, and Sociotech-
nical Work Systems.[2] Their common characteristics are that they involve small
groups of union members and/or officers in informal participation processes in
the workplace as supplements to the formal collective bargaining negotiations
and grievance-handling procedures. Some also modify the way jobs and work
are structured and organized at the workplace.[3]

The second form, productivity bargaining, is utilized to create economic benefits in which both parties may share. The focus here is on extrinsic rewards (i.e., wages and profits) rather than intrinsic rewards such as satisfaction and self-actualization. A common impetus for such cooperation is high labor cost subject to potential nonunion competition.

The third form, concession bargaining, has received a great deal of publicity in the 1980s. In this instance, management wishes the union to concede benefits previously agreed to by management. Presumably, management must have thought it could live with such terms when it agreed to them. What commonly has happened is that economic conditions have turned out worse for employers and unions than they had anticipated, and concessions must be granted to keep the employer competitive. For unions to agree to such concessions they must be convinced by economic data that such concessions are genuinely necessary. When such proof has been forthcoming, unions have generally made the concessions (albeit grumblingly) rather than forcing the bankruptcy of employers. It is probably safe to conclude that concessionary bargaining is a short-term phenomenon caused by adjustments to market mechanisms in the 1980s. A synopsis of concessions reached in that era between large companies and unions appears in Figure 16-1.

A fourth and somewhat different form of cooperation allies unions and management in attempts to create public concern and support for their mutual needs. These efforts are often organized as Area Wide Labor Management Committees.

In rare instances it has been proposed (but seldom acted on) that American unions become involved in corporate decision making and direction along the lines of European Works Councils.[4] Such a remarkable reformation has generally been opposed by both sides. Union leaders have likened sharing in corporate decision making (and responsibility for outcomes) to ''serving two masters,'' while management generally believes such issues as product development and market strategies to be beyond the proper concern of unions. Cooperation might arguably be appropriate on matters directly concerning employees, but in the opinion of many managers, ''managerial decisions'' should be the province solely of managers.

CONDITIONS REQUIRED FOR IMPLEMENTING COOPERATION

In the most basic sense, three conditions are required to implement cooperation. They are: (1) both parties must genuinely be committed to the project, (2) they must communicate openly with each other, and (3) they must trust each other not to exploit any advantage gained through open communication.[5] Obviously, these are not typical relationships in typical bargaining situations. They are generally resorted to only under the pressure of a mutual threat such as bankruptcy.

FIGURE 16–1 SELECTED CONTRACT CONCESSIONS

1982 Selected Concession Settlements Toned Boxes Show Where Contract Provisions Apply	Company got Wage/Benefit Freeze	Company got Scheduling Concessions	Company got Work/Rules Concessions	Union got Say in Company Decisions	Union got Job Security Provisions	Union got Future Wage/Benefit Hikes
Kelsey–Hayes/UAW	■	■	■		■	
Massey–Ferguson/UAW	■	■			■	
Budd Co./UAW	■	■				■
Chatham/Retail Clerks	■					
General Motors/Electricians	■	■				■
B.F. Goodrich/URW	■	■				
Nat'l. Auto Haulers/Teamsters			■			
In'tl. Harvester/UAW				■	■	■
Westinghouse/Electricians	■		■			
Detroit Schools/multi	■					
Michigan A&P/Teamsters and Retail Clks.	■				■	
Bormans/Teamsters and Retail Clks.	■	■				
Nat'l. Electric Contr./Elect. Wkrs.	■					
Hamody Bros./Food and Cmrc. Wkrs.		■				
San Diego Symphony/Musicians	■					
Ford/UAW	■	■	■		■	■
General Motors/UAW	■	■	■		■	■
Oregon Gen'l. Contr./Carpenters	■					
Wiedeman Brewing/Teamsters	■				■	■
Kroger (Mich.)/Teamsters and Retail Clks.	■	■			■	■
TWA/Airline Pilots	■		■			
Milwaukee Railroad/multi	■		■			
Union Steel/Teamsters	■	■				
Dana Corp./UAW	■				■	■
Trucking Mgmt./Teamsters	■		■			
Penn Dixie/Steelworkers	■					
Oscar Mayer/Food and Comm. Workers	■				■	■
Pan Am/Flight Attendants	■		■			
McLouth Steel/Steelworkers	■				■	■

SOURCE: Detroit Free Press, *May 9, 1982, 131.*

LIMITATIONS ON COOPERATION

Despite a great deal of publicity in the 1980s favoring cooperation as the preferable mode of conflict resolution, the idea is not a new one. The United States has dabbled in it at times in the past—times when countervailing power wasn't working well enough. Past experience has revealed that after the immediate threat has passed, the parties almost always revert to their traditional countervailing power strategies.[6] It appears that much of the concern for cooperation in the 1980s has been caused by an unusually high number of threats to traditional bargaining, rather than a sudden discovery of a new solution. Whether this new concern for cooperation will be longer-lasting than its predecessors remains to be seen.

SPECIFIC PROGRAMS

Quality of Work Life et al.

One's Quality of Work Life (QWL) is seen as representing not only job satisfaction but also an opportunity for growth and self-development, freedom from tension and stress, and an avenue to the fulfillment of basic needs.[7] Work environments offering security, equity in treatment, opportunities for individual adaptations, and democracy are assumed to be of high quality.[8]

A typical means to attempt to achieve these ends consists of forming teams of workers and giving them broad responsibilities, such as determining work rules and production standards. These programs are often conducted as experiments outside the constraints of the contract.

It is generally hoped that both employees and employers will derive benefits from QWL programs. Hoped-for benefits for employees include more satisfying work, better economic outcomes, and improved feelings of the quality of their employment. Employers hopefully may gain through reduction in absences, accidents, and strikes; improved productive volume and quality; enhanced abilities to transfer workers as skills improve; and reduced downtime to equipment.[9]

Productivity Bargaining and Concession Bargaining

The main goal in productivity bargaining is to reduce labor cost per unit, often by increasing the value added by employees. This is often accomplished through employee suggestion systems which propose more efficient utilization of capital and labor. The economic benefits derived are then shared in predetermined proportions by employees and management. Productivity bargaining differs from profit sharing in that the focus of financial improvement is labor costs (which can be directly affected by employees), rather than profits, which are subject to additional constraints beyond the control of employees.

Productivity bargaining is also not a new idea. Perhaps the best-known format, the Scanlon Plan, dates back to the 1930s.[10] It is, of course, of tremendous economic importance, because increasing productivity is the source of growth of real wages. Productivity bargaining is most useful where management has been unable to implement high productivity on its own. In many instances the goal may be to get the union to relax restrictive work rules in exchange for higher pay or greater job security.

EXAMPLE OF PUBLICITY ACCORDED PRODUCTIVITY BARGAINING IN THE EARLY 1980s

ANATOMY OF AN AUTO-PLANT RESCUE

One after another the big old Chrysler plants in Detroit shut down. Hamtramck Assembly, Eight Mile Stamping, and Huber Foundry closed in 1980, Lynch Road Assembly and part of Mack Stamping in 1981. It was the same each time. First the rumors on the factory floor. Then the stark announcement of the closing. That was it. Labor and management never tried to work together to keep a plant open. A year ago the familiar rumors flitted through the Detroit Trim plant, which makes seat covers for Chrysler cars. Figures shown to managers said Detroit Trim was hopelessly noncompetitive, and the plant seemed doomed. Surprisingly, not only is the plant still functioning today, but its productivity is up by more than 25 percent and it has prospects of enjoying prolonged good health.

This time, when the rumors started, the United Auto Workers went to Chrysler's management to find out if they were true, and if so, to see what the union could do to help. And this time Chrysler was responsive. Without any of the belligerent rhetoric that has characterized union management relations in the auto industry, the two sides worked out an agreement that completely altered the economics of the plant, the way it works, and the way it is managed. By March 1 the plant met the productivity goals Chrylser had set as a condition for keeping it open.

When finally drawn together by a mutual threat, labor and management discovered they both thought the plant's 709 employees, blue- and white-collar alike, were not putting in much of a day's work. Many sewing machine operators were finishing their quotas an hour or more before the whistle signaled the end of the day shift at 2:30 P.M. The two sides agreed that the plant's roster could be cut by 25 percent and the remaining employees given new quotas to keep them busy for a full eight hours—or 7-½ hours, to be more accurate, since the eight hours include two 12-minute breaks and a five-minute wash-up period.

Old Work Rules have been swept aside along with the old work standards. A foreman doesn't have to call a plant electrician to unplug a sewing machine. Anyone can unplug it. Managers now have the flexibility to change job assignments. Work teams are smaller.

The burden isn't falling all on the blue-collar worker, by any means. A large proportion of the managers, foremen, clerks, and skilled tradesmen have been dismissed, leaving those who remain with more to do. Even the number of company-paid union officers at the plant has been cut, from six to four, and one spends more time on plant work than union affairs.

The plant's employees, mostly women, aren't exactly happy about the new pace of work. Hunched tensely over their sewing machines and cutters, they grumble they're having trouble meeting the new quotas. But they accept the hard work as the price of keeping their jobs and saving the plant.

While they haven't become bosom buddies, management and labor have achieved a measure of trust and mutual respect that has been conspicuously missing in Detroit. Joe Zappa, 57, president of the once powerful UAW Local 212 that encompasses Detroit Trim, says of

Moe Teodosic, 43, the kinetic plant manager, "Without him, we would never have done it." Teodosic says the same of Zappa. Indeed, it almost seemed as if the plant management and union leaders formed an alliance aimed at dragging along their respective constituencies— corporate management and labor rank and file. Managers have learned not to use words like "concession," "featherbedding," or "giveback," and labor leaders are becoming comfortable with words like "productivity" and "competitiveness." Stephan Sharf, 62, Chysler's executive vice president for manufacturing, still can't resist the occasional reference to featherbedding, and that still annoys Zappa. But Zappa isn't the old fire-eating union boss he was when Local 212 had 12,000 members in 14 plants and he repeatedly won reelection by a wide margin. He's retiring as president, and membership is down to 3,000 dues payers in 11 remaining plants. "Zappa has changed a lot," says Sharf. "We are changing too." ...

SOURCE: Jeremy Main, FORTUNE, April 4, 1983, pp. 108–109. © 1983 Time, Inc. All rights reserved.

Concession bargaining follows basically the same format as productivity bargaining with a slightly different motivation.

CONCESSIONARY BARGAINING: WILL THE NEW COOPERATION LAST?

It has come more suddenly than almost anyone thought possible. And it holds staggering implications not only for worker-management relations but also for the competitiveness of U.S. industry, company profits, inflation, and the standard of living. The combination of the severest recession since the Great Depression, government deregulation, and intense world competition is reversing the automatic acceleration in wages and

(continued)

benefits that has become a fixture of the U.S. economy in the postwar period. What has been set in motion is a clear pattern of wage deceleration, the first real retreat on restrictive work rules, and greater worker participation in corporate decision-making

In recent months unions have agreed to freeze or cut base wages and benefits in airlines, trucking, autos, rubber, meat processing, steel, farm implements, and other industries. This has introduced a sharp reduction in compensation gains—perhaps the first major deceleration since the massive wage cuts in the largely non-union economy of the early 1930s. First-year wage increases in major settlements averaged only 2.2% in this year's first quarter, down from 9% in 1981. And the trend has now extended far beyond the well-publicized examples.

A poll of top executives in 600 large corporations, commissioned by BUSINESS WEEK and conducted by Louis Harris & Associates Inc. in mid-May, disclosed that 107, or 26%, of the 419 unionized companies have obtained wage and benefit concessions from their unions (page 19). Concessions have been granted by workers in hundreds of smaller companies. Every industrial town in the recession-scarred Midwest probably has some company, large or small, where workers have agreed to accept cutbacks to save their jobs or even to prevent bankruptcy.

These concessions are being widely heralded as a major step toward saving much of the traditional "smokestack industry" from foreign competition. But analysis of the impact of this new trend on the cost structure of U.S. industry indicates that this optimism is premature for the following reasons:

Although wage gains have decelerated sharply, wages would have to be cut deeply—an unlikely possibility—to close the labor cost gap in such U.S. industries as steel and autos and their foreign competitors (chart, page 72).

Labor is starting to give up restrictive work rules, but companies want still more flexibility to assign workers and change job functions—and their demands present fundamental conflicts that will not be easily resolved. Of the executives in unionized companies polled by Harris, 57% said they would prefer to ease work rules rather than win wage-and-benefit concessions.

Where "concession" bargaining has included giving something on both sides, it has shown a potential for creating a new structure of labor-management cooperation that could increase efficiency. But this movement is at a pivotal point and could collapse if either side becomes too rigid in its demands in the face of a continued economic slump. The shutdown of too many companies, such as Braniff International Corp., despite concessions, and the exploitation of the new trend by too many companies that are not in trouble could doom the move toward cooperation.

While labor costs did spiral inexorably during the 1970s in steel, autos, trucking, and rubber, they are not the sole or even the most important cause of the decline in these industries. Soaring energy costs and management errors have also been crucial and must be addressed.

For 35 years powerful unions and managements in the basic industries—insulated for much of that time from competition—have danced a happy jig as wages and prices spiraled. But the pain of adversity brought on by industry's problems has forced both sides to move away from what amounted to collusive behavior in wage- and price-setting.

This extraordinary trend is heightening conflicts in both companies and unions. A decades-old split is widening between large unionized corporations that want to live peacefully with their unions (although at reduced cost) and smaller, entrepreneurial companies that would rather fight to eliminate the unions. In the Harris poll, 57% of the executives in highly unionized companies said that instead of returning to adversary relations when the economy recovers, they would prefer to give workers "more of a voice in how the company is run in return for gearing their compensation to how well the company is doing." But in companies with less than 40% unionization, executives were much less willing to share decision-making or give job-security guarantees, and much more in favor of forcing concessions from workers even to the point of eliminating the union.

The old, anachronistic attitudes are also prevalent on the union side. Despite staggering job losses, building trades unions are still demanding and winning double-digit wage settlements where they have leverage. In the auto industry, an estimated 1 million jobs have been lost since 1978. Yet ratification of contract concessions by United Auto Workers members at General Motors Corp. won by only a 52%-48% vote; 105,000 workers voted against any "givebacks." One thoughtful UAW leader at the local level complains that workers lack faith in either the corporation or the union. "The American work force has to open its eyes and realize this is not a time we're going to grow, but a time to drop back and try to maintain some things we have," he says.

The pattern that has emerged from bellwether settlements—in the trucking and rubber industries, at GM and Ford, and at International Harvester Co.—includes the reduction of paid time-off and the elimination of future general wage increases. Wages will still go up, though more slowly, through cost-of-living adjustment (COLA) payments, which are in some cases deferred or capped. Most of these settlements raise labor costs only by roughly 75% of projected inflation.

If similar terms are adopted in other industries such as steel and aluminum, the economic impact could be large (charts). In critical industries such as steel, autos, and trucking, wage deceleration can generate hefty increases in net income over what would have been available if the high wage trend of the 1970s had persisted. The additional profits could be used to help make the industries more competitive.

Some critics contend that concessions by unions in the high-wage industries will have to cut more deeply before they constitue a fundamental change in bargaining behavior. The UAW, for example, hopes to restore its 3% annual wage increases when the auto industry recovers, and COLA is still firmly embedded in its contracts. To many management people, high-yielding COLAs—which increased the auto wage rate by $2.06 per hour from 1979 to this year—are the real cost villains at a time of high inflation. "The changes made by the UAW have a strong connotation of being short-term," says a disappointed management negotiator in a major metals company.

Indeed, some experts worry that many of the concessions that have been granted so far are merely recession-induced. When economic recovery takes hold and corporate profits rebound, some unions undoubtedly will demand a restoration of what they have given up. But the new realism on both sides of the table, along with cooperative mechanisms that are being put in place, likely will persist and hold down labor costs.

The new bargaining trend is by no means universal. Some unions, such as the International Association of Machinists and the Transport Workers Union, in-

(continued)

sist that a company prove to the last dec-
imal point that it will not fold if wage relief
is granted. UAW members merely "lent"
money to American Motors Corp. And at
Braniff, 8,000 employees were fired the
day before the company filed for reorganization under Chapter 11. Despite the
workers' effort to save Braniff by taking a
10% pay cut, Braniff used this tactic to
try to avoid dealing with the unions in reorganization.

A CHANGING ATTITUDE

But significant changes in union-management relations are also occurring. At
auto and steel plants, rank-and-file workers are becoming involved in programs to
improve productivity and quality through
joint decision-making teams. The United
Rubber Workers (URW) negotiated new
rubber-industry contracts without striking for the first time since 1965. Says Jack
W. Johnson, the chief negotiator for B. F.
Goodrich Co.: "Union leaders to one degree or another are realizing that it's not
'us against them' but 'we against the
world.'"

The nature of the relationship between
unions and corporations in the large basic
industries has contributed much to their
current predicament. This was first
pointed out nearly 30 years ago by John
Kenneth Galbraith. Many of these industries, he said, are really oligopolies, consisting of a few sellers that control the
market, and their power created the need
for a "countervailing" power to arise
among employees. The unions in these
industries developed the strength to bargain uniform wage patterns on an industrywide basis.

Indeed, standardized wage costs have
enabled the companies in autos and steel
to take wages out of competition, thus
eliminating a major factor that might have

kept prices lower. Unions, in turn, took
their share of the price rises in wage increases, and companies passed the costs
on to their customers. For the first 20
years or so after World War II, facing no
competition from abroad, these companies and unions developed "an arrogant
disregard of the consumer and changes
in consumption patterns, almost a willful
disregard of the potential for competition, and a macho attitude toward market
control," observes Audrey Freedman, a
labor economist at the Conference Board.

The airline, railroad, and trucking industries were similarly insulated against
wage and price competition by government regulation. Deregulation of the
trucking industry in 1980 allowed free entry into the industry—perhaps as many as
3,000 new carriers have started up—at the
same time that freight traffic was leveling
off in the recession. Theoretically, the industry should reach equilibrium as the
weak carriers fail. But under federal pension law, most of the assets of bankrupt
carriers would be needed to pay for un-
funded pension liabilities. Rather than
declare bankruptcy, owners of trucking
companies are holding on, hoping the
economy will improve. The problem, says
an industry insider, "is that you've let
everyone in, but you're not letting anyone
out."

Labor costs were not the primary
cause of trucking's current chaos, but
certainly large wage and benefit increases won by the International Broth-
erhood of Teamsters in the 1970s made
the carriers less able to withstand the
current shocks. Always fragmented in
bargaining, the truckers usually gave
what the Teamsters wanted, and the 1979
contract drove up labor costs by about
35% over 30 months even as profits were
being pinched. This year's new contract,
which will raise wages and benefits by

less than 15% over 37 months (assuming 8% inflation), may only help carriers survive a little longer in hopes that the economy will rebound.

HANGING ON

Steel, autos, rubber, machine tools, and agricultural implements have had other problems, including difficulties in competing with some foreign producers, especially those subsidized by government. They have also suffered from excess world capacity and the weakening of foreign currencies against the dollar. But high labor rates in the U.S. are a major factor. In the steel industry, hourly labor costs (wages plus benefits) last year averaged $19.42 per worker, compared with $10.15 in Japan, $11.46 in West Germany, and $9.74 in France. Total hourly compensation of about $20 at GM and Ford is about $8 higher than at Japanese auto producers.

These gaps are so wide that the UAW and the United Steelworkers would have to accept huge wage and benefit cuts to narrow them significantly—and even then the foreign producers might find ways to undersell the U.S. companies. In the case of autos, for example, Data Resources Inc. estimated that the domestic industry will realize wage savings of $2.7 billion in 1984 under the new UAW contracts. But John H. Hammond Jr., DRI's director of automotive services, says that Japanese auto makers "are already priced 30% above their underlying cost levels, which would suggest that the manufacturers can easily meet any price competition that would be effected through the lower wages in the U.S."

The same problem exists in the steel industry. The USW has not yet negotiated new steel contracts, although it is under great pressure to do so long before the pacts expire on Aug. 1, 1983. USW leaders are reluctant to admit that the union will concede anything, but their attitude is clearly conciliatory. Unemployment stands at 30% in steel, and a permanent contraction of the industry is under way. Most likely, the USW will open its contracts early—it needs rank-and-file approval to do so—and will grant at least as much as the UAW gave in autos.

The savings would be $1.4 billion in 1984, but Walter F. Carter, a steel analyst at DRI, says this amount would only keep the labor-cost gap from widening. "The Japanese have a lot of room to lower their steel prices," he says. If the wage savings will not immediately enhance the competitive posture of the U.S. industries, they could provide funds for modernization to prevent their demise and, in the auto industry, perhaps help to finance new-product development. "I don't think you can get enough money out of wage cuts in the long run to save the steel industry," concedes one steel executive. "But you can certainly get enough through wages, COLA, and cuts in manning to control the cost trend." Moreover, costs could be significantly reduced in the newest company strategy in concession bargaining: getting the unions to change or eliminate restrictive work rules.

GAINING FLEXIBILITY

Ford has already made considerable headway on this at several key parts plants by promising not to buy the parts elsewhere if workers cut production costs. So ripe for cost-cutting is this area that one GM insider estimates his company could reduce its labor bill by an average of $3.50 to $5 per hour. But GM concedes that it pulled a boner in announcing a new bonus plan—one that would
(continued)

have raised executives' compensation—shortly after UAW members barely ratified a new contract granting concessions to the company. This produced an explosion of rank-and-file anger, and GM's chances now of winning widespread work-rule changes in local bargaining are not good.

Nevertheless, company pressures and worker fears of job loss are likely to produce widespread changes in work practices in many industries. Work rules continue to be troublesome issues in the construction, railroad, and airline industries, where unions have fought against cuts in crew size and the assignment of workers outside their work classification. In manufacturing, shop-floor practices under union rules have always been a major contributor to operating costs, but until recent years management did not make a major effort to contest work-rule encroachments. In the no-strike period of World War II, the War Labor Board established many rules to settle disputes. For 25 or so years after that, the companies were more interested in meeting consumer demand than in fighting the unions. "Profits were up, and sales were up," recalls a negotiator at an auto company. "You hated to lose a sale."

But now companies are trying to reduce or eliminate relief time and coffee breaks, change seniority practices to gain more flexibility in transferring and assigning workers within a plant, and require workers to work out of classification. This increasing need for flexibility may be, in large part, stymied by methods introduced by management itself years ago, says Michael J. Piore, a labor economist at Massachusetts Institute of Technology. He contends that in applying the "scientific management" principles of Frederick W. Taylor in the first half of the 20th century, American management split already fragmented jobs into ever-narrower functions in the name of efficiency.

Unionists had fought this fragmentation, but after organizing manufacturing in the 1930s they adapted themselves to Taylorism by negotiating extensive job classification systems to prevent management from assigning jobs on the basis of favoritism. Such close union control of shop-floor practices did not arise in Japan, Germany, and other nations that provide the sharpest competition for U.S. manufacturers. This has become crucial, Piore says, because of changing technology. "Things are so much more fluid now that the rules are a real constraint on what management can do," he says. "Where technology is wide open, a set of rules negotiated last year or the year before may not fit the situation next year or the year after."

Piore's explanation does not cover the entire work-rule controversy, but it indicates how deeply embedded the problems are. The auto and steel companies would like, in particular, to collapse more than 15 skilled craft classifications into four or five broad categories, and this has already been done in a few plants. However, the companies themselves have raised barriers to more flexible work assignments: They do little training of workers. In Japan, a newly hired steelworker receives 60 days of training before he is put to work. In contrast, declares Sam Camens, an assistant to USW President Lloyd McBride, U.S. steelmakers tell new workers: "Buy a pair of work shoes, here's a hard hat, show up at the gate."

The ailing machine-tool industry has a special problem with old production standards that have too-liberal machine time allowances. At Acme-Cleveland Corp.'s National Acme Div., many workers needed to work only half a day to meet production quotas. "It got out of hand," admits Michael C. Willingham, chief negotiator of Local 19 of the Mechanics Educational Society of America. In January, with 600 of 1,200 workers laid off, the union agreed to change the standards. "Some stringent work rules, I'll admit, have strangled the company," he says.

In the rubber industry, the URW is now willing to try new approaches. With the union's cooperation, Firestone will experiment more with such things as seven-day operations, and it has reduced job categories significantly at several plants. The URW has also agreed to explore changes in piecework standards that enabled some workers to finish early. "The days of not doing a full day's work are behind us," says URW President Milan Stone.

The worst of the featherbedding practices exist in only isolated places in the basic manufacturing industries. But inefficient practices are widespread, testifying to management's failure to deal with plant-floor operations and its "people" problems. Perhaps the best prospect of improvement lies with the spreading worker-participation, or quality of work life (QWL), movement. There have been labor-management committees in the past, but mostly they involved union and company officials at levels remote from the workplace.

But rank and filers on the plant floor are now gaining a voice in decision-making, contributing their intimate knowledge of the production process to cut costs, eliminate waste, and improve quality. At Ford, the UAW has helped set up employee involvement committees at many plants, and it has conducted joint QWL programs with GM for several years. In addition, GM and the UAW recently agreed to set up local Joint Councils for Enhancing Job Security & the Competitive Edge. GM hopes to involve workers in discussions of how to improve its competitive position on a plant-by-plant, product-by-product basis. GM obviously is seeking worker commitment, and in return it is willing to share information on sales, profits, and investment plans that it previously kept secret. "When we sit down and talk about whether we're competitive or not," says a GM executive, "we're showing [workers] things we've never shown before."

In the steel industry, the USW and several large companies have set up labor-management participation teams—about 10 workers and supervisors trained in problem-solving techniques—at the departmental level within plants. For example, a team in the byproduct department at the Aliquippa (Pa.) plant of Jones & Laughlin Steel Corp. has been active only for a few months but already has found a way to save $449,000 a year in the cost of maintaining coke ovens. The rank-and-file members are enthusiastic about the team process. Says Tom Porter, a coke-oven heater with 15 years' service: "If all 10,000 workers in this plant went through the training we've had, this would be the lowest-cost steel producer in the U.S." The USW's Camens adds: "We are quietly taking over responsibility for quality and production. Management knows this and no longer insists on retaining management prerogatives."

GAINS-SHARING SYSTEMS

It is this kind of participation and information-sharing that will build trust between labor and management and involve workers more deeply in the circumstances of their individual plant and company. This process of binding workers more closely to the success of their plant is improved by provisions strengthening job security and pay systems, such as profit-sharing, that reflect the company's performance. Both unions and companies are showing increasing interest in so-called gains-sharing systems that link compensation directly to productivity or sales.

(continued)

The difficulties faced by unions in winning ratification of concessions reflect a strong distrust of management among rank and filers. But both unions and companies can do much to improve workers' understanding of a legitimate need for concessions. What happened in the GM and Ford ratification votes illustrate both points. For example, "resentment of local management" was the major reason that UAW Local 1776 in Ypsilanti, Mich., turned down the GM agreement by a 3-to-1 vote, says Billy Moon, chairman of the local's bargaining committee. Last Jan. 1, well before talks began at GM, plant management decided to make a change in a system for relieving workers who require first aid, thus unilaterally discontinuing a practice the union had won more than a decade ago. This angered rank and filers.

Workers were also alienated by GM Chairman Roger Smith's repeated threats of plant closings unless the UAW made concessions. Although GM insiders contend that early talks would not have started without such prodding, Smith "does not come off in any way, shape, or form as showing employees that he's concerned about their health and welfare and building a quality car," declares Richard Debs, president of Local 1776. He adds: "At GM, you feel like you're a cost factor and not a human being." GM's profit of $333 million in 1981 was a factor in the heavy vote against its contract.

On the other hand, Ford's loss of $1.5 billion in 1980 and $1 billion in 1981 helped account for a 75% rank-and-file approval of a pact similar to GM's. But another key element was a greater effort by the UAW's Ford Dept. to explain the package. GM executives contend that the UAW made only a token effort to sell its agreement, and that this explains why the rank and file approved the pact so narrowly even though UAW leaders approved it

overwhelmingly. By contrast, the UAW's Ford officials held more frequent bargaining meetings with local leaders and put more effort into selling the final package. One Ford bargaining committee member visited nine plants containing 13 bargaining units, won the support of local leaders first, and then explained the package to the membership. And Ford management believes its Employee Involvement program had produced a wider understanding of Ford's problems.

RISING LAYOFFS

Another factor limiting givebacks is the feeling by many unions that concessions acceptable to the rank and file will not prevent more layoffs during the recession. Indeed, despite the modest 37-month pact signed by the Teamsters last January, layoffs among the union's 300,000 trucking industry members have risen to about 30% from 20% last fall. "I can't see people going back to work as a result of the settlement," says one union insider.

Nevertheless, the potential for further concessions exists in several industries. Especially in the Upper Midwest, Teamsters locals are considering proposals from carriers that face imminent failure. The Ford and GM contracts both provide clauses giving workers at uneconomical plants the "opportunity" to accept further concessions rather than see their work given to other companies. And both UAW and GM officials note that where labor relations are good—such as in plants that have QWL programs—workers tend to be much more amenable to concessions.

Rank-and-file rejection of concessions, even at companies that are clearly in trouble, suggests that the level of economic education is not as high as it might be. But this may merely be another reflection of the old adversary relations in the workplace and the treatment of workers as having nothing more to contribute than their hourly labor. "When a worker's horizons are short-term and he is one of several hundred thousand workers, he doesn't feel a direct personal stake in a company, and he thinks short-term," says Jack Barbash, a former labor educator and now professor emeritus at the University of Wisconsin. The new bargaining trend, however, shows promise of moving workers and management alike well beyond that archaic attitude.

SOURCE: *Reprinted from June 14, 1982 issue of* Business Week *by special permission. Copyright © 1982 by McGraw-Hill.*

TABLE 16-1 SUMMARY OF OPPORTUNITIES CREATED BY COOPERATIVE UNION-MANAGEMENT PROGRAMS

Performance Indicators	Employee Outcomes	Relationship Changes
Productivity improvement	Increase job satisfaction	Attitude change among key actors
Reduce labor costs	Job influence and involvement	Union influence on key decisions
Quality improvements	Information about job and company	Reduce likelihood of future strikes
Product design changes	Commitment to company	Reduce grievances
Reduce absenteeism	Improve conditions of work	Better understanding of L-M issues
Reduce turnover	Improve supervision	Examine outdated contract language
Reduce tardiness	Reduce job frustration	Continuous study of on-going problems
Reduce accidents	Improve earnings	Facilitate technological change
Improve manpower utilization	Upgrade job characteristics	
	Increase trust	
	Increase job security	

SOURCE: *Schuster 1983:192. Reprinted with permission of the Industrial Relations Research Association © 1983.*

AREA WIDE LABOR-MANAGEMENT COMMITTEES

AWLMCs have a different thrust than the previous two forms of cooperation.[11] While some of their efforts are directed toward improving specific employment relationships, there is also an attempt to change the "system" surrounding the parties. AWLMCs are generally made up of equal numbers of management and labor representatives who try to improve the economic climate of their area. They generally wish to promote economic growth and forestall plant closings

TABLE 16-2 AREA LABOR-MANAGEMENT COMMITTEES IN THE UNITED STATES

Year Established	Committee	Year Established	Committee
1945	Toledo, Ohio	1979	Akron, Ohio
1946	Louisville, Kentucky		Beaumont, Texas
1953	Chattanooga, Tennessee		Duluth, Minnesota
1958	Jackson, Michigan		Haverhill, Massachusetts
1963	South Bend, Indiana		Portsmith, Ohio
1965	Green Bay, Wisconsin		Scranton, Pennsylvania
1969	Western Kentucky (Paducah)		Sioux City, Iowa
1970	Fox Cities, Wisconsin	1980	Elk County, Pennsylvania
	Upper Peninsula, Michigan	1981	Kankake, Illinois
1972	Jamestown, New York		Kenosha, Wisconsin
	Pittsburgh, Pennsylvania	1982	Chillicotche (Ross County), Ohio
1975	Buffalo/Erie County, New York		Danville, Illinois
	Chautauqua County, New York		Decatur, Illinois
	Clinton County, Pennsylvania		Manistee, Michigan
	Cumberland, Maryland		Norwalk (Fireland), Ohio
	Evansville, Indiana	1983	Aurora, Illinois
	Mahoning Valley (Youngstown), Ohio		Columbus, Ohio
1976	Elmira, New York		Des Moines, Iowa
	Springfield, Ohio		Memphis, Tennessee
1977	Lansing, Michigan		Mercy City, Pennsylvania
	Muskegon, Michigan		New Castle, Pennsylvania
	North Central, Wisconsin		
	Riverside/San Bernadino, California		
	St. Louis, Missouri		
	Western Virginia		

SOURCES: *Richard D. Leone et al.,* The Operation of Area Labor-Management Committees *(Washington, D.C.: U.S. Department of Labor, 1982); Irving Siegel and Edgar Weinberg,* Labor-Management Cooperation: The American Experience. *(Kalamazoo, Mich.: W. E. Upjohn Institute for Employment Research, 1982); and the National Association of Area Labor-Management Committees. Reprinted by permission of Sage Publications, Inc.*

for their mutual benefit. They are generally administered by a team of hired professional experts. They are most commonly found in the Northeast and Midwest and have had varying degrees of success.

EFFECTS OF COOPERATION

Quality of Work Life

One wide-ranging study of QWL programs observed the following effects:[12]

1. There is substantial interest in QWL among union members;
2. Some jobs are improved somewhat by QWL programs, but the result is neither uniformly positive nor extremely large;

3. Workers do not appear to believe that participation in QWL programs reduces their support of their union;

4. Local union leaders believe that QWL has a strong positive effect on union officer-plant management relationships, worker-supervisor relations, product quality, and productivity;

5. A majority of local union leaders believe QWL strengthens the local union;

6. There is no strong evidence to suggest that QWL programs improve members' opinions of their unions;

7. Local union leaders believe the biggest problems inhibiting the expansion of QWL programs are layoffs, management efforts to change work rules, and supervisory resistance. National union leaders believe management's desire to operate nonunion is the biggest impediment;

8. Local union leaders are split on the role they foresee QWL playing in the future. One group sees it as a limited supplement to traditional bargaining. The other sees an expansion of participation, where workers will carry out many responsibilities now held by management;

9. Workers are generally skeptical about QWL programs until they have experienced them. Enthusiasm generally rises with experience;

10. Enthusiasm declines over time as barriers to accomplishment or trust arise;

11. There must be economic as well as psychological success to sustain interest; and lastly, and perhaps very significantly to the long-term success of QWL (after the "new" wears off);

12. It does not appear that in most QWL programs workers actually experienced greater say or influence over workplace issues than did nonparticipants.

Productivity Bargaining

Among the observed consequences of productivity bargaining are the following:[13]

1. If management is already operating efficiently, productivity bargaining is not likely to produce great improvements; if management is operating inefficiently, there is more room for and greater likelihood of success;

2. Pay increases for employees sometimes result;

3. Employment levels are relatively unaffected;

4. Labor relations are seen as improved; and

5. Productivity improvements are more likely one-shot increases rather than a long, steady improvement.

IMPLICATIONS OF COOPERATION
IN THE AMERICAN SYSTEM

The most direct effect of expanded worker-participation efforts, especially those that involve work reorganization, is a movement away from the detailed job-control form of unionization characteristic of U.S. collective bargaining.[14] This can be expected to produce a more flexible and varied form of work, thereby implying changes in the role of local unions, supervisors, and management.[15]

For the union this would require relinquishing a traditional source of power in exchange for more joint planning and consultation.[16] For the worker it implies a wider variety of tasks, more training, and more skill enhancement. It also implies greater responsibilties for decisions.[17] For management it implies a reduction in prerogatives and a reformulating of the role of the supervisor in exchange for greater flexibility through reduced work rules and increasing versatility of the workforce. In summary, for all the parties, it implies a movement toward a more proactive form of labor-management relations based around more joint research and analysis, planning, and consultation.[18]

Notes

1. John A. Fossum, *Labor Relations*, 3d ed. (Plano, Tex.: Business Publications, Inc., 1985), pp. 368–69.
2. Thomas A. Kochan, Harry C. Katz, and Nancy R. Mower, ''Worker Participation in American Unions,'' in Thomas Kochan, *Challenges and Choices Facing American Labor* (Cambridge, Mass.: MIT Press, 1985), p. 271.
3. *Ibid.*
4. Thomas A. Kochan and Michael J. Piore, ''Will the New Industrial Relations Last? Implications for the American Labor Movement,'' in *The Future of American Unionism*, Louis A. Ferman, ed., in *The Annals*, May 1984, p. 189.
5. Richard E. Walton and Robert B. McKersie, *A Behavioral Theory of Labor Negotiations* (New York: McGraw-Hill, 1965), pp. 139–43.
6. Fossum, p. 350.
7. Fossum, p. 363.
8. *Ibid.*
9. Barry A. Macy and Phillip H. Mirvis, ''A Methodology for Assessment of Quality of Work Life and Organizational Effectiveness in Behavioral-Economic Terms,'' *Administrative Science Quarterly*, 1976, p. 214.
10. Fossum, p. 358.
11. Joel Cutcher-Gershenfeld, ''Labor-Management Cooperation in American Communities: What's in It for Unions?'' *The Annals*, May 1984, p. 78.
12. Kochan, Katz, and Mower, pp. 275–92.
13. Fossum, pp. 368–69.
14. Kochan, Katz, and Mower, p. 303.
15. *Ibid.*
16. *Ibid.*
17. *Ibid.*
18. *Ibid.*

Discussion Questions

1. Discuss the various forms of cooperation.
2. Discuss the conditions required for the implementation of cooperation.

3. Describe and evaluate the specific programs for cooperation reported in the text.
4. Evaluate the effects of cooperation.
5. Discuss the implications of cooperation.

Statements for Comment

1. "Cooperation is just another fad."
2. "QWL improvements should be made, even if they don't pay for themselves."
3. "Union participation on company boards of directors doesn't make much sense."
4. "Cooperation requires trusting the other side not to take advantage of you. That's un-American. It can be done, but only as an act of desperation."
5. "Productivity bargaining is great. Everyone wins. I don't know why we don't see it everywhere."
6. "Unless accompanied by a full sharing of responsibility, power, and profits, participative management techniques cannot provide rights and benefits that would cause labor to join management in genuine cooperation."
7. "Participative management gives workers no compelling reason to abandon the adversarial struggle for concrete improvements in wages and working conditions that in large part determine the quality of worklife in America."

Situations

Case 16–1 "Boy, it sure seems obvious to me that cooperation is the way to go in labor relations. I don't understand why the parties don't use it all the time," said Stacey Stephens.

Under what circumstances would you not recommend cooperation?

Case 16–2 "Stop working so hard, you'll kill the job," said Ben Stanley.

"If we don't get jobs like this done, management's going to close this place and we'll all be out of work," said Erv Jozwiak.

As a co-worker of Ben and Erv, what should you do? Why?

Case 16–3 "Things have gone from bad to worse," said Bobby Joe Ferguson, President of Midwest Meat Processors, Inc. Bobby Joe has just reviewed his company's latest financial statements for the third time, and they paint a grim picture indeed: sales are down 17 percent, costs have risen 5.6 percent in the last six months, and the plant faces the loss of an increasing share of the market to the Bolivians with each passing month. True, the company's QWL program has been a success—at least in terms of higher job satisfaction and less tension and stress in the workcenters, but the numbers don't lie. "We're happy, but broke," as Bobby Joe puts it. There seem to be only two solutions for the survival of Midwest: increase productivity or cut costs. Either way, *the workers* will be forced to bear the brunt of the coming hardships.

Bobby Joe is scheduled to meet with Jim Steinkopf, the company's union leader, in the morning. Although Bobby Joe has no idea how to approach this problem, one thing is for certain: Jim would rather eat Bolivian Spam than see even one of his union members laid off or have them lose a dollar off their next paycheck.

What routes are open to Bobby Joe in solving this problem? How could Jim accept the idea of concession bargaining? What would you suggest as a possible solution? Does Bolivian Spam taste good with sauerkraut?

Case 16–4 "You know, cooperation techniques do encourage worker identification with profit-maximization goals, but labor's priorities have to be ignored when they conflict with such efforts. Workers are allowed to participate in corporate decision making as long as it does not infringe upon management prerogatives. These techniques leave corporate power structures unchanged and give workers a voice only when they don't disagree with management. It's really a sham. It certainly is no alternative to confrontational methods for protecting and advancing employee interest. Cooperation techniques are just the latest management means of avoiding fair compensation or job security while giving workers no real ability to influence key corporate decisions or to exercise greater control over their work lives," said business student Rhonda Manchester.

How right is Rhonda?

Bibliography of Related Readings

Cutcher-Gershenfeld, Joel, "Labor-Management Cooperation in American Communities: What's in It for the Unions," *The Annals*, May 1984, pp. 76–87.

Freeman, Richard B., and James L. Medoff, "Trade Unions and Productivity: Some New Evidence on an Old Issue," *The Annals*, May 1984, pp. 149–64.

Kochan, Thomas A., Harry C. Katz, and Nancy R. Mower, "Worker Participation and American Unions," in Kochan, ed., *Challenges and Choices Facing American Labor* (Cambridge, Mass.: MIT Press, 1985), pp. 271–306.

Kornbluh, Hy, "Workplace Democracy and Quality of Work Life: Problems and Prospects," *The Annals*, May 1984, pp. 88–95.

Macy, Barry A., and Phillip H. Mirvis, "A Methodology for Assessment of Quality of Work Life and Organizational Effectiveness in Behavioral-Economic Terms," *Administrative Science Quarterly*, June 1976, pp. 212–26.

SEVENTEEN

EVALUATION

OF THE SYSTEM

This chapter examines the effects of unionization and assesses the effectiveness of our industrial relations system at meeting the needs of employees, employers, unions, customers, and the public. It also examines areas that some observers believe are under significant pressure to change.

EFFECTS OF UNIONIZATION

A very well researched and documented study has reached the following conclusions about the effects of unionization:[1]*

> 1. On the wage side, unions have a substantial monopoly wage impact, but there is no single union/nonunion wage differential. The union wage effect is greater for less educated than for more educated workers, for younger than for prime-age workers, and for junior than for senior workers, and it is greater in heavily organized industries and in regulated industries than in others. It increased in the 1970s as unionized workers won wage gains exceeding those of their nonunion peers. Most importantly, the social costs of the monop-

SOURCE: *From What Do Unions Do? by Richard B. Freeman and James L. Medoff. Copyright © 1984 by Basic Books, Inc., Publishers. Reprinted by permission of the publisher.*

423

oly wage gains of unionism appear to be relatively modest, of the order of .3 percent of gross national product, or less.

2. In addition to raising wages, unions alter the entire package of compensation, substantially increasing the proportion of compensation allotted to fringe benefits, particularly to deferred benefits such as pensions and life, accident, and health insurance, which are favored by older workers.

3. The claim that unions increase wage inequality is not true. It is true that unions raise the wages of organized blue collar workers relative to the wages of unorganized blue collar workers, and thus increase that aspect of inequality. But they also raise blue collar earnings relative to the higher white collar earnings, thus reducing inequality between those groups. Moreover, by adopting pay policies that limit managerial discretion in wage setting, they reduce inequality among workers in the same establishments and among different establishments. Quantitatively, the inequality-reducing effects of unionism outweigh the inequality-increasing effects, so that on balance unions are a force for equality in the distribution of wages among individual workers.

4. By providing workers with a voice in determining rules and conditions of work, by instituting grievance and arbitration procedures for appealing supervisors' decisions, and by negotiating seniority clauses desired by workers, unionism greatly reduces the probability that workers will quit their jobs. As a result, unionized workforces are more stable than nonunion workforces paid the same compensation.

5. Unionism alters the way in which firms respond to swings in the economy. In cyclical downturns, unionized firms make more use of temporary layoffs and less use of cuts in wage growth than do nonunion firms, while in cyclical upturns, unionized firms recall relatively more workers and nonunion firms tend to hire new employees. In a decline that threatens the jobs of senior employees, unions negotiate wage and work-rule concessions of substantial magnitude.

6. Union workplaces operate under rules that are both different from and more explicit than those in nonunion workplaces. Seniority is more important in union settings, with unionized senior workers obtaining relatively greater protection against job loss and relatively greater chance of promotion than nonunion senior workers. In addition, management in union companies generally operates more "by the book," with less subjectivity and also less flexibility, than does management in nonunion companies, and in more professional, less paternalistic or authoritarian ways.

7. Some nonunion workers, namely those in large nonunion firms that are trying to avoid unions through "positive labor relations," obtain higher wages and better working conditions as a result of the existence of trade unions. The average employed nonunion blue collar worker may enjoy a slight increase in well-being because the threat of unionism forces his or her firm to offer better wages and work conditions, but the average white collar worker appears essentially unaffected by the existence of blue collar unionization. Some workers, however, may suffer from greater joblessness as a result of higher union wages in their city or their industry.

8. Paradoxically, while unionized workers are less willing to leave their employers than nonunion workers, unionized workers often report themselves

less satisfied with their jobs than nonunion workers. Unionists are especially dissatisfied with their work conditions and their relations with supervisors. One explanation is that unions galvanize worker discontent in order to make a strong case in negotiations with management. To be effective, voice must be heard.

9. The view of unions as a major deterrent to productivity is erroneous. In many sectors, unionized establishments are more productive than nonunion establishments, while in only a few are they less productive. The higher productivity is due in part to the lower rate of turnover under unionism, improved managerial performance in response to the union challenge, and generally cooperative labor-management relations at the plant level. When labor-management relations are bad, so too is productivity in organized plants.

10. Unionized employers tend to earn a lower rate of return per dollar of capital than do nonunion employers. The return is lower under unionism because the increase in wages and the greater amount of capital used per worker are not compensated for by the higher productivity of labor associated with unionism. The reduction in profitability, however, is centered in highly concentrated and otherwise historically highly profitable sectors in the economy.

11. Unions have had mixed success in the political arena. Legislators representing highly unionized districts or receiving considerable union campaign support tend to support unions' political goals in the Congress, but legislators representing less unionized districts or receiving more support from business and other interest groups often oppose unions' political goals. In the important area of major labor legislation, bills opposed by unions have been enacted while bills favored by unions have been voted down. In general, unions have managed to preserve laws augmenting monopoly powers in specific sectors but have not been able to use the law to expand their monopoly power. Most union political successes have come in the areas of general labor and social goals that benefit workers as a whole rather than unionists alone.

12. The picture of unions as nondemocratic institutions run by corrupt labor bosses is a myth. Most unions are highly democratic, with members having access to union decision-making machinery, especially at the local level. While corruption exists in some unions, its occurrence seems to be highly concentrated in a few industries.

13. The percentage of the U.S. private-sector workforce that is in trade unions has declined precipitously since the mid-1950s. The decline is due largely to (1) a dramatic increase in the amount and sophistication of both legal and illegal company actions designed to forestall the organization of workers, and (2) reduced union organizing activity per nonunion worker.

ASSESSMENT OF THE SYSTEM

A successful industrial relations system should provide peace, freedom, prosperity, stability, efficiency, adaptability, economic growth and full employment, individual dignity and self-worth, and a safe and healthy working environment.

SOURCE: Top photo, *UPI/Bettman Newsphotos;* bottom photo, *American Airlines Photo*

On the whole, the American system is extraordinarily successful. Although not without areas of strain, it does remarkably well at fulfilling most of the needs of employees, employers, the consuming public, and the citizen public.

Labor relations in the United States are basically peaceful. When they aren't, it makes news. Certainly, picket-line violence in the United States is quite rare and is certainly less common than in the past. There is absolutely no violent "revolutionary" fervor, as there is in other economies of the world. While management may be exhibiting an increased desire to operate nonunion, it seldom resorts to physical violence to achieve that end.

Freedom is unexcelled in the United States. Employees are free to select their type of employment and particular employer, and the system as a whole operates with minimal regulation and interference from the government. This is certainly true in comparison to the more regulated economies of Europe.

Prosperity evaluations produce more mixed results. Certainly, on a macro level, the American industrial relations system generates great wealth for both income earners and investors. American labor is among the highest paid in the world, and American companies are the wealthiest, in aggregate, in the world, while customers are provided an incredible array of goods and services. Whether it would be possible to be even wealthier under different conditions is impossible to determine. It can be demonstrated without rebuttal, however, that it is possible for both employers and employees to get rich in the United States. On the down side, there are concerns for declines in the rate of productivity increases, foreign trade deficits, and an exodus of jobs to lower-wage-cost economies.

The American system is also remarkably stable, compared both to other countries and to our own past. Economic strikes are an almost trivial cost to productivity compared to other causes, such as alcohol abuse. In a typical year less than two-tenths of one percent of working time is lost to strikes.[2] Wildcat strikes have been greatly reduced, and grievance processing provides an orderly resolution of conflict in the unionized sector. Labor agreements provide predictability and stability for the life of the contract, while concessions are made when conditions require them. Bargaining is increasingly well-informed, professional, and data-oriented.

On the whole, American employment is tremendously efficient by world standards. This is due largely to good managerial practices and the intensive use of capital. Unions stimulate rational professional management practices that contribute to high productivity. In instances where union-negotiated practices result in restricted productivity there is usually an absence of market-pressure competition. How widespread and severe a problem this is is arguable.[3]

The adaptability of the system is also subject to some amount of dispute. One school of thought holds that many of the assumptions under which the present system was developed are no longer valid and that the system is becoming inappropriate.[4] Another school of thought argues that the system has always been subjected to attack and that its major characteristics remain basically unchanged over the long haul.[5] It is further alleged that the threats of the 1980s are not significantly different from those of previous decades and that stability has been the norm much more than change.

The system must also provide adequate opportunities for economic growth. Again, the American record is exemplary. Technological improvements, productive labor, and good managerial practices have combined to produce a steady growth of real wealth throughout our history. Furthermore, these increases have been achieved while hours of work and effort levels have decreased. Setbacks to growth, such as the petroleum crisis of the 1970s, have always been overcome in the long run. Based on past records of success in adaptation it is likely that our system will find ways to continue growth and prosperity.

Full employment has proved to be more of a problem. Economic recessions are, of course, always a problem for employees. But even in periods of relative prosperity, unemployment may remain naggingly high in the United States. Worse yet, it is not randomly distributed throughout the population. Some pockets of "structural unemployment" may exist among groups never assimilated into the workforce. "Frictional unemployment"—the unemployment of those who are changing jobs and will find another—may also be somewhat higher in the United States because the system presents so much freedom to change employment.

The American system also gets mixed reviews on producing dignity and self-worth. Critics claim that many jobs lack intrinsic value (as contrasted to extrinsic values such as high pay). This situation was largely brought about by the application of scientific management principles. On the good side, American unions have been very effective at promoting voice for employees in matters affecting them. This, combined with experiments (often jointly sponsored) in Quality of Work Life, are tending to ameliorate the problems that do exist. The problem is also reducing itself, as many menial jobs are disappearing and being replaced by jobs requiring more training and employee input.

Finally, efforts to provide safe and healthy workplaces, while not yet totally successful, are headed in the right direction. Certainly union pressure, governmental regulation, and changing managerial attitudes are all combining to make work in America less onerous.

One other aspect of the industrial relations system deserves mention. That is the role the government has played in upgrading employment conditions and opportunities. American unions have successfully intervened in political affairs to the benefit of employees in general, not just union members. This intervention has resulted in the reduction of many significant employment abuses.

AREAS OF STRESS AND POTENTIAL CHANGE

Two areas seem to be subject to long-term pressure to change. They are job-control unionism and taking wages out of competition.

Job-control unionism is under attack because it places many unionized employers at a cost disadvantage in competing with large nonunion firms.[6] These nonunion firms have pursued human resources management policies encouraging high levels of communication, involvement, commitment, and motivation of individual workers. They have emphasized broad-banded jobs with few job classifications, fewer work rules governing job assignments and transfers, and more active training programs.[7] The Japanese enjoy similar flexibility. This capability allows these employers to adapt more rapidly and appropriately to changing markets, products, and production methods. This advantage of nonunion employers is not likely to be overcome and will probably have to be adjusted to instead.

To implement these changes it may be necessary to change the role of the union on the shop floor. Instead of policing a set of preexisting strict rules, the union may need to engage in joint efforts with management to bring individual employees more directly into the process of communications, decision making on shop-floor issues that affect their jobs, and the adaptation of current rules to the demands for more flexible and productive work systems.[8] This may require the union to assume the role of providing access to the information and the power that workers will need to effectively influence their work environment and enhance their careers.[9] These union efforts will be needed to help produce the productivity and cost controls needed to support a high-wage industrial relations system.[10]

The second area of probable change is taking wages out of competition. To the extent that this was achieved in the past, high wages were being subsidized by consumers. While such an outcome was an affront to a free-enterprise model, it must be remembered that under New Deal Keynesian economics union wage-raising was believed desirable for the national interest. That belief, which was fueled by the immediate effects of the Depression, is considerably more questionable today. Besides, the issue of desirability is becoming close to moot, as economic reality restricts union attempts to take wages out of competition.

Several factors have hindered union success at taking wages out of competition. They include the growth of domestic nonunion competition, foreign nonunion competition, deregulation of leading sectors of transportation such as airlines, railroads, and trucking; and a trend toward smaller, more specialized markets.[11] These features have combined to force several conspicuous leading unions to engage in at least one round of concession bargaining to attempt to bring wages in line with effective competition.

Their inability to take wages out of competition may compel unions to live with variations in labor cost among employers and to rely more on contingent compensation systems tying pay to the performance of the firm.[12] It also may lead to significant reductions in pattern bargaining.[13] It can be further expected that various forms of profit sharing, employee stock ownership plans, and productivity gains sharing will take on added significance.[14] Finally, it can be expected that job-security protections will become more important as wage increases are subjected to more constraints.[15]

CONCLUSIONS

The American industrial relations system arose out of necessity. It exists as it does because it has responded to problems that had to be cured. It acted in response to the values and needs of our society. In many instances, these reponses have been largely unique to America.

Collective bargaining, a cornerstone of the system, arose because unacceptable problems existed without it. The problems of conflict of interest between employee and employer exist whether or not there are unions. Unions merely provide a framework for resolving those conflicts.

The system is, of course, subject to outside stimuli. Changing conditions render it occasionally inappropriate, but it has always adjusted over time. It seems reasonable to expect that the traditional focus of adversarialism balanced by countervailing power will continue to exist. It is the format most compatible with American values of competition, self-reliance, and individual gain. It is a system which has produced great benefits for all parties in the past. It remains to be seen whether it can continue to do so in the future.

Notes

1. Richard B. Freeman and James L. Medoff, *What Do Unions Do?* (New York: Basic Books, 1984), pp. 20–22.
2. *Ibid.*, p. 217.
3. Freeman and Medoff claim that union restrictions on productivity are greatly exaggerated. They also acknowledge that this claim is not widely accepted. See pages 173 and 180.
4. Thomas A. Kochan and Michael J. Piore, "Will the New Industrial Relations Last? Implications for the American Labor Movement," *The Annals*, May 1984, pp. 177–89.
5. John A. Fossum, Labor Relations 3rd ed. (Plano, Tex.: Business Publications, Inc., 1985), pp. 486–87.
6. Kochan and Piore, pp. 181–82.
7. *Ibid.*, p. 181.
8. *Ibid.*, p. 188.
9. *Ibid.*
10. *Ibid.*
11. *Ibid.*, pp. 182–83.
12. *Ibid.*, pp. 188–89.
13. *Ibid.*, p. 186.
14. *Ibid.*, p. 189.
15. *Ibid.*

Discussion Questions

1. Discuss and evaluate the effects of unionization.
2. Evaluate the success of the American industrial relations system.
3. Assess the areas of stress and potential change in the system.

Statements for Comment

1. "Unions are pricing their members out of jobs."
2. "Union effects on fringe benefits are a social plus."

3. "Unions reduce wage inequality. Unfortunately, that is bad."
4. "With the recent atypical exception of the early 1980s, unionization and high profits have gone hand-in-hand."
5. "The decline in union representation as a percentage of the total workforce is a problem for no one but unions."
6. "American unionized employees actually have very significant voice in organizations, notwithstanding the application of scientific management principles."
7. "America should be able to compete in the marketplace. It always has—and it has always had a high cost of labor—unionized or not."

Situations

Case 17–1 "Before I took this course, I was totally opposed to unions. Now I think they may be all right for other people," said Becky Selfridge.

"What about for yourself?" queried her friend Bob Schustor. "Aren't there any circumstances under which you would consider joining a union?"

Describe a reasonable set of conditions under which Becky should join a union. Create a set of circumstances under which you would join a union.

Case 17–2 "The purpose of American labor laws is to protect and promote the public's interest in employment. Our current laws are in some ways inadequate," said Abraham Smith.

If you could pass labor laws, what would you change and why?

Case 17–3 "You know, if it weren't for the union, I'd either be out of a job or my job wouldn't be worth having," said Stewart Simmons.

"Boy, that's quite a turnabout from what I hear and read about everyday," said Lisa Whitlock. "I thought unions were supposed to be costing people jobs."

Examine the extent to which each of these arguments has merit.

Bibliography of Related Readings

Addison, J. T., "Are Unions Good For Productivity?" *Journal of Labor Research*, 1982, pp. 125–38.

Angel, J., "White Collar and Professional Unionization," *Labor Law Journal*, February 1982, pp. 82–101.

Baker, J. G., and W. C. Appleton, "The Effect of Unionization on the Safety in Bituminous Deep Mines," *Journal of Labor Research*, 1984, pp. 139–47.

Bloch, F. E., "Formalization, Collectivization, and the Demand for Union Services," *Journal of Labor Research*, 1982, pp. 31–37.

Bright, D., et al., "Industrial Relations of Recession," *Industrial Relations Journal*, 1983, pp. 24–33.

Cameron, K., "The Relationship Between Faculty Unionism and Organizational Effectiveness," *Academy of Management Journal,* 1982, pp. 6–24.

Cappelli, P., "What Do Unions Get in Return for Concessions?" *Monthly Labor Review,* May 1984, pp. 40–41.

Chamberlain, J., "Unions and Politics: A Journalist's View," *Journal of Labor Research,* 1984, pp. 309–13.

Corby, S., "Civil Servant and Trade Union Member: A Conflict of Loyalties," *Industrial Relations Journal,* 1984, pp. 18–29.

Croft, J. A., "New Strategies in Union Organizing," *Journal of Labor Research,* 1983, pp. 19–32.

Eberts, R. W., "How Unions Affect Management Decisions: Evidence From Public Schools," *Journal of Labor Research,* 1983, pp. 239–47.

Eberts, R. W., "Union Effects on Teachers' Productivity," *Industrial and Labor Relations Review,* 1984, pp. 346–58.

Elliott, R. D., and J. R. Huffman, "The Impact of Right-To-Work Laws on Employer Unfair Labor Practices Charges," *Journal of Labor Research,* 1984, pp. 165–76.

Fiorito, J., "The Determinants of Occupational Unionization," *Journal of Labor Research,* 1982, pp. 473–85.

Hirsch, B. T., "The Interindustry Structure of Unionism, Earnings, and Earnings Dispersion," *Industrial and Labor Relations Review,* 1982, pp. 22–39.

Hirsch, B. T., and A. N. Link, "Unions, Productivity, and Productivity Growth," *Journal of Labor Research,* 1984, pp. 29–37.

Hogler, R. L., "Employee Involvement Programs and *NLRB* v. *Scott & Fetzer Co.:* The Developing Interpretations of Section 8(a)(2)," *Labor Law Journal,* January 1984, pp. 21–27.

Holzer, H. J., "Unions and the Labor Market Status of White and Minority Youth," *Industrial Relations Journal,* 1982, pp. 354–67.

Guzda, H. P., "Industrial Democracy: Made in the U.S.A.," *Monthly Labor Review,* May 1984, pp. 26–33.

Jacoby, S. M., "Union-Management Cooperation in the United States: Lessons from the 1920's," *Industrial and Labor Relations Review,* 1983, pp. 18–33.

Juris, H. A., *The Shrinking Perimeter: Unionism and Labor Relations in the Manufacturing Section* (Lexington, Ky.: Lexington Books, 1980).

Kilgour, J. G., *Preventative Labor Relations* (New York: Amacon, Division of American Management Association, 1981).

Kolchin, M. G., and T. Hyclak, "Participation in Union Activities: A Multivariate Analysis," *Journal of Labor Research,* 1984, pp. 255–62.

Lacombe II, J. J., "Collective Bargaining Calendar Crowded Again in 1984." *Monthly Labor Review,* January 1984, pp. 19–32.

Latta, G. W., "Union Organization Among Engineers: A Current Assessment," *Industrial and Labor Relations Review,* 1981, pp. 29–42.

Marchington, M., and R. Armstrong, "Employee Participation: Some Problems for Some Shop Stewards," *Industrial Relations Journal,* 1984, pp. 68–81.

Marett, P. C., "Japanese Owned Firms in the United States: Do They Resist Union-ization" *Labor Law Journal,* 1984, pp. 240–50.

Martin, S., and C. Rence, "Vertical Spillovers, Market Concentration, Union Coverage, and Wages," *Journal of Labor Research,* 1984, pp. 177–89.

Neumann, G. R., and M. W. Reder, "Output and Strike Activity in U.S. Manufacturing: How Large are the Losses?" *Industrial and Labor Relations Review,* 1984, pp. 197–211.

Northup, H. R., "The Rise and Demise of PATCO," *Industrial and Labor Relations Review,* 1984, pp. 167–84.

Nowark, M. F., "Worker Participation and Its Potential Applications in the United States," *Labor Law Journal,* March 1984, pp. 148–66.

Rueben, G., "Organized Labor in 1981: A Shifting of Priorities," *Monthly Labor Review,* January 1982, pp. 21–28.

Scheuch, R., *Labor in the American Economy: Labor Problems and Union-Management Relations* (New York: Harper and Row, 1980).

Smith, R. R., "From Bowen to Devine: The Quandary Facing Federal Unions," *Labor Law Journal,* July 1984, pp. 435–39.

Voos, P. B., "Union Organizing: Costs and Benefits," *Industrial and Labor Relations Review,* 1983, pp. 576–91.

APPENDIX

SELECTED PORTIONS

OF THE LABOR

MANAGEMENT RELATIONS

ACT, 1947

Act of June 23, 1947, 61 Stat. 136, as Amended by Act of September 14, 1959, 73 Stat. 519.*

KEY TO AMENDMENTS

Portions of the Act which have been eliminated by the Labor-Management Reporting and Disclosure Act of 1959, Public Law 86-257, are enclosed by black brackets; provisions which have been added to the Act are in italics, and unchanged portions are shown in roman type.

*Section 201 (d) and (e) of the Labor-Management Reporting and Disclosure Act of 1959 which repealed Section 9 (f), (g), and (h) of the Labor Management Relations Act, 1947, and Section 505 amending Section 302 (a), (b), and (c) of the Labor Management Relations Act, 1947, took effect upon enactment of Public Law 86-257, September 14, 1959. As to the other amendments of the Labor Management Relations Act, 1947, Section 707 of the Labor-Management Reporting and Disclosure Act provides:

The amendments made by this title shall take effect sixty days after the date of the enactment of this Act and no provision of this title shall be deemed to make an unfair labor practice, any act which is performed prior to such effective date which did not constitute an unfair labor practice prior thereto.

[Public Law 101—80th Congress]

An Act

To amend the National Labor Relations Act, to provide additional facilities for the mediation of labor disputes affecting commerce, to equalize legal responsibilities of labor organizations and employers, and for other purposes.

Be it enacted by the Senate and House of Representatives of the United States of America in Congress assembled,

SHORT TITLE AND DECLARATION OF POLICY

SEC. 1. (a) This Act may be cited as the "Labor Management Relations Act, 1947."

(b) Industrial strife which interferes with the normal flow of commerce and with the full production of articles and commodities for commerce, can be avoided or substantially minimized if employers, employees, and labor organizations each recognize under law one another's legitimate rights in their relations with each other, and above all recognize under law that neither party has any right in its relations with any other to engage in acts or practices which jeopardize the public health, safety, or interest.

It is the purpose and policy of this Act, in order to promote the full flow of commerce, to prescribe the legitimate rights of both employees and employers in their relations affecting commerce, to provide orderly and peaceful procedures for preventing the interfrence by either with the legitimate rights of the other, to protect the rights of individual employees in their relations with labor organizations whose activities affect commerce, to define and proscribe practices on the part of labor and management which affect commerce and are inimical to the general welfare, and to protect the rights of the public in connection with labor disputes affecting commerce.

TITLE I
AMENDMENT OF NATIONAL LABOR RELATIONS ACT

SEC. 101. The National Labor Relations Act is hereby amended to read as follows:

FINDINGS AND POLICIES

SEC. 1. The denial by some employers of the right of employees to organize and the refusal by some employers to accept the procedure of collective bargaining lead to strikes and other forms of industrial strife or unrest, which have the intent or the necessary effect of burdening or obstructing commerce by (a) impairing the efficiency, safety, or operation of the instrumentalities of commerce; (b) occurring in the current of commerce; (c) materially affecting, restraining, or controlling the flow of raw materials or manufactured or processed goods in commerce; or (d) causing diminution of employment and wages in such volume as substantially to impair or disrupt the market for goods flowing from or into the channels of commerce.

Unequal power hurts commerce

The inequality of bargaining power between employees who do not possess full freedom of association or actual liberty of contract, and employers who are organized in the corporate or other forms of ownership association substantially burdens and affects the flow of commerce, and tends to aggravate recurrent business depressions, by depressing wage rates and the purchasing power of wage earners in industry and by preventing the stabilization of competitive wage rates and working conditions within and between industries.

Collective bargaining helps commerce

Experience has proved that protection by law of the right of employees to organize and bargain collectively safeguards commerce from injury, impairment, or interruption, and promotes the flow of commerce by removing certain recognized sources of industrial strife and unrest, by encouraging practices fundamental to the friendly adjustment of industrial disputes arising out of differences as to wages, hours, or other working conditions, and by restoring equality or bargaining power between employers and employees.

Unions must also be regulated

Experience has further demonstrated that certain practices by some labor organizations, their officers, and members have the intent or the necessary effect of burdening or obstructing commerce by preventing the free flow of goods in such commerce through strikes and other forms of industrial unrest or through concerted activities which impair the interest of the public in the free flow of such commerce. The elimination of such practices is a necessary condition to the assurance of the rights herein guaranteed.

Policy of U.S. to encourage bargaining

It is hereby declared to be the policy of the United States to eliminate the causes of certain substantial obstructions to the free flow of commerce and to mitigate and eliminate these obstructions when they have occurred by encouraging the practice and procedure of collective bargaining and by protecting the exercise by workers of full freedom of association, self-organization, and designation of representatives of their own choosing, for the purpose of negotiating the terms and conditions of their employment or other mutual aid or protection.

DEFINITIONS. SEC. 2. When used in this Act—

Types or organizations covered

(1) The term "person" includes one or more individuals, labor organizations, partnerships, associations, corporations, legal representatives, trustees, trustees in bankruptcy, or receivers.

Employers not covered by the Act

(2) The term "employer" includes any person acting as an agent of an employer, directly or indirectly, but shall not include the United States or any wholly owned Government corporation, or any Federal Reserve Bank, or any State or political subdivision thereof, or any corporation or association operating a hospital, if no part of the net earnings inures to the benefit of any private shareholder or individual, or any person subject to the Railway Labor Act, as amended from time to time, or any labor organization (other than when acting as an employer), or anyone acting in the capacity of officer or agent of such labor organization.

Employees who are covered

(3) The term "employee" shall include any employee, and shall not be limited to the employees of a particular employer, unless the Act explicitly states otherwise, and shall include any individual whose work has ceased as a consequence of, or in connection with, any current labor dispute or because of any unfair labor practice, and who has not obtained any other regular and substantially equivalent employment, but

Types of employees not covered by the Act

shall not include any individual employed as an agricultural laborer, or in the domestic service of any family or person at his home, or any individual employed by his parent or spouse, or any individual having the status of an independent contractor, or any individual employed as a supervisor, or any individual employed by an employer subject to the Railway Labor Act, as amended from time to time, or by any other person who is not an employer as herein defined.

(4) The term "representatives" includes any individual or labor organization.

What constitutes a union

(5) The term "labor organization" means any organization of any kind, or any agency or employee representation committee or plan, in which employees participate and which exists for the purpose, in whole or in part, of dealing with employers concerning grievances, labor disputes, wages, rates of pay, hours of employment, or conditions of work.

Commerce defined

(6) The term "commerce" means trade, traffic, commerce, transportation, or communication among the several States, or between the District of Columbia or any Territory of the United States and any State or other Territory, or between any foreign country and any State, Territory, or the District of Columbia, or within the District of Columbia or any Territory, or between points in the same State but through any other State or any Territory or the District of Columbia or any foreign country.

Affecting commerce defined

(7) The term "affecting commerce" means in commerce, or burdening or obstructing commerce or the free flow of commerce, or having led or tending to lead to a labor dispute burdening or obstructing commerce or the free flow of commerce.

(8) The term "unfair labor practice" means any unfair labor practice listed in section 8.

Labor dispute defined

(9) The term "labor dispute" includes any controversy concerning terms, tenure or conditions of employment, or concerning the as-

sociation or representations of persons in negotiating, fixing, maintaining, changing, or seeking to arrange terms or conditions of employment, regardless of whether the disputants stand in the proximate relation of employer and employee.

(10) The term "National Labor Relations Board" means the National Labor Relations Board provided for in section 3 of this Act.

Supervisor defined

(11) The term "supervisor" means any individual having authority, in the interest of the employer, to hire, transfer, suspend, lay off, recall, promote, discharge, assign, reward, or discipline other employees, or responsibly to direct them, or to adjust their grievances, or effectively to recommend such action, if in connection with the foregoing the exercise of such authority is not of a merely routine or clerical nature, but requires the use of independent judgment.

Professional defined

(12) The term "professional employee" means—

(a) any employee engaged in work (i) predominantly intellectual and varied in character as opposed to routine mental, manual, mechanical, or physical work; (ii) involving the consistent exercise of discretion and judgment in its performance; (iii) of such a character that the output produced or the result accomplished cannot be standardized in relation to a given period of time; (iv) requiring knowledge of an advanced type in a field of science or learning customarily acquired by a prolonged course of specialized intellectual instruction and study in an institution of higher learning or a hospital, as distinguished from a general academic education or from an apprenticeship or from training in the performance of routine mental, manual, or physical processes; or

(b) any employee, who (i) has completed the courses of specialized intellectual instruction and study described in clause (iv) of paragraph (a), and (ii) is performing related work under the supervision of a professional person to qualify himself to become a professional employee as defined in paragraph (a).

Agent defined

(13) In determining whether any person is acting as an "agent" of another person so as to make such other person responsible for his acts, the question of whether the specific acts performed were actually authorized or subsequently ratified shall not be controlling.

Health care institution defined

(14) The term "health care institution" shall include any hospital, convalescent hospital, health maintenance organization, health clinic, nursing home, extended care facility, or other institution devoted to the care of sick, infirm, or aged persons.

NATIONAL LABOR RELATIONS BOARD

Sec. 3. (a) The National Labor Relations Board (hereinafter called the "Board") created by this Act prior to its amendment by the Labor Management Relations Act, 1947, is hereby continued as an agency of the United States, except that the Board shall consist of five instead of three members, appointed by the President by and with the advice and consent of the Senate. Of the two additional members so provided for, one

NLRB membership

shall be appointed for a term of five years and the other for a term of two years. Their successors, and the successors of the other members, shall be appointed for terms of five years each, excepting that any individual chosen to fill a vacancy shall be appointed only for the unexpired term of the member whom he shall succeed. The President shall designate one member to serve as Chairman of the Board. Any members of the Board may be removed by the President, upon notice and hearing, for neglect of duty or malfeasance in office, but for no other cause.

Delegation of Board authority(b) The Board is authorized to delegate to any group of three or more members any or all of the powers which it may itself exercise. *The Board is also authorized to delegate to its regional directors its powers under section 9 to determine the unit appropriate for the purpose of collective bargaining, to investigate and provide for hearings, and determine whether a question of representation exists, and to direct an election or take a secret ballot under subsection (c) or (e) of section 9 and certify the results thereof, except that upon the filing of a request therefor with the Board by any interested person, the Board may review any action of a regional director delegated to him under this paragraph, but such a review shall not, unless specifically ordered by the Board, operate as a stay of any action taken by the regional director.* A vacancy in the Board shall not impair the right of the remaining members to exercise all of the powers of the Board, and three members of the Board shall, at all times, constitute a quorum of the Board, except that two members shall constitute a quorum of any group designated pursuant to the first sentence hereof. The Board shall have an official seal which shall be judicially noticed.

(c) The Board shall at the close of each fiscal year make a report in writing to Congress and to the President stating in detail the cases it has heard, the decisions it has rendered, the names, salaries, and duties of all employees and officers in the employ or under the supervision of the Board, and an account of all moneys it has disbursed.

Duties of the General Counsel(d) There shall be a General Counsel of the Board who shall be appointed by the President, by and with the advice and consent of the Senate, for a term of four years. The General Counsel of the Board shall exercise general supervision over all attorneys employed by the Board (other than trial examiners and legal assistants to Board members) and over the officers and employees in the regional offices. He shall have final authority, on behalf of the Board, in respect of the investigation of charges and issuance of complaints under section 10, and in respect of the prosecution of such complaints before the Board, and shall have such other duties as the Board may prescribe or as may be provided by law. *In case of a vacancy in the office of the General Counsel the President is authorized to designate the officer or employee who shall act as General Counsel during such vacancy, but no person or persons so designated shall so act (1) for more than forty days when the Congress is in session unless a nomination to fill such vacancy shall have been submitted to the Senate, or (2) after the adjournment since die of the sessions of the Senate in which such nomination was submitted.*

SEC. 4. (a) Each member of the Board and the General Counsel of the Board shall receive a salary of $12,000* a year, shall be eligible for reappointment, and shall not engage in any other business, vocation, or employment. The Board shall appoint an executive secretary, and such attorneys, examiners, and regional directors, and such other employees as it may from time to time find necessary for the proper performance of its duties. The Board may not employ any attorneys for the purpose of reviewing transcripts of hearings or preparing drafts of opinions except that any attorney employed for assignment as a legal assistant to any Board member may for such Board member review such transcripts and prepare such drafts. No trial examiner's report shall be reviewed, either before or after its publication, by any person other than a member of the Board or his legal assistant, and no trial examiner shall advise or consult with the Board with respect to exceptions taken to his findings, rulings, or recommendations. The Board may establish or utilize such regional, local, or other agencies, and utilize such voluntary and uncompensated services, as may from time to time be needed. Attorneys appointed under this section may, at the direction of the Board, appear for and represent the Board in any case in court. Nothing in this Act shall be construed to authorize the Board to appoint individuals for the purpose of conciliation or mediation, or for economic analysis.

Establishment of staff positions and regulations

(b) All of the expenses of the Board, including all necessary traveling and subsistence expenses outside the District of Columbia incurred by the members or employees of the Board under its orders, shall be allowed and paid on the presentation of itemized vouchers therefore approved by the Board or by any individual it designates for that purpose.

SEC. 5. The principal office of the Board shall be in the District of Columbia, but it may meet and exercise any or all of its powers at any other place. The Board may, by one or more of its members or by such agents or agencies as it may designate, prosecute any inquiry necessary to its functions in any part of the United States. A member who participates in such an inquiry shall not be disqualified from subsequently participating in a decision of the Board in the same case.

Authority of Board to promulgate rules

SEC. 6. The Board shall have authority from time to time to make, amend, and rescind, in the manner prescribed by the Administrative

---

*AUTHORS' NOTE: All salaries quoted in this Act are now increased periodically as a result of the Government Employees Salary Reform Act of 1964, 88th Congress, Public Law 88-426, 78 Stat. 400.

Procedure Act, such rules and regulations as may be necessary to carry out the provisions of this Act.

Right of employees to form unions and/or engage in concerted activity RIGHTS OF EMPLOYEES. SEC. 7. Employees shall have the right to self-organization, to form, join, or assist labor organizations, to bargain collectively through representatives of their own choosing, or to engage in other concerted activities for the purpose of collective bargaining or other mutual aid or protection, and shall also have the right to refrain from any or all of such activities except to the extent that such right may be affected by an agreement requiring membership in a labor organization as a condition of employment as authorized in section 8(a)(3).

Employer unfair labor practices UNFAIR LABOR PRACTICES. SEC. 8. (a) It shall be an unfair labor practice for an employer—

(1) to interfere with, restrain, or coerce employees in the exercise of the rights guranteed in section 7;

Company union (2) to dominate or interfere with the formation or administration of any labor organization or contribute financial or other support to it: Provided, That subject to rules and regulations made and published by the Board pursuant to section 6, an employer shall not be prohibited from permitting employees to confer with him during working hours without loss of time or pay;

(3) by discrimination in regard to hire or tenure of employment or any term or condition of employment to encourage or discourage membership in any labor organization: Provided, That nothing in this Act, or in any other statute of the United States, shall preclude an employer from making an agreement with a labor organization (not established, maintained, or assisted by any action defined in section 8[a] of this Act as an unfair labor practice) to require as a condition of employ- Union shop permitted ment membership therein on or after the thirtieth day following the beginning of such employment or the effective date of such agreement, whichever is the later, (i) if such labor organization is the representative of the employees as provided in section 9 (a), in the appropriate collective-bargaining unit covered by such agreement when made [and has at the time the agreement was made or within the preceding twelve months received from the Board a notice of compliance with section 9 (f), (g), (h)], and (ii) unless following an election held as provided in section 9 (e) within one year preceding the effective date of such agreement, the Board shall have certified that at least a majority of the employees eligible to vote in such election have voted to rescind the authority of such labor organization to make such an agreement: Provided further, That no employer shall justify any discrimination against an employee for nonmembership in a labor organization (A) if he has reasonable grounds for believing that such membership was not available to the employee on the same terms and conditions generally applicable to

other members, or (B) if he has reasonable grounds for believing that membership was denied or terminated for reasons other than the failure of the employee to tender the periodic dues and the initiation fees uniformly required as a condition of acquiring or retaining membership;

(4) to discharge or otherwise discriminate against an employee because he has filed charges or given testimony under this Act;

(5) to refuse to bargain collectively with the representatives of his employees, subject to the provisions of section 9 (a).

(b) It shall be an unfair labor practice for a labor organization or its agents

(1) to restrain or coerce (A) employees in the exercise of the rights guaranteed in section 7: Provided, That this paragraph shall not impair the right of a labor organization to prescribe its own rules with respect to the acquisition or retention of membership therein; or (B) an employer in the selection of his representatives for the purposes of collective bargaining or the adjustment of grievances;

(2) to cause or attempt to cause an employer to discriminate against an employee in violation of subsection (a) (3) or to discriminate against an employee with respect to whom membership in such organization has been denied or terminated on some ground other than his failure to tender the periodic dues and the initiation fees uniformly required as a condition of acquiring or retaining membership;

(3) to refuse to bargain collectively with an employer, provided it is the representative of his employees subject to the provisions of section 9 (a);

(4) (i) to engage in, or to induce or encourage [the employees of any employer] *any individual employed by any person engaged in commerce or in an industry affecting commerce* to engage in, a strike or a [concerted] refusal in the course of [their] *his* employment to use, manufacture, process, transport, or otherwise handle or work on any goods, articles, materials, or commodities or to perform any services [,]; *or (ii) to threaten, coerce, or restrain any person engaged in commerce or in an industry affecting commerce,* where in *either case* an object thereof is:

(A) forcing or requiring any employer or self-employed person to join any labor or employer organization or [any employer or other person to cease using, selling, handling, transporting, or otherwise dealing in the products of any other producer, processor, or manufacturer, or to cease doing business with any other person] *to enter into any agreement which is prohibited by section 8 (e);*

(B) *forcing or requiring any person to cease using, selling, handling, transporting, or otherwise dealing in the products of any other producer, processor, or manufacturer, or to doing business with any other person, or* forcing or requiring any other employer to recognize or bargain with a labor organization as the representative of his employees unless such labor organization has been certified as the representative of such employees under the provisions of section 9 [;]: *Provided, That nothing contained in this clause (B) shall be construed to make unlawful, where not otherwise unlawful, any primary strike or primary picketing;*

Compelling recognition if another union is certified	(C) forcing or requiring any employer to recognize or bargain with a particular labor organization as the representative of his employees if another labor organization has been certified as the representative of such employees under the provisions of section 9;
Compelling assignment of work to certain employees	(D) forcing or requiring any employer to assign particular work to employees in a particular labor organization or in a particular trade, craft, or class rather than to employees in another labor organization or in another trade, craft, or class, unless such employer is failing to conform to an order or certification of the Board determining the bargaining representative for employees performing such work:

Right not to have to cross picket line

Provided, That nothing contained in this subsection (b) shall be construed to make unlawful a refusal by any person to enter upon the premises of any employer (other than his own employer), if the employees of such employer are engaged in a strike ratified or approved by a representative of such employees whom such employer is required to recognize under this Act [;]: *Provided further, That for the purposes of this*

May publicize disputes with secondary employers

paragraph (4) only, nothing contained in such paragraph shall be construed to prohibit publicity, other than picketing, for the purpose of truthfully advising the public, including consumers and members of a labor organization, that a product or products are produced by an employer with whom the labor organization has a primary dispute and are distributed by another employer, as long as such publicity does not have an effect of inducing any individual employed by any person other than the primary employer in the course of his employment to refuse to pick up, deliver, or transport any goods, or not to perform any services, at the establishment of the employer engaged in such distribution;

Excessive initiation fees barred

(5) to require of employees covered by an agreement authorized under subsection (a) (3) the payment, as a condition precedent to becoming a member of such organization, of a fee in an amount which the Board finds excessive or discriminatory under all the circumstances. In making such a finding, the Board shall consider, among other relevant factors, the practices and customs of labor organizations in the particular industry, and the wages currently paid to the employees affected; [and]

Featherbedding prohibited

(6) to cause or attempt to cause an employer to pay or deliver or agree to pay or deliver any money or other thing of value, in the nature of an exaction, for services which are not performed or not to be performed [.]; *and*

Recognitional picketing banned if . . .

(7) *to picket or cause to be picketed, or threaten to picket or cause to be picketed, any employer where an object thereof is forcing or requiring an employer to recognize or bargain with a labor organization as the representative of his employees, or forcing or requiring the employees of an employer to accept or select labor organization as their collective bargaining representative, unless such labor organization is currently certified as the representative of such employees:*

Other union is lawfully recognized

(A) where the employer has lawfully recognized in accordance with this Act any other labor organization and a question concerning representation may not appropriately be raised under section 9 (c) of this Act,

Election has been
held within 12
months
Petition has
not been filed
within 30 days
Expedited
elections
Protection
of publicity
picketing

(B) *where within the preceding twelve months a valid election under section 9 (c) of this Act has been conducted, or*

(C) *where such picketing has been conducted without a petition under section 9 (c) being filed within a reasonable period of time not to exceed thirty days from the commencement of such picketing: Provided, That when such a petition has been filed the Board shall forthwith, without regard to the provisions of section 9 (c) (1) or the absence of a showing of a substantial interest on the part of the labor organization, direct an election in such unit as the Board finds to be appropriate and shall certify the results thereof: Provided further, That nothing in this sub-paragraph (C) shall be construed to prohibit any picketing or other publicity for the purpose of truthfully advising the public (including consumers) that an employer does not employ members of, or have a contract with, a labor organization, unless an effect of such picketing is to induce any individual employed by any other person in the course of his employment, not to pick up, deliver or transport any goods or not to perform any services.*

Nothing in this paragraph (7) shall be construed to permit any act which would otherwise be an unfair labor practice under this section 8 (b).

Employer
(and others)
free speech

(c) The expressing of any views, argument, or opinion, or the dissemination thereof, whether in written, printed, graphic, or visual form, shall not constitute or be evidence of an unfair labor practice under any of the provisions of this Act, if such expression contains no threat of reprisal or force or promise of benefit.

Good faith
requirements
Scope of
bargaining
Concession
not required

(d) For the purposes of this section, to bargain collectively is the performance of the mutual obligation of the employer and the representative of the employees to meet at reasonable times and confer in good faith with respect to wages, hours, and other terms and conditions of employment, or the negotiation of an agreement, or any question arising thereunder, and the execution of a written contract incorporating any agreement reached if requested by either party, but such obligation does not compel either party to agree to a proposal or require the making of a concession: Provided, That where there is in effect a collective-bargaining contract covering employees in an industry affecting commerce, the duty to bargain collectively shall also mean that no party to such contract shall terminate or modify such contract, unless the party desiring such termination or modification—

Procedural
requirements
for contract
modification

(1) serves a written notice upon the other party to the contract of the proposed termination or modification sixty days prior to the expiration date thereof, or in the event such contract contains no expiration date, sixty days prior to the time it is proposed to make such termination or modification;

(2) offers to meet and confer with the other party for the purpose of negotiating a new contract or a contract containing the proposed modifications;

(3) notifies the Federal Mediation and Conciliation Service within thirty days after such notice of the existence of a dispute, and simultaneously therewith notifies any State or Territorial agency established to mediate and conciliate disputes within the State or Territory where the dispute occurred, provided no agreement has been reached by that time; and

(4) continues in full force and effect, without resorting to strike or lockout, all the terms and conditions of the existing contract for a period of sixty days after such notice is given or until the expiration date of such contract, whichever occurs later:

Special procedures for health care institutions

Whenever the collective bargaining involves employees of a health care institution, the provisions of this section 8 (d) shall be modified as follows:

(A) The notice of section 8 (d) (1) shall be ninety days; the notice of section 8 (d) (3) shall be sixty days; and the contract period of section 8 (d) (4) shall be ninety days.

(B) Where the bargaining is for an initial agreement following certification or recognition, at least thirty days' notice of the existence of a dispute shall be given by the labor organization to the agencies set forth in section 8 (d) (3).

(C) After notice is given to the Federal Mediation and Conciliation Service under either clause (A) or (B) of this sentence, the Service shall promptly communicate with the parties and use its best efforts, by mediation and conciliation, to bring them to agreement. The parties shall participate fully and promptly in such meetings as may be undertaken by the Service for the purpose of aiding in a settlement of the dispute.

Successor parties

The duties imposed upon employers, employees, and labor organizations by paragraphs (2), (3), and (4) shall become inapplicable upon an intervening certification of the Board, under which the labor organization or individual, which is a party to the contract, has been superseded as or ceased to be the representative of the employees subject to the provisions of section 9 (a), and the duties so imposed shall not be construed as requiring either party to discuss or agree to any modification of the terms and conditions contained in a contract for a fixed period, if such modification is to become effective before such terms and conditions can be reopened under the provisions of the contract. Any employee who engages in a strike within the sixty-day period specified in this subsection shall lose his status as an employee of the employer engaged in the particular labor dispute, for the purposes of sections 8, 9, and 10 of this Act, as amended, but such loss of status for such employee shall terminate if and when he is reemployed by such employer.

Hot cargo prohibition

(e) It shall be an unfair labor practice for any labor organization and any employer to enter into any contract or agreement, express or implied, whereby such employer ceases or refrains or agrees to cease or refrain from handling, using, selling, transporting or otherwise dealing in any of the products of any other employer, or to cease doing business with any other person, and any contract or agreement entered into heretofore or hereafter containing such an agreement shall be to such extent unenforceable and void: Provided, That nothing in this subsection (e) shall apply to an agreement between a labor organization and an employer in the construction industry relating to the contracting or subcontracting of work to be done at the site of the construction,

Exception for construction industry

alteration, painting, or repair of a building, structure, or other work: Provided further, That for the purposes of this subsection (e) and section 8 (b) (4) (B) the terms "any employer," "any person engaged in commerce or an industry affecting commerce" and "any person" when used in relation to the term "any other producer, processor, or manufacturer," "any other employer," or "any other person" shall not include persons in the relation of a jobber, manufacturer, contractor, or subcontractor working on the goods or premises of the jobber or manufacturer or performing parts of an integrated process of production in the apparel and clothing industry: Provided further, That nothing in this Act shall prohibit the enforcement of any agreement which is within the foregoing exception.

Liberalized union shop rules for construction industry

*(f) It shall not be an unfair labor practice under subsections (a) and (b) of this section for an employer engaged primarily in the building and construction industry to make an agreement covering employees engaged (or who upon their employment, will be engaged) in the building and construction industry with a labor organization of which building and construction employees are members (not established, maintained, or assisted by any action defined in section 8 [a] of this Act as an unfair labor practice) because (1) the majority status of such labor organization has not been established under the provisions of section 9 of this Act prior to the making of such agreement, or (2) such agreement requires as a condition of employment, membership in such labor organization after the seventh day following the beginning of such employment or the effective date of the agreement, whichever is later, or (3) such agreement requires the employer to notify such labor organization of opportunities for employment with such employer, or gives such labor organization an opportunities for employment with such employer, or gives such labor organization an opportunity to refer qualified applicants for such employment, or (4) such agreement specifies minimum training or experience qualifications for employment or provides for priority in opportunities for employment based upon length of service with such employer, in the industry or in the particular geographical area: Provided, That nothing in this subsection shall set aside the final proviso to section 8 (a) (3) of this Act: Provided further, That any agreement which would be invalid, but for clause (1) of this subsection, shall not be a bar to a petition filed pursuant to section 9 (c) or 9 (e). ***

Strike notification in health care industry

(g) A labor organization before engaging in any strike, picketing, or other concerted refusal to work at any health care institution shall, not less than ten days prior to such action, notify the institution in writing and the Federal Mediation and Conciliation Service of that

---

*Section 8 (f) is inserted in the Act by subsection (a) of Section 705 of Public Law 86-257. Section 705 (b) provides:
    Nothing contained in the amendment made by subsection (a) shall be construed as authorizing the execution or application of agreements requiring membership in a labor organization as a condition of employment in any State or Territory in which such execution or application is prohibited by State or Territorial law.

intention, except that in the case of bargaining for an initial agreement following certification or recognition the notice required by this subsection shall not be given until the expiration of the period specified in clause (B) of the last sentence of section 8 (d) of this Act. The notice shall state the date and time that such action will commence. The notice, once given, may be extended by the written agreement of both parties.

Majority election
Exclusive representation
Right to present grievances

REPRESENTATIVES AND ELECTIONS. SEC. 9. (a) Representatives designated or selected for the purposes of collective bargaining by the majority of the employees in a unit appropriate for such purposes, shall be the exclusive representatives of all the employees in such unit for the purposes of collective bargaining in respect to rates of pay, wages, hours of employment, or other conditions of employment: Provided, That any individual employee or a group of employees shall have the right at any time to present grievances to their employer and to have such grievances adjusted, without the intervention of the bargaining representative, as long as the adjustment is not inconsistent with the terms of a collective-bargaining contract or agreement then in effect: Provided further, That the bargaining representative has been given opportunity to be present at such adjustment.

Appropriate bargaining unit

(b) The Board shall decide in each case whether, in order to assure to employees the fullest freedom in exercising the rights guaranteed by this Act, the unit appropriate for the purposes of collective bargaining shall be the employer unit, craft unit, plant unit, or subdivision thereof: Provided, That the Board shall not (1) decide that any unit is appropriate for such purposes if such unit includes both professional employees and employees who are not professional employees unless a majority of such professional employees vote for inclusion in such unit;

Rights of professionals
Rights of craftsmen
Rights of guards

or (2) decide that any craft unit is inappropriate for such purposes on the ground that a different unit has been established by a prior Board determination, unless a majority of the employees in the proposed craft unit vote against separate representation; or (3) decide that any unit is appropriate for such purposes if it includes, together with other employees, any individual employed as a guard to enforce against employees and other persons rules to protect property of the employer or to protect the safety of persons on the employer's premises; but no labor organization shall be certified as the representative of employees in a bargaining unit of guards if such organization admits to membership, or is affiliated directly or indirectly with an organization which admits to membership, employees other than guards.

(c) (1) Whenever a petition shall have been filed, in accordance with such regulations as may be prescribed by the Board—

Representation procedures

(A) by an employee or group of employees or any individual or labor organization acting in their behalf alleging that a substantial number of employees (i) wish to be represented for collective bargaining and that their employer declines to recognize their representative as the representative defined in section 9 (a), or (ii) assert that the individual or labor organization, which has been certified or is being currently recognized by their employer as the bargaining representative, is no longer a representative as defined in section 9 (a); or

(B) by an employer, alleging that one or more individuals or labor organizations have presented to him a claim to be recognized as the representative defined in section 9 (a);

the Board shall investigate such petition and if it has reasonable cause to believe that a question of representation affecting commerce exists shall provide for an appropriate hearing upon due notice. Such hearing may be conducted by an officer or employee of the regional office, who shall not make any recommendations with respect thereto. If the Board finds upon the record of such hearing that such a question of representation exists, it shall direct an election by secret ballot and shall certify the results thereof.

(2) In determining whether or not a question of representation affecting commerce exists, the same regulations and rules of decision shall apply irrespective of the identity of the persons filing the petition or the kind of relief sought and in no case shall the Board deny a labor organization a place on the ballot by reason of an order with respect to such labor organization or its predecessor not issued in conformity with section 10 (c).

Election bar
Right of strikers to vote in representation election
(3) No election shall be directed in any bargaining unit or any subdivision within which, in the preceding twelve-month period, a valid election shall have been held. Employees [on] *engaged in an economic* strike who are not entitled to reinstatement shall [not] be eligible to vote [.] *under such regulations as the Board shall find are consistent with the purposes and provisions of this Act in any election conducted within twelve months after the commencement of the strike.* In any election where none of the choices on the ballot receives a majority, a run-off shall be conducted, the ballot providing for a selection between the two choices receiving the largest and second largest number of valid votes cast in the election.

Consent elections
(4) Nothing in this section shall be construed to prohibit the waiving of hearings by stipulation for the purpose of a consent election in conformity with regulations and rules of decision of the Board.

(5) In determining whether a unit is appropriate for the purposes specified in subsection (b) the extent to which the employees have organized shall not be controlling.

(d) Whenever an order of the Board made pursuant to section 10 (c) is based in whole or in part upon facts certified following an investigation pursuant to subsection (c) of this section and there is a petition for the enforcement or review of such order, such certification and the record of such investigation shall be included in the transcript of the entire record required to be filed under section 10 (e) or 10 (f), and thereupon the decree of the court enforcing, modifying, or setting aside in whole or in part the order of the Board shall be made and entered upon the pleadings, testimony, and proceedings set forth in such transcript.

Showing of interest

Secret ballot election; certification

(e)(1) Upon the filing with the Board, by 30 per centum or more of the employees in a bargaining unit covered by an agreement between their employer and a labor organization made pursuant to section 8 (a) (3), of a petition alleging they desire that such authority be rescinded, the Board shall take a secret ballot of the employees in such unit and certify the results thereof to such labor organization and to the employer.

Election bar

(2) No election shall be conducted pursuant to this subsection in any bargaining unit or any subdivision within which, in the preceding twelve-month period, a valid election shall have been held.

[(f) No investigation shall be made by the Board of any question affecting commerce concerning the representation of employees, raised by a labor organization under subsection (c) of this section, and no complaint shall be issued pursuant to a charge made by a labor organization under subsection (b) of section 10, unless such labor organization and any national or international labor organization of which such labor organization is an affiliate or constituent unit (A) shall have prior thereto filed with the Secretary of Labor copies of its constitution and bylaws and a report, in such form as the Secretary may prescribe, showing—

(1) the name of such labor organization and the address of its principal place of business;

(2) the names, titles, and compensation and allowances of its three principal officers and of any of its other officers or agents whose aggregate compensation and allowances for the preceding year exceding year exceeded $5,000, and the amount of the compensation and allowances paid to each such officer or agent during such year;

(3) the manner in which the officers and agents referred to in clause (2) were elected, appointed, or otherwise selected;

(4) the initiation fee or fees which new members are required to pay on becoming members of such labor organization;

(5) the regular dues or fees which members are required to pay in order to remain members in good standing of such labor organization;

(6) a detailed statement of, or reference to provisions of its constitution and bylaws showing the procedure followed with respect to, (a) qualification for or restrictions on membership, (b) election of officers and stewards, (c) calling of regular and special meetings, (d) levying of assessments, (e) imposition of fines, (f) authorization for bargaining demands, (g) ratification of contract terms, (h) authorization for strikes, (i) authorization for disbursement of union funds, (j) audit of union financial transactions, (k) participation in insurance or other benefit plans, and (l) expulsion of members and the grounds therefor;

and (B) can show that prior thereto it has—

(1) filed with the Secretary of Labor, in such form as the Secretary may prescribe, a report showing all of (a) its receipts of any kind and the sources of such receipts, (b) its total assets and liabilities as of the end of its last fiscal year, (c) the disbursements made by it during such fiscal year, including the purposes for which made; and

(2) furnished to all of the members of such labor organization copies of the financial report required by paragraph (1) hereof to be filed with the Secretary of Labor.]

[(g) It shall be the obligation of all labor organizations to file annually with the Secretary of Labor, in such form as the Secretary of Labor may prescribe, reports bringing up to date the information required to be supplied in the initial filing by subsection (f) (A) of this section, and to file with the Secretary of Labor and furnish to its members annually financial reports in the form and manner prescribed in subsection (f) (B). No labor organization shall be eligible for certification under this section as the representative of any employees, and no complaint shall issue under section 10 with respect to a charge filed by a labor organization unless it can show that it and any national or international labor organization of which it is an affiliate or constituent unit has complied with its obligation under this subsection.]

[(h) No investigation shall be made by the Board of any question affecting commerce concerning the representation of employees, raised by a labor organization under subsection (c) of this section, and no complaint shall be issued pursuant to a charge made by a labor organization under subsection (b) of section 10, unless there is on file with the Board an affidavit executed contemporaneously or within the preceding twelve-month period by each officer of such labor organization and the officers of any national or international labor organization of which it is an affiliate or constituent unit that he is not a member of the Communist Party or affiliated with such party, and that he does not believe in, and is not a member of or supports any organization that believes in or teaches, the overthrow of the United States Government by force or by any illegal or unconstitutional methods. The provisions of section 35 A of the Criminal Code shall be applicable in respect to such affidavits.]

Board procedure in unfair labor practice cases

PREVENTION OF UNFAIR LABOR PRACTICES. SEC. 10. (a) The Board is empowered, as hereinafter provided, to prevent any person from engaging in any unfair labor practice (listed in section 8) affecting commerce. This power shall not be affected by any other means of adjustment or prevention that has been or may be established by agreement, law, or otherwise: Provided, That the Board is empowered by agreement with any agency of any State or Territory to cede to such agency jurisdiction over any cases in any industry (other than mining, manufacturing, communications, and transportation except where predominantly local in character) even though such cases may involve labor disputes affecting commerce, unless the provision of the State or Territorial statute applicable to the determination of such cases by such agency is inconsistent with the corresponding provision of this Act or has received a construction inconsistent therewith.

(b) Whenever it is charged that any person has engaged in or is engaging in any such unfair labor practice, the Board, or any agent or agency designated by the Board for such purposes, shall have power to issue and cause to be served upon such person a complaint stating the charges in that respect, and containing a notice of hearing before the Board or a member thereof, or before a designated agent or agency, at a place therein fixed, not less than five days after the serving of said complaint: Provided, That no complaint shall issue based upon any unfair labor practice occurring more than six months prior to the filing of the charge with the Board and the service of a copy thereof upon the person against whom such charge is made, unless the person aggrieved thereby was prevented from filing such charge by reason of service in the armed forces, in which event the six-month period shall be computed from the day of his discharge. Any such complaint may be amended by the member, agent, or agency conducting the hearing or the Board in its discretion at any time prior to the issuance of an order based thereon. The person so complained of shall have the right to file an answer to the original or amended complaint and to appear in person or otherwise and give testimony at the place and time fixed in the complaint. In the discretion of the member, agent, or agency conducting the hearing or the Board, any other person may be allowed to intervene in the said proceeding and to present testimony. Any such proceeding shall, so far as practicable, be conducted in accordance with the rules of evidence applicable in the district courts of the United States under the rules of civil procedure for the district courts of the United States, adopted by the Supreme Court of the United States pursuant to the Act of June 19, 1934 (U.S.C., title 28, secs. 723-B, 723-C).

(c) The testimony taken by such member, agent, or agency or the Board shall be reduced to writing and filed with the Board. Thereafter, in its discretion, the Board upon notice may take further testimony or hear argument. If upon the preponderance of the testimony taken the Board shall be of the opinion that any person named in the complaint has engaged in or is engaging in any such unfair labor practice, then the Board shall state its findings of fact and shall issue and cause to be served on such person an order requiring such person to cease and desist from such unfair labor practice, and to take such affirmative action including reinstatement of employees with or without back pay, as will effectuate the policies of this Act: Provided, That where an order directs reinstatement of an employee, back pay may be required of the employer or labor organization, as the case may be, responsible for the discrimination suffered by him: And provided further, That in deter-

Margin notes (adjacent to paragraph (c)):
Preponderance of evidence
Cease and desist remedy
Reinstatement for discharged employees

mining whether a complaint shall issue alleging a violation of section 8 (a) (1) or section 8 (a) (2), and in deciding such cases, the same regulations and rules of decision shall apply irrespective of whether or not the labor organization affected is affiliated with a labor organization national or international in scope. Such order may further require such person to make reports from time to time showing the extent to which it has complied with the order. If upon the preponderance of the testimony taken the Board shall not be of the opinion that the person named in the complaint has engaged in or is engaging in any such unfair labor practice, then the Board shall state its findings of fact and shall issue an order dismissing the said complaint. No order of the Board shall require the reinstatement of any individual as an employee who has been suspended or discharged, or the payment to him of any back pay, if such individual was suspended or discharged for cause. In case the evidence is presented before a member of the Board, or before an examiner or examiners thereof, such member, or such examiner or examiners, as the case may be, shall issue and cause to be served on the parties to the proceeding a proposed report, together with a recommended order, which shall be filed with the Board, and if no exceptions are filed within twenty days after service thereof upon such parties, or within such further period as the Board may authorize, such recommended order shall become the order of the Board and become effective as therein prescribed.

Discharge for cause

(d) Until the record in a case shall have been filed in a court, as hereinafter provided, the Board may at any time, upon reasonable notice and in such manner as it shall deem proper, modify or set aside, in whole or in part, any finding or order made or issued by it.

Judicial enforcement

(e) The Board shall have power to petition any court of appeals of the United States, or if all the courts of appeals to which application may be made are in vacation, any district court of the United States, within any circuit or district, respectively, wherein the unfair labor practice in question occurred or wherein such person resides or transacts business, for the enforcement of such order and for appropriate temporary relief or restraining order, and shall file in the court the record in the proceedings, as provided in section 2112 of title 28, United States Code. Upon the filing of such petition, the court shall cause notice thereof to be served upon such person, and thereupon shall have jurisdiction of the proceeding and of the question determined therein, and shall have power to grant such temporary relief or restraining order as it deems just and proper, and to make and enter a decree enforcing, modifying, and enforcing, as so modified, or setting aside in whole or in part the order of the Board. No objection that has not been urged before the Board, its member agent, or agency, shall be considered by the court, unless the failure or neglect to urge such objection shall be excused because of extraordinary circumstances. The findings of the Board with respect to questions of fact if supported by substantial evidence on the record considered as a whole shall be conclusive. If either party shall apply to the court for leave to adduce additional evidence and shall show to the satisfaction of the court that such additional evidence is material and that there were reasonable grounds for the failure to adduce such evidence in the hearing before the Board, its member, agent, or agency, the court may order such additional evidence to be taken before the Board, its member, agent, or agency, and to be made a part of the record. The Board may modify its findings as to the facts, or make new findings, by reason of additional evidence so taken and filed, and it shall file such modified or new findings, which findings with respect to questions of fact if supported by substantial evidence on the record considered as a whole shall be conclusive, and shall file its recommendations, if any, for the modification or setting aside of its original order. Upon the filing of the record with it the jurisdiction of the court shall be exclusive and its judgment and decree shall be final, except that the same shall be subject to review by the appropriate United States court of appeals if application was made to the district court as hereinabove provided, and by the Supreme Court of the United States upon writ of certiorari or certification as provided in section 1254 of title 28.

(f) Any person aggrieved by a final order of the Board granting or denying in whole or in part the relief sought may obtain a review of such order in any circuit court of appeals of the United States in the circuit wherein the unfair labor practice in question was alleged to have been engaged in or wherein such person resides or transacts business, or in the United States Court of Appeals for the District of Columbia, by filing in such court a written petition praying that the order of the Board be modified or set aside. A copy of such petition shall be forthwith transmitted by the clerk of the court to the Board, and thereupon the aggrieved party shall file in the court the record in the proceeding, certified by the Board, as provided in Section 2112 of title 28, United States Code. Upon the filing of such petition, the court shall proceed in the same manner as in the case of an application by the Board under subsection (e) of this section, and shall have the same jurisdiction to grant to the Board such temporary relief or restraining order as it deems just and proper, and in like manner to make and enter a decree enforcing, modifying, and enforcing as so modified, or setting aside in whole or in part the order of the Board; the findings of the Board with respect to questions of fact if supported by substantial evidence on the record considered as a whole shall in like manner be conclusive.

(g) The commencement of proceedings under subsection (e) or (f) of this section shall not, unless specifically ordered by the court, operate as a stay of the Board's order.

(h) when granting appropriate temporary relief or a restraining order, or making and entering a decree enforcing, modifying, and enforcing as so modified, or setting aside in whole or in part an order of the Board, as provided in this section, the jurisdiction of courts sitting in equity shall not be limited by the Act entitled "An Act to amend the Judicial Code and to define and limit the jurisdiction of courts sitting in equity, and for other purposes," approved March 23, 1932 (U.S.C., Supp. VII, title 29, secs. 101–115).

(i) Petitions filed under this Act shall be heard expeditiously, and if possible within ten days after they have been docketed.

(j) The Board shall have power, upon issuance of a complaint as provided in subsection (b) charging that any person has engaged in or is engaging in an unfair labor practice, to petition any district court of the United States (including the District Court of the United States for the District of Columbia), within any district wherein the unfair labor practice in question is alleged to have occurred or wherein such person resides or transacts business, for appropriate temporary relief or restraining order. Upon the filing of any such petition the court shall cause notice thereof to be served upon such person, and thereupon shall have jurisdiction to grant to the Board such temporary relief or restraining order as it deems just and proper.

(k) Whenever it is charged that any person has engaged in an unfair labor practice within the meaning of paragraph (4) (D) of section 8 (b), the Board is empowered and directed to hear and determine the dispute out of which such unfair labor practice shall have arisen, unless, within ten days after notice that such charge has been filed, the parties to such dispute submit to the Board satisfactory evidence that they have adjusted, or agreed upon methods for the voluntary adjustment of the dispute. Upon compliance by the parties to the dispute with the decision of the Board or upon such voluntary adjustment of the dispute, such charge shall be dismissed.

Priority cases; Injunction proceedings

(l) Whenever it is charged that any person has engaged in an unfair labor practice within the meaning of paragraph (4) (A), (B), or (C) of section 8 (b), *or section 8 (e) or section 8 (b)(7)*, the preliminary investigation of such charge shall be made forthwith and given priority over all other cases except cases of like character in the office where it is filed or to which it is referred. If, after such investigation, the officer or regional attorney to whom the matter may be referred has reasonable cause to believe such charge is true and that a complaint should issue, he shall, on behalf of the Board, petition any district court of the United States (including the District Court of the United States for the District of Columbia) within any district where the unfair labor practice in question has occurred, is alleged to have occurred, or wherein such person resides or transacts business, for appropriate injunctive relief pending the final adjudication of the Board with respect to such matter. Upon the filing of any such petition the district court shall have jurisdiction to grant such injunctive relief or temporary restraining order as it deems just and proper, notwithstanding any other provision of law: Provided further, That no temporary restraining order shall be issued without notice unless a petition alleges that substantial and irreparable injury to the charging party will be unavoidable and such temporary restraining order shall be effective for no longer than five days and will become void at the expiration of such period [.]: Provided further, That such officer or regional attorney shall not apply for any restraining order under section 8 (b)(7) if a charge against the employer under section 8 (a) (2) has been filed and after the preliminary investigation, he has reasonable cause to believe that such charge is true and that a complaint should issue. Upon filing of any such petition the courts shall cause notice thereof to be served upon any person involved in the charge and such person, including the charging party, shall be given an opportunity to appear by counsel and present any relevant testimony: Provided further, That for the purposes of this subsection district courts shall be deemed to have jurisdiction of a labor organization (1) in the district in which such organization maintains its principal office, or (2) in any district in which its duly authorized officers or agents are engaged in promoting or protecting the interests of employee members. The service of legal process upon such officer or agent shall constitute service upon the labor organization and make such organization a party to the suit. In situations where such relief is appropriate the procedure specified herein shall apply to charges with respect to section 8 (b) (4) (D).

(m) Whenever it is charged that any person has engaged in an unfair labor practice within the meaning of subsection (a) (3) or (b) (2) of section 8, such charge shall be given priority over all other cases except cases of like character in the office where it is filed or to which it is referred and cases given priority under subsection (1).

INVESTIGATORY POWERS

Sec. 11. For the purpose of all hearings and investigations, which, in the opinion of the Board, are necessary and proper for the exercise of the powers vested in it by section 9 and section 10—

(1) The Board, or its duly authorized agents or agencies, shall at all reasonable times have access to, for the purpose of examination, and the right to copy any evidence of any person being investigated or proceeded against that relates to any matter under investigation or in

question. The Board, or any member thereof, shall upon application of any party to such proceedings, forthwith issue to such party subpenas requiring the attendance and testimony of witnesses or the production of any evidence in such proceeding or investigation requested in such application. Within five days after the service of a subpena on any person requiring the production of any evidence in his possession or under his control, such person may petition the Board to revoke, and the Board shall revoke, such subpena if in its opinion the evidence whose production is required does not relate to any matter under investigation, or any matter in question in such proceedings, or if in its opinion such subpena does not describe with sufficient particularity the evidence whose production is required. Any member of the Board, or any agent or agency designated by the Board for such purposes, may administer oaths and affirmations, examine witnesses, and receive evidence. Such attendance of witnesses and the production of such evidence may be required from any place in the United States or any Territory or possession thereof, at any designated place of hearing.

(2) In case of contumacy or refusal to obey a subpena issued to any person, any district court of the United States or the United States courts of any Territory or possession, or the District Court of the United States for the District of Columbia, within the jurisdiction of which the inquiry is carried on or within the jurisdiction of which said person guilty of contumacy or refusal to obey is found or resides or transacts business, upon application by the Board shall have jurisdiction to issue to such person an order requiring such person to appear before the Board, its member, agent, or agency, there to produce evidence if so ordered, or there to give testimony touching the matter under investigation or in question; and any failure to obey such order of the court may be punished by said court as a contempt thereof.

(3) [Repealed.]

(4) Complaints, orders, and other process and papers of the Board, its member, agent, or agency, may be served either personally or by registered mail or by telegraph or by leaving a copy thereof at the principal office or place of business of the person required to be served. The verified return by the individual so serving the same setting forth the manner of such service shall be proof of the same, and the return post office receipt or telegraph receipt therefor when registered and mailed or telegraphed as aforesaid shall be proof of service of the same. Witnesses summoned before the Board, its member, agent, or agency, shall be paid the same fees and mileage that are paid witnesses in the courts of the United States, and witnesses whose depositions are taken and the persons taking the same shall severally be entitled to the same fees as are paid for like services in the courts of the United States.

(5) All process of any court to which application may be made

under this Act may be served in the judicial district wherein the defendant or other person required to be served resides or may found.

(6) The several departments and agencies of the Government, when directed by the President, shall furnish the Board, upon its request, all records, papers, and information in their possession relating to any matter before the Board.

SEC. 12. Any person who shall willfully resist, prevent, impede, or interfere with any member of the Board or any of its agents or agencies in the performance of duties pursuant to this Act shall be punished by a fine of not more than $5,000 or by imprisonment for not more than one year, or both.

LIMITATIONS

Affirmation of right to strike

SEC. 13. Nothing in this Act, except as specifically provided for herein, shall be construed so as either to interfere with or impede or diminish in any way the right to strike, or to affect the limitations or qualifications on that right.

Limited right of supervisors

SEC. 14. (a) Nothing herein shall prohibit any individual employed as a supervisor from becoming or remaining a member of a labor organization, but no employer subject to this Act shall be compelled to deem individuals defined herein as supervisors as employees for the purpose of any law, either national or local, relating to collective bargaining.

"Right-to-work" provision

(b) Nothing in this Act shall be construed as authorizing the execution or application of agreements requiring membership in a labor organization as a condition of employment in any State or Territory in which such execution or application is prohibited by State or Territorial law.

Jurisdictional limits. Authority to decline jurisdiction

(c) (1) The Board, in its discretion, may, by rule of decision or by published rules adopted pursuant to the Administrative Procedure Act, decline to assert jurisdiction over any labor dispute involving any class or category of employers, where, in the opinion of the Board, the effect of such labor dispute on commerce is not sufficiently substantial to warrant the exercise of its jurisdiction: Provided, That the Board shall not decline to assert jurisdiction over any labor dispute over which it would assert jurisdiction under the standards prevailing upon August 1, 1959.

(2) Nothing in this Act shall be deemed to prevent or bar any agency or the courts of any State or Territory (including the Commonwealth of Puerto Rico, Guam, and the Virgin Islands), from assuming and asserting jurisdiction over labor disputes over which the Board declines, pursuant to paragraph (1) of this subsection, to assert jurisdiction.

Relationship to bankruptcy laws

SEC. 15. Wherever the application of the provisions of section 272 of chapter 10 of the Act entitled "An Act to establish a uniform system of bankruptcy throughout the United States," approved July 1, 1898, and Acts amendatory thereof and supplementary thereto (U.S.C., title 11, sec. 672), conflicts with the application of the provisions of this Act, this Act shall prevail: Provided, That in any situation where the provisions of this Act cannot be validly enforced, the provisions of such other Acts shall remain in full force and effect.

SEC. 16. If any provision of this Act, or the application of such provision to any person or circumstances, shall be held invalid, the remainder of this Act, or the application of such provision to persons or circumstances other than those as to which it is held invalid, shall not be affected thereby.

SEC. 17. This Act may be cited as the "National Labor Relations Act."

SEC. 18. No petition entertained, no investigation made, no election held, and no certification issued by the National Labor Relations Board, under any of the provisions of section 9 of the National Labor Relations Act, as amended, shall be invalid by reason of the failure of the Congress of Industrial Organizations to have complied with the requirements of section 9 (f), (g), or (h) of the aforesaid Act prior to December 22, 1949, or by reason of the failure of the American Federation of Labor to have complied with the provisions of section 9 (f), (g), or (h) of the aforesaid Act prior to November 7, 1947: Provided, That no liability shall be imposed under any provision of this Act upon any person for failure to honor any election or certificate referred to above, prior to the effective date of this amendment: Provided, however, That this proviso shall not have the effect of setting aside or in any way affecting judgments or decrees heretofore entered under section 10 (e) or (f) and which have become final.

INDIVIDUALS WITH RELIGIOUS CONVICTIONS

Religious exception   SEC. 19. Any employee of a health care institution who is a member of and adheres to established traditional tenets or teachings of a bona fide religion, body, or sect which has historically held conscientious objections to joining or financially supporting labor organizations shall not be required to join or financially support any labor organization as a condition of employment; except that such employee may be required, in lieu of periodic dues and initiation fees, to pay sums equal to such dues and initiation fees to a nonreligious charitable fund exempt from taxation under section 501 (c) (3) of the Internal Revenue Code, chosen by such employee from a list of at least three such funds, designated in a contract between such institution and a labor organization, or if the contract fails to designate such funds, then to any such fund chosen by the employee.

EFFECTIVE DATE OF CERTAIN CHANGES*

SEC. 102. No provision of this title shall be deemed to make an unfair labor practice any act which was performed prior to the date of the enactment of this Act which did not constitute an unfair labor practice prior thereto, and the provisions of section 8 (a) (3) and section 8 (b) (2) of the National Labor Relations Act as amended by this title shall not make an unfair labor practice the performance of any obligation under a collective-bargaining agreement entered into prior to the date of the enactment of this Act, or (in the case of an agreement for a period of not more than one year) entered into on or after such date of enactment, but prior to the effective date of this title, if the performance of such obligation would not have constituted an unfair labor practice under section 8 (3) of the National Labor Relations Act prior to the effective date of this title, unless such agreement was renewed or extended subsequent thereto.

SEC. 103. No provisions of this title shall affect any certification of representatives or any determination as to the appropriate collective-bargaining unit, which was made under section 9 of the National Labor Relations Act prior to the effective date of this title until one year after the date of such certification or if, in respect of any such certification, a collective-bargaining contract was entered into prior to the effective date of this title, until the end of the contract period or until one year after such date, whichever first occurs.

SEC. 104. The amendments made by this title shall take effect sixty days after the date of the enactment of this Act, except that the authority of the President to appoint certain officers conferred upon him by section 3 of the National Labor Relations Act as amended by this title may be exercised forthwith.

TITLE II
CONCILIATION OF LABOR DISPUTES IN INDUSTRIES AFFECTING COMMERCE: NATIONAL EMERGENCIES

SEC. 201. That it is the policy of the United States that—

Public policy to settle disputes peacefully

(a) sound and stable industrial peace and the advancement of the general welfare, health, and safety of the Nation and of the best interest of employers and employees can most satisfactorily be secured

The effective date referred to in Sections 102, 103, and 104 is August 22, 1947.

by the settlement of issues between employers and employees through the processes of conference and collective bargaining between employers and the representatives of their employees;

(b) the settlement of issues between employers and employees through collective bargaining may be advanced by making available full and adequate governmental facilities for conciliation, mediation, and voluntary arbitration to aid and encourage employers and the representatives of their employees to reach and maintain agreements concerning rates of pay, hours, and working conditions, and to make all reasonable efforts to settle their differences by mutual agreement reached through conferences and collective bargaining or by such methods as may be provided for in any applicable agreement for the settlement of disputes; and

(c) certain controversies which arise between parties to collective bargaining agreements may be avoided or minimized by making available full and adequate governmental facilities for furnishing assistance to employers and the representatives of their employees in formulating for inclusion within such agreements provision for adequate notice of any proposed changes in the terms of such agreements, for the final adjustment of grievances or questions regarding the application or interpretation of such agreements, and other provisions designed to prevent the subsequent arising of such controversies.

Creation
of FMCS

SEC. 202. (a) There is hereby created an independent agency to be known as the Federal Mediation and Conciliation Service (herein referred to as the "Service," except that for sixty days after the date of the enactment of this Act such term shall refer to the Conciliation Service of the Department of Labor). The Service shall be under the direction of a Federal Mediation and Conciliation Director (hereinafter referred to as the "Director"), who shall be appointed by the President by and with the advice and consent of the Senate. The Director shall receive compensation at the rate of $12,000* per annum. The Director shall not engage in any other business, vocation, or employment.

(b) The Director is authorized, subject to the civil-service laws, to appoint such clerical and other personnel as may be necessary for the execution of the functions of the Service, and shall fix their compensation in accordance with the Classification Act of 1923, as amended, and may, without regard to the provisions of the civil service laws and the Classifiction Act of 1923, as amended, appoint and fix the compensation of such conciliators and mediators as may be necessary to carry out the functions of the Service. The Director is authorized to make such

---

*AUTHORS' NOTE: All salaries quoted in this Act are now increased periodically as a result of the Government Employees Salary Reform Act of 1964, 88th Congress, Public Law 88-426, 78 Stat. 400.

expenditures for supplies, facilities, and services as he deems necessary. Such expenditures shall be allowed and paid upon presentation of itemized vouchers therefor approved by the Director or by any employee designated by him for that purpose.

(c) The principal office of the Service shall be in the District of Columbia, but the Director may establish regional offices convenient to localities in which labor controversies are likely to arise. The Director may by order, subject to revocation at any time, delegate any authority and discretion conferred upon him by this Act to any regional director, or other officer or employee of the Service. The Director may establish suitable procedures for cooperation with State and local mediation agencies. The Director shall make an annual report in writing to Congress at the end of the fiscal year.

(d) All mediation and conciliation functions of the Secretary of Labor or the United States Conciliation Service under section 8 of the Act entitled "An Act to create a Department of Labor," approved March 4, 1913 (U.S.C., title 29, sec. 51), and all functions of the United States Conciliation Service under any other law are hereby transferred to the Federal Mediation and Conciliation Service, together with the personnel and records of the United States Conciliation Service. Such transfer shall take effect upon the sixtieth day after the date of enactment of this Act. Such transfer shall not affect any proceedings, pending before the United States Conciliation Service or any certification, order, rule, or regulation theretofore made by it or by it or by the Secretary of Labor. The Director and the Service shall not be subject in any way to the jurisdiction or authority of the Secretary of Labor or any official or division of the Department of Labor.

FUNCTIONS OF THE SERVICE

SEC. 203. (a) It shall be the duty of the Service, in order to prevent or minimize interruptions of the free flow of commerce growing out of labor disputes, to assist parties to labor disputes in industries affecting commerce to settle such disputes through conciliation and mediation.

Right of FMCS to intervene in labor disputes

(b) The Service may proffer its services in any labor dispute in any industry affecting commerce, either upon its own motion or upon the request of one or more of the parties to the dispute, whenever in its judgment such dispute threatens to cause a substantial interruption of commerce. The Director and the Service are directed to avoid attempting to mediate disputes which would have only a minor effect on interstate commerce if State or other conciliation services are available to the parties. Whenever the Service does proffer its services in any dispute, it shall be the duty of the Service promptly to put itself in communication with the parties and to use its best efforts, by mediation and conciliation, to bring them to agreement.

(c) If the Director is not able to bring the parties to agreement by conciliation within a reasonable time, he shall seek to induce the parties voluntarily to seek other means of settling the dispute without resort to strike, lockout, or other coercion, including submission to the employees in the bargaining unit of the employer's last offer of settlement for approval or rejection in a secret ballot. The failure or refusal of either party to agree to any procedure suggested by the Director shall not be deemed a violation of any duty or obligation imposed by this Act.

(d) Final adjustment by a method agreed upon by the parties is hereby declared to be the desirable method for settlement of grievance disputes arising over the application or interpretation of an existing collective-bargaining agreement. The Service is directed to make its conciliation and mediation services available in the settlement of such grievance disputes only as a last resort and in exceptional cases.

SEC. 204. (a) In order to prevent or minimize interruptions of the free flow of commerce growing out of labor disputes, employers and employees and their representatives, in any industry affecting commerce, shall—

(1) exert every reasonable effort to make and maintain agreements concerning rates of pay, hours, and working conditions, including provision for adequate notice of any proposed change in the terms of such agreements;

(2) whenever a dispute arises over the terms or application of a collective-bargaining agreement and a conference is requested by a party or prospective party thereto, arrange promptly for such a conference to be held and endeavor in such conference to settle such dispute expeditiously; and

(3) in case such dispute is not settled by conference, participate fully and promptly in such meetings as may be undertaken by the Service under this Act for the purpose of aiding in a settlement of the dispute.

SEC. 205. (a) There is hereby created a National Labor-Management Panel which shall be composed of twelve members appointed by the President, six of whom shall be selected from among persons outstanding in the field of management and six of whom shall be selected from among persons outstanding in the field of labor. Each member shall hold office for a term of three years, except that any member appointed to fill a vacancy occurring prior to the expiration of the term for which his predecessor was appointed shall be appointed for the remainder of such term, and the terms of office of the members first taking office shall expire, as designated by the President at the time of appointment, four at the end of the first year, four at the end of the second year, and four at the end of the third year after the date of appointment. Members of the panel, when serving on business of the panel, shall be paid compensation at the rate of $25 per day, and shall also be entitled to receive an allowance for actual and necessary travel and subsistence expenses while so serving away from their places of residence.

(b) It shall be the duty of the panel, at the request of the Director, to advise in the avoidance of industrial controversies and the manner in which mediation and voluntary adjustment shall be administered, particularly with reference to controversies affecting the general welfare of the country.

NATIONAL EMERGENCIES

Emergency dispute procedures

SEC. 206. Whenever in the opinion of the President of the United States, a threatened or actual strike or lockout affecting an entire industry or a substantial part thereof engaged in trade, commerce, transportation, transmission, or communication among the several States or with foreign nations, or engaged in the production of goods for commerce, will, if permitted to occur or to continue, imperil the national health or safety, he may appoint a board of inquiry to inquire into the issues involved in the dispute and to make a written report to him within such time as he shall prescribe. Such report shall include a statement of the facts with respect to the dispute, including each party's statement of its position but shall not contain any recommendations. The President shall file a copy of such report with the Service and shall make its contents available to the public.

SEC. 207. (a) A board of inquiry shall be composed of a chairman and such other members as the President shall determine, and shall have power to sit and act in any place within the United States and to conduct such hearings either in public or in private, as it may deem necessary or proper, to ascertain the facts with respect to the causes and circumstances of the dispute.

(b) Members of a board of inquiry shall receive compensation at the rate of $50 for each day actually spent by them in the work of the board, together with necessary travel and subsistence expenses.

(c) For the purpose of any hearing or inquiry conducted by any board appointed under this title, the provisions of sections 9 and 10 (relating to the attendance of witnesses and the production of books, papers, and documents) of the Federal Trade Commission Act of September 16, 1914, as amended (U.S.C. 19, title 15, secs. 49 and 50, as amended), are hereby made applicable to the powers and duties of such board.

SEC. 208. (a) Upon receiving a report from a board of inquiry the President may direct the Attorney General to petition any district court of the United States having jurisdiction of the parties to enjoin such strike or lockout or the continuing thereof, and if the court finds that such threatened or actual strike or lockout—

(i) affects an entire industry or a substantial part thereof engaged in trade, commerce, transportation, transmission, or communication among the several States or with foreign nations, or engaged in the production of goods for commerce; and

(ii) if permitted to occur or to continue, will imperil the national health or safety, it shall have jurisdiction to enjoin any such strike or lockout, or the continuing thereof, and to make such other orders as may be appropriate.

(b) In any case, the provisions of the Act of March 23, 1932, entitled "An Act to amend the Judicial Code and to define and limit the jurisdiction of courts sitting in equity, and for other purposes," shall not be applicable.

(c) The order or orders of the court shall be subject to review by the appropriate circuit court of appeals and by the Supreme Court upon writ of certiorari of certification as provided in sections 239 and 240 of the Judicial Code, as amended (U.S.C., title 29, secs. 346 and 347).

SEC. 209. (a) Whenever a district court has issued an order under section 208 enjoining acts or practices which imperil or threaten to imperil the national health or safety, it shall be the duty of the parties to the labor dispute giving rise to such order to make every effort to adjust and settle their differences, with the assistance of the Service created by this Act. Neither party shall be under any duty to accept, in while or in part, any proposal of settlement made by the Service.

(b) Upon the issuance of such order, the President shall reconvene the board of inquiry which has previously reported with respect to the dispute. At the end of a sixty-day period (unless the dispute has been settled by that time), the board of inquiry shall report to the President the current position of the parties and the efforts which has (sic) been made for settlement, and shall include a statement by each party of its position and a statement of the employer's last offer of settlement. The President shall make such report available to the public. The National Labor Relations Board, within the succeeding fifteen days, shall take a secret ballot of the employees of each employer involved in the dispute on the question of whether they wish to accept the final offer of settlement made by their employer as stated by him and shall certify the results thereof to the Attorney General within five days thereafter.

SEC. 210. Upon the certification of the results of such ballot or upon a settlement being reached, whichever happens sooner, the Attorney General shall move the court to discharge the injunction, which motion shall then be granted and the injunction discharged. When such motion is granted, the President shall submit to the Congress a full and comprehensive report of the proceedings, including the findings of the board of inquiry and the ballot taken by the National Labor Relations Board, together with such recommendations as he may see fit to make for consideration and appropriate action.

Record keeping of
Bureau of Labor
Statistics

COMPILATION OF COLLECTIVE-BARGAINING AGREEMENTS, ETC. SEC. 211. (a) For the guidance and information of interested representatives of employers, employees, and the general public, the Bureau of Labor Statistics of the Department of Labor shall maintain a file of copies of all available collective-bargaining agreements and other available agreements and actions thereunder settling or adjusting labor disputes. Such file shall be open to inspection under appropriate conditions prescribed by the Secretary of Labor, except that no specific information submitted in confidence shall be disclosed.

(b) The Bureau of Labor Statistics in the Department of Labor is authorized to furnish upon request of the Service, or employers, employees, or their representatives, all available data and factual information which may aid in the settlement of any labor dispute, except that no specific information submitted to confidence shall be disclosed.

EXEMPTION OF RAILWAY LABOR ACT. SEC. 212. The provisions of this title shall not be applicable with respect to any matter which is subject to the provisions of the Railway Labor Act, as amended from time to time.

CONCILIATION OF LABOR DISPUTES
IN THE HEALTH CARE INDUSTRY

Special provisions
for conciliation in
health care
industry

SEC. 213 (a) If, in the opinion of the Director of the Federal Mediation and Conciliation Service a threatened or actual strike or lockout affecting a health care institution will, if permitted to occur or to continue, substantially interrupt the delivery of health care in the locality concerned, the Director may further assist in the resolution of the impasse by establishing within 30 days after the notice to the Federal Mediation and Conciliation Service under clause (A) of the last sentence of section 8 (d) [which is required by clause (3) of such section 8 (d)], or within 10 days after the notice under clause (B), an impartial Board of Inquiry to investigate the issue involved in the dispute and to make a written report thereon to the parties within fifteen (15) days after the establishment of such a Board. The written report shall contain the findings of fact together with the Board's recommendations for settling the dispute. Each such Board shall be composed of such number of individuals as the Director may deem desirable. No member appointed under this section shall have any interest or involvement in the health care institutions or the employee organizations involved in the dispute.

(b) (1) Members of any board established under this section who are otherwise employed by the Federal Government shall serve without compensation but shall be reimbursed for travel, subsistence, and other necessary expenses incurred by them in carrying out its duties under this section.

(2) Members of any board established under this section who are not subject to paragraph (1) shall receive compensation at a rate prescribed by the Director but not to exceed the daily rate prescribed for GS-18 of the General Schedule under section 5332 of title 5, United States Code, including travel for each day they are engaged in the performance of their duties under this section and shall be entitled to reimbursement for travel, subsistence, and other necessary expenses incurred by them in carrying out their duties under this section.

(c) After the establishment of a board under subsection (a) of this section and for 15 days after any such board has issued its report, no change in the status quo in effect prior to the expiration of the contract in the case of negotiations for a contract renewal, or in effect prior to the time of the impasse in the case of an initial bargaining negotiation, except by agreement, shall be made by the parties to the controversy.

TITLE III
SUITS BY AND AGAINST LABOR ORGANIZATIONS

Enforcement
of contracts
through law suits

SEC. 301. (a) Suits for violation of contracts between an employer and a labor organization representing employees in an industry affecting commerce as defined in this Act, or between any such labor organizations, may be brought in any district court of the United States having jurisdiction of the parties, without respect to the amount in controversy or without regard to the citizenship of the parties.

(b) Any labor organization which represents employees in an industry affecting commerce as defined in this Act and any employer whose activities affect commerce as defined in this Act shall be bound by the acts of its agents. Any such labor organization may sue or be sued as an entity and in behalf of the employees whom it represents in the courts of the United States. Any money judgment against a labor organization in a district court of the United States shall be enforceable only against the organization as an entity and against its assets, and shall not be enforceable against any individual member or his assets.

(c) For the purposes of actions and proceedings by or against labor organizations in the district courts of the United States, district courts shall be deemed to have jurisdiction of a labor organization (1) in the district in which such organization maintains its principal office, or (2) in any district in which its duly authorized officers or agents are engaged in representing or acting for employee members.

(d) The service of summons, subpena, or other legal process of any court of the United States upon an officer or agent of a labor organization, in his capacity as such, shall constitute service upon the labor organization.

(e) For the purposes of this section, in determining whether any person is acting as an ''agent'' of another person so as to make such other person responsible for his acts, the question of whether the specific acts performed were actually authorized or subsequently ratified shall not be controlling.

RESTRICTIONS ON PAYMENTS TO EMPLOYEE REPRESENTATIVES. SEC. 302. (a) It shall be unlawful for any employer *or association of employers or any person who acts as a labor relations expert, adviser, or consultant to an employer or who acts in the interest of an employer* to pay, *lend,* or deliver, or [to] agree to pay, *lend,* or deliver, any money or other thing of value—

(1) to any representative of any of his employees who are employed in an industry affecting commerce[.]; *or*

(2) to any labor organization, or any officer or employee thereof, which represents, seeks to represent, or would admit to membership, any of the employees of such employer who are employed in an industry affecting commerce; or

(3) to any employee or group or committee of employees of such employer employed in an industry affecting commerce in excess of their normal compensation for the purpose of causing such employee or group or committee directly to indirectly to influence any other employees in the exercise of the right to organize and bargain collectively through representatives of their own choosing; or

(4) to any officer or employee of a labor organization engaged in an industry affecting commerce with intent to influence him in respect to any of his actions, decisions, or duties as a representative of employees or as such officer or employee of such labor organization.

(b) (1) It shall be unlawful for any [representative of any employees who are employed in an industry affecting commerce] *person* to *request, demand,* receive, or accept, or [to] agree to receive or accept, [from the employer of such employees] *any payment, loan, or delivery* of any money or other thing of value[.] *prohibited by subsection* (a).

(2) It shall be unlawful for any labor organization, or for any person acting as an officer, agent, representative, or employee of such labor organization, to demand or accept from the operator of any motor vehicle (as defined in part II of the Interstate Commerce Act) employed in the transportation of property in commerce, or the employer of any such operator, any money or other thing of value payable to such organization or to an officer, agent, representative or employee thereof as a fee or charge for the unloading, or in connection with the unloading, of the cargo of such vehicle: Provided, That nothing in this paragraph whall be construed to make unlawful any payment by an employer to any of his employees as compensation for their services as employees.

(c) The provisions of this section shall not be applicable (1) [with] in respect to any money or other thing of value payable by an employer *to any of his employees whose established duties include acting openly for such employer in matters of labor relations or personnel administration or* to any representative *of his employees, or to any officer or employee of a labor organization* who is *also* an employee or former employee of such employer, as compensation for, or by reason of, his service[s] as an employee of such employer; (2) with respect to the payment or delivery of any money or other thing of value in satisfaction of a judgment of any court or a decision or award of an arbitrator or impartial chairman or in compromise, adjustment, settlement, or release of any claim, complaint, grievance, or dispute in the absence of fraud or duress; (3) with respect to the sale or purchase of an article or commodity at the prevailing market price in the regular course of business; (4) with respect to money deducted from the wages of employees in payment of membership dues in a labor organization: Provided, That the employer has received from each employee, on whose account such deductions are made, a written assignment which shall not be irrevocable for a period of more than one year, or beyond the termination date of the applicable collective agreement, whichever occurs sooner; [or] (5) with respect to money or other thing of value paid to a trust fund established by such representative, for the sole and exclusive benefit of the employees of such employer, and their families and dependents (or of such employees, families, and dependents jointly with the employees of other employers making similar payments, and their families and dependents): Provided, That (A) such payments are held in trust for the purpose of paying, either from principal or income or both, for the benefit of employees, their families and dependents, for medical or hospital care, pensions on retirement or death of employees, compensation for injuries or illness resulting from occupational activity or insurance to provide any of the foregoing, or unemployment benefits or life insurance, disability and sickness insurance, or accident insurance; (B) the detailed basis on which such payments are to be made is specified in a written agreement with the employer, and employees and employers are equally represented in the administration of such fund, together with such neutral persons as the representatives of the employers and the representatives of [the] employees may agree upon and in the event the employer and employee groups deadlock on the administration of such fund and there are no neutral persons empowered to break such deadlock, such agreement provides that the two groups shall agree on an impartial umpire to decide such dispute or in event of their failure to agree within a reasonable length of time an impartial umpire to decide such dispute shall, on petition of either group, be appointed by the district court of the United States for the district where the trust fund has its principal office, and shall also contain provisions for an annual audit of the trust fund, a statement of the results of which shall be available for inspection by interested persons at the principal office of the trust fund and at such other places as may be designated in such written agreement; and (C) such payments as are intended to be used for the purpose of providing pensions or annuities for employees are made to a separate trust which provides that the funds held therein cannot be used for any purpose other than paying such pensions or annuities [.]; *or (6) with respect to money or other thing of value paid by any employer to a trust fund established by such representative for the purpose of pooled vacation, holiday, severance or similar benefits, or defraying costs of apprenticeship or other training programs; Provided, That the requirements of clause (B) of the proviso to clause (5) of this subsection shall apply to such trust funds.* [; or] (7) With respect to money or other thing of value paid by any employer to a pooled or individual trust fund established by such representative for the purpose of (A) scholarships for the benefit of employees, their families, and dependents for study at educational institutions, or (B) child care centers for preschool and school age dependents of employees: Provided, That no labor organization or employer shall be required to bargain on the establishment of any such trust fund, and refusal to do so shall not constitute an unfair labor practice: Provided further, That the requirements of clause (B) of the proviso to clause (5) of this subsection shall apply to such trust funds; or (8) with respect to money or any other thing of value paid by any employer to a trust fund established by such representative for the purpose of defraying the costs of legal services for employees, their families, and dependents for counsel or plan of their choice: Provided, That the requirements of clause (B) of the proviso to clause (5) of this subsection shall apply to such trust funds: Provided further, That no such legal services shall be furnished: (A) to initiate any proceeding directed (i) against any such employer or its officers or agents except in workman's compensation cases, or (ii) against such labor organizations, or its parent or subordinate bodies, or their officers or agents, or (iii) against any other employer or labor organization, or their officers or agent, in any matter arising under the National Labor Relations Act, as amended, or this Act; and (B) in any proceeding where a labor organization would have been prohibited from defraying the costs of legal services by the provisions of the Labor-Management Reporting and Disclosure Act of 1959.

(d) Any person who willfully violates any of the provisions of this section shall, upon conviction thereof, be guilty of a misdemeanor and be subject to a fine of not more than $10,000 or to imprisonment for not more than one year, or both.

(e) The district courts of the United States and the United States courts of the Territories and possessions shall have jurisdiction, for cause shown, and subject to the provisions of section 17 (relating to notice to opposite party) of the Act entitled "An Act to supplement existing laws against unlawful restraints and monopolies, and for other purposes," approved October 15, 1914, as amended (U.S.C., title 28, sec. 381), to restrain violations of this section, without regard to the provisions of sections 6 and 20 of such Act of October 15, 1914, as amended (U.S.C., title 15, sec. 17, and title 29, sec. 52), and the provisions of the Act entitled "An Act to amend the Judicial Code and to define and limit the jurisdiction of courts sitting in equity, and for other purposes," approved March 23, 1932 (U.S.C., title 29, secs. 101–115).

(f) This section shall not apply to any contract in force on the date of enactment of this Act, until the expiration of such contract, or until July 1, 1948, whichever first occurs.

(g) Compliance with the restrictions contained in subsection (c) (5) (B) upon contributions to trust funds, otherwise lawful, shall not be applicable to contributions to such trust funds established by collective agreement prior to January 1, 1946, nor shall subsection (c) (5) (A) be construed as prohibiting contributions to such trust funds if prior to January 1, 1947, such funds contained provisions for pooled vacation benefits.

BOYCOTTS AND OTHER UNLAWFUL COMBINATIONS. SEC. 303. (a) It shall be unlawful, for the purpose [s] of this section only, in an industry or activity affecting commerce, for any labor organization to engage in [, or to induce or encourage the employees of any employer to engage in, a strike or a concerted refusal in the course of their employment to use, manufacture, process, transport, or otherwise handle or work on any goods, articles, materials, or commodities or to perform any services, where an object thereof is—]

[(1) forcing or requiring any employer or self-employed person to join any labor or employer organization or any employer or other person to cease using, selling, handling, transporting, or otherwise dealing in the products of any other producer, processor, or manufacturer, or to cease doing business with any other person;]

[(2) forcing or requiring any other employer to recognize or bargain with a labor organization as the representative of his employees unless such labor organization has been certified as the representative of such employees under the provisions of section 9 of the National Labor Relations Act;]

[(3) forcing or requiring any employer to recognize or bargain with a particular labor organization as the representative of his employees if another labor organization has been certified as the representative of such employees under the provisions of section 9 of the National Labor Relations Act;]

[(4) forcing or requiring any employer to assign particular work to employees in a particular labor organization or in a particular trade, craft, or class rather than to employees in another labor organization or in another trade, craft, or class unless such employer is failing to conform to an order or certification of the National Labor Relations Board determining the bargaining representative for employees performing

such work. Nothing contained in this subsection shall be construed to make unlawful a refusal by any person to enter upon the premises of any employer (other than his own employer), if the employees of such employer are engaged in a strike ratified or approved by a representative of such employees whom such employer is required to recognize under the National Labor Relations Act.]
any activity or conduct defined as an unfair labor practice in section 8 (b) (4) of the National Labor Relations Act, as amended.

(b) Whoever shall be injured in his business or property by reason of any violation of subsection (a) may sue therefor in any district court of the United States subject to the limitations and provisions of section 301 hereof without respect to the amount in controversy, or in any other court having jurisdiction of the parties, and shall recover the damages by him sustained and the cost of the suit.

RESTRICTION ON POLITICAL CONTRIBUTIONS

SEC. 304. Section 313 of the Federal Corrupt Practices Act, 1925 (U.S.C., 1940 edition, title 2, sec. 251; Supp. V, title 50, App., sec. 1509), as amended, is amended to read as follows:

SEC. 313. It is unlawful for any national bank, or any corporation organized by authority of any law of Congress, to make a contribution or expenditure in connection with any election to any political office, or in connection with any primary election or political convention or caucus held to select candidates for any political office, or for any corporation whatever, or any labor organization to make a contribution or expenditure in connection with any election at which Presidential and Vice Presidential electors or a Senator or Representative in, or a Delegate or Resident Commissioner to Congress are to be voted for, or in connection with any primary election or political convention or caucus held to select candidates for any of the foregoing offices, or for any candidate, political committee, or other person to accept or receive any contribution prohibited by this section. Every corporation or labor organization which makes any contribution or expenditure in violation of this section shall be fined not more than $5,000; and every officer or director of any corporation, or officer of any labor organization, who consents to any contribution or expenditure by the corporation or labor organization, as the case may be, in violation of this section shall be fined not more than $1,000 or imprisoned for not more than one year, or both. For the purposes of this section "labor organization" means any organization of any kind, or any agency or employee representation committee or plan, in which employees participate and which exists for the purpose, in whole or in part, of dealing with employers concerning grievances, labor disputes, wages, rates of pay, hours of employment, or conditions of work.

STRIKES BY GOVERNMENT EMPLOYEES

Strikers outlawed for federal employees

SEC. 305. It shall be unlawful for any individual employed by the United States or any agency thereof including wholly owned Government corporations to participate in any strike. Any individual employed by the United States or by any such agency who strikes shall be discharged immediately from his employment, and shall forfeit his civil-service status, if any, and shall not be eligible for reemployment for three years by the United States or any such agency. . . .

INDEX

(Note: Union names may be inverted so as to be found under descriptive craft or industry, i.e. Mine Workers, United.)